PENGUIN BOOKS
Pears Ultimate Quiz Companion

Jim Hensman was born in Sri Lanka and has a degree in Mathematics and Electronics, and a Research Degree in Computer Science. He is a self-confessed information addict and collector of facts on all sorts of strange subjects. He is the author of *Pears Ultimate Quiz Companion* as well as a number of quiz, trivia and puzzle features in national newspapers. He also helped to research the television series *Notes and Queries* (with Clive Anderson). In real life he works with computers and attempts to indulge his diverse interests, which range from playing guitar to politics.

Jim Hensman is married with three children and lives in Coventry.

D0309839

JIM HENSMAN

PEARS ULTIMATE QUIZ
COMPANION

PENGUIN BOOKS

PENGUIN BOOKS

Published by the Penguin Group
Penguin Books Ltd, 27 Wrights Lane, London W8 5TZ, England
Penguin Putnam Inc., 375 Hudson Street, New York, New York 10014, USA
Penguin Books Australia Ltd, Ringwood, Victoria, Australia
Penguin Books Canada Ltd, 10 Alcorn Avenue, Toronto, Ontario, Canada M4V 3B2
Penguin Books (NZ) Ltd, 182–190 Wairau Road, Auckland 10, New Zealand

Penguin Books Ltd, Registered Offices: Harmondsworth, Middlesex, England

First published by Pelham Books 1989
Updated and published in Signet 1992
Published in Penguin Books 1998
1 3 5 7 9 10 8 6 4 2

Printed in England by Clays Ltd, St Ives plc

Introduction

Pears Ultimate Quiz Companion is a unique reference work for anyone taking part in or setting quizzes, as a complement to crossword dictionaries for word game enthusiasts, and as a reference book of general knowledge.

It differs from most reference books in three ways. First in its coverage, which includes as wide and diverse a range of topics as possible, from serious to trivial, from Astronomy and Philosophy to Crime and Pop Music, including many subjects not covered by most works of reference. Secondly, it is different in the type of information it contains. In order to cover as wide a field as possible within the space of one volume, only information that is of a form suitable for quizzes is included. Thus the populations and areas of countries for instance are not to be found in its pages (though the largest countries and those with the highest population are listed in order). Of course a work of this size must of necessity be extremely selective, but the aim has been to pick the essential core of the most quizzable information from as wide a spectrum as possible. The third and most significant way this book differs from other reference works is in the way it is organised. The aim has been to structure and list the information contained in it in a way that reflects the way that quiz questions are normally asked, not alphabetically or by arbitrary categories. So if you want to know who played in a FA Cup Final with a broken neck, which king died on the toilet or what the lightest metal is, the information is easily and quickly accessible.

Overall, *Pears Ultimate Quiz Companion* is an ideal book not only for quiz and puzzle enthusiasts, but also for anyone as a unique reference source for those tantalizingly hard to find pieces of information, and as a fascinatingly browseable general compendium of facts.

Contents

How to Use this Book	ix	TV, General	106
Notes	xi	TV and Radio Personalities	107
Acknowledgements	xii	TV Programmes	108
Art, Craft and Architecture	1	**Geography and Places**	125
Architectural Terms	3	Man Made Constructions	128
Art Terms	4	Bridges	128
Artistic Movements and Schools	5	Buildings and Constructions	128
Artists	6	Canals	132
Buildings	8	Houses, Famous	133
Crafts	9	Natural Features	133
Galleries and Collections	10	Bays and Gulfs	133
Paintings	10	Capes	134
Photographers	12	Deserts	134
Sculptors	13	Geographical Terms	134
Sculptures	13	Islands	136
Entertainment	15	Lakes	139
Cinema	17	Mountain Ranges	139
Characters from Films	17	Mountains	140
Cinema, General	21	Natural Disasters	141
Films	23	Other Natural Sites and Places	142
Film Quotes and Publicity Blurbs	49	Rivers	144
Musical Themes	50	Seas and Oceans	145
Songs from Films	51	Straits	146
Stars and Directors	52	Volcanoes	147
Music	56	Waterfalls	147
Backing Groups	56	Weather	148
Classical Music, General	57	Places	149
Composers	57	Capitals	149
Musical Instruments	58	Capitals, Former	152
Musical Terms	58	Cities	152
Musical Works	59	Cities on Lakes	153
Musical Works, Common Names	61	Cities on Rivers	154
Musicians	62	Countries	155
Musicians, Instruments played	62	Exploration and Discovery	158
Opera Characters	63	Extremities	159
Operas	65	Flags	160
Pop Groups/Singers	67	Historical Territories	161
Pop LPs/Albums	80	Inhabitants	161
Pop Music, Other	82	National Anthems	161
Pop Records	83	National Symbols	162
Pop Singles	84	Other Places	162
Singers, Classical	94	Peoples and Tribes	163
Songs and Tunes	94	Place Name Changes	164
Stage Entertainment	96	Place Name Derivations	166
Ballets	96	Place Name Parts, Meaning	167
Dance and Ballet	96	Place Nicknames	167
Musicals	97	Places, Latitude and Longitude	168
Musicals, Songs from	99	Roman Names	168
Theatre, Variety, etc.	99	Territories, Sovereignty	169
TV and Radio	100	United Kingdom	169
Catchphrases	100	United States	170
Radio, General	102	**Health and the Body**	171
Radio Programmes	102	The Body	173
TV and Radio Characters	104	Disease and Medicine	178

Diseases, Common Names	181	Habitations	284
Diseases, Effects	182	Horses	284
Medical Specialities	183	Insects (and Related Creatures)	285
Mental Illnesses and Conditions	183	Land Animals	286
Psychology and Psychiatry	184	Male and Female	291
Ideas and Beliefs	**185**	Other Names	292
The Bible	187	Scientific Names	293
Christianity	189	Young	293
Mythological Gods and Goddesses	192	Biology	294
Mythology	194	Plants	295
The Occult and Parapsychology	197	Common Names	295
Philosophy and Philosophers	198	Other Names	295
Religion	199	Plant Families	296
Language and Literature	**203**	Plant Varieties and Types	297
Language	205	Plants, General	298
Abbreviations	205	Plants, Products obtained from	300
American English	207	**People**	**303**
Codes and Ciphers	208	Biography	305
Derivations	209	Awards and Prizes	305
Foreign Phrases	210	Biographical Quotations	306
Languages	211	Brothers and Sisters	306
Mottoes	213	Children	307
Phrases and Terms	213	Death	308
Quotations	214	Death, After	311
Rhyming Slang	222	Diseases and Disabilities	311
Slang	222	Executions	312
Words and Letters	223	Last Words	313
Words from other Languages	223	Marriages	314
Literature	224	Miscellaneous	319
Authors	224	Nationality and Origin	321
Autobiography	226	Occupations	322
Biography	227	Pairs and Partnerships	325
Cartoons and Comics	227	Parents	325
Fiction, Books	229	Relations	326
Fictional Characters and Things	242	Relationships	327
Fictional Detectives	249	Suicide	328
Legendary Characters and Things	250	Names	329
Literary Movements	251	Christian Names	329
Literature	252	Initials	330
Literature and Books, Other	254	Maiden Names	331
Newspapers and Magazines	255	Middle Names	331
Non Fiction	256	Names, General	331
Nursery Rhymes	257	Nicknames	332
Plays	258	Real (First) Names	336
Poetry	263	Real Names	337
The Living World	**267**	Surnames	345
Animals	269	Titles	345
Animal Sounds	269	**Science and Technology**	**347**
Animal Life, General	269	General	349
Animals, Products from	271	Chemical Names	349
Birds	271	Chemistry and Materials	350
Breeds	274	Communications	353
Collections	277	Computers	354
Dogs	277	Discoveries and Theories	354
Families	278	Energy Technology	355
Famous Animals	280	Inventions	356
Fish and Sea Creatures	282	Mathematics	358

Measurement	359	International Politics and	
Miscellaneous	360	Institutions	407
Ores	361	Military	408
Physics	362	Parliaments, Names of	410
Printing	363	People	411
Rocks and Gems	364	Royalty	413
Sciences and Studies	365	Royalty, UK	415
Scientific Instruments	366	Rulers, Names for	419
Scientists and Inventors	366	Social and Welfare Issues	419
Time and Calendars	367	Society, Other	420
Weapons and Military		Trade Unions	420
Technology	368	Treaties	421
Weapons, Famous	369	United Kingdom	422
Transport	370	United States	428
Air Transport	370	Wars and Battles	431
Aircraft, Famous Models	372	World Politics and History	437
Airlines, National	373	**Sport and Leisure**	**453**
Cars, Countries from	374	Leisure	455
Cars, Famous Models	374	Coins	455
Motorcycles, Famous	375	Cookery, Dishes	456
Other Transport	375	Cookery, Food	459
Rail Transport	376	Cookery, Terms	461
Road Transport	377	Drink	462
Roads	379	Drink, Cocktails	463
Sea and Water Transport	380	Drink, Made from	464
Ships, Famous	381	Fashion and Dress	464
Trains and Engines, Famous	382	Games	465
Society and Politics	**385**	Games, Terms from	467
Crime	387	Holidays and Festivals	467
Assassination and Murder	387	Leisure Activities and Skills	468
Assassination and Murder,		Stamps	469
Attempted	390	Sport	470
Crime Detection and Punishment	390	American Football	470
Crime, Other	391	Association Football	470
Fraud and Forgery	392	Athletics	474
Gangs and Gangsters	393	Awards and Trophies	477
Kidnapping	394	Badminton	477
Law	395	Baseball	478
Murderers	396	Basketball	478
Pirates	397	Bowling (Ten pin)	479
Robbery and Robbers	397	Bowls	479
Wild West, Outlaws and		Boxing	479
Highwaymen	398	Bullfighting	481
Economics and Business	399	Cricket	481
Advertising Slogans	399	Cycling	483
Companies and Business	400	Darts	484
Currencies	402	Equestrian Events	484
Currency, Slang	402	Fencing	485
Economics and Finance	403	Golf	485
Occupations, Traditional	404	Greyhound Racing	486
Politics and History	404	Gymnastics	486
Archaeology	404	Horse Racing	487
Colonies, Former	404	Motor Racing	489
Customs and Superstitions	405	Motorcycle Racing	491
Education	405	Olympic Games	491
Espionage	406	Other Sports	495
Heraldry	407	Rowing	497

Rugby League	497	Squash	508
Rugby Union	498	Swimming	508
Sailing	500	Table Tennis	509
Skating	500	Tennis	509
Skiing and Winter Sports	501	**The Universe and Space**	
Snooker	501	**Exploration**	**513**
Speedway	502	Astronomy and the Universe	515
Sport, General	502	Constellations	517
Sporting Terms	503	Space Exploration	517
Sportspeople	506	**Subject Index**	**521**

How to Use this Book

Guidelines Used in Selecting Information

What makes a good Quiz question? Obviously it has to be capable of being asked and replied to fairly concisely. It has to be capable of an unambiguous answer or set of answers. It has to be reasonably interesting and entertaining without being too obscure or difficult.

The main criterion used to select information for this book has been to aim to cover as wide a range of subjects as possible but, for reasons of space, be necessarily very selective in what information on any particular topic is included. Although the emphasis is inevitably on the unusual and surprising, care has been taken not to select items for these reasons alone. Though much of the information in the book could be classified as Trivia, and the main focus of the book is towards 'Popular' knowledge, an attempt has been made to preserve a balance with the inclusion of 'serious' subject matter as well.

In some cases, Pop Music for example, the shortage of space means that the information in this book might be considered fairly arbitrary and subjective. However, rather than leave out a topic like this entirely, an attempt has been made to select the most noteworthy and 'quizzable' information for inclusion in this volume.

Many shorter items as well are deliberately selective to allow the widest number of topics to be covered. Thus full lists of FA Cup Winners or International Number Plate Letters are not included, only a selected number of particularly noteworthy cases.

Information in numeric form is rarely suitable for quizzes, except when part of a multiple choice question, and thus is only included in exceptional cases. In some cases information such as dates are included as these may form part of the question which is asked. Information of a topical nature or which tends to change often is only included in a small number of cases.

Although a good quiz question should have a single answer or set of answers, some of the items of information in the book may be ambiguous or have many answers, not all of which may be given. This is intended for the type of quiz question or word game clue where several different pieces of information help to identify uniquely a person or thing. Consider, for example the entry in the 'Deaths' section of the People chapter, under Drowning.

Drowning Barbarossa, Harold Holt, Amy Johnson, Brian Jones (in swimming pool), Mary Jo Kopechne (at Chappaquidick), King Ludwig of Bavaria, Shelley (sailing off Italian coast), Dennis Wilson, Natalie Wood

This information could form part of a question such as:

Which member of the Rolling Stones was drowned?

to which of course there is only one answer. Many of the facts in the book similarly need to be combined with others to produce suitable quiz questions.

How the Book is Organised

The key to the successful use of this book is an understanding of how the information in it is organised, which is different from any other reference book and expressly designed for easy access to a particular item of information. The twelve Subject chapters are divided into narrower categories, e.g. the Entertainment chapter is divided into Cinema, Music, etc. These units are in turn divided into sections, such as Stars, Characters from Films, etc. Within the sections, in many cases, information on important topics is grouped together for easy reference. In order to avoid duplication of information, items are normally included in one section only.

The large number of individual items of information in the book would make a full index too long for inclusion, but a Subject Index is provided and is the first place to look if the section you want is not readily apparent from the Table of Contents.

For many topics, information is listed in two or more different ways, corresponding to the type of question that would most often be asked. For example, in the Table of Contents for the Entertainment chapter the entry under Film reads:

Films
  By: Description
  By: Title

Thus, for example, the film Chariots of Fire is listed in the Films by Title section as follows:

Chariots of Fire
  Harold Abrahams   Ben Cross
  Eric Liddell   Ian Charleson
  Olympics   1924, Paris

It is also listed by its main theme in the Film by Description section as:

Olympic Runners; Competition between   Chariots of Fire

This system of listing items of information in different ways corresponding to the type of question that might be asked about a particular topic is the key to finding the answer to those frustrating questions which defy conventional classification.

The heading for a section that appears as follows, for instance:

Association Football

By: General

indicates that the topic is presented as a single list. In some cases, examples of the format of the type of question the section provides answers for is given. Additional notes at the start of some sections give an indication of its area of coverage and other information that may be helpful. The *See Also:* heading at the start of a section, as in the example below, provides cross references with other sections, which can be referred to if the information you require is not in this particular one.

Military

See also: Wars and Battles/Science and Technology; Weapons

In many cases, information could fit into several categories and the reader may have to examine several sections of the book to find the required fact or facts. In general, items of information are listed under the most specific section that is relevant. Consider the question, for example:

What was the name of Queen Victoria's eldest daughter?

The answer to this is found in the Children section of the People chapter rather than under Royalty in the Politics and Society chapter. Similarly, within a section, a particular fact will tend to be listed under the most specific heading applicable. If you want to know what the longest snake is, for example, look for it first in the Land Animals section under Snake, rather than under Longest. This principle usually makes a particular fact easier to locate and also allows the type of information that is buried deep in conventional reference books to be easily accessible.

Although the book is divided into chapters under fairly conventional subject headings, these categories have deliberately been interpreted in a flexible way to incorporate the kind of information often wanted, but seldom available in works of reference. Thus, for instance, the Living World chapter includes a section on Famous Animals covering Animals from Literature and the Screen. Again the Transport category of the Science and Technology chapter contains a section on Famous Ships, and so on.

Notes

Ambiguous Entries

Because of the need to be as concise as possible, some entries may be ambiguous with regard to which is the subject in the entry. The Convention adopted in these cases is that the word the entry is listed under is the subject. For example, the entry:

Father; Shot   Marvin Gaye

means that (Marvin Gaye's) Father shot Marvin Gaye, not the other way round.

Errors and Omissions

As has already been mentioned, restrictions of size mean that the information in this book is unavoidably extremely selective and represents a very subjective choice in many cases. Nevertheless I am only too aware that many Quiz classics and notable facts warranting inclusion have been left out. In addition, in the course of the book's preparation, despite attempts to verify the information in it, errors of facts, spelling, etc. have inevitably crept in. Corrections and suggestions for additions and alterations would be most gratefully received and hopefully will be incorporated in future editions of the book. These can be sent to the author, care of the publishers, Pelham Books Ltd.

List Order, Multiple Items

Multiple word item headings and items with subsections are listed alphabetically by the first word and then subsequent words. Where a number of answers are listed for a particular item, these are generally in some meaningful order such as Alphabetical, or Chronological for Sports Achievements, etc.

List Order, Names

Names are normally listed by Surname. Where names of non-standard types are included, they are listed by the most relevant word, e.g. Mickey Mouse by Mickey.

List Order, Numbers

Numbers are listed by their alphabetic equivalent, e.g. 1984 is listed as if it were Nineteen Eighty-Four.

List Order, Titles

Items are listed alphabetically by the word most iikely to identify them. Where Titles are preceded by 'A' or 'The', these are ignored in the alphabetical sequence.

References to 'Title'

The word Title, as in:

The Singing Detective
   Title   Michael Gambon

indicates that the role of The Singing Detective was played by Michael Gambon, and is used for reasons of brevity.

Acknowledgements

It would be impossible to list the hundreds of books and periodicals that were used in the preparation of this book. However the following were particularly useful and repeatedly referred to in the course of writing the book.

Encyclopaedia Britannica
Pears Cyclopaedia
The Random House Encyclopedia
The Guinness Book of Records
The Guinness Book of British Hit Singles
The Book of Lists (Corgi)
The People's Almanac (Bantam Press)

Many people have helped with suggestions and encouragement during the preparation of this book. Special thanks to Amanda Hartley, Kevin Giles and Keith Eardley, to my wife Beth and family, to Ros Munro and Jennifer Bull – my editors at Pelham Books, and to Sharon Twyneham, Cherry Gaylard and Jane Bishop for typing the manuscript.

Art, Craft and Architecture

Contents

Architectural Terms 3
Art Terms 4
Artistic Movements and Schools
  By: Artist 5
Artists
  By: Description 6
Buildings
  By: Building name 8
Crafts 9
Galleries and Collections
  By: Gallery Name 10

Paintings
  By: Name of painting 10
  By: Description 12
Photographers
  By: Description 12
Sculptors
  By: Description 13
Sculptures
  By: Description 13
  By: Name 13

Architectural Terms

By: General

Arch(es);-	
Ends in a point	Ogee
Intersection, Curve of	Groin
Space between two with moulding on	Spandrel
Bauhaus;-	
Founder	Walter Gropius
Location	Weimar, then Dessau
Beam; Lowest below roof	Architrave
Bell Tower; Not attached to church	Campanile
Bond; Brickwork; Most common	English, Flemish
Buddhist Burial Mound	Stupa
Castle;-	
Court inside	Bailey
Inner tower	Keep
Iron gate which opens vertically	Portcullis
Tower at gate or drawbridge	Barbican
Church;-	
Central aisle	Nave
Gateway to churchyard with coffin resting place	Lych Gate
Screen sculptured, behind altar	Reredos
Seat; Bracket on for leaning	Misericord
Seat; For priests cut into chancel	Sedilia
Column(s);-	
Crowning feature	Capital
Human figure in form of	Caryatid
Supporting a handrail	Balustrade
Geodesic Dome; Inventor	Buckminster Fuller
Glass; Decorated over door	Fanlight
Gothic;-	
English styles	Early English, Decorated, Perpendicular
Main Feature	Point of Arch
Greek Orders;-	Doric, Ionic, Corinthian

Based on	Columns used
Oldest	Doric
Moulding; Zigzagged	Chevron
Plaster finish on walls	Stucco
Projecting part on top of building, etc.	Cornice
Roman Orders	Tuscan, Composite
Roof; Support for rafters	Purlin
Space in church for altar or statues	Apse
Spiral form used in decoration	Volute
Spout for rainwater, grotesquely carved	Gargoyle
Style(s);	
George IV; During reign	Regency
Heavy; Elaborately decorated, Renaissance	Baroque
Inigo Jones; Style of	Palladian
Light, early 18th Century, often with shell motif	Rococo
1920s and '30s	International
Wall;-	
Recess in	Niche
Support	Buttress
Support; Half Arch	Flying Buttress
Window;-	
Bar dividing glass vertically	Mullion
Stonework pattern in	Tracery
Tax on; 18th and 19th Centuries; Levied on	More than 6 windows
Wren; Inscription on tomb in St Paul's	'If you seek his monument, look around'

Art Terms

By: General

Altar piece;-	
2 panels	Diptych
3 panels	Triptych
More than 3 panels	Polyptych
Art Gallery; Largest	Hermitage, Leningrad
Balance of Light and Shade	Chiaroscuro
Cire Perdue	'Lost wax' technique for casting
Dada; Originated in	Zurich
Drawing; Preliminary for painting, etc.	Cartoon
Fauvism; Name from	Fauves (Wild Beasts)
Fired clay used for statues	Terracotta
Futurism; Painters' manifesto, Author of	Umberto Boccioni
Gothic; Name coined by	Giorgio Vasari
Impressionism;-	
Name from	Monet painting 'Impression: Sunrise'
Term invented by	Louis Leroy
Inanimate objects; Painting of	Still Life
Low relief sculpture	Bas relief
Paint made using egg yolk	Tempera

Picture made from various materials stuck together	Collage
Pointillism; Characteristic	Fine dots
Pop Art; Term invented by	Lawrence Alloway (critic)
Post-Impressionism; Term invented by	Roger Fry
Pre-Raphaelite Brotherhood; Critic who defended	John Ruskin
Religious Image	Icon
Royal Academy;-	
1st President	Sir Joshua Reynolds
Founded	1768
Statue, base	Podium
Stick used to rest brush hand when painting	Maulstick
Surface alteration on statue caused by age	Patina
Surrealism; Term invented by	Apollinaire (from title of play)
USSR; Post Revolution, Style associated with	Socialist Realism
Wall decoration; Design scratched through plaster layer	Sgraffito
Wall or Ceiling; Painting on	Fresco
Water Colour using opaque paint	Gouache

Artistic Movements and Schools

By: Artist → Movement

E.g.: What movement was associated with the Painter . . .

Arp	Dada
Aubrey Beardsley	Art Nouveau
Bomberg	Kitchen Sink School
Braque	Cubism
Bratby	Kitchen Sink School
Brueghel (the Elder)	Antwerp School
Burne-Jones	Pre-Raphaelite Brotherhood
Cézanne	Cubism, Impressionism
Corbet	Realism
Dali	Surrealism
De Kooning	Abstract Expressionism
Degas	Impressionism
Robert Delaunay	Orphism
Derain	Fauvism
Marcel Duchamp	Dada
El Greco	Mannerism
Max Ernst	Surrealism
Gauguin	Pont-Aven School
Grandma Moses	Primitivism, Naive Art
David Hockney	Pop Art (Originally)
Holman Hunt	Pre-Raphaelite Brotherhood
Kandinsky	Der Blaue Reiter (Blue Rider)

Ernst Kirchner	Die Brücke (The Bridge)
Klee	Der Blaue Reiter (Blue Rider)
Wyndham Lewis	Vorticism
Roy Lichtenstein	Pop Art
Magritte	Surrealism
Cazimir Malevich	Suprematism
Manet	Impressionism
Matisse	Fauvism
Millais	Pre-Raphaelite Brotherhood
Mondrian	De Stijl (The Style)
Monet	Impressionism
William Morris	Pre-Raphaelite Brotherhood, Arts and Crafts Movement
Parmigianino	Mannerism
Picasso	Cubism
Pissaro	Impressionism
Jackson Pollock	Action Painting, Abstract Expressionism
Renoir	Impressionism
Bridget Riley	Op Art
Dante Gabriel Rossetti	Pre-Raphaelite Brotherhood
Mark Rothko	Abstract Expressionism
Roualt	Fauvism
Rousseau	Barbizon School, Primitivism, Naive Art
Rubens	Antwerp School, Baroque
George Seurat	Pointillism
Tristan Tzara	Dada
Van Doesburg	De Stijl (The Style)
Van Dyck	Antwerp School, Baroque
Velasquez	Baroque
Vlaminck	Fauvism
Andy Warhol	Pop Art
Watteau	Rococo

Artists

By: Description → Artist

Autobiography; First written by artist	Lorenzo Ghiberti
Baker held paintings because of unpaid bill	Vermeer
Ballet *Parade*; Did stage design for	Picasso
Bankrupt; Declared	Rembrandt
Bed; Shared with poet, Max Jacob	Picasso
Birth; Abandoned as stillborn by midwife	Picasso
Brush strapped to hand, painted with	Renoir
Buried inside city despite dying of plague	Titian
Circle; Drew for Pope to show skill	Giotto
Court Painter;-	
Charles I	Van Dyck
Charles IV (of Spain)	Goya
Charles V (of Spain)	Titian

Henry VIII	Hans Holbein (the Younger)
Philip IV (of Spain)	Velasquez
Crete; Came from	El Greco
Critic; Marriage annulled because of non-consummation	John Ruskin
Death; 1987, Pop Artist	Andy Warhol
Ear; Cut off his own	Van Gogh
Faker;-	
Samuel Palmer paintings	Tom Keating
Vermeer paintings	Hans van Meegeren
Forged; Most of all artists	Corot
Horses; Known for portraits of	George Stubbs
Imprisoned;-	
Accused of destroying monument	Courbet
For cartoon	Daumier
Over homosexuality charge	Leonardo da Vinci
Insane at end of life	Van Gogh
Inventions; Drew numerous	Leonardo da Vinci
Knighted;-	
By Britain and Spain	Rubens
English painter: 1st	Lord Leighton
Legs; Broken, leaving deformed	Toulouse Lautrec
Matchstick people and objects, Known for	L.S.Lowry
Military Engineer (for Cesare Borgia)	Leonardo da Vinci
Mirror writing; Wrote notes in	Leonardo da Vinci
Monk; Runs off with nun	Fra Filippo Lippi
Moulin Rouge; Pictures of	Toulouse Lautrec
Murder; Exiled for	Caravaggio
Name; Changes 33 times	Hokusai
Name Means;-	
Hulking Tom	Masaccio
Little Barrel	Botticelli
Little Dyer (from father's occupation)	Tintoretto
Nose; Permanently broken after quarrel	Michelangelo
Obscene; Only exhibition closed as	Modigliani
Paintings; Most	Picasso
Paints over most pictures	Francis Bacon
Patron(ess);-	
Lord Egremont of Petworth	Turner
Archduchess Isabella	Rubens
Queen Maria Luisa of Spain	Goya
Medici family	Michelangelo
Periods; Blue, Rose (Pink)	Picasso
Perspective; Believed discoverer of	Brunelleschi
Priest; To Belgian mining district, Sent as	Van Gogh
Rubens; Chief assistant to	Van Dyck
Ruskin accused of 'Throwing a pot of paint in the Public's face'	Whistler
Saturday Evening Post covers; Famous for	Norman Rockwell
Sold only one painting (Red Vineyard)	Van Gogh
Storm; Tied to ship's mast during, to paint	Turner
Subject;-	
American Revolutionary leaders	Charles Willson Peale

Ballet	Edgar Degas
Birds	John Audubon
Comic strip based pictures	Roy Lichtenstein
Landscapes	Constable
Portraits	Gainsborough
US Flag	Jasper Johns.
Tahiti; Lived in	Paul Gauguin
Titian's verdict on: 'He will never be anything but a dauber'	Tintoretto
Wellington; Threw plaster cast at	Goya

Buildings

By: Building name → Architect, General

See Also: Geography and Places; Houses, Famous

Adelphi	Robert Adam
Albert Memorial	George Gilbert Scott
The Bauhaus, Dessau	Walter Gropius
Blenheim Palace	Vanbrugh
Brasilia	Oscar Niemeyer (Buildings), Lucio Costa (Town Design)
Brighton Pavilion	John Nash
Built for	George IV
Buckingham Palace (Remodelled)	John Nash
Canterbury Cathedral	William of Sens
Cenotaph, London	Sir Edwin Lutyens
Chandigarh	Le Corbusier
Chiswick House	Lord Burlington
Colonnade, St Peter's Rome	Bernini
Coventry Cathedral	Sir Basil Spence
Crystal Palace	Sir Joseph Paxton
Built in	Hyde Park
Destroyed by fire	1936
Moved to	Sydenham Hill
Duomo (Campanile), Florence	Giotto
'Falling Water' Bear Run, Pennsylvania	Frank Lloyd Wright
Built for	Kaufmann family
Florence Cathedral, Dome	Brunelleschi
Fontainebleau	Primaticcio, Serlio
Foreign Office	George Gilbert Scott
Glasgow School of Art	Charles Rennie Mackintosh
Guggenheim Museum, New York	Frank Lloyd Wright
Houses of Parliament	Charles Barry, Augustus Pugin
Kings Cross Station	Lewis Cubitt
Church of La Sagrada Familia, Barcelona	Antonio Gaudi
Leaning Tower of Pisa	Bonnano, Buschetto
Luton Hoo	Robert Adam
Marble Arch	John Nash
Nelson's Column (Lions)	Edward Landseer
New Delhi, Government Buildings	Edwin Lutyens
Notre Dame Du Maut, Ronchamp	Le Corbusier
Paris Opera	Charles Garnier
Portmeirion	Clough Williams Ellis

Based on	Portofino, Italy
Regent Street	John Nash
Regent's Park	John Nash
Rijksmuseum	P.J.H.Cuypers
Royal Crescent, Bath	John Wood
Royal Exchange	Sir Christopher Wren
Royal Pavilion, Brighton	John Nash
Seagram Building, New York	Mies Van der Rohe
Somerset House	Sir William Chambers
St Pancras Station	George Gilbert Scott
St Paul's Cathedral	Sir Christopher Wren
St Peter's, Rome	Donato Bramante
Strawberry Hill	Horace Walpole
Sydney Opera House	Joern Utzon
Syon House	John Adam
Turin Exhibition Hall	Pier Nervi
United Nations Building, New York	Le Corbusier
Versailles Palace	Louis Le Vau
Decorator	Le Brun
Gardens	Le Notre
Hall of mirrors	Massart
Villa Rotunda, Vicenta	Palladio
Washington	Major Pierre L'Enfant
Westminster Cathedral	J.F.Bentley

Crafts

By: General

See Also: Sports and Leisure; Leisure Activities and Skills

Arts and Crafts movement; Founder	William Morris
Bayeux Tapestry; Why misnomer	Embroidered
Carved stone (often oval), On background of	Cameo
China; Dresden; Where made	Meissen
Cutouts; Glued to furniture and varnished	Découpage
Decorative style;-	
1880s–1910, Flower motifs	Art Nouveau
1920s and '30s	Art Deco
Enamelling;-	
Base	Flux
Types	Champlève, Cloisonné, Basse-taille, Pliqué-a-jour
Engraver; German; 15th–16th Century	Albrecht Dürer
Engraving; Cut into a material	Intaglio
Furniture;-	
Decoration using inlay of wood of different colours	Intarsia
English Designers; Famous	Chippendale, Hepplewhite, Sheraton
Gems; Cutting and polishing; Craft of	Lapidary
Gilded mountings on furniture and clocks, 18th Century France	Ormolu

Gold and precious metal ware; Official stamp on	Hallmark
Goldsmith; Italian; Famous	Benvenuto Cellini
Greek drinking cup	Cylix
Greek vase or storage jar	Amphora
Hallmarks; Hall that name derives from	Goldsmith's Hall
Hallmarks; UK;-	
Anchor	Birmingham
Castle	Edinburgh
Leopard's Head	Goldsmith's Hall, London
Rose	Sheffield
Inlay work in Wood, Metal, Ivory, etc.	Marquetry
Lacquered decoration on furniture; Craft of	Japanning
Porcelain; Name from	Porcellus – Little Pig
Tapestry;-	
French 17th Century workshop	Gobelins
Largest	Christ in Glory, Coventry Cathedral
Tool; Cutting designs in gold, used for	Burin
Wedgwood; Factory at	Etruria
Wire;-	
Beaten into engraving	Damascening
Gold or silver applied to a surface in fine pattern	Filigree
Woodcarver; Decorated Windsor Castle, Hampton Court	Grinling Gibbons
Writing; Art of	Calligraphy

Galleries and Collections

By: Gallery Name → Location, General

Guggenheim Museum	New York
Hermitage	St Petersburg
Kunsthistorisches Museum	Vienna
Louvre	Paris. World's Largest
Metropolitan Museum of Art	New York
Museum of Modern Art	New York
National Gallery	London
Pitti Palace	Florence
Prado	Madrid
Rijksmuseum	Amsterdam
Tate Gallery	London
Uffizi Gallery	Florence
Wallace Collection	Hertford House, London
Originator	Marquess of Hertford

Paintings

By: Name of painting → Artist, General

Adoration of the Lamb,The	Van Eyck
Adoration of the Shepherds,The	Correggio
Arnolfini Wedding,The	Van Eyck

Arrangement in Grey and Black	James Whistler
Popular Name	*Whistler's Mother*
Assumption of the Virgin,The	Correggio
Location	On Dome of Parma Cathedral
Assumption,The	Titian
At the Moulin Rouge (and others of	
Moulin Rouge)	Toulouse-Lautrec
Birth of Venus,The	Sandro Botticelli
Blue Boy,The	Thomas Gainsborough
Breaking Wave of Kahagaura,The	Hokusai
Bubbles	Sir John Millais
Subject	Grandson, later Admiral William
	James
Used as advertisement by	Pears Soap
Campbell's Soup Tins	Andy Warhol
Children's Games	Pieter Brueghel (the Elder)
Cornfield	Constable
Coventry Cathedral, Windows	John Piper
Death of Marat	Jacques-Louis David
Déjeuner sur l'Herbe	Manet
Demoiselles d'Avignon	Picasso
Fighting Temeraire,The	Turner
Flatford Mill	Constable
Flight into Egypt	Jacopo Bassano
Garden of (Earthly) Delights,	
The	Hieronymus Bosch
Parts	*Creation, The Flood, Hill*
Gleaners,The	Millet
Guernica	Picasso
Hay Wain,The	Constable
Location	National Gallery
Farm	Willy Lott's
Hundred Views of Mt Fuji,A	Hokusai
I Want You (US Recruitment Poster,	
WWI)	James Montgomery Flagg
Judgement of Paris,The	Rubens
Last Supper,The	Leonardo Da Vinci
On	Walls of St Maria delle Grazie,
	Milan
Laughing Cavalier,The	Franz Hals
Les Parapluies	Renoir
Marriage à la mode	William Hogarth
Marriage Feast at Cana of Galilee,The	Veronese
Mona Lisa	Leonardo da Vinci
Eyebrows	None
Location	The Louvre
Real Title	*La Gioconda*
Mona Lisa (with a moustache)	Marcel Duchamp
Naked Maja,The	Goya
Night Watch,The	Rembrandt
Nude Descending a Staircase	Marcel Duchamp
Potato Eaters,The	Van Gogh
Primavera	Botticelli
Raft of the Medusa,The	Gericault
Rake's Progress,The	William Hogarth
Rokeby Venus,The	Velasquez
Scream (The Cry)	Edvard Munch

Sistine Chapel ceiling (Vatican) Time taken	Michelangelo 4 years
Sunday Afternoon on the Grand-Jatte	George Seurat
Twittering Machine	Paul Klee
Venus of Urbino	Titian
View of Toledo	El Greco
Water Seller,The	Velasquez
Whaam!	Roy Lichtenstein

Paintings

By: Description → Painting, Painter

Cubism; Picture that began	*Les Demoiselles d'Avignon* (Picasso)
Medici Family; Portayed as Magi	*Adoration of the Magi* (Botticelli)
Portrait;-	
Destroyed by subject's wife	Graham Sutherland's portrait of Churchill
Head sewn on for, after execution	Duke of Monmouth
Made Henry VIII marry	Anne of Cleves (Holbein)
Naked and Clothed version	*Naked Maja, Clothed Maja* (Goya)
Wellington; Stolen 1961 and later found	Goya
Spanish Civil War; Bombed village inspired	*Guernica*
Spanish revolt against French, 1808; Painted	*Second of May, Third of May* (Goya)
Suffragette slashed in National Gallery	*Rokeby Venus* (Velasquez)
Upside down; Picture displayed	Matisse's *Le Bateau* at New York Museum of Modern Art
Value; Highest	*Mona Lisa*

Photographers

By: Description → Photographer

Blow Up (Film); Photographer in, based on (reputedly)	David Bailey
Book of Photographs; 1st	Fox Talbot (*The Pencil of Nature*)
Child Labour in US; Photographs exposed	Lewis Hine
Harper's Bazaar; Fashion Photographer with	Richard Avedon
How the Other Half Lives; Book of photographs	Jacob Riis
Human and animal movement; Photographic study of	Edward Muybridge
Let us now praise famous men; Pictures of sharecroppers	Walker Evans, James Agee (text)
Paris by Night; Book of photographs	Brassai
Photo Session Group; Formed	Alfred Steiglitz
Royal Family; Prominent Photographer	Lord Lichfield

Surrealist Painter also; Noted	Man Ray
Trouble and Strife; Photographs of Wife, Marie Helvin	David Bailey
US Depression; Photographs of	Dorothea Lange
War Photographer; 1st	Roger Fenton

Sculptors

By: Description → Name

Holes in Sculptures; Known for	Henry Moore, Barbara Hepworth
Household Objects, Huge sculptures of; Known for	Claes Oldenberg
Mobiles; Known for	Alexander Calder
Ready Mades; Known for	Marcel Duchamp
Refused entrance to French Academy 3 times	Auguste Rodin
Soft Sculptures; Known for	Claes Oldenberg
Sticklike Figures; Known for	Giacometti
Wrapping buildings and natural objects; Known for	Christo

Sculptures

By: Description → Sculpture, Sculptor

Court case takes place over refusal of Work of Art Status on entry to US	*Bird in Space* (Brancusi)
Nude; First since Roman times	*David* (Donatello)
Parthenon, Mainly from; In British Museum	Elgin Marbles
Urinal; Entered in exhibition	*Fountain* (Marcel Duchamp)

Sculptures

By: Name of → Sculptor, General

Aphrodite	Praxiteles
Baptistry doors, Florence	Lorenzo Ghiberti. Two sets, including 'Gates of Paradise'
Material	Bronze
Bird in Space	Constantin Brancusi
Burghers of Calais, The	Rodin
Cathedra Petri, St Peter's, Rome	Bernini
Crazy Horse	Korczak Ziolkowski
David, Florence	Michelangelo, Donatello (Bronze)
Discobolus (Discus Thrower)	Myron
Ecce Homo	Jacob Epstein
Ecstasy of St Theresa	Bernini
Eros, Piccadilly Circus	Sir Alfred Gilbert
Proper Name	*Shaftesbury Memorial*
Gate of Hell, The	Rodin (Unfinished bronze door,

	Paris)
Kiss,The	Rodin
Lovers	Paulo Malatesta, Francesca Da Rimini
Lions, Trafalgar Square	Sir Edwin Landseer
Monument to the Third International	Tatlin ('Tatlin's Tower')
Moses, Rome	Michelangelo
Mount Rushmore; *Presidents*	Gutzon Borglum
Presidents	Washington, Jefferson, Lincoln, Theodore Roosevelt
Nelson, Trafalgar Square	Edward Hodges Baily
Parthenon	Pheidias
Perseus and the Head of Medusa	Benvenuto Cellini
Pieta, St Peter's, Rome	Michelangelo
Statue of Liberty	Augusto Bartholdi (Copy by Gustave Eiffel)
Official name	*Liberty Enlightening the World*
Gift from	France
Thinker,The	Rodin
Originally meant to be	Dante
Trevi Fountain, Rome	Nicola Salvi
Venus de Milo;-	
Discoverer	Dumond D'Urville
Found on	Melos
Location	Louvre
Missing	Arms

Entertainment

Contents:

Cinema	**17**
Characters from Films	
By: Name	17
Cinema, General	21
Films	
By: Description	23
By: Title	26
Film Quotes and Publicity Blurbs	
By: Quote	49
Musical Themes	
By: Film	50
Songs from Films	
By: Song	51
Stars and Directors	
By: Description	52
By: Name	54
Music	**56**
Backing Groups	
By: Singer	56
Classical Music, General	57
Composers	57
Musical Instruments	58
Musical Terms	58
Musical Works	
By: Description	59
By: Title	60
Musical Works, Common Names	
By: Title	61
Musicians	62
Musicians, Instruments played	
By: Name	62
Opera Characters	
By: Character	63
Operas	
By: Description	65
By: Title	65
Pop Groups/Singers	
By: Description	67
By: Name	68
Pop LPs/Albums	
By: Title	80
Pop Music, Other	82
Pop Records	
By: Description	83
Pop Singles	
By: Title	84
Singers, Classical	94
Songs and Tunes	
By: Title	94
Stage Entertainment	**96**
Ballets	
By: Name	96
Dance and Ballet	96
Musicals	
By: Description	97
By: Title	97
Musicals, Songs from	
By: Title	99
Theatre, Variety, etc.	99
TV and Radio	**100**
Catchphrases	
By: Catchphrase	100
Radio, General	102
Radio Programmes	
By: Name	102
TV and Radio Characters	
By: Character	104
TV, General	106
TV and Radio Personalities	
By: Description	107
By: Name	108
TV Programmes	
By: Description	108
By: Name	109

CINEMA

Characters from Films

By: Name → Film, General

Charlie Allnut	*The African Queen*
Norman Bates	*Psycho*
C.C.Baxter	*The Apartment*
Max Bialystock	*The Producers*
Travis Bickle	*Taxi Driver*
Don Birnam	*The Lost Weekend*
Rick Blaine	*Casablanca* (Café Owner)
Leo Bloom	*The Producers*
Blue Meanies	*Yellow Submarine*
James Bond	
Cover company	**Universal import and export**
David Niven as	*Casino Royale* ('Sir James')

Elder brother	Henry
Favourite drink	Vodka Martini (Shaken not stirred)
1st Film	*Dr No*
George Lazenby as	*On Her Majesty's Secret Service*
Guns	Beretta, Walther PPK, .38 Smith & Wesson
Number	007 (00 is licence to kill)
Played by	Sean Connery (7 times), David Niven, George Lazenby, Roger Moore, Timothy Dalton
Roger Moore; 1st	*Live and Let Die*
Sean Connery; Comeback	*Never Say Never Again*
Secret Service Chief	M (Bernard Lee)
Timothy Dalton	*The Living Daylights, Licence to Kill*
Wife for one day	Tracy
Betty Boop	Creator: Max Fleischer
Sally Bowles	*Cabaret*
Johnny Boy	*Mean Streets*
Benjamin Braddock	*The Graduate*
Velvet Brown	*National Velvet*
Joe Buck	*Midnight Cowboy*
Bugs Bunny	
Creator	Chuck Jones
Hunter	Elmer J.Fudd
Voice	Mel Blanc
C3PO	*Star Wars*
Harry Callahan	
Films	*Dirty Harry, Magnum Force, The Enforcer, Sudden Impact*
Gun	.44 Colt Magnum
Played by	Clint Eastwood
Cisco Kid	
Horse	Diablo
Sidekick	Pancho
Inspector Clouseau	
Played by	Peter Sellers (*Pink Panther* films). Alan Arkin in *Inspector Clouseau*
Valet	Kato (Burt Kwouk)
Rooster Cogburn	*True Grit*
Vito Corleone	*The Godfather*
Cornelius	*Planet of the Apes*
Jack Crabb	*Little Big Man*
Apollo Creed	*Rocky II*
Ann Darrow	*King Kong*
D'Ascoyne Family	*Kind Hearts and Coronets*
Norma Desmond	*Sunset Boulevard*
Cruella De Ville	*101 Dalmatians*
Donald Duck	
1st Film	*The Little Wise Hen*
Girlfriend	Daisy
Nephews	Huey, Dewey, Louie
Voice	Clarence Nash
Michael Dorsey	*Tootsie*
Elwood P.Dowd	*Harvey*
Popeye Doyle	*The French Connection*
Dracula	
Based on	Bram Stoker story
From	Transylvania

Original choice	Lon Chaney (Senior)
Played by	Bela Lugosi (1st Hollywood film)
Bulldog Drummond	Played by: Richard Johnson
Dumbo	Disney's Flying Elephant
Falstaff	Played by: Orson Welles (*Chimes at Midnight*)
Fat Man, The	*The Maltese Falcon*
Fast Eddie Felson	*The Hustler*
Flint	Played by: James Coburn
Frankenstein	
Assistant	Igor
Creator of monster	Dr Victor Frankenstein
Director; 1st Film	James Whale
From	Mary Shelley story
Monster played by; 1st	Boris Karloff
Miss Froy	*The Lady Vanishes*
Dorothy Gale	*The Wizard of Oz*
Pussy Galore	*Goldfinger* (Honor Blackman)
Chauncey Gardner	*Being There*
Godzilla	Radioactive Tyrannosaurus Rex
Holly Golightly	*Breakfast at Tiffany's* (Audrey Hepburn)
Flash Gordon	Played by: Buster Crabbe (1930s)
Grandier	*The Devils* (Oliver Reed)
Grusinskaya	*Grand Hotel*
Hal	*2001* (Computer)
Andy Hardy	Played by: Mickey Rooney
Alec Harvey	*Brief Encounter*
Harvey	Invisible giant rabbit
Friend of	Elwood P.Dowd (James Stewart)
Billy Hayes	*Midnight Express*
Herbie	Volkswagen in Disney films: *The Love Bug*, etc.
Sherlock Holmes	1930s–1940s, played by: Basil Rathbone (Dr Watson – Nigel Bruce)
Robin Hood	Played by: Errol Flynn (1938)
Hotlips Hoolihan	*M.A.S.H.*
Hunchback of Notre Dame	Played by: Lon Chaney, Anthony Quinn, James Cagney, Charles Laughton
Adenoid Hynkel	*The Great Dictator*
Oliver Barrett IV	*Love Story*
Lucas Jackson	*Cool Hand Luke*
Cody Jarrett	*White Heat*
Jaws	*The Spy Who Loved Me* (1st)
Played by	Richard Kiel
Laura Jesson	*Brief Encounter*
Tom Joad	*The Grapes of Wrath*
Sugar Kane	*Some Like it Hot*
Will Kane	*High Noon*
Obi Ben Kenobi	*Star Wars*
Keystone Cops	
Creator	Mack Sennett
Leader	Ford Sterling
Colonel Kurtz	*Apocalypse Now*
Clubber Lang	*Rocky III*
Flower Belle Lee	*My Little Chickadee*

19

Princess Leia	*Star Wars*
Harry Lime	*The Third Man*
Don Lockwood	*Singin' in the Rain*
Lola Lola	*The Blue Angel*
Tracy Lord	*The Philadelphia Story*
Ilsa Lund	*Casablanca*
John McClane	*Die Hard* (and sequel)
Man with no name, The	Clint Eastwood in Spaghetti Westerns
Tony Manero	*Saturday Night Fever*
Randall McMurphy	*One flew Over the Cuckoo's Nest*
John Merrick	*The Elephant Man*
Mickey Mouse	
Created	1928
1st Film; Made	*Plane Crazy*
1st Film; Released	*Steamboat Willie*
1st Film; Sound	*Steamboat Willie*
Originally called	Mortimer Mouse
Voice; 1st	Walt Disney
Minnesota Fats	*The Hustler*
Terry Molloy	*On the Waterfront*
Mr Moto	
Creator	John Marquand
Played by	Peter Lorre
Harry Palmer	
Based on	Len Deighton books
Films	*Ipcress File, Funeral in Berlin, Billion Dollar Brain*
Played by	Michael Caine
Phantom of the Opera	Title: Lon Chaney (1925 version)
Dr Phibes	Vincent Price
Hawkeye Pierce	*M.A.S.H.*
Popeye	
Enemy	Bluto
Food	Spinach
Girlfriend	Olive Oyl
Harry Powell	*Night of the Hunter*
Tom Powers	*Public Enemy*
R2D2	*Star Wars*
Rambo	1st film: *First Blood*
Nurse Ratched	*One flew Over the Cuckoo's Nest*
Ratso	*Midnight Cowboy*
Ringo Kid	*Stagecoach*
Road Runner, The	
Chased by	Wile E.Coyote
Says	'Beep Beep' (name)
Robby the Robot	*Forbidden Planet*
Mrs Robinson	*The Graduate*
Rose Sayer	*The African Queen*
Tony Scamonte	*Scarface*
Shaft	
First Name	John
Played by	Richard Roundtree
Simon Sparrow, the Doctor	Played by: Dirk Bogarde
Han Solo	*Star Wars*
Jim Stark	*Rebel Without a Cause*
Rocky Sullivan	*Angels with Dirty Faces*
Superman	
Girlfriend	Lois Lane

Lives in	Metropolis
Newspaper	*Daily Planet*
Secret identity	Clark Kent
Vulnerable to	Kryptonite
Tarzan	
Chimpanzee	Cheta
1st	Elmo Lincoln
1st, with sound	Johnny Weismuller
Swimmers who played	Weismuller, Buster Crabbe
Thin Man	
Based on	Dashiel Hammett stories
Nick Charles	William Powell
Nora	Myrna Loy
Original part	Edward Ellis
Roger Thornhill	*North by Northwest*
Virgil Tibbs	*In the Heat of the Night*
Tinkerbell	Walt Disney's Peter Pan
Modelled on	Marilyn Monroe
Caleb Trask	*East of Eden*
Cuthbert J.Twillie	*My Little Chickadee*
Darth Vader	*Star Wars*
Sarah Woodruff	*The French Lieutenant's Woman*
Woody Woodpecker	Laugh: Mel Blanc
Zorro	
Deaf servant	Bernardo
Ended by	Censorship Office
Real identity	Don Diego de Vega

Cinema, General

By: General

Academy of Motion Picture Arts and Sciences; 1st President	Douglas Fairbanks
Age categories; Former	AA, over 14
Animals, Award to	Patsy
Cannes; Best film award	Golden Palm
Cannon Pictures; Owners	Yoram Globus, Menahem Golam
Censor; 1st British; Unusual attribute	Blind
Censorship:-	
US Code	Hay's Code
Western country without	Belgium
Children's story; Most filmed	*Cinderella*
Cinema; 1st US name for	Nickelodeon
Cinemascope:-	
1st Film	*The Robe*
Lens used for	Anamorphic
Dynamation; Creator	Ray Harryhausen
Extras; Most	*Gandhi*
Feature film; 1st	*The Squaw Man*
Fictional character; Most portrayed	Sherlock Holmes
Gossip columnists; Hollywood 1930s	Hedda Hopper, Louella Parsons
Historical character; Most portrayed	Napoleon
India; 1st screen kiss	1978 (Shashi Kapoor)
Keystone Studios; Director associated with	Mack Sennett
Kiss; Longest; Commercial Film	Regis Toomey, Jane Wyman (*You're in the army now*)
Moneymaker; Top; 1960s	*Sound of Music*

Neo-realism; 1st Film	*Rome, Open City* (Rosselini)
Oscar;	Award made by (US) Academy of Motion Picture Arts & Science (Academy Awards)
Best Actor; 1st	Emil Jannings
Best Actor; 1st black	Sidney Poitier (*Lilies of the Field*)
Best Actor/Actress; Same film	Clarke Gable, Claudette Colbert (*It Happened One Night*)
	Jack Nicholson, Louise Fletcher (*One Flew Over the Cuckoo's Nest*)
	Peter Finch, Faye Dunaway (*Network*)
	Jon Voight, Jane Fonda (*Coming Home*)
	Henry Fonda, Katharine Hepburn (*On Golden Pond*)
Best Actress; 1st	Janet Gaynor
Best Actress; 1st black (Supporting)	Hattie McDaniel (*Gone with the Wind*)
Cartoon character	Mickey Mouse
Consecutive years; Best Actor	Spencer Tracy
Father and Son, Same film	John and Walter Huston, *Treasure of the Sierra Madre*
Film; 1st	*Wings* (1927–1928)
Film; 1st British	*Hamlet* (1948)
Film; Most	*Ben Hur* (11)
Film; Most nominations	*All About Eve*
Husband and Wife; 1st	Lawrence Olivier, Vivien Leigh
Most	Walt Disney
Most (Acting)	Katherine Hepburn (4)
Oldest	George Burns
Posthumous	Peter Finch
Refusal; 1st	Walter Wanger (Director)
Refusal; Actor	George C.Scott (*Patton*), Marlon Brando (*The Godfather*)
Size	13 inches high, 8 pounds weight
Theatrical equivalent	Tony
Youngest	Shirley Temple (5 – Special Oscar), Tatum O'Neal (10 – Full Oscar)
President; Most portrayed	Lincoln
Road pictures;-	
Stars of	Bob Hope, Bing Crosby, Dorothy Lamour
Titles	*Bali, Hong-Kong, Morocco, Rio, Singapore, Utopia, Zanzibar*
Sound film; 1st	*The Jazz Singer*, with Al Jolson. 1st words: 'Wait a minute, you ain't heard nothing yet'
Sport; Most films about	Boxing
Stars' Feet and other prints	In cement outside Grauman's Chinese Theatre, Hollywood
Story for film; Most paid for	*The Clansman* (*Birth of a Nation*)
20th Century Fox; Founder	William Fox
United Artists; Formed by	Chaplin, D.W.Griffiths, Fairbanks, Pickford
Worst Actress of the Year award	Natalie Wood Award (*Harvard Lampoon*)
X Certificate; Introduced	1950

Films

By; Description → Title

Notes: Includes Themes, Famous Scenes, etc.

Airforce Pilots; Rivalry between two	*Top Gun*
Alcoholism	*The Lost Weekend*
Alien comes to earth seeking water supply	*The Man Who Fell to Earth*
Angel stops businessman from committing suicide	*It's a Wonderful Life*
Amish (Religious group)	*Witness*
Assassination of a Greek politician	*Z*
Barrel; Bath in	*Red Dust* (Jean Harlow)
Baseball Team saved by female pitcher	*The Bad News Bears*
Billie Holliday; Life of	*Lady Sings the Blues* (Diana Ross)
Blind girl;-	
In house; Terrorised by criminals	*Wait Until Dark* (Audrey Hepburn)
Sight restored by operation	*City Lights*
Blood; Submarine sails in; Inside body	*Fantastic Voyage*
Books; All confiscated and burned	*Fahrenheit 451*
Boots; Prospector eats	*The Gold Rush*
Bra; Cantilevered; Designed for Jane Russell	*The Outlaw*
Brainwashed Korean War veteran carries out assassinations	*The Manchurian Candidate*
Bread Rolls and forks; Dance with	*The Gold Rush*
Broken Leg; Journalist with, sees murder	*Rear Window*
Bus balanced on edge of cliff; Ends with	*The Italian Job*
Butter; Sex scene with	*Last Tango in Paris*
Cabin, on a ship; Filled up with people	*A Night at the Opera*
Canoe party face fight for survival	*Deliverance*
Carry on film; 1st	*Carry on Sergeant*
Cartoon;-	
Accused of Immorality (1930s)	*Betty Boop*
X Certificate; 1st	*Fritz the Cat* (Ralph Bakshi)
Ceiling and Walls; Dances on	*Royal Wedding* (Fred Astaire)
Chameleon; Human	*Zelig* (Woody Allen)
Chariot Race	*Ben Hur*
Chess; Knight plays with death	*The Seventh Seal*
Child Prostitute in New Orleans	*Pretty Baby*
Children only; Gangster musical	*Bugsy Malone*
Chile; Parents try to find disappeared son	*Missing*
Chopin; Life of	*A Song to Remember*
Chorus Girl Sequences; Filmed from above	*Busby Berkeley Musicals*
Churchill; Plot to assassinate, in WWII	*The Eagle has Landed*
Clock, on side of building; Clings to hand	*Safety Last* (Harold Lloyd)
Cloning; Nazi attempts at	*The Boys from Brazil*
Conman assisted by little girl	*Paper Moon*
Criminals released for WWII operation	*The Dirty Dozen*
Crop Dusting Aeroplane attacks hero	*North by Northwest*
Cynthia Payne; Based on life of	*Personal Services*
Dance Marathons; 1930s	*They Shoot Horses – Don't They*

23

D-Day Landings	*The Longest Day*
Dentist;-	
Former; Tortures victim	*The Marathon Man* (Laurence Olivier)
Mistaken for gunfighter	*The Paleface* (Bob Hope)
Devil; Makes pregnant	*Rosemary's Baby* (Mia Farrow)
Devil's Island; Escape from	*Papillon*
Director pretends to be a tramp	*Sullivan's Travels*
Disk Jockey; Phoned by disturbed fan	*Play Misty for Me* (Clint Eastwood)
Dockland, New York; Corruption in	*On the Waterfront*
Douglas Bader; Life of	*Reach for the Sky*
Drag; Actor dresses in, to get part	*Tootsie*
Drug smuggler's ordeal in Turkish jail	*Midnight Express*
Eggs; Eats 50 hard boiled, for a bet	*Cool Hand Luke*
Eiffel Tower models used to smuggle gold	*The Lavender Hill Mob*
Electric Chair; Gangster feigns fear when facing	*Angels with Dirty Faces*
Elephant;	
Taken across Alps	*Hannibal Brooks*
Water skiing	*Honky Tonk Freeway*
Empire State Building; Aircraft attack on	*King Kong*
Eskimo Life; Documentary on	*Nanook of the North*
Explosion; Petrol tank; Dies on top of	*White Heat* (James Cagney)
Explosives; Four drivers have to Transport, in South America	*The Wages of Fear*
Eye; Sliced with razor; Opening sequence	*Un Chien Andalou*
Fanny Brice; Life of	*Funny Girl*
Food; People made into	*Soylent Green*
Game; In the future; Used to work off aggressions	*Rollerball*
Gardener becomes Presidential Advisor	*Being There*
George Cohan; Life of	*Yankee Doodle Dandy*
Grapefruit; Pushes in girlfriend's face	*Public Enemy* (James Cagney to Mae Clarke)
Gunfighter faces twin brother	*Cat Ballou* (Lee Marvin)
Hairdresser in Beverly Hills	*Shampoo* (Warren Beatty)
Headmaster; Race to get to conference	*Clockwise*
Heroin Shipment; Locating	*The French Connection*
Horse race; 1000 mile	*Bite the Bullet*
Idiot Savant	*Rain Man*
Insurance Fraud; Lovers attempt, after murdering husband	*Double Indemnity*
I.R.A. Gunman on the run	*Odd Man Out*
Irving Thalberg; Film based on (Reputedly)	*The Last Tycoon*
Jake La Motta (Boxer); Based on	*Raging Bull*
Jesuit Missionaries in South America	*The Mission*
Jesus Christ; Children mistake criminal for	*Whistle Down the Wind*
Jewish girl dresses as a boy to study to be a rabbi	*Yentl* (Barbra Streisand)
Jockey's fight against cancer	*Champions*
John Reed; Life of	*Reds*
Juror disagrees with rest of jury	*Twelve Angry Men* (Henry Fonda – Number 8)

Kampuchea; War in	*The Killing Fields*
Kleptomaniac	*Marnie*
Korean War; Medical unit	*M.A.S.H.*
Peter Kurten (Dusseldorf murderer)	*M*
Landru (Murderer)	*Monsieur Verdoux*
Lion Tamer; Female	*I'm No Angel* (Mae West)
Letters; Boy delivers between lovers	*The Go-Between*
Locomotive; US Civil War	*The General*
London; Part of; Found belonging to France	*Passport to Pimlico*
Lord Mountbatten; Inspired by	*In Which We Serve*
Loretta Lynn; Life of	*Coal Miner's Daughter*
Lovers die in each other's arms after gun-fight	*Duel in the Sun*
Ma Barker	*Bloody Mama* (Shelley Winters)
Macbeth; Kurosawa film based on	*Throne of Blood*
Meal; Attempt by 6 friends to have	*The Discreet Charm of the Bourgeoisie*
Michelangelo; Life of	*The Agony and the Ecstasy* (Charlton Heston)
Mirrors; Shootout in hall of	*The Lady from Shanghai*
Missionary helps children through enemy lines in China	*Inn of the Sixth Happiness*
Monaco; Cat burglar in	*To Catch a Thief*
Motorcycle Gang invade town; Banned in UK when released	*The Wild Ones*
Mount Rushmore; Climax on	*North by Northwest*
Multiple Personality	*Three Faces of Eve*
Murderer;-	
Disguises himself in 7 ways	*No Way to Treat a Lady* (Rod Steiger)
Kills 8 members of aristocratic family	*Kind Hearts and Coronets*
Musical; *Springtime for Hitler*; Production of	*The Producers*
Musicians dress up as women to escape gangsters	*Some Like it Hot*
Mutiny; Russian Navy, 1905	*Battleship Potemkin*
Nazis impersonated by actors	*To Be Or Not To Be*
Night Club Singer; Teacher gets infatuated with	*The Blue Angel*
Nuclear Bomb; 'Rides' as launched	*Dr. Strangelove*
Nuclear power station accident	*The China Syndrome*
Nude appearance; 1930s; Causes scandal	*Ecstasy* (Hedy Lamarr)
Nuremberg Nazi Rally; 1934	*Triumph of the Will* (Leni Riefenstahl)
Odessa steps sequence	*Battleship Potemkin*
Office workers; Female; Revenge against sexist boss	*9 to 5*
Olympic Games; 1936	*Olympia* (Leni Riefenstahl)
Olympic Runners; Competition between	*Chariots of Fire*
Opera House on the Amazon; Attempt to build	*Fitzcarraldo*
Pacific Island; US and Japanese soldier on in WWII	*Hell in the Pacific*
Panthers; Brother and sister turn into	*Cat People*
Paranoid Girl	*Repulsion*
Party line; Shared by songwriter and girl	*Pillow Talk*
Photograph; Enlarged; Shows murder	*Blow Up*

Policeman fights corruption in New York	*Serpico* (Al Pacino)
Pool Shark	*The Hustler*
Power and the Glory; Based on the novel	*The Fugitive*
Preacher; Psychopathic; Hunts children	*Night of the Hunter*
Priest; Told of murder in confessional	*I Confess* (Mongomery Clift)
Princess; Anonymous, with reporter in Rome	*Roman Holiday* (Audrey Hepburn)
Prison Governor; Idealistic	*Brubaker* (Robert Redford)
Prisoners form American football team	*The Mean Machine*
Public School; Rebellion in	*If*
Rosebud; Dies saying	*Citizen Kane* (Charles Foster Kane)
Russian Roulette; Scenes of	*The Deer Hunter*
School; Boys', Has Girls' school billeted on it	*The Happiest Days of your Life*
Scissors; Stabbing with	*Dial M for Murder*
Scopes Monkey Trial	*Inherit the Wind*
Screen; Characters walk out of	*The Purple Rose of Cairo*
Sewers of Vienna; Final scene in	*The Third Man*
Sextuplets; Girl gives birth to	*The Miracle of Morgan's Creek*
Ship; Overturned by tidal wave	*The Poseidon Adventure*
Shower; Murder in	*Psycho*
Sioux Indians; English aristocrat initiated into	*A Man Called Horse*
Sniper meets aging horror actor	*Targets*
Soldiers; Set themselves up as Gods	*The Man Who Would Be King*
Split Screen; Pioneering film	*Napoleon*
Submarine versus destroyer in WWII	*The Enemy Below*
Tchaikovsky; Life of	*The Music Lovers*
Tempest; Based on (Science Fiction)	*Forbidden Planet*
Train; Lady disappears on, in spy intrigue	*The Lady Vanishes*
Transvestite Nightclub Singer	*Victor/Victoria* (Julie Andrews)
Trapp family escape from Nazis	*The Sound of Music*
Twenty-second Century; Man frozen returns in	*Sleeper* (Woody Allen)
Venice; Couple in, during murders	*Don't Look Now*
Vietnam; Search for mad colonel	*Apocalypse Now*
Vigilante; New York avenges attack on family	*Death Wish*
Violette Szabo, Spy; Life of	*Carve Her Name with Pride*
Wagon Train of Women	*Westward the Women*
Watergate; Exposure of	*All The President's Men*
Wedding; Arrives on horse to stop	*The Graduate*
Whisky Laden Ship; Wrecked on Scottish shore	*Whisky Galore*
Windmill; Turns the wrong way	*Foreign Correspondent*
Wrestling; Nude male scene	*Women in Love*
WWI; Anti-war film	*All Quiet on the Western Front*
WWII; Returning to midwest town	*The Best Years of our Lives*
Xanadu; Lives in	*Citizen Kane* (Charles Foster Kane)

Films

By: Title → Actors, General

A Nous La Liberté	Director: René Clair
Abbott and Costello Go to Mars	Setting: Venus
Addams Family, The	

Gomez	Raul Julia
Morticia	Anjelica Huston
Admirable Crichton, The	Title: Kenneth More
African Queen, The	
Based on	C.S.Forester novel
Charlie Allnut, Boat owner	Humphrey Bogart
Location	German East Africa
Rose Sayer, the Missionary	Katherine Hepburn
Title	A Boat
Agony and the Ecstasy, The	
Based on	Irving Stone novel
Michelangelo	Charlton Heston
Pope Julius II	Rex Harrison
Alamo, The	
Jim Bowie	Richard Widmark
Davy Crockett	John Wayne
Smitty	Frankie Avalon
Travis	Laurence Harvey
Alfie	Title: Michael Caine
Alien	
Director	Ridley Scott
Spawns in	John Hurt
All about Eve	Eve: Anne Baxter
All Quiet on the Western Front	Director: Lewis Milestone
All The President's Men	
Carl Bernstein	Dustin Hoffman
Director	Alan Pakula
Bob Woodward	Robert Redford
Amadeus	
Based on	Peter Schaffer play
Director	Milos Forman
Mozart	Tom Hulce
Salieri	F.Murray Abraham
American Gigolo	Title: Richard Gere
American Graffiti	Director: George Lucas
And God Created Woman	Woman: Brigitte Bardot
Angels with Dirty Faces	
Father Connolly, Priest	Pat O'Brien
Rocky Sullivan, Gangster	James Cagney
Annie	
Annie	Aileen Quinn
Daddy Warbucks	Albert Finney
Annie Hall	
Director/Alvy Singer	Woody Allen
Title	Diane Keaton
Apartment	
C.C.Baxter, Apartment owner	Jack Lemmon
Director	Billy Wilder
Apocalypse Now	
Based on (theme)	Heart of Darkness (Joseph Conrad story)
Director	Frances Ford Coppola
Colonel Kilgore	Robert Duvall
Colonel Kurtz	Marlon Brando
Lieutenant Willard (hunts down Kurtz)	Martin Sheen
Apu Trilogy	*Pather Panchali, Aparajito, The World of Apu*
Director	Satyajit Ray

27

Around the World in 80 Days
  Princess Aouda   Shirley MacLaine
  Phileas Fogg   David Niven
  Passepartout   Cantinflas
Arsenic and Old Lace
  Based on   Joseph Kesselring play
  Dr Einstein   Peter Lorre
  Nephew   Cary Grant
Ashes and Diamonds   Director: Andrzej Wajda
Back to the Future   Marty McFly: Michael J.Fox
Bad Day at Black Rock
  Director   John Sturges
  John J McReedy, One armed stranger   Spencer Tracy
Bad News Bears,The
  Coach   Walter Matthau
  Pitcher   Tatum O'Neal
  Title   Baseball Team
Badlands   Martin Sheen, Sissy Spacek
Bambi   Marries: Faline
Barbarella
  Based on Comic Strip by   Jean Claude Forest
  Director   Roger Vadim
  Title   Jane Fonda
Batman (1989)
  Batman   Michael Keaton
  The Joker   Jack Nicholson
  Vickie Vale   Kim Basinger
Batman, The Return
  Catwoman   Michelle Pfeiffer
  The Penguin   Dannie DeVito
Battleship Potemkin   Director: Eisenstein
Beauty and the Beast   Director: Jean Cocteau
Bedtime for Bonzo
  Bonzo   Peggy
  Professor Boyd   Ronald Reagan
Being There   Chauncey Gardner, the Gardener: Peter
                       Sellers

Ben Hur
  Ben Hur   Charlton Heston (1959 version), Ramon
                       Navarro (Silent version)

  Messala   Stephen Boyd (1959 version), Francis
                       X.Bushman (Silent version)
Beverly Hills Cop   Axel Foley, Title: Eddie Murphy
Bicycle Thief,The   Director: Vittorio De Sica
Big Heat,The
  David Bannion,the Detective   Glenn Ford
  Director   Fritz Lang
Big Sleep,The
  Based on   Raymond Chandler novel
  Director   Howard Hawks
  Philip Marlowe   Humphrey Bogart
  Vivian   Lauren Bacall
Billy Liar   Title: Tom Courtenay
Birdman of Alcatraz,The   Title: Burt Lancaster
Birds,The   Director: Alfred Hitchcock
Birth of a Nation
  Based on   *The Clansman* (Thomas Dixon)
  Director   D.W.Griffith

Makes famous	Lilian Gish
Blade Runner	
Based on	*Do Androids dream of Electric Sheep* (novel)
Detective	Harrison Ford
Director	Ridley Scott
Blazing Saddles	Director: Mel Brooks
Blood and Sand (1922)	Juan, the Bullfighter: Rudolph Valentino
Blow Up	
Director	Antonioni
Jane	Vanessa Redgrave
Thomas, the Photographer	David Hemmings
Blue Angel (1929 version)	
Director	Von Sternberg
Lola Lola	Marlene Dietrich
Lola's Man	Emil Jannings
Title	A Night Club
Blue Thunder	
Pilot	Roy Scheider
Title	A Reconnaissance Helicopter
Blues Brothers,The	
Elwood	Dan Ackroyd
Jake	John Belushi
Bonnie and Clyde	
Clyde Barrow	Warren Beatty
Director	Arthur Penn
Bonny Parker	Faye Dunaway
Born on the Fourth of July	
Director	Oliver Stone
Ron Kovic (War Veteran)	Tom Cruise
Bout de Souffle	Jean Paul Belmondo, Jean Seberg
Director	Jean Luc Godard
Remade	1983
Boys from Brazil,The	
Based on	Ira Levin novel
Mengele, Nazi Doctor	Gregory Peck
Nazi Hunter	Laurence Olivier
Bridge on the River Kwai	
Based on	Pierre Boulle novel
Colonel Nicholson	Alec Guinness
Colonel Saito	Sessue Hayakawa
Brief Encounter	
Based on	*Still Life* (Noel Coward play)
Director	David Lean
Alec Harvey	Trevor Howard
Laura Jesson	Celia Johnson
Theme Music	Rachmaninov Piano Concerto No. 2
Brighton Rock	Pinkie: Richard Attenborough
Bringing up Baby	
Baby	A Leopard
David Huxley	Cary Grant
Susan	Katherine Hepburn
Butch Cassidy and the Sundance Kid	
Butch Cassidy	Paul Newman
Etta Place	Katherine Ross
Sequel/Prequel	*Butch and Sundance, The Early Days*
The Sundance Kid	Robert Redford

Cabaret
Based on · *I am a Camera* (Isherwood play)
Sally Bowles · · · · · · · · · · · · · · · · · Liza Minnelli
Club · Kit Kat Club
Director · Bob Fosse
Nightclub Master of Ceremonies · · · Joel Grey

Cabin in the Sky
Georgia Brown · · · · · · · · · · · · · · · · Lena Horne
Little Joe · Eddie (Rochester) Anderson
Petunia · Ethel Waters

Camille
Armand's Father · · · · · · · · · · · · · · · Lionel Barrymore
Armand Duval · · · · · · · · · · · · · · · · · Robert Taylor
Marguerite Gautier · · · · · · · · · · · · · Greta Garbo

Carnal Knowledge
Bobbie · Ann Margret
Script · Jules Feiffer

Carrie
Based on · Stephen King novel
Title · Sissy Spacek

Casablanca
Based on · *Everybody goes to Ricks* (Play)
Rick Blaine · · · · · · · · · · · · · · · · · · · Humphrey Bogart
Director · Michael Curtiz
Café · Rick's Café Americain
Victor Laszlo · · · · · · · · · · · · · · · · · Paul Henreid
Lead role turned down · · · · · · · · · · George Raft
Ilsa Lund · Ingrid Bergman
Rick's part, originally intended for · · Ronald Reagan
Sam (Dooley Wilson) sings · · · · · · · 'As time goes by'
Ugarte · Peter Lorre

Casanova
Director · Fellini
Title · Donald Sutherland

Cat People
Theme · People turning into panthers
Title · Nastassja Kinski, Malcolm McDowell

Catch-22
Director · Mike Nichols
Yossarian · Alan Arkin

Champions
Bob Champion · · · · · · · · · · · · · · · · John Hurt
Theme · Bob Champion's (Jockey) fight against cancer

Chariots of Fire
Harold Abrahams · · · · · · · · · · · · · · Ben Cross
Eric Liddell · · · · · · · · · · · · · · · · · · Ian Charleson
Olympics · 1924, Paris

Chinatown
Detective · Jack Nicholson
Director · Roman Polanski

Chitty Chitty Bang Bang · · · · · · · · · Based on: Ian Fleming story

Citizen Kane
Character based on · · · · · · · · · · · · · William Randolph Hearst
Director · Orson Welles
Charles Foster Kane · · · · · · · · · · · · Orson Welles
Kane dies saying · · · · · · · · · · · · · · 'Rosebud' (Opening lines)
Jedediah Leland · · · · · · · · · · · · · · · Joseph Cotten

Newspaper	*The Inquirer*
Cleopatra (1963 version)	
Anthony	Richard Burton
Caesar	Rex Harrison
Director	Joseph Mankiewicz
Title	Elizabeth Taylor
Clockwise	Mr Stimpson, Headmaster: John Cleese
Clockwork Orange,A	
Alex	Malcolm McDowell
Based on	Anthony Burgess novel
Director	Stanley Kubrick
Close Encounters of the 3rd Kind	Director: Steven Spielberg
Color of Money,The	Paul Newman, Tom Cruise
Color Purple,The	
Based on	Alice Walker novel
Celie	Whoopi Goldberg
Director	Steven Spielberg
Coming Home	
Affair with Veteran	Jane Fonda
Paraplegic Veteran	Jon Voight
Conan the Barbarian	Title: Arnold Schwarzenegger
Cool Hand Luke	
Bet	Will eat 50 eggs in an hour
Imprisoned for	Sawing off parking meter
Lucas Jackson (Luke)	Paul Newman
Creature Comforts	
Animator	Nick Park
Crocodile Dundee	Michael Dundee: Paul Hogan
Cry Freedom	
Steve Biko	Denzel Washington
Director	Richard Attenborough
Donald Woods, the Journalist	Kevin Kline
Cyrano de Bergerac (1990)	
Title	Gerard Depardieu
Dam Busters, The	Barnes Wallis: Michael Redgrave
Dances with Wolves	
Lieutenant John Dunbar	Kevin Costner
Day at the Races, A	The Marx Brothers
Day for Night	Director: Francois Truffaut
Day of the Jackal, The	Assassin: Edward Fox
Dead Poets Society	
John Keating (Teacher)	Robin Williams
Death in Venice	
Based on	Thomas Mann novel
Director	Luchino Visconti
Von Aschenbach	Dirk Bogarde
Death Wish	
Director	Michael Winner
Paul Kersey, Vigilante	Charles Bronson
Deer Hunter,The	
Director	Michael Cimino
Stars	Robert de Niro, Meryl Streep, Christopher Walken
Deliverance	
Based on	James Dickey novel
Director	John Boorman
Set in	Bottleneck
Destry Rides Again	

Tom Destry	James Stewart
Frenchy	Marlene Dietrich
Dial M for Murder	
Director	Alfred Hitchcock
Husband	Ray Milland
Wife	Grace Kelly
Dick Tracy	
Big Boy Caprice	Al Pacino
Breathless Mahoney	Madonna
Title	Warren Beatty
Die Hard	
John McClane	Bruce Willis
Dirty Dancing	
Johnny Castle	Patrick Swayze
Dirty Dozen,The	
Major Reisman, Leader	Lee Marvin
Only member also in Magnificent	
Seven	Charles Bronson
Dirty Harry	Harry Callahan: Clint Eastwood
Discreet Charm of the Bourgeoisie,The	Director: Luis Bunuel
Don't Look Now	
Based on	Daphne Du Maurier novel
Parents	Julie Christie, Donald Sutherland
Set in	Venice
Doors, The	
Jim Morrisson	Val Kilmer
Double Indemnity	
Based on	James Cain story
Burton Keys, Insurance Assessor	Edward G.Robinson
Director	Billy Wilder
Lovers	Fred MacMurray, Barbara Stanwyck
Dr No	Title: Joseph Wiseman
Dr Strangelove	
Director	Stanley Kubrick
Music when bomb dropped	'We'll meet again'
Title	Peter Sellers
Dr Zhivago	
Director	David Lean
Lara	Julie Christie
Score	Maurice Jarre
Strelnikov	Tom Courtenay
Tanya	Geraldine Chaplin
Title	Omar Sharif
Dresser,The	
The Actor	Albert Finney
Title	Tom Courtenay
Driving Miss Daisy	
Morgan Freeman (The Chauffeur)	Hoke Colburn
Boolie Werthan	Dan Aykroyd
Miss Daisy Werthan	Jessica Tandy
Duck Soup	
Country	Freedonia
Rufus T.Firefly	Groucho Marx
Duel	
Director	Steven Spielberg
Theme	Lorry chases a car
Duel in the Sun	
Pearl Chavez	Jennifer Jones

Director	King Vidor
Lewt and Jesse McCanles, Rivals for her	Gregory Peck, Joseph Cotten
Earth	Director: Alexander Dovzhenko
East of Eden	
Based on	John Steinbeck novel
Caleb Trask	James Dean
Director	Elia Kazan
Easy Rider	
Billy	Dennis Hopper
Wyatt	Peter Fonda
Educating Rita	
Frank Bryant, the Professor	Michael Caine
Rita	Julie Walters
Edward Scissorhands	
Edward	Johnny Depp
El Cid	
Chimene	Sophia Loren
Title	Charlton Heston
Elephant Boy	Title: Sabu
Elephant Man,The	
Director	David Lynch
Title (John Merrick)	John Hurt
Frederick Treves, Doctor	Anthony Hopkins
Elmer Gantry	
Based on	Sinclair Lewis novel
Title	Burt Lancaster
Emily	Title: Koo Stark
Emmanuelle	Title: Sylvia Kristel
Enemy Below,The	
Captain Murrell (Destroyer)	Robert Mitchum
Captain Von Stolles (Submarine)	Curt Jurgens
Enter the Dragon	Bruce Lee
ET	
Director	Steven Spielberg
Elliott, Friend	Henry Thomas
ET played by	3 People
Working title	'A Boy's Life'
Exorcist,The	
Based on	Peter Blatty novel
Girl	Linda Blair
Set in	Georgetown
Fahrenheit 451	
Based on	Ray Bradbury book
Director	Francois Truffaut
Name from	Temperature at which paper catches fire
Fantasia	Walt Disney
Musical Collaborator	Leopold Stokowski
Orchestra	Philadelphia Orchestra
Sorcerer's Apprentice	Mickey Mouse
Fantastic Voyage	Submarine: *Proteus*
Fatal Attraction	
Dan Gallagher	Michael Douglas
Alex Forest	Glenn Close
Fish Called Wanda, A	
Director	Charles Crichton
Wanda Gerschwitz	Jamie Lee Curtis

Ken	Michael Palin
Otto	Kevin Kline
Fisher King, The	
Jack Lucas (DJ)	Jeff Bridges
Parry	Robin Williams
Fistful of Dollars, A	
Director	Sergio Leone
Man with no name	Clint Eastwood
Fly, The (1987)	
Director	David Cronenberg
Seth Brindle, The Fly	Jeff Goldblum
Fool There Was, A	Theda Bara
Foolish Wives	Director: Erich Von Stroheim
Forbidden Planet	
Based on	*The Tempest* (Shakespeare)
Morbius, Mad Scientist	Walter Pidgeon
Planet	Altair 4
Robot	Robby
Foreign Correspondent	
Director	Alfred Hitchcock
Reporter	Joel McCrea
42nd Street	
Billy Lawler	Dick Powell
Ann Lowell	Ginger Rogers
Peggy Sawyer	Ruby Keeler
Frankenstein (1931)	
Director	James Whale
Monster	Boris Karloff
Freaks	Director: Todd Browning
French Connection, The	
Director	William Friedkin
French Setting	Marseilles
Popeye Doyle, Detective	Gene Hackman
US setting	New York
French Lieutenant's Woman, The	
Based on	John Fowles novel
Charles	Jeremy Irons
Sarah Woodruff, Title	Meryl Streep
From Here to Eternity	
Maggio	Frank Sinatra
Prewitt	Montgomery Clift
Sergeant Warden	Burt Lancaster
Funny Girl	Fanny Brice: Barbra Streisand
Gandhi	
Director	Richard Attenborough
Gandhi	Ben Kingsley
General, The	Buster Keaton
Title	A Locomotive
Gentlemen Prefer Blondes	Marilyn Monroe, Jane Russell
Get Carter	Carter: Michael Caine
Ghost	
Sam	Patrick Swayze
Molly	Demi Moore
Gigi	
Title	Leslie Caron
Honore Lachaille	Maurice Chevalier
Girl Can't Help It, The	The Girl (Jerri Jordan): Jane Mansfield
Glenn Miller Story, The	Glenn Miller: James Stewart

Go-Between,The
  Based on   L.P.Hartley novel
  Director   Joseph Losey
  Lovers   Julie Christie, Alan Bates
  Lee Colston (Title)   Dominic Guard, Michael Redgrave
                                                   (when old)

Godfather,The
  Based on   Mario Puzo novel
  Director   Francis Ford Coppola
  Don Vito Corleone (Title)   Marlon Brando
  Michael Corleone   Al Pacino
  Offered Lead Role   Laurence Olivier
  Sonny   James Caan
Godfather II   Don Vito Corleone (as a young man):
                  Robert De Niro

Godzilla   From: Odo Island
Gold Rush,The   Charlie Chaplin
Goldfinger
  Painted gold   Shirley Eaton
  Oddjob   Harold Sakata (has lethal hat)
  Title   Gert Frobe
Gone With The Wind
  Rhett Butler   Clark Gable
  Rhett Butler part, turned down   Gary Cooper
  Scarlett O'Hara   Vivien Leigh
  Scarlett O'Hara part, turned down   Bette Davis
  Ashley Wilkes   Leslie Howard
Good the Bad and the Ugly,The
  Bad   Lee Van Cleef
  Good   Clint Eastwood
  Ugly   Eli Wallach
Gorillas in the Mist
  Dian Fossey   Sigourney Weaver
Gothic
  Director   Ken Russell
  Setting   Villa Diodati, Switzerland
Graduate,The
  Benjamin Braddock (Title)   Dustin Hoffman
  Mrs Robinson   Anne Bancroft
Grand Hotel
  Billed as   'Garbo Speaks'
  Grusinskaya, the Ballerina   Greta Garbo
  Secretary   Joan Crawford
Grapes of Wrath,The   Tom Joad: Henry Fonda
Grease   John Travolta, Olivia Newton-John
Great Dictator,The   Adenoid Hynkel, dictator of Tomania:
                  Charlie Chaplin

Greed
  Based on   McTeague (Frank Norris novel)
  Director   Erich Von Stroheim
  Makes Famous   Zasu Pitts
Guess Who's Coming to Dinner
  Comes to Dinner   Sidney Poitier
  Parents   Spencer Tracy, Katharine Hepburn
Hallowe'en
  Director   John Carpenter
  Doctor Loomis   Donald Pleasance
  Michael Myers, the Maniac   Tony Moran

Hannah and Her Sisters
  Director — Woody Allen
  Hannah — Mia Farrow
  Lee — Barbara Hershey
  Molly — Dianne Wiest
Hannibal Brooks — Title: Oliver Reed
Happiest Days of Your Life,The
  Headmaster — Alistair Sim
  Headmistress — Margaret Rutherford
  School — Nutbourne
Harder They Come,The — Ivan Martin: Jimmy Cliff
Harvey
  Elwood P.Dowd — James Stewart
  Title — Invisible Rabbit
Heat and Dust — Director: James Ivory
Heaven's Gate
  Director — Michael Cimino
  Marshal — Kris Kristofferson
  Set in — Johnson County, Wyoming
Hell in the Pacific
  American Soldier — Lee Marvin
  Japanese Soldier — Toshiro Mifune
Hello Dolly
  Director — Jean Kelly
  Dolly — Barbra Streisand
Hell's Angels — Jean Harlow
  Director — Howard Hughes
High Noon
  Amy Kane — Grace Kelly
  Will Kane, retiring Sheriff — Gary Cooper
  Music — Dimitri Tiomkin
  Set in — Hadleyville
Home Alone
  Kevin — Macaulay Culkin
Hook
  Captain Hook — Dustin Hoffman
  Peter Pan/Banning — Robin Williams
  Smee — Bob Hoskins
  Tinkerbell — Julia Roberts
How to Marry a Millionaire — Marilyn Monroe, Lauren Bacall, Betty Grable

Hustler,The
  (Fast) Eddie Felson — Paul Newman
  Minnesota Fats — Jackie Gleason
  Sequel — *The Colour of Money*
I Am A Fugitive From a Chain Gang
  Director — Mervyn Le Roy
  Fugitive — Paul Muni
I Was a Male War Bride
  Female Lead — Ann Sheridan
  Title — Cary Grant
I,Claudius (Unfinished)
  Claudius — Charles Laughton
  Director — Joseph Von Sternberg
If
  Director — Lindsay Anderson
  Nick — Malcolm McDowell
I'm Allright Jack

Fred Kite, Shop Steward	Peter Sellers
Production	Boulting Brothers
In the Heat of the Night	
Chief Gillespie	Rod Steiger
Virgil Tibbs	Sydney Poitier
In Which We Serve	
Shorty Blake	John Mills
Captain 'D'	Noel Coward
Inherit the Wind	
Based on	The Scopes Monkey Trial
William Jennings Bryan	Frederick March
Clarence Darrow	Spencer Tracy
Scopes	Dick York
Inn of the Sixth Happiness,The	
Gladys Aylward, the Missionary	Ingrid Bergman
Based on	*The Small Woman* (biography)
Mandarin	Robert Donat
Intolerance	Director: D.W.Griffiths
Invisible Man,The	
Title	Claude Rains
It Happened One Night	Clark Gable, Claudette Colbert
Director	Frank Capra
Meet on	Bus
It's a Wonderful Life	James Stewart, Donna Reed
Director	Frank Capra
Ivan the Terrible	Director: Sergei Eisenstein
Jaws	
Based on	Peter Benchley novel
Director	Steven Spielberg
Hooper, Icthyologist	Richard Dreyfuss
Music	John Williams
Police Chief, Brody	Roy Scheider
Quint, Shark Hunter	Robert Shaw
Set in	Amity
Shark's nickname	Bruce
J.F.K.	
Director	Oliver Stone
Jim Garrison	Kevin Costner
Jules et Jim	Director: Francois Truffaut
Julia	
Director	Fred Zinnemann
Lillian Hellman	Jane Fonda
Julia	Vanessa Redgrave
Kagemusha	Director: Kurosawa
Karate Kid,The	
Instructor, Miyagi	Pat Morita
Daniel (Title)	Ralph Macchio
Kelly's Heroes	Kelly: Clint Eastwood
Khartoum	
General Gordon	Charlton Heston
The Mahdi	Lawrence Olivier
Kid,The	
The Kid	Jackie Coogan
The Kid (as a baby)	Baby LeRoy (2)
The Tramp	Charlie Chaplin
Killers,The	
Based On	Ernest Hemingway story
Browning	Ronald Reagan

Charlie, Lee (Title)	Lee Marvin, Clu Gulager
Killing Fields,The	
Director	Roland Joffe
Dith Pran, Guide	Haing Ngor
Sydney Schanberg, the Journalist	Sam Waterston
Set in	Kampuchea
Kind Hearts and Coronets	
D'Ascoyne Family	Alec Guinness (8 members)
Louis, the Murderer	Dennis Price
King and I,The	
I (the Governess)	Deborah Kerr
King Mong Kut	Yul Brynner
King Kong	
Ann Darrow	Fay Wray, Jessica Lange (Remake)
Final sequence	King Kong holds girl at the top of the Empire State Building
King Kong; Found on	Skull Island
Kiss of the Spider Woman	William Hurt
Kramer v Kramer	Dustin Hoffman, Meryl Streep
Based on	Avery Corman novel
Son	Justin Henry
La Dolce Vita	
Director	Fellini
Marcello	Marcello Mastroianni
La Grande Illusion	Director: Jean Renoir
Lady Vanishes,The	
Based on	*The Wheel Spins* (Ethel White novel)
Director	Alfred Hitchcock
English Gentlemen	Charters and Caldicott
Title role	Miss Froy (May Whitty)
Ladykillers,The	Title: Alec Guinness, Peter Sellers
Last Tango in Paris	
Director	Bernardo Bertolucci
Jeanne	Maria Schneider
Paul	Marlon Brando
Last Temptation of Christ, The	
Christ	Willem Dafoe
Director	Martin Scorsese
Judas Iscariot	Harvey Keitel
Mary Magdalene	Barbara Hershey
Last Tycoon,The	Title: Robert De Niro
Last Year at Marienbad	Director: Alain Resnais
Lavender Hill Mob,The	Crooks: Alec Guinness (Leader), Stanley Holloway, Alfie Bass, Sid James
Lawrence of Arabia	
Director	David Lean
First choice for part	Albert Finney
Title	Peter O'Toole
Les Enfants du Paradis	
Director	Marcel Carne
Mime, Debureau	Jean-Louis Barrault
Limelight	Calvero, the Comedian: Charlie Chaplin
Lion in Winter,The	
Eleanor of Aquitaine	Katherine Hepburn
Henry II	Peter O'Toole
Lisztomania	

Director — Ken Russell
Liszt — Roger Daltrey

Little Big Man
  Jack Crabb (Title) — Dustin Hoffman
  Crabb's final age — 121
  Director — Arthur Penn
Little Caesar
  Caesar, Enrico Bandello: Edward G.Robinson

Little Lord Fauntleroy (1936) — Title: Freddy Bartholomew
Lola Montes
  Director — Max Ophuls
  Title — Martine Carol
Lolita
  Charlotte Haze, Mother — Shelley Winters
  Humbert — James Mason
  Title — Sue Lyon
Long Goodbye,The
  Based on — Raymond Chandler novel
  Philip Marlowe — Elliot Gould
Look Back in Anger
  Helena Charles, Mistress — Claire Bloom
  Jimmy Porter — Richard Burton
Look Who's Talking
  Mikey's Voice — Bruce Willis
Lost Horizon (1937)
  Conway — Ronald Colman
  Director — Frank Capra
Lost Weekend,The
  Based on — Charles Jackson novel
  Director — Billy Wilder
  Don Birman, the Alcoholic — Ray Milland
Love Story
  Oliver Barrett IV — Ryan O'Neal
  Based on — Erich Segal novel
  Jennifer Cavallieri — Ali McGraw
Lust for Life
  About — Vincent Van Gogh
  Based on — Irving Stone biography
  Paul Gauguin — Anthony Quinn
  Van Gogh — Kirk Douglas
M
  Director — Fritz Lang
  Murderer — Peter Lorre
Mad Max
  Director — George Miller
  Max — Mel Gibson
Madigan — Title: Richard Widmark
Magnificent Seven
  Bad Guy — Eli Wallach
  Based on — *Seven Samurai* (Kurosawa film)
  Knife thrower — James Coburn
  Seven — Charles Bronson, Yul Brynner, Horst Bucholz, James Coburn, Brad Dexter, Steve McQueen, Robert Vaughn

Maltese Falcon,The
  Based on — Dashiell Hammett novel
  Joel Cairo — Peter Lorre

Director	John Huston
Falcon contains	Precious stones
The Fat Man	Sydney Greenstreet
Lead role turned down	George Raft
Sam Spade	Humphrey Bogart
Man and a Woman,A	
Man	Jean Louis Trintignant (Racing driver)
Woman	Anouk Aimée
Man Called Horse,A	Title: Richard Harris
Man For All Seasons,A	
Director	Fred Zinnemann
Henry VIII	Robert Shaw
Sir Thomas More (Title)	Paul Scofield
Man of Marble	Director: Andrzej Wajda
Man Who Fell To Earth,The	Title: David Bowie
Man Who Would Be King,The	
Based on	Rudyard Kipling story
Danny	Sean Connery
Director	John Huston
Peachy	Michael Caine
Setting	Kariristan
Manchurian Candidate,The	Raymond Shaw (Title): Laurence Harvey
Mary Poppins	Julie Andrews, Dick Van Dyke
Address	17, Cherry Tree Lane
Based on	P.L.Travers book
Children	Jane and Michael Banks
M.A.S.H	
Based on	Richard Hooker novel
Director	Robert Altman
Major Hot Lips Houlihan	Sally Kellerman
Hawkeye Pierce	Donald Sutherland
Title, Stands for	Mobile Army Surgical Hospital
Trapper John McIntyre	Elliott Gould
Mean Streets	
Johnny Boy	Robert de Niro
Charlie	Harvey Keitel
Director	Martin Scorsese
Meet me in St Louis	Esther Smith, Judy Garland
Director	Vincente Minnelli
Metropolis	Director: Fritz Lang
Midnight Cowboy	
Joe Buck	Jon Voight
Rico Rizzo (Ratso)	Dustin Hoffman
Midnight Express	Billy Hayes, Drug smuggler: Brad Davis
Misfits,The	Clark Gable, Marilyn Monroe (Last film of both)
Director	John Huston
Modern Times	Charlie Chaplin, Paulette Goddard
Monsieur Hulot's Holiday	Jacques Tati
Mummy,The	Title: Boris Karloff
Music Lovers,The	
About	Tchaikovsky
Director	Ken Russell
Nina, Wife	Glenda Jackson
Tchaikovsky	Richard Chamberlain
Mutiny on the Bounty	
Captain Bligh	Charles Laughton (1935), Trevor

	Howard (1962)
Fletcher Christian	Clark Gable (1935), Marlon Brando (1962)
My Darling Clementine	
Director	John Ford
Wyatt Earp	Henry Fonda
Doc Holliday	Victor Mature
My Fair Lady	
Eliza Doolittle	Audrey Hepburn
Professor Higgins	Rex Harrison
Set design	Cecil Beaton
My Left Foot	
Christy Brown	Daniel Day Lewis
Mrs Brown	Brenda Fricker
My Little Chickadee	
Flower Belle Lee (Title)	Mae West
Cuthbert J.Twillie	W.C.Fields
Nanook of the North	Director: Robert Flaherty
Napoleon	Director: Abel Gance
National Velvet	
Auditioned for Velvet's part	Shirley Williams
Velvet Brown	Elizabeth Taylor
Sequel	*International Velvet* (Tatum O'Neal)
Trainer	Mickey Rooney
Never Give a Sucker an Even Break	W.C.Fields
Never on Sunday	
Director	Jules Dassin
Homer, the Tourist	Jules Dassin
The Prostitute	Melina Mercouri
Night at the Opera,A	The Marx Brothers
Night of the Hunter	
Director	Charles Laughton
Harry Powell, Psychopathic Preacher	Robert Mitchum
Wife	Shelley Winters
Night of the Living Dead	Director: George Romero
Nightmare on Elm Street	Maniac, Freddy Krueger: Robert Englund
9 to 5	Jane Fonda, Dolly Parton, Lily Tomlin
1984	Winston Smith: John Hurt (1984 version), Edmund O'Brien (1955)
Ninotchka	
Director	Ernst Lubitsch
Publicity	'Garbo Laughs'
Title	Greta Garbo
North by Northwest	
Director	Alfred Hitchcock
Eve Kendall	Eve Marie Saint
Roger Thornhill	Cary Grant
Nosferatu	Director: F.W.Murnau
October	Director: Sergei Eisenstein
Odd Couple,The	Title: Walter Matthau, Jack Lemmon
Officer and a Gentleman,An	
Girlfriend	Debra Winger
Pilot, Zack Mayo	Richard Gere
Oh, Mr Porter	Will Hay
Oliver	
Director	Carol Reed
Fagin	Ron Moody

Title	Mark Lester
Omen,The	
Boy's Name	Damien
Father, US Ambassador	Gregory Peck
Mother	Lee Remick
On Golden Pond	
Daughter	Jane Fonda
Professor, Norman Thayer	Henry Fonda
Wife	Katherine Hepburn
One Hundred Men and a Girl	
About	An Orchestra
Girl	Deanna Durbin
On the Waterfront	
Edie Doyle	Eve Marie Saint
Charley Molloy	Rod Steiger
Terry Molloy	Marlon Brando
One Flew Over the Cuckoo's Nest	
Based on	Ken Kesey novel
Director	Milos Forman
Randall McMurphy	Jack Nicholson
Nurse Ratched	Louise Fletcher
Ordinary People	Donald Sutherland, Mary Tyler Moore
Director	Robert Redford
Out of Africa	
Baron Blixen	Klaus Brandauer
Karen Blixen	Meryl Streep
Denys Finch-Hatton	Robert Redford
Outlaw,The	Jane Russell
Passage to India,A	
Director	David Lean
Adela Quested	Judy Davis
Passion of Joan of Arc,The	
Director	Carl Dreyer
Title	Maria Falconetti
Paths Of Glory	
Based on	Humphrey Cobb novel
Colonel Dax	Kirk Douglas
Director	Stanley Kubrick
Patton	
Omar Bradley	Karl Malden
General Patton	George C.Scott
Performance	
Chas	James Fox
Turner	Mick Jagger
Perils of Pauline,The	Title: Pearl White
Philadelphia Story,The	
Mike Connor, Journalist	James Stewart
Director	George Cukor
Dexter Haven, 1st Husband	Cary Grant
Tracy Lord	Katherine Hepburn
Picnic at Hanging Rock	Director: Peter Weir
Pillow Talk	Rock Hudson, Doris Day
Pink Panther,The	
Inspector Clouseau	Peter Sellers
Jewel Thief	David Niven
Title	A Jewel
Planet of the Apes	

Based on	Monkey Planet (Pierre Boulle novel)
Cornelius, the Ape	Roddy McDowall
Platoon	Director: Oliver Stone
Police Academy	Police Group: D-Squad
Pretty Baby	
Director	Louis Malle
Violet	Brooke Shields
Pretty Woman	
Edward Lewis	Richard Gere
Vivian Ward	Julia Roberts
Prime of Miss Jean Brodie,The	
Based on	Muriel Spark novel
Jean Brodie	Maggie Smith
School	Marcia Blaine School for Girls
Private Benjamin	Title: Goldie Hawn
Private Life of Henry VIII,The	
Director	Alexander Korda
Henry VIII	Charles Laughton
Prizzi's Honor	
Director	John Huston
Mafia Killers	Jack Nicholson, Kathleen Turner
Producers,The	
Max Bialystock, the Producer	Zero Mostel
Leo Bloom, the Accountant	Gene Wilder
Director	Mel Brooks
Musical	*Springtime for Hitler*
Psycho	
Norman Bates	Anthony Perkins
Marion Crane	Janet Leigh
Motel	Bates' Motel
Public Enemy	Tom Powers, the Gangster: James Cagney
Queen Christina	Title: Greta Garbo
Raging Bull	Jake La Motta, the Boxer: Robert De Niro
Raiders of the Lost Ark	
Director	Steven Spielberg
Indiana Jones	Harrison Ford
Rain Man	
Charles Babbitt	Tom Cruise
Raymond Babbitt	Dustin Hoffman
Ran	Director: Akira Kurosawa
Rashomon	Director: Akira Kurosawa
Reach for the Sky	Douglas Bader: Kenneth Moore
Rear Window	
Director	Alfred Hitchcock
Jeff	James Stewart
Lisa	Grace Kelly
Rebecca	
Director	Alfred Hitchcock
Maxim De Winter	Laurence Olivier
Mrs De Winter	Joan Fontaine
Rebel Without a Cause	
Director	Nicholas Ray
Father	Jim Bacchus
Girlfriend	Natalie Wood
Jim Stark (Title)	James Dean
Red River	

Tom Dunson, Trail Boss	John Wayne
Matthew Garth, Adopted Son	Montgomery Clift
Red Shoes,The	Moira Shearer
Reds	
Louise Bryant	Diane Keaton
John Reed	Warren Beatty
Repulsion	
Director	Roman Polanski
Girl	Catherine Deneuve
Reversal of Fortune	
Claus von Bülow	Jeremy Irons
Rififi	Director: Jules Dassin
Rio Bravo	
Colorado	Ricky Nelson
Director	Howard Hawks
Dude, Drunken Deputy	Dean Martin
Sheriff	John Wayne
Robe,The	
Demetrius	Victor Mature
Diana	Jean Simmons
Marcellus	Richard Burton
Sequel	*Demetrius and the Gladiators*
Robin and Marian	
Marian	Audrey Hepburn
Robin	Sean Connery
Robin Hood, Prince of Thieves	
Robin	Kevin Costner
Will Scarlett	Christian Slater
Rocky	
Rocky Balboa	Sylvester Stallone
Director	John Avildsen
Rocky II	
Director	Sylvester Stallone
Rocky's Opponent, Apollo Creed	Carl Weathers
Rocky III	Rocky's Opponent (Clubber Lang): Mr T
Rocky IV	Rocky's Opponent (Ivan Drago): Dolph Lundgren
Roman Holiday	
Joe Bradley, the Journalist	Gregory Peck
Princess Ann	Audrey Hepburn
Romeo and Juliet	
Director	Franco Zefferelli
Title	Leonard Whiting, Olivia Hussey
Room at the Top	
Alice	Simone Signoret
Joe Lambton	Laurence Harvey
Room With a View	Director: James Ivory
Rosemary's Baby	
Based on	Ira Levin novel
Director	Roman Polanski
Mother	Mia Farrow
Rose,The	Bette Middler
Safety Last	Harold Lloyd
Saturday Night and Sunday Morning	
Arthur	Albert Finney
Director	Karel Reisz
Doreen	Shirley Ann Field
Saturday Night Fever	

Based on	New York Magazine article
Gangs	Faces, Barracudas
Tony Manero	John Travolta
Music	The Gibb Brothers
Stephanie	Karen Lynn Gorney
Tony's Job	Sells paint
Scarface	
Director	Howard Hughes
Tony Scamonte (Title)	Paul Muni
Scarlet Empress,The	Catherine II (Title): Marlene Dietrich
Seven Samurai	
Director	Akira Kurosawa
Seven Year Itch,The	Marilyn Monroe
Director	Billy Wilder
Seventh Seal,The	
Director	Ingmar Bergman
The Knight	Max Von Sydow
Shane	
Director	George Stephens
Title	Alan Ladd
Wilson, the 'Baddie'	Jack Palance
Sheik	Ahmed Ben Hassan (Title): Rudolph Valentino
Shirley Valentine	
Joe Bradshaw	Bernard Hill
Shirley Valentine Bradshaw	Pauline Collins
Costas Caldes (Greek Hotelier)	Tom Conti
Silence of the Lambs, The	
Dr Hannibal Lecter	Anthony Hopkins
Clarice Starling (FBI Agent)	Jodie Foster
Silent Movie	
Director	Mel Brooks
Only Speech	'No' – Marcel Marceau
Silkwood	Title: Meryl Streep
Singin' in the Rain	
Director	Stanley Donen
Don Lockwood	Gene Kelly
Kathy Selden (Female lead)	Debbie Reynolds
Sleep	Director: Andy Warhol
Sleuth	
Milo	Michael Caine
Andrew Wyke, Detective Story Writer	Lawrence Olivier
Smokey and the Bandit	
The Bandit	Burt Reynolds
Burford T.Justice, the Sheriff	Jackie Gleason
Snow White and the Seven Dwarfs (Disney)	
Dwarfs	Bashful, Doc, Dopey, Grumpy, Happy, Sleepy, Sneezy
No Beard	Dopey
Wears Glasses	Doc
Some Like it Hot	
Director	Billy Wilder
Jerry/Daphne	Jack Lemmon
Joe/Josephine	Tony Curtis
Sugar Kane	Marilyn Monroe
Sophie's Choice	

Based on	William Styron novel
Sophie	Meryl Streep
Sound of Music,The	
Director	Robert Wise
Maria	Julie Andrews
Captain Von Trapp	Christopher Plummer
Spartacus	
Based on	Howard Fast novel
Director	Stanley Kubrick
Karinia	Jean Simmons
Title	Kirk Douglas
Spy Who Came in From the Cold,The	Title: Richard Burton
Stagecoach	
Director	John Ford
Ringo Kid	John Wayne
Star is Born,A (1954)	
Husband	James Mason
Title	Judy Garland
Star Wars	
C3PO	Anthony Daniels
Director	George Lucas
Ben Kenobi	Alec Guinness
Music	John Williams
Princess Leia	Carrie Fisher
R2D2	Kenny Baker
Robots	R2D2, C3PO
Sequels	*The Empire Strikes Back, Return of the Jedi*
Luke Skywalker	Mark Hamill
Hans Solo	Harrison Ford
Solo's Spaceship	Millennium Falcon
Darth Vader	David Prowse (Voice: James Earl Jones)
Wookie	Chewbacca
Sting,The	
The Conmen	Robert Redford, Paul Newman
Gets Stung	Robert Shaw
Streetcar Named Desire,A	
Blanche Du Bois	Vivien Leigh
Director	Elia Kazan
Stanley Kowalski	Marlon Brando
Sullivan's Travels	
Director	Preston Sturges
John L.Sullivan	Joel McCrea
Sunset Boulevard	
Butler	Erich Von Stroheim
Norma Desmond, Former Star	Gloria Swanson
Director	Billy Wilder
Joe Gillis, Norma's Lover	William Holden
Superman	
Clark Kent (Title)	Christopher Reeve
Lex Luthor	Gene Hackman
Suspicion	
Director	Alfred Hitchcock
Hanna, the Wife	Joan Fontaine
Johnnie	Cary Grant
Taming of the Shrew,The	
Katharina	Elizabeth Taylor
Petruchio	Richard Burton

Targets
  Director — Peter Bogdanovich
  Byron Orlock, Horror Actor — Boris Karloff
Taste of Honey,A — Pregnant girl (Jo): Rita Tushingham
Taxi Driver
  Director — Martin Scorsese
  Travis Bickle, the Taxi Driver — Robert De Niro
Ten
  Girl — Bo Derek
  Songwriter — Dudley Moore
  Title from — Marks he awards Bo Derek
Ten Commandments,The
  Director — Cecil B.De Mille
  Moses — Charlton Heston
  Prince — Yul Brynner
Terminator
  The Terminator — Arnold Schwarzenegger
  Sarah Connor — Linda Hamilton
Terms of Endearment
  Astronaut — Jack Nicholson
  Daughter — Debra Winger
  Director — James Brooks
  Mother — Shirley MacLaine
They Shoot Horses Don't They — Michael Sarrasin, Jane Fonda
Thin Man,The
  Based on — Dashiell Hammett novel
  Dog — Asta
  Nick — William Powell
  Nora — Myrna Loy
Third Man,The
  Based on — Graham Greene novel
  Director — Carol Reed
  Harry Lime — Orson Welles
Thirty Nine Steps,The
  Director — Alfred Hitchcock (1935)
  Richard Hannay — Robert Donat (1935), Kenneth More (1959), Robert Powell (1978)

Thoroughly Modern Millie — Title: Julie Andrews
Three Faces of Eve — Eve: Joanne Woodward
Three Men and a Baby/Little Lady
  Men — Ted Danson, Steve Guttenberg, Tom Selleck

To Catch a Thief
  Cat Burglar — Cary Grant
  Director — Alfred Hitchcock
  Female lead — Grace Kelly
To Have and Have Not
  Harry Morgan — Humphrey Bogart
  Setting — Martinique
  Slim — Lauren Bacall
Tommy
  The Acid Queen — Tina Turner
  Director — Ken Russell
  Title — Roger Daltrey
Tootsie — Michael Dorsey/Dorothy (Title): Dustin Hoffman

Top Gun
  Female lead — Kelly McGillis

Maverick	Tom Cruise
Top Hat	
Dale	Ginger Rogers
Jerry	Fred Astaire
Music	Irving Berlin
Total Recall	
Doug Quaid	Arnold Schwarzenegger
Touch of Class,A	Glenda Jackson, George Segal
Touch of Evil	
Brothel Madam	Marlene Dietrich
Quinlan, the Police Chief	Orson Welles
Vargas, the Narcotics Inspector	Charlton Heston
Towering Inferno,The	
Architect	Paul Newman
Electrical Contractor	Richard Chamberlain
Trading Places	Eddie Murphy, Dan Aykroyd
Treasure Island (1950)	Long John Silver: Robert Newton
Trouble with Harry,The	
Director	Alfred Hitchcock
Trouble	He's dead
True Grit	The Sheriff (Rooster Cogburn): John Wayne
2001 – A Space Odyssey	
Based on	Arthur C.Clarke story, 'The Sentinel'
Computer	Hal
Destination	Moon of Jupiter
Director	Stanley Kubrick
Spaceship	Discovery 1
Un Chien Andalou	
Collaborator	Salvador Dali
Director	Luis Bunuel
Valentino	
Director	Ken Russell
Title	Rudolf Nureyev
Vertigo	
Director	Alfred Hitchcock
Female lead	Kim Novak
Scottie (who suffers vertigo)	James Stewart
Way out West	Laurel and Hardy
Way We Were,The	Barbra Streisand, Robert Redford
West Side Story	
Gangs	Jets, Sharks
Maria	Natalie Wood
Tony	Richard Beymer
Whatever Happened to Baby Jane	Bette Davis, Joan Crawford
What's Up Doc?	
Director	Peter Bogdanovich
Female leads	Madeline Kahn, Barbra Streisand
Professor	Ryan O'Neal
Who Framed Roger Rabbit	
Eddie Valiant	Bob Hoskins
Whisky Galore	
Based on	Compton Mackenzie novel (derived from real wreck of the *Politician*)
Director	Alexander Mackendrick
Whistle Down the Wind	Hayley Mills
Criminal	Alan Bates

White Heat	The Gang Leader (Cody Jarrett): James Cagney
Who's Afraid of Virginia Woolf	
Director	Mike Nichols
Martha	Elizabeth Taylor
Professor	Richard Burton
Wild at Heart	
Director	David Lynch
Lula	Laura Dern
Sailor	Nicholas Cage
Wild Bunch,The	
Director	Sam Peckinpah
Pile Bishop, the Leader	William Holden
Wild One,The	
Chino, Leader of the Beetles	Lee Marvin
Johnny, Leader of Black Rebels Motorcycle Gang	Marlon Brando
Town	Wrightsville
Witness	Harrison Ford
Theme	Religious sect (The Amish)
Wizard of Oz,The	
Book by	L.Frank Baum
Dog	Toto
Dorothy Gale	Judy Garland
Hickory, the Tin Man wants	A Heart
Hunk, the Scarecrow wants	A Brain
Midgets	The Munchkins
Songs	'Over the Rainbow', 'Follow the Yellow Brick Road'
Wizard lives in	The Emerald City
Zeke, the Lion wants	Courage
Women in Love	
Birkin	Alan Bates
Director	Ken Russell
Gerald	Oliver Reed
Gudrun	Glenda Jackson
Ursula	Jennie Linden
Wuthering Heights	
Cathy	Merle Oberon
Heathcliff	Laurence Olivier
Yellow Submarine	
Baddies	Blue Meanies
Director	George Dunning
Kingdom	Pepperland
Young Frankenstein	
Director	Mel Brooks
Title	Gene Wilder
Zorba the Greek	
The Englishman	Alan Bates
Music	Mikis Theodorakis
Set in	Crete
Title	Anthony Quinn

Film Quotes and Publicity Blurbs

By: Quote → Actor/Actress, Film

'After all, tomorrow is another day'	Vivien Leigh (Scarlett O'Hara) in *Gone with the Wind*

'Beulah, peel me a grape'	Mae West in *I'm no Angel*
'Come with me to the Casbah'	Charles Boyer in *Algiers* (Attributed, never said)
'Excuse me while I slip into something more comfortable'	Jean Harlow in *Hell's Angels*
'Frankly, my dear, I don't give a damn'	Clark Gable (Rhett Butler) in *Gone with the Wind* (His last words)
'Garbo Laughs'	*Ninotchka*
'Garbo Talks'	*Anna Christie*
'Gif me a viskey, ginger ale on the side, and don't be stingy, baby'	Greta Garbo in *Anna Christie* (Her first screen words)
'Here's looking at you kid'	Humphrey Bogart to Ingrid Bergman in *Casablanca*
'I coulda had class, I coulda been somebody, I coulda been a contender'	Marlon Brando in *On the Waterfront*
'If you want anything, all you have to do is whistle'	Lauren Bacall to Humphrey Bogart in *To Have and Have Not*
'I'll be back'	Arnold Schwarzenegger in *Terminator*
'In space no one can hear you scream'	*Alien*
'Just when you thought it was safe to go back in the water'	*Jaws 2*
'Last night I dreamt I went to Manderley again'	*Rebecca*
'Love means never having to say you're sorry'	Ali McGraw to Ryan O'Neal in *Love Story*
'Made it Ma – Top of the world!'	James Cagney in *White Heat*
'Nobody's Perfect'	Joe E.Brown to Jack Lemmon in *Some Like it Hot* (last line)
'Play it (again) Sam'	Humphrey Bogart in *Casablanca*
'Rosebud'	*Citizen Kane* (Kane's last words)
'This is another fine mess you've gotten me into'	Oliver Hardy to Stan Laurel
'When you call me that, smile'	Gary Cooper to Walter Brennan in *The Virginian*
'Why don't you come up sometime and see me'	Mae West to Cary Grant in *She done him Wrong*
'You ain't heard nothin' yet'	Al Jolson in *The Jazz Singer* (First spoken words on film)

Musical Themes

By: Film → Artiste

See Also: Songs from Films

'Addams Family, The'	Hammer
'Absolute Beginners'	David Bowie
'Against All Odds'	Phil Collins
'Alfie'	Cilla Black
'Ben'	Michael Jackson
'Car Wash'	Rose Royce
'Chariots of Fire'	Vangelis
'Diamonds are Forever'	Shirley Bassey
'Fame'	Irene Cara
'For Your Eyes Only'	Sheena Easton

'From Russia With Love'	Matt Monro
'Georgy Girl'	The Seekers
'Ghostbusters'	Ray Parker Jnr.
'Goldfinger'	Shirley Bassey
'Good the Bad and the Ugly,The'	Hugo Montenegro
'In the Heat of the Night'	Ray Charles
'Live and Let Die'	Paul McCartney and Wings
'Living Daylights,The'	A-ha
'Man With the Golden Gun,The'	Lulu
'Moonraker'	Shirley Bassey
'Move Over Darling'	Doris Day
'Never on a Sunday'	Manos Hadjidakis. Hit Song: Melina Mercouri
'9 to 5'	Dolly Parton
'Octopussy'	Rita Coolidge
'Romancing the Stone'	Eddie Grant
'Shaft'	Isaac Hayes
'Soldier Blue'	Buffy Sainte-Marie
'Stand by Me'	Ben E.King
'Tender Trap,The'	Frank Sinatra
'Thunderball'	Tom Jones
'To Sir With Love'	Lulu
'View to a Kill'	Duran Duran
'Way We Were,The'	Barbra Streisand
'What's New Pussycat?'	Tom Jones
'You Only Live Twice'	Nancy Sinatra

Songs from Films

By: Song → Film

Notes: Singers are given for songs that were hits.
See Also: Musical Themes

'All Come High' (Rita Coolidge)	*Octopussy*
'As Time Goes By' (Dooley Wilson)	*Casablanca*
'Bachelor Boy' (Cliff Richard)	*Summer Holiday*
'Boys in the Backroom,The' (Marlene Dietrich)	*Destry Rides Again*
'Bright Eyes' (Art Garfunkel)	*Watership Down*
'Call Me' (Blondie)	*American Gigolo*
'Can't Help Falling In Love' (Elvis Presley)	*Blue Hawaii*
'Cheek to Cheek' (Fred Astaire)	*Top Hat*
'Chim Chim Cheree' (Julie Andrews, Dick Van Dyke)	*Mary Poppins*
'Colonel Bogey March'	*Bridge on the River Kwai*
'Consider Yourself'	*Oliver*
'Diamonds are a Girl's Best Friend'	*Gentlemen Prefer Blondes*
'Edelweiss'	*The Sound of Music*
'Entertainer,The' (Scott Joplin)	*The Sting*
'Everything I do (I do it for You)' (Bryan Adams)	*Robin Hood, Prince of Thieves*
'Eye of the Tiger' (Survivor)	*Rocky 3*
'Falling in Love Again' (Marlene Dietrich)	*The Blue Angel*
'Foggie Mountain Breakdown' (Flatt and Scruggs)	*Bonnie and Clyde*
'God Gave Rock and Roll to You' (Kiss)	*Bill and Ted's Bogus Journey*
'Harry Lime Theme' (Anton Karas)	*The Third Man*

'High Hopes' (Frank Sinatra)	*A Hole in the Head*
'Hopelessly Devoted To You' (Olivia Newton-John)	*Grease*
'I Just Called to Say I Love You' (Stevie Wonder)	*Woman in Red*
'Jean' (Rod McKuen)	*The Prime of Miss Jean Brodie*
'Lara's Theme'	*Dr Zhivago*
'Let's Call The Whole Thing Off' (Fred Astaire, Ginger Rogers)	*Shall We Dance*
'Memo to Turner' (Mick Jagger)	*Performance*
'Moonriver' (Henry Mancini)	*Breakfast at Tiffany's*
'Mrs Robinson' (Simon and Garfunkel)	*The Graduate*
'Nobody Does it Better' (Carly Simon)	*The Spy Who Loved Me*
'On The Good Ship Lollipop' (Shirley Temple)	*Bright Eyes*
'One and Only' (Chesney Hawkes)	*Buddy's Song*
'Over the Rainbow' (Judy Garland)	*Wizard of Oz*
'Power of Love,The' (Huey Lewis)	*Back to the Future*
'Que Sera Sera' (Doris Day)	*The Man Who Knew Too Much (Hitchcock)*
'Raindrops Keep Falling on my Head' (B.J.Thomas)	*Butch Cassidy and the Sundance Kid*
'Return to Sender' (Elvis Presley)	*Girls! Girls! Girls!*
'Rock Around the Clock' (Bill Haley)	*Blackboard Jungle (1st)*
'Say You Say Me' (Lionel Ritchie)	*White Nights*
'Secret Love' (Doris Day)	*Calamity Jane*
'Shoop Shoop Song' (Cher)	*Mermaids*
'Singin' in the Rain' (Fred Astaire)	*Broadway Revue of 1929 (1st)*
'A Spoonful of Sugar' (Julie Andrews)	*Mary Poppins*
'Stayin' Alive' (The Beegees)	*Saturday Night Fever*
'Suicide is Painless'	*M.A.S.H.*
'Summer Nights' (John Travolta, Olivia Newton-John)	*Grease*
'Supercalifragilisticexpialidocious' (Julie Andrews)	*Mary Poppins*
'Talk to the Animals' (Rex Harrison)	*Dr Doolittle*
'Thank Heaven for Little Girls' (Maurice Chevalier)	*Gigi*
'Tubular Bells' (Mike Oldfield)	*The Exorcist*
'Up Where We Belong' (Joe Cocker, Jennifer Warnes)	*An Officer and a Gentleman*
'Wanderin' Star' (Lee Marvin)	*Paint Your Wagon*
'We're in the Money'	*Gold Diggers of 1933 (1st)*
'When The Going Gets Tough' (Billy Ocean)	*Jewel of the Nile*
'When You Wish Upon a Star'	*Pinnochio*
'Whistle While You Work'	*Snow White and the Seven Dwarfs*
'White Christmas' (Bing Crosby)	*Holiday Inn (1st)*
'Windmills of your Mind' (Noel Harrison)	*The Thomas Crown Affair*
'Wooden Heart' (Elvis Presley)	*G.I. Blues*
'You're the One That I Want' (Olivia Newton-John, John Travolta)	*Grease*

Stars and Directors

By: Description → Name

Ambassador to Ghana; Became	Shirley Temple

Animal Rights; Noted campaigner for	Brigitte Bardot
Arrested as a suspected terrorist	Robert de Niro
Art Collection; Owned large	Edward G.Robinson
Bank accounts; Had over 700	W.C.Fields
Banned from US in 1950s	Charlie Chaplin
Banned in Germany, Italy, USSR in 1930s	Mickey Mouse
Biographical Film about; 1st	Charlie Chaplin
Boxer; Competed in Olympics as	Errol Flynn
Bridge Player; International	Omar Sharif
Brigadier General; Retired as	James Stewart
Brothel; Brought up in	Richard Pryor
Car Racing; Amateur champion	Paul Newman
Centrefold in *Cosmopolitan* magazine; 1st male	Burt Reynolds
Chain Gang; Worked in	Robert Mitchum
Circus; Ran away to in youth	Fellini
Clog Dancing Act; Stage appearance in	Chaplin
Concentration Camp; Sent to	Curt Jurgens
Death; 100,000 filed past coffin	Rudolph Valentino
Died in Jean Harlow's arms	Rin Tin Tin
Discovered; Sitting at a soda fountain	Lana Turner
Dutch Baroness; Daughter of	Audrey Hepburn
Earnings; Over $1 million per year; 1st	Fatty Arbuckle
Ears; Noted for large	Clark Gable, Bing Crosby
Elle magazine; Appeared on cover at 15	Brigitte Bardot
Embezzlement; Accused studio chief of	Cliff Robertson
Father; Olympic Gold medallist	Charlotte Rampling (Athletics), Grace Kelly (Rowing)
Fingers; Lost in explosion	Harold Lloyd
Great Danes; Kept 300	Francis X.Bushman
Harpers Bazaar cover; Appeared on before acting career	Lauren Bacall
Hitler invited to be his mistress	Marlene Dietrich
Jailed for;-	
Assault on newspaper editor	Ryan O'Neal
Cocaine smuggling into UK	Stacy Keach
Income tax evasion	Sophia Loren, Richard Pryor
Marijuana possession (1948)	Robert Mitchum
Non-payment of alimony	Michael Caine
Libel; Sued Graham Greene for	Shirley Temple
Life Jacket; Has named after	Mae West
Lift; Born in	Jack Lemmon
Marriages; Never consummated	Rudolph Valentino
Mayor of Carmel	Clint Eastwood
Mexicans; Played in first films	David Niven
Miss Hungary; Stripped of title	Zsa Zsa Gabor
MP; Greek	Melina Mercouri
Mr Scotland; Former	Sean Connery
Opera; English National; Sang with as soprano	David Hemmings
Opposite sex; Always played	Lassie (Dog, Pal, was male)
Oscar Ceremony; American Indian girl read statement as Oscar rejection	Marlon Brando
Oscars; Didn't turn up to receive 3	Woody Allen
Pain Killer; Addicted to	Jerry Lewis
Parents deaf mutes	Lon Chaney
Parents music hall entertainers	Chaplin

Parliamentary candidate/MP (Labour Party)	Glenda Jackson
Parliamentary candidate (Workers' Revolutionary Party)	Vanessa Redgrave
Philosophy Student at University	Bruce Lee
Pin-up; WWII US favourite	Betty Grable
Plastic Surgery after wartime crash	Jack Palance
Portrayed by other actors; Most	Charlie Chaplin
Ran away from home at 11	W.C.Fields
Reward offered for killing or capture by Germans in WWII	Clark Gable
Royal Command Performance at the age of 3	Elizabeth Taylor (with ballet class)
Russell Harty; Actress hit on television	Grace Jones
Scandal over starlet's death ruins career	Fatty Arbuckle
Short; Had to stand on boxes when filming	Alan Ladd
60 Pounds; Put on to play role	Robert de Niro (In *Raging Bull*)
Spectacles: No glass	Harold Lloyd
Squeaky voice caused failure when sound arrived	John Gilbert
Squint; Insured	Ben Turpin
Stabbed; Lover (Johnny Stompanato), by daughter	Lana Turner
Stamp; Actress; 1st on	Grace Kelly
Suicide; Business Manager; Committed in her hotel room	Sarah Miles
Tattoos; Hidden when filming	Sean Connery
Vamp; 1st	Theda Bara
Voice dubbed as vocal cords removed	Jack Hawkins

Stars and Directors

By: Name → General

Julie Andrews	
Fred Astaire	Bared breasts in: SOB
Ginger Rogers,1st Film with	*Flying Down to Rio*
Ginger Rogers, Films with	11
Brigitte Bardot	
Magazine Cover appears on, causing discovery	*Elle*
Western in	Shalako
Jack Benny	Instrument played: Violin
Humphrey Bogart	
Films with Lauren Bacall	5
1st Film	*To Have and Have Not*
Last Film	*The Harder They Fall*
Oscar for	*African Queen*
Charles Bronson	Played part without moving: Dummy in *House of Wax*
Richard Burton	Films with Elizabeth Taylor: 11
Charlie Chaplin	
Banned in US	*Limelight*
Born in	Lambeth, London
Buster Keaton, Film with	*Limelight*
Last Film	*A Countess from Hong Kong* (plays a steward)
Roger Corman	Associated with: Edgar Allan Poe films

James Dean	
Died	20th September, 1955
Last Film	*Giant*
Disney	
Full length Film; 1st	*Snow White*
Non-Cartoon; 1st	*Treasure Island*
Clint Eastwood	Mayor of: Carmel
Douglas Fairbanks	House with Mary Pickford: 'Pickfair'
Greta Garbo	
'Garbo Laughs'	Publicity for *Ninotchka*
'Garbo Talks'	Publicity for *Anna Christie*, her 1st sound film
Judy Garland	Co-star in 10 films: Mickey Rooney
Katherine Hepburn	
Films with Spencer Tracy	9
Last Film	*Guess Who's Coming To Dinner?*
Alfred Hitchcock	
Appeared in Lifeboat	In Newspaper Advertisement
1st Film	*The Pleasure Gardens*
Remake of own film	*The Man Who Knew Too Much*
Bob Hope	
Dentist in the West	*Son of Paleface*
Theme tune	'Thanks for the memory'
Buster Keaton	1st talking film: *Free and Easy*
Harry Langdon	Directed by: Frank Capra
Laurel and Hardy	
Go to University	*A Chump at Oxford*
Victim	Jimmy Finlayson
Harold Lloyd	Leading ladies: Bebe Daniels, Mildred Davis
Sophia Loren	Jailed for: Income tax evasion
Jeanette MacDonald	Screen partner: Nelson Eddy
Lee Marvin	Palimony case with: Michele Triola
Groucho Marx	
Animal Crackers; Plays	Captain Spalding
At the Circus; Plays	J.Cheever Loophole
A Day at the Races; Plays	Doctor Hugo Hackenbush
Duck Soup; Plays	Rufus T.Firefly
Horse Feathers; Plays	Professor Wagstaff
Marx Brothers	
Female lead	Margaret Dumont
1st Film	*The Cocoanuts*
Last Film	*Love Happy*
Names	Groucho, Harpo, Chico, Zeppo, Gummo
Steve McQueen	Last Film: *The Hunter*
Marilyn Monroe	Wind blows up skirt: *The Seven Year Itch*
Morecambe and Wise	Films: *The Intelligence Men, That Riviera Touch, The Magnificent Two*
Mary Pickford	Mother and Daughter in: *Little Lord Fauntleroy*
Ronald Reagan	
Last Film	*The Killers*
Union Post	President of Screen Actors Guild, 1940s and 1950s
With Nancy in	*Hellcats of the Navy*
Robert Redford	
1st Film directed	*Ordinary People*

Rin Tin Tin	Dies in: Jean Harlow's arms
Brooke Shields	Age in Pretty Baby: 12
Frank Sinatra	Oscar (Best Supporting Actor): *From Here To Eternity*
Steven Spielberg	Actor in: *The Blues Brothers*
Gloria Swanson	Last Film: *Airport 1975*
Elizabeth Taylor	
Oscar	*Butterfield 8*
Richard Burton, 1st Film with	*Cleopatra*
Rudolf Valentino	Last Film: *Son of Sheik*
Warner Brothers	Names: Albert, Harry, Jack, Sam
John Wayne	
Directed	*The Alamo*
Last Film	*The Shootist*

MUSIC
Backing Groups

By: Artist → Backing Group

Herb Alpert	Tijuana Brass
Captain Beefheart	Magic Band
Booker T	MG's
James Brown	Famous Flames
Joe Cocker	Grease Band
Elvis Costello	Attractions
Desmond Decker	Aces
Dion	Belmonts
Ian Dury	Blockheads
Georgie Fame	Blue Flames
Wayne Fontana	Mindbenders
Freddy	Dreamers
Gerry	Pacemakers
Bill Haley	Comets
Steve Harley	Cockney Rebel
Herman	Hermits
Buddy Holly	Crickets
Tommy James	Shondells
Joan Jett	Blackhearts
Country Joe	Fish
KC	Sunshine Band
Johnny Kidd	Pirates
Gladys Knight	Pips
Kool	The Gang
Billy J.Kramer	Dakotas
Lulu	Luvvers
Marky Mark	Funky Bunch
Bob Marley	Wailers
Martha (Reeves)	Vandellas
John Mayall	Bluesbreakers
Gary Numan	Tubeway Army
Tom Petty	Heartbreakers
Brian Poole	Tremeloes
Gary Puckett	Union Gap
Paul Revere	Raiders
Cliff Richard	Shadows
Smokey Robinson	Miracles
Diana Ross	Supremes

Mitch Ryder	Detroit Wheels
Bob Seger	Silver Bullet Band
Sam the Sham	Pharaohs
Sly	Family Stone
Bruce Springsteen	E Street Band
Shakin Stevens	Sunsets
Gene Vincent	Blue Caps
Junior Walker	All Stars

Classical Music, General

By: General

Festivals;-	
Benjamin Britten; Associated with	Aldeburgh
Mozart; in Germany	Salzburg
Mozart Operas; in Britain	Glyndebourne
Wagner's music	Bayreuth
Indonesia: Traditional Orchestra	Gamelan
Manchester; Orchestra	Hallé Orchestra
Opera House: On Amazon	Manaus Opera House, Brazil. Film based on: *Fitzcarraldo*
Proms;-	
1st	1895, Queens Hall, London
Founder	Sir Henry Wood
Royal Opera House; Location	Covent Garden

Composers

By: General

Anti-Semitic	Wagner
Beethoven; Operas	Fidelio (only one)
Buried in unmarked Pauper's grave	Mozart
Children; Had 20	J.S.Bach
Cothen, Prince of; Musician to	J.S.Bach
Deaf; Became	Beethoven
Fatness; Known for	Rossini
First work; Opus 62	Eric Satie
Five,The	Russian 18th Century Nationalist composers (Rimsky-Korsakov, Borodin, Mussorgski, Balakirev, César Cui)
GPO film unit; Member of	Benjamin Britten
Haydn; Patron	Esterházy family
Head removed after death	Haydn
Heart in Poland; Body in France	Chopin
Impressionist music; Founder	Debussy
Imprisoned for conscientious objection	Sir Michael Tippett
Insane; Became	Schumann, Smetana
Mozart;-	
Birthplace	Salzburg
Cataloguer of works	Ludwig Von Köchel
Claimed to have poisoned Mozart	Antonio Salieri
Opera; Closed by police for obscenity	Rossini
Patron;-	
Queen Anne	Handel
Ludwig II of Bavaria	Wagner
Widow he was not allowed to meet	Tchaikovsky
Paid women to faint in concerts	Liszt

Peer; Made	Benjamin Britten
Peter Pears; Friend of and accompanist to	Benjamin Britten
Songs; Famous for	Schubert
Walked long distances	Bach

Musical Instruments

By: General

Balalaika; Strings (Normal)	3
Bass Guitar; Strings tuned	G (top),D,A,E
Bell;-	
Lutine	Rung at Lloyds', London, after a disaster
St Paul's Cathedral	'Great Paul'
Brass; Lowest	Tuba
Celesta; 1st orchestral use	'Dance of the Sugar Plum Fairy' in 'The Nutcracker Suite'
Cello;-	
Full name	Violoncello
Strings tuned	A (top), D,G,C (Octave below Viola)
Double Bass; Strings tuned	G,D,A,E
English Horn; Type	Woodwind
Exhaling and Inhaling; Played by	Harmonica
Glockenspiel; Played from Keyboard	Celesta
Guitar;-	
Plucked with	Plectrum
Strings tuned	E (top),B,G,D,A,E
Harp	Strings: 46. Pedals: 7
Keyboard; First mechanical stringed instrument	Clavichord
Piano	Keys: 88
Piccolo	Pitch: Octave above Flute
Recorder	Sizes: Bass, Tenor, Treble (Alto), Descant (Soprano) Finger holes: 8
Sousaphone; Inventor	John Sousa
Spinet	Piano-like, Keyboard instrument
Steam-operated Keyboard Instrument	Calliope
Strings	Violin, Viola, Cello, Double Bass (Lowest)
Timpani; Other name	Kettledrums
Tuba Family; Largest	Sousaphone
Viola; Strings tuned	A(top), D, G, C
Violin;-	
Famous makes	Stradivarius, Amati, Guarneri (from Cremona)
Strings tuned	E(top), A, D, G
Woodwind;-	
Double reed	Oboe, Bassoon
Highest	Piccolo
Lowest	Bassoon
Single reed	Clarinet
Zither; Origin	China

Musical Terms

By: General

Accent on off beat	Syncopation

Catholic Church; Chant	Gregorian
Chord	Notes played in succession: Arpeggio
Clefs	Treble, Bass
Concerto; Movements	Usually 3
Do-Re-Mi . . .; Originally	Ut-Re-Mi . . .
Musical Staff; Inventor	Guido D'Arezzo (Monk)
Notes; Length;-	
Breve	8 crotchets (longest)
Crochet	2 quavers
Minim	2 crotchets
Quaver	Half a crotchet
Semibreve	4 crotchets
Semiquaver	Half a quaver
Octave; Interval	8 notes
Opera;-	
Solo song	Aria
Text of	Libretto
Pitch; Small fluctuations	Vibrato
Singer; Main female	Prima Donna
Singing; Above normal voice	Falsetto
Singing Voices	Soprano or Treble (Highest), Mezzo-soprano, Contralto (Alto)/Countertenor, Tenor, Baritone, Bass
Songs; German, with piano accompaniment	Lieder
Symphony; Movements	Usually 4
Tempo, Terms for;-	
Adagio	Slowly
Allegro	Quickly
Andante	Fairly slowly
Crescendo	Getting louder
Diminuendo	Getting softer
Forte	Loud
Fortissimo	Very loud
Largo	Slow
Legato	Smoothly connected
Lento	Slowly
Pianissimo	Very softly
Presto	Quick
Rallentando	Getting slower
Rubato	At a different speed than marked

Musical Works

By: Description → Work

Car Horns; Includes	Ballet Mecanique by George Antheil
Dedicated to Napoleon, then revoked	'Eroica' (Beethoven)
Dedicated to Violinist, who refused to play it	'Kreutzer Sonata' (Beethoven)
Music; Repeated 840 times	'Vexations' (Erik Satie)
Riot at Première	'Rite of Spring' (Stravinsky)
Silence; Composition consists of	4'3" (John Cage)
Symphony; 1st to use singers	Beethoven's 9th ('Choral') Symphony

Musical Works

By: Title → Composer

'Air on a G String'	J.S.Bach. Other name: 'Air from Suite No.3'
'Also Sprach Zarathustra'	Richard Strauss
'An American in Paris'	George Gershwin
'Ave Maria'	Schubert
'Ave Verum'	Mozart
'Belshazzar's Feast'	Sir William Walton
'Blue Danube Waltz'	Johann Strauss
'Bolero'	Ravel. Written for: Ida Rubenstein (Dancer)
'Brandenburg Concertos'	J.S.Bach
'Bridal Chorus' ('Here comes the Bride')	Wagner. From: Lohengrin
'Carmina Burana'	Orff
'Carnival of the Animals'	Saint-Saens
'Cavalleria Rusticana'	Mascagni
'Christmas Oratorio'	J.S.Bach
'Clair de Lune'	Debussy (from 'Suite Bergamasque')
'Creation,The'	Haydn
'Dance of the Hours,The'	Ponchielli
'Dance of the Sugar Plum Fairy,The'	Tchaikovsky (from 'The Nutcracker Suite')
'Danse Macabre'	Saint-Saens
'Dido and Aeneas'	Purcell
'Donkey Serenade,The'	Friml
'Dream of Gerontius,The'	Elgar
'1812 Overture,The'	Tchaikovsky
'Eine Kleine Nachtmusik'	Mozart
'Elijah' (Oratorio)	Mendelssohn
'Enigma Variations'	Elgar
'Eroica'	Beethoven's 3rd Symphony. Originally dedicated to: Napoleon
'Fairy Queen,The'	Purcell
'Faust Symphony'	Liszt
'Fingal's Cave'	Mendelssohn
'Flight of the Bumble Bee,The'	Rimsky-Korsakov (from 'Tsar Sultan')
'Für Elise'	Beethoven
'Goldberg Variations,The'	J.S.Bach
'Harold in Italy'	Berlioz
'Hungarian Rhapsodies'	Liszt
'Invitation to the Dance'	Weber
'Jesu Joy of Man's Desiring'	J.S.Bach
'Karelia Suite'	Sibelius
'Leningrad'	Shostakovich's 7th Symphony
'Let's Make an Opera'	Benjamin Britten
'March of the Toreadors'	Bizet (from Carmen)
'Mass in B Minor'	J.S.Bach
'La Mer'	Debussy
'Messiah'	Handel. Contains: 'Hallelujah Chorus'
'Missa Solemnis'	Beethoven
'New World Symphony,The'	Dvorak
'Peer Gynt Suites'	Edvard Grieg
'Peter and the Wolf'	Prokofiev
'Pictures at an Exhibition'	Mussorgsky
'Pierrot Lunaire'	Schoenberg

'Planets,The'	Holst
'Pomp and Circumstance'	Elgar
'Prelude a L'Après-midi d'un Faune'	Debussy
'Requiem'	Verdi (In honour of novelist Alessandro Manzoni). Fauré
'Rhapsody in Blue'	George Gershwin
'Ride of the Valkyries'	Wagner
'Rite of Spring'	Stravinsky. Riot at Première
'Royal Fireworks Music'	Handel
'Sabre Dance'	Aram Khachaturian (from ballet Gayane)
'Scheherezade'	Rimsky-Korsakov
'Seasons,The'	Haydn
'Sorcerer's Apprentice,The'	Paul Dukas
'St Matthew Passion'	J.S.Bach
'Stars and Stripes Forever,The'	Sousa
'Symphonie Fantastique'	Berlioz
'Tales from the Vienna Woods'	Johann Strauss
'Toccata and Fugue'	J.S.Bach
'Trout,The'	Schubert
'Trumpet Voluntary'	Jeremiah Clarke. Originally attributed to: Purcell
'Warsaw Concerto'	Richard Addinsell
'Water Music'	Handel
'Wedding March'	Mendelssohn. From: 'A Midsummer Night's Dream'
'Well Tempered Clavier,The'	J.S.Bach
'Young Person's Guide to the Orchestra,The	Benjamin Britten

Musical Works, Common Names

By: Title → *Common Name*

Beethoven;-

Piano Concerto No 5 in E Flat	'Emperor'
Piano Sonata No 8 in C Minor	'Pathetique'
Piano Sonata No 14 in C Sharp Minor	'Moonlight'
Piano Sonata No 23 in F Minor	'Appassionata'
Piano Trio No 9 in B Flat	'Archduke'
Symphony No 6 in F	'Pastoral'
Symphony No 9 in D minor	'Choral'
Synphony No 3 in E Flat	'Eroica'
Violin Sonata No 9 in D	'Kreutzer'

Chopin;-

Etude in G Flat, No 5	'Black Key'
Waltz in D Flat, No 1	'Minute Waltz'
Waltz No 3 in F	'Cats Waltz'

Dvorak;-

String Quartet No 6	'American'
Symphony No 9	'New World'

Handel; Harpsichord Suite No 5 in E   'Harmonious Blacksmith'

Haydn;-

No 100 in G	'Military'
No 104 in D	'London'
Symphony No 94 in 6	'Surprise'
Symphony No 101 in D	'Clock'

Mozart;-
Piano Concerto No 21 in C	'Elvira Madigan'
Serenade in 6	'Eine Kleine Nachtmusik'
Symphony No 38 in D	'Prague'
Symphony No 41 in C	'Jupiter'
Prokofiev; Symphony No 1	'Classical'

Schubert;-
Piano Quintet in A	'Trout'
Symphony No 8 in B minor	'Unfinished'
Shostakovich; Symphony No 7 in C	'Leningrad'
Tchaikovsky; Symphony No 6	'Pathétique'

Musicians

By: General

Benjamin Britten; Accompanied on piano	Peter Pears
Concert Career; Longest	Artur Rubenstein (Over 75 years)
Conductor;-	
Berlin Philharmonic Orchestra	Herbert Von Karajan
London Symphony Orchestra (and Founder)	Sir Thomas Beecham
NBC Symphony Orchestra; Created for	Toscanini
New York Philharmonic, Hallé Orchestra	Sir John Barbirolli
Considered in league with the devil	Paganini
Covent Garden; Musical Directors; Recent	George Solti, Colin Davis
Drug millionaire; Son of	Thomas Beecham
Knighthood; 1st	Henry Rowley Bishop (1823)
Master of the Queen's Music	Sir Malcolm Williamson
Musical Director; New York Philharmonic	Leonard Bernstein
Proms; Associated with	Henry Wood
Score; Never used	Toscanini
Violinist; Composed pieces purporting to be by various composers	Fritz Kreisler

Musicians, Instruments played

By: Name → Instrument played

Covers: Classical, Jazz.
Larry Adler	Harmonica
Louis Armstrong	Trumpet
Count Basie	Piano
Beethoven	Piano
Bix Biederbecke	Trumpet/Cornet
Julian Bream	Guitar
Pablo Casals	Cello
Charlie Christian	Guitar
Ornette Coleman	Alto Sax
John Coltrane	Tenor Sax
Johnny Dankworth	Alto Sax
Miles Davis	Trumpet
Duke Ellington	Piano
Mischa Elman	Violin
Erroll Garner	Piano
Stan Getz	Tenor Sax

Dizzy Gillespie	Trumpet
Benny Goodman	Clarinet
Coleman Hawkins	Tenor Sax
Jascha Heifetz	Violin
Myra Hess	Piano
Vladimir Horowitz	Piano
Milt Jackson	Vibraphone
Fritz Kreisler	Violin
Wanda Landowska	Harpsichord
Wynton Marsalis	Trumpet
Yehudi Menuhin	Violin
Charlie Mingus	Bass
Thelonius Monk	Piano
Jelly Roll Morton	Piano
Kid Ory	Trombone
Paganini	Violin
Charlie Parker	Alto Sax
Django Reinhardt	Guitar
Sonny Rollins	Tenor Sax
Artur Rubinstein	Piano
Domenico Scarlatti	Harpsichord
Schnabel	Piano
Ronnie Scott	Tenor Sax
Andres Segovia	Guitar
Wayne Shorter	Saxophone
Jack Teagarden	Trombone
Rosalyn Tweck	Harpsichord
John Williams	Guitar
Lester Young	Tenor Sax

Opera Characters

By: Characters → Opera

Alberich	*Das Rheingold*
Alfia	*Cavalleria Rusticana*
Don Alfonso	*Cosi Fan Tutte*
Alfredo	*La Traviata*
Count Almaviva	*Barber of Seville, Marriage of Figaro*
Amfortas	*Parsifal*
Princess Amneris	*Aida*
Donna Anna	*Don Giovanni*
Azucena	*Il Trovatore*
Bartolo	*Barber of Seville, Marriage of Figaro*
Calaf	*Turandot*
Canio	*I Pagliacci*
Count de Luna	*Il Trovatore*
Crown	*Porgy and Bess*
Daland	*The Flying Dutchman*
Dorabella	*Cosi Fan Tutte*
Elsa	*Lohengrin*
Escamillo	*Carmen*
Esmeralda	*The Bartered Bride*
Eva	*The Mastersingers of Nuremberg*
False Dimitri,The	*Boris Godunov*
Feodor	*Boris Godunov*
Ferrando	*Cosi Fan Tutte*
Figaro	*Barber of Seville, Marriage of Figaro*
Filch	*The Beggar's Opera*

63

Fiordiligi	*Cosi Fan Tutte*
Florestan	*Fidelio*
Gilda	*Rigoletto*
Godfrey	*Lohengrin*
Golaud	*Pelleas et Melisande*
Guglielmo	*Cosi Fan Tutte*
Don José	*Carmen*
Kundry	*Parsifal*
Lenski	*Eugene Onegin*
Leonora	*Fidelio, Il Trovatore*
Leporello	*Don Giovanni*
Lindorf	*The Tales of Hoffman*
Macheath	*The Beggar's Opera*
Manrico	*Il Trovatore*
Duke of Mantua,The	*Rigoletto*
Marcello	*La Bohème*
Marcellina	*Fidelio*
Mad Margaret	*Ruddigore*
Marguerite	*Don Giovanni*
Marie (The Prostitute)	*Wozzeck*
Mario	*Tosca*
King Mark	*Tristan and Isolde*
Micha	*The Bartered Bride*
Mimi	*La Bohème*
Dr Miracle	*The Tales of Hoffman*
Musetta	*La Bohème*
Nedda	*I Pagliacci*
Count Octavian	*Der Rosenkavalier*
Olga	*Eugene Onegin*
Ellen Orford	*Peter Grimes*
Pamina	*The Magic Flute*
Papageno	*The Magic Flute*
Mr Peachum	*The Beggar's Opera*
Lieut. Pinkerton	*Madame Butterfly*
Pizarro	*Fidelio*
Rhadames	*Aida*
Robbins	*Porgy and Bess*
Rocco	*Fidelio*
Rosina	*Barber of Seville, Marriage of Figaro*
Rudolpho	*La Bohème*
Cio Cio San	*Madame Butterfly*
Santuzza	*Cavalleria Rusticana*
Sarastro	*The Magic Flute*
Baron Scarpia	*Tosca*
Senta	*The Flying Dutchman*
Sharpless	*Madame Butterfly*
Silvio	*I Pagliacci*
Sophie	*Der Rosenkavalier*
Sportin' Life	*Porgy and Bess*
Stella	*The Tales of Hoffman*
Tatiana	*Eugene Onegin*
Telramund	*Lohengrin*
King Titurel	*Parsifal*
Turiddu	*Cavalleria Rusticana*
Violetta	*La Traviata*
Walter Von Stolzing	*The Mastersingers of Nuremberg*
Wenzel	*The Bartered Bride*
Wolfram	*Tannhauser*

Operas

By: Description

Figaro; Operas with central character	Barber of Seville, Marriage of Figaro
1st	Daphne (Jacopo Peri)
Gilbert and Sullivan; Opera company associated with	D'Oyly Carte
Première in Egypt	Aida
Puccini; Uncompleted	Turandot
Suez Canal Opening; Written for	Aida

Operas

By: Title → Composer, Other

Aida	Verdi
Lovers' fate	Burned alive
Written for	Suez Canal opening
Amahl and the Night Visitors	Menotti
Appalachian Spring	Aaron Copland
Barber of Seville,The	Rossini
Barber	Figaro
Based on	De Beaumarchais story
Lovers	Count Almaviva, Rosina
Rosina's Guardian	Bartolo
Bartered Bride,The	Smetana
Title	Marenka
Beggar's Opera,The	John Gay (Libretto)
Hero	Highwayman MacHeath
Music arranged by	Pepusch
Billy Budd	Benjamin Britten
Based on	Herman Melville story
Commander	Captain Vere
Libretto	E.M.Forster, Eric Crozier
Master at arms	Claggart
Ship	HMS Indomitable
Billy the Kid	Aaron Copland
Bluebeard's Castle	Bartok
Boris Godunov	Mussorgsky
Based on	Pushkin play
Carmen	Bizet
Based on	Merimée novel
Carmen's Death	Stabbed by Don José
Toreador	Escamillo
Coppelia	Delibes
Cosi Fan Tutte	Mozart
Der Rosenkavalier	Richard Strauss
Dido and Aeneas	Purcell
Die Fledermaus	Johann Strauss
Based on	Le Reveillon (Meilhat and Halevy story)
Main Character	Baron Von Eisenstein
Wife	Rosalinde
Don Giovanni	Mozart
Eugene Onegin	Tchaikovsky
Falstaff	Verdi (His last)
Faust	Gounod
Fidelio	Beethoven
Original name	Leonore

Setting	Prison
Flying Dutchman, The	Wagner
Gondoliers, The	Gilbert and Sullivan
Hansel and Gretel	Humperdinck
HMS Pinafore	Gilbert and Sullivan
I Pagliacci	Leoncavallo
Idomineo	Mozart
Il Trovatore	Verdi
Title	Manrico
Iolanthe	Gilbert and Sullivan
La Bohème	Puccini
La Traviata	Verdi
Based on	*The Lady of the Camelias* (Dumas novel)
La Traviata dies from	Consumption
Title	Violetta
Lohengrin	Wagner
Madame Butterfly	Puccini
Madam Butterfly	Cio Cio San
US Naval Officer	Pinkerton
Magic Flute, The	Mozart
Theme	Freemasonry
Marriage of Figaro, The	Mozart
Based on	De Beaumarchais story
Merry Widow, The	Franz Lehar
Mikado, The	Gilbert and Sullivan
Nabucco	Verdi
Orpheus and Eurydice	Gluck
Otello	Verdi
Parsifal	Wagner
Pearl Fishers, The	Bizet
Set in	Sri Lanka
Pelleas et Mellisande	Debussy
Peter Grimes	Benjamin Britten
Set in	The Borough, a fishing village
Pirates of Penzance, The	Gilbert and Sullivan
Porgy and Bess	George Gershwin
Pulcinella	Stravinsky
Scenery and Costumes	Picasso
Rake's Progress, The	Stravinsky
Rape of Lucretia, The	Benjamin Britten
Rigoletto	Verdi
Ring, The	Wagner (4 Opera cycle)
Operas	Das Rheingold, Die Valkyrie, Siegfried, Gotterdamerung
Rise and fall of the City of Mahagonny, The	Kurt Weill
Rose Marie	Rudolf Friml
Salome	Richard Strauss
Based on	Oscar Wilde play
Samson and Delilah	Saint-Saens
Tales of Hoffman	Offenbach
Tannhauser	Wagner
Thieving Magpie, The	Rossini
Threepenny Opera, The	Brecht and Weill
Based on	*The Beggar's Opera*
Tosca	Puccini
Tristan and Isolde	Wagner

Vagabond King,The	Rudolf Friml
War and Peace	Prokofiev
William Tell	Rossini

Pop Groups/Singers

By: Description → Name

Covers: All Non-Classical.
Notes: All charts referred to are UK charts unless otherwise stated.

African Instrument; Named after	Bo Diddley
Albino	Johnny and Edgar Winter
Anorexia related death	Karen Carpenter
Arrested for indecent exposure	Jim Morrison
Atlantic, both sides; Played on same day	Phil Collins ('Live Aid')
Bats' Heads, biting off; Famous for	Ozzy Osbourne
Beards; Long	ZZ Top
Be-Bop; Founders	Charlie Parker, Dizzie Gillespie
Black Artist; Jazz; 1st recordings	Kid Ory
Blind; Acoustic guitarist	José Feliciano
Buddy Holly Songs; Bought rights	Paul McCartney
Burning Headdress; Appeared wearing	Arthur Brown
Busker	Don Partridge
Charles Manson; Friend of	Dennis Wilson (Beach Boys)
Charts;-	
Longest period in	Elvis Presley
Longest period in; 2nd	Cliff Richard
Most records in	Elvis Presley
Most records in; 2nd	Cliff Richard
Child Stars; Former	Phil Collins, Petula Clark, Micky Dolenz
Cousin; Married 13-year-old, causing scandal	Jerry Lee Lewis
Dolls; Chopped up	Alice Cooper
Duck Walk; Famous for	Chuck Berry
Eye make-up, black; Known for	Dusty Springfield
Father;-	
English Army Captain	Bob Marley
Joe Loss band vocalist	Elvis Costello
Shot	Marvin Gaye
Final Concert: 'The Last Waltz'	The Band
Foreign Legion; Served in	Cole Porter
Glasses; Bizarre wears	Elton John
Glove; One, wears	Michael Jackson
Gold Lamé Suits; Wore	Liberace
Guitar;-	
Set fire to	Jimi Hendrix
Smashing; Noted for	Jimi Hendrix, Pete Townshend
Hair caught fire	Michael Jackson
Hospitals; Spent years of childhood in	Ringo Starr
Islam; Converted to	Cat Stevens
Israeli Couple; Had No 1 hit	Esther and Abi Ofarim
Jehovah's Witness	Michael Jackson
London School of Economics Student	Mick Jagger
LP Charts;-	
Most records in	Elvis Presley
Most records in; 2nd	Frank Sinatra
Mad Max III; Appears in	Tina Turner

Make-up; US group with	Kiss
Mayor of Palm Springs	Sonny Bono
Mormon	Osmonds
MP; Greek Communist	Mikis Theodorakis
No 1;-	
Most	Beatles, Elvis Presley (17)
Most; Consecutive	Beatles (11)
Oldest artiste	Louis Armstrong, 'Hello Dolly' (63)
Straight in at; Most	Slade, Jam (3)
US; Most	Beatles (20)
Norwegian Group; No 1; 1st	A-ha ('The Sun always Shines on TV')
Parliament adjourned to hear radio show	Gracie Fields
Petrol Ration Fraud; Fined for; WWII	Ivor Novello
Piano; Stands on	Little Richard
Plastic Surgery to improve face	Michael Jackson
Polio; Crippled by	Ian Dury
Pop Journalist; Former	Neil Tennant
Red Wedge; Prominent with	Billy Bragg
Rhodes Scholar at Oxford University	Kris Kristofferson
Russian Roulette; Died playing	Terry Kath (Chicago)
Scarecrow; Appeared as in a film	Michael Jackson
Schoolboy; Dresses as on stage	Angus Young (AC/DC)
Snake; Part of stage act	Alice Cooper
Songwriter; Cannot read or write music	Irving Berlin
Straw Hat; Usually appeared in	Maurice Chevalier
Sued by Harold Wilson	The Move
Surfing Sound; Famous for	Beach Boys
Swimming Pool; Piano shaped	Liberace
Tom and Jerry; Recorded as	Simon and Garfunkel
Top 10;-	
Most records simultaneously	Frankie Laine (4 in 1953)
Most records simultaneously; US	Beatles (Top 5 in 1964)
Trousers; Split on stage	P.J.Proby
Margaret Trudeau; Involved with	Rolling Stones
Twangy Sound; Associated with	Duane Eddy
Twelve Children; One of	Dolly Parton
USSR; 1st foreign rock concert in	Elton John
Waist up; Only shown from, when first televised	Elvis Presley
Watford Football Club; Former Chairman	Elton John
Wombles; Music for	Mike Batt
Yachts; Races	Simon Le Bon

Pop Groups/Singers

By: Name → General

Notes: *For individuals, prominent groups they play/have played with are normally given. Hits, unless otherwise stated, are UK Top 20 hits. Those under individual names are solo hits.*

Abba	Bjorn Ulvaeus, Agnetha Faltskog (were married), Anni-Frid Lyngstad, Benny Andersson (were married)
Bjorn Ulvaeus musical	Chess
No 1, 1st	'Waterloo' (Eurovision Song Contest Winner)

ABC	Vocals: Martin Fry
AC/DC	
From	Australia
Lead Guitarist	Angus Young
Singer died	Bon Scott
Adam and the Ants	No 1, 1st: 'Stand and Deliver'
Marc Almond	Soft Cell
Benny Andersson	Abba
Ian Anderson	Jethro Tull
Plays	Flute
Jon Anderson	Yes
Animals	
No 1, only	'House of the Rising Sun'
Vocals	Eric Burden
Rod Argent	Zombies, Argent
Joan Armatrading	
Born	St Kitts
Home	Birmingham
Randy Bachman	Guess Who, Bachman Turner Overdrive
Tom Bailey	Thompson Twins
Florence Ballard	Supremes
Syd Barrett	Pink Floyd
Bay City Rollers	
From	Edinburgh
No 1, 1st	'Bye Bye Baby'
Beach Boys	Brian, Dennis, Carl Wilson, Mike Love, Al Jardine
No 1, 1st	'Good Vibrations'
Beatles	John Lennon (Rhythm Guitar, Vocals), Paul McCartney (Bass Guitar, Vocals), George Harrison (Lead Guitar), Ringo Starr (Drums)
Biggest selling single	'I Wanna Hold Your Hand'
Earlier name	The Quarrymen
From	Liverpool
Guru	Maharishi Mahesh Yogi
Hit, 1st	'Love Me Do'
Managers	Allan Williams, Brian Epstein, Allan Klein
Name Derived from	The Crickets
No 1, 1st	'From Me To You' (1963)
No 1, 1st, US	'Love Me Do' (1962)
No 1, 1st by another artist	World Without Love (Peter and Gordon)
No 1s, number of	17
Original members	Lennon, McCartney, Harrison, Stu Sutcliffe, Pete Best (Drums)
Played at	Cavern Club, Liverpool
Record Label, 1st	Polydor (Germany)
Record Label, 1st UK	Parlaphone
Record Label, US	Capitol
Jeff Beck	Yardbirds
Walter Becker	Steely Dan
Bee Gees	Barry, Maurice, Robin Gibb
Hit, 1st	'New York Mining Disaster'
No 1, 1st	'Massachusetts'

Oldest	Barry
Twins	Maurice, Robin
Madeline Bell	Blue Mink
Robert Bell	Kool and the Gang
Brian Bennett	Shadows
Chuck Berry	No 1: 'My Ding a Ling'
Nuno Bettencourt	Extreme
Bev Bevan	ELO
Beverley Sisters	Names: Babs, Joy, Teddy
Cindy Birdsong	Supremes
Jet Black	Stranglers
Black Sabbath	Vocalists: Osbourne, Dio, Gillan
Ritchie Blackmore	Deep Purple, Rainbow
Blind Faith	Eric Clapton, Ginger Baker, Stevie Winwood, Rick Grech
Blondie	
No 1, 1st	'Heart of Glass'
Singer	Debbie Harry
Buster Bloodvessel	Bad Manners (Vocals)
Mike Bloomfield	Paul Butterfield Blues Band, Electric Flag (Guitarist)
Blues Brothers	John Belushi (Jake), Dan Akroyd (Elwood)
Colin Blunstone	Zombies
Marc Bolan	T.Rex
Simon Le Bon	Duran Duran
Boney M	No 1, 1st: 'Rivers of Babylon'
Bono	U2
Boomtown Rats	
Formed in	Dun Laoghaire
No 1, 1st	'Rat Trap'
David Bowie	
Hit, 1st	'Space Oddity' (1969)
Hit, with Bing Crosby	Peace on Earth
No 1, 1st	'Space Oddity' (1975)
No 1, With others	Queen ('Under Pressure'), Mick Jagger ('Dancing in the Street')
Brian and Michael	Names: Kevin Parrott, Mick Coleman
Gary Brooker	Procol Harum
Elkie Brooks	Vinegar Joe
Hit, 1st	'Pearl's a Singer'
Errol Brown	Hot Chocolate
Lindsey Buckingham	Fleetwood Mac
Dewey Bunnell	America
Eric Burden	Animals (Vocalist), War
Chris De Burgh	
From	Ireland
No 1	The Lady in Red
Kate Bush	No 1, 1st: 'Wuthering Heights'
Biff Byford	Saxon
Byrds	No 1, only: 'Mr Tambourine Man'
David Byrne	Talking Heads
Randy California	Spirit
Ali Campbell	UB40
Captain Sensible	Damned
Kim Carnes	New Christy Minstrels
Carpenters,The	Richard, Karen
David Cassidy	TV show appeared on: *The Partridge Family*

Roger Chapman	Family
Chas and Dave	Surnames: Hodges, Peacock
Chipmunks	Creator: David Seville
Eric Clapton	Yardbirds, John Mayalls
	Bluebreakers, Cream, Blind Faith,
	Derek and the Dominoes
Gene Clark	Byrds
Dave Clark Five	Dave Clark played: Drums
Allan Clarke	Hollies
Stanley Clarke	Plays: Bass Guitar
Vince Clarke	Yazoo, Erasure
Adam Clayton	U2
Con Clusky	Bachelors
Declan Clusky	Bachelors
Leonard Cohen	From: Canada
Phil Collins	
Acts in	Oliver Twist
Formerly with	Genesis
Plays	Drums, Piano
Communards	Jimmy Somerville, Richard Coles
	(Piano)
Ry Cooder	Plays: Slide Guitar
Julian Cope	The Teardrop Explodes
Stewart Copeland	Curved Air, Police
Hugh Cornwell	Stranglers
Country Joe and the Fish	Country Joe: Joe McDonald
David Coverdale	Deep Purple, Whitesnake
Cream	Eric Clapton, Jack Bruce, Ginger Baker
Lol Creme	10 CC, Godley and Creme
David Crosby	Byrds, Crosby Stills Nash and Young
Mike D'Abo	Manfred Mann
Roger Daltrey	Who
Jerry Dammers	Specials
August Darnell	Kid Creole and the Coconuts
Dave Davies	Kinks
Ray Davies	Kinks
John Deacon	Queen
Carol Decker	T'Pau
Delaney and Bonnie	Surname: Bramlett
Sandy Denny	Fairport Convention, Fotheringay
Depeche Mode	Name from: French fashion
	magazine
Dexy's Midnight Runners	
No 1, 1st	'Geno'
Vocalist/Leader	Kevin Rowland
Bruce Dickinson	Iron Maiden
Mickey Dolenz	Monkees
Duran Duran	
Name from	Film *Barbarella*
No 1, 1st	'Is There Something I Should Know'
Judith Durham	Seekers
Echo and the Bunnymen	From: Liverpool
The Edge	U2
Dave Edmunds	Groups: Love Sculpture, Rockpile
Cass Elliott	Mamas and the Papas
Keith Emerson	Nice, Emerson Lake and Palmer
Brian Eno	Roxy Music
John Entwhistle	Who

Equals	No 1, only: 'Baby Come Back'
Erasure	Vince Clark, Andy Bell
David Essex	Musical starred in: Godspell
Eurhythmics	Annie Lennox, Dave Stewart
Hit, 1st	'Sweet Dreams (Are made of this)'
No 1, 1st	'There must be an Angel (Playing with my heart)'
Little Eva	
Babysitter for	Carole King, Gerry Goffin
Hit	'Locomotion'
Everly Brothers	
Names	Don (Elder), Phil
No 1, 1st	'All I Have To Do Is Dream'
Donald Fagen	Steely Dan
Adam Faith	No 1, 1st: 'What Do You Want'
Agnetha Faltskog	Abba
Bryan Ferry	Roxy Music
Fine Young Cannibals	David Steele, Roland Gift, Andy Cox, formerly in: The Beat
Five Star	Pearsons (Doris, Lorraine, Deniece, Stedman, Delroy)
Mickey Finn	T.Rex
Fish	Marillion (Vocals)
Mick Fleetwood	Fleetwood Mac
John Fogerty	Creedence Clearwater Revival
Four Seasons	
Hit, 1st	'Sherry'
Vocals	Frankie Valli
Four Tops	No 1, 1st: 'Reach Out I'll Be There'
Peter Frampton	Herd, Humble Pie
Frankie Goes To Hollywood	
From	Liverpool
No 1, 1st	'Relax'
Aretha Franklin	Hit, 1st: 'Respect'
Freddy and the Dreamers	Freddy: Freddy Garrity
Robert Fripp	King Crimson
Edgar Froese	Tangerine Dream
Martin Fry	ABC (Vocals)
Fun Boy Three	Terry Hall, Lynval Golding, Neville Staples
Billy Fury	Hit, 1st: 'Maybe Tomorrow'
Peter Gabriel	Genesis
Gallagher and Lyle	First Names: Benny, Graham
Gerry Garcia	Grateful Dead
Art Garfunkel	No 1, 1st: 'I Only Have Eyes For You'
Freddy Garrity	Freddy and the Dreamers
David Gates	Bread
Marvin Gaye	Records with: Tammy Tyrell, Mary Wells, Kim Weston, Diana Ross
Bob Geldof	Boomtown Rats
Boy George	Bow Wow Wow, Culture Club
No 1, only	'Everything I Own'
Lowell George	Little Feat
Gerry and the Pacemakers	No 1, 1st: 'How Do You Do It'
Gibb Brothers	Barry, Maurice, Robin (Bee Gees), Andy (Solo)
Billy Gibbons	ZZ Top

Gary Glitter	
1st Stage Name	Paul Raven
No 1, 1st	'I'm the Leader of the Gang'
Kevin Godley	10 CC, Godley and Creme
Eddy Grant	Equals
From	Guyana
No 1, 1st solo	'I Don't Wanna Dance'
Peter Green	Fleetwood Mac
Woody Guthrie	Written on Guitar: 'This Machine Kills Fascists'
Steve Hackett	Genesis
Tony Hadley	Spandau Ballet
Bill Haley and the Comets	No 1: 'Rock Around The Clock'
Terry Hall	Specials, Fun Boy Three
Hall and Oates	First Names: Daryl, John
George Harrison	Beatles
Hit, 1st solo (No 1)	My Sweet Lord
Debbie Harry	Blondie
Bobby Hatfield	Righteous Brothers
Jimi Hendrix Experience	Hendrix, Mitch Mitchell (Drums), Noel Redding (Bass)
Hit, 1st	'Hey Joe'
No 1, only	'Voodoo Chile'
Woody Herman Band	Theme tune: 'Blue Flame'
Herman's Hermits	
Hit, 1st (No 1)	'I'm Into Something Good'
Vocals	Peter Noone
Nick Heyward	Haircut 100
Tony Hicks	Hollies
Dusty Hill	ZZ Top
Chris Hillman	Byrds
Bob (The Bear) Hite	Canned Heat
Noddy Holder	Slade
Jools Holland	Squeeze
Hollies	No 1, only: 'I'm Alive'
Buddy Holly	Hit, 1st (No 1): 'That'll Be The Day'
Adam Horowitz	Beastie Boys
Hot Chocolate	Vocals: Errol Brown
Housemartins	From: Hull
Whitney Houston	No 1, 1st: 'Saving All My Love For You'
Steve Howe	Yes, Asia
Mick Hucknall	Simply Red
Alan Hull	Lindisfarne
Human League	No 1, only: 'Don't You Want Me'
Humble Pie	Hit, only: 'Natural Born Boogie'
Humblebums	Billy Connolly, Gerry Rafferty
Ian Hunter	Mott the Hoople
Michael Hutchence	Inxs
Ashley Hutchings	Fairport Convention, Steeleye Span
Chrissie Hynde	Pretenders
No 1, solo	'I Got You Babe' (with UB40)
Billy Idol	Generation X
Tony Iommi	Black Sabbath
Isley Brothers	
Hit, 1st	'This Old Heart of Mine'
Names	O'Kelly, Ronald, Rudolph
J. Geils Band	No 1, only: 'Centrefold'
Michael Jackson	No 1, 1st: 'One Day In Your Life'

Jackson Five	Hit, 1st: 'I Want You Back'
Mick Jagger	Rolling Stones
Jam,The	
No 1, 1st	'Going Underground'
Vocals	Paul Weller
Jan and Dean	Surnames: Berry, Torrence
Bert Jansch	Pentangle
Al Jardine	Beach Boys
Jethro Tull	Vocals: Ian Anderson
Billy Joel	No 1, only: 'Uptown Girl'
Elton John	
Hit, 1st	'Your Song'
Lyric Writer	Bernie Taupin
No 1, Only	'Don't Go Breaking My Heart' (with Kiki Dee)
Holly Johnson	Frankie Goes to Hollywood
Brian Jones	Rolling Stones
Davy Jones	Monkees
From	England
Kenny Jones	Small Faces, Who
Mick Jones	Clash, Big Audio Dynamite
Paul Jones	Manfred Mann, Blues Band
Tom Jones	Hit, 1st (No 1): 'It's Not Unusual'
Janis Joplin	Big Brother and the Holding Company
Steve Katz	Blood, Sweat and Tears
KC and the Sunshine Band	KC: Harry Casey
Eddie Kendricks	Temptations
Jim Kerr	Simple Minds
Nik Kershaw	Fusion
Hit, 1st	'Wouldn't It Be Good'
Kid Creole and the Coconuts	Kid Creole: August Darnell
B.B.King	Guitar: Lucille
Ben E.King	Drifters
Mark King	Level 42
Kinks,The	No 1, 1st: 'You Really Got Me'
Mark Knopfler	Dire Straits
Kool and the Gang	
Kool	Robert Bell
Hit, 1st	'Ladies Night'
Al Kooper	Blood, Sweat and Tears
Paul Kossoff	Free
Kraftwerk	No 1, only: 'The Model/Computer Love'
Denny Laine	Moody Blues, Wings
Greg Lake	King Crimson, Emerson Lake and Palmer
Ronnie (Plonk) Lane	Small Faces, Slim Chance
Jimmy Lea	Slade
Led Zeppelin	John Bonham (Drums), John Paul Jones (Bass), Jimmy Page (Guitar), Robert Plant (Vocals)
Film	*The Song Remains the Same*
Originally called	New Yardbirds
Alvin Lee	Ten Years After
Arthur Lee	Love
Lemmy	Motorhead
John Lennon	Beatles
Bed in (during honeymoon)	Amsterdam Hilton
Hit, 1st solo	'Give peace a Chance'

No 1, 1st solo	'Starting Over'
Annie Lennox	Tourists, Eurhythmics
Def Leppard	From: Sheffield
Jerry Lee Lewis	
Hit, 1st	'Whole Lotta Shakin Goin' On'
No 1, only	'Great Balls of Fire'
Limahl	Kajagoogoo
Little Richard	Hit, 1st: 'Tutti Frutti'
Mike Love	Beach Boys
Lovin' Spoonful	Hit, 1st: 'Daydream'
Chris Lowe	Pet Shop Boys
Lulu	Hit, 1st: 'Shout'
Annabella Lwin	Bow Wow Wow (Vocals)
Anni-Frid Lyngstad	Abba
Jeff Lynne	ELO
Phil Lynott	Thin Lizzy
Shane MacGowan	Pogues
Madness	No 1, only: 'House of Fun'
Madonna	
Hit, 1st	'Holiday'
No 1, 1st	'Into the Groove'
Russell Mael	Sparks
Manfred Mann	
Hit, 1st	'5-4-3-2-1'
No 1, 1st	'Doo Wah Diddy Diddy'
Manhattan Transfer	No 1, only: 'Chanson D'Amour'
Barry Manilow	Hit, 1st: 'Mandy'
Phil Manzanera	Roxy Music
Marillion	Name from: *Silmarillion* (Tolkien novel)
Bob Marley	Hit, 1st: 'Exodus'
Steve Marriott	Small Faces, Humble Pie
Gerry Marsden	Gerry and the Pacemakers
Hank Marvin	Shadows
Dave Mason	Traffic
Ian Matthews	Fairport Convention, Matthews Southern Comfort
Brian May	Queen
John Mayall's Bluesbreakers	Guitarists: Eric Clapton, Peter Green, Mick Taylor
Glenn Miller Band	Theme Tune: 'Moonlight Serenade'
Dan McCafferty	Nazareth
Paul McCartney	Beatles, Wings
Film	*Give My Regards To Broadstreet*
Plays	Bass Guitar
Roger McGuinn	Byrds
Leslie McKeown	Bay City Rollers
Pigpen McKernan	Grateful Dead
John McLaughlin	Mahavishnu Orchestra
Don McLean	
Hit, 1st	'American Pie'
No 1, 1st	'Vincent'
John McVie	Fleetwood Mac
Bill Medley	Righteous Brothers
Men at Work	
From	Australia
No 1, only	'Down Under'
Freddie Mercury	Queen

George Michael	Wham!
Glenn Miller Band	Theme Tune: 'Moonlight Serenade'
Joni Mitchell	Hit, 1st: 'Big Yellow Taxi'
Mitch Mitchell	Jimi Hendrix Experience
Monkees,The	Mickey Dolenz, Davy Jones, Mike Nesmith, Peter Tork
Hit, 1st (No 1)	'I'm a Believer'
Moody Blues	Hit, 1st (No 1): 'Go Now'
Keith Moon	Who
Stephen Morrissey	Smiths
Jim Morrison	Doors
Van Morrison	Them
Move,The	
Hit, 1st	'Night of Fear'
No 1, only	'Blackberry Way'
Alison Moyet	Yazoo
Nickname	Alf
Larry Mullen	U2
Graham Nash	Hollies, Crosby Stills Nash and Young
Johnny Nash	No 1, only: 'Tears On My Pillow'
Mike Nesmith	Monkees
Olivia Newton-John	
Hit, 1st	'If Not For You'
No 1, 1st	'You're The One That I Want' (with John Travolta)
Stevie Nicks	Fleetwood Mac
Harry Nilsson	No 1: 'Without You'
Peter Noone	Herman's Hermits (Herman)
Gary Numan	No 1, 1st: 'Are Friends Electric?'
Phil Oakey	Human League
Hazel O'Connor	Film, Starred in: *Breaking Glass*
Roy Orbison	Hit, 1st (No 1): 'Only the Lonely'
Roland Orzabel	Tears for Fears
Ozzy Osbourne	Black Sabbath
Donny Osmond	
Hit, 1st (No 1)	'Puppy Love'
Hit, 1st with Marie	'I'm Leaving It All Up To You'
Jimmy Osmond	Hit, 1st (No 1): 'Long-Haired Lover From Liverpool'
Marie Osmond	Hit: 'Paper Roses'
Osmonds,The	No 1, only: 'Love Me For A Reason'
Jimmy Page	Yardbirds, Led Zeppelin
Robert Palmer	Power Station
Pearsons	Five Star
Marti Pellow	Wet Wet Wet
Mike Pender	Searchers
Pepsi and Shirlie	Surnames: Demacque, Holliman
Pet Shop Boys	Neil Tennant, Chris Lowe
Peter and Gordon	Surname: Asher, Waller
Peter, Paul and Mary	Peter Yarrow, Paul (Noel) Stookey, Mary Travers
Slim Jim Phantom	Stray Cats
Michelle Philips	Mamas and the Papas
Wilson Pickett	Hit, 1st: 'In the Midnight Hour'
Pink Floyd	
Hit, 1st	'Arnold Layne'
No 1, only	'Another Brick in the Wall'
Gene Pitney	Hit, 1st: '24 hours from Tulsa'

Robert Plant	Led Zeppelin
Police,The	Sting (Vocals, Bass), Andy Summers (Guitar), Stewart Copeland (Drums)
Hit, 1st	'Roxanne'
No 1, 1st	'Message in a Bottle'
Elvis Presley	
Hit, 1st	'Heartbreak Hotel'
House	'Graceland'
Manager	'Colonel' Tom Parker
No 1, 1st	'All Shook Up'
Record Label, 1st	Sun
Reg Presley	Troggs
Pretenders,The	Hit, 1st (No 1): 'Brass in Pocket'
Alan Price	Animals
Procol Harum	
Follow up to 1st hit	'Homburg'
Hit, 1st (No 1)	'A Whiter Shade of Pale'
Jim Pursey	Sham 69
Suzy Quatro	
From	Detroit
Hit, 1st (No 1)	'Can the Can'
Queen	Freddy Mercury (Vocals), Brian May (Guitar), John Deacon (Bass), Roger Taylor (Drums)
Hit, 1st	'Seven Seas of Rhye'
No 1, 1st	'Bohemian Rhapsody'
Originally named	Smile
With David Bowie	'Under Pressure'
Roddy Radiation	Specials
Noel Redding	Jimi Hendrix Experience
Otis Redding	Hit, 1st: 'My Girl'
Lou Reed	Velvet Underground
Hit	'Walk on the Wild Side'
Jim Reeves	No 1, only: 'Distant Drums'
Keith Relf	Yardbirds, Renaissance
John Renbourn	Pentangle
Cliff Richard	
Hit, 1st	'Move It'
No 1, 1st	'Livin' Doll'
Keith Richard	Rolling Stones
Lionel Richie	Commodores
Hit, 1st	'All Night Long'
No 1	'Hello'
Andrew Ridgeley	Wham!
Righteous Brothers	Bill Medley, Bobby Hatfield
Robbie Robertson	The Band
Lee Rocker	Stray Cats
Nile Rodgers	Chic
Paul Rodgers	Free, Bad Company
Rankin Roger	Beat
Rolling Stones	
Beatles song recorded	'I Wanna Be Your Man'
Hit, 1st	'I Wanna Be Your Man'
Murder at concert	Altamont
Name From	'Rolling Stone Blues' (Muddy Waters)
No 1, 1st	'It's all Over Now'
Original members	Mick Jagger (Vocals), Keith Richard (Guitar), Brian Jones

	(Guitar), Bill Wyman (Bass), Charlie Watts (Drums)
W.Axl Rose	Guns N' Roses
Diana Ross	Supremes
No 1, 1st	'I'm Still Waiting'
Francis Rossi	Status Quo
David Lee Roth	Van Halen
Johnny Rotten	Sex Pistols
Demis Roussos	Aphrodite's Child
Kevin Rowland	Dexy's Midnight Runners
Roxy Music	
Hit, 1st	'Virginia Plain'
No 1, only	'Jealous Guy'
David Ruffin	Temptations
Sam and Dave	Surnames: Moore, Prater
Leo Sayer	
Hit, 1st	'The Show Must Go On'
No 1, only	'When I Need You'
Rat Scabies	Damned
Michael Schenker	Scorpions, MSG
Searchers,The	Hit, 1st (No 1): 'Sweets for my Sweet'
John Sebastian	Lovin' Spoonful
Neil Sedaka	Hit, 1st: 'I Go Ape'
Sex Pistols,The	
Hit, 1st	'God Save The Queen'
Manager	Malcolm McLaren
Vocals	Johnny Rotten
Shadows,The	
Hit, 1st (No 1)	'Apache'
Lead Guitar	Hank Marvin
Original Name	Drifters
Feargal Sharkey	Undertones
Wayne Shorter	Weather Report
Paul Simon	Hit, 1st: 'Mother and Child Reunion'
Simon and Garfunkel	No 1, only: 'Bridge Over Troubled Water'
Frank Sinatra	No 1, 1st: 'Strangers in the Night'
Sky	Guitarist: John Williams
Slade	
Hit, 1st	'Get Down and Get With It'
Manager	Chas Chandler
No 1, 1st	'Coz I Luv You'
Vocals	Noddy Holder
Grace Slick	Jefferson Airplane/Starship
Sly and the Family Stone	Hit, 1st: 'Dance to the Music'
Chas Smash	Madness
Curt Smith	Tears for Fears
Smokey Robinson and the Miracles	No 1, 1st: 'Tears of a Clown'
Soft Cell	Marc Almond, Dave Ball
Hit, 1st (No 1)	'Tainted Love'
Soft Machine	Name from: William Burroughs novel
Jimmy Somerville	Bronski Beat, Communards
Sonny and Cher	Hit, 1st (No 1): 'I Got You Babe'
Sparks	Hit, 1st: 'This Town Ain't Big Enough For The Both Of Us'
Specials,The	
Hit, 1st	'Gangsters'
No 1, 1st	'Too Much Too Young'

Dusty Springfield	Hit, 1st: 'I Only Want to Be With You'
Bruce Springsteen	Hit, 1st: 'Dancing in the Dark'
Viv Stanshall	Bonzo Dog Doo Dah Band
Ringo Starr	Beatles
Hit, 1st solo	'It Don't Come Easy'
Status Quo	
Hit, 1st	'Pictures of Matchstick Men'
No 1, 1st	'Down Down'
Chris Stein	Blondie
Shakin' Stevens	
Hit, 1st	'Marie Marie'
No 1, 1st	'This Ole House'
Dave Stewart	Tourists, Eurhythmics
Rod Stewart	Jeff Beck Group, Faces
Hit, 1st solo (No 1)	'Maggie May'
Steven Stills	Buffalo Springfield
Sting	Police
Barbra Streisand	
Hit, 1st	'Second Hand Rose'
No 1, only	'Woman in Love'
Joe Strummer	Clash
Levi Stubbs	Four Tops
Suggs	Madness
Donna Summer	No 1, only: 'I Feel Love'
Andy Summers	Police
Supremes,The	Originally called: Primettes
David Sylvian	Japan
T.Rex	
Leader	Marc Bolan
Original Name	Tyrannosaurus Rex
Mick Taylor	John Mayall's Bluesbreakers, Rolling Stones (replaced Brian Jones)
Philthy Phil Taylor	Motorhead
Roger Taylor	Queen, Duran Duran (Different people, both drummers)
Tears for Fears	Roland Orzabel, Curt Smith
Hit, 1st	'Mad World'
10 CC	No 1, 1st: 'Rubber Bullets'
Neil Tennant	Pet Shop Boys
Them	
From	Ireland
Vocals	Van Morrison
Thin Lizzy	
Hit, 1st	'Whiskey in the Jar'
Leader	Phil Lynott
Thompson Twins	Name from: Tin Tin cartoon characters
Peter Tork	Monkees
Pete Townshend	Who
Travelling Wilburys	Bob Dylan, George Harrison, Jeff Lynne, Roy Orbison, Tom Petty
Troggs	
Hit, 1st	'Wild Thing'
No 1, only	'With A Girl Like You'
U2	Hit, 1st: 'New Years Day'
Ultravox	Hit, 1st: 'Vienna'
Bjorn Ulvaeus	Abba

Midge Ure	Ultravox
No 1, solo	'If I Was'
Frankie Valli	Four Seasons
Vangelis	Aphrodite's Child
Sid Vicious	Sex Pistols
Accused of murdering	Nancy Spungen
Vinegar Joe	Vocals: Elkie Brooks, Robert Palmer
Donnie Wahlberg	New Kids on the Block
Rick Wakeman	Yes
Walker Brothers	Gary Leeds, Scott Engel, John Maus
No 1, 1st	'Make it Easy on Yourself'
Joe Walsh	James Gang, Eagles
Roger Waters	Pink Floyd
Charlie Watts	Rolling Stones
Carl Wayne	Move
Bruce Welch	Shadows
Paul Weller	Jam, Style Council
Wham!	George Michael, Andrew Ridgeley
Hit, 1st	'Young Guns (Go for It)'
No 1, 1st	'Wake Me Up (Before you Go Go)'
Maurice White	Earth, Wind and Fire
Who,The	Pete Townshend (Guitar), Roger Daltrey (Vocals), John Entwhistle (Bass), Keith Moon (Drums) – replaced by Kenny Jones
Hit, 1st	'I Can't Explain'
John Williams	Sky
Al (Blind Owl) Wilson	Canned Heat
Brian Wilson	Beach Boys
Mary Wilson	Supremes
Stevie Winwood	Spencer Davis Group, Blind Faith
Stevie Wonder	
Hit, 1st	'Uptight'
No 1, 1st (with Paul McCartney)	'Ebony and Ivory'
No 1, 1st solo	'I Just Called To Say I Love You'
Ron Wood	Faces, Rolling Stones
Roy Wood	Move, ELO, Wizzard
Stuart (Woody) Wood	Bay City Rollers
Bill Wyman	Rolling Stones
Yazoo	Alison Moyet, Vince Clark
Hit, 1st	'Only You'
Angus Young	AC/DC (Guitar)
Neil Young	Buffalo Springfield, Crosby Stills Nash and Young
Hit, solo	'Heart of Gold'
Paul Young	Q-Tips
Hit, 1st solo (No 1)	'Wherever I Lay My Hat'
Ronnie Van Zant	Lynyrd Skynyrd
Frank Zappa	Mothers of Invention
Joe Zawinul	Weather Report
ZZ Top	From: Texas

Pop LPs/Albums

By: Title → Group/Artiste

Abbey Road	Beatles
Achtung Baby	U2
Aftermath	Rolling Stones

Aladdin Sane	David Bowie
Alf	Alison Moyet
Are you Experienced?	Jimi Hendrix Experience
Astral Weeks	Van Morrison
Atlantic Crossing	Rod Stewart
Bad	Michael Jackson
Band on the Run	Wings
Bat Out of Hell	Meat Loaf
Beggars Banquet	Rolling Stones
Blonde on Blonde	Bob Dylan
Bookends	Simon & Garfunkel
Brothers in Arms	Dire Straits
Business as Usual	Men at Work
But Seriously	Phil Collins
Can't Slow Down	Lionel Richie
Colour by Numbers	Culture Club
Dangerous	Michael Jackson
Dark Side of the Moon	Pink Floyd
Discovery	Electric Light Orchestra
Don't Shoot Me, I'm Only the Piano Player	Elton John
Electric Ladyland	Jimi Hendrix Experience
Electric Warrior	T.Rex
Every Picture Tells a Story	Rod Stewart
Exile on Main Street	Rolling Stones
Face Value	Phil Collins
Fantastic	Wham!
Fog on the Tyne	Lindisfarne
Forever Changes	Love
Ghost in the Machine	Police
Going to a Go-Go	Smokey Robinson and the Miracles
Goodbye Yellow Brick Road	Elton John
Help!	Beatles
Hergest Ridge	Mike Oldfield
Highway 61 Revisited	Bob Dylan
Horses	Patti Smith
Hotel California	Eagles
Hunky Dory	David Bowie
Immaculate Collection, The	Madonna
Innervisions	Stevie Wonder
John Wesley Harding	Bob Dylan
Joshua Tree,The	U2
L.A. Woman	Doors
Last Waltz,The	The Band
Legend	Bob Marley and the Wailers
Let it Bleed	Rolling Stones
Lie	Charles Manson
Love Over Gold	Dire Straits
Makin' Movies	Dire Straits
Mr Fantasy	Traffic
Music from Big Pink	The Band
My Aim is True	Elvis Costello
Nashville Skyline	Bob Dylan
Night At The Opera,A	Queen
No Jacket Required	Phil Collins
No Parlez	Paul Young
Off the Wall	Michael Jackson. Wears on sleeve: Dinner Jacket

On Every Street	Dire Straits
On the Threshold of a Dream	Moody Blues
Out of Time	R.E.M.
Outlandos D'Amour	Police
Oxygene	Jean Michael Jarre
Paranoid	Black Sabbath
Pearl	Janis Joplin
Physical Graffiti	Led Zeppelin
Pin Ups	David Bowie
Piper at the Gates of Dawn	Pink Floyd
Private Dancer	Tina Turner. On LP Sleeve: Cat
Regatta de Blanc	Police
Revolver	Beatles
Rubber Soul	Beatles
Rumours	Fleetwood Mac
Sergeant Pepper's Lonely Hearts Club Band	Beatles. Group Name on Cover: In Flowers
Slippery When Wet	Bon Jovi
Smoker you drink the player you get, The	Joe Walsh
Songs in the Key of Life	Stevie Wonder
Stars	Simply Red
Stranger, The	Billy Joel
Surrealistic Pillow	Jefferson Airplane
Synchronicity	Police
Talking Book	Stevie Wonder
Tapestry	Carole King
Ten Good Reasons	Jason Donovan
Thriller	Michael Jackson
Transformer	Lou Reed
Trout Mask Replica	Captain Beefheart and his Magic Band
Tubular Bells	Mike Oldfield
Welcome to the Pleasure Dome	Frankie Goes to Hollywood
X	Inxs
Young Americans	David Bowie
Zenyatta Mondatta	Police

Pop Music, Other

By: General

Charts;-

UK; First Published	November 1952
US; Magazine	Billboard
Concert Halls; US; Promoter, Bill Graham	Fillmore East and West
Heavy Metal; Term from	*Naked Lunch* (William Burroughs novel)
Island Records; Founded by	Chris Blackwell
'Live Aid'	July 13th, 1985. UK: Wembley Stadium. US: JFK Stadium, Philadelphia

Motown;-

Founded by	Berry Gordy
Name from	Motor City (Detroit)
Virgin Records; Founded by	Richard Branson
Woodstock Pop Festival; Land owner	Max Yasgur

Pop Records

By: Description → Title

Air Crash; About	'Ebony Eyes' (Everly Brothers)
Bagpipes; Million seller with	'Amazing Grace' (Royal Scots Dragoon Guards)
Banned	'Je T'aime', 'God Save the Queen' (Sex Pistols), 'Relax', 'My Ding a Ling'
Warren Beatty; About (allegedly)	'You're So Vain' (Carly Simon)
Biggest Selling	'White Christmas'
Not No 1	'Last Christmas' (Wham!)
UK	'Do They Know It's Christmas?' ('Band Aid')
Boston Strangler; About	'Midnight Rambler' (Rolling Stones)
Angela Bowie; About	'Angie' (Rolling Stones)
Jennifer Boyd; About	'Jennifer Juniper' (Donovan)
Patti Boyd; About	'Layla'
Car Crash	'Tell Laura I Love Her' (Rickie Valance)
Clarinet; Record featuring	'Stranger on the Shore'
Coca Cola Advertisement; Song used for	'I'd Like to Teach the World to Sing'
Communications Satellite; Title	'Telstar'
Copeland (Classical) piece; Based on	'Fanfare for the Common Man' (Emerson Lake and Palmer)
Eurovision Song Contest; Double Winner	Johnny Logan (1980, 1987)
Eurovision Song Contest; UK Winners:-	
1967	Sandie Shaw ('Puppet on a String')
1969	Lulu (shared) ('Boom, Bang a Bang')
1976	Brotherhood of Man ('Save Your Kisses for Me')
1981	Bucks Fizz ('Making Your Mind Up')
Eyes; About actress's	'Bette Davis Eyes'
Geno Washington, Tribute to	'Geno' (Dexy's Midnight Runners)
Gold Disc: 1st	'Chattanooga Choo Choo' (Glen Miller)
Buddy Holly; About his death	'American Pie'
'It Ain't Half Hot Mum' stars; Song by	'Whispering Grass'
Khachaturian piece; Based on	'Sabre Dance' (Love Sculpture)
Carol King; About	'O Carol'
Julian Lennon; About	'Hey Jude' (The Beatles)
Lincoln, Martin Luther King, Kennedy; About	'Abraham,Martin and John' (Marvin Gaye)
Longest in Chart (All releases)	'My Way'
Sara Lowndes (Dylan's wife); About	'Sad Eyed Lady of the Lowlands'
LP:-	
Biggest Selling; Live	*Frampton Comes Alive*
No 1; Longest	*South Pacific*
No 1; Longest; Rock	*Bat out of Hell*
Don McLean; About	'Killing me Softly with his Song'
Marilyn Monroe; About	'Candle in the Wind
Motorcycle Crash; About	'Terry' (Twinkle), 'Leader of the Pack' (Shangri Las)
No 1:-	
Also No 2 on different label	'Je T'Aime'
Father and daughter	'Somethin' Stupid' (Frank and Nancy Sinatra)

1st	'Here in my Heart' (Al Martino)
1st 3 releases	Gerry and the Pacemakers, Frankie Goes to Hollywood
Straight in at; 1st	'Jailhouse Rock'
Longest; Consecutive	'Everything I Do (I Do it for You)', Bryan Adams (16 weeks)
Longest; Total	'I Believe', Frankie Laine (18 weeks)
TV Show; Songs from	'Chicken song' (Spitting Image), 'Fame' (Kids from Fame)
US; 1st British Group	'Telstar' (Tornados)
Novel; Title of	'Wuthering Heights'
Nude; Singers appear on sleeve	Two Virgins (John Lennon, Yoko Ono)
Painter; About	'Vincent' (Van Gogh), 'Matchstalk Men and Matchstalk Cats and Dogs' (L.S. Lowry)
Painting, Famous; Title	'Mona Lisa'
Prison; Recorded in	Johnny Cash (Folsom and St Quentin)
Rats, Killer; Theme to film about	Ben (Michael Jackson)
Release to Number 1; Longest gap	'Reet Petite' (Jackie Wilson)
Russian visit inspires	'Nikita' (Elton John)
South Pacific; Song from	'Happy Talk'
Sued (Writer) for similarity to 'She's So Fine'	'My Sweet Lord'
Top 10; British only records in	March 7th, 1964
Vietnam War soldiers	'19'
Wife; Written for	'Annie's Song', 'Lady in Red'

Pop Singles

By: Title → Group/Artiste

Notes: If several groups are given, the records are in chronological order. Only selected versions of songs are listed.

'Agadoo'	Black Lace
'Albatross'	Fleetwood Mac
'All I Have To Do Is Dream'	Everly Brothers
'All Kinds of Everything'	Dana
'All or Nothing'	Small Faces
'All Right Now'	Free
'All Shook Up'	Elvis Presley
'Always on My Mind'	Elvis Presley, Pet Shop Boys
'Always Something There to Remind Me'	Sandie Shaw
'Amazing Grace'	Judy Collins, Royal Scots Dragoon Guards
'American Pie'	Don McLean. 'The Day the Music Died': Buddy Holly's death
'Annie's Song'	John Denver, James Galway (Instrumental)
'Another Brick in the Wall'	Pink Floyd
'Anyone Who Had A Heart'	Cilla Black
'Any Dream Will Do'	Jason Donovan
'Apache'	Shadows
'Are Friends Electric?'	Gary Numan
'As Tears Go By'	Marianne Faithfull
'Atomic'	Blondie
'Baby Come Back'	Equals
'Baby Love'	Supremes
'Baby Now That I've Found You'	Foundations

'Back Home'	England World Cup Squad (1970)
'Bad'	Michael Jackson
'Bad Moon Rising'	Creedence Clearwater Revival
'Banana Boat Song'	Harry Belafonte
'Band of Gold'	Freda Payne
'Barcelona'	Freddie Mercury, Montserrat Caballé
'Beat it'	Michael Jackson. Guitar solo: Eddie Van Halen
'Begin the Beguine'	Julio Iglesias. Written by: Cole Porter
'Believe'	Frankie Laine
'Bette Davis Eyes'	Kim Carnes
'Big Bad John'	Jimmy Dean
'Billie Jean'	Michael Jackson
'Billy Don't Be a Hero'	Paper Lace
'Birdie Song,The'	Tweets
'Black is Black' (1966)	Los Bravos
'Blackberry Way'	Move
'Black or White'	Michael Jackson
'Blockbuster'	Sweet
'Blue Suede Shoes'	Carl Perkins (1st Version)
'Blueberry Hill'	Fats Domino
'Bohemian Rhapsody'	Queen
'Boogie Nights'	Heatwave
'Born in the USA'	Bruce Springsteen
'Born to be Wild'	Steppenwolf
'Boy Named Sue,A'	Johnny Cash
'Brass in Pocket'	Pretenders
'Bridge Over Troubled Water'	Simon and Garfunkel
'Bright Eyes'	Art Garfunkel
'Butterfly'	Andy Williams
'Bye Bye Baby'	Bay City Rollers
'Bye Bye Love'	Everly Brothers
'Call Up the Groups'	Barron Knights
'Can the Can'	Suzi Quatro
'Candy Girl'	New Edition
'Captain Beaky'	Keith Michell
'Caravan of Love'	Housemartins
'Carnival is Over,The'	Seekers
'Catch the Wind'	Donovan
'Cathy's Clown'	Everly Brothers
'Chain Reaction'	Diana Ross
'Chanson D'Amour'	Manhattan Transfer
'Chicken Song,The'	Spitting Image
'China In Your Hand'	T'Pau
'Chirpy Chirpy Cheep Cheep'	Middle of the Road
'Christmas Alphabet'	Dickie Valentine
'Cinderella Rockefella'	Esther and Abi Ofarim
'Clapping Song,The'	Shirley Ellis
'Clare'	Gilbert O'Sullivan
'Combine Harvester'	Wurzels
'Come on Eileen'	Dexy's Midnight Runners
'Computer Love'	Kraftwerk
'Concrete and Clay'	Unit Four Plus Two
'Congratulations'	Cliff Richard
'Convoy'	C.W.McCall
'Convoy G.B'	Laurie Lingo and the Dipsticks (Dave Lee Travis, Paul Burnett)
'Coward of the County'	Kenny Rogers

'Coz I Luv You'	Slade
'Crocodile Rock'	Elton John
'Crying'	Don McLean
'Dancing in the Street'	Martha and the Vandellas, David Bowie and Mick Jagger
'Day Trip to Bangor'	Fiddler's Dram
'Daydream'	Lovin' Spoonful
'Daydreamer'	David Cassidy
'Deck of Cards'	Wink Martindale
'Delilah'	Tom Jones
'Diana'	Paul Anka
'Diane'	Bachelors
'D.I.S.C.O.'	Ottawan
'Distant Drums'	Jim Reeves
'D.I.V.O.R.C.E.'	Tammy Wynette, Billy Connolly (Take off)
'Dizzy'	Tommy Roe, Vic Reeves and The Wonderstuff
'Do the Bartman'	The Simpsons
'Do They Know It's Christmas?'	Band Aid
'Do Wah Diddy Diddy'	Manfred Mann
'Do You Love Me'	Brian Poole and the Tremeloes
'Dock of the Bay,The'	Otis Redding
'Dominique'	The Singing Nun
'Don't Cry for me Argentina'	Julie Covington
'Don't Give Up On Us'	David Soul
'Don't Go Breaking My Heart'	Elton John and Kiki Dee
'Don't Leave Me This Way'	Harold Melvin and the Blue Notes, Communards
'Don't Let the Stars Get in your Eyes'	Perry Como
'Don't You Want Me'	Human League
'Down Under'	Men at Work
'Dreadlock Holiday'	10 CC
'Dream Lover'	Bobby Darin
'Dreamboat'	Alma Cogan
'Easy Lover'	Philip Bailey with Phil Collins
'Ebony and Ivory'	Paul McCartney with Stevie Wonder
'Edelweiss'	Vince Hill
'Ernie (The Fastest Milkman in the West)'	Benny Hill
'Eve of Destruction'	Barry McGuire
'Everlasting Love'	Love Affair
'Every Breath You Take'	Police
'Every Loser Wins'	Nick Berry
'Everything I Do (I Do it for You)'	Bryan Adams
'Everything I Own'	Ken Boothe, Boy George
'Eye Level'	Simon Park
'Fame'	Irene Cara
'Fernando'	Abba
'Final Countdown'	Europe
'Fire'	Crazy World of Arthur Brown
'First Time Ever I Saw Your Face,The'	Roberta Flack
'For What It's Worth'	Buffalo Springfield
'Free'	Deniece Williams
'Garden of Eden'	Frankie Vaughan
'Geno'	Dexy's Midnight Runners. Geno is: Geno Washington
'Get Away'	Georgie Fame

'Get It On'	T.Rex
'Ghost Town'	Specials
'Glad All Over'	Dave Clark Five
'Go Now'	Moody Blues
'God Save the Queen'	Sex Pistols
'Going Underground'	Jam
'Gonna Make You A Star'	David Essex
'Good Golly Miss Molly'	Little Richard
'Good Heart,A'	Feargal Sharkey
'Good Vibrations'	Beach Boys
'Goody Two Shoes'	Adam Ant
'Grandad'	Clive Dunn
'Great Balls of Fire'	Jerry Lee Lewis
'Green Door'	Frankie Vaughn, Shakin' Stevens
'Green Green Grass of Home'	Tom Jones
'Halfway to Paradise'	Billy Fury
'Hang on Sloopy'	McCoys
'Happy Talk'	Captain Sensible
'Have I The Right'	Honeycombs
'Heart of Glass'	Blondie
'Hello'	Lionel Richie
'Hello Dolly'	Louis Armstrong
'Here in my Heart'	Al Martino
'He's So Fine'	Chiffons
'Hey Girl Don't Bother Me'	Tams
'Hi Ho Silver Lining'	Jeff Beck
'Hippy Hippy Shake'	Swinging Blue Jeans
'Hit Me With Your Rhythm Stick'	Ian Dury and the Blockheads
'Hold Me Close'	David Essex
'Honey'	Bobby Goldsboro
'Honky Tonk Woman'	Rolling Stones
'Hoots Mon'	Lord Rockingham XI
'Hot Love'	T.Rex
'House of the Rising Sun,The'	Animals
'How Much Is That Doggie in the Window'	Lita Roza (No 1)
'I Believe in Father Christmas'	Greg Lake
'I Can't Get No Satisfaction'	Rolling Stones
'I Can't Help Myself'	Four Tops
'I Can't Stop Loving You'	Ray Charles
'I Don't Like Mondays'	Boomtown Rats
'I Don't Want To Dance'	Eddy Grant
'I Feel Love'	Donna Summer, Communards
'I Get Around'	Beach Boys
'I Got You Babe'	Sonny and Cher, UB40 with Chrissie Hynde
'I Hear you Knocking'	Dave Edmunds
'I Heard it Through the Grapevine'	Marvin Gaye
'I Just Called to Say I Love You'	Stevie Wonder
'I Knew You Were Waiting For Me'	Aretha Franklin and George Michael
'I Know Him So Well'	Elaine Paige and Barbara Dickson. From: Musical *Chess*
'I Like It'	Gerry and the Pacemakers
'I Love To Love'	Tina Charles
'I Love You Love Me Love'	Gary Glitter
'I Only Have Eyes For You'	Art Garfunkel
'I Pretend'	Des O'Connor
'I Remember You'	Frank Ifield

'I Should be so Lucky'	Kylie Minogue
'I Wanna Dance With Somebody'	Whitney Houston
'I Want To Know What Love Is'	Foreigner
'I Want to Wake Up With You'	Boris Gardiner
'I Will Survive'	Gloria Gaynor
'I'd Like To Teach The World To Sing'	New Seekers
'If'	Telly Savalas
'If I Had a Hammer'	Trini Lopez
'If I Was'	Midge Ure
'If Paradise is Half as Nice'	Amen Corner
'If You Leave Me Now'	Chicago
'I'll Be Home'	Pat Boone
'I'll Never Fall In Love Again'	Bobbie Gentry
'I'll Never Find Another You'	Seekers
'I'm a Believer'	Monkees
'I'm Alive'	Hollies
'I'm Into Something Good'	Herman's Hermits
'I'm Not in Love'	10 CC
'I'm the Leader of the Gang'	Gary Glitter
'I'm the Urban Spaceman'	Bonzo Dog Doo Dah Band
'I'm too Sexy'	Right Said Fred
'Imagine'	John Lennon
'In the Summertime'	Mungo Jerry
'In the Year 2525 (Exordium and Terminus)'	Zager and Evans
'Into the Groove'	Madonna
'Is There Something I Should Know'	Duran Duran
'Israelites'	Desmond Dekker and the Aces
'It Aint What You Do It's The Way That You Do It'	Fun Boy Three and Bananarama
'It Doesn't Matter Anymore'	Buddy Holly
'It's a Sin'	Pet Shop Boys
'It's All Over Now'	Rolling Stones
'It's My Party'	Leslie Gore, Dave Stewart with Barbara Gaskin (No 1)
'It's Not Unusual'	Tom Jones
'It's Now or Never'	Elvis Presley. Based on: 'O Sole Mio'
'It's Only Make Believe'	Conway Twitty
'It's Over'	Roy Orbison
'Itsy Bitsy Teeny Weeny Yellow Polka Dot Bikini'	Brian Hyland, Bombalurina
'I've Never Been to Me'	Charlene
'Jailhouse Rock'	Elvis Presley
'January'	Pilot
'Japanese Boy'	Aneka
'Je T'Aime . . . moi non plus'	Jane Birkin and Serge Gainsbourg
'Jealous Guy'	Roxy Music. Written by: John Lennon
'Jealous Mind'	Alvin Stardust
'Jilted John'	Jilted John (Line: 'Gordon is a Moron')
'Joy To The World'	Three Dog Night
'Juliet'	Four Pennies
'Jumping Jack Flash'	Rolling Stones
'(Just Like) Starting Over'	John Lennon
'Just Walkin in the Rain'	Johnny Ray
'Karma Chameleon'	Culture Club
'Keep on Running'	Spencer Davis Group
'Kids in America'	Kim Wilde
'Killing Me Softly With His Song'	Roberta Flack

'King of the Road'	Roger Miller
'Knock Three Times'	Dawn
'Kung Fu Fighting'	Carl Douglas
'La Isla Bonita'	Madonna
'Lady in Red, The'	Chris De Burgh
'Land of Make Believe'	Bucks Fizz
'Last Train to San Fernando'	Johnny Duncan and the Blue Grass Boys
'Last Waltz,The'	Englebert Humperdinck
'Laughing Gnome,The'	David Bowie
'Legend of Xanadu'	Dave Dee, Dozy, Beaky, Mick and Tich
'Let It Be' (1987)	Ferry Aid
'Let's Dance'	Chris Montez, David Bowie (Different songs)
'Let's Twist Again'	Chubby Checker
'Letter,The'	Box Tops
'Like a Virgin'	Madonna
'Lily the Pink'	Scaffold
'Lion Sleeps Tonight,The'	Tight Fit
'Little Arrows'	Leapy Lee
'Little Children'	Billy J.Kramer and the Dakotas
'Little Donkey'	Nina and Frederick
'Living Doll'	Cliff Richard, Cliff Richard and the Young Ones
'Locomotion,The'	Little Eva, Kylie Minogue
'Lola'	Kinks
'Lonely this Christmas'	Mud
'Long Haired Lover from Liverpool'	Little Jimmy Osmond
'Long Tall Sally'	Little Richard
'Love Grows (Where My Rosemary Goes)'	Edison Lighthouse
'Love Letters in the Sand'	Pat Boone
'MacArthur Park'	Richard Harris, Donna Summer
'Mack the Knife'	Bobby Darin
'Maggie May'	Rod Stewart
'Magic Moments'	Perry Como
'Make it Easy on Yourself'	Walker Brothers
'Make Me Smile (Come Up and See Me)'	Steve Harley and Cockney Rebel
'Man from Laramie,The'	Jimmy Young
'Mary's Boy Child'	Harry Belafonte, Boney M
'Massachusetts'	Bee Gees
'Matchstalk Men and Matchstalk Cats and Dogs'	Brian and Michael
'Matthew and Son'	Cat Stevens
'Memories are Made of this'	Dean Martin
'Merry Xmas Everybody'	Slade
'Message in a Bottle'	Police
'Michelle'	Overlanders. Written by: Lennon/McCartney
'Mickey'	Tony Basil
'Mighty Quinn'	Manfred Mann
'Mississipi'	Pussycat
'Mistletoe and Wine'	Cliff Richard
'Mona Lisa'	Nat King Cole
'Monday Monday'	Mamas and the Papas
'Monster Mash'	Bobby Pickett and the Crypt Kickers
'Mony Mony'	Tommy James and the Shondells

'Moon River'	Danny Williams
'Mouldy Old Dough'	Lieutenant Pigeon
'Mr Tambourine Man'	Byrds. Written by: Bob Dylan
'Mull of Kintyre'	Paul McCartney
'Music (Was my first love)'	John Miles
'My Ding a Ling'	Chuck Berry
'My Generation'	Who
'My Old Man's a Dustman'	Lonnie Donegan
'My Sharona'	The Knack
'My Son My Son'	Vera Lynn
'My Sweet Lord'	George Harrison. Sued for similarity to: 'She's So Fine'
'My Way'	Frank Sinatra
'Needles and Pins'	Searchers
'Never Gonna Give You Up'	Rick Astley
'Nikita'	Elton John
'19'	Paul Hardcastle
'99 Red Balloons'	Nena
'96 Tears'	Question Mark and the Mysterians
'No One Quite Like Grandma'	St Winifred's School Choir
'No Woman No Cry'	Bob Marley and the Wailers
'Nothing Compares 2 U'	Sinead O'Connor
'Nothing's Gonna Stop Us Now'	Starship
'Nutbush City Limits'	Ike and Tina Turner
'Ob-la-di Ob-la-da'	Marmalade. Written by: Lennon/McCartney
'Ode To Billie Joe'	Bobbie Gentry
'Oh Carol'	Neil Sedaka. Reply: Carole King's 'Oh Neil'
'Oh Happy Day'	Edwin Hawkins Singers
'Oh Pretty Woman'	Roy Orbison
'One Day At A Time'	Lena Martell
'One Day In Your Life'	Michael Jackson
'1-2-3'	Len Barry
'Only Sixteen'	Craig Douglas
'Only the Lonely'	Roy Orbison
'Only You'	Yazoo, Flying Pickets
'Only Way is Up, The'	Yazz and the Plastic Population
'Oops Up Side Your Head'	Gap Band
'Out of Time'	Chris Farlowe
'Papa Don't Preach'	Madonna
'Part of the Union'	Strawbs
'Pass the Dutchie'	Musical Youth
'Peggy Sue'	Buddy Holly
'Perfect'	Fairground Attraction
'Pipes of Peace'	Paul McCartney
'Poetry in Motion'	Johnny Tillotson
'Power of Love,The'	Jennifer Rush
'Pretty Flamingo'	Manfred Mann
'Price of Love,The'	Everly Brothers
'Prince Charming'	Adam and the Ants
'Puff the Magic Dragon'	Peter,Paul and Mary. Land: Honalee
'Pump up the Volume'	M/A/R/R/S
'Puppet on a String'	Sandie Shaw
'Puppy Love'	Paul Anka, Donny Osmond
'Raindrops Keep Fallin' On My Head'	B.J.Thomas
'Rat Trap'	Boomtown Rats
'Reach Out, I'll Be There'	Four Tops

'Red Red Wine'	Johnny James and the Vagabonds, UB40
'Reet Petite'	Jackie Wilson
'Reflex,The'	Duran Duran
'Relax'	Frankie Goes to Hollywood
'Release Me'	Englebert Humperdinck
'Respect'	Aretha Franklin
'Return to Sender'	Elvis Presley
'Rhinestone Cowboy'	Glen Campbell
'Ride on Time'	Black Box
'Ring My Bell'	Anita Ward
'River Deep, Mountain High'	Ike & Tina Turner
'Rivers of Babylon'	Boney M
'Rock Around the Clock'	Bill Haley and The Comets
'Rock Me Amadeus'	Falco
'Rock Your Baby'	George McCrae
'Rocket Man'	Elton John
'Rose Marie'	Slim Whitman
'Roses are Red'	Bobby Vinton
'Rosie'	Don Partridge
'Rubber Bullets'	10 CC
'Runaway'	Del Shannon
'Running Bear'	Johnny Preston
'Sabre Dance'	Love Sculpture
'Sacrifice'	Elton John
'Sailing'	Rod Stewart
'San Francisco'	Scott McKenzie
'Save the Last Dance for Me'	Drifters
'Save Your Love'	Renée and Renato
'Saving All My Love For You'	Whitney Houston
'School's Out'	Alice Cooper
'Sealed with a Kiss'	Brian Hyland, Jason Donovan
'Seasons in the Sun'	Terry Jacks
'See My Baby Jive'	Wizzard
'See You Later, Alligator'	Bill Haley and the Comets
'Seven Tears'	Goombay Dance Band
'Shaddap You Face'	Joe Dolce Music Theatre
'Shakin' All Over'	Johnny Kidd and the Pirates
'She'	Charles Aznavour
'Shoop Shoop Song'	Cher (Betty Everett, Linda Lewis as 'It's in His Kiss')
'Shout'	Lulu
'Side Saddle'	Russ Conway
'Silence is Golden'	Tremeloes
'Silver Lady'	David Soul
'Silver Machine'	Hawkwind
'Simon Says'	1910 Fruitgum Company
'Singing the Blues'	Guy Mitchell, Tommy Steele, Dave Edmunds
'Sledgehammer'	Peter Gabriel
'Sloop John B'	Beach Boys
'Smoke Gets in Your Eyes'	Platters, Bryan Ferry
'Smurf Song,The'	Father Abraham (and the Smurfs)
'So You Win Again'	Hot Chocolate
'Softly Softly'	Ruby Murray
'Somethin' Stupid'	Nancy and Frank Sinatra
'Something's Gotten Hold of my Heart'	Gene Pitney, Mark Almond with Gene Pitney

'Something in the Air'	Thunderclap Newman
'Space Oddity'	David Bowie
'Spanish Flea'	Herb Alpert
'Speedy Gonzales'	Pat Boone
'Spirit in the Sky'	Norman Greenbaum, Doctor and the Medics
'Stand By Me'	Ben E.King
'Stand By Your Man'	Tammy Wynette
'Star Trekkin'	The Firm
'Stop the Cavalry'	Jona Lewie
'Stranger on the Shore'	Acker Bilk
'Strangers in the Night'	Frank Sinatra
'Streak,The'	Ray Stevens
'Streets of London'	Ralph McTell
'Sugar Baby Love'	Rubettes
'Sugar Sugar'	Archies
'Sultans of Swing'	Dire Straits
'Summer Holiday'	Cliff Richard
'Summer Nights'	John Travolta and Olivia Newton-John
'Sun Ain't Gonna Shine Anymore,The'	Walker Brothers
'Sun Always Shines on TV,The'	A-ha
'Sunday Girl'	Blondie
'Sunny Afternoon'	Kinks
'Super Trouper'	Abba
'Suspicious Minds'	Elvis Presley, Fine Young Cannibals
'Sweet Dreams (Are Made of This)'	Eurhythmics
'Swing the Mood'	Jive Bunny and the Master Mixers
'Tainted Love'	Soft Cell
'Take Five'	Dave Brubeck Quartet
'Tears'	Ken Dodd
'Tears of a Clown'	Smokey Robinson and the Miracles
'Tears on my Pillow'	Johnny Nash, Kylie Minogue (Different songs)
'Telegram Sam'	T.Rex
'Tell Laura I Love Her'	Ricky Valance
'Telstar'	Tornados
'That'll Be The Day'	Crickets (Buddy Holly)
'Theme from a Summer Place'	Percy Faith
'There Must Be An Angel (Playing With My Heart)'	Eurhythmics
'These Boots are Made for Walking'	Nancy Sinatra
'This Old Heart of Mine'	Isley Brothers, Rod Stewart
'This Ole House'	Rosemary Clooney, Shakin' Stevens
'This Wheel's on Fire'	Julie Driscoll, Brian Auger and the Trinity (Together)
'Those Were The Days'	Mary Hopkin
'Three Coins in the Fountain'	Frank Sinatra
'Three Times a Lady'	Commodores
'Tie a Yellow Ribbon Round the Ole Oak Tree'	Tony Orlando with Dawn
'Tiger Feet'	Mud
'Times They are a Changin',The'	Bob Dylan
'To Know Him Is To Love Him'	Teddy Bears
'To Sir With Love'	Lulu
'Together We Are Beautiful'	Fern Kinney
'Too Shy'	Kajagoogoo
'Total Eclipse of the Heart'	Bonny Tyler
'Town Called Malice,A'	Jam

'Trail of the Lonesome Pine,The'	Laurel and Hardy
'Trains and Boats and Planes'	Burt Bacharach
'True Blue'	Madonna
'Twelfth of Never'	Donny Osmond
'Two Little Boys'	Rolf Harris
'Two Tribes'	Frankie Goes To Hollywood
'Under Pressure'	Queen and David Bowie
'Up Town Top Ranking'	Althia and Donna
'Uptown Girl'	Billy Joel
'Venus'	Frankie Avalon
'Video Killed the Radio Star'	Buggles
'Vienna'	Ultravox'
'Vincent'	Don McLean. About: Vincent Van Gogh
'Voodoo Chile'	Jimi Hendrix Experience
'Wake Me Up Before You Go Go'	Wham!
'Walk in the Black Forest,A'	Horst Jankowski
'Walk Like an Egyptian'	Bangles
'Walk on the Wild Side'	Lou Reed
'Walkin' Back to Happiness'	Helen Shapiro
'Walking on the Moon'	Police
'Wanderin' Star'	Lee Marvin
'Waterloo'	Abba (Eurovision Song Contest Winner)
'Way We Were,The'	Barbra Streisand
'We Are The World'	USA for Africa. Written by: Michael Jackson, Lionel Richie
'Wedding,The'	Julie Rogers
'Welcome Home'	Peters and Lee
'Well I Ask You'	Eden Kane
'West End Girls'	Pet Shop Boys
'What a Wonderful World'	Louis Armstrong
'What Do You Want'	Adam Faith
'What Do You Want To Make Those Eyes At Me For'	Emile Ford and the Checkmates
'Whatever Will Be'	Doris Day
'When a Child Is Born'	Johnny Mathis
'When a Man Loves a Woman'	Percy Sledge
'When I Need You'	Leo Sayer
'When Will I See You Again'	Three Degrees
'When You're in Love with a Beautiful Woman'	Dr Hook
'Where Are You Now My Love'	Jackie Trent
'Where Do You Go To My Lovely'	Peter Sarstedt
'Wherever I Lay My Hat'	Paul Young
'Whispering Grass'	Windsor Davies and Don Estelle
'Whiter Shade of Pale,A'	Procol Harum
'Who's Sorry Now'	Connie Francis
'Why Do Fools fall in Love'	Frankie Lymon and the Teenagers
'Wild Thing'	Troggs
'Winchester Cathedral'	New Vaudeville Band
'Windmills of Your Mind'	Noel Harrison
'Winds of Change'	Scorpions
'With A Little Help From My Friends'	Joe Cocker. Written by: Lennon/McCartney
'Without You'	Nilsson
'Woman'	John Lennon
'Woman in Love'	Barbra Streisand

'Wonderful Land'	Shadows
'Woodstock'	Matthews Southern Comfort
'Wooly Bully'	Sam the Sham and the Pharaohs
'Words'	F.R.David
'World in Union'	Kiri Te Kanawa
'World Without Love'	Peter and Gordon. Written by: Lennon/McCartney
'Wuthering Heights'	Kate Bush
'Xanadu'	Olivia Newton-John and ELO
'Yeh Yeh'	George Fame
'Yellow River'	Christie
'Yes Sir, I Can Boogie'	Baccara
'YMCA'	Village People
'You Can't Hurry Love'	Supremes, Phil Collins
'You Don't Have To Say You Love Me'	Dusty Springfield
'You Really Got Me'	Kinks
'You Spin Me Round'	Dead or Alive
'You Wear It Well'	Rod Stewart
'You Win Again' (1987)	Bee Gees
'You'll Never Walk Alone'	Gerry and the Pacemakers
'Young Gifted and Black'	Bob and Marcia
'Young Girl'	Gary Puckett and the Union Gap
'Young Love'	Tab Hunter, Donny Osmond
'Young Ones,The'	Cliff Richard
'You're Driving Me Crazy'	The Temperance Seven
'You're My World'	Cilla Black
'You're So Vain'	Carly Simon
'You're The First The Last My Everything'	Barry White
'You're The One That I Want'	John Travolta and Olivia Newton-John
'You've Lost That Loving Feelin'	Righteous Brothers

Singers, Classical

By: General

Benjamin Britten; Accompanies	Peter Pears
Caruso; Succeeded by at New York Met.	Benjamin Gigli
Highest Paid	Caruso
La Scala; Principal soprano, 1950s	Maria Callas
Prince Charles' wedding, Sings at	Kiri Te Kanawa
Singing Voice;-	
Caruso	Tenor
Chaliapin	Bass
Gigli	Tenor
Pavarotti	Tenor
Paul Robeson	Bass
Strauss Operas; Premières many	Lotte Lehmann
Wagnerian Singer; Norwegian	Kirsten Flagstad

Songs and Tunes

By: Title → Writer, General

Notes: Excludes Modern Pop.
See Also: Musicals, Songs from / Records, Singles / Songs from films

'Alexander's Ragtime Band'	Irving Berlin
'Any Old Iron'	Singer: Harry Champion
'Auld Lang Syne'	Words: Robert Burns
'Begin the Beguine'	Cole Porter. From: *Jubilee*

'Bicycle Built for Two,A (Daisy Bell)'	Harry Dacre
'Biggest Aspidistra in the World,The'	Singer: Gracie Fields
'Blue Moon'	Rodgers and Hart
'Camptown Races'	Stephen Foster
'Colonel Bogey'	Major F.J.Ricketts
'Entertainer,The'	Scott Joplin
'Georgia on my Mind'	Hoagy Carmichael and Stuart Gorrell
'Give My Regards to Broadway'	George Cohan
'God Bless America'	Irving Berlin
'Goodnight Irene'	Leadbelly
'Greensleeves'	Henry VIII (Attributed to)
'Happy Birthday to you'	Mildred and Patty Hill
'Home Sweet Home'	Words: John Howard Payne. Music: Henry Rowley Bishop
'I Got Rhythmn'	George and Ira Gershwin
'I'm A Yankee Doodle Dandy'	George Cohan
'Internationale,The'	Pierre Degeyter and Eugene Pottier
'It's a Long way to Tipperary'	Music: Jack Judge. Lyrics: Harry Williams
'I've Got You Under My Skin'	Cole Porter
'Jeanie with the Light Brown Hair'	Stephen Foster
'Jerusalem'	Words: William Blake
'Jingle Bells'	James Pierpoint
'Keep the Home Fires Burning'	Ivor Novello
'Land of Hope and Glory'	Music: Elgar. Lyrics: Arthur Benson
'Lilli Marlene'	Norbert Schultze
'Lilliburlero'	Music: Purcell (Attributed to)
'Mad About the Boy'	Noel Coward
'Mad Dogs and Englishmen'	Noel Coward
'Maple Leaf Rag'	Scott Joplin
'Marsellaise,The'	Claude de Lisle
'Minnie the Moocher'	Singer: Cab Calloway
'Mood Indigo'	Duke Ellington
'Moon River'	Henry Mancini
'My Old Kentucky Home'	Stephen Foster
'Nessun Dorma'	Puccini. From: *Turandot*
'Onward Christian Soldiers'	Sir Arthur Sullivan
'Pack up your Troubles in your Old Kit Bag'	Felix Powell and George Asaf
'Policeman's lot is not a happy one,A'	Gilbert and Sullivan (*Pirates of Penzance*)
'Rock Island Line'	Leadbelly
'Rule Britannia'	Thomas Arne
'Star Spangled Banner'	Words: Francis Scott Key. Music: John Stafford Smith (English)
'Stars and Stripes Forever,The'	Composer: John Sousa
'Swanee River'	Original Title: 'Yazoo River'
'Thank Heaven for Little Girls'	Singer: Maurice Chevalier
'This Land is your Land'	Woody Guthrie
'Twelve Days of Christmas,The'	(Carol)
2nd	Turtle Doves
3rd	French Hens
4th	Calling Birds
5th	Gold Rings
6th	Geese-a-laying
7th	Swans-a-swimming
8th	Maids-a-Milking
9th	Ladies Dancing

10th	Lords-a-leaping
11th	Pipers Piping
12th	Drummers Drumming
'Underneath the Arches'	Bud Flanagan
'Waltzing Matilda'	Marie Cowan
'When I Survey the Wonderous Cross'	Isaac Watts
'Yes, We have no Bananas'	Frank Silver and Irving Cohn

STAGE ENTERTAINMENT
Ballets

By: Name → Composer

Billy the Kid	Aaron Copland
Coppelia	Delibes
Daphnis et Chloe	Ravel
Firebird,The	Stravinsky
Giselle	Adolphe Adam (Music)
L' Apres-midi d'un Faune	Debussy
La Sylphide	Schneitzhoeffer
Midsummer Night's Dream,A	Mendelssohn
Nut Cracker,The	Tchaikovsky (French name: Casse-Noisette)
Petrushka	Stravinsky
Pierrot Lunaire	Schoenberg
Rite of Spring,The	Stravinsky. Choreography: Massine
Romeo and Juliet	Prokofiev
Sleeping Beauty,The	Tchaikovsky
Swan Lake	Tchaikovsky
Three Cornered Hat,The	Falla

Dance and Ballet

By: General

Ballet; 1st formal	*Ballet Comique de la Reine*
Ballet Rambert; Recent Anniversary	60th Anniversary, 1986
Ballet Russe;-	
Choreographer	Michel Fokine
Founder	Sergei Diaghilev
Ballet Terms;-	
Dance for two	Pas de deux
Leap from one foot to the other	Jeté
Leap striking heels together	Entrechat
Positions; Number	5
Spin around on one foot	Pirouette
Black Dancer; Became famous in Paris	Josephine Baker
Can Can; 1st Performed in	Paris, Offenbach's *Orpheus in the Underworld*
Choreographer; 'Father of Classical Ballet'	Marius Petipa
Court Dance; Marie Antoinette popularized	Gavotte
Dancer;-	
Born on a train	Rudolf Nureyev
Greek art; Dances based on	Isadora Duncan
1st in a film	Anna Pavlova
Kirov Ballet; Defected to West	Mikhail Baryshnikov (1974), Rudolf Nureyev (1961)

Elephants; Ballet for	*Circus Polka* (Stravinsky)
Eurhythmics; Developer	Emile Jacques-Dalcroze
Flamenco; Prominent	Jose Greco, Vincente Escudero
Folk Dance; Introduced into ballet	*Coppelia*
Imprisoned as a spy	Nijinsky
Lambeth Walk; From originally	*Me and My Gal* (Lupino Lane)
Leopard, pet, takes for walks	Josephine Baker
New York City Ballet; Choreographer associated with	George Ballanchine
Rudolf Nureyev; Russian Ballet with	Kirov
Poland; National dance	Mazurka
Royal Ballet;-	
Choreographer till 1960s	Sir Frederick Ashton
Director	Sir Frederick Ashton
Former Name	Sadlers Wells
Sailor's Dance	Hornpipe
Schizophrenia forced retirement	Nijinsky
Symphonies; Dance often included in classical	Minuet
Toes; 1st ballerina to dance on	Marie Taglioni
Tutu; 1st ballerina to wear	Marie Taglioni
Vienna; Dance associated with	Waltz

Musicals

By: Description → Title

Ingmar Bergman film; Musical based on	*A Little Night Music*
Fanny Brice, Life of; Based on	*Funny Girl*
Carmen; Set in wartime US	*Carmen Jones*
Cyclist fights gambling syndicate	*The Girl Friend*
T.S.Eliot book; Based on	*Cats*
Fellini film; Musical based on	*Sweet Charity*
Girl in gold rush town	*Paint Your Wagon*
Governess at Siamese king's court	*The King and I*
King Arthur legend; Based on	*Camelot*
Liliom (Ferenc Molnar play); Based on	*Carousel*
New Testament theme	*Jesus Christ Superstar*
Nudity; Features	*Hair*
Oliver Twist; Based on Dickens novel	*Oliver*
Eva Peron, Life of; Based on	*Evita*
Pygmalion; Based on G.B.Shaw play	*My Fair Lady*
Don Quixote; Based on Cervantes novel	*Man of La Mancha*
Railway; Setting	*Starlight Express*
Romeo and Juliet in New York Slums	*West Side Story*
Damon Runyon story; Based on	*Guys and Dolls*
San Franciso's Chinatown; Set in	*Flower Drum Song*
Taming of the Shrew; Based on	*Kiss Me Kate*
Trapp Family Singers	*The Sound of Music*
H.G.Wells novel; Based on	*Half a Sixpence*
P.G.Wodehouse collaborated on	*Show Boat*

Musicals

By: Title → Composers, General

Annie Get Your Gun	Irving Berlin
Anything Goes	Cole Porter
Aspects of Love	Andrew Lloyd-Webber, Don Black and Charles Hunt
Based on	David Garnett novel

Barnum	Star: Michael Crawford
Boy Friend,The	Sandy Wilson
Cabaret	John Kander, Fred Ebb
Based on	I am a Camera (Play)
Original source	Goodbye to Berlin (Christopher Isherwood novel)
Camelot	Loewe and Lerner
Can Can	Cole Porter
Carmen Jones	Bizet, Hammerstein
Carousel	Rodgers and Hammerstein
Based on	Liliom (Ferenc Molnar play)
Cats	Lloyd-Webber and Tim Rice
Based on	Old Possum's Book of Practical Cats (T.S.Eliot poems)
Chorus Line, A	Marvin Hamlisch, Michael Bennett
Evita	Lloyd-Webber and Rice
Fiddler on the Roof	Sheldon Harnick, Jerry Bock
Based on	The Milkman and Other Stories (Shalom Aleichem)
Flower Drum Song	Rodgers and Hammerstein
Girlfriend,The	Rodgers and Hart
Godspell	Stephen Schwartz
Guys and Dolls	Frank Loesser
Hair	Galt McDermott
Half a Sixpence	Based on: Kipps (H.G.Wells novel)
Hello Dolly	Jerry Herman
Based on	The Matchmaker (Thornton Wilder Play)
Jesus Christ Superstar	Lloyd-Webber and Rice
Joseph and his Amazing Technicolour Dreamcoat	Lloyd-Webber and Rice
King and I, The	Rodgers and Hammerstein
Kiss me Kate	Cole Porter
Lady be Good	George and Ira Gershwin
Les Miserables	Claude-Michel Schonberg and Alain Boublil
Little Night Music, A	Stephen Sondheim
Based on	Smiles of a Summer Night (Ingmar Bergman film)
Miss Saigon	Schonberg and Boublil
My Fair Lady	Loewe and Lerner
Based on	Pygmalion (G.B.Shaw play)
Costumes and sets	Cecil Beaton
Oklahoma	Rodgers and Hammerstein
Based on	Green Grow the Lilacs (Lynn Riggs play)
Oliver	Lionel Bart
Paint Your Wagon	Loewe and Lerner
Phantom of the Opera	Lloyd-Webber and Rice
Porgy and Bess	George and Ira Gershwin
Show Boat	Jerome Kern, Hammerstein (with P.G.Wodehouse)
Based on	Edna Ferber novel
Sound of Music,The	Rodgers and Hammerstein
Based on	The Trapp Family Singers (Maria Trapp autobiography)
South Pacific	Rodgers and Hammerstein
Based on	Tales of the South Pacific (James Mitchener short stories)

Starlight Express	Lloyd-Webber and Richard Stilgoe
Sweet Charity	Cy Coleman
Based on	*Nights of Cabiria* (Federico Fellini film)
West Side Story	Leonard Bernstein, Stephen Sondheim

Musicals, Songs from

By: Title → Musical

'Ain't got no/I got Life'	*Hair*
'America'	*West Side Story*
'Any Dream Will Do'	*Joseph and his Amazing Technicolour Dreamcoat*
'Anything You Can Do'	*Annie Get Your Gun*
'Big Spender'	*Sweet Charity*
'Can't Help Lovin that Man'	*Show Boat*
'Climb every Mountain'	*The Sound of Music*
'Consider Yourself'	*Oliver*
'Diamonds are a Girl's Best Friend'	*Gentlemen Prefer Blondes*
'Do-re-mi'	*The Sound of Music*
'Edelweiss'	*The Sound of Music*
'Everything's Coming up Roses'	*Gypsy*
'Get Me to the Church on Time'	*My Fair Lady*
'Happy Talk'	*South Pacific*
'Hopelessly Devoted to you' (Olivia Newton-John)	*Grease*
'I could have Danced all Night'	*My Fair Lady*
'I get a Kick out of You'	*Anything Goes*
'I got Rhythm'	*Girl Crazy*
'If I Ruled the World'	*Pickwick*
'If I were a Rich Man'	*Fiddler on the Roof*
'I'm Forever Blowing Bubbles'	*The Passing Show*
'Indian Love Call'	*Rose Marie*
'It Ain't Necessarily So'	*Porgy and Bess*
'Lady is a Tramp, The'	*Babes in Arms, Pal Joey*
'Love Changes Everything'	*Aspects of Love*
'Money Money'	*Cabaret*
'Oh What a Beautiful Morning'	*Oklahoma*
'Ol' Man River'	*Showboat*
'Second Hand Rose'	*Funny Girl*
'Send in the Clowns'	*A Little Night Music*
'Seventy Six Trombones'	*The Music Man*
'Sixteen going on Seventeen'	*The Sound of Music*
'Somewhere'	*West Side Story*
'Stranger in Paradise'	*Kismet*
'Summertime'	*Porgy and Bess*
'Tea for Two'	*No, No, Nanette*
'There's no Business like Show Business'	*Annie Get your Gun*
'Wanderin' Star'	*Paint your Wagon*
'You're the Top'	*Anything Goes*

Theatre, Variety, etc.

By: General

Covers: Actors/Actresses, Circus, Music Hall, etc.

Actress;-	
Leg amputated, acted after	Sarah Bernhardt

Public; 1st	Margaret Hughes (1660)
Slept in coffin	Sarah Bernhardt
Aldwych Farces; Writer	Ben Travers
Clowns; Face copyrighted by	Painting on an eggshell
Crazy Gang,The	Members: Flanagan and Allan, Naughton and Gold, Nervo and Knox
Drury Lane; Manager; 18th Century	David Garrick
Electrically lit; Theatre; 1st	Savoy, London
Eliza Doolittle (*Pygmalion*); Part written for	Mrs Patrick Campbell
Equity; Founder; Actress	Dame May Whitty
Female Impersonator; Famous	Danny La Rue
Females; Stage; Legalised	1662 (By Charles II)
France; National Theatre	Comédie Francaise
Gang Show; Creator	Ralph Reader
Henry Irving; Partner	Ellen Terry
Ireland; National Theatre; Former name	Abbey Theatre
Italy; Popular renaissance theatre	Commedia dell Arte
Japanese Theatre; Classical	No
Japanese Theatre; Popular	Kabuki
Jester; Henry I's; Famous	Rahere
Knighted; Actor; 1st	Henry Irving
Longest Run	*The Mousetrap* (Agatha Christie)
Longest Run; Comedy	*No Sex Please We're British*
Magician; 19th Century UK; Most famous	Nevil Maskelyne
Marcel Marceau; Character	Bip
Method Acting; Founder	Stanislavsky
Mime; French	Marcel Marceau
Motto; 'We never close'	Windmill Theatre
Music Hall;-	
Edwardian; Male impersonators, famous	Hetty King, Vesta Tilley
Edwardian; Most popular performer	Marie Lloyd
Theatre, London; Oldest still in use	Drury Lane
Theatre Royal; Common name	Drury Lane
Tight Rope Walker; Niagara, 1st to cross	Blondin
Tight Rope Walker; World Trade Centre towers; Walks between	Philippe Petit
Trapeze artist; 1st	Jules Leotard
Unlucky to mention, Play Name	*Macbeth* (called 'The Scottish Play')
Ventriloquist's dummy; Gets honorary degree	Charlie McCarthy
Whitehall Farces; Producer	Brian Rix

TV AND RADIO
Catchphrases

By: Catchphrase → Person associated with

'All in the best possible taste'	Kenny Everett
'And now for something completely different'	John Cleese in 'Monty Python's Flying Circus'
'Are you sitting comfortably?'	'Listen with Mother'
'Beam me up Scotty'	William Shatner (Captain Kirk) in 'Star Trek'

'Before your very eyes'	Arthur Askey
'Book em, Danno'	Steve McGarrett (Jack Lord) to Danno Williams (James MacArthur) in 'Hawaii Five O'
'Can I do you now, sir'	Mrs Mopp (Dorothy Summers) in 'ITMA'
'Can we talk?'	Joan Rivers
'Can you hear me, mother?'	Sandy Powell
'Didn't he do well!'	Bruce Forsyth
'Dodgy'	Norman Vaughan
'Evening All'	Jack Warner (George Dixon) in 'Dixon of Dock Green'
'Everybody out'	Miriam Karlin (Paddy, the shop steward) in 'The Rag Trade'
'Gi's a job'	Yosser Hughes in 'Boys from the Blackstuff'
'Hello, Good Evening and Welcome'	David Frost
'Hello, my darlings'	Charlie Drake
'Hello possums'	Dame Edna Everage
'Hi there pop-pickers'	Alan Freeman
'How tickled I am'	Ken Dodd
'How's about that then, guys and gals?'	Jimmy Savile
'I mean that most sincerely, friends'	Hughie Green in 'Opportunity Knocks'
'I only arsked'	Bernard Bresslaw in 'The Army Game'
'I thang yew'	Arthur Askey
'I wanna tell you a story'	Max Bygraves
'I'll give it foive'	Janice Nicholls in 'Thank Your Lucky Stars'
'I'm a little worried about Jim'	Mrs Dale in 'Mrs Dale's Diary'
'I'm in charge'	Bruce Forsyth
'It's goodnight from me, and it's goodnight from him'	Ronnie Barker, Ronnie Corbett in 'The Two Ronnies'
'I've started so I'll finish'	Magnus Magnusson in 'Mastermind'
'Just give me the facts, Ma'am'	Sergeant Joe Friday in 'Dragnet'
'Just like that'	Tommy Cooper
'Left hand down a bit'	Leslie Phillips in 'The Navy Lark'
'Loadsamoney'	Harry Enfield
'Nice to see you – to see you nice'	Bruce Forsyth
'Not a lot'	Paul Daniels
'Ooh, Betty!'	Michael Crawford (Frank Spencer) in 'Some Mothers do 'ave em'
'Ooh, you are awful, but I like you'	Dick Emery
'Open the box'	Audience in 'Take Your Pick'
'Orft we jolly well go'	Jimmy Young
'Rock on, Tommy'	Bobby Ball (to Tommy Cannon)
'Silly Moo'	Warren Mitchell (Alf Garnett) in 'Till Death Us Do Part'
'Sock it to me'	Judy Carne in 'Rowan and Martin's Laugh In'
'Soopersonic'	'Little and Large'
'Swinging'	Norman Vaughan
'Ta Ta for now (TTFN)'	Mrs Mopp in 'ITMA'
'Ten Four'	Broderick Crawford (Dan Matthews) in 'Highway Patrol'
'There's no answer to that'	Eric Morecambe
'Up and under'	Eddie Waring (Rugby League commentator)

'Wakey Wakey!'	Billy Cotton
'Walkies'	Barbara Woodhouse (Dog trainer)
'Who loves ya, baby'	Telly Savalas (Theo Kojak) in 'Kojak'
'You dirty old man'	Harry H.Corbett (Harold Steptoe) in 'Steptoe and Son'
'You lucky people'	Tommy Trinder
'Your starter for ten'	Bamber Gascoigne (Questionmaster) in 'University Challenge'

Radio, General

By: General

Address in Keynsham	Horace Batchelor
Children's stories	'Listen with Mother'
Factory entertainment in WWII	'Workers' Playtime'
Home Service	Became: Radio 4 (1967)
Light programme	Became: Radio 2 (1967)
Local Radio Stations;-	
Aire	Leeds
Beacon	Wolverhampton
BRMB	Birmingham
Centre	Leicester
Chiltern	Luton, Bedford
City	Liverpool
Hallam	Sheffield
Hereward	Peterborough
Mercia Sound	Coventry
Orwell	Ipswich
Pennine	Bradford
Piccadilly	Manchester
Trent	Nottingham
2CR	Bournemouth
West	Bristol
Wyvern	Hereford, Worcester
Panic caused by radio play	War of the Worlds, US, 1938 (Orson Welles)
Pirate; 1st	Radio Caroline (1964)
Programme; Longest run;-	
Serial	'The Archers' (from 1950)
Series	'The Week's Good Cause'
Solo	'Letter from America', Alistair Cooke (from 1946)
Schools Quiz	'Top of the Form'

Radio Programmes

By: Name → General

'Any Questions/Any Answers'	Presenters: Freddy Grisewood, David Jacobs, Jonathan Dimbleby
'Archers,The'	
Actor; Longest in	Norman Painting
Doris Archer (1st – for 30 years)	Gwen Berryman
Philip Archer (1st)	Norman Painting
Archers' address	Brookfield Farm
Billing	'Everyday Story of Country Folk'
1st broadcast	January 1st, 1951
Pub	The Bull
Royal Family member appeared	Princess Margaret

Set in	Ambridge
Signature Tune	'Barwick Green'
Starts	1950
'Beyond Our Ken'	Kenneth Horne
Billing	'A Sort of Radio Show'
'Billy Cotton Band Show'	Opening: 'Wakey Wakey!'
'Brains Trust,The'	
Chairman	Donald McCullough, Gilbert Harding
Panel; 1st	Julian Huxley, C.E.M.Joad, Commander A.B.Campbell
'Charlie McCarthy Programme,The'	Ventriloquist: Edgar Bergen
'Clitheroe Kid,The'	Jimmy Clitheroe
'Desert Island Discs'	Presenter: Roy Plomley (1st), Michael Parkinson, Sue Lawley
'Educating Archie'	
Surname	Andrews
Ventriloquist	Peter Brough
'Flying Doctor,The'	
Terry O'Donnell	Bill Kerr
Dr Chris Rogers (Title role)	James McKecknie
'Glums,The'	
Eth	June Whitfield
Originally in	'Take it from Here'
Pa	Jimmy Edwards
Ron	Dick Bentley
'Goon Show,The'	
Eccles, Minnie Bannister, Moriarty	Spike Milligan
Neddy Seagoon	Harry Secombe
Major Bloodnock, Grytpype-Thynne, Bluebottle	Peter Sellers
'Have a Go'	
Presenter	Wilfred Pickles
At the Table	Mable
'I'm Sorry I'll Read That Again'	TimBrookeTaylor,JohnCleese,BillOddie
Music	'The Angus Prune Tune'
'It's That Man Again (ITMA)'	
Main Character	Tommy Hanley
Mrs Mopp	Dorothy Summers
'Letter from America'	Alistair Cooke
'Life with the Lyons'	Ben Lyon, Bebe Daniels
Children	Barbara, Richard (Real life children)
'Men from the Ministry,The'	
Roland Hamilton-Jones	Wilfred Hyde-White
Richard Lamb	Richard Murdock
'Mrs Dale's Diary'	
Mr Dale's occupation	Doctor
Mrs Dale	Jessie Matthews (final)
'My Word'	
Team members	Frank Muir, Denis Norden
Umpire	John Arlott (1st), Michael O'Donnel (current)
'Navy Lark,The'	
No 1	Dennis Price (later Stephen Murray)
Chief Petty Officer Pertwee	John Pertwee
'Ray's a Laugh'	Ted Ray
'Round the Horne'	Kenneth Horne
Rambling Syd Rumpo	Kenneth Williams
'Take it from Here'	Jimmy Edwards, Dick Bentley

Introduces	The Glums
Writers	Frank Muir, Dennis Norden
'Twenty Questions'	
Chairman	Stewart McPherson (1st), Gilbert Harding, Kenneth Horne, Cliff Michelmore
Mystery Voice	Norman Hackforth
'Variety Playhouse'	MC: Vic Oliver

TV and Radio Characters

By: Character → Programme

Major Seth Adams	'Wagon Train'
David Addison	'Moonlighting'
Alexis	'Dynasty'
Sergeant 'Pepper' Anderson	'Police Woman'
Archie Andrews	'Educating Archie'
Sir Humphrey Appleby	'Yes Minister/Prime Minister'
Ashton Family	'Family at War'
Steve Austin	'The Six Million Dollar Man'
B.A.Baracus	'The A Team'
David Banner	'The Incredible Hulk'
Inspector Barlow	'Z Cars'
Ken Barlow	'Coronation Street'
Nora Batty	'Last of the Summer Wine'
Bert and Ernie	'Sesame Street'
Big Bird	'Sesame Street'
Sergeant Ernie Bilko	'The Phil Silvers Show'
Major Bloodnock	'The Goon Show'
Bluebottle	'The Goon Show'
Bodie	'The Professionals'
Boo Boo	'Yogi Bear'
Bootsie	'The Army Game' (1st)
Bungle	'Rainbow'
Cain	'Kung Fu'
Big John Cannon	'The High Chaparral'
Blake Carrington	'Dynasty'
Cartwright Family,The	'Bonanza'
Clampett Family,The	'The Beverly Hillbillies'
Clegg	'Last of the Summer Wine'
Jimmy Clitheroe	'The Clitheroe Kid'
Terry Collier	'The Likely Lads'
Compo	'Last of the Summer Wine'
Cookie Monster	'Sesame Street'
Sonny Crockett	'Miami Vice'
Crystal	'Dynasty'
Jed 'Kid' Curry	'Alias Smith and Jones'
Arthur Daley	'Minder'
Del Boy	'Only Fools and Horses'
Richard De Vere	'To The Manor Born'
Officer Dibble	'Top Cat'
Marshall Matt Dillon	'Gunsmoke' ('Gun Law')
Dirty Den	'Eastenders'
Doyle	'The Professionals'
Eccles	'The Goon Show'
J.R.Ewing	'Dallas'
Fallon	'Dynasty', 'The Colbys'
Fletcher	'Porridge'

Fonz,The	'Happy Days'
Detective Inspector Maggie Forbes	'The Gentle Touch'
Audrey Forbes-Hamilton	'To The Manor Born'
Sergeant Joe Friday	'Dragnet'
Alf Garnett	'Till Death Us Do Part'
Dr Gillespie	'Dr Kildare'
Glums,The	'Take It From Here'
Godber	'Porridge'
Bobby Grant	'Brookside'
Jim Hacker	'Yes Minister/Yes Prime Minister'
Hackett	'Target'
Hannibal	'The A Team'
Bradley Hardacre	'Brass'
Jim Hardy	'Wells Fargo'
Jess Harper	'Laramie'
Maddie Hayes	'Moonlighting'
Hannibal Heyes	'Alias Smith and Jones'
Mr Humphreys	'Are You Being Served'
Charlie Hungerford	'Bergerac'
Jess	'Postman Pat'
Dr Richard Kimble	'The Fugitive'
Captain Kirk	'Star Trek'
Kookie	'77 Sunset Strip'
Ilya Kuryakin	'The Man From U.N.C.L.E.'
Ma and Pop Larkin	'The Darling Buds of May'
Superintendent Lockhart	'No Hiding Place'
Lofty	'Eastenders'
Lurcio	'Up Pompeii'
Captain Mainwaring	'Dad's Army'
Mrs Mangle	'Neighbours'
Manuel	'Fawlty Towers'
Dan Matthews	'Highway Patrol'
Terry McCann	'Minder'
Steve McGarrett	'Hawaii Five-O'
Mrs Mopp	'I.T.M.A.'
Moriarty	'The Goon Show'
Muldoon	'Car 54, Where are you?'
Tony Nelson	'I Dream of Jeannie'
Elliott Ness	'The Untouchables'
Hilda Ogden	'Coronation Street'
Oscar the Grouch	'Sesame Street'
Paladin	'Have Gun Will Travel'
Parker	'Thunderbirds'
Lady Penelope	'Thunderbirds'
Colonel Oreste Pinto	'Spycatcher'
Popeye Popplewell	'The Army Game'
Wilbur Post	'Mr Ed'
Mr Rigsby	'Rising Damp'
Megan Roberts	'The District Nurse'
Kelly Robinson	'I Spy'
Dr Chris Rogers	'The Flying Doctor'
George Roper	'George and Mildred'
Rambling Syd Rumpo	'Round the Horne'
Samantha	'Bewitched'
Alexander Scott	'I Spy'
Neddie Seagoon	'The Goon Show'
Seymour	'Last of the Summer Wine'
Ena Sharples	'Coronation Street'

Mrs Slocombe	'Are You Being Served?'
Snudge	'The Army Game' (1st)
Napoleon Solo	'The Man From U.N.C.L.E.'
Frank Spencer	'Some Mothers Do 'Ave 'Em'
Mr Spock	'Star Trek'
John Steed	'The Avengers'
Darren Stephens	'Bewitched'
Lieutenant Mike Stone	'The Streets of San Francisco'
Jaime Summers	'The Bionic Woman'
Elsie Tanner	'Coronation Street'
Jessica Tate	'Soap'
Toody	'Car 54, Where are you?'
Trampas	'The Virginian'
David Vincent	'The Invaders'
Waldorf and Statler	'The Muppet Show'
Annie Walker	'Coronation Street'
Wicksy	'Eastenders'
Danny Williams	'Hawaii Five-O'
Rowdy Yates	'Rawhide'
Yosser	'The Boys from the Black Stuff'
Zippy	'Rainbow'

TV, General

By: *General*

Advertisement; 1st	Gibbs SR Toothpaste
BBC;-	
Announcer; 1st	Leslie Mitchell
Director General; 1st	Lord Reith
Chairman of Governors; Appointed 1986	Marmaduke Hussey
Ordinary transmission; 1st	1932; featured Louis Frecar singing 'I want to be a Lady'
Regular service; 1st	1936
Test Card girl	Carol Hersey ('Most Seen Person On TV')
BBC 2; Started	April 20th, 1964
Breakfast TV; 1st	BBC Breakfast Time, January 17th, 1983
Channel 4; Started	1982
Colour Transmission; 1st	1967
Four Letter Word; 1st use	Kenneth Tynan
Independent TV Companies (Former);-	
East England	Anglia
Lancashire	Granada
London	London Weekend, Thames
Midlands	Central
North East England	Tyne Tees
North East Scotland	Grampian
Wales	HTV (Harlech)
ITN Newscaster; 1st	Chris Chataway
TV Announcer; 1st; UK	Leslie Mitchell
Regular Service; 1st country	Germany
Royal Wedding; 1st in colour	Princess Anne, Captain Mark Philips
Sky television;-	
Merges with	British Satellite Broadcasting (1990)
Starts Broadcasting	1989
Studios; Founded by Lucille Ball and Desi Arnaz	Desilu

Teletext;-
BBC	Ceefax
ITV	Oracle
TV Licences; 1st	1946

TV Newscaster;-
1st	Richard Baker
1st; Black	Trevor McDonald
TV; Not on Thursday; Country	Iceland
US; Major systems	ABC, CBS, NBC, PBS
Viewdata service	Prestel

TV and Radio Personalities

By: Description → Name

See Also: TV, General (for Announcers, etc.)

Australia; Went to on million dollar contract	Michael Parkinson
Bird Watcher	Bill Oddie
Boxer; Amateur	Eamonn Andrews
Boxing; Commentator	Harry Carpenter
Cook; 1st TV	Philip Harben
Cricket Commentator; Liberal Parliamentary candidate	John Arlott
Father; Violinist; (1st Violinist with London Symphony Orchestra)	David McCallum
Fez; Comedian wore	Tommy Cooper
Googly; Father invented	Reginald Bosanquet
Horse Racing; Commentator	Peter O'Sullivan
Hospital Porter; Works as	Jimmy Savile
Interviewers; Liberal Parliamentary candidates	Robin Day, Ludovic Kennedy
Little Lord Fauntleroy; Played as a child	Richard O'Sullivan
Mastermind; Taxi driver wins	Fred Housego
News Team; US Top, '60s and '70s	Chet Huntley and David Brinkley
Newsreader; ITN; 1st; Female	Anna Ford
Nixon; Famous interview with	David Frost
Nose; Prominent	Jimmy Durante
Mr Pastry	Richard Hearne
Poetry; Homespun doggerel	Pam Ayres
Politicians; Former	Brian Walden, Robert Kilroy-Silk
Polo; Plays	Ted Rogers
Queen; Look-alike	Geanette Charles
Rugby League; Commentator	Eddie Waring
Spitfire Pilot; Former	Raymond Baxter
Sports Commentator;-	
Former middle distance runner	David Coleman
Has played at Wembley	Frank Bough
US, Top	Howard Cosell
Tennis Commentator; Former professional tennis champion	Dan Maskell
Territorial Army paratrooper; Former	Billy Connolly
Tickling Stick; Associated with	Ken Dodd
Underwater Series; Couple	Hans and Lotte Haas
William (In Just William); Played as a child	Denis Waterman
Wrestling; Commentator	Kent Walton

TV and Radio Personalities

By: Name → General

Jack Benny	Feud with: Fred Allen
Cannon and Ball	Former Name: The Harper Brothers
Billy Connolly	Group with: The Humblebums
Harry Corbett	Puppets: Sooty and Sweep
Jimmy Durante	Nose, called: 'Schnozzola'
Larry Grayson	Female Backup: Isla St Clair
Lenny Henry	DJ character: Delbert Wilkins
Krankies	Real Name: Tough
Morecambe and Wise	Signature Tune: 'Bring Me Sunshine'
Eric Sykes	Screen Sister: Hattie Jacques
Mary Whitehouse	Organisation: National Viewers' and Listeners' Association

TV Programmes

By: Description → Title

Antiques	'Going for a Song', 'Antiques Roadshow'
Beat the Clock, Included	'Sunday Night at the London Palladium'
Black Drama series, UK	'Empire Road'
Boatyard, Set in	'Howard's Way'
Bowls Competition	'Jack High'
Charades	'Give us a Clue'
Clapometer; 1st used in	'Opportunity Knocks'
Corner Shop, Set in	'Open All Hours'
Dead Private Eye; Helps partner	'Randall and Hopkirk (deceased)'
Diplomatic rift between Britain and Saudi Arabia; Causes	'Death of a Princess'
Dressmaking Factory, Set in	'The Rag Trade'
Frogmen	'Sea Hunt'
Gossip Columnist	'Lytton's Diary'
Home Guard	'Dad's Army'
Homeless Family	'Cathy Come Home'
Horse, Talking	'Mr Ed'
Longest Run (without a break)	'The Sky at Night' (since 1957)
Oil Company (UK)	'Mogul', 'The Troubleshooters'
Pathologist, Police	'The Expert'
Pop Music Show; Longest run	'Top of the Pops'
Prison, Comedy	'Porridge'
Rag and Bone Business	'Steptoe and Son'
Road Haulage Business	'The Brothers'
Satire Show; 1st	'That was the Week that Was'
Serial:-	
1st; Daily	'Sixpenny Corner'
1st; Regular (Twice weekly)	'Emergency Ward 10'
Longest run	'Coronation Street' (since 1960)
Sheepdog Trials	'One Man and his Dog'
Snooker Competition	'Pot Black'
Soap Opera:-	
Australian	'Neighbours', 'Home and Away'
Magazine; Set at	'Compact'
Spies; Travel as tennis players	'I Spy'
Tailor	'Never Mind the Quality, Feel the Width'

Tarmac laying gang	'Boys from the Blackstuff'
Variety Programme, Longest run	'The Good Old Days'
Variety Show; Top US, '50s and '60s	'Ed Sullivan Show'
Wheelchair; Detective in	'Ironside'
Yes/No Game; Included in	'Take Your Pick'

TV Programmes

By: Name → Stars, General

'A Team,The'	
B.A.Baracus (Bad Attitude)	Mr T
Faceman	Dirk Benedict
Hannibal	George Peppard
Murdock	Dwight Schultz
'Addams Family,The'	
Based on	Charles Addams Cartoons
Butler	Lurch
Uncle Fester	Jackie Coogan
'Alias Smith and Jones'	
Hannibal Heyes ('Smith')	Pete Duel (1st)
Jed 'Kid' Curry ('Jones')	Ben Murphy
'All Creatures Great and Small'	
Siegfried Farnon	Robert Hardy
Helen	Carol Drinkwater, Linda Bellingham
James Herriott	Christopher Timothy
Tristran	Peter Davison
'All Gas and Gaiters'	
The Bishop	William Mervyn
The Curate	Derek Nimmo
''Allo'Allo'	
Café	René's Cafe
René	Gordon Kaye
'America'	Alistair Cooke
'Andy Pandy'	Girlfriend: Looby Loo
'Angels'	Set in: St Angela's Hospital
'Are You Being Served?'	
Miss Brahms	Wendy Richards
Mr Humphreys	John Inman
Mrs Slocombe	Molly Sugden
Store	Grace Brothers
'Army Game,The'	
Bootsie	Alfie Bass
Snudge	Bill Fraser
Spin off	'Bootsie and Snudge'
'Around the World in 80 Days'	
Traveller	Michael Palin
'Ascent of Man,The'	Presenter: Jacob Bronowski
'Ask the Family'	Presenter: Robert Robinson
'Auf Wiedersehen, Pet'	Theme tune: 'That's Living All right'
'Avengers,The'	
Cathy Gale	Honor Blackman
New Avengers	Gareth Hunt, Joanna Lumley
Tara King	Linda Thorson
Emma Peel	Diana Rigg
John Steed	Patrick Macnee
'Banacek'	Title: George Peppard
'Baretta'	Title: Robert Blake
'Batman'	
Based on	Bob Kane comic

Batman	Adam West
Batman's real identity	Bruce Wayne
Butler	Alfred
House	Wayne Manor
Robin	Burt Ward, Jason Todd
Robin's real identity	Dick Grayson
Set in	Gotham City
'Bergerac'	
Jim Bergerac	John Nettles
Charlie Hungerford	Terence Alexander
Set in	Jersey
'Beverly Hillbillies,The'	
Address	5/8, Crestview Drive
Family	The Clampetts
'Bewitched'	
Daughter	Tabitha
Samantha	Elizabeth Montgomery
Darren Stephens	Dick York (1st), Dick Sargent
'Billy Bunter'	Title: Gerald Campion
'Bionic Woman,The'	Jaime Summers (Title): Lindsay Wagner
'Bird of Prey'	Title: Richard Griffiths
'Blackadder'	
Baldrick	Tony Robinson
Title	Rowan Atkinson
'Blankety Blank'	Presenter: Terry Wogan (1st), Les Dawson
'Blind Date'	
Presenter	Cilla Black
'Blockbusters'	Presenter: Bob Holness
'Bonanza'	
Ben (father)	Lorne Green
Brothers	Adam, Hoss, Little Joe
Family	The Cartwrights
Ranch	Ponderosa
'Botanic Man'	Presenter: David Bellamy
'Boys from the Blackstuff,The'	
Catchphrase	'Gi's a Job'
Theme	Gang of tarmac layers
Writer	Alan Bleasdale
Yosser	Bernard Hill
'Brass'	Bradley Hardacre: Timothy West
'Bread'	
Author	Carla Lane
Nellie Boswell	Jean Boht
'Brideshead Revisited'	Sebastian: Jeremy Irons
'Bronco'	Bronco Lane: Ty Hardin
'Brookside'	
Creator	Phil Redmond
Miss UK, actress	Dinah May
Set in	Liverpool (Croxteth)
'Budgie'	Title: Adam Faith
'Burke's Law'	
Amos Burke	Gene Barry
Each episode	'Who killed ?'
'Cagney and Lacey'	
Christine Cagney	Sharon Gless
Mary Beth Lacey	Tyne Daly
'Call My Bluff'	Chairman: Robert Robinson

'Callan'	Edward Woodward
'Candid Camera'	
UK Compere; 1st	Bob Monkhouse
UK Stunts	Jonathon Routh
US Host	Allen Funt
'Cannon'	William Conrad
'Car 54, Where Are You'	
Muldoon	Fred Gwynne
Toody	Joe E.Ross
'Casualty'	
Hospital	Holby General
'Cathy Come Home'	
Cathy	Carol White
Director	Ken Loach
'Celebrity Squares'	Presenter: Bob Monkhouse
'Charlie's Angels'	
Angels	Kate Jackson, Farrah Fawcett Majors, Jaclyn Smith (Original 3), Cheryl Ladd
Charlie Townsend (never appears); Voice	John Forsythe
'Cheyenne'	Cheyenne Bodie: Clint Walker
'Child's Play'	Presenter: Michael Aspel
'Chinese Detective,The'	Title: David Yip
'Cisco Kid,The'	Title: Duncan Renaldo
'Civilization'	Presenter: Kenneth Clark
'Colbys,The'	
Jason Colby	Charlton Heston
Fallon	Emma Samms
'Colditz'	Commandant: Bernard Hepton
'Columbo'	
Columbo	Peter Falk
First name	Never mentioned
'Coronation Street'	
Janet Barlow; Died from	Suicide by drug overdose
Ken Barlow	William Roache
Ken Barlow's twin children	Peter and Susan
Ken Barlow's wives	Valerie Tatlock, Janet Reid, Deidre Langton
Valerie Barlow; Died from	Electrocution when mending a hairdryer
Bigamous marriage	Emily Bishop, Arnold
Violet Carson	Ena Sharples
Creator	Tony Warren
Deidre's ex-husband	Ray Langton
Deirdre's daughter	Tracy
1st words	'Now the next thing you've got to do is to get the sign-writer in', Elsie Lappin (Maudie Edwards)
Bet Lynch	Julie Goodyear
Bet Lynch; Married	Alec Gilroy
Mayor of Weatherfield; Became	Alf Roberts
Newsagents	The Kabin
Hilda Ogden	Jean Alexander
Original character, only	Ken Barlow
Pop singers; Formerly in serial	Davy Jones, Peter Noone
Pub	Rover's Return
Mavis Riley; Failed to turn up to marry	Derek Wilton

Rover's Return brewery	Newton and Ridley
Rover's Return Manager	Alec Gilroy
Alma Sedgewick	Amanda Barrie
Started	December 9th, 1960
Leonard Swindley	Arthur Lowe
Elsie Tanner	Pat Phoenix
Elsie Tanner's Husbands	Arnold Tanner, Sergeant Steve Tanner, Alan Howard
Curly Watts; Real name	Norman
Annie Walker	Doris Speed
'Criss Cross Quiz'	
Presenter	Jeremy Hawk
US equivalent	Tic Tac Dough
'Crossroads'	
Benny	Paul Henry
Creators	Hazel Adair, Peter Ling
1st words	'Crossroads Motel, can I help you?'
Ends	1988
Location	King's Oak
Meg; Jailed for	Dangerous driving
Original title, intended	Midland Road
Meg Richardson	Noele Gordon (Leaves 1981)
Sandy Richardson, (Paralysed)	Roger Tonge
Setting	Midland's Motel
Started	1964
Test tube baby, Had	Glenda Banks
Theme music	Tony Hatch
'Crown Court'	Set in: Fulchester
'Dad's Army'	
Lance Corporal Jones	Clive Dunn
Captain Mainwaring, Bank Manager	Arthur Lowe
Set in	Walmington-on-Sea
Sergeant Wilson	John Le Mesurier
'Dallas'	
Cliff Barnes's father	Digger Barnes
Bobby	Patrick Duffy
Bobby; 'Killed by'	Katherine Wentworth
Bobby; Returns	In a shower
Miss Ellie	Barbara Bel Geddes (1st), Donna Reed (temporarily)
Miss Ellie; Remarried	Clayton Farlow
Ewing brother, 3rd	Gary
Jock Ewing	Jim Davies
J.R.Ewing	Larry Hagman
Ewing's house	Southfork
Jock killed in	Helicopter crash in South America
JR, stands for	John Ross
JR's son	John Ross
Pam	Victoria Principal
Pam and Bobby, adopted son	Christopher
Shot JR	Kirsten
Spin off	'Knott's Landing'
Sue Ellen	Linda Gray
Jenna Wade	Priscilla Beaulieu Presley
'Dame Edna Everage'	Barry Humphries
Husband	Norm
'Dangerman'	John Drake: Patrick McGoohan

'Darling Buds of May, The'
  Based on — H.E.Bates Stories
  Ma Larkin — Pam Ferris
  Pop Larkin — David Jason
'Death of a Princess' — Theme: Execution of Saudi Arabian princess and lover

'Dempsey and Makepeace'
  Dempsey — Michael Brandon
  Makepiece — Glynis Barber
'District Nurse,The'
  Dog — Scratch
  Megan Roberts (Title) — Nerys Hughes
'Dixon of Dock Green'
  Based on — *The Blue Lamp* (film)
  Creator — Ted Willis
  Dixon — Jack Warner
  Runs — 1955–1976
  Jack Warner; Age — 80 at end
'Doctor in the House' — Hospital: St Swithin's
'Doctor Kildare'
  Dr Gillespie — Raymond Massey (original)
  Hospital — Blair General
  Title — Richard Chamberlain
'Double Your Money'
  Based on — $64,000 Question
  Presenter — Hughie Green
'Dr Finlay's Casebook'
  Dr Cameron — Andrew Cruickshank
  Dr Finlay — Bill Simpson
  Janet, the Housekeeper — Barbara Mullen
  Set in — Tannochbrae
'Dr Who'
  Daleks from — Skaro
  Dog — K9
  Spaceship — Tardis (Time and Relative Dimensions in Space)
  Title — William Hartnell, Jon Pertwee, Patrick Troughton, Tom Baker, Peter Davison, Colin Baker, Sylvester McCoy

'Dragnet'
  At end — 'The story you have just seen is true, only the names have been changed to protect the innocent'

  Sergeant Joe Friday — Jack Webb
'Duchess of Duke Street,The' — Title: Gemma Jones
'Dukes of Hazzard,The'
  Car — General Lee
  Theme music — Waylon Jennings
'Duty Free'
  Linda Cochrane — Joanna Van Gyseghem
  Robert Cochrane — Neil Stacy
  Amy Pearce — Gwen Taylor
  David Pearce — Keith Barron
'Dynasty'
  Adam attempted to kill Jeff Colby with — Poisonous office paint
  Alexis — Joan Collins

113

Alexis's company	Colby Co
Alexis's daughter	Amanda Bedford
Bisexual	Steven Carrington
Blake Carrington	John Forsythe
Blake killed	Ted Dinard
Blake's former wife	Alexis
Ben Carrington	Christopher Cazenove
Dominique Devereaux	Diahann Carroll (Blake's half sister)
Fallon	Pamela Sue Martin (1st), Emma Samms
Fallon's Club	Le Mirage
Kidnapped when a baby	Adam
Krystle	Linda Evans
Krystle's former husband	Mark Jennings
Original title	'Oil'
Politicians who appeared in	Gerald Ford, Kissinger
Producer	Aaron Spelling
Spin off	'The Colbys'

'Eastenders'

Angie	Anita Dobson
Brewery	Luxford and Copley
Café	Ali's Café (run by Ali and Sue Osman)
Creators	Julia Smith, Tony Holland
Den's children	Sharon (adopted), Vicki (with Michelle)
HIV Positive, Diagnosed as	Mark Fowler
Lofty Holloway	Tom Watt
Michelle	Susan Tully
Newspaper	*Walford Gazette*
Pub	Queen Victoria (Queen Vic)
Dennis Watts (Dirty Den)	Leslie Grantham
Simon Wicks (Wicksy)	Nick Berry

'Edna the Inebriate Woman' — Title: Patricia Hayes

'Edward and Mrs Simpson'

Edward VIII	Edward Fox
Mrs Simpson	Cynthia Harris

'Emmerdale'

Annie Sugden	Sheila Mercier
Joe Sugden	Frazer Hines
Gamekeeper	Seth Armstrong
Pub	The Woolpack
Publican	Amos Brearly
Set in	Beckindale, Yorkshire

'Equalizer,The' — Title: Edward Woodward
'Expert,The' — Title: Marius Goring
'Face to Face' — Interviewer: John Freeman

'Falcon Crest'

Angie Channing	Jane Wyman (Reagan's ex-wife)
Clare	Robert Foxworth
Family	The Channings
Setting	Vine estate in the Napa Valley

'Fall and Rise of Reginald Perrin,The'

C.J., Boss	John Barron
Company	Sunshine Desserts
Perrin	Leonard Rossiter

'Fame' — Set in: High School for the Performing Arts, New York
'Family at War' — Family: The Ashtons
'Father Brown' — Title: Kenneth More
'Fawlty Towers'

Basil Fawlty	John Cleese
Sybil Fawlty	Prunella Scales
Manuel	Andrew Sachs
Manuel; From	Barcelona
Polly	Connie Booth
Written by	John Cleese, Connie Booth
'Flinstones,The'	
Dinosaur	Dino
Flintstone's Baby	Pebbles
Names	Fred and Wilma
Neighbours	Barney and Betty Rubble
Rubble's baby	Bam Bam
'Flowerpot Men,The'	Bill and Ben
'Flying Nun,The'	Sally Field
'Forsyte Saga,The'	
Based on	John Galsworthy novels
Irene	Nyree Dawn Porter
Soames	Eric Porter
'Fraggle Rock'	Only human: Fulton Mackay
'Fugitive,The'	
Searches for	One armed man who killed his wife
Title	David Janssen
'Galloping Gourmet'	Title: Graham Kerr (Cookery programme)
'Gardener's World'	Presenter (1st): Percy Thrower
'GBH'	
Michael Murray	Robert Lindsay
Jim Nelson (Headmaster)	Michael Palin
Writer	Alan Bleasdale
'Generation Game'	
Presenter	Bruce Forsyth (with Anthea Redfern), Larry Grayson (with Isla St Clair)
'Gentle Touch,The'	Detective Inspector Maggie Forbes: Jill Gascoigne
'George and Mildred'	
George Roper	Brian Murphy
Mildred	Yootha Joyce
'Get Smart'	Maxwell Smart: Don Adams
'Gideon's Way'	Inspector Gideon: John Gregson
'Girls on Top'	Dawn French, Jennifer Saunders, Tracey Ullman, Ruby Wax (original)
'Give Us A Clue'	
Team Captains	Lionel Blair, Una Stubbs
Chairman	Michael Aspel (1st), Michael Parkinson
'Glittering Prizes'	Tom Conti
'Going for a Song'	Resident Expert: Arthur Negus
'Golden Shot,The'	
Crossbow, loads	Bernie the Bolt
Presenter	Bob Monkhouse
'Good Life,The'	
Tom and Barbara Good	Richard Briers, Felicity Kendal
Jerry and Margot Leadbetter	Paul Eddington, Penelope Keith
'Good Old Days,The'	Chairman: Leonard Sachs
'Goodies,The'	Tim Brooke-Taylor, Graeme Garden, Bill Oddie
'Gunsmoke'	
Blacksmith	Burt Reynolds

Matt Dillon, Marshall of Dodge City	James Arness
'Hancock's Half Hour'	Address: Railway Cuttings, East Cheam
'Happy Days'	Arthur Fonzerelli, the Fonz: Henry Winkler
'Happy Ever After'	
The Medfords	Terry Scott, June Whitfield
Sequel	'Terry and June'
'Harry O'	Title: David Janssen
'Hart to Hart'	
Dog	Freeway
Title	Robert Wagner, Stefanie Powers
'Have Gun Will Travel'	
On calling card	'Have gun will travel, Wire Paladin'
Paladin	Richard Boone
'Hawaii Five-O'	
McGarrett	Jack Lord
Detective Danny Williams	James McArthur
'Hazell'	Title: Nicholas Ball
'Hi-de-Hi'	
Ted Bovis	Paul Shane
Peggy	Su Pollard
Gladys Pugh	Ruth Madoc
'High Chaparral,The'	Big John Cannon: Leif Erickson
'History Man,The'	Title: Antony Sher
'Hogan's Heroes'	Hogan: Bob Crane
'Home and Away'	
Bobby	Nicole Dixon
Matt	Greg Benson
Grant Mitchell	Craig McLachlan
'Hopalong Cassidy'	William Boyd
'Howard's Way'	Title: Boatyard, Mermaid Yard
'I Dream of Jeannie'	
Jeannie	Barbara Eden
Tony Nelson	Larry Hagman
'I Love Lucy'	
Later becomes	'The Lucy Show'
Lucy Ricardo	Lucille Ball
Ricky Ricardo	Desi Arnaz
'I Spy'	
Kelly Robinson	Robert Culp
Alexander Scott	Bill Cosby
'In at the Deep End'	Presenters: Paul Heiney, Chris Searle
'Incredible Hulk, The'	
David Banner	Bill Bixby
Title	Lou Ferrigno
'Inspector Morse'	
Sergeant Lewis	Kevin Whateley
Title	John Thaw
'Invaders,The'	
David Vincent	Roy Thinnes
Distinguishing feature of invaders	Crooked little finger
'Irish RM,The'	Title: Peter Bowles
'Ironside'	Title: Raymond Burr
'It's a Knockout'	International name: Jeux Sans Frontières
'Juke Box Jury'	Presenter: David Jacobs, Jools Holland (New Series)

'Juliet Bravo'	Stephanie Turner, Anna Carteret
'Just William'	William (1st): Dennis Waterman
'Knots Landing'	
Abby Ewing	Donna Mills
Gary Ewing	Ted Shackleford
'Kojak'	
Telly's brother	George (Stavros)
Theo Kojak (Title)	Telly Savalas
'Krypton Factor,The'	Woman Winner (1st): Marian Chanter, 1987
'Kung Fu'	
Cain	David Carradine
Looks for	Brother Daniel
'Laramie'	Jess Harper: Robert Fuller
'Last of the Summer Wine,The'	
Compo	Bill Owen
Clegg	Peter Sallis
Seymour	Michael Aldridge
'Life and Loves of a She Devil,The'	She Devil: Julie T.Wallace
'Life on Earth'	Presenter: David Attenborough
'Likely Lads,The'	
Bob	Rodney Bewes
Terry Collier	James Bolam
Sequel	'Whatever happened to the Likely Lads?'
'Lillie'	Lillie Langtry: Francesca Annis
'Liver Birds,The'	Polly James, Nerys Hughes, Elizabeth Estensen (later)
'Lone Ranger,The'	
Lone Ranger's horse	Silver
Real identity	John Reid
Theme tune	William Tell Overture
Title	Clayton Moore (Later John Hart)
Tonto	Jay Silverheels
Tonto; Calls Lone Ranger	'Kemo Sabe' (Trusty Scout)
Tonto's horse	Scout
'Look'	Presenter: Peter Scott
'Lou Grant'	
Lou Grant	Ed Asner
Newspaper	Los Angeles Tribune
'Magnum P.I.'	Title: Tom Selleck
'Maigret'	Inspector Maigret: Rupert Davies
'Main Chance,The'	The Solicitor: John Stride
'Man about the House'	Spin offs: 'Robin's Nest', 'George and Mildred'
'Man from U.N.C.L.E.,The'	
Ilya Kuryakin	David McCallum
Napoleon Solo	Robert Vaughn
Stands for	United Network Command for Law Enforcement
Mr Waverly	Leo G.Carroll
'Marriage Lines'	Prunella Scales, Richard Briers
'Mary Hartman, Mary Hartman'	Louise Lasser
'Mary Tyler Moore Show'	Spin offs: 'Lou Grant', 'Phyllis', 'Rhoda'
'M.A.S.H'	
Hawkeye Pierce	Alan Alda
Hot Lips (Margaret) Houlihan	Loretta Swit
Trapper John	Wayne Rogers

'Mastermind'	Questionmaster: Magnus Magnusson
'Masterteam'	Presenter: Angela Rippon
'Maverick'	Bret Maverick: James Garner
'McCloud'	Title: Denis Weaver
'McMillan and Wife'	
McMillan	Rock Hudson
Wife	Susan St James
'Miami Vice'	
Sonny Crockett	Don Johnson
Ricardo Tubbs	Philip Michael Thomas
'Minder'	
Arthur Daley	George Cole
Ray Daley	Gary Webster
Terry McCann	Dennis Waterman
Theme tune	'I could be so good for you'
'Miss Marple'	Title: Joan Hickson
'Mission Impossible'	Catchphrase: 'This tape will self destruct in 5 (10) seconds'
'Mister Ed'	Wilbur Post: Alan Young
'Mogul'	
About	Oil company
Later	'The Troubleshooters'
'Monkees,The'	Micky Dolenz, Davy Jones (British), Mike Nesmith, Peter Tork
'Moonlighting'	
David Addison	Bruce Willis
Maddie Hayes	Cybill Shepherd
'Mr Bean'	
Title	Rowan Atkinson
'Munsters,The'	
Herman	Fred Gwynne
Lily	Yvonne De Carlo
'Muppet Show,The'	
Creator	Jim Henson
Miss Piggy; Surname	Lee
Theatre hecklers	Statler and Waldorf
'Naked Civil Servant,The'	Quentin Crisp, the Homosexual: John Hurt
'Neighbours'	
Harold Bishop	Ian Smith
Madge Bishop	Anne Charleston
Joe Mangle	Mark Little
Charlene Robinson	Kylie Minogue
Scott Robinson	Jason Donovan (1st: Darius Perkins)
Twins (Caroline and Christina Alessi)	Gillian and Gayle Blakeney
'No Hiding Place'	
Sergeant Baxter	Eric Lander
Superintendent Lockhart	Raymond Francis
'Not In Front Of The Children'	The Mother: Wendy Craig
'Not Only But Also'	Dudley Moore, Peter Cook ('Dud' and 'Pete')
'Not the Nine O'Clock News'	Rowan Atkinson, Griff Rhys-Jones, Mel Smith, Pamela Stephenson
'Oh no, it's Selwyn Froggatt'	Title: Bill Maynard
'On Safari'	Armand and Michaela Denis
'On the Buses'	
Inspector Blake	Stephen Lewis

Butler	Reg Varney
'One Man and his Dog'	Presenter: Phil Drabble
'Only Fools and Horses'	
Rodney	Nicholas Lyndhurst
Del Boy Trotter	David Jason
'Only When I Laugh'	
Figgis	James Bolam
Glover	Peter Bowles
'Open All Hours'	Ronnie Barker, David Jason
'Opportunity Knocks'	
Presenter	Hughie Green
Revived with	Bob Monkhouse
'Pallisers,The'	Susan Hampshire
'Panorama'	
Presenters	Pat Murphy (1st), Richard Dimbleby, Malcolm Muggeridge, David Dimbleby
'Perry Mason'	
Della Street, Secretary	Barbara Hale
Title	Raymond Burr
'Persuaders,The'	Roger Moore, Tony Curtis
'Peyton Place'	
Based on	Grace Metalious novel
Rodney Harrington	Ryan O'Neal
Alison McKenzie	Mia Farrow
Constance McKenzie	Dorothy Malone
'Phil Silvers Show,The'	
Army Camp	Fort Baxter
Sergeant Ernie Bilko	Phil Silvers
'Phyllis'	Title: Cloris Leachman
Spin off from	'Mary Tyler Moore Show'
'Play Your Cards Right'	Presenter: Bruce Forsyth
'Please Sir'	
Spin off	'The Fenn Street Gang'
The Teacher	John Alderton
(Agatha Christie's) 'Poirot'	
Title	David Suchet
'Police Five'	Presenter: Shaw Taylor
'Police Woman'	Sergeant Pepper Anderson: Angie Dickinson
'Porridge'	
Fletcher	Ronnie Barker
Godber	Richard Beckinsale
Mr McKay, Prison Warder	Fulton McKay
Sequel	'Going Straight'
'Postman Pat'	
Cat	Jess (black and white)
Post Office Owner	Mrs Goggins
Set in	Greendale
Twins	Katie and Tom Pottage
'Power Game,The'	John Wilder: Patrick Wymark
'Price is Right,The'	
Catchphrase	'Come on down'
Presenter	Leslie Crowther
'Prisoner,The'	
Filmed in	Portmeirion, Wales
Title	Patrick McGoohan
'Professionals,The'	

Bodie	**Lewis Collins**
Doyle	**Martin Shaw**
'Protectors,The'	**Robert Vaughn, Nyree Dawn Porter, Tony Arnholz**
'Question of Sport,A'	**Questionmaster: David Coleman**
'Quincy'	**Title: Jack Klugmann**
'Rag Trade,The'	
Catchphrase	**'Everybody out'**
Company	**Fenner Fashions**
Paddy, the Shop Steward	**Miriam Karlin**
'Rawhide'	
Rowdy Yates	**Clint Eastwood**
Theme song sung by	**Frankie Laine**
'Ready Steady Go'	**Presenters: Cathy McGowan, Keith Fordyce**
'Rebecca'	
Mrs Danvers	**Anna Massey**
Maxim De Winter	**Jeremy Brett**
Mrs De Winter	**Joanna David**
'Rhoda'	
Spin off from	**'The Mary Tyler Moore Show'**
Title	**Valerie Harper**
'Rich Man, Poor Man'	**Peter Strauss, Nick Nolte**
Based on	**Irwin Shaw novel**
'Ripping Yarns'	**Writer and Star: Michael Palin**
'Rising Damp'	
Hallam	**Richard Beckinsale**
Miss Jones	**Frances De La Tour**
Philip	**Don Warrington**
Mr Rigsby	**Leonard Rossiter**
'Rock Follies'	**Charlotte Cornwell, Julie Covington, Rula Lenska**
Group	**The Little Ladies**
'Rockford Files,The'	**James Garner**
Lives in	**A Trailer**
'Roots'	
Based on	**Alex Haley novel**
Story of	**Kunte Kinte**
'Rowan and Martin's Laugh In'	
Presenters	**Dan Rowan, Dick Martin**
Set in	**Beautiful Downtown Burbank**
'Sock it to me' Girl	**Judy Carne**
'Rumpole of the Bailey'	
Rumpole	**Leo McKern**
Writer	**John Mortimer**
'Saint'	
Drove	**Volvo P1800S**
Sequel	**'Return of the Saint' (Ian Ogilvy)**
Simon Templar	**Roger Moore**
'Sale of the Century'	**Presenter: Nicholas Parsons**
'Sapphire and Steel'	
Sapphire	**Joanna Lumley**
Silver	**David Collings**
Steel	**David McCallum**
'Secret Diary of Adrian Mole, Aged 13¾,The'	
Adrian	**Gian Sammarco**
Mr Mole	**Stephen Moore**
Mrs Mole	**Julie Walters (1st), Lulu**

'Seventy-Seven Sunset Strip'	Efrem Zimbalist Jnr, Roger Smith
Kookie	Ed Byrnes
'Sherlock Holmes'	Title: Jeremy Brett
'Shoestring'	Eddie Shoestring: Trevor Eve
'Shogun'	Blackthorne: Richard Chamberlain
'Simpsons, The'	
Children	Maggie (Baby), Lisa, Bart
Parents	Homer, Marge
'Singing Detective,The'	
Disease	Psoriasis
Title	Michael Gambon
'Six Million Dollar Man,The'	Title, Colonel Steve Austin: Lee Majors
'$64,000 Question,The'	Presenter (US): Hal March
'Smiley's People'	
Based on	John Le Carré novel
Smiley	Alec Guinness
'Softly Softly'	Spin off from: 'Z Cars'
'Some Mothers Do 'Ave 'Em'	
Betty	Michele Dotrice
Frank Spencer	Michael Crawford
'South Bank Show,The'	Presenter: Melvyn Bragg
'Spitting Image'	Peter Fluck, Roger Law
'Spycatcher'	Colonel Oreste Pinto: Bernard Archard
'St Elsewhere'	Hospital: St Eligius, Boston
'Starsky and Hutch'	
Kenneth Hutch	David Soul
David Starsky	Paul Michael Glaser
'Startrek' (Original Series)	
Catchphrase	'To boldly go where no man has gone before'
Captain Kirk	William Shatner
Dr Leonard McCoy ('Bones')	De Forest Kelly
Mr Spock	Leonard Nimoy (Half Vulcan)
Spock's Mother	T'Pau
'Steptoe and Son'	
Horse	Hercules
Setting	Rag and Bone business
Son	Harry H.Corbett
Steptoe	Wilfred Bramble
US equivalent	Sanford and Son
'Streets of San Francisco,The'	Lieutenant Mike Stone: Michael Douglas (1st), Karl Malden, Richard Hatch
'Sutherland's Law'	Procurator Fiscal: Iain Cuthbertson
'Sweeney,The'	John Thaw, Dennis Waterman
'Taggart'	Mark McManus
'Take Three Girls'	Angela Down, Liza Goddard, Susan Jameson
'Take your Pick'	Presenter: Michael Miles
'Target'	Hackett: Patrick Mower
'Taxi'	Taxi Company: Sunshine Cab Company
'Telford's Change'	Peter Barkworth, Hannah Gordon
'That Was the Week that Was (TW3)'	First satire show
Producer	Ned Sherrin
Presenter	David Frost
'That's Life'	
Odd Odes	Cyril Fletcher
Presenter	Esther Rantzen

'Third Man,The'	Harry Lime: Michael Rennie
'This is Your Life'	
First Subject	Eamonn Andrews
Presenter	Eamonn Andrews (1st)
Refuse to appear	Danny Blanchflower, Richard Gordon
US presenter	Ralph Edwards
'Thorn Birds,The'	
Based on	Colleen McCullough novel
Meggie Cleary	Rachel Ward
Cardinal de Bricassart	Richard Chamberlain
'Three of a kind'	Lenny Henry, Tracy Ullman, David Copperfield
'3 – 2 – 1'	Presenter: Ted Rogers
'Thunderbirds'	
Butler	Parker
Creators	Gerry and Sylvia Anderson
'Till Death Us Do Part'	
Else	Dandy Nichols
Alf Garnett	Warren Michell
Rita	Una Stubbs
Rita's Husband	Anthony Booth
Sequel	'In Sickness and in Health'
US version	'All in the Family' (Archie Bunker – Carroll O'Connor)
Writer	Johnny Speight
'Tinker, Tailor, Soldier, Spy'	
Based on	John Le Carré novel
George Smiley	Alec Guinness
'TISWAS'	Stands for: Today is Saturday, wear a smile
'T.J.Hooker'	Title: William Shatner
'To The Manor Born'	
Audrey Forbes-Hamilton	Penelope Keith
Richard De Vere	Peter Bowles
'Tomorrow's World'	Presenter (1st): Raymond Baxter
'Tonight'	Presenter: Cliff Michelmore
'Top Cat'	Policeman: Officer Dibble
'Top of the Pops'	Started: 1963
'Treasure Hunt'	In helicopter: Anneka Rice
'Troubleshooters,The'	Original title: Mogul
'Tumbledown'	
Lieutenant Robert Lawrence	Colin Firth
'Twin Peaks'	
Agent Dale Cooper	Kyle Maclachlan
Audrey Horn	Sherilyn Fenn
'University Challenge'	Questionmaster: Bamber Gascoigne
'Untouchables,The'	Elliot Ness: Robert Stack
'Up Pompeii'	Lurcio: Frankie Howard
'Upstairs Downstairs'	
Address	165, Eaton Place
James Bellamy (Commits suicide)	Simon Williams
Mr Bellamy	David Langton
Mrs Bridges, the Cook	Angela Baddeley
Hudson, the Butler	Gordon Jackson
Rose	Jean Marsh
Sarah, the Parlourmaid	Pauline Collins
Spin off	'Thomas and Sarah'
Thomas, the Chauffeur	John Alderton

'Van Der Valk'　　　　　　　　　　　Title: Barry Foster
'Virginian,The'
　Ranch　　　　　　　　　　　　　　Shiloh
　Title　　　　　　　　　　　　　　　James Drury
　Trampas　　　　　　　　　　　　　Doug McClure
'Wagon Train'
　Major Seth Adams, Wagonmaster　　Ward Bond
'Weekend World'　　　　　　　　　　Presenters: Peter Jay, Brian Walden
'Wells Fargo'　　　　　　　　　　　　Jim Hardy: Dale Robertson
'Whacko'
　Headmaster　　　　　　　　　　　　Jimmy Edwards
　School　　　　　　　　　　　　　　Chiselbury
'What's My Line'
　Chairman　　　　　　　　　　　　　Eamonn Andrews (1st)
　Original panel　　　　　　　　　　Isobel Barnett, David Nixon, Gilbert
　　　　　　　　　　　　　　　　　　　　Harding, Barbara Kelly
　Revived with　　　　　　　　　　　David Jacobs
'When The Boat Comes In'　　　　　James Bolam, Susan Jameson
　Family　　　　　　　　　　　　　　The Seatons
'World of Sport'　　　　　　　　　　Presenter (1st): Eamonn Andrews
'Worzel Gummidge'
　Aunt Sally　　　　　　　　　　　　Una Stubbs
　Title　　　　　　　　　　　　　　　Jon Pertwee
'Wyatt Earp'　　　　　　　　　　　　Title: Hugh O'Brian
'Yes, Minister'
　Sir Humphrey Appleby　　　　　　Nigel Hawthorne
　Jim Hacker '　　　　　　　　　　　Paul Eddington
　Sequel　　　　　　　　　　　　　　'Yes, Prime Minister'
'Yogi Bear'
　Friend　　　　　　　　　　　　　　Boo boo
　Setting　　　　　　　　　　　　　Jellystone Park
'Young Ones,The'　　　　　　　　　Rick Mayall, Adrian Edmundson, Nigel
　　　　　　　　　　　　　　　　　　　　Planer, Christopher Ryan

'Z Cars'
　Inspector Barlow　　　　　　　　　Stratford Johns
　Created by　　　　　　　　　　　　Troy Kennedy Martin
　Set in　　　　　　　　　　　　　　Newtown, Liverpool
　Spin off　　　　　　　　　　　　　'Softly Softly'
　Sergeant Watt　　　　　　　　　　Frank Windsor
'Zoo Quest'　　　　　　　　　　　　Presenter: David Attenborough
'Zorro'　　　　　　　　　　　　　　Horses: Phantom, Tornado

Geography and Places

Contents

Man Made Constructions	**128**
Bridges	
By: Description	128
By: Name	128
Buildings and Constructions	
By: Description	128
By: Name	130
Canals	132
Houses, Famous	
By: House Name	133
Natural Features	**133**
Bays and Gulfs	
By: Description, Location	133
Capes	134
Deserts	134
Geographical Terms	134
Islands	
By: Description, Location	136
By: Name	137
Lakes	
By: Description	139
By: Name	139
Mountain Ranges	
By: Description, Location	139
By: Name	140
Mountains	
By: Description, Location	140
By: Name	141
Natural Disasters	141
Other Natural Sites and Places	
By: Description	142
By: Name	142
Rivers	
By: Description, Location	144
By: Name	144
Seas and Oceans	
By: Description, Location	145
By: Name	146
Straits	
By: Location	146
Volcanoes	
By: Description	147
By: Name	147
Waterfalls	147
Weather	148

Places	**149**
Capitals	
By: Country	149
Capitals, Former	
By: Country	152
Cities	
By: Description	152
By: Name	153
Cities on Lakes	
By: City	153
Cities on Rivers	
By: City	154
Countries	
By: Description	155
By: Name	157
Exploration and Discovery	158
Extremities	
By: Place	159
Flags	160
Historical Territories	
By: Territory	160
Inhabitants	
By: Place	161
National Anthems	
By: Country	161
National Symbols	
By: Country	162
Other Places	
By: Description	162
By: Name	162
Peoples and Tribes	
By: Name	163
Place Name Change	
By: Original Name	164
Place Name Derivations	
By: Place	166
Place Name Parts, Meaning	
By: Name Part	167
Place Nicknames	
By: Nickname	167
Places, Latitude and Longitude	168
Roman Names	
By: Roman Name	168
Territories, Sovereignty	
By: Territory	169
United Kingdom	169
United States	170

MAN MADE CONSTRUCTIONS
Bridges

By: Description → Name, General

Disaster:-	
Scotland, 1879	Tay Bridge
US, 1940	Tacoma Narrows Bridge; Puget Sound
Floating; Military	Bailey Bridge
London; Opens and closes	Tower Bridge
Longest; Britain	Humber
New York; Staten Island, Brooklyn	Verrazano Narrows Bridge
Tunnel; Includes	Chesapeake Bay, US
Types; Main	Arch, Girder, Cantilever, Suspension

Bridges

By: Name → Location, General

Bridge of Sighs	Venice, Italy
Clifton Suspension Bridge	Bristol
Built by	I.K.Brunel
Over	River Avon
Golden Gate Bridge	San Francisco, US
Howrah Bridge	Calcutta
London Bridge	Present location: Lake Havasu City, Arizona, US
Ponte Vecchio	Florence, Italy
Over	River Arno
Rialto	Venice

Buildings and Constructions

By: Description → Name

Abbey commemorating Norman Conquest	Battle Abbey, Sussex
Artificial Hill; Europe; Biggest	Silbury Hill, Wiltshire
Building; Pillars don't touch roof	Windsor Town Hall
Capacity; Biggest	Vehicle Assembly building, Cape Canaveral, Florida
Casino; Oldest	Monte Carlo
Castle:-	
British; Stone built; 1st	Chepstow, Gwent
Leaning keep	Bridgnorth, Shropshire
Oldest inhabited; Britain	Berkeley, Gloucestershire
Cathedral:-	
Clock with no face	Salisbury Cathedral
Inverted arches	Wells Cathedral
Separate bell-tower; UK	Chichester Cathedral
Three spires	Lichfield Cathedral
Church:-	
Crooked spire	Chesterfield Cathedral
Highest spire	Ulm Cathedral, Germany
Highest spire; UK	Salisbury Cathedral
Largest	St Peter's, Rome
Cinema; Largest	Radio City Music Hall, New York
Coronations take place; UK	Westminster Abbey

Crown Jewels; Repository	Tower of London, Corfe Castle (under King John)
Door; Cannot be opened from outside	No 10, Downing Street
Font; Largest	Mormon Tabernacle, Salt Lake City
Footprints; Stars leave	Grauman's Chinese Theatre (Los Angeles) 1st: Norma Talmadge
French President; Summer residence	Fontainebleau
Gladiatorial Contests in	Colosseum, Rome
Great Fire of London; Marks start	The Monument
Hospital; Albert Schweitzer's	Lambarene, Gabon
Man-made structure; Largest	Great Wall of China (2486 miles)
Museum; British; First public	Ashmolean Museum, Oxford
Palace;-	
Given to Henry VIII by Wolsey	Whitehall Palace
Largest	Imperial Palace, Beijing
Prime Minister; Country house	Chequers
Pub; Name; Most popular	Red Lion
Pyramid; Largest	Cholula de Rivadabia, Mexico
Royal Coaches; Kept	Royal Mews, Buckingham Palace
Stadium;-	
Largest	Strahov Stadium, Prague
Largest; Historical	Circus Maximus, Rome (250,000 capacity)
Largest; Indoor	Superdrome, New Orleans
Stone Statues; Pacific Islands; Mysterious	Easter Island
Stupa; Largest	Borobudur, Java, Indonesia
Tallest;-	Sears Tower, Chicago
Britain	Canary Wharf Tower
Historical;	
2580 BC–AD 1307	Great Pyramid
AD 1307–AD 1548	Lincoln Cathedral spire
1930–1971	Empire State Building
Second	World Trade Center, New York
Structure	Warszawa Radio Mast, Poland
Structure; UK	IBA Mast, Lincolnshire
Temple; Moved to a higher location	Abu Simbel, Egypt
Tunnels;-	
Alps; 1st through	Mont Cenis
Longest; Rail	Seikan, Japan
Longest; Road	St Gotthard, Switzerland
Water Wheel; Largest	Lady Isabella, Isle of Man
Wonders of the World; Ancient:-	
Colossus of Rhodes	Greece
Hanging Gardens of Babylon	Iraq. Built By: Nebuchadnezzar for wife Semiramis
Mausoleum at Halicarnassus	Turkey. Built for King Mausolus (from which 'Mausoleum')
Pharos at Alexandria (Lighthouse)	Egypt
Pyramid of Cheops	Egypt
Temple of Artemis, Ephesus	Turkey. Burnt down by: Herostratus to immortalize himself. Rebuilt
Temple of Zeus, Olympia	Greece
Wonders of the World; Ancient; Remaining	Pyramid of Cheops

Buildings and Constructions

By: Name → Location, General

See Also: Art and Craft; Buildings (for Architects)

Abu Simbel, Temple at	Egypt. Moved to higher position when Aswan high dam built
Acropolis	Athens, Greece. Citadel on hill
Buildings	Propylaea, Erectheum, Parthenon
Alcazar	Seville, Spain. Palace
Alhambra	Granada, Spain. Palace
Angkor Wat	Kampuchea. Hindu Temple
Aswan Dam	Egypt. On the Nile
Athar Mosque	Cairo, Egypt
Balmoral Castle	Scotland. On River Dee
Big Ben	London. Bell in Clock Tower of Houses of Parliament
Name commonly applied to	Clock
Named after	Benjamin Hall, Commissioner of Works
Blue Mosque	Istanbul, Turkey
Brandenburg Gate	East Berlin
Bull Ring	Birmingham, Britain. Shopping Centre
Cabora Bassa Dam	Mozambique. On Zambezi River
Capitol	Washington DC, US. (US Senate and House of Representatives)
Catacombs	Rome
Cathedral of the Holy Family	Barcelona, Spain
Chamber of Horrors	Madame Tussaud's Waxworks, London
Christ of the Andes	Argentina/Chile border. Statue
Church of St Basil	Moscow
Circus Maximus	Rome
Cleopatra's Needle	Thames Embankment, London
Contains	Books, artifacts brought from Alexandria
Connection to Cleopatra	None
Colosseum	Rome
Alternative name	Flavian Amphitheatre
Conservative Party HQ	Smith Square, London
Crystal Palace	Hyde Park, then Sydenham
Built for	London Exhibition, 1851
Demolished	1941
Disneyland (Original)	Anaheim, California
Disney World	Near Orlando, Florida
Doge's Palace	Venice, Italy
Duomo	Florence, Italy
Eddystone Lighthouse	Near Plymouth, UK
Eiffel Tower	Paris
Built by	Gustave Eiffel, 1889, for Paris Exhibition
Escorial	Spain. Palace
Fontainebleau	France. Palace
Built for	Francis I
Forbidden City	Beijing. Site of Imperial Palace
Forum	Rome. Market and meeting place
Giotto's Tower	Florence, Italy
Golden Temple	Amritsar, India

Grand Coulee Dam	Washington, US
On	Columbia River
Great Tom	Christ Church, Oxford. Bell
G.U.M.	Moscow. Largest shop
Hadrian's Wall	England. Wallsend to Bowness on Solway. Built by: Romans to keep out Picts and Scots
Hagia Sophia	Istanbul. Church, then Mosque
Built by	Emperor Justinian
Hampton Court Palace	Near London
Built by	Cardinal Wolsey
Hoover Dam	Colorado
On	Colorado River
Name change	Boulder Dam (1933–47)
Houses of Parliament	London
Proper name	Palace of Westminster
Itaipu Dam	Brazil/Paraguay
On	Parana River
Kailasa Temple	Ellura, India. Carved out of rocks
Kariba Dam	Zambia/Zimbabwe
On	Zambezi River
Khaba	Mecca. Sacred black stone
Kremlin	Moscow (Means 'Citadel')
Labour Party HQ	Walworth Road, London
Liberty Bell	Philadelphia, US
Little Mermaid Statue	Copenhagen Harbour, Denmark (Memorial to Hans Andersen)
Longships Lighthouse	Off Lands End, Britain
Loop	Chicago. Central District
Marble Arch	Hyde Park, London
Original location	Buckingham Palace
Mezquita	Córdoba, Spain. Mosque
National Agricultural Centre	Stoneleigh, Warwickshire
National Exhibition Centre	Birmingham
Nazca Lines	Peru. Figures drawn in pebbles
Nelson's Column	Trafalgar Square, London
Neuschwanstein Castle	Germany. (Fairy tale Castle)
Built by	Ludwig II of Bavaria
Notre Dame Cathedral	Paris, France
Pagan Pagoda	Burma
Palace of Versailles	Outside Paris
Built for	Louis XIV
Contains	Hall of Mirrors
Pantheon	Rome. Temple
Parthenon	Athens. Temple of Athene
Peterhof Palace	Near St Petersburg
Poets' Corner	Westminster Abbey, London (Poets buried there)
Potala	Lhasa, Tibet. Palace
Pyramid of the Sun	Teotihuacan, Mexico
Pyramids of Giza	Egypt
Largest	Pyramid of Cheops (Khufu)
Others	Chephren, Mycerinus
Quetzalcoatl Pyramid	Mexico
Royal Mint	Llantrisant, Wales
Royal Observatory	Greenwich, UK
Shway Dagon Pagoda	Rangoon, Burma

Spanish Riding School	Hofburg Palace, Vienna
Sphinx	Giza, Egypt. Head of Pharaoh, Chephren on lion's body
Statue of Liberty	Liberty Island, New York
Inscription	'Give me your tired, your poor, your huddled masses, yearning to breathe free.'
St Mark, Cathedral of	Venice
Stonehenge	On Salisbury Plain, Wiltshire, UK
St Paul's Cathedral	London
St Peter's Church	Rome
Taj Mahal	Agra, India. Mausoleum
Built by	17th Century Emperor Shah Jehan
Built for	Wife, Mumtaz Mahal
Tarbela Dam	Pakistan
On	Indus River
Temple of Amon-Ra	Karnak, Egypt
Temple of Heaven	Beijing
Terracotta Army	Xian, China ('Guarding' tomb)
Tien An Men Square	Beijing
Tivoli Gardens	Copenhagen
Topkapi Palace	Istanbul
Trevi Fountain	Rome, Italy (Wish after throwing coins in)
Wailing Wall	Jerusalem
Westminster Abbey	London
Proper name	Collegiate Church of St Peter
Contains	Poets' Corner (Shakespeare, etc., buried)
Whispering Gallery	St Paul's Cathedral, London
Winter Palace	St Petersburg
Zimbabwe ruins	Series of walls (Gives country its name)

Canals

By: General

Albert Canal	Belgium
Built by	George Goethals
Busiest; Ship	Panama Canal
Links;-	
Atlantic, Mediterranean; Through France	Canal Du Midi
Baltic, North Sea	Kiel Canal
Beijing, Hangchow (Yellow River to Yangtze); China	Grand Canal
Gothenburg, Stockholm; Sweden	Gota Canal
Ionian, Aegean Seas; Greece	Corinth Canal
Lake Superior, Lake Huron; US/Canada	Soo Canals (Sault Ste. Marie)
London, Liverpool	Grand Union Canal
Mediterranean, Red Sea	Suez Canal
Montreal, Lake Ontario	St Lawrence Seaway
North Sea, Atlantic; North West Scotland	Caledonian Canal

Pacific, Atlantic	Panama Canal
Longest:-	White Sea – Baltic Canal
Ancient	Grand Canal, China
Ship	Suez Canal
UK	Grand Union Canal
Niagara Falls; Bypasses	Welland Canal
Panama Canal	
Alternative location, proposal	
narrowly defeated	Nicaragua
Locks	6
Western end	Pacific
Suez Canal	Built by: Ferdinand De Lesseps
Venice; Main Canal	Grand Canal

Houses, Famous

By: Name, Place → Occupant

E.g. Who lived in . . .
See Also: Art and Craft; Buildings (for Architects)

Alloway	Robert Burns
Apsley House (Called No.1, London)	Duke of Wellington
Badminton Hall	Duke of Beaufort
Batemans, Sussex	Rudyard Kipling
Blenheim Palace	Duke of Marlborough
Chawton	Jane Austen
Clarence House	The Queen Mother
Clivedon	The Astors
Dove Cottage, Grasmere	Wordsworth
Gatcombe Park	Princess Anne
Graceland	Elvis Presley
Haworth Parsonage	Bronte Family
Highgrove	Prince Charles
Hill Top, Cumbria	Beatrix Potter
Houghton Hall	Robert Walpole
Hughenden Manor	Disraeli
Kirriemuir	James Barrie
San Simeon	William Randolph Hearst
Strawberry Hill	Horace Walpole
Sutton Place	Paul Getty
Walmer Castle	Duke of Wellington

NATURAL FEATURES
Bays and Gulfs

By: Description, Location, → Name

E.g.: What Gulf lies between . . . and . . .

Africa (West); South	Gulf of Guinea
Australia:-	
Captain Cook landed at	Botany Bay
North	Gulf of Carpentaria
South	Great Australian Bight
Finland, Sweden	Gulf of Bothnia
France; South West	Gulf of Lions
Greenland, Canada	Baffin Bay

India, Burma	Bay of Bengal
Iran;-	
Arabian Peninsula	Gulf of Oman
Saudi Arabia	Persian Gulf
Italy; Southern end	Gulf of Taranto
Jamaica; Holiday centre	Montego Bay
Largest;-	
Bay	Hudson Bay
Gulf	Gulf of Mexico
Mexico, Baja California	Gulf of California
Newfoundland, Canadian	
mainland	Gulf of St Lawrence
Nova Scotia; West	Bay of Fundy
Saudi Arabia, Sinai Peninsula	Gulf of Aqaba
South Africa; Near Cape Town	Table Bay
South Yemen, Somalia	Gulf of Aden
Spain (North), South West France	Bay of Biscay
Vietnam, South China	Gulf of Tongking

Capes

By: Location → Name

Greenland; South tip	Cape Farewell
Portugal; South West	Cape Saint Vincent
South Africa; Near Cape Town	Cape of Good Hope
South America; South	Cape Horn
South Georgia	Cape Disappointment
Spain; North West	Cape Finisterre

Deserts

By: General

Death Valley	California
Driest	Atacama Desert, Chile
Great Sandy Desert	Australia
Kalahari	Botswana
Kara Kum	Turkmenistan
Largest	Sahara
2nd	Australian Desert
Mojave	California, US
Negev	Israel
Northernmost	Gobi
Nubian	Sudan
Painted Desert	Arizona, US
Sahara	North Africa
Only recorded snowfall	1979
Taklamakan	China
Thar	India/Pakistan

Geographical Terms

By: General

Angle between magnetic line and latitude line	Magnetic declination
Cave; Opening in roof	Sink hole

Coast; Flat sea bed lying off	Continental shelf
Col	Mountain pass
Continent, Original;-	Pangaea
Northern:	Laurasia
Southern:	Gondwanaland
Continental Drift;-	
Pioneer	Alfred Wegener
Theory explaining	Plate tectonics
Coral Island: Ring shaped	Atoll
Day;-	
Longest	Summer Solstice
Shortest	Winter Solstice
Day and Night; Equal	Spring and Autumn Equinoxes
Daylight Saving;-	
Country; 1st	Germany, 1915
Proponent; 1st	Benjamin Franklin
UK; 1st	1916
Dictionary of Places	Gazetteer
Earth;-	
Circumference; 1st calculation	Eratosthenes
Crust; Discontinuity at	Moho
Structure; Parts	Crust, Mantle, Core
Eclipse of the Sun; Caused by	Moon between Earth and the Sun
Flat topped mountain	Mesa
Force on object due to Earth's rotation	Coriolis Effect
Forest; Cold, Siberia	Taiga
Geological Eras	Pre-Cambrian (1st), Palaeozoic, Mesozoic, Cenozoic (Latest)
Glacier;-	
Crack in	Crevasse
Debris from	Moraine
Hill created by	Drumlin
Grassland; South Africa	Veldt
Hole; Project to bore through Earth's crust, abandoned	Project Mohole
Ice; Thin floating sheet	Floe
Igneous Rocks; Molten material making	Magma
International Date Line; Change when crossing	Moving East gains a day
International Geophysical Year	1957–1958
Islands; Group of	Archipelago
Light; Proportion reflected from a surface	Albedo
Map;-	
Fixed bearing on	Rhumb line or Loxodrome
Part containing scale, legend, etc.,	Cartouche
Map Symbols;-	
Dashed line	Bridleway
Dotted line	Footpath
Flag	Golf Course
Red triangle	Youth Hostel
Tent	Camp Site
Mountain;-	
Precipitous bare place	Scar
Side away from wind	Lee side
Side; Loose rocks on	Scree
Narrow strip connecting 2 land areas	Isthmus

Opposite points on the Earth's surface	Antipodes
Plain;-	
Central South America	Chaco
Frozen, northern	Tundra
North Asia	Steppes
Reclaimed from sea; Land in Holland	Polders
River;-	
Bank; Relating to	Riparian
Sediments	Alluvium
Tidal mouth	Estuary
Riverbed or Valley, North Africa	Wadi
Rock Basin with steep walls	Cirque
Rock;-	
Downward fold	Syncline
Types; Main	Igneous, Metamorphic, Sedimentary
Upward fold	Anticline
Sea Inlet caused by glaciation	Fjord
Shallow water; Land under; bordering continents	Continental shelf
Snow; Overhanging edge on mountain ridge	Cornice
Stalactites	From roof
Stalagmites	Up from ground
Stalagmites and Stalactites; Made of	Calcium Carbonate (Calcite)
Subsoil; Permanently frozen	Permafrost
Sun; Crosses equator	Equinox (Vernal: Going North. Autumnal: Going South)
Swampy area; Southern US	Bayou
Tarn	Lake (northern England)
Theory of geological change through violent upheavals	Catastrophism
Tor	Hill
Triangular shaped land at mouth of river	Delta
Tropics	Cancer: North. Capricorn: South
Volcanic gases; Vent for	Fumarole
Waterhole; Australia	Billabong

Islands

By: Description, Location → Name

Alaska; Across Bering Sea	Aleutian Islands
Bought for trinkets worth $24 from Indians	Manhattan Island
Clyde, Firth of; Large	Arran
Corsica, Italy; Between	Elba
Granite; Made out of	Seychelles
Greece; Largest	Crete
Japan, Taiwan; Chain between	Ryukyu Islands
Largest;-	Australia (normally discounted, considered a Continent), Greenland
2nd	New Guinea
3rd	Borneo
4th	Madagascar
5th	Baffin Island

Mediterranean; Largest	Sicily
New York;-	
Bay	Staten Island
Harbour, Immigration station	Ellis Island
Paris; Islands in Seine	Ile de la Cité, Ile St Louis
Penal Colony (Former); French Guiana	Devil's Island
Pirate Treasure supposedly on; Nova	
Scotia	Oak Island
Prison (Former); San Francisco Bay	Alcatraz
Remotest	Bouvet Island
Remotest: Inhabited	Tristan da Cunha
Sicily; North of	Lipari Islands
Sweden; East of (Baltic)	Gotland, Oland
Wales; North West	Anglesey

Islands

By: Name → Location, General

Aleutian Islands	Alaska
Main	Andreanof, Fox, Near, Rat
Alexander Archipelago	Alaska
Balearic Islands	Mediterranean
Main	Majorca, Minorca, Ibiza
Bimini	Bahamas
Bismarck Archipelago	Near New Guinea
Main	New Britain, New Ireland, Admiralty Islands
Canary Islands	Atlantic
Main	Gran Canaria, Lanzarote, Fuerteventura, Tenerife
Chagos Archipelago	Indian Ocean
Most important	Diego Garcia
Channel Islands	English Channel
Main	Jersey, Guernsey, Alderney, Sark
Cyclades	Greece
Centre	Delos
Desolation Island	South America (southern tip)
Djerba	Tunisia
Dodecanese	Greece
Main	Rhodes
Dry Tortugas	Florida (7 Islands)
Easter Island	Pacific
Discovered by	Dutch Admiral Jacob Roggeven, on Easter Day, 1722
Falkland Islands	South Atlantic
Other name	Malvinas
Florida Keys	Off Florida
Includes	Key Largo, Key West
Greater Antilles	Main: Cuba, Dominican Republic, Haiti, Jamaica, Puerto Rico
Hainan Island	China. Second largest island off
Hawaii	Main Island: Oahu (Honolulu on)
Hebrides	Off Scotland (North West)
Main, Outer	Lewis, Harris, North and South Uist
Main, Inner	Skye, Mull, Jura, Islay
Heligoland	Germany
Former possession of	Denmark, Britain

Holy Island	(England) Berwick on Tweed, other name: Lindisfarne (Scotland) in Firth of Clyde (Wales) off Anglesey
Ionian Islands	Main: Corfu, Paxos, Ithaca, Zante
Isle of Man	Owned by: (in historical order) Norway, Earls of Derby, Crown
Jersey	Official language: French
Juan Fernandez Islands	South Pacific
Main	Mas a Tierra, Mas a Fuera, Santa Clara
Kodiak Island	Alaska
Laccadive Islands	Off India (South West)
Leeward Islands	West Indies
Main	Antigua (Largest), Guadeloupe, Montserrat, St Kitts-Nevis, Virgin Islands
Lipari Islands	Off Sicily
Main	Lipari, Stromboli, Vulcano, Salina
Mariana Islands	Western Pacific
Largest	Guam
Marquesas Islands	Pacific
Main	Fatuhiva, Hivaoa, Nukuhiva
Marshall Islands	Pacific
Main chains	Ralik, Ratak
Mascarene Islands	Indian Ocean
Main	Mauritius, Réunion, Rodriguez
Moluccas	Indonesia
Mustique	Grenadines
Owner	Colin Tennant
Netherlands Antilles	Main Islands: Curaçao (Largest), Bonaire, St Eustativa
New Guinea	Parts: Irian Barat (Indonesia), Papua-New Guinea
Nicobar Islands	Bay of Bengal
Orkney Islands	Off Scotland (North East)
Main	Pomona (mainland)
Pribilof Islands	Bering Sea
Main	St Paul, St George
Prince Edward Island	Canada
Queen Elizabeth Islands	Arctic
Rat Islands	Alaska
Ryukyu Islands	Japan
Main	Okinawa
Saint Pierre and Miquelon	Newfoundland (South). French Department
Scilly Isles	Off Cornwall, UK
Main	St Mary's, St Martin's, St Agnes, Tresco, Bryher
Sheppey	Thames Estuary, UK
Shetland Islands	Off Scotland (North East)
Main	Mainland, Uist, Yell
Solomon Islands	Pacific Ocean
Main	Bougainville (Largest), Guadalcanal
Spitsbergen	Arctic
Sulawesi	Indonesia
Sulu Archipelago	Philippines
Sunda Islands	Indonesia

Thousand Islands	US, Canada (in St Lawrence River)
Tierra del Fuego	South America, southern tip
Sovereignty	Chile/Argentina
Windward Islands	West Indies
Main	Martinique, Grenada, Dominica, St Lucia, St Vincent

Lakes

By: Description → Name

Deepest;-	Lake Baykal, Russia
Britain	Loch Morar, Scotland
England	Wastwater
US	Crater Lake
Great Lake(s);-	Erie, Huron, Michigan, Ontario, Superior
In US only	Lake Michigan
Highest (Navigable)	Lake Titicaca, Bolivia/Peru
Largest;-	Caspian Sea
Africa	Lake Victoria
England	Windermere
Europe	Lake Ladoga, Russia
Freshwater	Lake Superior, US
Freshwater; 2nd	Lake Victoria, Tanzania/Uganda/Kenya
Great Britain	Loch Lomond
UK	Lough Neagh, Northern Ireland
Monster; Famous for	Loch Ness
Villages; Built on floating reed beds	Lake Titicaca

Lakes

By: Name → Location, General

Bitter Lakes	Egypt
Constance	West Germany/Switzerland. Other name: Bodensee
Crater Lake	Oregon, US
Dead Sea	Israel/Jordan. Saltiness: 9 × that of Ocean
Disappointment	Australia
Great Bear Lakes	Canada
Great Salt Lake	Utah, US
Great Slave Lake	Canada
Ladoga	Russia
Maracaibo	Venezuela
Onega	Russia
Sea of Galilee	Israel. Other Names: Lake Kinneret, Lake Tiberias
Surprise	Australia
Xochimilco	Mexico

Mountain Ranges

By: Description, Location → Name

Adriatic coast (Yugoslavia, Albania)	Dinaric Alps
Australia; East	Great Dividing Range

Czechoslovakia, East Germany	Ore Mountains
Czechoslovakia, Poland	Sudeten Mountains
England;-	
Avon and Somerset	Mendips
Backbone of, called	Pennine Chain
Gloucestershire	Cotswolds
Hereford and Worcestershire	Malverns
Scotland boundary	Cheviots
France, Italy	Alps
France, Spain	Pyrenees
Germany; East, West	Harz Mountains
Iran; On Caspian Sea	Elbruz Mountains
Italy; Backbone of	Apennines
Longest;-	Andes
Underwater included	Mid-Atlantic Ridge (10,000 miles)
Same Name; US, Spain	Sierra Nevada
South America; North to South	Andes
Spain;-	
North West	Cantabrian Mountains
South coast	Sierra Nevada
US;-	
East	Appalachians
North to South West	Rocky Mountains
Wales; North and Central	Cambrian Mountains

Mountain Ranges

By: Name → Location

Aleutians	Alaska
Altai	Mongolia
Black	South Wales
Brecon Beacons	South Wales
Cascade	US, Canada
Drakensberg	South Africa
Ghats, Western and Eastern	India
Pamirs	Tajikistan
Quantocks	Somerset, England
Sierra Madre	Mexico
Taurus	Turkey
Zagros	Iran

Mountains

By: Description, Location → Name

Greece: Sacred to Apollo	Parnassus
Highest;-	Everest, Nepal/China
Africa	Kilimanjaro, Tanzania
Australia	Kosciusko
Base to summit	Mauna Kea, Hawaii (Base underwater)
Britain	Ben Nevis, Scotland
Britain; 2nd	Ben Macdhui, Scotland
Canada	Logan
England	Scafell Pike
Europe	Elbruz, Georgia
Europe, Western	Mont Blanc

Germany	Zugspitze
Greece	Olympus
North America	McKinley
Peak; 2nd	Everest (2 highest peaks)
2nd	K2
South America	Aconcagua
Switzerland	Monte Rosa
3rd	Kanchenjunga, Sikkim/Nepal
Unclimbed	Zemu Gap Peak, Sikkim/Nepal
Wales	Snowdon
Western Hemisphere	Aconcagua
'Meanest mountain on Earth'; Called	Eiger. Most difficult climb: North face
Monolith; Largest	Ayers Rock, Australia
Noah's Ark; Finishes on (Bible)	Ararat, Turkey
Rio de Janeiro, Overlooks	Sugar Loaf Mountain
Tower built to increase height	Zugspitze, Germany

Mountains

By: Name → Location, General

Adam's Peak	Sri Lanka
Annapurna	Nepal
1st climbed	Maurice Herzog
Ararat	Turkey
Atlas	Algeria
Egmont	New Zealand
Everest	Nepal/Tibet
1st climbed	Edmund Hillary (New Zealand), Sherpa Tenzing Norgay (Nepal – Sherpa) (May 29th, 1953). Expedition Leader: John Hunt
1st climbed; British	Dougal Haston, Doug Scott (1976)
1st climbed; Solo	Reinhold Messner
1st climbed; Woman	Junko Tabei (Japanese) (1976)
Height	29,028 feet
Name from	Surveyor General of India
Range	Himalayas
Surveying Team calls	Peak XV
Hermon	Syria
K2	Pakistan
Also known as	Godwin Austen
Range	Karakoram
Matterhorn	Switzerland
Also known as	Mont Cervin
1st climbed	Edward Whymper
Mont Blanc	France/Italy
1st climbed	Balmat Paccard (1776)
Table Mountain	South Africa (Near Cape Town)

Natural Disasters

By: General

Crater Lake; Formed by	Eruption of Mazama

141

Earthquakes; Important:-
San Francisco	1906, 1989
Lisbon	1755
Mexico City	1985
Tangshan, China	1976

Earthquakes; Scales	Magnitude: Richter, Kanamori. Intensity: Mercalli
Landslide; Aberfan; 1966	Caused by: Slag Heap. School: Pantglas Junior School
Pompeii; Destroyed by	Eruption of Vesuvius (AD 79)
Tidal Wave; Correct name	Tsunami

Volcanoes; Eruption, Important;-
Biggest	Tambora, Indonesia (1815)
Biggest; Explosion	Santorini, Aegean Sea 470 BC (estimated). Destroyed Thera
Krakatoa	Between Java and Sumatra (1883)
Mont Pelee	Destroyed St Pierre, Martinique (1902)
Mount St Helens	Washington State, US (1980)

Other Natural Sites and Places

By: Description → Name

Archipelago; Largest	Malay Archipelago
Continent(s);-	Africa, Antarctica, Asia, Australia, Europe, North America, South America
Flattest	Australia
No native population	Antarctica (thus 1st to be 'discovered')
Wider in the South	Antarctica
Driest Place	In Atacama Desert, Chile
Earth's Surface; Sea; Proportion	70%
Fault; Divides California	San Andreas Fault
Forest; Nearest to London	Epping Forest
Glacier; Largest; Europe	Aletsch Glacier
Icebergs; Proportion above water	1/9th
Lowest Point-;	Marianas Trench, Pacific
Land	Dead Sea, Jordan (coast)
Land; Europe	Caspian Sea (coast)
Land; Western Hemisphere	Death Valley, California
Living things; Made by; Largest structure	Great Barrier Reef
Pole, Coldest	South

Valleys and Canyons;-
Colorado River	Grand Canyon
East Africa; Crosses	Great Rift Valley
Kenya; Fossil Site	Olduvai Gorge
Park; US National; Largest, Oldest	Yellowstone Park
Utah/Arizona; John Ford films set in	Monument Valley
Wettest place (over 1 year)	Cherrapunji, India

Other Natural Sites and Places

By: Name → Location, General

Ajanta Caves	India
Altamira Caves	Spain

Known for	Prehistoric Paintings
Blue Grotto,The	Capri, Italy
Bodmin Moor	Cornwall, UK
Highest point	Brown Willy
Bois De Boulogne	Paris (Park)
Bondi Beach	Sydney, Australia
Carlsbad Caverns	New Mexico, US
Central Park	New York
Coromandel Coast	India
Craters of the Moon,The	Idaho
Dartmoor	Devon, UK
Highest point	High Willays
Deccan,The	India (Plateau)
Diamond Head	Oahu Island, Hawaii
Dismal Swamp	US
Dogger Bank	North Sea
Ergs	Algeria
Exmoor	Somerset and Devon, UK
Highest point	Dunkery Beacon
Fingal's Cave	Isle of Staffa, Scotland
Garden of the Gods,The	Colorado, US
Giant's Causeway,The	Northern Ireland
Golden Horn,The	Turkey (Inlet forming Istanbul Harbour)
Goodwin Sands	Straits of Dover, Britain
Gower,The	South Wales (Peninsula). Near Swansea
Gran Chaco	South America (Plain)
Grand Canyon	Arizona/Colorado, US
Formed by	Colorado River
Great Barrier Reef	Australia, off East Coast of Queensland
Great Geyser	Iceland
Hyde Park	London
Horse track	Rotten Row
Lake	Serpentine
Khyber Pass	Pakistan/Afghanistan (Connects)
Lascaux Caves	France
Known for	Prehistoric paintings
Lido	Italy, Near Venice (Island beach)
Mammoth Cave	Kentucky, US
Mull of Kintyre	West Scotland (Headland). Close to Northern Ireland
Needles	Solent, UK (Chalk stacks)
Ninety Mile Beach	Victoria, Australia
Nullarbor Plain	Australia
Okefenokee Swamp	Florida/Georgia
Okovango Swamp	Botswana
Old Faithful	Yellowstone Park, Colorada (Geyser)
Old Man of Hoy	Orkney, Scotland (Rock)
Petrified Forest,The	Arizona, US
Pillars of Hercules,The	Entrance to Mediterranean (Gibraltar, Mt.Aisha)
Pitch Lake	Trinidad (Asphalt)
Plain of Jars	Laos (Prehistoric jars found)
Serengeti National Park	Tanzania
Sudd	Sudan (Swamp area)
Treptower Park	East Berlin
Waikiki Beach	Honolulu, Hawaii
Wookey Hole	Near Wells, Somerset, UK

Yellowstone Park	US (Mostly Wyoming)
Yorkshire Moors	UK
Highest point	Urra Moor
Yosemite National Park	Sierra Nevada Mountains, California, US

Rivers

By: Description, Location → Name

Afghanistan, Northern border	Amu Darya
Devon, Cornwall	Tamar
England, Scotland border	Tweed
Europe; Six countries, Flows through	Danube
France, Germany border	Rhine
Germany; Divides Former East and West	Elbe
Julius Caesar; Crossed from Gaul to Italy to declare war on Republic	Rubicon
Korea (North), China border	Yalu
Longest;-	Nile
2nd	Amazon
3rd	Mississippi–Missouri
Asia (Non-USSR)	Mekong
Australia	Murray–Darling
Britain	Severn
China	Yangtze
England, Solely in	Thames
Europe	Volga. 2nd: Danube
France	Loire
Italy	Po
North America	Mississippi–Missouri
Poland	Vistula
Scotland	Tay
South America	Amazon
Spain	Guadalquivir
Mexico, US Border	Rio Grande
Sacred; India	Ganges
George Washington; Crossed to fight at Trenton	Delaware
Water; Most	Amazon

Rivers

By: Name → Location

Amazon	Brazil
Brahmaputra	Bangladesh (Mainly)
Don	Russia
Ebro	Spain
Fraser	Canada
Humber	UK
Estuary of	Trent, Ouse
Indus	Pakistan
Irrawaddy	Burma

Kwai	Thailand
Lena	Russia
Mackenzie	Canada
Nile	Africa
White and Blue meet at	Khartoum
First Cataract	Aswan
Ob-Irtysh	Russia
Orange	South Africa
Orinoco	Venezuela
Parana	Brazil
Peace	Canada
Plate	Argentina/Uruguay
Local name	Rio del la Plata
Merging of	Panama, Uruguay rivers
Red	US
San Francisco	Brazil
St Lawrence	Canada
Tagus	Portugal/Spain
Thames	England
Bridges over	27
Rises	In Cotswolds
Tiber	Italy
Tocantins	Brazil
Weser	Germany
Yellow	China
Other name	Hwang Ho
Yenisei	Russia
Yukon	US/Canada

Seas and Oceans

By: Description, Location → Name

Arctic; Chief Port: Murmansk	Barents Sea
Australia (North East), New Guinea	Coral Sea
Barents Sea, Part of; Chief Port: Archangel	White Sea
Biggest;-	Pacific Ocean (Greater than total land area of the Earth)
Non Ocean	Mediterranean
Corsica, France	Ligurian Sea
Crimea; Connected to Black Sea	Sea of Azev
Current; Fishing off South America dependent on	Humboldt Current
Deepest	Pacific (Marianas Trench)
Greece, Italy	Ionian Sea
Greece, Turkey	Aegean Sea
Hottest	Persian Gulf
Korea, China	Yellow Sea
New Zealand, Australia	Tasman Sea
Polluted; Most	Mediterranean
Salty;-	
Least	Baltic Sea
Most	Red Sea
Sardinia, Italy	Tyrrhenian Sea

Shoreline; None	Sargasso Sea
Tidal Bore; Britain; Biggest	Severn
Tides:-	
Daily cycle	Ebb, Flood
Highest	Bay of Fundy, Newfoundland
Twice monthly cycle	Neap, Spring
Turkey; European, Asian	Sea of Marmara
Yugoslavia, Italy	Adriatic Sea

Seas and Oceans

By: Name → Location, General

Banda Sea	Indonesia
Barents Sea	Arctic
Beaufort Sea	Arctic (off Canada/Alaska)
Bismarck Sea	New Guinea
Flores Sea	Indonesia
Kara Sea	Arctic (off Russia)
Laptev Sea	Arctic (off Russia)
Ross Sea	Antarctic
The Wash	North Sea (Lincolnshire, Norfolk)
Weddell Sea	South Atlantic, Near Antarctic

Straits

By: Location → Name

E.g.: What Strait separates . . . and . . .

Australia, Tasmania	Bass Strait
Baffin Island	
Canada (Hudson Bay, Atlantic)	Hudson Strait
Greenland	Davis Strait
Baltic Sea, Kattegat	Oresund
Corfu, Italy (Ionian, Adriatic Seas)	Straits of Otranto
Corsica, Sardinia	Straits of Bonifacio
Cuba	
Mexico	Yucatan Channel
US	Straits cf Florida
England, France	Straits of Dover
Japan; Hokkaido, Honshu Islands	Tsugaru Strait
Ireland, South Wales	St George's Channel
Isle of Wight, mainland Britain	The Solent
Java, Sumatra	Sunda Strait
Madagascar, mainland Africa	Mozambique Channel
Malaysia, Sumatra	Straits of Malacca
New York; Manhattan Island, Long Island	East River
New Zealand; North, South Island	Cook Straits
Norway, Denmark	Skaggerak
Nova Scotia, Newfoundland	Cabot Strait
Orkney	
Pomona (mainland), Hoy	Scapa Flow
Scotland	Pentland Firth
Outer Hebrides, Scotland	The Minch
Persian Gulf; Entrance to	Straits of Hormuz
Prince Edward Island, Canadian mainland	Northumberland Strait

Russia, Alaska	Bering Straits
Sicily, Italy (Ionian, Tyrrhenian Sea)	Straits of Messina
Spain, Morocco	Straits of Gibraltar
Sri Lanka, India	Palk Strait
Sumatra, Malaya	Malacca Strait
Sweden, Denmark	Kattegat
Taiwan	
China	Formosa Strait
Philippines	Luzon Strait
Tasmania, Australia	Bass Strait
Tierra Del Fuego, Chile (South America, tip of)	Straits of Magellan
Turkey; European – Asian	
Black Sea, Sea of Marmara	Bosphorus
Sea of Marmara, Aegean	Dardanelles

Volcanoes

By: Description → Name

Highest:-	
Active; Europe	Mount Etna, Sicily
Extinct	Aconcagua, Argentina
Name from	Vulcano Island (named after Vulcanus – Greek fire god)
New; 1963	Surtsey, Near Iceland

Volcanoes

By: Name → Location

Cotopaxi	Ecuador
Erebus	Antarctica
Hekla	Iceland
Kilauea	Hawaii
Mauna Loa	Hawaii
Paricutin	Mexico
Popocatapetl	Mexico
Ruapehu	New Zealand
St Helens	US (Washington State)
Stromboli	Lipari Islands, off Sicily

Waterfalls

By: General

Angel Falls	Venezuela
Named from	Jimmy Angel (Discoverer)
Biggest Flow	Boyoma, Zaire
Guaira Falls	Brazil/Paraguay
Highest	Angel Falls, Venezuela
Iguazu Falls	Brazil
Minnehaha Falls	Minnesota, US
Niagara Falls	US/Canada
Between	Lake Erie, Lake Ontario
Cataracts	Horseshoe (Canadian), American (US)
Tightrope Crossing; 1st	Blondin
Ribbon Falls	Nevada, US
Sherlock Holmes; Disappeared over	Riechenbach Falls, Switzerland

Widest	Khône, Laos
Yosemite Falls	US

Weather

By: General

Atmosphere;-	
Lowest region	Troposphere
Radio waves; Reflecting area	Ionosphere
Ultra-violet radiation absorbed	Stratosphere
Atmospheric Pressure; Unit	Millibar
Balloon Ascents; Used to study stratosphere; Scientist	Auguste Piccard
Britain; Why warm	Gulf Stream
Calm Seas and Winds; Equatorial regions	Doldrums
Clouds;-	
Highest	Cirrus
Sign of bad weather	Nimbus
High Pressure area	Anticyclone
Meeting of different air bodies	Front
Monsoon; Direction	From South West (Summer); North East (Winter)
Northern Lights; Proper name	Aurora Borealis
Roaring 40s	Rough area in North (and sometimes South) Atlantic from 40–50 degrees latitude
Southern Lights; Proper name	Aurora Australis
Storm; Tropical; China Sea	Typhoon
Temperature;-	
Biggest Variation	Russia (Siberia)
Highest recorded	Libya
Lowest recorded	Antarctic
Tides; Caused by	Moon
Tornadoes; Direction	Anticlockwise in Northern Hemisphere
Weather Areas;-	
Northernmost	South East Iceland
Northernmost, off mainland	Fair Isle
Off Cornwall	Lundy
Southernmost	Finisterre
Weather Map;-	
Line linking same pressure	Isobar
Line linking same temperature	Isotherm
Whirlpool;-	
Between Italy and Sicily	Charybdis
Off Norway	Maelstrom
Wind;-	
Scale	Beaufort
Scale; Highest value	12 (Hurricane), 17 (US Modified Scale)
Windiest Place	Antarctic
Winds;-	
Adriatic; From Central Europe	Bora
African Coast, North; From Sahara	Harmattan (Other name: The Doctor)
Alps; North	Föhn
Egypt; From Sahara	Khamsin
France; South	Mistral
Iran	Samoon

Italy and Mediterranean; From
    Sahara   Sirocco
Rocky Mountains   Chinook
South Asia   Monsoon

PLACES
Capitals

By: Country → Capital

Country	Capital
Afghanistan	Kabul
Albania	Tirana
Algeria	Algiers
Angola	Luanda
Antigua	St John's
Argentina	Buenos Aires
Armenia	Yerevan
Australia	Canberra
Austria	Vienna
Azerbaijan	Baku
Bahamas	Nassau
Bahrain	Manama
Bangladesh	Dacca
Barbados	Bridgetown
Belgium	Brussels
Belize	Belmopan
Benin	Porto Novo
Bermuda	Hamilton
Bhutan	Thimphu
Bolivia	La Paz (Seat of government), Sucre (Legal)
Botswana	Gaborone
Brazil	Brasilia
Bulgaria	Sofia
Burkina Faso	Ouagadougou
Burma	Rangoon
Burundi	Bujumbura
Byelorussia	Minsk
Cameroon	Yaoundé
Canada	Ottawa
Cayman Islands	Georgetown
Central African Republic	Bangui
Chad	Ndjamena
Chile	Santiago
China	Beijing
Colombia	Bogota
Congo, People's Republic of	Brazzaville
Costa Rica	San José
Cuba	Havana
Cyprus	Nicosia
Czechoslovakia	Prague
Denmark	Copenhagen
Dominican Republic	Santo Domingo
Egypt	Cairo
El Salvador	San Salvador

Equador	Quito
Equatorial Guinea	Malabo
Estonia	Tallinn
Ethiopia	Addis Ababa
Falkland Islands	Port Stanley
Fiji	Suva
Finland	Helsinki
France	Paris
French Guiana	Cayenne
Gabon	Libreville
Gambia	Bathurst
Georgia	Tbilisi
Germany	Bonn (Berlin over phased period)
Ghana	Accra
Greece	Athens
Greenland	Godthaab
Grenada	St George's
Guatemala	Guatemala
Guernsey	St Peter Port
Guinea	Conakry
Guyana	Georgetown
Haiti	Port-au-Prince
Honduras	Tegucigalpa
Hong Kong	Victoria
Hungary	Budapest
Iceland	Reykjavik
India	New Delhi
Indonesia	Jakarta
Iran	Tehran
Iraq	Baghdad
Ireland	Dublin
Isle of Man	Douglas
Israel	Jerusalem
Italy	Rome
Ivory Coast	Abidjan
Jamaica	Kingston
Japan	Tokyo
Jersey	St Helier
Jordan	Amman
Kampuchea	Phnom Penh
Kazakhstan	Alma Ata
Kenya	Nairobi
Kirgizia	Frunze
Korea, North	Pyongyang
Korea, South	Seoul
Kuwait	Kuwait
Laos	Vientiane
Latvia	Riga
Lebanon	Beirut
Lesotho	Maseru
Liberia	Monrovia
Libya	Tripoli
Liechtenstein	Vaduz
Lithuania	Vilnius
Luxembourg	Luxembourg
Macao	Macao
Madagascar	Tananarive

Malawi	Lilongwe
Malaysia	Kuala Lumpur
Maldives	Malé
Mali	Bamako
Malta	Valletta
Martinique	Fort-de-France
Mauritania	Nouakchott
Mauritius	Port Louis
Mexico	Mexico City
Moldavia	Kishinev
Monaco	Monaco Ville
Mongolia	Ulan Bator
Morocco	Rabat
Mozambique	Maputo
Namibia	Windhoek
Nepal	Katmandu
Netherlands	Amsterdam
New Zealand	Wellington
Nicaragua	Managua
Niger	Niamey
Nigeria	Lagos
Northern Ireland	Belfast
Norway	Oslo
Oman	Muscat
Pakistan	Islamabad
Panama	Panama
Papua New Guinea	Port Moresby
Paraguay	Asunción
Peru	Lima
Philippines	Manila
Poland	Warsaw
Portugal	Lisbon
Qatar	Doha
Réunion	Saint-Denis
Romania	Bucharest
Russia	Moscow
Rwanda	Kigali
Saudi Arabia	Riyadh
Scotland	Edinburgh
Senegal	Dakar
Seychelles	Victoria
Sierra Leone	Freetown
Sikkim	Gangtok
Singapore	Singapore
Somalia	Mogadishu
South Africa	Pretoria (Administrative), Cape Town (Legislative)
Spain	Madrid
Sri Lanka	Colombo
Sudan	Khartoum
Surinam	Paramaribo
Swaziland	Mbabane
Sweden	Stockholm
Switzerland	Berne
Syria	Damascus
Taiwan	Taipei
Tajikistan	Dushanbe

Tanzania	Dodoma
Thailand	Bangkok
Togo	Lome
Tonga	Nuku'alofa
Trinidad and Tobago	Port of Spain
Tunisa	Tunis
Turkey	Ankara
Turkmenistan	Ashkhabad
Uganda	Kampala
Ukraine	Kiev
United Arab Emirates	Abu Dhabi
United Kingdom	London
United States	Washington D.C.
Uruguay	Montevideo
Uzbekhistan	Tashkent
Venezuela	Caracas
Vietnam	Hanoi
Yemen Arab Republic	Sana'a
Yemen, South	Aden
Zaire	Kinsasha
Zambia	Lusaka
Zimbabwe	Harare

Capitals, Former

By: Country → Capital

Australia	Melbourne
Belize	Belize
Brazil	Rio de Janeiro
Burma	Mandalay
China	Nanking
England	Winchester (Middle Ages)
India	Calcutta
Japan	Kyoto
Malawi	Zomba
Pakistan	Karachi
South Vietnam	Saigon
Tanzania	Dar Es Salaam
Turkey	Istanbul
Uganda	Entebbe (till 1962)
US	Philadelphia

Cities

By: Description → Name

Aeroplane; Designed in shape of	Brasilia
Alexander the Great; Founded by	Alexandria
Arctic Circle; Largest City	Murmansk, Russia
Australia; Centre of	Alice Springs
Canals; Most Mileage	Birmingham, UK
Capital:-	
Coldest	Ulan Bator, Mongolia
Highest	La Paz, Bolivia (Lhasa was once)
Hottest	Khartoum, Sudan
Northernmost	Reykjavik, Iceland

Cars; None	Venice
China; Largest City	Shanghai
Diamond; Production centre	Kimberley, South Africa
Dying; See before	Naples
Eloping Couples; Former centre	Gretna Green, Scotland (Village)
French Speaking; 2nd Largest City	Montreal
Highest City	Lhasa, Tibet
India; Largest City	Bombay
Marble; Supplier of	Carrara, Italy
Nickname; 'Pearl of the Desert'	Damascus
Pakistan; Largest City	Karachi
Population; Highest;-	Mexico City (Tokyo – Yokohama is a larger agglomeration)
Britain	London. 2nd: Birmingham
Over 1 million; Western; 1st	London
Southern Hemisphere	São Paulo
'Rose red city, half as old as time'	Petra, Jordan (Quote: Dean Burgon)
Salt; City built of	Wieliczka, Poland
Sinking	Venice, Mexico City (Fastest)
Statue of Christ overlooks	Rio de Janeiro
Union Jack; Built in the shape of	Khartoum

Cities

By: Name → General

Aachen; Alternative name	Aix La Chapelle
Athens; Port of	Piraeus
Bangkok; Proper name	Krung Thep
Brasilia; Public Buildings designed by	Oscar Niemeyer
Chichen Itza	Mexico (Mayan city)
Copenhagen; Island	Sjaelland
Edinburgh; Port of	Leith
Machu Picchu	Peru (Inca city in the Andes)
Mecca	Saudi Arabia
Mexico City; Built on ruins of	Tenochtitlan
New York	
Largest borough	Queens
Street Names East and West, divided By	5th Avenue
Paris; Separate Commune	Montmartre
Sydney; Founded as	Penal Colony
Tel Aviv; Joined with	Jaffa
Tikal	Guatemala (Mayan city)
Timbuktu	Mali
Washington; State in	None; In District of Columbia (Federal District)

Cities on Lakes

By: City → Lake

Astrakhan	Caspian Sea
Baku	Caspian Sea
Buffalo	Erie
Chicago	Michigan
Detroit	St Clair
Geneva	Geneva

Kampala	Victoria
Lausanne	Geneva
Milwaukee	Michigan
Toronto	Ontario
Zurich	Zurich

Cities on Rivers

By: City → River

Amsterdam	Amstel
Antwerp	Scheldt
Babylon	Euphrates
Baghdad	Tigris
Bangkok	Chao Phraya
Bangui	Ubangi (Anagram of name)
Basel	Rhine
Belfast	Lagan
Belgrade	Danube, Sava
Benares	Ganges
Bonn	Rhine
Bordeaux	Garonne
Bristol	Avon
Brussels	Senne
Bucharest	Dimbovita
Budapest	Danube
Buenos Aires	Rio de la Plata
Cairo	Nile
Calcutta	Hooghly
Cambridge	Cam (Known locally as Granta)
Cardiff	Gaff, Rhymney, Ely
Cologne	Rhine
Cork	Lee
Dublin	Liffey
Dundee	Tay
Florence	Arno
Frankfurt (West Germany)	Main
Glasgow	Clyde
Guangzhou (Canton)	Zhujiang
Hamburg	Elbe
Hyderabad	Indus
Ipswich	Orwell
Kiev	Dnieper
Lahore	Ravi
Lima	Rimac
Lisbon	Tagus
London	Thames
Londonderry (Derry)	Foyle
Lyons	Rhone
Madrid	Manzanares
Mandalay	Irrawaddy
Moscow	Moskva
New Orleans	Mississippi
New York	Hudson
Northampton	Nene
Oporto	Douro
Oxford	Isis, Cherwell (Local name for Thames)

Paris	Seine
Phnom Penh	Mekong
Pisa	Arno
Prague	Vltava
Reading	Thames, Kennet
Rome	Tiber
São Paulo	Tiete
Shanghai	Yangtze
St Petersburg (Russia)	Neva
Turin	Po
Vienna	Danube
Warsaw	Vistula
Washington	Potomac

Countries

By: Description → Country

Alcohol Consumption; Highest	Japan
Aliens; Highest proportion	Kuwait
Apes; Famous for	Gibraltar
Armed Forces; Biggest	China
Army; None	Costa Rica
Awarded George Cross	Malta (1942)
Battles; Most in; Europe	Belgium
Biggest;-	Russia
2nd	Canada
3rd	China
4th	US
5th	Brazil
6th	Australia
7th	India
Africa	Sudan
Europe	France (Discounting Russia)
South America	Brazil
Bird Droppings; Main financial source	Nauru
Books; Most read per person	Iceland
Border(s);-	
Longest	China
Most countries	China
Cashew Nuts; Largest producer	Mozambique
Cattle; Most	India
Christians; Most	US
Churches; Have 2 clocks	Malta
Cloves; Largest producer	Zanzibar (Tanzania)
Coastline;-	
Longest	Canada. 2nd: Indonesia
Shortest	Monaco
Cocoa Production; Highest	Ghana
Coffee; Largest producer	Brazil
Colonised; Black African state; Not	Liberia
Continent; Smallest	Australia
Cork; Largest supplier	Portugal
Dependencies in Arctic and Antarctic	Norway
Film Production; Highest	India
Frontier; Shortest	Spain/Gibraltar

Gold;-
Largest producer	South Africa
Private stock; Largest	India

Head of State; No single person;
Western country	Switzerland

Hispaniola;-
Eastern part	Dominican Republic
Western part	Haiti

Independence; Will lose if no heir to
throne	Monaco

Independent State; Smallest; Western Hemisphere	Grenada
Islamic State; Highest population	Indonesia
Jews; Most	US

Landlocked;-
Asia	Mongolia, Afghanistan
Largest	Mongolia
South America	Paraguay, Bolivia

Literacy; Highest	Iceland
Low Point; Highest	Lesotho
Merchant Navy; Largest	Liberia

Monkeys;-
Most per population	Lesotho
Wild in Europe	Gibraltar

National Anthem; No words	Spain
Northernmost; Europe	Norway

Oil;-
Importer; Biggest	USA
Production; Biggest	Saudi Arabia

Oldest; Europe	San Marino
Pigs; Most	China

Population;-
Density; Highest	Macau
Density; Lowest	Mongolia
Highest	China. 2nd: India. 3rd: USA. 4th: Indonesia
Highest: Africa	Nigeria
Highest; Europe	Germany (Discounting Russia)
Smallest	Vatican City

Republic; Oldest	San Marino
Rice; Largest producer	China
Roads; Most	US
Rubber Production; Highest	Malaysia
Shipbuilding; Most	Japan
Shipping; Largest registered	Liberia
Slaves; Freed; Founded by	Liberia

Smallest;-
Republic	Nauru
Republic; Europe	San Marino
South America	Uruguay
Sovereign State	Vatican City

Snakes; None	Ireland (Among many others)
South Africa; Surrounded by	Lesotho

South American; Atlantic and Pacific
shores	Colombia

Spanish Speaking; Highest population	Mexico
'32 religions and only one sauce'	US (Quote: Talleyrand)
Tin; Largest producer	Malaysia
Tourists; Most	Spain
Vanilla; Largest producer	Madagascar
Wealth; Highest	US

Countries

By: Name → General

Andorra	
Between	France, Spain
Ruled by	President of France, Bishop of Urgel (Spanish)
Australia	States: New South Wales, Queensland, South Australia, Tasmania, Victoria, Western Australia
Belgium	Official Languages: Flemish, Walloon, German
Brazil	Language: Portuguese
Canada	
Largest province	Quebec
Provinces	10
Cyprus	Peoples: Greek (Majority – in South), Turkish
Czechoslovakia	Traditionally disputed area with Germany: Sudetenland
Egypt	Local Name: Misr
Equatorial Guinea	Provinces: Biako, Rio Muni
Ethiopia	Disputed area with Somalia: Ogaden
Fiji	Largest Island: Viti Levu
Finland	Lakes: About 60,000
France	Traditionally disputed area with Germany: Alsace Lorraine, Saarland
Gambia	Within: Senegal
Haiti	Official Language: French
Indonesia	
Islands	Over 13,000
Main	Java, Sumatra, Kalimantan (South Borneo), Sulawesi, West Irian
Israel	
East Europe, Asia, Africa born	Ashkenazim
Israeli born	Sabra
N.Africa, Spain, Portugal born	Sephardim
Japan	
Main islands	Hokkaido, Honshu, Shikoku, Kyushu
Local name	Nippon
Korea	Divided at: 38th Parallel
Liechtenstein	Between: Austria, Switzerland
Malta	Main Islands: Malta, Gozo, Comino

New Zealand	Islands: North, South (Largest)
Nigeria	Official Language: English
Pakistan	Provinces: Punjab, Sind, Baluchistan, North West Frontier Province
Panama	Formerly part of: Colombia
Paraguay	Borders: Argentina, Brazil, Bolivia
Philippines	Main Islands: Luzon (North), Mindanao (South)
San Marino	
Title	Most Serene Republic of
Within	Italy
Seychelles	Indian Ocean
Main island	Mahé
Spain	
South Mediterranean coast	Costa del Sol
Territories in Africa	Ceuta, Melilla (within Morocco)
Sri Lanka	
Main crop before tea	Coffee
Main groups	Sinhalese and Tamils
Swaziland	Between: South Africa, Mozambique
Switzerland	
Borders	Austria, France, Germany, Italy, Liechtenstein
Official name	Confederation Helvetique
Tonga	Also called: Friendly Islands
USSR	
Republics	15
Republics with UN Seats	Ukraine, Byelorussia
Vietnam	French Divisions: Annam, Cochin China, Tonkin

Exploration and Discovery

By: General

Alaska	Vitus Bering
Amazon;-	
Discovered	Amerigo Vespucci
Explored	Francisco de Orellana
America; 1st European (disputed)	Leif Eriksson
Angkor Wat	Henri Mouhot
Antarctic Circle; 1st to cross	Captain James Cook
Antarctic; Crossing	Vivian Fuchs
Argonaut's Voyage; Retraced, 1984	Tim Severin
Around world in 80 days; US Reporter	Nelly Bly (72 days – 1889)
Atlantic Crossing;-	
In leather boat, 1977	Brendan Voyage, Tim Severin
In papyrus boat, 1969–1970	Ra Expedition, Thor Heyerdahl
Australia	Willem Jansz
Brazil	Pedro Cabral
Cape Horn; Discovered and rounded	Willem Schouten
Cape of Good Hope; 1st European to round	Bartholomew Diaz
Cape of Good Hope; Rounding Westward	Phoenicians (Navigator – Hanno)
China (Visited)	Marco Polo
Circumnavigation of globe;-	Ferdinand Magellan (killed during voyage. Juan Cano completed)

UK	Sir Francis Drake
Columbus	
Goal when sailing	Japan
Nationality	Italian
Sponsor	Ferdinand II and Isabella of Spain
Congo River	Diego Cam
Falkland Islands	John Davis
Greenland	Eric the Red
Hawaii	Captain James Cook
Hudson River	Giovanni Verrazona
India; 1st European to sail to	Vasco Da Gama
Lake Tanganyika	Burton and Speke
Lake Victoria	Speke
Magellan	
Nationality	Portuguese
Sponsored by	Spain
Mississipi	Hernando De Soto
New Zealand	Abel Tasman
Newfoundland	John Cabot
Niagara Falls	Louis Hennepin
Niger River	Mungo Park
North Pole;-	Admiral Robert Peary, 1909 (with black servant Matthew Henson and 4 Eskimos)
1st to fly over	Admiral Richard Byrd. Plane: Miss Josephine Ford
Solo; 1st	Naomi Uemura, 1978
Woman; 1st	Fran Phillips, 1971
North West Passage; Completed	Captain Roald Amundsen
Oceanographic Expedition; 1st round globe	HMS Challenger
Pacific Ocean;-	
Crossing on a raft, 1947	Kon Tiki Expedition, Thor Heyerdahl
1st European to see	Balboa
Sinbad's Voyage; Recreated, 1980–1981	Tim Severin
South Pole	Captain Roald Amundsen, 1911
1st to fly over	Admiral Richard Byrd
2nd	Captain Scott
St Lawrence River; 1st European to sail up	Jacques Cartier
Victoria Falls	David Livingstone
West Indies	Christopher Columbus, 1492

Extremities

By: Place → Extreme Point

E.g.: What is the Southernmost point of . . .

Africa;-	
East	Cape Guardafui, Somalia
North	Cape Bon, Tunisia
South	Cape Agulhas (not Cape of Good Hope)
West	Cape Verde, Senegal
Britain;-	
East	Lowestoft, Suffolk
North (mainland)	Dunnet Head, Caithness
South	Lizard Point, Cornwall

West (mainland)	Ardnamurchan Point, Argyll
Europe;-	
West (Continental)	Cape Roca, Portugal
North	Cape Nordkyn, Norway
South	Point Marroqui, Spain
South America;-	
South	Cape Horn, off Tierra del Fuego
South (mainland)	Fuerte Bulnes, Chile
West	Aguja Point, Peru
UK; South	Les Minquiers, Channel Islands
US (Continental); South	Key West
Western Hemisphere; South	Cape Horn off Tierra Del Fuego, South America

Flags

By: General

Note: Includes Non National Flags

Different Sides	Paraguay
France; Nickname	Tricolour
Italy; Designer	Napoleon
Merchant Navy: UK	Red Ensign
Monaco; Colours reversed	Poland
National; Oldest	Denmark
Navy: UK	White Ensign
Netherlands; Colours reversed	Yugoslavia
Not Rectangular	Nepal
Outline of Country on	Cyprus
Pan African Colours	Red, Green, Yellow
Parts of;-	
Furthest from pole	Fly
Nearest to pole	Hoist
Raised and lowered with	Halyard
Queen's; Personal flag	Royal Standard
Red Circle, White Background	Japan (Circle represents the Sun)
Red Cross; Inverse	Switzerland
Ship before sailing	Blue Peter
Single Colour	Libya (Green)
Union Jack; Created	1801
US;-	
1st Flag; Maker (reputedly)	Mrs Betsy Ross
Nickname	Stars and Stripes, Old Glory
Stars	50 (States)
Stripes	6 (White), 7 (Red) (Original States)
USSR (Former)	Gold Hammer and Sickle on Red Background
Words on	Brazil

Historical Territories

By: Territory → Country now in

E.g.: What Country is . . . now part of

Babylonia	Iraq
Barbary (Coast)	Algeria, Libya, Morocco, Tunisia
Bessarabia	Moldavia (formerly Romania)
Bohemia	Czechoslovakia
Carthage	Tunisia
Dacia	Romania
Gaul	France
Illyria	Albania
Karelia	Finland/Russia
Khmer Empire	Kampuchea
Lusitania	Portugal
Mashonaland	Zimbabwe
Matabeleland	Zimbabwe
Moravia	Czechoslovakia
Numidia	Algeria
Phoenicia	Lebanon/Syria
Phrygia	Turkey
Prussia	Germany
Ruthenia	Ukraine (formerly Czechoslovakia)
Silesia	Czechoslovakia
Spanish Main	West Indies, South American Coast
Sumer	Iraq
Thrace	Bulgaria
Transylvania	Romania
Troy	Turkey
Vinland	North America (Viking name)
Wallachia	Romania
Westphalia	Germany

Inhabitants

By: Place → Inhabitant

E.g.: What is Someone from . . . called

Aberdeen	Aberdonian
Brittany	Breton
Glasgow	Glaswegian
Liverpool	Liverpudlian
Manchester	Mancunian
Monaco	Monagasque
Newcastle	Novocastrian
Sardinia	Sard
Shropshire	Salopian

National Anthems

By: Country → Title

Belgium	'The Brabançonne'
France	'The Marseillaise'
Germany	'Deutschland über Alles'

Ireland	'The Soldier's Song'
Netherlands	'Wilhelmus Van Nassouwe'
Scotland	'Scots Wha Hae'
US	'The Star Spangled Banner'
Wales	'Land of my Fathers'

National Symbols

By: Country → Symbol

Australia	Wattle
Canada	Maple
England	Rose
France	Fleur de lys (Lily)
Germany	Cornflower
India	Lotus
Ireland	Shamrock
Japan	Chrysanthemum
Scotland	Thistle
South Africa	Springbok
Spain	Pomegranate
US	Bald Eagle
Wales	Leek, Daffodil

Other Places

By: Description → Place

Female; Person or animal not allowed	Mount Athos, Greece
Named after 1 Person; Places; Most	Humboldt
North America; French Sovereignty	St Pierre and Miquelon
Welsh settlement in South America	Patagonia, Argentina
White Rajahs; Former rulers of	Sarawak (Brooke Family)

Other Places

By: Name → Location, General

Alaska	US State
Bought from	Russia, 1867, by William Seward (Secretary of State)
Atlantis (mythical)	Popularised by: Plato
Benelux countries	Belgium, Netherlands, Luxembourg
Bowery	Manhattan, New York
Known for	Tramps
Bronx	New York. Borough
Brooklyn	New York. Borough
Cabinda	Angola
Surrounded by	Zaire
Camargue	Rhone Delta, France
Casbah (Famous)	Algiers, Algeria
Empty Quarter	Saudi Arabia/Oman (Desert Area)
Eritrea	North Ethiopia
Florida	US State
Bought from	Spain, for $5 million
Gallipoli	Turkey (Peninsula)
Ginza District	Tokyo
Golan Heights	Syria

Golden Triangle	Burma, Laos, Thailand (opium growing area)
Gorbals	Glasgow. Former slum area
Guadalcanal	Solomon Islands (Island)
Harlem	New York
Known for	Black ghetto
Iberian Peninsula	Spain, Portugal
Jutland	Denmark (Peninsula)
Karroo	South Africa (Plateau area)
Kashmir	India/Pakistan
Capital	Srinagar
Kurdistan	Iran/Iraq/Turkey
Lapland	
Made up of parts of	Finland, Norway, Sweden, Russia (Kola Peninsula)
Most Lapps in	Norway
Levant	Syria, Lebanon
Patagonia	Argentina
Pemba	Tanzania (Island)
Rann of Kutch	India (Marsh area)
Reeperbahn	Hamburg, Germany (Red Light district)
Sahel	Area South of the Sahara
Scandinavia	Denmark, Norway, Sweden
Soho	London. Nightclub Centre
Ulster, Provinces;-	
Eire	Cavan, Donegal, Monaghan
North	Antrim, Armagh, Down, Fermanagh, Londonderry, Tyrone

Peoples and Tribes

By: Name → Where from

Aborigines	Australia
Ainu	Japan
Bedouin	Middle East, North Africa
Berbers	North Africa (Morocco, Algeria, Tunisia)
Bushmen	Kalahari Desert, Southern Africa
Chicanos	Mexican Americans
Cockneys	London (Born within hearing of Bow Bells)
Dayaks	Borneo
Dinka	Sudan
Flemings	Belgium (Flemish speaking)
Gauchos	Argentina (Cowboys)
Gegs	Albania
Gonds	India
Harijans	India (formerly Untouchables)
Hausa	Nigeria
Ibo	Nigeria
Jats	India
Kabyle	Algeria
Karen	Burma
Khalkha	Mongolia
Kikuyu	Kenya
Luo	Kenya

Magyars	Hungary
Maoris	New Zealand
Masai	East Africa (Kenya/Tanzania)
Mossi	Burkina Faso
Nagas	India/Burma
Ndebele (Matabele)	Zimbabwe
Nuer	Sudan
Ovimbundu	Angola
Pashtun	Afghanistan/Pakistan
Pathans	Afghanistan/Pakistan
Pygmies	Zaire
Shan	Burma
Sherpas	Nepal
Shona	Zimbabwe/Mozambique
Sinhalese	Sri Lanka
Tamils	India/Sri Lanka
Tosks	Albania
Walloons	Belgium (French dialect speaking)
Wolof	Senegal
Yanomamo	South America (Venezuela, Brazil)
Yoruba	Nigeria

Place Name Changes

By: *Original Name → Current Name*

See Also: Roman Names

Absecon	Atlantic City
Abyssinia	Ethiopia
Adrianople	Edirne
Angora	Ankara
Angostura	Ciudad Bolivar
Asia Minor	Anatolia
Basutoland	Lesotho
Batavia	Djakarta
Bathurst	Banjul
Bechuanaland	Botswana
Belgian Congo	Zaire
Benares	Varanasi
Bourbon Island	Reunion
Brighthelmstone	Brighton
British Honduras	Belize
Byzantium	Constantinople (Now: Istanbul)
Cambodia	Kampuchea
Canton	Guangzhou
Cathay	China
Cawnpore	Kanpur
Ceylon	Sri Lanka
Christiania	Oslo
Ciudad Trujillo	Santo Domingo
Cologne	Koln
Congo (Kinshasa)	Zaire
Constantinople	Istanbul

Dagon	Rangoon
Dahomey	Benin
Danzig	Gdansk
East Pakistan	Bangladesh
Edo	Tokyo
Ekaterinburg	Sverdlovsk
El-Kahira	Cairo
Ellis Islands	Tuvalu
Formosa	Taiwan
Fort Dearborn	Chicago
Fort Snelling	Minneapolis
Fort Washington	Cincinnati
French Equatorial Africa	Chad
French Sudan	Mali
Gilbert Islands	Kiribati
Gold Coast	Ghana
Hellespont	Dardanelles (Strait)
Leopoldville	Kinsasha
Lourenço Marques	Maputo
Madagascar	Malagasy Republic (Now: Madagascar)
Mesopotamia	Iraq
Netherlands-Indies	Indonesia
New Amsterdam	New York
New Granada	Colombia
New Hebrides	Vanuatu
Nizhni Novgorod	Gorki
Northern Rhodesia	Zambia
Nyasaland	Malawi
Oxus	Amu Darya (River)
Peking	Beijing (Also once called: Peiping)
Persia	Iran
Pleasant Island	Nauru
Port Natal	Durban
Porto Rico	Puerto Rico
Rabbath Ammon	Amman
Rhodesia	Zimbabwe
Saigon	Ho Chi Minh City
Salisbury	Harare
Sandwich Islands	Hawaiian Islands
Siam	Thailand
Smyrna	Izmir
Somers Islands	Bermuda
South West Africa	Namibia
Spitzbergen	Svalbard Island
St Domingue	Haiti
St Petersburg	Petrograd (Next: Leningrad, Now: St Petersburg)
Stalingrad	Volgograd
Stanleyville	Kisangani (Zaire)
Sulphur Island	Iwo Jima
Tripolitania	Libya
Tsaritsyn	Stalingrad (Now: Volgograd)
Ubangi-Shan	Central African Republic
Upper Peru	Bolivia
Upper Volta	Burkina Faso

Van Diemens Land	Tasmania
Vernyi	Alma-Ata
Yathrib	Medina
Zuider Zee	Ijselmeer (Reservoir)

Place Name Derivations

By: Place → Derivation

E.g.: Where did . . . get its name from

Addis Ababa	New Flower
Albania	Land of the Eagle
America	Amerigo Vespucci. Italian Navigator. Named by: Martin Waldseemuller
Anguilla	Eel (French)
Argentina	Land of Silver
Australia	Terra Australis Incognita (the 'Unknown Southern Land')
Austria	'Osterreich' – Eastern Empire
Barbados	Bearded (Portuguese)
Bermuda	Juan Bermudez (Spanish Discoverer)
Calcutta	Goddess Kali
Cameroon	Shrimp (Portuguese)
Canary Islands	Dogs (Roman Name: Canariae Insulae – Isles of Dogs)
Caribbean	Caribs, Indian peoples
Colombia	Christopher Columbus
Costa Rica	Rich Coast
England	Angle Land
Equador	The Equator, which runs through it
Faroes	Sheep Islands
Florida	The Easter Season (Discovered on Easter Sunday)
Himalayas	Place of Snow
India	Indus River
Kuala Lumpur	Muddy Estuary
Liechtenstein	Ruling Dynasty
Mesopotamia	Between the Rivers (Euphrates and Tigris)
Monrovia	James Monroe (US President)
Montreal	Mont Real (Mount Royal)
New York	James, Duke of York (Brother of Charles II)
New Zealand	New Sea Land (Sea Land – The Netherlands)
Nova Scotia	New Scotland
Pakistan	Made up of 5 province names
Panama	Many fish
Peking	Northern Capital
Pennsylvania	**William Penn (Founder)**
Phoenicia	**Purple (Dye obtained there)**
Punjab	**Five Rivers**
Sahara Desert	**Desert (Arabic)**
Saudi Arabia	**King Ibn Saud**
Sierra Leone	**Lion**
Spain	**Land of Rabbits**

Tasmania	Abel Tasman (Discoverer)
Tierra del Fuego	Land of Fire
Uruguay	River
Venuzuela	Little Venice
Zaire	River Zaire (Meaning: River)
Zimbabwe	Houses of Stone

Place Name Parts, Meaning

By: *Name Part → Meaning*

E.g. What does the Word . . . mean in a place name

Aber	Mouth of river (Welsh)
Borough, Burg	Defended place
Brae	Hillside (Scots)
Burn	Stream (Scots)
By	Village (Norse)
Caster, Chester	Walled
Chipping	Market
Ford	River crossing
Glen	Valley (Scots)
Ham	Homestead
Inver	River Mouth (Scots)
Kirk	Church (Scots)
Kyle	Strait (Scots)
Lee	Meadow
Llan	Church (Welsh)
Loch	Lake (Scots)
Rio	River (Spanish)
Sex	Saxon
Shan	Mountain (Chinese)
Thorpe	Farm
Ton	Town
Wick, Wich	Village (Scots)

Place Nicknames

By: *Nickname → Place*

Auld Reekie	Edinburgh
Backbone of England,The	Pennines
Backbone of Italy,The	Appennines
Big Apple,The	New York City
Cockpit of Europe,The	Belgium
Emerald Isle,The	Ireland
Empire State,The	New York
Eternal City,The	Rome
Forbidden City,The	Lhasa
Fortunate Islands,The	Canary Islands
Golden State,The	California
Granite City,The	Aberdeen
Land of the Rising Sun,The	Japan
Lone Star State,The	Texas
Motor City (Motown)	Detroit
The Smoke	London
Spice Island	Zanzibar
Spice Islands	Moluccas

167

Sunshine State,The	Florida
Switzerland of Africa, The	Swaziland
Windy City	Chicago

Places, Latitude and Longitude

By: *General*

E.g: Where would you reach if you travelled East from . . .

Cape Horn; Next East/West	Cape Horn
Equator;-	
Asian Country on	Indonesia
South American Countries on	Brazil, Colombia, Ecuador
Europe; Capitals, East to West	Moscow, Istanbul, Bucharest, Helsinki, Athens, Sofia, Warsaw, Belgrade, Tirana, Budapest, Stockholm, Vienna, Prague, Berlin, Copenhagen, Rome, Oslo, Bern, Bonn, Amsterdam, Brussels, Paris, London, Edinburgh, Madrid, Dublin, Lisbon
Iceland (Reykjavik); Next South	Antarctic
Melbourne; Next West	Argentina
Miami; Next East	Western Sahara
Same Latitude;-	
Edinburgh	Labrador (West), Moscow (East)
Florida	Sahara Desert
London	Newfoundland, Hudson Bay
Los Angeles	Fez, Rabat
Naples	New York
San Francisco	Sicily
Shetland Islands	Greenland (West), St Petersburg (East)
Washington	Lisbon
Sydney; Next North (Excluding Australia, Islands)	Siberia
UK; Towns, East to West	London, Leicester, Sheffield, Leeds/Newcastle, Birmingham, Manchester, Bristol, Liverpool, Cardiff/Edinburgh, Glasgow

Roman Names

By: *Roman Name → Current Name*

Albion	England
Aquae Sulis	Bath
Aquincum	Budapest
Caledonia	Scotland
Camulodonum	Colchester
Clausentum	Southampton
Danum	Doncaster
Deva	Chester
Dubris	Dover
Durovernum	Canterbury
Eboracum	York
Glevum	Gloucester
Granta	Cambridge

Hibernia	Ireland
Isca Dumnoniorum	Exeter
Lindum	Lincoln
Londinium	London
Lugdunum	Lyons
Lutecia	Paris
Mancurium	Manchester
Massilia	Marseilles
Mediolanum	Milan
Olisipo	Lisbon
Ratae (Coritanorum)	Leicester
Sarbiodunum	Salisbury
Turicum	Zurich
Venta Belgarum	Winchester
Verulamium	St Albans
Vindobona	Vienna

Territories, Sovereignty

By: Territory → Sovereign Country

E.g.: Which country rules . . .
See Also: Society and Politics; Colonies

Admiralty Islands	Papua New Guinea
Andaman Islands	India
Ascension Islands	Britain
Azores	Portugal
Bismarck Archipelago	Papua New Guinea
Canary Islands	Spain
Easter Island	Chile
Faroe Islands	Denmark
Galapagos Islands	Ecuador
Gotland	Sweden
Greenland	Denmark
Guadeloupe	France
Guam	USA
Heligoland	Germany
Juan Fernandez	Chile
Kurile Islands	Japan
Macao	Portugal
Madeira	Portugal
Martinique	France
Nicobar Islands	India
Pescadores	Taiwan
Puerto Rico	US
Réunion	France
Ross Dependency (Antarctic)	New Zealand
St Pierre and Miquelon	France
Socotra	South Yemen
Tristan Da Cunha	Britain
Virgin Islands	Britain, US

United Kingdom

By: General

Canals; Most	Birmingham (More than Venice)

Channel Ports; Closest	Dover–Calais
County;-	
Became part of GLC, 1965	Middlesex
Largest	North Yorkshire
Nickname: Garden of England	Kent
Orchards; Most	Kent
Population; Largest	Greater London
Population; Smallest	Isle of Wight
Potatoes; Most grown	Lincolnshire
Smallest	Isle of Wight
Smallest; Before change	Rutland (excluding London)
Westernmost	Fermanagh
Deaths exceed Births; 20th Century; 1st time	1976
Flower Bulbs; County associated with	Lincolnshire
Hottest (Average)	Penzance, Scilly Isles
Italianate Village	Portmeirion, Wales
John O'Groats to Lands End; Distance	603 miles (in straight line)
Kent; Occupant	East of Medway: Man of Kent, West of Medway, Kentish Man
Lowest Area	Fens (Cambridgeshire, Norfolk)
Name;-	
Place; Longest	Llanfairpwllgwyngyll-gogerychwyrndrobwll-llantysiliogogogoch
Place; Shortest	As, Oa, Ba
Shortest	E.O (Rivers)
Population; Highest	London, 2nd: Birmingham
Raspberries; Centre	Blairgowrie, Scotland
Sea; Furthest point from	Near Meriden (75 miles)
Wiltshire; Inhabitant; Nickname	Moonraker

United States

By: General

California;-	
Capital	Sacramento
Peninsula attached to	Baja California
City;-	
Highest population	New York. 2nd: Chicago
Largest area	Los Angeles. 2nd: New York
New York State; Capital	Albany
Russia; Closest Point to	Diomede Islands, Bering Straits
State;-	
Largest	Alaska
Largest; 2nd	Texas
Population; Lowest	Alaska
Population; Highest	California
Smallest	Rhode Island
States; Four meeting at one point	Arizona, Colorado, New Mexico, Utah
States; Rectangular	Colorado, Wyoming

Health and the Body

Contents

The Body	173	By: Disease	182
Disease and Medicine	178	Medical Specialities	
Diseases, Common Names		By: Term	183
By: Technical Name	181	Mental Illnesses and Conditions	183
Diseases, Effects		Psychology and Psychiatry	184

The Body

By: General

Adam's Apple	Larynx
Adrenaline; Other name; US	Ephinephrine
Allergic Reaction; Causes	Histamine
Appetite; Abnormal loss of	Anorexia Nervosa
Armpit; Anatomical Term	Axilla
Artery(ies);-	
Function	Carry Blood from the Heart
Largest	Aorta
Neck	Carotid Artery
Babies;-	
Can do what adults cannot	Breathe and Swallow at same time
Soft spot on head	Fontanelle
Balance; Maintained by	Labyrinth (in ear)
Bile; Made by	Liver
Birth;-	
Feet first	Breech
Period after; Term for	Puerperium
Blood;-	
Circulation; Duration	About 23 seconds
Clotting; Substance in	Fibrin
Factor named after type of Monkey	Rhesus
Fats in	Lipids
Liquid Portion	Plasma
Oxygen Carrier	Haemoglobin
Pressure; Constituents	Systolic and Diastolic Pressures
Quantity; Average	Men: 7 litres (12 pints). Women: 4 litres (7 pints)
Vessels; Smallest	Capillaries
Blood Cells;-	
Destroyed every second	About 15 Million
Red; Function	Carry Oxygen and Waste Materials around Body
Red; Where made	Bone Marrow
White; Function	Combat infection
White; Main types	Leukocyte, Lymphocyte
Blood Group(s);-	A, B, AB, O, Rhesus negative, Rhesus positive
Can give to others	O
Can receive from any blood group	AB
Most Common	O
Body;-	
Build; Classification	Somatotype
Build; Types	Ectomorph (Tall), Endomorph (Fat), Mesomorph (Muscular)

Hardest Substance	Tooth Enamel
No Blood Supply, only part	Cornea
Part; Increases to 8 times its size	Pupil
Percentage Water	About 60%

Bone(s);-

Constituent; Main	Collagen
Longest	Femur
Most; Where	Nearly half in Hands and Feet
Not in contact with any other, only one	Hyoid bone (Throat)
Number	206 (Adult), 330 (New Born Baby)
Process of formation	Ossification
Smallest	Stapes (in the Ear)

Bones; Common names;-

Clavicle	Collar Bone
Cranium	Skull
Femur	Thigh Bone
Hallux	Big Toe
Mandible	Lower Jawbone
Maxilla	Upper Jaw Bone
Patella	Knee Cap
Pelvis	Hip Bone
Scapula	Shoulder Blade
Sternum	Breast Bone
Tibia	Shin Bone

Bones; Location;-

Anvil (Incus)	Ear
Calcaneus	Heel
Carpals	Wrist
Fibula	Lower Leg
Hammer (Malleus)	Ear
Humerus	Upper Arm
Metacarpals	Hand
Metatarsals	Foot
Phalanges	Fingers, Toes
Radius	Forearm
Sacrum	Lower Spine
Stirrup (Stapes)	Ear
Talus	Ankle
Tarsals	Ankle
Ulna	Forearm

Brain;-

Bone Case	Cranium (8 Bones)
Lobes	Frontal, Parietal, Temporal, Occipital
Oxygen used	20% Supply
Rational side	Left
Size; Average	Man: 1.45 litres. Woman: 1.3 litres.
Weight, Average	1.4 kg (3 lbs)

Catalyst: Biological	Enzyme

Cell;-

Largest	Female Ovum
Smallest	Male Sperm
Chest Cavity; Membrane lining	Pleura
Chest; Anatomical term	Thorax

Chromosomes;-

Females	Two X sex chromosomes

Male–Female difference	Male has one dissimilar pair (XY sex chromosomes)
Number	46 (23 pairs)
Colon; Other name	Large Intestine
Digestion; Food moves by	Peristalsis
Ear;-	
Inner	Cochlea, Labyrinth
Sound receptor	Organ of Corti
Sound turned into nerve impulses in	Cochlea
Throat Connection	Eustachian Tube
Endocrine Glands	Pituitary, Thyroid, Parathyroid, Thymus, Adrenal, Hypothalamus, Sex Glands
Function	Make Hormones
Eye(s);-	
Blood Vessels; Where Enter and Leave	Blind Spot
Coloured Part	Iris
Light Sensitive Cells; Types	Rods (black and white), Cones (colour)
Light Sensitive Portion	Retina
Protective Shield	Cornea
Weight	About 7g (¼ ounce)
While open, Cannot do	Sneeze
White of	Sclera
Female Sex Hormones	Oestrogen, Progesterone
Filter Body Water	Kidneys
Foetus;-	
Connection to Mother in womb	Placenta and Umbilical Cord (Afterbirth – at birth)
Fluid Surrounding	Amniotic Fluid
Funny Bone	A Nerve
Gall Bladder; Function	Stores Bile
Gland;-	
Largest	Liver
Top of Skull	Pineal gland
Producing Hormones	Endocrine
Gullet; Anatomical term for	Oesophagus
Hair;-	
Body; Total	About 5 million
Head, Growth Rate	About 12 cm (4.75 inches) per year
Head; Number	About 100,000
Head; Measure	Cephalic Index
Heart;-	
Chambers	4
Each side; Division	Auricle and Ventricle
Lower Chambers	Ventricles
Pacemaker; Internal	Sinoatrial Node
Pumping Capacity	About 4.5 litres (1 gallon) per minute
Sac surrounding	Pericardium
Upper Chambers	Auricles
Wall dividing	Septum
Weight	About 350 g (¾ lb)
Heat; Body; Amount	Same as 120 Watt Bulb
Heel; Tendon in	Achilles Tendon
Hormone; Stimulates Nervous System, Raises Heart Rate	Adrenaline

Human Being; Observed characteristics	Phenotype
Insulin; Gland produces	Islets of Langerhans, Pancreas
Intestine;-	
First section; Horseshoe-shaped	Duodenum
Small; Parts	Duodenum, Jejunum, Ileum
Sizes	Large shorter than Small
Joints;-	
Fixed	Sutures
Fluid lubricating	Synovial fluid
Kidney;-	
Function	Remove Waste Material from the blood
Substituting for function	Artificial Dialysis
Tubes in	Nephrons
Left Handed; Proportion	About 5%
Liver;-	
Weight of	About 1.8kg (4 pounds)
Lungs;-	
Air Sacs	Alveoli
Bones enclosing	Thoracic Cage
Heavier	Right
Lymph Glands; Function	Make White Blood Cells
Male Sex Hormone; Main	Testosterone
Menstrual Period;-	
First	Menarche
Last	Menopause
Milk; Mother's; First after birth	Colostrum
Mouth;-	
Passageway at back of	Pharynx
Separated from Nasal cavity by	Uvula
Separated from Windpipe by	Epiglottis
Muscle(s);-	
Largest	Buttock
Not attached at both ends	Tongue
Percentage Body Weight	About 40%
Smile or Frown; Which uses more	Frown
Muscles; Where (Function);-	
Biceps	Arm (bends)
Buccinator	Head (eating)
Deltoid	Shoulder (arm movement)
Extensor Digitorum	Arm (opens hand)
Gastrocnemius	Lower Leg (straightens ankle)
Gluteus Maximus	Buttocks (keeps upright)
Gracilis	Upper Leg (bends)
Hamstring	Upper Leg (bends)
Latissimus Dorsi	Back (arm movement)
Lumbricals	Hand (finger movement)
Masseter	Head (chewing)
Occipito Frontalis	Head (frowning)
Pectoralis Major	Chest (arm movement)
Quadriceps	Upper Leg (straightens)
Sartorius	Upper Leg (bends)
Soleus	Lower Leg (straightens ankle)
Temporalis	Head (chewing)
Trapezius	Neck, Shoulder (arm movement)
Triceps	Arm (straightens)
Nerve(s);-	
Carries impulse to	Dendrite

Connection away from	Axon
Chemical responsible for transmission	Acetylcholine
Junction between cells	Synapse
Parathyroid Gland; Function	Calcium Metabolism
Physique; Classification System	Somatotyping
Pituitary Gland; Function	Controls production of Hormones
Pulse; Artery used	Radial Artery
Red Blood Corpuscles; Function	Carry Oxygen
Ribs;-	
Number	12 pairs
Types	True, False, Floating
Salivary Gland; Largest	Parotid Gland
Selective Breeding; Humans; Proposer	Francis Galton (Eugenics)
Sense; Most Sensitive	Smell
Sex Glands	Gonads
Female	Ovaries
Male	Testes
Skin;-	
Area, Average	Man: 20 sq ft. Woman: 17 sq ft.
Constituent; Main	Collagen
Parts of	Epidermis (Outer), Dermis
Pigment; Absence of	Albinism
Pigment; Filters sun	Melanin
Replaced	About every 28 days
Skull; Only Movable Bone	Lower Jaw
Sperm; First seen by	Anton Leuwenhoek
Spine; Bones making up	Vertebrae
Stomach;-	
Acid in	Hydrochloric Acid
Capacity	About 2.5 Pints
Dissolves food	Gastric Juices
Lives with hole in	Alexis St Martin
Substance secreted for Sexual Attraction, etc.	Pheromone
Substance; Skin, Hair, Nails; Component of	Keratin
Taste; Receptors	Taste Buds
Tears; Produced by	Lacrymal Glands
Teeth;-	
Film on	Plaque
Materials	Enamel (Surface), Dentine
Number	32 (Adult), 20 (Child)
Types	Incisors, Canines, Premolars, Molars
Temperature;-	
Highest (Survived)	116 degrees F
Lowest (Survived)	60.8 degrees F
Regulates	Hypothalamus
Throat; Anatomical term for	Pharynx
Thymus	Gland in Chest
Thyroid Gland; Function	Regulates Growth and Metabolism
Twins; Frequency; Britain	About 1 in 80
Veins; Function	Carry Blood to the Heart
Vertebra(e);-	
Lowest	Coccyx
Neck; Number	7
Number	33

White Corpuscles; Function — Combat infection

Windpipe;-
   Divides into — Bronchi
   Proper name — Trachea

Womb; Anatomical term for — Uterus

Disease and Medicine

By: General

Accumulation of Air in Tissues — Emphysema

AIDS, Stands for — Acquired Immune Deficiency Syndrome

Alcoholism; Liver disease caused by — Cirrhosis

Anaesthesia; Use of, in childbirth made acceptable — Queen Victoria

Anatomy; Pioneer; Condemned to death by the Inquisition — Versalius

Antibiotic; 1st — Penicillin

Appetite and Weight Loss; Condition characterised by — Anorexia Nervosa

Artificial Body Part — Prosthetic

Artificial Heart; Inventor — Dr Barney Clark (1982)

Aspirin; Made from (originally) — Tree Bark

Athlete's Foot; Cause — Ringworm

Barbiturates — Sedative

BCG, Stands for — Bacillus of Calmette and Guérin

Beriberi; Cause — Vitamin B1 deficiency

Beta Blocker; Effect — Lowers Blood Pressure

Birth Control Clinic; Founder of 1st in London — Marie Stopes

Birth Control Pioneer; Imprisoned for sending Birth Control information through the mail — Margaret Sanger

Black Death — Plague (Bubonic)

Blackwater Fever; Complication of — Malaria

Bleeding; Medical term — Haemorrhage

Blindness; Major cause in Third World — Trachoma

Blood Cells; Red; Deficiency — Anaemia

Blood Clotting; Preventer — Anticoagulant

Blood Vessel; Blockage — Embolism

Body Fluid; Drug to reduce — Diuretic

Body Tissue; Used for analysis — Biopsy

Bone; Most often broken — Collar Bone

Brain; Treatment using electric current — Electroconvulsive Therapy (ECT)

Brain Waves; Recording equipment — Electro-encephalograph (EEG)

Cancer; Major types — Carcinoma, Sarcoma

Cancer-producing substance — Carcinogen

Capillaries; Function — Connect Arteries and Veins, carry blood deep into the tissues

CAT Scanner; Stands for — Computerised Axial Tomography

Chinese Restaurant Syndrome; Believed caused by — Monosodium Glutamate

Chiropodist; Treats — Feet

Colour Blindness; Most common — Red and Green Confused

Dead Body; Examination — Post Mortem or Autopsy

Death of tissue in body — Gangrene

Deformed Births; Drug that caused	Thalidomide
Diabetes; Cause	Insulin deficiency
Digitalis; Obtained from	Foxglove
Diphtheria; Immunity test	Schick Test
Discovery; By accident when mould settled on laboratory culture	Penicillin
Disease:-	
Causes compulsive eating	Bulimia
Infectious; Most	Measles
Most Widespread	Tooth and Gum disease
Period between infection and symptoms	Incubation Period
Saint; Named after	St Vitus' Dance, St Anthony's Fire
Doctor; Executed for refusing to charge patients	St Pantaleon
Doctor; Greek; Earliest known	Aeschylapus
Down's Syndrome; Cause	Extra Chromosome
Drug:-	
Blood Vessels; Narrows	Vasoconstrictor
Blood Vessels; Widens	Vasodilator
Derived from rye fungus	Ergometrine
Prevention of disease; Used for	Prophylactic
Drugs; Common names:-	
Acetylsalicylic Acid	Aspirin
Acetaminophen	Paracetamol
Lysergic Acid Diethylamide	LSD
Chlordiazepoxide	Librium
Diazepam	Valium
Nitrazepam	Mogadon
Drinamyl	Purple Hearts
Amphetamines	Pep Pills, Speed
Secobarbital	Seconal
Pentobarbital	Nembutal
Barbiturates	Tranquillisers, Sedatives
Ear:-	
Instrument to look down	Otoscope
Ringing in	Tinnitus
Egyptian Mummy; Medical use	Used as drug component in 18th Century
Elephant Man; Disease	Neurofibromatosis
Epilepsy; Categories	Grand Mal, Petit Mal, Psychomotor
Ether; Pioneer as anaesthetic	Morton
Eye:-	
Chart; Standard	Snellen
Dilating Pupil; Drug used for	Atropine
Disease makes Lens opaque	Cataract
Father of Medicine; Known as	Hippocrates
Fluid; Excessive in tissues	Oedema
Folic Acid	Vitamin B
Foods; Unnatural; Craving for	Pica
Goitre; Cause	Iodine deficiency
Haemophilia; Victims	Men Only
Heart and Lungs; Instrument for listening to	Stethoscope
Heart Transplant; 1st:-	
At	Groote Schuur Hospital, Capetown, South Africa (1967)

By	Dr Christiaan Barnard
On	Louis Washkansky
Heartbeat; Recording equipment	Electrocardiograph (ECG)
Heroin; Made from	Morphine
Hiccough; Cause	Spasm of the Diaphragm
Homeopathy; Populariser	C.F.S.Hahnemann
Hospital; Entering when not ill; Most common reason	Childbirth
Hyoscyamine; Source	Henbane
Hypoglycemia	Low Blood Sugar
Infants; Disease affecting Protein metabolization	Phenylketonuria (PKU)
Influenza; Name from	Supposed influence of stars
Instrument; Body Cavities, for looking into	Endoscope
Insulin Deficiency; Disease caused by	Diabetes
Insulin; Discoverer	(Sir) Frederic Banting (1922)
Iron Lung; Proper name	Drinker Respirator
Jaundice; Cause	Excessive Bile Pigment
Kala-azar; Transmitted by	Sandfly
Kidney Transplant; 1st	(Dr) Richard Lawler (1950)
Kwashiorkor; Cause	Protein Deficiency
Leprosy Bacteria; Discoverer	Hansen
Leukemia; Characterised by	Abnormal White Blood Cells
'Magic Bullet' (Chemotherapy); Pioneer	Paul Ehrlich
Malaria;-	
Carrier	Anopheles Mosquito
Cause isolated by	(Sir) Ronald Ross (1902)
Organism causing	Plasmodium
Medicine; Greek pioneer	Galen
Medicine; No physical effect	Placebo
Medicines; Reference book of	Pharmacoepeia
Memory; Loss of; Term for	Amnesia
Mescaline; Source	Peyote (Cactus)
Miners; Disease through inhaling coal dust	Pneumoconiosis
Muscle; Instrument to record electrical impulses from	Electromyograph
Nausea; Preventer	Anti-emetic
Needles; Treatment using; Ancient Chinese	Acupuncture
Nickname: The English Disease	Bronchitis
Operations;-	
Uterus; Removal of	Hysterectomy
Brain; Removal of Frontal Lobe	Lobotomy
Breast; Removal of	Mastectomy
Abdominal Wall	Laparotomy
Ear, Middle	Myringotomy
Spleen	Splenectomy
Gall Bladder	Cholecystectomy
Tendon	Tenotomy
Sterilization, Male	Vasectomy
Tonsils; Removal	Tonsillectomy
Appendix; Removal	Appendectomy
Opium Tincture; Once used to treat Diarrhoea	Laudanum
Pain Killing; Term for	Analgesic

Parasitic Infection; Most widespread	Malaria
Pellagra; Cause	Nicotinic Acid (Vitamin B2) deficiency
Penicillin; Commercial developers	Florey and Chain
Penicillin; Discoverer	(Sir) Alexander Fleming
Phlegm; Medical term for	Sputum
Pill, Contraceptive; Developer	Gregory Pincus
Plague; Types	Bubonic, Pneumonic
Polio; Inactivated Vaccine; Developer	Jonas Salk
Polio; Live Vaccine; Developer	Sabin (Oral)
Pregnancy;-	
Disease dangerous to foetus	German Measles
Fluid extraction from womb	Amniocentesis
Fluid surrounding foetus	Amniotic Fluid
Quinine; Made from	Cinchona Bark
Rickets; Cause	Vitamin D deficiency
Royal Disease; Known as	Haemophilia
Royal Touch; Supposedly cured by	Scrofula ('King's Evil')
Schistosomiasis; Parasite carried by	Snails
Scurvy; Cause	Vitamin C deficiency
Sex Change Operation; 1st	George (Christine) Jorgensen
Siamese Twins; 1st	Chang and Eng Bunker
Sleeping Sickness; Carrier	Tsetse Fly
Smallpox; Inoculation developer	Edward Jenner
Smallpox; Vaccine developed from	Cowpox
Surgery; Using extreme cold	Cryosurgery
Syphilis; Test for	Wassermann Test
TB; Test for	Heaf Test, Mantoux Test
TB; Vaccine against	BCG (Bacille Calmette-Guerin)
Temperature; Drug to lower	Antipyretic
Test Tube Birth; 1st;-	
Baby	Louise Brown (1978)
Doctors	Edwards and Steptoe
Treatment; Using Exercise, Massage, etc.	Physiotherapy
Tube for withdrawing/introducing fluid	Catheter
Tuberculosis Bacillus; Discoverer	Robert Koch
Venereal Disease, Main	Gonorrhea, Syphilis
Venereal Disease, Most common	Gonorrhea
Viruses; Substance destroying; Made by body	Interferon
Vision; Deterioration through age	Presbyopia (longsightedness)
Vitamin C; Present in	Fruit and Fresh Vegetables
Yellow Fever; Carrier	Mosquito

Diseases, Common Names

By: Technical Name → Common Name

Alopecia	Baldness
Bovine Spongiform Encephalopathy	Mad Cow Disease
Brucellosis	Undulant Fever
Bursitis	Housemaid's Knee
Cerebral Palsy	Spastic (sufferer)
Comedo	Blackhead
Coronary Thrombosis	Heart Attack
Down's Syndrome	Mongolism
Dysmenorrhoea	Period Pains

Enuresis	Bed Wetting (Involuntary urination)
Erysipelas	St Anthony's Fire
Haemorrhoids	Piles
Hansen's Disease	Leprosy
Hernia	Rupture
Herpes Labialis	Cold Sore
Herpes Zoster	Shingles
Hydrophobia	Rabies
Hypermetropia	Long Sight
Hypertension	High Blood Pressure
Hypotension	Low Blood Pressure
Infectious Mononucleosis	Glandular Fever
Myocardial Infarction	Heart Attack
Myopia	Short Sight
Nyctalopia	Night Blindness
Pertussis	Whooping Cough
Plague	Black Death
Polio(Myelitis)	Infantile Paralysis
Pyrexia	High Temperature
Pyrosis	Heartburn
Rubella	German Measles
Rubeola	Measles
Scabies	The Itch
Schistosomiasis	Bilharzia
Seborrheic Dermatitis	Dandruff
Strabismus	Squint
Sydenham's Chorea	St Vitus' Dance
Syphilis	Pox
Tachycardia	Increased Pulse Rate
Tetanus	Lockjaw
Tinea Pedis	Athletes Foot
Urticaria	Hives or nettle rash
Varicella	Chicken Pox
Variola	Smallpox

Disease, Effects

By: Disease → Body Part Affected

Aneurysm	Artery
Arthritis	Joints
Blepharitis	Eyelids
Bursitis	Joints
Cholecystitis	Gall Bladder
Cirrhosis	Liver
Conjunctivitis	Eye
Cystitis	Bladder
Dermatitis	Skin
Encephalitis	Brain
Enteritis	Bowel, Intestine
Gingivitis	Gums
Glaucoma	Eye
Glossitis	Tongue
Haemophilia	Blood Clotting
Hepatitis	Liver
Lumbago	Small of Back

Mastitis	Breast
Meningitis	Meninges (Membranes Covering Brain)
Nephritis	Kidney
Osteomyelitis	Bones, Bone Marrow
Phlebitis	Veins
Pneumonia	Lungs
Proctitis	Rectum
Psoriasis	Skin
Pyorrhea	Gums
Rhinitis	Nose

Medical Specialities

By: Term → Area or Speciality

Cardiology	Heart
Cerebral (Medicine)	Brain
Dermatology	Skin
Geriatrics	Old People
Gynaecology	Female Reproduction
Haematology	Blood
Histology	Cells
Neurology	Brain and Nerves
Ophthalmology	Eyes
Orthodontics	Teeth, Straightening and Correcting
Orthopaedics	Bones and Joints
Otology	Ear
Paediatrics	Children
Periodontics	Gums
Proctology	Rectum and Lower Intestine
Renology	Kidney
Rheumatology	Joints
Rhinology	Nose
Thoracic (Medicine)	Chest
Toxicology	Poisons
Urology	Urinary Tract, Male Reproduction

Mental Illness and Conditions

By: General

Children; Condition of, Characterised by Inability to Communicate	Autism
Disease; Chronic concern with	Hypochondria
Dressing Up in Clothing of Opposite Sex	Transvestism
Manias:-	
Alcohol, Craving for	Dipsomania
Fire	Pyromania
Food	Phagomania, Sitomania
One Idea	Monomania
Power	Megalomania

Sex (Woman)	Nymphomania
Stealing	Kleptomania
Masochism; Name from	Sacher-Masoch (Austrian novelist)
Mental Institutions; Women/Men	Women many times Men
Phobias;-	
Animals	Zoophobia
Closed Places	Claustrophobia
Crossing Roads	Dromophobia
Crowds	Ochlophobia
Dark	Nyctophobia
Death	Thanatophobia
Dirt	Mysophobia
Eating	Sitophobia, Phagophobia
Foreigners	Xenophobia
Heights	Acrophobia
Insects	Entomophobia
Open Places	Agoraphobia
Pain	Algophobia
Thirteen	Triskaidekaphobia
Thunder and Lightening	Astraphobia
Water	Hydrophobia
Pleasure in being Hurt	Masochism
Pleasure in Hurting others	Sadism
Sadism; Name from	Marquis De Sade
Suicides; Men/Women	More Men

Psychology and Psychiatry

By: General

Behaviourism; Founder	John B.Watson
Child; Desire of Parent of Opposite Sex	Boy: Oedipus Complex. Girl: Electra Complex
Collective Unconscious; Put forward	Carl Jung
Conditioned Reflexes; Associated with	Pavlov (Work with Dogs)
Development Psychology; Swiss Pioneer	Jean Piaget
'Individual Psychology' School	Alfred Adler
Inferiority Complex; Proponent	Alfred Adler
Ink Blot Test; Introducer	Rorschach
Intelligence Test; Pioneer	Alfred Binet
Operant Conditioning; Associated with	B.F.Skinner (Work with Rats)
Personality; Deepest level	Id
Psychoanalysis; Pioneer	Freud
Repressed Feelings; Expression of in psychoanalysis	Catharsis
Whole Personality; Study	Gestalt Psychology

Ideas and Beliefs

Contents

The Bible 187
Christianity 189
Mythological Gods and Goddesses
  By: Category 192
Mythology, General 194
The Occult and Parapsychology 197
Philosophy and Philosophers 198
Religion 199

The Bible

By: General

Aaron: Tribe	Levites
Abraham;-	
Birthplace	Ur
Children	Ishmael (Mother: Hagar), Isaac (Mother: Sarah)
Wives	Sarah, Keturah
Adam and Eve; Children	Cain and Abel
Angels; Mentioned	Michael, Gabriel
Ascension; Traditional site of	Bethany
Baby; Found in Bulrushes by Pharoah's daughter	Moses
Battle; End of World	Armageddon
Beatitudes; Part of	Sermon on the Mount
Bible;-	
Authorised Version, authorised by	King James VI
Books not included in Main	Apocrypha
English translation; 1st	John Wycliffe
Latin translation of	Vulgate
Printed; 1st	Gutenberg Bible
Printed; 1st; English	Coverdale Bible
Roman Catholic; Authorised	Douai or Rheims Bible
Birth; 1st in Bible	Cain
Cain; Eldest son	Enoch
Chariot Driver; Fast	Jehu, King of Israel
Coat of Many Colours; Receives	Joseph
Crucifixion;-	
Place	Calvary/Golgotha
Roman Governor who orders	Pontius Pilate
David;-	
Father	Jesse
Giant kills	Goliath
Kills Goliath with	Stone from Sling
Sons: Well known	Solomon, Absalom, Adonijah
Wives: Well known	Michal, Bathsheba (formerly wife of Uriah)
Destroyed for Disobeying God; Cities	Sodom and Gomorrah
Disciple, doubts resurrection	Thomas
Disciples	Andrew, Bartholomew, James(2), Judas, Judas Iscariot, Mathias, Matthew, Peter, Philip, Simon, Thomas
Donkey; Commanded by God through	Balaam
Elijah; Driven from Israel by	Jezebel
Epistles; Main writer	St Paul
Feast; King of Babylon slain during	Belshazzar
Fiery Furnace; Cast into	Shadrach, Meshach, Abednego

Four Horsemen of the Apocalypse:-

Horsemen	War (Conquest), Famine, Pestilence, Death
Horses	White, Red, Black, Pale (Rider: Death)

Gifts of the Magi	Gold, Frankincense and Myrrh
Gospels; 8th Century; Found in Ireland	Book of Kells

Herod;-

Wife	Herodias
Step-daughter	Salome
Hunter; Great	Nimrod
Isaac; Sons (Twins)	Esau, Jacob
Israel; King; 1st	Saul

Jacob;-

Son; Youngest	Benjamin
Wives	Leah, Rachel

Jesus;-

Baptised	In: River Jordan. By: John the Baptist
Betrayed	By: Judas. In: The Garden of Gethsemane
Birthplace	Bethlehem
Body; Receives, for burial	Joseph of Arimithea
Brings back to life	Lazarus
Home Town	Nazareth
Parents	Mary, Joseph
Resurrection; 1st to see after	Mary Magdalene
Robber; Released in place of	Barabbas

Jezebel; Husband	Ahab
John the Baptist beheaded by	Herod Antipas
Judaea; Independence Movement, 2nd Century BC	Maccabees
King; Commits suicide	King Saul
Lions Den; Escapes from	Daniel
Midianites; Destroys	Gideon
Miracle; 1st according to St John	Turning Water into Wine (Marriage at Cana)
Moses; Elder brother	Aaron
Murder; 1st in Bible	Cain kills Abel
Nebuchadnezzar's Dreams; Interprets	Daniel

New Testament;-

Books	27
English translation; 1st	William Tyndale
Non Jewish author	St Luke

Noah;-

Sons	Shem, Ham, Japheth
Wife	Name never mentioned

Noah's Ark;-

Humans	8
Lands at	Mount Ararat, Turkey
Made from	Gopher wood
Old Testament; 1st Greek Version	Septuagint
Oldest Man	Methuselah (969 years)
Pentateuch	1st 5 books (Genesis, Exodus, Leviticus, Numbers, Deuteronomy)

Psalms;-

Main Author (Attributed)	David
Number	150

Ravens; Feed   Elijah
Sacrifice Son; God commands to   Abraham (to sacrifice Isaac)
Salome; Dance   Dance of the Seven Veils
Salt; Pillar of; Turned into for looking back   Lot's Wife. Looks back at: Sodom and Gomorrah

Samson;-
  Hair cut off by order of   Delilah
  Kills Philistines with   Jaw bone of an ass
  Source of strength   Long hair
Samuel; Tutor   Eli
Shortest Verse   'Jesus Wept'
Slavery; Sold into by brothers   Joseph
St Peter; Original name   Simon (Peter from Petros – Rock)
Synoptic Gospels   Matthew, Mark, Luke
Ten Commandments;-
  Other name   Decalogue
  Received by   Moses
  Written on   Two stone tablets
Tower; Built to reach Heaven   Babel
Tribes of Israel; Descended from Jacob's sons   12
Tricks Father to obtain blessing   Jacob
Twins   Jacob and Esau
Whale; Swallowed by   Jonah
Whirlwind; Carries from Earth   Elijah
Wise Men; Traditional names   Caspar, Melchior, Balthazar
Wrestles to get God's blessing   Jacob
Writing on the Wall   At: Belshazzar's Feast in Babylon. Read by: Daniel

Christianity

By: General
Archbishop of Canterbury;-
  Father and Son   Frederick Temple, William Temple
  1st   St Augustine
  Post War   Fisher, Ramsey, Runcie, Carey
  Protestant; 1st   Thomas Cranmer
Archbishop of York   John Habgood
Benedictines; Robes   Black
Bibles; Put in hotels, etc.; Group   Gideons International
Black Friars; Official name   Dominicans
Cardinal, addressed as   Eminence
Catharist Heresy; Followers   Albigenses
Christian Science; Founder   Mary Baker Eddy
Christmas; When abolished   1647, by Puritan Parliament
Christmas Day, December 25th; Established by   Dionysus, AD 525
Church of England;-
  Doctrines   39 Articles
  1st (legendary)   Glastonbury
  Governing body   General Synod
Clergy; Register of   *Crockford's Clerical Directory*

Coptic Church;-	
Centre	Egypt
Claimed founder	St Mark
Covenanters, term used for	Scottish Presbyterians
Deadly Sins	7. Avarice, Envy, Gluttony, Lust, Pride, Sloth, Wrath
Dominicans; Robes	White Habits, Black Capes
Durham, Bishop of; Controversial	David Jenkins
Ecumenical Council; 1st	Council of Nicaea
Egypt; Church of	Coptic
Encyclical; Pope Paul, 1968	Condemned artificial birth control
Ethiopia; Church of	Coptic
Excommunication; Objects used	Bell, Book and Candle
Fatima (Portugal); Vision of	Lucia dos Santos and cousins, 1917
Festivals;-	
Advent	4th Sunday before Christmas
All Saints Day	November 1st. Former name: All Hallows
Ash Wednesday	1st day of Lent
Candlemas	February 2nd (Purification of the Virgin Mary)
Christmas	Celebrates Jesus' birth
Easter	Commemorates resurrection. Date: 1st Sunday following full moon on or after March 21st (latest April 25th)
Epiphany	Celebrates coming of 3 Wise Men. Date: January 6th
Good Friday	Commemorates Jesus' crucifixion
Lent	Period of 40 days before Easter
Low Sunday	Sunday after Easter
Palm Sunday	Sunday before Easter. Celebrates Jesus' entry to Jerusalem
Pentecost	Descent of Holy Spirit on Apostles
Remembrance Sunday	Sunday closest to Armistice Day. Common name: Poppy Day
Shrove Tuesday	Pancake Day. Day preceding Ash Wednesday
Whitsun	2nd Sunday after Ascension
Franciscans; Other name	Order of Friars Minor
God; Worship abolished	France, 1793
Grey Friars; Official name	Franciscans
Honest to God Debate; Originator	John Robinson
Hymn Writer; Most prolific	Charles Wesley
Inquisition; Ceremony before execution	Auto-da-fe
Iona, Monastery; Founder	St Columba
Jehovah's Witnesses;-	
Founder	C.T.Russell
Magazine	*The Watch Tower*
Jesuits;-	
1st missionary	Francis Xavier
Founder	Ignatius Loyola
Lourdes: Vision of	St Bernadette, 1858
Luther: Theses	95, nailed to door of Wittenberg Church
Lutheranism; Dominant church in	Scandinavia
Martyr: 1st English	St Alban

Meat on Friday; Vatican allows	1966
Methodists; Founder	John Wesley
Monastic Order;-	
English origin (only one)	Gilbertines
Largest; Male	Jesuits
Speaking not allowed (till 1960s)	Trappists
Monk; 1st	St Anthony
Moral Rearmament;-	
Former name	The Oxford Group
Founder	Frank Buchman
Mormons;-	
Also known as	Latter Day Saints
1st leader	Joseph Smith
Subsequent leader	Brigham Young
Patron Saints;-	
Children	St Nicholas
Doctors	St Luke
England	St George
Fishermen	St Peter
France	St Denis
Germany	St Boniface
Ireland	St Patrick
Lost causes	St Jude
Lovers	St Valentine
Scotland	St Andrew
Soldiers	St Michael
Travellers	St Christopher
Wales	St David
Pillars; Ascetics living on	Stylites
Plymouth Brethren; Founder	J.N.Darby
Papacy; Split in	The Great Schism, 1378
Pope;-	
Abdicates; 1st to	Celestine V
Alleged murdered	John Paul I, 1978. Book about: *In God's Name*, by David Yallop
Assassinated	26
Rodrigo Borgia	Alexander VI
Britain; 1st to visit	John Paul II (1982)
British (only one)	Adrian IV, Nicholas Breakspear
Death; Official; Ceremony	Secretary calls name 3 times. Taps head with silver hammer
Directive from	Papal Bull
Double name; 1st	John Paul I (1978)
Escort	Swiss Guard
Female (legendary)	Pope Joan
Infallibility; Promulgated	1870
John Paul II; Former position	Archbishop of Cracow
John Paul II; Name	Karol Wojtyla
Letter sent to churches	Encyclical
Longest reign	Pius IX, 32 years
Non Italian; Last before John Paul II	Adrian VI (1522), Dutch
Selection; Made known by	White smoke from Vatican chimney means selected
Special blessing	Urbi et Orbi
Term 1st used for head of Roman Catholic Church	Gregory VII
Throne	Sedes Gestatoria

Tried and executed after death	Formosus
Youngest	Benedict IX, 12
Prayer book; Compiler; 1st	Thomas Cranmer
Presbyterianism; Founder	John Calvin. In Scotland; John Knox
Priest; Shaven head	Tonsure
Primates	Archbishop of Canterbury ('All England'), Archbishop of York ('England')
Quakers;-	
Founder	George Fox
Proper name	Society of Friends
Roman Catholic Church;-	
Council to correct abuses, 16th Century	Council of Trent
List of forbidden books	*Index Librorum Prohibitorum*
Offices barred to; UK	Sovereign, Lord Chancellor
Roman Emperor; Makes Christianity the official religion	Constantine
Saint;-	
French King	Louis IX
US; 1st	Elizabeth Seton, 1975
Salvation Army; Founder	William Booth
Scotland; Reformation leader	John Knox
Sect; 2nd Century, Promised special knowledge of God	Gnostics
Seventh Day Adventists; Founder	William Miller
Shroud of Christ; Once supposed	Turin Shroud
St Alban, martyred for	Sheltering Amphibalus
St Francis; Birthplace	Assisi
St Nicholas; Bishop of	Myra (by tradition)
St Patrick;-	
Buried at	Downpatrick, Ireland
From	Not Ireland, probably Wales
St Thomas; Martyred at (legendary)	Madras, India
Sunday Schools; Founder	Robert Raikes
Symbol; Early Christian	Fish
Trappists; Proper name	Cistercians of the Strict Observance
Unification Church; Founder	Sun Myung Moon
Vatican Bank; President	Archbishop Marcinkus
White Friars; Proper name	Carmelites
Worldwide Church; Founder	Garner Ted Armstrong

Mythological Gods and Goddesses

By: Category → God, Goddess

Agriculture (Goddess)	
Greek	Demeter
Roman	Ceres
Chief of	
Egyptian	Ammon
Greek	Zeus

Norse	Odin
Roman	Jupiter
Sumerian	Anu
Dawn (Goddess)	
Greek	Eos
Roman	Aurora
Dead	
Egyptian	Anubis
Destruction	
Hindu	Shiva
Domestic Life (The Hearth)	
Greek	Hestia
Roman	Vesta
Earth (Goddess)	
Sumerian, Babylonian	Ninhursag
Earth (God)	
Egypt	Geb
Fertility	
Phoenician	Baal
Fire	
Greek	Hephaestus
Roman	Vulcan
Vedic	Agni
Flowers	
Roman	Flora
Heaven	
Sumerian, Babylonian	Anu
Hunting and the Moon	
Greek	Artemis
Roman	Diana
Love (God)	
Greek	Eros
Roman	Cupid
Love (Goddess)	
Greek	Aphrodite
Norse	Freya
Phoenician	Astarte
Roman	Venus
Marriage	
Greek and Roman	Hymen
Motherhood	
Egyptian	Isis
Peace (Goddess)	
Greek	Irene
Roman	Pax
Poetry and Music	
Greek	Apollo
Sea (Goddess)	
Greek	Amphitrite
Sea	
Greek	Poseidon
Roman	Neptune
Sky (Goddess)	
Egypt	Nut
Sleep	
Greek	Hypnos
Roman	Somnus

Spring (Goddess)	
Greek	Persephone
Roman	Proserpina
Sun	
Egyptian	Ra
Greek	Helios
Hindu	Surya
Roman	Sol
Thunder	
Norse	Thor
Underworld	
Greek	Pluto
Roman	Tartarus
Victory	
Greek	Nike
Roman	Victoria
War	
Greek	Ares
Norse	Tyr
Roman	Mars
Water	
Sumerian, Babylonian	Ea
Wine	
Greek	Dionysus
Roman	Bacchus
Wisdom and Learning	
Egyptian	Thoth
Wisdom (Goddess)	
Greek	Athene
Roman	Minerva
Witchcraft and Magic	
Greek	Hecate
Woods and Fields	
Greek	Pan
Roman	Faunus
Youth (Goddess)	
Greek	Hebe

Mythology, General

By: General

Agamemnon;-	
Killed by	Wife, Clytemnestra
Son, daughter, son-in-law, avenge murder	Orestes, Electra, Pylades
Antigone	Daughter of Oedipus and Jocasta
Aphrodite;-	
Loved by	Adonis
Son	Eros (Greek), Cupid (Roman)
Apollo; Sister of	Diana
Asses ears; Given	King Midas
Assyrians; National God	Ashur
Babylonian Mythology; Supreme God	Anu
Bed; Robber fits captives to it	Procrustes
Boatman to Underworld	Charon

Carries World on his shoulders — Atlas
Carthage; Founder of — Dido
Castor and Pollux; Become on death — Constellation Gemini
Chained to Rock with eagle picking liver — Prometheus
Charybdis — Whirlpool opposite monster Scylla
Children of Uranus and Gaea — Titans
Chimaera; Killer of — Bellerophon
Clytemnestra; Lover — Aegisthus
Cup Bearer — Hebe, Ganymede
Cupid; Portrayed as — Winged boy, with bow and arrow
Deirdre; Kidnapped by (Irish) — King Conchobar. Flees with lover: Naoise

Demeter and Persephone; Rites to honour — Eleusinian Mysteries
Demons; Prince of (Hebrew) — Asmodeus
Doctor; 1st — Aesculapius
Dog; Guarding entrance to Hades — Cerberus (3 headed)
Execution; Friend agrees to take place at — Pythias (Damon takes place)
Eyes; 100 — Argus (half always open)
Fairies; King of — Oberon
Fastest Mortal — Atalanta (beaten by Melanion dropping 3 golden apples)

Fates — 3. Lachesis, Clotho, Atropos
Female Warriors; Race of — Amazons
Fire; Stealer of from Heaven — Prometheus
Fly with Wings — Daedalus and Son, Icarus
Food of the Gods — Ambrosia and Nectar
Furies — 3. Alecto, Megaera, Tisiphone
Giants; Father of (Teutonic) — Ymir
Gold; Everything touched turns to — King Midas
Golden Fleece; Sail in quest of — Jason and Argonauts. Number: 50. Ship: Argo

Gorgons — Euryale, Medusa, Sthena
Graces — 3. Aglaia, Thalia, Euphrosyne
Hall; Souls of heroes go (Norse) — Valhalla
Hawk/Falcon headed; Egyptian God — Horus
Heel; Only vulnerable place — Achilles (held by heel when dipped in River Styx)

Home of Gods — Mount Olympus, Asgard (Norse)
Ibis headed; Egyptian God — Thoth
Invisible; Turns things he touches — Autolycus
Io; Guardian of — Argus (100 eyed)
Jackal headed; Egyptian God — Anubis
Jason; Wife — Medea
Kills with a look; Animal — Basilisk
Kingfishers; Turned into, by Gods — Halcyon and Ceyx
Labours of Hercules/Heracles — 12

Apples from Garden of Hesperides; Stealing
Augean Stables; Cleansing
Cattle of Geryon; Stealing
Cerberus; Bringing Back
Ceryneian Hind; Capturing
Cretan Bull; Capturing
Erymanthian Boar; Capturing
Girdle of Hippolyta; Obtaining

Horses of Diomedes; Fetching
Hydra of Lerna; Killing
Nemean Lion; Fetching pelt of
Stymphalian Birds; Driving off

Labyrinth;-	
Builder of	Daedalus
Creature	Minotaur (slain by Theseus)
Laurel Tree; Transformed into	Daphne
Lohengrin; Father	Parsifal
Loud voice	Stentor (Greek Herald)
Marry; Only man stronger than herself (Germanic)	Brunhild
Medusa; Killer of	Perseus (Using reflection in shield to look at)
Messenger of the Gods	Mercury (Roman), Hermes (Greek)
Minotaur; Killed by	Theseus
Monster; Forest dwelling (Scandinavian)	Troll
Murders Father, Marries Mother	Oedipus
Muses; Parents of	Zeus, Mnemosyne
Muses:-	
Astronomy	Urania
Comedy	Thalia
Dance	Terpsichore
Epic Poetry	Calliope
History	Clio
Love Poetry	Erato
Lyric Poetry	Euterpe
Song and Oratory	Polymnia
Tragedy	Melpomene
Mythical Animals;-	
Basilisk	Can kill with a look
Centaur	Head of a Man, Body and Legs of a Horse
Chimaera	Part Lion, part Goat, part Serpent
Griffin	Head of an Eagle, Body of a Lion
Harpy	Body and Head of a Woman, Feet and Wings of a Vulture
Minotaur	Bull; Head of
Pegasus	Winged Horse
Phoenix	Bird, Rises from its ashes
Satyr	Legs, Ears and Horns of a Goat
Narcissus; Pines away to a voice for	Echo
Nine headed Monster	Hydra
Nymph; Lures ships onto rocks	Siren
Odin; Handmaidens of	Valkyries
Odysseus; Home	Ithaca
Oedipus;-	
Daughter	Antigone
Father	Laius
Mother	Jocasta
One-eyed Giant	Cyclops
Orpheus; Loses Eurydice; Reason	Turns back to look at her
Pandora's Box; Remains after opening	Hope
Paradise for Heroes	Elysium or Elysian Fields
Pegasus; Tamer of	Bellerophon
Penelope; Delays suitors by	Unravelling sewing of canopy
Plumed Serpent; Ruling God (Mexican)	Quetzalcoatl

Poet and Musician; Finest	Orpheus
Poet; Follows wife to Underworld	Orpheus. Wife: Eurydice
Priam; Wife	Hecuba
Procrustes; Killed by	Theseus
Prophecy; Condemned not to be heeded	Cassandra
Race; Promises to marry anyone who beats her	Atalanta
Reflection; Falls in love with own	Narcissus
River; Underworld	Styx
Roll a stone up a hill; Condemned to	Sisyphus
Shield; Made for Jupiter by Vulcan	Aegis
Sphinx, Riddle of; Answers	Oedipus
Statue; Falls in love with	Pygmalion (King of Cyprus)
Stone; Anyone who looks at turns to	Medusa (Gorgon)
Sun Chariot; Loses control of, causing Zeus to strike with thunderbolt	Phaeton
Supreme God (Babylonian)	Marduk
Swims Hellespont to visit Hero	Leander
Swine; Changes Odysseus' men into	Circe
Sword hangs over during feast	Damocles (Courtier of Dionysus)
Trojan War;-	
Cause of	Paris abducts Helen, wife of Menelaus
Greek hero	Ulysses
Greek leader	Agamemnon. Wife: Clytemnestra. Son: Orestes
Greek trick to enter Troy	Trojan Horse. Priest who argues against: Laocoon
Trojan hero	Hector (killed by Achilles)
Twins: Sons of Zeus and Leda	Castor and Pollux
Ulysses; Wife	Penelope
Underworld; Queen of	Persephone
Vishnu; Wife (Hindu)	Lakshmi
Winged Horse	Pegasus
Wise Old Man of the Sea	Nereus. Daughters: Nereids
Woman; 1st	Pandora

The Occult and Parapsychology

By: General

Automatic Writing; Board used for	Planchette
Board used in Spiritualism	Ouija board
Book of Changes, Confucian	I Ching
Divination; Means of:-	
Animal entrails	Haruspicy
Smoke	Capnomancy
Dreams	Oneiromancy
Fire, looking at	Pyromancy
Animal behaviour	Zoomancy
Water	Hydromancy
Double that haunts somebody	Doppelganger
Hypnotic Regression; Irish woman from 'past life' of Virginia Tighe	Bridey Murphy

Lines; Supposedly linking Prehistoric Sites	Ley lines
Metal bending; Famous for	Uri Geller
Moving objects at a distance; Term for	Psychokinesis
Number of the beast	666
Parapsychology; 1st Laboratory researcher	J.B. Rhine, Duke University
Parapsychology Experimental Cards	Zener Cards (Square, Circle, Cross, Star, Wavy Line)
Seer; 16th Century; Prophecy in Verse	Nostradamus
Tarot Cards;-	
Main Division	Major and Minor Arcanas
Number	78
Suits	Wands, Cups, Swords, Pentacles
Theosophical Society; Founder	Helen Blavatsky
Transcendental Meditation; Introduced	Maharishi Mahesh Yogi
Zodiac; Signs	
Aquarius	Water Carrier
Aries	Ram
Cancer	Crab
Capricorn	Goat
Gemini	Twins
Leo	Lion
Libra	Scales
Pisces	Fish
Sagittarius	Archer
Scorpio	Scorpion
Taurus	Bull
Virgo	Virgin

Philosophy and Philosophers

By: General

Anthroposophy; Founder	Rudolf Steiner
Aryan Superiority; French Proponent of	Count Gobineau
Asylum; Spent last years in	Nietzsche
Chinese Philosophy: Opposing Cosmic Modes	Yin (Earth), Yang (Heaven)
Christian Existentialism; Regarded as Founder	Soren Kierkegaard
Cynics; Founder of	Diogenes
Dialectical Logic; Introduced by	George Hegel
Eleatic School; Founder	Parmenides
Four Freedoms (F.D.Roosevelt)	Speech and expression, religion, from fear, from want
Functionalism; Founder	John Dewey
'Greatest happiness of the greatest number'; Put forward	Jeremy Bentham
Knowledge; Philosophical system based on	Gnosticism
Lantern; Carried round to find an honest man	Diogenes

Laughing Philosopher; Known as	Democritus
Linguistic Philosopher; Famous	Ludwig Wittgenstein
Lord Chancellor of England	Francis Bacon
Marx; Philosophy associated with	Dialectical Materialism
Nickname; 'The Dog'	Diogenes
Nominalists; Leader	William of Occam
Occam's Razor	'Entities should not be needlessly multiplied' (Principle of Simplicity)
Parkinson's Law	Work expands so as to fill the time available for its completion.
Peripatetic Philosophers; Leader	Aristotle
Peter Principle	'In a hierarchy every employee tends to rise to his level of incompetence.'
Positivism; Founder	Auguste Comte
Pragmatism; Proponents	William James, C.S.Pierce
Socrates, Pericles; Teacher of	Anaxagoras
Social Contract; Concept; Proponents	Rousseau, Hobbes
Stoicism: Founder	Zeno
Syndicalism; Proponent of	George Sorel
Theosophy; Leading British Proponent	Annie Besant
Tub; Lived in	Diogenes
Utilitarianism; Originator	Jeremy Bentham
Weeping Philosopher; Known as	Heraclitus

Religion

By: General

Note: Excludes Christianity

Ark of the Covenant; Contains	Two Tablets of the Ten Commandments
Baha'i;-	
Founders	Husayn Ali (Baha'u'llah), Ali Mohammed (The Bab)
Holy Book	*Katabi Ikan*
Buddhism;-	
Buddha attains Nirvana under	Bo Tree
Festival; Buddha's birth	Vesak
Founder	Siddhartha Gautama
Indian Emperor; Sponsors	Asoka
Japanese school	Zen
Main schools	Mahayana, Theravada (Hinayana)
State of enlightenment	Nirvana
Tibetan form	Lamaism
Celtic Priests; Ancient Britain	Druids
Confucianism; *Book of Changes*	I Ching
Dionysus; Religion worshipping	Orphism
Hinduism;-	
Caste; Highest	Brahman
Caste; Lowest	Sudras
Epic	*Mahabharata (Bhagavadgita*, Part of)
Festival of light	Divali
1st Book of Scriptures	*Rig Veda*
Incarnation of God	Avatar
Sacred city	Varanasi (Benares)

Sacred duty	Dharma
Sacred river	Ganges
Trinity	Brahma, Shiva, Vishnu
Women; Secluding of	Purdah

Islam;-

Calendar	From Hegira, AD 622, flight of Mohammed from Mecca to Medina
European Country with majority adherence to	Albania
Fasting; Month of	Ramadan
Holy book	Koran
Holy War	Jihad
Ismaili sect; Members in Lebanon	Druze
Main groups	Sunnis (Majority – 90%), Shia
Mohammed; Flight from Mecca to Medina	Hejira
Mohammed; Successors	Caliphs
Prayer; Caller	Muezzin
Prayer; Requirement	5 times a day, Facing Mecca
Requirement for devout, at least once	Pilgrimage to Mecca (Hadj)
Sect; Saudi Arabia	Wahhabi
Sect; Union with God through ecstasy	Sufism
Shia; Main country	Iran
Shia; Main sects	Imam's, Ismailis
Trance obtained by Dancing; Practitioner	(Whirling) Dervish

Jainism; Founder	Mahavira
Japan; Religion of	Shinto

Judaism;-

Bible and teachings; Term for	Torah
Ceremony of adulthood	Bar Mitzvah (At 13 years, 1 day)
Community outside Israel	Diaspora
Ethiopian Jews	Falashas
Excommunicated for heresy, 1656	Spinoza
Extreme Nationalist Party in Biblical times	Zealots
Feast of dedication	Hanukkah
Ghetto; Jewish; Original	Venice
Historian of, in Biblical times	Josephus
Jews who settled in N.W. Europe	Ashkenazim
Jews who settled in Spain and Portugal	Sephardim
Leather Boxes containing scriptures worn during prayers	Phylacteries
Mystical numerological Bible interpretation	Kabbala
New Year	Rosh Hashhanah
Sabbath	Saturday
Sect, Lived by Dead Sea (in Biblical times)	Essenes
State; First to adopt as state religion	Khazars (8th Century AD)
Talmud; Parts	*Mishnah* (Oral tradition), *Gemara* (Interpretations)

Krishna Consciousness; Founder	Swami Prabhupada, 1965
Lamaism; Sects	Red Hat, Yellow Hat
Light and Darkness; Religion based on opposition of	Manichaeism

Natural Spirits; Worship of	Animism
Rome; Priest worshipping a single God	Flamen (Hat: Apex)
Scientology; Founder	Lafayette Ron Hubbard
Sikhism;-	
Founder	Guru Nanak
Holy book	*Granth*
Religious centre	Amritsar (Golden Temple)
Taoism; Founder	Lao-Tze
Theosophy; Founder	Madam Blavatsky
Zen Buddhism;-	
Founder	Bodhidharma
Riddle	Koan
Zoroastrianism;-	
Angel of light	Ahura Mazda (Ormuzd)
Hymns	Gathas
Origin	Persia
Sacred book	*Avesta*
Spirit of Evil	Ahriman or Angra Mainyu

Language and Literature

Contents

Language	**205**
Abbreviations	
By: Abbreviation	205
American English	
By: English Word	207
Codes and Ciphers	208
Derivations	
By: Word	209
Foreign Phrases	
By: Phrase	210
Languages	
By: General	211
By: Language	212
Mottoes	
By: Motto	213
Phrases and Terms	
By: Phrase	213
Quotations	
By: Description	214
By: Quotation	215
Rhyming Slang	
By: Expression	222
Slang	
By: Word	222
Words and Letters	223
Words from Other Languages	
By: Word	223
Literature	**224**
Authors	
By: Description	224
By: Name	226
Autobiography	
By: Title	226
Biography	
By: Title	227
Cartoons and Comics	227
Fiction, Books	
By: Title	229
Fictional Characters and Things	
By: Character	242
By: Description	248
By: Name	248
Fictional Detectives	
By: Name	249
Legendary Characters and Things	
By: Name	250
Literary Movements	
By: Writer	251
Literature	
By: Description	252
Literature and Books,Other	254
Newspapers and Magazines	255
Non Fiction	
By: Title	256
Nursery Rhymes	257
Plays	
By: Title	258
Poetry	
By: Title	263

LANGUAGE
Abbreviations

By: Abbreviations → Meaning

ACAS	Advisory, Conciliation and Arbitration Service
ANZAC	Australia and New Zealand Army Corps
AWACS	Airborne Warning and Control System
AWOL	Absent Without Leave
BAFTA	British Academy of Film and Television Arts
BAOR	British Army of the Rhine (formally 'on')
BBC	British Broadcasting Corporation (originally 'Company')
CAMRA	Campaign for Real Ale
CAP	Common Agricultural Policy
CBI	Confederation of British Industry
COMECON	Council for Mutual Economic Assistance
DERV	Diesel Engine Road Vehicle (diesel-fuel)
ECG	Electro Cardiograph/gram
ECT	Electroconvulsive Therapy
EDP	Electronic Data Processing

EEG	Electro Encephalograph/gram
EFTA	European Free Trade Association
ENSA	Entertainments to National Service Association
EPNS	Electroplated Nickel Silver
ER	Elisabetha Regina (Queen Elizabeth)
ERNIE	Electronic Random Number Indicating Equipment
FAO	Food and Agricultural Organisation
FIFA	Federation Internationale de Football Association
GATT	General Agreement on Tariffs and Trade
GCHQ	Government Communications Headquarters
GCSE	General Certificate of Secondary Education
GESTAPO	Geheime Staatspolizei
GNP	Gross National Product
HGV	Heavy Goods Vehicle
HMSO	Her Majesty's Stationery Office
IBA	Independent Broadcasting Authority
ICBM	Intercontinental Ballistic Missile
INRI	Jesus Nazarenus Rex Judaeorum (Jesus of Nazareth, King of the Jews)
INTERPOL	International Criminal Police Organisation
IQ	Intelligence Quotient
LORAN	Long Range Navigation
MBE	Member of (the Order of) the British Empire
MEP	Member of the European Parliament
MIDI	Musical Instrument Digital Interface
MIRV	Multiple Independently Targetable Re-entry Vehicle
NAAFI	Navy, Army and Air Force Institutes
NASA	National Aeronautics and Space Administration
NATO	North Atlantic Treaty Organisation
NEDC	National Economic Development Council (nickname: Neddy)
NSPCC	National Society for the Prevention of Cruelty to Children
OBE	Officer of (the Order of) the British Empire
OECD	Organisation for Economic Cooperation and Development
OHMS	On Her Majesty's Service
OPEC	Organisation of Petroleum Exporting Countries
OXFAM	Oxford Committee for Famine Relief
P&O	Peninsular and Oriental (Steam Navigation Co.)
PAYE	Pay As You Earn
PDSA	Peoples Dispensary for Sick Animals
PLC	Public Limited Company
PLR	Public Lending Right
PMT	Pre Menstrual Tension

POW	Prisoner of War
PSBR	Public Sector Borrowing Requirement
QED	Quod Erat Demonstrandum ('Which was to be proved')
QUANGO	Quasi Autonomous Non Governmental Organisation
RAC	Royal Automobile Club
RADA	Royal Academy of Dramatic Art
REME	Royal Electrical and Mechanical Engineers
RNLI	Royal National Lifeboat Institution
ROSPA	Royal Society for the Prevention of Accidents
RSPCA	Royal Society for the Prevention of Cruelty to Animals
RUC	Royal Ulster Constabulary
SALT	Strategic Arms Limitation Talks
SAS	Special Air Service
SDI	Strategic Defense Initiative (Star Wars)
SEN	State Enrolled Nurse
SERPS	State Earnings-Related Pension Scheme
SONAR	Sound, Navigation and Radar
SPG	Special Patrol Group
SRN	State Registered Nurse
SS	Schutzstaffel
STD	Subscriber Trunk Dialling
STOL	Short Take off and Landing
SWAT	Special Weapons and Tactical Team
TUC	Trades Union Congress
UFO	Unidentified Flying Object
UNCTAD	United Nations Commission on Trade and Development
UNESCO	United Nations Educational Scientific and Cultural Organisation
UNRRA	United Nations Relief and Rehabilitation Administration
USSR	Union of Soviet Socialist Republics
VDU	Visual Display Unit
VE (Day)	Victory in Europe
VJ (Day)	Victory over Japan
VSO	Voluntary Service Overseas
WAAF	Women's Auxiliary Air Force
WRAC	Women's Royal Army Corps
YMCA	Young Men's Christian Association
YWCA	Young Women's Christian Association

American English

By: English Word → American Equivalent

E.g.: What is the American term for ...?

Aluminium	Aluminum
Autumn	Fall
Bonnet (car)	Hood
Boot (car)	Trunk
Bowler (hat)	Derby

Candy floss	Cotton candy
Cashier	Teller
Chemist's shop	Drug store
Cupboard	Closet
Curtains	Drapes
Dinner jacket	Tuxedo
Draughts	Checkers
Drawing pin	Thumb tack
Estate agent	Realtor
Estate car	Station wagon
Fan light	Transom
Flannel/Face cloth	Wash cloth/rag
Flat	Apartment
Garage (mechanic's)	Body shop
Handbag	Purse
Jumble sale	Rummage sale
Lift	Elevator
Lorry	Truck
Maize	Corn
Motorway	Freeway
Nappy	Diaper
Noughts and Crosses	Tic Tac Toe
Oven	Range
Paraffin	Kerosene
Pavement	Sidewalk
Petrol	Gasoline
Pimple	Zit
Post code	Zip code
Queue	Line
Skirting board	Base board
Solicitor	Attorney
Spanner	Wrench
Suitcase	Valise
Tap	Faucet
Tennis shoes	Sneakers
Toilet	Restroom
Torch	Flashlight
Tram	Streetcar
Trousers	Pants
Truncheon	Nightstick
Underpants	Shorts
Undertaker	Mortician
Verruca	Planter's wart
Vest	Undershirt
Waistcoat	Vest
Wallet	Billfold
Windscreen	Windshield
Zed (letter)	Zee

Codes and Ciphers

By: General

Cipher Machine; German; Used in WWII	Enigma
Distress Code	SOS (formerly CQD)
International Radio Code:-	
A	Alpha (was Able)

B	Bravo (was Baker)
C	Charlie
D	Delta

Morse Code;-

A	–
E	.
O	– – –
S	. . .
T	–
V	. . . –(for Victory)

Derivations

By: Word → Derivation

Algorithm	Arab mathematician Al-Khwarizmi
Armageddon	Biblical scene of battle at end of World. From 'Hill of Megiddo'
Assassin	Hashish used by Middle Eastern Sect
Atlas	1st atlas had picture of Greek God on frontispiece
Bedlam	St Mary of Bethlehem – early lunatic asylum
Bikini	Nuclear test at Bikini atoll in the Pacific
Biscuit	Baked twice
Blurb	Piece written by Gelett Burgess featuring Miss B. Blurb
Bobby (policeman)	Sir Robert Peel, founder of Metropolitan Police
Bob's your uncle	M.J.Balfour, promoted by Lord Robert Salisbury (his uncle)
Bowdlerize	Thomas Bowdler, publisher of expurgated edition of Shakespeare
Boxing Day	Distribution of alms from church boxes
Boycott	Captain Boycott, Irish land agent
Cabal	Charles II's advisers: Clifford, Arlington, Buckingham, Ashley Cooper, Lauderdale
Chauvinism	Nicholas Chauvin, Napoleonic soldier
Cloud-Cuckoo Land	Aristophanes' The Birds
Countdown	Invented by Fritz Lang (film director)
Duffel Coat	Belgian town
Dunce	Duns Scotus, Scottish scholar
Eskimo	Eater of raw flesh
Exchequer	Chess board
Fascism	Fasces, bundle of rods
Fifth Column	Spanish Civil War (General Mola)
Gerrymander	US Vice-President Elbridge Gerry
GI	Government Issue
Great Scott	General Winfield Scott
Grog	Admiral Vernon, who wore a Grogram coat, responsible for diluting rum
Gypsy	Egypt (Believed came from)
Hobson's Choice	Cambridge horse hirer (Always gave horse closest to the stable door)
Hooker	Camp followers of US Civil War General, Joseph Hooker

209

Humble Pie	Umbles, deer's entrails
Jingoism	Musical Hall song ('We don't want to fight but by Jingo if we do')
Juggernaut	Hindu god, Jagganath
Jumbo	Elephant at Barnum and Bailey's circus
Left (and Right) Wing	Positions in French National Convention (1791)
Leotard	Jules Leotard, trapeze artist
Lynch	Captain Lynch, Virginia
Maverick	Sam Maverick
Moron	Invented by Molière (*La Princesse D'Elide*)
Namby Pamby	Ambrose Philips' poetry
Nicotine	Jean Nicot, French diplomat
Nosey Parker	Matthew Parker, Archbishop of Canterbury
Pandemonium	Invented by Milton (*Paradise Lost*)
Pants	St Pantaleon
Philosophy	Love of wisdom
Pommie	Property Of His Majesty (on British convicts' shirts)
Pyrrhic Victory	Pyrrhus, King of Epirus, after disastrous 'victory' at Asculum
Quarantine	Original duration of 40 days
Quisling	Vidkund Quisling, Norwegian traitor in WWII
Quiz	(Supposed) Irish theatre manager's invention for a bet
Red Indians	Believed country to be India when discovered
Robot	Used by Karel Capek (*R.U.R.*)
Sabotage	Sabots, wooden shoes
Salary	Payment in salt
Sandwich	4th Earl of Sandwich, ate while gambling
Saxophone	Antoine Sax, inventor
Serendipity	Horace Walpole; From Serendib, name for Sri Lanka
Sweet Fanny Adams	Murdered 19th Century girl
Teddy Bear	Theodore Roosevelt
Thug	Indian religious cult to goddess Kali
Trilby	George Du Maurier novel
Tureen	Viscount De Turenne
Uncle Sam	Samuel Wilson, US meat packer
Whisky	'Water of Life' (Gaelic)
Writing on the wall	Belshazzar's palace (Bible)

Foreign Phrases

By: *Phrase → Meaning*

A fortiori	With stronger reason
A la mode	According to the fashion
A priori	From cause to effect
Ab initio	From the beginning
Ad infinitum	To infinity
Ad nauseam	To excess
Al fresco	In the open air

Alter ego	The other self
Au fait	Well acquainted with
Bête noir	Black beast – what one hates
Blitzkrieg	Lightning war
Bon mot	Witty saying
Bon vivant	A good liver, one who enjoys life
Bona fide	Genuine
Carte blanche	A blank paper – full authority
Cause célèbre	Well known legal case
Caveat emptor	Let the buyer beware
Ceteris paribus	Other things being equal
Compos mentis	In right mind
Contretemps	An accident
Coup de grâce	Finishing stroke
De facto	Actual
De jure	By law
De rigueur	Required by etiquette
Dei gratia	By God's grace
Déjà vu	'Already seen'
En bloc	In a lump
En famille	With one's family
En masse	All together
En passant	In passing
Esprit de corps	Group spirit
Eureka	I have found it
Ex cathedra	From the chair
Ex officio	By virtue of office
Fait accompli	Already done
Faux pas	False step – an error of behaviour
Hors de combat	Out of the fight
In camera	In secret
Incognito	Unrecognised
Kamikaze	A suicidal attack (Literally: Divine wind)
Modus operandi	Method of working
Mutatis mutandis	With required changes
Nom de guerre	An assumed name
Nom de plume	Pen name
Non sequitur	Something that doesn't follow
Pari passu	Together
Prima facie	On the first view
Sine qua non	The indispensable condition
Sotto voce	In an undertone
Sub judice	Under legal consideration
Sui generis	Of its own kind
Ultra vires	Beyond one's powers
Vice versa	The other way round
Viva voce	By word of mouth
Vox populi	The popular opinion

Languages

By: General

Australian English; Name	Strine
Chinese; Romanised Alphabet	Pinying
Code in WWII; Used as	Navajo Indian language
Egyptian; Ancient; Writing	Hieroglyphics

Esperanto;-	
Inventor	Ludwik Zamenhof
Meaning	One who hopes
French;-	
Alphabet; Letters	25
Latin American country speaking	Haiti
Greek;-	
Alphabet; Letters	24
1st letters	Alpha, Beta, Gamma, Delta, Epsilon
Last letter	Omega
Gypsy language	Romany
India;-	
Classical language	Sanskrit
Official language	Hindi
Ireland; Historic language	Gaelic or Erse
Japanese	Script: Kanji (ideographs), Katagana, Hiragana
Jesus: Main language	Aramaic
Jewish language; Based on German	Yiddish
Latin; Languages derived from	Romance Languages
Letters; Least	Rotokas (Bourgainville Island), 11
Most Spoken	Mandarin Chinese
2nd	English
Oldest; Living	Chinese
Oldest; Written	Sumerian
Pakistan;-	
Main language	Punjabi
Official language	Urdu
Portuguese; South American country speaking	Brazil
Right to Left; Written	Arabic, Mandarin, Hebrew
Romance languages	French, Italian, Spanish, Portuguese Provencal, Rumanian
Script; Downwards	Chinese, Japanese
Serbo Croat; Script	Cyrillic (Serb), Roman (Croats)
Singapore; Official languages	English, Chinese, Malay, Tamil
South Africa; Official languages	Afrikaans, English
South American Indian language; Most spoken	Quechua
Spanish; African country speaking	Equatorial Guinea
Speech; Smallest unit of meaning	Morpheme
Speech: Smallest unit of sound	Phoneme
Switzerland;-	
Most Spoken	German
Official languages	4. French, German, Italian, Romansch

Languages

By: Language → Where spoken

Amharic	Ethiopia
Bengali	Bangladesh, East Bengal
Breton	Brittany
Divehi	Maldive Islands
Dzonghka	Bhutan
Farsi	Iran
Guarani	Paraguay

Kannada	Mysore, India
Khmer	Kampuchea
Kikuyu	Kenya
Malayalam	Kerala, India
Marathi	Maharashtra, India
Portuguese	Portugal, Brazil
Pushtu	Afghanistan
Romansch (Rhaeto-Romanic)	Graubunden, Switzerland
Serbo Croat	Yugoslavia
Sindhi	Pakistan
Sinhalese	Sri Lanka
Siswati	Swaziland
Swahili	East Africa
Tagalog	Philippines (now called Filipino)
Tamil	Tamilnadu, South India. Sri Lanka
Telegu	Andhra Pradesh, India
Urdu	Pakistan
Wolof	West Africa
Yoruba	West Africa

Mottoes

By: Motto → Institution

Ars Gratia Artis	MGM (Art for the sake of Art)
Be prepared	Boy Scouts
Blood and Fire	Salvation Army
Citius, Altius, Fortius	The Olympics (Swifter, Higher, Stronger)
Dieu et Mon Droit	English Royal Motto, Richard I adopted (My God and my Right)
Domine Dirige Nos	City of London (Lord Guide Us)
E Pluribus Unum	On US seal, back of US coins (One out of many)
Honi Soit qui Mal y Pense	Order of the Garter (Evil to him who evil thinks)
In God We Trust	US National Motto (Liberty – In God We Trust, on front of US coins)
My word is my Bond	The Stock Exchange
Nemo me impune lacessit	Order of the Thistle (No one touches me with impunity)
Per ardua ad astra	R.A.F. (Through struggle to the stars)
Power to the People	Black Panthers
Think	IBM
Ubique	The Royal Artillery (Everywhere)
Who Dares Wins	The SAS

Phrases and Terms

By: Phrase → Meaning

Baker's dozen	13
Beefeater	Guard at Tower of London
Cat o' nine tails	Whip with 9 knots
China's Sorrow	Yellow River
Cross the Rubicon	Make an irreversible decision (Julius Caesar taking army into Italy)

Cut the Gordian knot	Overcome a great difficulty (from Alexander the Great cutting knot impossible to untie)
Forty-Niners	Californian gold mines (gold rush of 1849)
Fourth Estate,The	The press
Greatest Show on Earth,The	Barnum and Bailey's circus
Hoi Polloi,The	The mass of people
Mounties,The	Royal Canadian Mounted Police
Old Lady of Threadneedle Street,The	Bank of England (Gilray phrase)
Shank's pony	On foot
Ship of the Desert,The	Camel
Sick Man of Europe,The	Turkey (19th Century)
Splicing the mainbrace	Taking a drink of alcohol
Sublime Porte,The	Turkish government
Take the King's shilling	Enlist in the armed forces
Thin Red Line,The	93rd Highlanders during the Battle of Balaklava
Thunderer,The	*Times* newspaper

Quotations

By: Description → Quotation

E.g.: What did . . . say when . . .

Marie Antoinette; Told the people hadn't enough bread to eat (reputedly)	'Let them eat cake'
Captain Oates; Leaving shelter to commit suicide	'I am just going outside and may be some time'
Cato, Roman Senator; Ending speeches	'Carthage must be destroyed'
Oliver Cromwell; Asking to be painted	'Warts and everything'
Euclid; Asked by Ptolemy for an easy route to his teachings	'There is no royal road to geometry'
W.C.Fields; Asked if he liked children	'I do, if they are properly cooked'
W.C.Fields; Asked why reading Bible at deathbed	'I'm looking for a loophole'
George II; Told General Wolfe is mad	'Mad is he? Then I hope he will bite some of my other Generals'
Pope Gregory; Seeing slaves who he is told are Angles	'Not Angles but Angels'
Nathan Hale; Facing execution	'I only regret that I have but one life to lose for my country'
Edward Heath; On Lonrho	'Unpleasant and unacceptable face of Capitalism'
John Paul Jones; Asked to surrender by a British Captain	'I have not yet begun to fight'
Liberace; After bad reviews	'I cried all the way to the bank'
Lincoln; To General McLellan, not engaging enemy	'If you don't want to use the army I should like to borrow it for a while'
Luther; Before the Diet of Worms	'Here I stand, I cannot do anything else'
Macmillan; When Khruschev banged shoe on table	'I'd like that translated, If I may'

Mallory; Asked why he wanted to climb Everest	'Because it's there'
Sir Charles Napier; Telegram on capturing Sind, 1834	'Peccavi (I have sinned)'
Tsar Nicholas I; Stating best Allies against Britain and France in Crimea	'Generals January and February'
Dorothy Parker; Told President Coolidge is dead	'How can they tell?'
Sheridan; When Edmund Burke ended Commons speech by sticking knife in desk	'The honourable gentleman has brought his knife with him, but where's his fork'
Stanley; When finding Livingstone	'Dr Livingstone I presume'
Sir Philip Sydney; Giving a soldier his water at the battle of Zutphen	'Thy need is greater than mine'
Mark Twain; When his death is mistakenly reported	'Reports of my death have been greatly exaggerated'
Cornelius Vanderbilt; Asked didn't he run a train for the Public's benefit	'The Public be damned'
Oscar Wilde; At US Customs	'I have nothing to declare but my genius'
Oscar Wilde; When told by poet of conspiracy of silence against him (the poet)	'Join it'

Quotations

By: Quotation → Source

E.g.: *Who said . . . / Which work does . . . come from*
Note: *Covers Literature, Sayings*

'Abandon all hope, you who enter here'	Dante (*Divine Comedy*)
'All (animals) are equal, but some (animals) are more equal than others'	George Orwell (*Animal Farm*)
'All children except one grow up'	J.M.Barrie (*Peter Pan* – opening)
'All men are created equal'	US Declaration of Independence
'All the World's a stage, and all the men and women merely players'	Shakespeare (*As You Like It* – Jaques)
'Any man who hates dogs and children can't be all bad'	W.C.Fields (attributed to, actually said of)
'Ask not what your country can do for you, but what you can do for your country'	President Kennedy (Inaugural Address)
'Balance of power'	Sir Robert Walpole
'Beauty is truth, truth beauty'	John Keats (*Ode on a Grecian Urn*)
'The Best laid plans of mice and men'	Robert Burns (*To a Mouse*)
'The Better part of valour is discretion'	Shakespeare (*Henry IV*)
'Big Brother is watching you'	George Orwell (*1984*)
'The Bigger they are the harder they fall'	Bob Fitzsimmons (Asked about forthcoming fight with Jim Jeffreys)
'Blood is thicker than water'	Commodore Tattnall

'The Boy stood on the burning deck' — Felicia Hemans (*Casablanca*). About: Battle of the Nile

'Brevity is the soul of wit' — Shakespeare (*Hamlet*)

'The Buck stops here' — President Truman (notice on desk)

'The Child is Father of the Man' — Wordsworth (*My Heart Leaps Up*)

'The Cinema is truth 24 times a second' — Jean Luc Godard

'The Course of true love never did run smooth' — Shakespeare (*A Midsummer Night's Dream*)

'Cruel, only to be kind' — Shakespeare (*Hamlet*)

'The Curfew tolls the knell of passing day' — Gray (*Elegy written in a Country Churchyard*)

'Don't count your chickens before they are hatched' — Aesop

'Don't waste any time in mourning, organise' — Joe Hill

'Drink to me only with thine eyes' — Ben Jonson

'Each man kills the thing he loves' — Oscar Wilde (*The Ballad of Reading Gaol*)

'East is East and West is West and never the twain shall meet' — Kipling (*The Ballad of East and West*)

'Et tu, Brute' — Shakespeare (*Julius Caesar*)

'The Evil that men do lives after them' — Shakespeare (*Julius Caesar*)

'Faint heart ne'er won a fair lady' — Colman (*Love laughs at Locksmiths*)

'The Female of the species is more deadly than the male' — Kipling (*The Female of the Species*)

'Fight, fight and fight again' — Hugh Gaitskell

'Fools rush in where angels fear to tread' — Alexander Pope (*An Essay on Criticism*)

'For men must work and women must weep' — Charles Kingsley (*The Three Fishers*)

'For whom the bell tolls' — John Donne (*Meditation XVII*)

'Fresh woods and pastures new' — Milton (*Lycidas*)

'Friends, Romans, countrymen, lend me your ears' — Shakespeare (*Julius Caesar*)

'Full many a flower is born to blush unseen' — Gray (*Elegy written in a Country Churchyard*)

'Genius is 1% Inspiration and 99% Perspiration' — Edison

'Genius is an infinite capacity for taking pains' — Carlyle

'The Ghost in the machine' — Gilbert Ryle

'Give me a lever long enough, and I will move the World' — Archimedes

'Give me liberty or give me death' — Patrick Henry

'Global Village' — Marshall McLuhan

'Go West, young man' — Horace Greeley

'God is always on the side of the heaviest batallions' — Voltaire

'God is dead' — Nietzsche

'God moves in a mysterious way' — William Cowper (Hymn)

'God's in his heaven – all's right with the world' — Browning (*Pippa Passes*)

'Government of the people, by the people, for the people'	Lincoln
'Great fleas have little fleas upon their backs to bite 'em'	De Morgan
'The Greatest happiness of the greatest number'	Jeremy Bentham
'He can run but he can't hide'	Joe Louis (about Billy Conn)
'He speaks to me as if I were a public meeting'	Queen Victoria (of Gladstone)
'He who binds to himself a joy, Does the winged life destroy'	William Blake (*Auguries of Innocence*)
'Hell hath no fury like a woman scorned'	Congreve (derived from)
'Hell is other people'	Jean-Paul Sartre (*In Camera*)
'History is bunk'	Henry Ford
'The History of the World is but the biography of great men'	Thomas Carlyle
'History will absolve me'	Fidel Castro (when on trial)
'Hope springs eternal in the human breast'	Pope (*An Essay on Man*)
'A horse a horse my kingdom for a horse'	Shakespeare (*Richard III*)
'How do I love thee? Let me count the ways'	Elizabeth Barrett Browning (*Sonnets from the Portuguese*)
'How doth the little busy bee'	Isaac Watts
'I am monarch of all I survey'	Cowper (*The Solitude of Alexander Selkirk*)
'I am on the side of the angels'	Disraeli (criticising Darwin)
'I am the greatest'	Muhammad Ali
'I am the master of my fate, I am the Captain of my soul'	William Henley (*Invictus*)
'I cannot and will not cut my conscience to fit this year's fashion'	Lillian Hellman
'I come to bury Caesar not to praise him'	Shakespeare (*Julius Caesar* – Anthony)
'I could not love thee, dear, so much, lov'd I not honour more'	Richard Lovelace (*To Lucasta on going to the wars*)
'I don't know what effect they will have upon the enemy, but by God they frighten me'	Duke of Wellington (of New Officers)
'I have a dream'	Martin Luther King (speech in Washington)
'I have nothing to offer but blood, toil, tears and sweat'	Churchill
'I have seen the future and it works'	Lincoln Steffens (of USSR)
'I know I have the body of a weak and feeble woman, but I have the heart and stomach of a King'	Queen Elizabeth I
'I married beneath me, all women do'	Nancy Astor
'I must go down to the sea again'	John Masefield (*Sea Fever*)
'I think, therefore I am'	Descartes
'Ich bin ein Berliner'	J.F.Kennedy (speech in Berlin)
'If God did not exist it would be necessary to invent him'	Voltaire
'If I have seen further, it is by standing on the shoulders of giants'	Isaac Newton

'If I should die think only this of me' — **Rupert Brooke** (*The Soldier*)

'If music be the food of love, play on' — **Shakespeare** (*Twelfth Night* – opening)

'If they come for me in the morning, they will come for you at night' — **Angela Davis**

'If Winter comes, can Spring be far behind' — **Shelley** (*Ode to the West Wind*)

'Ignorance is bliss' — **Thomas Gray** (*Ode on a Distant Prospect of Eton College*)

'I'm going to spend, spend, spend' — **Vivian Nicholson** (Pools winner)

'In the future, everyone will be famous for 15 minutes' — **Andy Warhol**

'In the long run we are all dead' — **J.M. Keynes**

'In the Spring a young man's fancy lightly turns to thoughts of love' — **Tennyson** (*Locksley Hall*)

'In two words, Impossible' — **Sam Goldwyn** (attributed)

'Include me out' — **Sam Goldwyn** (attributed)

'Into each life some rain must fall' — **Longfellow** (*The Rainy Day*)

'Into the valley of death rode the six-hundred' — **Tennyson** (*The Charge of the Light Brigade*)

' "Is there anybody there ?" said the traveller, knocking on the moonlit door' — **De la Mare** (*The Listeners*)

'It is a wise father that knows his own child' — **Shakespeare** (*Merchant of Venice*)

'It is better to die on your feet than live on your knees' — **La Pasionaria** (Spanish Civil War)

'It is magnificent but it is not war' — **General Pierre Bosquet** (French General – referring to Charge of the Light Brigade)

'It will be years – and not in my time – before a woman will lead the Party and become Prime Minister' — **Margaret Thatcher** (1974)

'It's worse than a crime, it's a blunder' — **Talleyrand** (of Napoleon)

'Kind hearts are more than coronets' — **Tennyson** (*Lady Clara Vere de Vere*)

'Knowledge is Power' — **Francis Bacon**

'The Lady's not for turning' — **Margaret Thatcher**

'The Lamps are going out all over Europe' — **Edward Gray** (Foreign Secretary; WWI)

'Laugh and the world laughs with you, weep, and you weep alone' — **Ella Wilcox** (*Solitude*)

'Let no man write my epitaph' — **Robert Emmett** (sentenced to death)

'L'Etat c'est moi' (I am the State) — **Louis XIV**

'Liberty, Equality, Fraternity' — **(French) Declaration of the Rights of Man**

'Lies, damned lies and statistics' — **Disraeli**

'The Life of man (in a state of nature) is solitary, poor, nasty, brutish and short' — **Thomas Hobbes**

'Lions led by donkeys' — **Max Hoffman** (of British Soldiers, WW1)

'A little learning is a dangerous thing' — **Pope** (*An Essay on Criticism*)

'Loves young dream' — **Thomas Moore**

'Mad dogs and Englishmen, Go out in the noon-day sun' — **Noel Coward**

'Man is born free and everywhere he is in chains' — **Rousseau**

'Manners maketh man'	William of Wykeham
'Mass of men lead lives of quiet desperation'	Thoreau (*Walden*)
'The Medium is the message'	Marshall McLuhan
'Men seldom make passes, At girls who wear glasses'	Dorothy Parker
'The Moving finger writes and having writ moves on'	*Rubaiyat of Omar Khayyam*
'Mr Balfour's Poodle'	Lloyd George (of House of Lords)
'Music has charms to sooth a savage breast'	Congreve (*The Mourning Bride*)
'My heart leaps up when I behold, A rainbow in the sky'	Wordsworth (*My Heart Leaps Up*)
'Necessity is the mother of invention'	Kingsley (*The Twin Rivals*)
'Neither a borrower or a lender be'	Shakespeare (*Hamlet*)
'Never in the field of human conflict was so much owed by so many to so few'	Churchill (referring to Battle of Britain pilots)
'Nice guys finish last'	Leo Durocher (baseball manager)
'No man is an island'	John Donne (*Meditation XVII*)
'Nothing is certain but death and taxes'	Benjamin Franklin
'Now is the winter of our discontent made glorious summer'	Shakespeare (*Richard III* – Opening)
'O what a tangled web we weave, when first we practise to deceive'	Sir Walter Scott (*Marmion*)
'Oh liberty, what crimes are committed in your name'	Madame Roland
'Oh to be in England now that April's there'	Browning (*Home-Thoughts, from Abroad*)
'Old Soldiers never die, they simply fade away'	General McArthur (Quoting a song)
'Once more into the breach dear friends'	Shakespeare (*Henry V*)
'One swallow does not make a Summer'	Aristotle
'The Only good Indians I ever saw were dead'	General Philip Sheridan (US)
'The Only thing we have to fear is fear itself'	F.D.Roosevelt
'Our (My) country right or wrong'	Stephen Decatur
'Out damned spot'	Shakespeare (*Macbeth*)
'The Paths of glory lead but to the Grave'	Gray (*Elegy written in a Country Churchyard*)
'Patriotism is the last refuge of a scoundrel'	Samuel Johnson
'Peace for our time'	Neville Chamberlain (returning from Munich, 1938)
'The Pen is mightier than the sword'	Bulwer Lytton
'The People are like water and the army is like a fish'	Mao Tse Tung
'Politics is the art of the possible'	Rab Butler
'Power tends to corrupt and absolute power corrupts absolutely'	Lord Acton
'Power without responsibility, the privilege of the harlot throughout the ages'	Baldwin (about the Press)

'Property is theft'	Proudhon
'The Public be damned'	Cornelius Vanderbilt
'Publish and be damned'	Duke of Wellington
'Put your trust in God and keep your powder dry'	Oliver Cromwell
'The Quality of mercy is not strained'	Shakespeare (*Merchant of Venice*)
'Quoth the Raven, Nevermore'	Edgar Allan Poe (*The Raven*)
'Religion is . . . the opium of the people'	Karl Marx
'Reports of my death are greatly exaggerated'	Mark Twain
'The Rest is silence'	Shakespeare (*Hamlet* – his last words)
'A Riddle wrapped in a mystery inside an enigma'	Churchill (of Soviet Union)
'Ring out the old, Ring in the new'	Tennyson (*In Memoriam*)
'Rivers of blood'	Enoch Powell
'A Rose by any other name would smell as sweet'	Shakespeare (*Romeo and Juliet*)
'Rose is a rose is a rose'	Gertrude Stein
'Season of mists and mellow fruitfullness'	Keats (Ode to Autumn)
'Shall I compare thee to a Summer's day'	Shakespeare (Sonnet No.18)
'Ships that pass in the night'	Longfellow (*Tales of a Wayside Inn*)
'Shoot, if you must, this old grey head but spare your country's flag, she said'	John Whittier (*Barbara Frietchie*)
'Some are born great, some achieve greatness, some have greatness thrust upon them'	Shakespeare (*Twelfth Night* – Malvolio)
'Speak softly and carry a big stick'	Theodore Roosevelt
'Stone walls do not a prison make, Nor iron bars a cage'	Richard Lovelace (*To Althea, from prison*)
'Tell truth and shame the devil'	Shakespeare (*Henry IV*)
'Theirs not to reason why, theirs but to do and die'	Tennyson (*Charge of the Light Brigade*)
'There are more things in heaven and earth (Horatio) than are dreamt of in your philosophy'	Shakespeare (*Hamlet*)
'There is no such thing as a free lunch'	J.K.Galbraith
'There is some corner of a foreign field, that is forever England'	Rupert Brooke (*The Soldier*)
'There's a sucker born every minute'	P.T.Barnum
'They also serve who only stand and wait'	Milton (*On his Blindness*)
'A Thing of beauty is a joy forever'	Keats (*Endymion*)
'This above all, To thine own self be true'	Shakespeare (*Hamlet*)
'This is the way the world ends, Not with a bang but a whimper'	T.S.Eliot (*The Hollow Men*)
'This sceptred isle'	Shakespeare (*Richard II*)
'Tis better to have loved and lost, than never to have loved at all'	Tennyson (*In Memoriam*)
'To be or not to be, that is the question'	Shakespeare (*Hamlet*)
'To each according to his needs, from each according to his abilities'	Louis Blanc

'To err is human, to forgive divine' — Pope (*An Essay on Criticism*)

'To make Britain a fit country for heroes to live in' — Lloyd George (1918)

'Tread softly, because you tread on my dreams' — W.B.Yeats (*Cloths of Heaven*)

'Two nations' — Disraeli

'Under a spreading chestnut tree, the village smithy stands' — Longfellow (*The Village Blacksmith*)

'Uneasy lies the head that wears a crown' — Shakespeare (*King Henry IV Part 2*)

'Unhand me, sir' — Trollope (*Barchester Towers* – Mrs Proudie)

'The Unspeakable in pursuit of the uneatable' — Oscar Wilde (of foxhunting)

'Variety's the spice of life' — Cowper (*The Task*)

'Veni Vidi Vici (I came, I saw, I Conquered)' — Julius Caesar

'A Verbal contract isn't worth the paper it's written on' — Sam Goldwyn (attributed)

'Virtue is its own reward' — Prior (*Imitations of Horace*)

'War is hell' — General Sherman

'War is the continuation of policy by other means' — Von Clausewitz

'Water, Water everywhere nor any drop to drink' — Coleridge (*The Rhyme of the Ancient Mariner*)

'We are not amused' — Queen Victoria

'We are such stuff as dreams are made on' — Shakespeare (*The Tempest* – Prospero)

'We must indeed all hang together or, most assuredly, we shall all hang separately' — Benjamin Franklin (Signing Declaration of Independence)

'We're more popular than Jesus now' — John Lennon

'What this country needs is a good five cent cigar' — Marshall (US Vice-President)

'What's good for General Motors is good for the country' — Charles Wilson

'When a man knows he is to be hanged in a fortnight, it concentrates his mind wonderfully' — Samuel Johnson

'White heat . . . of this revolution' — Harold Wilson

'White man's burden' — Rudyard Kipling

'Who steals my purse steals trash' — Shakespeare (*Othello*)

'Will no one rid me of this turbulent priest?' — Henry II (of Becket)

'Wind of Change' — Harold Macmillan (Speech to South African Parliament)

'Winning isn't everything, It's the only thing' — Vince Lombardi

'A Woman is only a woman, but a good cigar is a smoke' — Rudyard Kipling (*The Betrothed*)

'Woodman spare that tree' — George Pope Morris

'The World is so full of a number of things, I'm sure we should all be as happy as kings' — R.L. Stevenson (*Happy Thought*)

'The World must be made safe for democracy'	Woodrow Wilson (1917)
'Yes, Virginia, there is a Santa Claus'	New York Sun (Reply to 8 year old Virginia O'Hanlon)
'You are all of a lost generation'	Gertrude Stein (to Hemingway)
'You can fool all the people some of the time, but you cannot fool all the people all the time'	Lincoln
'You can have it any colour as long as it's black'	Henry Ford (of cars)
'You cannot be serious'	John McEnroe (to Wimbledon umpire)
'Youth is wasted on the young'	G.B.Shaw

Rhyming Slang

By: Expression → Meaning

Apples and pears	Stairs
April showers	Flowers
Barnet Fair	Hair
Cain and Abel	Table
Daisy roots	Boot
Dicky (Dirt)	Shirt
Half inch	Pinch (steal)
Hampstead Heath	Teeth
Jam jar	Car
Loaf (of bread)	Head
Pen and ink	Stink
Pig's ear	Beer
Plates (of meat)	Feet
Rosy lea	Tea
Sausage (and mash)	Cash
Tit for tat	Hat
Tommy Tucker	Supper

Slang

By: Word → Meaning

Ack-ack	Anti-aircraft guns
Ackers	Money
Banger	Sausage
Beak	Magistrate
Billabong	Waterhole (Australia)
Blue-stocking	Very educated woman
Bobby	Policeman (from Sir Robert Peel)
Butty	Sandwich
Chow	Food
Dinkum	Honest (Australia)
G Men	FBI agents
Gaffer	Boss, foreman
Honkey	White person
Matilda	Knapsack (Australia)
Monicker	Name
Pompey	Portsmouth
Spud	Potato
Sweeney,The	Flying squad

Words and Letters

By: General

Letters; Frequency;-

1st	E
2nd	T
3rd	A
4th	O
5th	N
6th	R

Longest; In *Oxford English Dictionary*	Floccipaucinihilipilification
Rhyme; Common word without	Oblige
Typewriter; Top line; Longest common word using letters	Proprietory
Vowels; In correct order	Abstemiously, Facetiously
Word; Consonants; Highest proportion of	(Y counted as vowel) Strengths
Words; Spoken; Most common	I

Words; Written; Frequency;-

1st	The
2nd	Of
3rd	And
4th	A
5th	To
6th	In

Words from Other Languages

By: Word → Language of Origin

E.g: From what language did the word . . . originate

Admiral	Arabic
Almanac	Arabic
Anorak	Eskimo
Bazaar	Persian
Bizarre	Basque
Budgerigar	Australian (Aborigine)
Caravan	Persian
Coffee	Turkish
Curry	Tamil
Divan	Persian
Dungarees	Hindi
Hammock	Taino (West Indies)
Jungle	Hindi
Ketchup	Malay
Khaki	Persian
Kiosk	Turkish
Marmalade	Portuguese
Mattress	Arabic
Ombudsman	Norwegian
Pyjamas	Hindi
Raffia	Malay
Shampoo	Hindi
Taboo	Polynesian (Tonga)
Tattoo	Polynesian (Tahiti)
Tycoon	Japanese/Chinese
Ukelele	Hawaiian
Yoghurt	Turkish

LITERATURE
Authors

By: Description → Author

Abandoned Novels because of adverse reaction	Thomas Hardy
Abandoned Writing at 19 to be a salesman	Rimbaud
Asylum; At Charenton; Ended life in	Marquis De Sade
Asylum; In Paris; Died in	Guy de Maupassant
Banished;-	
By Napoleon III	Victor Hugo
To Black Sea	Ovid
Bear; Kept	Lord Byron
Bicycle; Learned to ride at 67	Tolstoy
Biographist; French	Andre Maurois
Book; 1st English printer	William Caxton
Botanist; Noted	Beatrix Potter
Bottles; Stuck labels on, at 12	Charles Dickens
Buried Poems with wife; Later retrieved	Dante Gabriel Rossetti
Couldn't Speak English till 19; English novelist	Joseph Conrad
Channel Islands; Forced to leave France for	Victor Hugo
Dean;-	
of St Patrick's Cathedral, Dublin	Jonathan Swift
of St Paul's	John Donne
Deported from Britain as IRA member	Brendan Behan
Detective novelist; 1st; Considered	Wilkie Collins (*The Moonstone*)
Detective story; 1st writer of; Considered	Edgar Allan Poe
Disappeared for several weeks, 1926	Agatha Christie
Drury Lane Theatre; Manager of	Sheridan
Duke of Weimar, Minister of State	Goethe
Enslaved, then ransomed	Cervantes
Exile; Spent last 20 years of life in	Dante
Expelled From Eton for stabbing	Shelley
Expelled From Oxford	Shelley
Family; Broke with when 82	Tolstoy
Farces; French playwright famous for	Feydeau
Fascist Supporting Broadcasts from Italy; Made	Ezra Pound
Father:-	
Imprisoned for debt	Charles Dickens
Miner	D.H.Lawrence
Napoleonic General	Alexandre Dumas, Victor Hugo
Fatwa (Islamic Death Sentence); Issued against	Salman Rushdie
Fire; Morbid fear of	Thomas Gray
Fled Country to avoid creditors	Dostoyevsky
Folk Tales; Compiler of; French	Charles Perrault
France; Minister of Culture	Andre Malraux
Gambler, compulsive	Dostoyevsky
Governor General of Canada	John Buchan
Halley's Comet; Born and died during	Mark Twain
Hard Labour; 4 years; Served in Siberia	Dostoyevsky

Heart; Stolen by cat	Thomas Hardy
Horse Racing; Background to books	Dick Francis
Illustrator; Bizarre pictures, including Dante's *Inferno*	Gustave Doré
Imprisoned for;-	
Attempted murder	Brendan Behan
Debt	Daniel Defoe
Embezzlement	O.Henry
Shooting Rimbaud	Paul Verlaine
Inspiration; Never met	Dante (Beatrice)
Henry Irving; Secretary to	Bram Stoker
Jockey; Former	Dick Francis
Kennedy Inauguration; Recited poem at	Robert Frost
Killed by Fascists, 1936; Spanish poet	Federico Garcia Lorca
Killed;-	
Actor in duel	Ben Jonson
Mother	Mary Lamb
Lepanto; Battle of; Fought at	Cervantes
Lesbos; Greek love poet, lived on	Sappho
Most Written About person	Shakespeare
Mother; Slave	Alexandre Dumas (Père)
MP	Sheridan
Murder; Branded for	Ben Jonson
Murderer and Thief	Francois Villon
Mussolini; Charged with treason for supporting	Ezra Pound
New York Mayor, Candidate for	Norman Mailer
Nobel Prize; Refused	Jean-Paul Sartre
Nobel Prize Winner; Literature, 1st, US	Sinclair Lewis
Novelist; 1st Woman	Mrs Aphra Behn (Oroonoko)
Novelist; Wrote only poetry for last 32 years of life	Thomas Hardy
Olympic Games, Ancient; Composed odes to	Pindar
Opium Addict	Coleridge
Orphanage; Abandoned at	Harold Robbins
Pillory; Sentenced to	Daniel Defoe
Play; More than 1 character in; 1st to include	Aeschylus
Poet; 1st known; English	Caedmon
Poet Laureate	Ted Hughes
1st (Official)	John Dryden
Previous	John Betjeman
Writes no poetry as	Wordsworth
Poet's Corner; 1st to be buried at	Chaucer
Postbox; Credited with inventing	Anthony Trollope
Punctuation and Spelling; Ignores	E.E. Cummings
QC, Divorce Barrister	John Mortimer
Quoted; Most	Shakespeare
Rags to Riches stories	Horatio Alger
Ransomed after capture as soldier	Chaucer
Reprieved from execution at last minute	Dostoyevsky
Samoa; Died in	R.L. Stevenson
Sentenced;-	
For letter in defence of Dreyfus	Emile Zola (*J'Accuse*)
To death for murdering a priest	Francois Villon
Shakespeare; Expurgator of works	Bowdler

Shot wife by accident	William Burroughs
Skull Cap, Cycle Clips; Wears when writing	Frank Richards
Stammer; Noted	Charles Lamb
Stamp Distributor in Westmorland	Wordsworth
Stillborn; Left at birth as	Thomas Hardy
Suicide; Forced to commit by Nero	Seneca
Trieste; Responsible for seizing, 1919	Gabriele D' Annunzio
Trousers Worn (by Female) shocked society	George Sand
U and Non U; Classified	Nancy Mitford
Unpublished; Nearly all work at death	Emily Dickinson
Wrote most work before breakfast	Trollope
WWII; Broadcast from Germany during	P.G.Wodehouse

Authors

By: Name → General

Aesop	Slave. Writer of fables
Brontës	
Brother	Branwell
Home	Haworth, Yorkshire
Sisters	Anne, Charlotte, Emily
Chaucer	Patron: John of Gaunt
Dickens	
Father imprisoned in	Marshalsea prison
Favourite novel	*David Copperfield*
Illustrator	Phiz
Semi-autobiographical novel	*David Copperfield*
Unfinished novel	*The Mystery of Edwin Drood*
Worked at	Warren's Boot-Blacking Factory
Samuel Beckett	
From	Ireland
Lives in	France
Lord Byron	Died: Fighting for Greek independence
Shakespeare	
Account used for historical plays	Holinshed's *Chronicles*
Birthplace	Stratford on Avon
Children	3
1st Play	*Henry VI*
Inspiration for sonnets	'Dark Lady' (Supposedly Mary Fitton)
Last complete play	*The Tempest*
Lived in reigns of	Elizabeth I, James I
Shortest Play	*The Comedy of Errors*
Wordsworth	
Great friendship	Coleridge
Lived most of life in	Grasmere

Autobiography

By: Title → Author

Autobiography of Alice B.Toklas,The	Gertrude Stein
Bound for Glory	Woody Guthrie
Brief Lives	John Aubrey

Chronicles of Wasted Time	Malcolm Muggeridge
Coal Miner's Daughter	Loretta Lynn
Confessions	Rousseau
Dear Me	Peter Ustinov
Every Other Inch A Lady	Beatrice Lilley
Goodbye to All That	Robert Graves
Happy Hooker,The	Xaviera Hollander
I Paid Hitler	Baron Von Thyssen
Inside the Third Reich	Albert Speer
Love is a Many Splendoured Thing	Han Suyin
Mein Kampf	Hitler
Moon's a Balloon,The	David Niven (1st volume)
Moonwalk	Michael Jackson
My Double Life	Sarah Bernhardt
My Wicked Wicked Ways	Errol Flynn
Naked Civil Servant,The	Quentin Crisp
Ordeal	Linda Lovelace
Polly Wants a Zebra	Michael Aspel
Spend, Spend. Spend	Vivian Nicholson (Pools winner)
Summoned by Bells	John Betjeman (in verse)
Testament of Youth	Vera Brittain (1st volume)
To Hell and Back	Audie Murphy
Where's the Rest of Me?	Ronald Reagan
World Within World	Stephen Spender
Yes I Can	Sammy Davis Jnr.

Biography

By: Title → Author, Subject

Death of a President	William Manchester. About: J.F.Kennedy
Eminent Victorians	Lytton Strachey
Life and Memorable Acts of George Washington,The	Mason Weems
Life of Samuel Johnson,The	James Boswell
Lives of the Noble Greeks and Romans	Plutarch
Lives of the Caesars	Suetonius
Mommie Dearest	Christina Crawford. About: Joan Crawford
Profiles in Courage	John Kennedy, About: Famous Americans
Salad Days	Douglas Fairbanks Jnr.
Young Man with a Horn	Dorothy Baker. About: Bix Biederbecke

Cartoons and Comics

By: Title → Creator, General

Absurd Mechanical Contrivances; Drawings of	William Heath Robinson
Alfred E.Neumann	Appears in: *Mad* magazine
Andy Capp	Reg Smythe
Wife	Florrie (Flo')
Asterix the Gaul	Rene Goscinny and Albert Uderzo
Barry McKenzie	Barry Humphries
Fred Basset	Graham

Beano	
Founded	1938
Original cartoon still in	Lord Snooty and his Pals
Beetle Bailey	Mort Walker
Camp	Camp Swampy
Believe It or Not	Robert Ripley
Blondie	Chic Young
Married to	Dagwood Bumstead
Boss Tweed; Cartoons about	Thomas Nast
Bringing up Father	George McManus
Father	Jiggs
Married to	Maggie
Bristow	Frank Dickens
Captain Marvel	Billy Batson
Comics; Main publisher; UK	DC Thompson, Dundee
Dandy	
Founded	1937
Original cartoons still in	Korky the Cat, Desperate Dan
Daughter Nina's name in cartoons;	
Hides	Al Hirschfeld
Dennis the Menace	Frank Ketcham
Surname	Mitchell
Dick Tracy	Chester Gould
Doonesbury	Garry Trudeau
Dropping the pilot	Sir John Tenniel
About	Kaiser Wilhelm II dismissing Bismarck (the pilot)
Felix the Cat	Otto Mesmer
1st; strip	Mutt and Jeff
Flash Gordon	Alex Raymond
Flook	Wally Fawkes, Peter Lewis
Fosdyke Saga,The	Bill Tidy
The Gambols	Barry Appleby
Garfield	Jim Davis
If	Steve Bell
Jane	Norman Pett
Katzenjammer Kids	Rudolf Dirks
Names	Hans and Fritz
Lil Abner	Al Capp
Lives in	Dogpatch
Parents	Mammy and Pappy Yokum
Little Orphan Annie	Harold Grey
Dog	Sandy
Guardian	Daddy Warbucks
Servant	Punjab
Modesty Blaise	Peter O'Donnell
Mutt and Jeff	Bud Fisher
Peanuts	Charles Schulz
Beagle	Snoopy
Bird	Woodstock
Charlie in love with	Little red haired girl
Main characters	Charlie Brown, Lucy Van Pelt
Piano player	Schroeder
Uses blanket	Linus
The Perishers	Maurice Dodd
Pogo	Walt Kelly
Pogo; Animal	Possum

Lives in	Okefenokee swamp
Popeye	Elzie Siegar
Pullitzer Prize winner	Doonesbury
Superman	Jerry Siegel, Joe Shuster
1st appears in	Action Comics No 1
Terry and the Pirates	Milton Caniff
Tintin	Hergé (Georges Remi)
TUC Carthorse	Low
Wizard Of Id,The	Brant Parker, Johnny Hart

Fiction, Books

By: Title → Author, Other Information

Adam Bede	George Eliot
Admirable Crichton,The	Sir James Barrie
Master	Lord Loam
Title	Butler
Adventures of Huckleberry Finn,The	Mark Twain
Aeneid,The	Virgil
African Queen,The	C.S.Forester
Title	Boat
Agony and the Ecstasy,The	Irving Stone
Alexandria Quartet,The	Lawrence Durrell
Books	Justine, Balthazar, Mountolive, Clea
Ali Baba and the 40 Thieves	
Slave Girl	Morgana
Words to open the cave	'Open Sesame'
Alice in Wonderland	Lewis Carroll
Croquet	Mallets – Flamingoes, Balls – Hedgehogs
Illustrator	Sir John Tenniel
Smokes Hookah	Caterpillar
Vanishes, leaving smile	Cheshire Cat
Written for	Alice, Lorina, Edith Liddell
All Creatures Great and Small	James Herriot
Theme	Yorkshire vet
All Quiet on the Western Front	Erich Maria Remarque
American Tragedy,An	Theodore Dreiser
Central character	Clyde Griffiths
Amorous Adventures of Moll Flanders, The	Daniel Defoe
Moll Flanders born in	Newgate Prison
Transported to	Virginia
And Quiet Flows the Don	Mikhail Sholokhov
Angel Pavement	J.B.Priestley
Animal Farm	George Orwell
Farm	Manor Farm
Farmer	Jones
Leader	Napoleon (the pig)
Published	1949
Anna of the 5 Towns	Arnold Bennett
Anna Karenina	Leo Tolstoy
Anne of Green Gables	L.M.Montgomery
Set in	Prince Edward Island, Canada
Surname	Shirley

Arabian Nights,The
   Collector — Sir Richard Burton
   Husband — Shalimar
   Original Title — *Alf Layla Wa Layla*
   Storyteller — Scheherezade
   Theme — Tells stories for 1001 nights to prevent execution

Armageddon — Leon Uris
Armies of the Night — Norman Mailer
Around the World in 80 days — Jules Verne
   Indian Widow — Aouda
   Central Character — Phileas Fogg
   Starts at — Reform Club
   Valet — Passepartout
Arrowsmith — Sinclair Lewis
Atlas Shrugged — Ayn Rand
Barchester Towers — Anthony Trollope
Barnaby Rudge — Charles Dickens
   Set during — Gordon riots
Ben Hur — Lew Wallace
   Accused of — Attempted murder of Governor
   Chariot Race with — Messala
   Mother and Sister cured by Jesus of — Leprosy
   Title — Judah Ben Hur
Big Sleep,The — Raymond Chandler
Billy Budd — Herman Melville
   Antagonist — Petty Officer Claggart
Billy Bunter — Frank Richards
   Sister — Bessie
Black Beauty — Anna Sewell
   Title — Horse
Bleak House — Charles Dickens
   Court case — Jarndyce v Jarndyce
   Rag and Bone Man — Krook
   Title — John Jarndyce's home
Bonjour Tristesse — Francoise Sagan
Book of Nonsense,The — Edward Lear
Borrowers,The — Mary Norton
Bostonians,The — Henry James
Box of Delights,The — John Masefield
Brave New World — Aldous Huxley
Breakfast at Tiffany's — Truman Capote
   Central Character — Holly Golightly
Brideshead Revisited — Evelyn Waugh
   Central Character — Captain Charles Ryder
   Children — Brideshead, Julia, Cordelia
   Stationed at — Brideshead, home of the Marchmains
Brighton Rock — Graham Greene
   Gang leader — Pinkie Brown
Brothers Karamazov,The — Fyodor Dostoyevsky
   Brothers — Dmitri, Alyosha, Ivan, Smeryakov
Buddenbrooks — Thomas Mann
Call of the Wild,The — Jack London
   Dog — Buck
Cancer Ward — Alexander Solzhenitsyn
   Central Character — Kostoglotov
Candide — Voltaire

Canterbury Tales,The	Geoffrey Chaucer
Captains Courageous	Rudyard Kipling
Captain	Diska Troop
Central Character	Harvey Cheyne
Ship	We're Here
Catch 22	Joseph Heller
Set in	Pianosa, Mediterranean Island
Affected by Catch 22	Captain Yossarian
Catcher in the Rye,The	J.D.Salinger
Central Character	Holden Caulfield
Charlie and the Chocolate Factory	Roald Dahl
Charlie's Surname	Bucket
Factory Owner	Willy Wonka
Chérie	Colette
Children of the New Forest,The	Captain Marryat
Christmas Carol,A	Charles Dickens
Cratchit's Son	Tiny Tim (lame)
Ghost	Marley's
Last Line	'God bless us, every one'
Miser	Scrooge
Scrooge's Clerk	Bob Cratchit
Spirits	Ghost of Christmas Past, Present, Yet to Come
Chronicles of Thomas Covenant,The	Stephen Donaldson
Claudine	Colette
Clayhanger Trilogy,The	Arnold Bennett
Trilogy	*Clayhanger, Hilda Lessways, These Twain*
Cloister and the Hearth,The	Charles Reade
Central Character	Gerard
Collector,The	John Fowles
Title	Clegg
Collects	Butterflies
Color Purple,The	Alice Walker
Central Character	Celie
Comédie Humaine	Balzac
Confessions of an Opium Eater	Thomas De Quincey
Connecticut Yankee in King Arthur's Court,A	Mark Twain
Coral Island	R.M.Ballantyne
Corridors of Power,The	C.P.Snow
War Minister	Roger Quaife
Count of Monte Christo,The	Alexandre Dumas (Père)
Count	Edmond Dantes
Imprisoned in	Chateau d'If
Left Fortune by	Abbe Faria
Country Diary of an Edwardian Lady, The	Edith Holden
Cranford	Mrs Gaskell
Crime and Punishment	Fyodor Dostoyevsky
Crime	Murders woman pawnbroker
Criminal	Raskolnikov
Inspector	Petrovitch
Cry the Beloved Country	Alan Paton
Country	South Africa
Darkness at Noon	Arthur Koestler
Central Character	Nicholas Rubashov

David Copperfield	**Charles Dickens**
Aunt	**Betsy Trotwood**
David's Stepfather	**Edward Murdstone**
David's Wives	**Dora Spenlow, Agnes Wickfield**
Full Title	**The Personal History of David**
	Copperfield
Day of the Jackal,The	**Frederick Forsyth**
Day of the Triffids,The	**John Wyndham**
Dead Souls	**Nikolai Gogol**
Hero	**Chichikov**
Death in the Afternoon	**Ernest Hemingway**
Theme	**Bullfighting**
Death in Venice	**Thomas Mann**
Death of	**Gustav Von Aschenbach (Writer)**
Dies of	**Cholera**
Young Boy	**Tadzio**
Decameron	**Boccaccio**
Number of stories	**100**
Decline and Fall	**Evelyn Waugh**
Devil Rides Out,The	**Dennis Wheatley**
Devils of Loudon,The	**Aldous Huxley**
Dharma Bums,The	**Jack Kerouac**
Diary of a Madman,The	**Nikolai Gogol**
Dombey and Son	**Charles Dickens**
Son	**Paul**
Don Quixote	**Miguel de Cervantes**
Horse	**Rosinante**
Lady	**Dulcinea**
Squire	**Sancho Panza**
Dr Doolittle	**Hugh Lofting**
Lives in	**Puddleby on Marsh**
Taught by	**Polynesia, the Parrot**
Two Headed Animal	**Pushme-Pullyu**
Dr Faustus	**Thomas Mann**
Dr Jekyll and Mr Hyde	**Robert Louis Stevenson**
Hyde murders	**Sir Danvers Carew**
Dr Zhivago	**Boris Pasternak**
Lover	**Lara Antipova**
Title	**Yuri Zhivago**
Wife	**Tania Gromeko**
Dubliners	**James Joyce (short stories)**
Dune	**Frank Herbert**
East of Eden	**John Steinbeck**
Emma	**Jane Austen**
Marries	**Henry Knightley**
Title	**Emma Woodhouse**
Erewhon	**Samuel Butler**
Title	**Anagram of Nowhere**
Essays of Elia	**Charles Lamb**
Eugénie Grandet	**Honoré De Belzac**
Eugene Onegin	**Alexander Pushkin**
Lady	**Tatiana**
Exodus	**Leon Uris**
Eyeless in Gaza	**Aldous Huxley**
Fall of the House of Usher,The	**Edgar Allan Poe**
Fanny Hill	**John Cleland**
Far from the Madding Crowd	**Thomas Hardy**

Bathsheba marries	Sergeant Troy, Gabriel Oak
Central Character	Bathsheba Everdene
Farewell, My Lovely	Raymond Chandler
Set during	WWI
Farewell to Arms,A	Ernest Hemingway
Fathers and Sons	Ivan Turgenev
Central Character	Bazarov
Faust	Goethe
Finnegans Wake	James Joyce
Central Character	Humphrey Chimpden Earwicker (publican)
Takes place during	One night
First Among Equals	Jeffery Archer
First Circle	Alexander Solzhenitsyn
For Whom the Bell Tolls	Ernest Hemingway
Central Character	Robert Jordan
Set during	Spanish Civil War
Forsyte Saga,The	John Galsworthy
Central character	Soames Forsyte
1st Book	The Man of Property
Irene's Love	Bosinney (architect)
Sequels	*A Modern Comedy, End of the Chapter*
Trilogy	*The Man of Property, In Chancery, To Let,* + 2 stories
Wife	Irene
Foundation Trilogy	Isaac Asimov
Fourth Protocol,The	Frederick Forsyth
Frankenstein	Mary Shelley
Title	Monster's creator
Subtitle	*Or the Modern Prometheus*
From Here to Eternity	James Jones
Boxer	Private Prewitt
Fungus the Bogeyman	Raymond Briggs
Wife	Mildew
Son	Mold
Gamesmanship	Stephen Potter
Gargantua	Rabelais
Gentlemen Prefer Blondes	Anita Loos
Sequel	*Gentlemen Marry Brunettes*
Georgics,The	Virgil
Germinal	Emile Zola
Central Character	Etienne
Gigi	Colette
Gil Blas	Alain Le Sage
Golden Bowl,The	Henry James
Gone with the Wind	Margaret Mitchell
Central Character	Scarlet O'Hara
Marries	Charles Hamilton, Frank Kennedy, Rhett Butler
Plantation	Tara
Scarlett's Neighbour	Ashley Wilkes
Good Companions,The	J.B.Priestley
Title	Travelling players
Good Earth,The	Pearl Buck
Central Characters	Wang Lung, O-Lan
Set in	China in 1920s
Good Soldier Svejk,The	Jaroslav Hajek

Goodbye Columbus	Philip Roth
Goodbye, Mr Chips	James Hilton
Title	Mr Chipping (teacher)
Goodbye to All That	Robert Graves
Gormenghast	Mervyn Peake
Grapes of Wrath,The	John Steinbeck
Theme	Joad family leaving Oklahoma dust bowl for California
Gravity's Rainbow	Thomas Pynchon
Title	V2 rocket trajectory
Great Expectations	Charles Dickens
Blacksmith	Joe Gargery
Convict	Magwitch
Central Characters	Pip (Philip Pirrip), Miss Havisham
Pip's Love	Estella
Great Gatsby,The	F.Scott Fitzgerald
Gatsby's Real Name	James Gatz
His Love	Daisy Buchanan
Title	Jay Gatsby
Greenmantle	John Buchan
Group,The	Mary McCarthy
Title	8 girls from Vassar
Gulliver's Travels	Jonathan Swift
Houyhnyms	Horses ruling Yahoos (humans)
Lands visited	Lilliput (small people), Brobdingnag (giants), Laputa (flying island)
Guys and Dolls	Damon Runyon
Hard Times	Charles Dickens
Central Character	Gradgrind
Motto	'Facts, Facts, Facts'
Hawaii	James Michener
Heart of Midlothian,The	Sir Walter Scott
Title	Tolbooth Jail, Edinburgh
Heidi	Johanna Spyri
Set in	Switzerland
Hereward the Wake	Charles Kingsley
Herzog	Saul Bellow
History Man,The	Malcolm Bradbury
Title	Howard Kirk
History of Mr Polly,The	H.G.Wells
Hobbit,The	J.R.R.Tolkien
Title	Bilbo Baggins
Horseman Riding By,A	R.F.Delderfield
Hound of the Baskervilles,The	Sir Arthur Conan Doyle
How Green Was My Valley	Richard Llewellyn
Family	The Morgans
Set in	Welsh pit village
Howard's End	E.M.Forster
Hunchback of Notre Dame,The	Victor Hugo
Gypsy Girl	Esmeralda
Hunchback (Bell Ringer)	Quasimodo
Villain	Archdeacon Frollo (Quasimodo kills)
Hundred Years of Solitude,A	Gabriel Garcia Marquez
I, Claudius	Robert Graves
Sequel	*Claudius the God*
I, the Jury	Mickey Spillane
Idiot,The	Fyodor Dostoyevsky

Title	Prince Myshkin
Incident at Owl Creek Bridge	Ambrose Bierce
Inferno	Dante
Invisible Man,The	H.G.Wells
Title	Griffin
Ivanhoe	Sir Walter Scott
Ivanhoe's Love	Rowena
Set in	12th Century England
Title	Wilfred of Ivanhoe
Jamaica Inn	Daphne Du Maurier
Heroine	Mary Yellan
Jane Eyre	Charlotte Bronte
House	Thornfield
Jane's Husband	Rochester
Jonathan Livingston Seagull	Richard Bach
Journal of the Plague Year,A	Daniel Defoe
Journey to the Centre of the Earth	Jules Verne
Jude the Obscure	Thomas Hardy
Aspires to go to	Christminster (Oxford)
Title	Jude Fawley
Jungle Book,The	Rudyard Kipling
Bear	Baloo
Boy	Mowgli
Mongoose	Rikki-Tikki Tavi
Panther	Bagheera
Tiger	Shere Khan
Jungle,The	Upton Sinclair
Theme	Meat packing in the US
Just So Stories	Rudyard Kipling
Just William	Richmal Crompton
Justine	Marquis De Sade
Kenilworth	Sir Walter Scott
Set during	Queen Elizabeth I's reign
Kidnapped	Robert Louis Stevenson
David's Friend	Alan Breck
Hero	David Balfour
Ship	The Covenant
Kim	Rudyard Kipling
Kim's Occupation	Spy
Set in	India
King Solomon's Mines	H.Rider Haggard
King Solomon's Ring	Konrad Lorenz
Kipps	H.G.Wells
Lace	Shirley Conran
Lady Chatterley's Lover	D.H.Lawrence
Title	Gamekeeper, Mellors
Last Days of Pompeii,The	Edward Bulwer-Lytton
Last Tycoon,The	F.Scott Fitzgerald
Based on (supposed)	Irving Thalberg
Leatherstocking Stories,The	James Fenimore Cooper
Hero	Natty Bumppo (Scout, Hawkeye)
Last of the Mohicans	Uncas
Parts	5 (including, *The Deerslayer, Last of the Mohicans*)
Uncas' Father	Chingachook
Les Misérables	Victor Hugo
Central Character	Jean Valjean

Sent to gallows for	Stealing bread
Let us now Praise Famous Men	James Agee, Walker Evans
Lion the Witch and the Wardrobe,The	C.S.Lewis
Set in	Narnia
Little Dorrit	Charles Dickens
Title	Amy Dorrit
Born at	Marshalsea Prison
Little Lord Fauntleroy	Frances Hodgson Burnett
Title	Cedric Errol
Little Women	Louisa May Alcott
Family	March family
Sisters	Amy, Beth, Jo, Meg
Lolita	Vladimir Nabokov
Lolita's Age	12
Marries Lolita's mother to be near Lolita	Humbert Humbert
Title	Dolores Haze
Loneliness of the Long Distance Runner,The	Alan Sillitoe
Central Character	Smith
Set in	Borstal
Long Goodbye,The	Raymond Chandler
Lord Jim	Joseph Conrad
His Crime	Deserts pilgrims on sinking ship
Lord of the Flies	William Golding
Leader	Ralph
Lord of the Rings	J.R.R.Tolkien
Bilbo's Nephew	Frodo
Hobbit	Bilbo Baggins
Maker of the ring	Sauron
Quest	To destroy the ring in the Volcano where it was made
Sauron's Land	Mordor
Set in	Middle Earth
Wizard	Gandalf
Lorna Dorne	R.D.Blackmore
Hero	John Ridd
Set in	Exmoor
Lost Horizon	James Hilton
Location	Shangri La
Lost World,The	Arthur Conan Doyle
Explorer	Professor Challenger
Love Story	Eric Segal
Jenny dies of	Leukaemia
Lovers	Oliver Barrett IV, Jenny Cavillieri
Sequel	*Oliver's Story*
Lucky Jim	Kingsley Amis
Title	James Dixon (university history lecturer)
Lust for Life	Irving Stone
Madame Bovary	Gustave Flaubert
Title	Emma Roualt
Magic Mountain,The	Thomas Mann
Set in	TB Hospital in Switzerland
Magus,The	John Fowles
Mansfield Park	Jane Austen
Heroine	Fanny Price

Martian Chronicles,The	Ray Bradbury
Martin Chuzzlewit	Charles Dickens
Nurse	Mrs Sarah Gamp (drunk with umbrella)
Hypocrite	Mr Pecksniff
Mayor of Casterbridge,The	Thomas Hardy
Set in	Wessex
Title	Michael Henchard
Memoirs of a Foxhunting Man,The	Siegfried Sassoon
Men at Arms	Evelyn Waugh
Central Character	Guy Crouchback
Other parts of trilogy	*Officers and Gentlemen, Unconditional Surrender*
Metamorphosis	Franz Kafka (short story)
Theme	Man changes into an insect
Middlemarch	George Eliot
Midwich Cuckoos,The	John Wyndham
Title	Alien children
Mill on the Floss,The	George Eliot
Central Characters	Tom and Maggie Tulliver
Set at	Dorlcote Mill
Tom and Maggie's Gravestone	'In their death they were not divided'
Moby Dick	Herman Melville
Captain	Ahab
Ship	Pequod
Survivor	Ishmael
Title	White whale (has bitten off Ahab's leg)
Moon and Sixpence,The	Somerset Maugham
Morte d'Arthur	Sir Thomas Mallory
Mother	Maxim Gorki
Murders in the Rue Morgue,The	Edgar Allan Poe
Mystery of Edwin Drood,The	Charles Dickens (unfinished)
Naked and the Dead,The	Norman Mailer
Naked Lunch,The	William Burroughs
Name of the Rose,The	Umberto Eco
Nana	Emile Zola
Nicholas Nickleby	Charles Dickens
Job with	Cheeryble Brothers (counting house)
Nicholas befriends	Smike
Nicholas marries	Madeline Bray
Nicholas' Uncle	Ralph
Schoolmaster	Wackford Squeers
School Nicholas teaches at	Dotheboys Hall
1984	George Orwell
Central Characters	Winston Smith, Julia O'Brien
City	London
Country	Airstrip 1
Intended Title	*The Last Man in Europe*
Leader	Big Brother
Winston's Fear	Rats
Northanger Abbey	Jane Austen
Heroine	Catherine Morland
Marries	Henry Tilney
Nostromo	Joseph Conrad
Set in	South American country in revolution
Oblomov	Ivan Goncharov
Of Human Bondage	Somerset Maugham

Of Mice and Men	John Steinbeck
Central Characters	George Milton, Lennie Small (giant)
Old Curiosity Shop, The	Charles Dickens
Central Character	Little Nell
Dwarf	Quilp
Nell's Friend	Kit Nupples
Old Man and The Sea, The	Ernest Hemingway
Old Possum's Book of Practical Cats	T.S.Eliot
Old Possum	Eliot
Old Wives' Tales	Arnold Bennett
Oliver Twist	Charles Dickens
Artful Dodger's Name	Jack Dawkins
Beadle	Mr Bumble
Born in	Workhouse
Murder	Bill Sikes of Nancy
Pickpocket Leader	Fagin
On the Beach	Nevil Shute
Theme	Nuclear War
On the Road	Jack Kerouac
Central Character	Dean Moriarty
One Day in the Life of Ivan Denisovich	Alexander Solzhenitsyn
One Hundred Years of Solitude	Gabriel Garcia Marquez
Our Man in Havana	Graham Greene
Title	Wormold (vacuum cleaner representative)
Our Mutual Friend	Charles Dickens
Marries	Bella Wilfer
Title	John Harmon
Villain	Silas Wegg (wooden leg)
Pantagruel	Rabelais
Paradise Postponed	John Mortimer
Passage to India, A	E.M.Forster
Aziz's Accuser	Adela Quested
Central Characters	Cyril Fielding, Dr Aziz
Pickwick Papers	Charles Dickens
Christmas Party at	Dingley Dell
Servant	Sam Weller
Sued by	Landlady, Mrs Bardell
Title	Samuel Pickwick, founder of the Pickwick Club
Pilgrim's Progress, The	John Bunyan
Goal	Celestial City
Hero	Christian
Pinnochio	Collodi (Carlo Lorenzini)
Creator	Gepetto
When lying	Nose grows
Pit and the Pendulum, The	Edgar Allan Poe
Setting	Spanish Inquisition
Plague, The	Albert Camus
Portnoy's Complaint	Philip Roth
Portrait of a Lady	Henry James
Title	Isobel Archer
Portrait of the Artist as a Young Dog	Dylan Thomas
Power and the Glory, The	Graham Greene
Set in	Mexico
Pride and Prejudice	Jane Austen
Family	The Bennetts
Prime of Miss Jean Brodie, The	Muriel Spark

Aims to create	Crème de la Crème
Art Teacher	Teddy Lloyd
Prince and the Pauper,The	Mark Twain
Pauper	Tom Canty
Prince	Edward, Prince of Wales (later Edward VI)
Prisoner of Zenda,The	Anthony Hope
Imprisoned by	Duke Michael
Kingdom	Ruritania
Title	King Rudolf
Puck of Pook's Hill	Rudyard Kipling
Quentin Durward	Sir Walter Scott
Quentin marries	Isabelle de Croye
Set in	France under Louis XI
Quo Vadis	Henryk Sienkiewicz
Set in	Rome under Nero
Heroine	Ligia
Rabbit, Run	John Updike
Rabbit's Job	Magipeel Salesman
Sequel	*Rabbit Redux*
Title	Harry 'Rabbit' Angstrom
Railway Children,The	E.Nesbit
Names	Peter, Phylis, Roberta
Raj Quartet,The	Paul Scott
Rebecca	Daphne Du Maurier
Central Character	Maxim De Winter
House	Manderley
Housekeeper	Mrs Danvers
Red and the Black,The	Stendhal
Hero	Julien Sorel
Red Badge of Courage,The	Stephen Crane
Set during	US Civil War
Redgauntlet	Sir Walter Scott
Remembrance of Things Past	Marcel Proust
1st part	*Swann's Way*
Rewards and Fairies	Rudyard Kipling
Riders of the Purple Sage	Zane Grey
Rip Van Winkle	Washington Irving
Lives in	Catskill Mountains
Sleeps for	20 years
Rob Roy	Sir Walter Scott
Title	Rob Roy McGregor
Robinson Crusoe	Daniel Defoe
Based on	Alexander Selkirk, marooned on Juan Fernandez
Crusoe's Servant	Man Friday (found on a Friday)
Room With A View	E.M.Forster
Roots	Alex Haley
Original African	Kunte Kinte
Sailor Who Fell From Grace With The Sea,The	Yukio Mishima
Satanic Verses, The	Salman Rushdie
Satyricon	Petronius
Includes	*Feast of Tremalchio*
Scarlet Letter,The	Nathaniel Hawthorne
Central Character	Hester Prynne
Title	A for Adultery

Scarlet Pimpernel,The	Baroness Orczy
Title	Sir Percy Blakeney
Secret Agent,The	Joseph Conrad
Secret Garden,The	Frances Hodgson Burnett
Secret Life of Walter Mitty,The	James Thurber
Sense and Sensibility	Jane Austen
Original Title	*Elinor and Marianne*
Sisters	Elinor (Sense), Marianne (Sensibility)
Severed Head,A	Iris Murdoch
She	Rider Haggard
Name	Ayesha
Shogun	James Clavell
Siddhartha	Herman Hesse
Sign of Four,The	Sir Arthur Conan Doyle
Silas Marner	George Eliot
Occupation	Weaver
Slaughterhouse Five	Kurt Vonnegut
Hero	Billy Pilgrim
Sons and Lovers	D.H.Lawrence
Son	Paul Morel
Sound and the Fury,The	William Faulkner
Family	The Compson family
Spy Who Came in from the Cold,The	John Le Carré
Title	Leamas
Stalky and Co	Rudyard Kipling
Steppenwolf	Herman Hesse
Central Character	Harry Haller
Stranger,The	Albert Camus
Studs Lonigan	James Farrell
Set in	Chicago's Irish slums
Sun Also Rises,The	Ernest Hemingway
Uses Term	'The Lost Generation'
Swallows and Amazons	Arthur Ransome
Swiss Family Robinson	J.R. Wyss
Sybil	Benjamin Disraeli
Tale of Genji,The	Lady Murasaki
Tale of Two Cities,A	Charles Dickens
Sacrifices himself for Darnay	Sydney Carton
Sentenced to Guillotine	Charles Darnay
Title	Paris, London
Tales from Shakespeare	Charles and Mary Lamb
Tales of Mystery and Imagination	Edgar Allan Poe
Tanglewood Tales	Nathaniel Hawthorne
Tarka the Otter	Henry Williamson
Taste of Honey,A	Shelagh Delaney
Tenant of Wildfell Hall,The	Anne Brontë
Tender is the Night	F.Scott Fitzgerald
Tess of the D'Urbervilles	Thomas Hardy
Tess marries	Angel Clare
Tess murders	Alec D'Urberville
Title	Tess Durbeyfield
Testament of Youth	Vera Brittain
Thirty Nine Steps,The	John Buchan
Hero	Richard Hannay
This Sporting Life	David Storey
Sport	Rugby League
Three Men in a Boat	Jerome K.Jerome

In the boat	George, Harris, J, and Montmorency (dog)
Three Musketeers,The	Alexandre Dumas
Motto	'All for one and one for all!'
Musketeers	Athos, Porthos, Aramis, (and 4th musketeer: D'Artagnan)
Through the Looking Glass	Lewis Carroll
Time Machine,The	H.G.Wells
Tin Drum,The	Günter Grass
Hero	Oskar Matzerath (dwarf)
Set in	Germany from Fascist times
Tinker, Tailor, Soldier, Spy	John Le Carré
Titus Groan	Mervyn Peake
To Serve Them All My Days	R.F.Delderfield
To the Lighthouse	Virginia Woolf
Tobacco Road	Erskine Caldwell
Jeeter's Wife	Ada
Sharecropper	Jeeter Lester
Tom Jones	Henry Fielding
Tom marries	Sophia Western
Tom Sawyer	Mark Twain
Murderer	Injun Joe
Set in	St Petersburg, Mississippi
Tom's Love	Becky Thatcher
Town Like Alice,A	Nevil Shute
Treasure Island	Robert Louis Stevenson
Hero/Narrator	Jim Hawkins
Jim's Home	Admiral Benbow Inn
Notice of Death	Black spot
One Legged Pirate	Long John Silver
Parrot	Captain Flint
Title in Serial form	The *Sea Cove*
Treasure	Captain Flint's
Treasure found by	Ben Gunn
Trial,The	Frank Kafka
Character	Joseph K.
Tropic of Cancer	Henry Miller
Tunc	Lawrence Durrell
Turn of the Screw,The	Henry James (short story)
Children	Miles, Flora
Ghosts	Quint, Mrs Jessel
Twenty Thousand Leagues Under The Sea	Jules Verne
Captain	Nemo
Submarine	Nautilus
Two Years Before the Mast	Richard Dana
Ulysses	James Joyce
Central Characters	Leopold Bloom, Stephen Daedalus
Set during	18 hours in Dublin
Uncle Tom's Cabin	Harriet Beecher Stowe
Sadistic Slave Owner	Simon Legree
Subtitle	Life among the Lowly
Under Milk Wood	Dylan Thomas
Intended as	Radio play
Title	A forest
Under the Volcano	Malcolm Lowry
Valley of the Dolls,The	Jacqueline Susann

Vanity Fair	William Makepeace Thackeray
Amelia marries	Captain Dobbin
Becky marries	Rawdon Crawley
Becky's Friend	Amelia Sedley
Central Character	Becky Sharp
Vathek	William Beckford
Vicar of Wakefield,The	Oliver Goldsmith
Villette	Charlotte Brontë
Walden	Henry Thoreau
War and Peace	Leo Tolstoy
Set during	Napoleonic Wars
War of the Worlds,The	H.G.Wells
Washington Square	Henry James
Water Babies,The	Charles Kingsley
Central Character	Tom (chimney sweep)
Watership Down	Richard Adams
Rabbits	Hazel, Fiver, Bigwig, General Wormwort
Waverley	Sir Walter Scott
Way of All Flesh,The	Samuel Butler
Westward Ho!	Charles Kingsley
Hero	Amyas Leigh
Love	Rose of Torridge
What Katy Did	Susan Coolidge
Full name	Katy Carr
White Company,The	Sir Arthur Conan Doyle
Wind in the Willows,The	Kenneth Grahame
Characters	Toad, Mole, Water Rat, Badger
House	Toad Hall
Winnie the Pooh	A.A.Milne
Bear	Pooh (real name – Edward)
Boy	Christopher Robin (after Milne's son)
Donkey	Eeyore
Elephant called	Heffalump
Illustrator	Ernest Shepard
Kidnapped	Roo
Sequel	The House at Pooh Corner
Wuthering Heights	Emily Brontë
Central Characters	Catherine Earnshaw, Heathcliff
Title	House

Fictional Characters and Things

By: Character → Work

E.g.: What book does . . . appear in

Captain Absolute	The Rivals
Sir Andrew Aguecheek	Twelfth Night
Captain Ahab	Moby Dick
Squire Allworthy	Tom Jones
Harry Angstrom	Rabbit, Run
Antipholus	The Comedy of Errors
Lara Antipova	Doctor Zhivago
Antonio	The Merchant of Venice
Aramis	The Three Musketeers
Isobel Archer	Portrait of a Lady
Artful Dodger,The	Oliver Twist

Athos	*The Three Musketeers*
Ayesha	*She*
Dr Aziz	*Passage to India*
Belinda	*The Rape of the Lock*
Bilbo Baggins	*The Hobbit, Lord of the Rings*
David Balfour	*Kidnapped*
Banquo	*Macbeth*
Mrs Bardell	*Pickwick Papers*
Barkis	*David Copperfield*
Bassanio	*The Merchant of Venice*
Bazarov	*Fathers and Sons*
Beatrice	*Much Ado About Nothing*
Sir Toby Belch	*Twelfth Night*
Benedick	*Much Ado About Nothing*
Margot Beste-Chetwynde	*Decline and Fall*
John Blackthorne	*Shogun*
Sir Percy Blakeney	*The Scarlet Pimpernel*
Leopold Bloom	*Ulysses*
Bottom	*A Midsummer Night's Dream*
Jack Boyle	*Juno and the Paycock*
Lady Bracknell	*The Importance of Being Ernest*
Dorothea Brooke	*Middlemarch*
Pinkie Brown	*Brighton Rock*
Beatrice Bryant	*Roots*
Daisy Buchanan	*The Great Gatsby*
Bucket	*Bleak House*
Natty Bumppo	*The Leatherstocking Stories*
Rhett Butler	*Gone With The Wind*
Sergeant Buzfuz	*Pickwick Papers*
Caliban	*The Tempest*
Tom Canty	*The Prince and the Pauper*
William Carey	*Of Human Bondage*
Richard Carstone	*Bleak House*
Sidney Carton	*A Tale of Two Cities*
Captain Cat	*Under Milk Wood*
Holden Caulfield	*The Catcher in the Rye*
Mr Chadband	*Bleak House*
Professor Challenger	*The Lost World*
Jack Chesney	*Charlie's Aunt*
Harvey Cheyne	*Captains Courageous*
Chichikov	*Dead Souls*
Chingachook	*Leatherstocking Saga*
Christian	*Pilgrim's Progress*
Angel Clare	*Tess of the D'Urbervilles*
Claudio	*Much Ado About Nothing*
Hugh Conway	*Lost Horizon*
Cordelia	*King Lear*
Bob Cratchit	*A Christmas Carol*
Guy Crouchback	*Men at Arms*
Edmond Dantes	*The Count of Monte Christo*
Mrs Danvers	*Rebecca*
Charles Darnay	*A Tale of Two Cities*
D'Artagnan	*The Three Musketeers*
Desdemona	*Othello*
Maxim De Winter	*Rebecca*
James Dixon	*Lucky Jim*
Captain Dobbin	*Vanity Fair*

Eliza Doolittle	*Pygmalion*
Dromeo	*The Comedy of Errors*
Blanche Du Bois	*A Streetcar Named Desire*
Duncan	*Macbeth*
H.C.Earwicker	*Finnegan's Wake*
Cathy Earnshaw	*Wuthering Heights*
Eeyore	*Winnie the Pooh*
Mrs Erlynne	*Lady Windermere's Fan*
Cedric Errol	*Little Lord Fauntleroy*
Esmeralda	*The Hunchback of Notre Dame*
Estragon	*Waiting for Godot*
Bathsheba Everdene	*Far From the Madding Crowd*
Fagin	*Oliver Twist*
Falstaff	*Henry IV, The Merry Wives of Windsor*
King Ferdinand	*Love's Labours Lost*
Cyril Fielding	*Passage to India*
Fiver	*Watership Down*
Pegeen Flaherty	*Playboy of the Western World*
Flashman	*Tom Brown's Schooldays*
Phileas Fogg	*Around the World in 80 days*
Frodo	*Lord of the Rings*
Mrs Sarah Gamp	*Martin Chuzzlewit*
Gandalf	*Lord of the Rings*
Joe Gargery	*Great Expectations*
Marguerite Gautier	*Camille*
Holly Golightly	*Breakfast at Tiffany's*
Gollum	*Lord of the Rings*
Goneril	*King Lear*
Gradgrind	*Hard Times*
Grendel	*Beowulf*
Jack Griffin	*The Invisible Man*
Clyde Griffiths	*An American Tragedy*
Captain Grimes	*Decline and Fall*
Guildenstern	*Hamlet*
Ben Gunn	*Treasure Island*
Harry Haller	*Steppenwolf*
Basil Hallward	*The Picture of Dorian Gray*
Ham	*David Copperfield*
Richard Hannay	*The Thirty-Nine Steps*
Miss Hardcastle	*She Stoops to Conquer*
John Harmon	*Our Mutual Friend*
Miss Havisham	*Great Expectations*
Jim Hawkins	*Treasure Island*
Dolores Haze	*Lolita*
Heathcliff	*Wuthering Heights*
Uriah Heep	*David Copperfield*
Nora Helmer	*A Doll's House*
Michael Henchard	*The Mayor of Casterbridge*
Frederic Henry	*A Farewell to Arms*
Hero	*Much Ado About Nothing*
Hickey	*The Iceman Cometh*
Professor Henry Higgins	*Pygmalion*
Captain Hook	*Peter Pan*
Humbert Humbert	*Lolita*
Iago	*Othello*
Injun Joe	*Tom Sawyer*
John Jarndyce	*Bleak House*

Mrs Jessel	*The Turn of the Screw*
Tom Joad	*The Grapes of Wrath*
Jocasta	*Oedipus the King*
Robert Jorden	*For Whom the Bell Tolls*
Joseph K.	*The Trial*
Monsieur Jourdain	*Le Bourgeois Gentilhomme*
Katherina	*Taming of the Shrew*
Khlestakov	*The Inspector General*
Kostoglotov	*Cancer Ward*
Stanley Kowalsky	*A Streetcar Named Desire*
Krook	*Bleak House*
Laertes	*Hamlet*
Lydia Languish	*The Rivals*
Leamas	*The Spy Who Came In From the Cold*
Simon Legree	*Uncle Tom's Cabin*
Amyas Leigh	*Westward Ho!*
Leontes	*A Winter's Tale*
Jeeter Lester	*Tobacco Road*
Levin	*Anna Karenina*
Little Emily	*David Copperfield*
Little Nell	*The Old Curiosity Shop*
Lord Loam	*The Admirable Crichton*
Willy Loman	*Death of a Salesman*
Long John Silver	*Treasure Island*
Lucky	*Waiting for Godot*
Macduff	*Macbeth*
Mad Hatter,The	*Alice in Wonderland*
Magwitch	*Great Expectations*
Christie Mahon	*Playboy of the Western World*
Major Major	*Catch-22*
Mrs Malaprop	*The Rivals*
Captain Charles Mallison	*Lost Horizon*
Malvolio	*Twelfth Night*
Man Friday	*Robinson Crusoe*
Amy, Beth, Joe, Meg March	*Little Women*
Oskar Matzerath	*The Tin Drum*
Mellors	*Lady Chatterley's Lover*
Messala	*Ben Hur*
Mr Micawber	*David Copperfield*
Millamont	*The Way of the World*
George Milton	*Of Mice and Men*
Minnehaha	*Hiawatha*
Mirabell	*The Way of the World*
Algernon Moncrieff	*The Importance of Being Ernest*
Paul Morel	*Sons and Lovers*
Dean Moriarty	*On The Road*
Catherine Morland	*Northanger Abbey*
Mowgli	*Jungle Book*
Prince Myshkin	*The Idiot*
Nana	*Peter Pan*
Captain Nemo	*20,000 Leagues Under the Sea*
Gabriel Oak	*Far From the Madding Crowd*
Oberon	*A Midsummer Night's Dream*
Kitty Oblonsky	*Anna Karenina*
Mrs Ogmore-Pritchard	*Under Milk Wood*
Scarlett O'Hara	*Gone With The Wind*
O-Lan	*The Good Earth*

Oompa Loompas,The	*Charlie and the Chocolate Factory*
Orlando	*As You Like It*
Duke Orsino	*Twelfth Night*
Doctor Panglon	*Candide*
Panurge	*Gargantua & Pantagruel*
Sancho Panza	*Don Quixote*
Passepartout	*Around the World in 80 days*
Mr Pecksniff	*Martin Chuzzlewit*
Clara Peggoty	*David Copperfield*
Paul Pennyfeather	*Decline and Fall*
Petrovitch	*Crime and Punishment*
Petruchio	*The Taming of the Shrew*
Piggy	*Lord of the Flies*
Billy Pilgrim	*Slaughterhouse Five*
Pip	*Great Expectations*
Polixenes	*A Winter's Tale*
Maggie Pollitt	*Cat on a Hot Tin Roof*
Polonius	*Hamlet*
Jimmy Porter	*Look Back in Anger*
Porthos	*The Three Musketeers*
Portia	*The Merchant of Venice*
Pozzo	*Waiting for Godot*
Private Prewitt	*From Here to Eternity*
Fanny Price	*Mansfield Park*
Miss Prism	*The Importance of Being Ernest*
Prospero	*Tempest*
Proteus	*Two Gentlemen of Verona*
Mrs Proudie	*Barchester Towers*
Hester Prynne	*The Scarlet Letter*
Puck	*A Midsummer Night's Dream*
Quasimodo	*The Hunchback of Notre Dame*
Mistress Quickly	*Henry IV*
Quilp	*The Old Curiosity Shop*
Quint	*The Turn of the Screw*
Captain Rawdon	*Bleak House*
Paul Ray	*The Second Mrs Tanqueray*
Regan	*King Lear*
Archie Rice	*The Entertainer*
John Ridd	*Lorna Doone*
Rikki Tikki Tavi	*Jungle Book*
Rochester	*Jane Eyre*
Rosalind	*As You Like It*
Rose of Torridge	*Westward Ho!*
Rosencrantz	*Hamlet*
Emma Roualt	*Madame Bovary*
Rowena	*Ivanhoe*
Roxane	*Cyrano de Bergerac*
Nicholas Rubashov	*Darkness at Noon*
King Rudolf	*The Prisoner of Zenda*
Captain Charles Ryder	*Brideshead Revisited*
Sauron	*Lord of the Rings*
Scrooge	*A Christmas Carol*
Sebastian	*Twelfth Night*
Amelia Sedley	*Vanity Fair*
Becky Sharp	*Vanity Fair*
Shylock	*The Merchant of Venice*
Bill Sikes	*Oliver Twist*

Obediah Slope	*Barchester Towers*
Lennie Small	*Of Mice and Men*
Smike	*Nicholas Nickleby*
Winston Smith	*1984*
Lady Sneerwell	*School for Scandal*
Augustus Snodgrass	*Pickwick Papers*
Julian Sorel	*The Red and the Black*
Wackford Squeers	*Nicholas Nickleby*
Bertie Stanhope	*Barchester Towers*
James Steerforth	*David Copperfield*
Steerpike	*Titus Groan*
Alan Strang	*Equus*
Subtle	*The Alchemist*
Joseph Surface	*The School for Scandal*
Svengali	*Trilby (George Du Maurier)*
Tadzio	*Death in Venice*
John Tanner	*Man and Superman*
Lady Teazle	*The School for Scandal*
Teiresias	*Oedipus the King*
Professor George Tessman	*Hedda Gabbler*
Becky Thatcher	*Tom Sawyer*
The Three Witches	*Macbeth*
Henry Tilney	*Northanger Abbey*
Tinker Bell	*Peter Pan*
Tiny Tim	*A Christmas Carol*
Titania	*A Midsummer Night's Dream*
Toad	*The Wind in the Willows*
Topsy	*Uncle Tom's Cabin*
Touchstone	*As You Like It*
Trigorin	*The Seagull*
Disko Troop	*Captains Courageous*
Betsey Trotwood	*David Copperfield*
Sergeant Troy	*Far From the Madding Crowd*
Tom & Maggie Tulliver	*The Mill on the Floss*
Tracy Tupman	*Pickwick Papers*
Uncas	*The Leatherstocking Saga*
Valentine	*Two Gentlemen of Verona*
Jean Valjean	*Les Miserables*
Dolly Varden	*Barnaby Rudge*
Lord Verisopht	*Nicholas Nickleby*
Viola	*Twelfth Night*
Vladimir	*Waiting for Godot*
Gustav Von Aschenbach	*Death in Venice*
Count Vronsky	*Anna Karenina*
Wang Lung	*The Good Earth*
Silas Wegg	*Our Mutual Friend*
Sam Weller	*Pickwick Papers*
White Rabbit,The	*Alice in Wonderland*
Ann Whitefield	*Man and Superman*
Ashley Wilkes	*Gone With The Wind*
Willy Nilly	*Under Milk Wood*
Nathaniel Winkle	*Pickwick Papers*
Jack Worthing	*The Importance of Being Ernest*
Charley Wykeham	*Charley's Aunt*
Captain Yossarian	*Catch-22*

Fictional Characters and Things

By: Description → Character

Animals; Talks to	Dr Doolittle
Asks for more	Oliver Twist
Foundling	Tom Jones
Jilted by Lover on wedding day	Miss Havisham (*Great Expectations*)
'Just Growed'	Topsy (*Uncle Tom's Cabin*)
Lies; Told dreadful	Matilda
Lion; Spared by, for once removing thorn	Androcles
Long Words; Uses incorrectly	Mrs Malaprop
'Nevermore'; Says	The Raven
Nose; Grows when lying	Pinnochio
Shakespeare;-	
Most Lines	Hamlet
Most Lines; 2nd	Richard II
Smile; Remains after vanishing	Cheshire cat
Very 'Umble	Uriah Heep (*David Copperfield*)
Waiting for something to turn up	Mr Micawber (*David Copperfield*)
(Is) Willing	Barkis (*David Copperfield*)

Fictional Characters and Things

By: Name → Creator, Other Information

See Also: Entertainment; Characters from Films

Batwoman	Secret identity: Kathy Kane
Biggles	Captain W.E.Johns
Full Name	Major James Bigglesworth
Billy Bunter	Frank Richards
School	Greyfriars
Sister	Bessie
Bobbsey Twins	Laura Lee Hope
Real Author	Edward Stratemeyer and Syndicate
Brer Rabbit	Joe Chandler Harris
'Brer'; Meaning	Brother
Narrator	Uncle Remus
Bulldog Drummond	Sapper
Cat in the Hat	Dr Seuss
Chad	Character in WWII Graffiti with 'Wot no . . .'
Cinderella	Slipper made of: Fur (incorrectly translated as glass)
Dark Lady of the Sonnets	Shakespeare
Dick and Jane (Readers)	Zerna Sharp
Dracula	Bram Stoker
Based on	Vlad V (the impaler), King of Wallachia (15th Century)
Inspiration	Nightmare (after eating crabs)
Nancy Drew	Carolyn Keene
Real Author	Edward Stratemeyer and Syndicate
Famous Five	Names: Anne, Dick, George (Georgina), Julian, Timmy (dog)
Five Towns	Towns (6) in Potteries setting of Arnold Bennett stories
Now parts of	Stoke-on-Trent
Fu Manchu	Sax Rohmer

Adversary	Nayland-Smith
Organisation	Si Fan
Grinch	Dr Seuss. Steals Christmas
Hardy Boys	Franklin W.Dixon
Names	Frank, Joe
Real Author	Edward Stratemeyer and Syndicate
Hoppalong Cassidy	Clarence E.Mulford
Horatio Hornblower	C.S.Forester
1st Book	*The Happy Return*
Novels	12
James Bond	Ian Fleming
1st Book	*Casino Royale*
Jeeves	P.G.Wodehouse
Master	Bertie Wooster
J.G.Reeder	Edgar Wallace
Laura	Petrarch. Subject of poems
Mother Goose	Charles Perrault (narrator of Fairy Tales)
Paddington Bear	Michael Bond
Likes	Marmalade
Peter Rabbit	Beatrix Potter
Phantom of the Opera	Gaston Leroux
Title	Eric Claudin
Prydain	Imaginary land of Lloyd Alexander stories
Punch and Judy	
Dog	Toby
Hangman	Jack Ketch
Raffles	E.W.Hornung (gentleman burglar)
Secret Seven	Enid Blyton
Dog	Scamper
Names	Barbara, Janet, Pam, Colin, George, Jack, Peter
St Trinians	Ronald Searle
Tarzan	
Creator	Edgar Rice Burroughs
Father	Lord Greystoke
Real Name	John Clayton
Worzel Gummidge	Barbara Todd

Fictional Detectives

By: Name → Creator, Other Information

Lew Archer	Ross MacDonald
Sexton Blake	Harry Blyth
Father Brown	G.K.Chesterton
Modelled on	Father O'Connor
Father Cadfael	Ellis Peters
Max Carrados	Ernest Bramah (blind)
Charlie Chan	Earl Biggers
Dr Gideon Fell	John Dickson Carr
Mike Hammer	Mickey Spillane
1st Novel	*I, the Jury*
Sherlock Holmes	Sir Arthur Conan Doyle
Arch Enemy	Professor Moriarty
Assistant	Dr John Watson
Based on	Surgeon Joseph Bell
Brother	Mycroft

'1st appears in	*The Strand* magazine
1st Published Case	*A Study in Scarlet*
Hobby in Retirement	Bee-keeping
House	221B Baker Street
Landlady	Mrs Hudson
Last Case	Shoscombe Old Place
Name from	Oliver Wendell Holmes
Inspector Maigret	George Simenon
Philip Marlowe	Raymond Chandler
Jane Marple	Agatha Christie
1st Story	*Murder in the Vicarage*
Lives in	St Mary Mead
Perry Mason	Erle Stanley Gardner
Detective	Paul Drake
Secretary	Della Street
Inspector Morse	Colin Dexter
Hercule Poirot	Agatha Christie
1st Story	*The Mysterious Affair at Styles*
Last Story	*Curtain*
Nationality	Belgian
Solar Pons	August Derleth
Ellery Queen	Ellery Queen (Frederic Dannay, Manfred Lee)
The Saint (Simon Templar)	Leslie Charteris
Sam Spade	Dashiell Hammett
Paul Temple	Francis Durbridge
Dick Tracy	Chester Gould
Philo Vance	S.S.Van Dine
Lord Peter Wimsey	Dorothy Sayers
Other Names	Peter Death Bredon
Nero Wolfe	Rex Stout

Legendary Characters and Things

By: Name → General

See Also: Ideas and Beliefs; Mythology

Baba Yaga	Russian. Steals and eats children, house on one chicken leg
Bishop Hatto	Archbishop of Mainz
Burns	Starving peasants in his barn
Eaten by	Mice
Brigadoon	Scottish town that appears for 1 day every 100 years
Flying Dutchman	Ship that haunts seas around Cape of Good Hope and causes wrecks
Gog and Magog	Giants
Effigies in	Guildhall, London
Holy Grail	Cup used at Last Supper
John Henry	US railroad worker. Beats steam drill with a hammer
King Arthur	
At Death taken to	Avalon
Burial place	Glastonbury
Court at	Camelot
Finds Holy Grail	Sir Galahad
Galahad, Test	Siege Perilous
Lady of the Lake	Vivien
Lancelot's Son	Galahad

Quest for	Holy Grail
Sword	Excalibur
Wife	Guinevere

Lady Godiva
Looked at by	Peeping Tom (struck blind)
Rides Naked through	Coventry
To protest	Husband Leofric's taxes

Robin Hood
Enemy	Sheriff of Nottingham
Friar	Friar Tuck
Love	Maid Marian
Minstrel	Allan A Dale

Vampires
Distinguishing Feature	No reflection
Fear	Garlic, Cross
Killed by	Stake through heart

Werewolves
| Identification | Ring finger longest |
| Killed by | Silver bullet |

William Tell
| Enemy | Gessler |
| Shoots Apple from | Son's head |

Literary Movements

By: Writer → Movement

E.g.: Which movement was . . . associated with?

Kingsley Amis	Angry Young Men, The Movement
Baudelaire	Symbolism
Samuel Beckett	Theatre of the Absurd
Robert Benchley	Algonquin Round Table
Boswell	Literary Club (Founder)
Andre Breton	Surrealists
Rupert Brooke	Georgian Poets
Coleridge	Lake Poets
W.H.Davies	Georgian Poets
Ernest Dowson	Georgian Poets
John Donne	Metaphysical Poets
Ralph Waldo Emerson	Transcendentalists
Lawrence Ferlinghetti	Beat Poets
Garrick	Literary Club (Founder)
Allan Ginsberg	Beat Poets
Goethe	Sturm und Drang (Storm and Stress)
Goldsmith	Literary Club (Founder)
Robert Graves	Georgian Poets
Thom Gunn	The Movement
Ionesco	Theatre of the Absurd
Samuel Johnson	Literary Club (Founder)
Jack Kerouac	Beat Poets
Philip Larkin	The Movement
Amy Lowell	Imagism
Mallarmé	Decadents, Symbolism
Masefield	Georgian Poets
Walter De La Mare	Georgian Poets
John Osborne	Angry Young Men
Dorothy Parker	Algonquin Round Table
Ezra Pound	Imagism

Rimbaud	Decadents, Symbolism
Alain Robbe-Grillet	Nouvelle Roman
Schiller	Sturm und Drang (Storm and Stress)
Alan Sillitoe	Angry Young Men
Southey	Lake Poets
Thoreau	Transcendentalists
Valéry	Symbolism
Verlaine	Decadents, Symbolism
John Wain	The Movement
Wordsworth	Lake Poets

Literature

By: Description → Title

E.g.: What book deals with . . ./Which book is set in . . .?
Notes: Covers Books, Plays, Poems, Non Fiction.

Agincourt; Setting	*Henry V*
Albatross; Shooting causes bad luck	*The Ancient Mariner*
Alien Children in a village	*The Midwich Cuckoos*
Auctions Family	*The Mayor of Casterbridge*
Banned till 1960	*Lady Chatterley's Lover*
Best Selling Book	Bible
Best Selling Book; Copyright	*The Guinness Book of Records*
Boxer in US Army,WWII	*From Here to Eternity*
Bulgaria; Set in	*Arms and the Man*
Bullfighting in Spain	*Death in the Afternoon*
Burns Globe Theatre to the ground on 1st performance	*Henry VIII*
Burnt by mistake	*History of the French Revolution (Carlyle)*
Butler, when shipwrecked becomes leader	*The Admirable Crichton*
California; Family migrate to, during depression	*The Grapes of Wrath*
Car Industry, US; Condemns safety record	*Unsafe at any Speed*
Children; Eating; Advocates	*A Modest Proposal* (Swift)
Children's Nurse; Book given to	*Jungle Book*
Clutter Family; Murders of	*In Cold Blood*
Code; Written in; Not deciphered for 150 years	Samuel Pepys' Diary
De Gaulle; Plot to assassinate	*The Day of the Jackal*
Detective Novel; 1st, Considered	*The Moonstone* (Wilkie Collins)
Dresden Bombing; Set during	*Slaughterhouse Five*
Edition took 48 years to complete	*Oxford English Dictionary*
Elsa, the Lioness; About	*Born Free* (and sequels)
English Epic Poem; Oldest	*Beowulf*
E (letter); Book without any	*Gadsby* (Ernest Vincent Wright)
Finnish Epic	*Kalevala*
Flood; Tells of; Sumerian epic	*Gilgamesh*
French Revolution	*A Tale of Two Cities*
Ghost Story Competition between Shelleys and Byrons; Written for	*Frankenstein*
Gordon Riots; Set in	*Barnaby Rudge*
Gothic Novel; Parody of	*Northanger Abbey*
Grand Inquisitor story in	*The Brothers Karamazov*
Hanging; Takes place in the instant of	*Incident at Owl Creek Bridge*

Heroin Addiction	*The Man with The Golden Arm* (Nelson Algren)
Horses; Boy blinds 6	*Equus*
Indian Epic Poem	*Mahabharata, Ramayana*
Insect; Man changes into	*Metamorphosis*
Instructions left for the work to be burnt on author's death	*Aeneid* (Virgil)
Interruption causes poet to forget part of	*Kubla Khan*
Labour Camp in Soviet Union	*One Day in the Life of Ivan Denisovich*
Lavinium's founding, by Aeneas	*Aeneid*
'Lost Generation'; Term used in	*The Sun Also Rises*
Mad Hatter's Tea Party; Scene in	*Alice in Wonderland*
Manderley; House in	*Rebecca*
Meat Packing Plants in Chicago	*The Jungle*
Michelangelo; Life of	*The Agony and the Ecstasy*
Miners' Strike in 19th Century France	*Germinal*
Mountjoy Prison, Dublin; Set in	*The Quare Fellow*
Nihilists in 19th Century Russia	*Fathers and Sons*
No Characters or dialogue; Play	*Breath* (Samuel Beckett)
Novel; Oldest (considered)	*Tale of Genji* (Lady Murasaki)
Nymphet, 12 years old	*Lolita*
Overthrow of Government; Author attempts to recreate plot in real life	*The Dogs of War* (Frederick Forsyth)
Peru; Spanish conquest of	*The Royal Hunt of the Sun*
Picture, changes and ages	*The Picture of Dorian Gray*
Porteous Riots; Set during	*Heart of Midlothian*
Prince exchanges clothes with his double	*The Prince and the Pauper*
Prison; Written in	*Pilgrims Progress, Don Quixote, Mein Kampf*
Prosecuted for Immorality;-	
Banned for 20 years	*Mrs Warren's Profession* (Shaw)
Director (National Theatre)	*The Romans in Britain*
French Novel	*Madame Bovary*
Rabbits; Escape from old warren to new	*Watership Down*
Rugby League Player	*This Sporting Life*
Russian Capture of Berlin	*Armageddon*
School in Edinburgh	*The Prime of Miss Jean Brodie*
Schoolboys on Uninhabited Island	*Lord of the Flies*
Seagull	*Jonathan Livingston Seagull*
Sex Strike by Greek women	*Lysistrata*
Shakespeare Play; Most filmed	*Romeo and Juliet*
Shanghai Uprising, 1927	*Man's Fate*
Sharecroppers during US depression	*Let Us Now Praise Famous Men*
Shipwreck off Chile	*Don Juan*
Soldier; US Civil War	*The Red Badge of Courage*
South America; Revolution in	*Nostromo*
Spanish Civil War	*For Whom the Bell Tolls*
Spanish Inquisition, prisoner	*The Pit and the Pendulum*
Stepson; Written for	*Treasure Island*
Stolen from Public Libraries; Most	*Guinness Book of Records*
Taxi Drivers' strike	*Waiting for Lefty*
Vacuum Cleaner Representative, recruited into the Secret Service	*Our Man in Havana*
Valuable; Most	Gutenberg Bible
Vet; Yorkshire	James Herriot stories

Vietnam War; Demonstrations against in Washington	*Armies of the Night*
Vincent Van Gogh; Life of	*Lust for Life*
Whale; Quest for	*Moby Dick*
Whisky Drinking Priest in Mexico	*The Power and the Glory*
Windmill; Knight Imagines to be a giant	*Don Quixote*
Witchcraft Trials in Salem, Massachusetts	*The Crucible*
WWI; German anti-war novel	*All Quiet on the Western Front*
WWII; Mediterranean Island air force base	*Catch-22*
Xanadu; Set in	*Kubla Khan*

Literature and Books, Other

By: *General*

Booker Prize; Sponsored by	Booker McConnell Limited
Booker Prize Winners;-	
1983	J.M.Coetzee (*The Life and Times of Michael K*)
1984	Anita Brookner (*Hotel Du Lac*)
1985	Keri Hulme (*The Bone People*)
1986	Kingsley Amis (*The Old Devils*)
1987	Penelope Lively (*Moon Tiger*)
1988	Peter Carey (*Oscar & Lucinda*)
1989	Kazuo Ishiguro (*Remains of the Day*)
1990	A.S.Byatt (*Possession*)
1991	Ben Okri (*The Famished Road*)
Bound Volume, as against scrolled manuscript	Codex
Hotel with Round Table; Writers and critics meet at	Algonquin Hotel
Letter; Shortest	Victor Hugo to Publisher ('?'. Reply: '!')
Library(ies);-	
Classification; Pioneer	Melvil Dewey
France, National	Bibliothèque Nationale
Payment to Author for borrowing	Public Lending Right
Literature; Designed to instruct	Didactic
Manuscript written on 2nd hand vellum	Palimpsest
Material, originally made from calfskin	Vellum
MSS, Abbreviation for	Manuscripts
Nobel Prize for Literature; Winners;-	
1985	Claude Simon (France)
1986	Wole Soyinka (Nigeria)
1987	Joseph Brodsky (US)
1988	Naguib Mahfouz (Egypt)
1989	Camilo Jose Cela (Spain)
1990	Octavio Paz (Mexico)
1991	Nadine Gordimer (South Africa)
Poetry;-	
Feet; Types of	Anapest, Dactyl, Iambic, Trochee
Japanese form with 17 syllables	Haiku
Unit of metre	Foot
Without rhyme	Blank verse
Printed before 1500	Incunabula
Prize; Children's Book Illustration; UK	Kate Greenaway Medal

Newspapers and Magazines

By: General

Al Ahram	Country from: Egypt
Asahi Shimbun	Country from: Japan
Colour Magazine; 1st	*Sunday Times*, 1962
Corriere della Sera	Country from: Italy
Cosmopolitan; Editor from 1960s	Helen Gurley Brown
Daily Express; Proprietor from 1919	Lord Beaverbrook
Daily Mail; Founder	Alfred Harmsworth (Lord Northcliffe)
Daily Mirror; Founders	Alfred, Harold Harmsworth
Die Welt	Country from: Germany
El Pais	Country from: Spain

1st Appeared;-

1978	*Daily Star*
1986, March	*Today*
1986, October	*Independent*
1987, April	*News on Sunday*
Front Page; News for 1st time	*Times*, 1966
Guardian; Former name	*Manchester Guardian*
Haaretz	Country from: Israel
Headline; 'Dewey defeats Truman'	*Chicago Tribune* (Truman won)
Iszvetzia	Country from: Russia (The News)
Jen-min Jihbao	Country from: China
La Prensa	Country from: Argentina
La Stampa	Country from: Italy
Le Figaro	Country from: France
Le Monde	Country from: France
Mail on Sunday; Colour supplement	You
Morning Star; Former name	*Daily Worker* (till 1966)
National Review (US); Editor	William Buckley
New York Times; Slogan	'All the news that's fit to print'

News Agencies, Countries based in;-

Associated Press (AP)	US
Reuters	UK
TASS	USSR
United Press International (UPI)	US
Notice Restricting Publication for secrecy reasons	D-Notice
Opens and Closes, 1987	*Evening Post*
Penthouse	Publisher: Bob Guccione
People's Daily	Country from: China
Pigeon Post; News agency 1st uses	Reuters

Playboy

Founder	Hugh Hefner
Intended name	*Stag Party*
Motto	'Entertainment for Men'
Pravda	Country from: Russia (The Truth)
Publisher; Former Labour MP	Robert Maxwell
Readers Digest; Founder	DeWitt Wallace
Science fiction; 1st	*Amazing stories*
Spectator; Founders	Addison and Steele
Time Magazine; Cover, Woman most on	Virgin Mary
Time Magazine; Founder	Henry Luce
Times; Original name	*London Daily Universal Register*
Workers' Co-operative; Formed in 1975	*Scottish Daily News*
Yomiuri Shimbun	Country from: Japan

Non Fiction

By: Title → Author, Other Information

Affluent Society,The	J.K.Galbraith
Anabasis	Xenophon. Account of Greek expedition against Persians, under Cyrus
Art of Love,The	Ovid
Being and Nothingness	Sartre
Born Free	Joy Adamson
Brief History of Time, A	Stephen Hawking
City of God,The	St Augustine
Common Sense Book of Baby and Child Care,The	Benjamin Spock
Communist Manifesto,The	Marx and Engels
Compleat Angler,The	Izaak Walton. Dialogue between Fisherman, Hunter and Falconer
Concerning the Revolutions of the Heavenly bodies	Copernicus
Confessions	St Augustine
Critique of Pure Reason,The	Immanuel Kent
Das Kapital	Karl Marx
Decline and Fall of the Roman Empire,The	Edward Gibbon
Decline of the West,The	Oswald Spengler
Descent of Man,The	Charles Darwin
Devil's Dictionary,The	Ambrose Bierce
Dialogues on the Two Chief Systems of the Universe	Galileo
Diary	Samuel Pepys
Diary of Anne Frank,The	Diary of Girl in Amsterdam under Nazi occupation
Dictionary	Samuel Johnson
Dictionary of Modern English Usage	Henry Fowler
Discourse on Method	René Descartes
Divided Self,The	R.D.Laing
Ecclesiastical History of the English Nation	Venerable Bede
Elements	Euclid (on geometry)
Encyclopedia Brittanica	1st published in Edinburgh
Essay on The Principle of Population	Thomas Malthus. Argues that population outruns food
Female Eunuch,The	Germaine Greer
French Revolution,The	Thomas Carlyle
Future Shock	Alvin Toffler
Gallic Wars	Julius Caesar
Games People Play	Eric Byrne
General Theory of Employment, Interest and Money,The	J.M.Keynes
Golden Bough,The	Sir James Frazer
Gulag Archipelago	Alexander Solzhenitsyn
History of England,The	Thomas Macaulay
History of Rome,The	Livy
History of the English Speaking Peoples,A	Winston Churchill
History of the Kings of Britain	Geoffrey of Monmouth
How the Other Half Lives	Jacob Riis

Imitation of Christ,The	Thomas à Kempis
Interpretation of Dreams,The	Sigmund Freud
Lays of Ancient Rome,The	Macaulay
L'Encyclopédie	Denis Diderot and other
Leviathan	Thomas Hobbes
Meditations	Marcus Aurelius
Mein Kampf	Adolf Hitler. Written in jail (Meaning: My Struggle)
My Family and Other Animals	Gerald Durrell. Set in Corfu
New Industrial State,The	J.K.Galbraith
Novum Organum	Francis Bacon
On Aggression	Konrad Lorenz
On Liberty	John Stuart Mill
One Dimensional Man	Herbert Marcuse
Organisation Man,The	W.H.Whyte
Origin of Species,The	Charles Darwin
Oxford English Dictionary,The	James A.M.Murray (1st compiler)
Philippics	Demosthenes
Poor Richard's Almanac	Benjamin Franklin
Power Elite,The	C.Wright Mills
Prince,The	Machiavelli. Modelled on: Cesare Borgia
Principia Mathematica	Bertrand Russell
Protestant Ethic and the Spirit of Capitalism, The	Max Weber
Republic,The	Plato
Revolt of the Masses,The	Jose Ortega y Gasset
Rights of Man,The	Tom Paine
Second Sex,The	Simone De Beauvoir
Seven Pillars of Wisdom	T.E.Lawrence. Arab revolt against Turkey in WWI
Sex and the Single Girl	Helen Gurley Brown
Sexual Behaviour in the Human Male	Alfred Kinsey (The Kinsey Report)
Sexual Politics	Kate Millett
Silent Spring	Rachel Carson. Effects of pollution and insecticides
Soul on Ice	Eldridge Cleaver
Souls of Black Folk,The	W.E.B.Du Bois
Study of History,The	Arnold Toynbee
Summa Theologica	Saint Thomas Aquinas
Syntactic Structures	Noam Chomsky
Thus Spake Zarathustra	Friedrich Nietzsche
Two Cultures and the Scientific Revolution,The	C.P.Snow
Unsafe at Any Speed	Ralph Nader
Utopia	Sir Thomas More
Wealth of Nations,The	Adam Smith
Year in Provence, A	Peter Mayle

Nursery Rhymes

By: General

Child

Monday's	Fair of face
Tuesday's	Full of grace
Wednesday's	Full of woe
Thursday's	Far to go
Friday's	Loving and giving

Saturday's	Works hard for a living
Sabbath Day	Blithe, bonny, good and gay
Little Boy Blue; Where	Under a haystack fast asleep
Little Boys; Made of	Slugs and snails and puppy dogs' tails
Little Girls; Made of	Sugar and spice and all things nice
Little Miss Muffet; Eats	Curds and whey
Lucky Locket; Pocket; Who finds	Kitty Fisher
Nut tree; Bears	Silver nutmeg, golden pear
Shoe, Woman in; Gives children	Broth without any bread
St Ives; How many going to	1
Tarts; Who steals	Knave of Hearts

Plays

By: Title → Author, General

Admirable Crichton,The	J.M.Barrie
Title	Butler
Master	Lord Loam
After the Fall	Arthur Miller
Central Character	Quentin
Former Wife	Maggie (modelled on Marilyn Monroe)
Alchemist,The	Ben Jonson
Title	Subtle
All for Love	John Dryden
All's Well That Ends Well	Shakespeare
Central Characters	Count Bertram of Rousillon, Helena
Amadeus	Peter Schaffer
Theme	Salieri's claim to have murdered Mozart
Androcles and the Lion	G.B.Shaw
Andromaque	Racine
Antigone	Sophocles, Jean Anouilh
Arms and the Man	G.B.Shaw
Family	The Petkoffs
Set in	Bulgaria
Arsenic and Old Lace	Joseph Kesselring
As You Like It	Shakespeare
Clown	Touchstone
Lovers	Rosalind and Orlando
Set in	Forest of Arden
Balcony,The	Jean Genet
Bald Prima Donna,The	Eugène Ionesco
Barefoot in the Park	Neil Simon
Bartholomew Fair	Ben Jonson
Beaux Stratagem,The	George Farquhar
Becket	Jean Anouilh
Birthday Party,The	Harold Pinter
Boarding House Owners	Meg and Petey
Party for	Stanley
Blithe Spirit	Noel Coward
Blue Bird,The	Maurice Maeterlinck
Bluebird, whereabouts	At home
Children	Tyltyl, Mytyl
Cactus Flower	Abe Burrows
Caesar and Cleopatra	G.B.Shaw
Camille	Alexandre Dumas (Fils)
Central Character	Marguerite Gautier

Candida	G.B.Shaw
Candida's Husband	Morell (clergyman)
Poet	Marchbanks
Caretaker,The	Harold Pinter
Title	Davies
Cat on a Hot Tin Roof	Tennessee Williams
Husband	Brick
Location	St Louis
Title	Maggie Pollitt
Caucasian Chalk Circle,The	Bertold Brecht
Charley's Aunt	Brandon Thomas
Charley	Charley Wykeham
Title	Dona Lucia d'Alvadores
Cherry Orchard,The	Anton Chekhov
Cherry Orchard at end	Gets chopped down
Chips with Everything	Arnold Wesker
Theme	RAF conscripts' treatment
Cocktail Party,The	T.S.Eliot
Comedy of Errors,The	Shakespeare
Merchant of Syracuse	Aegeon
Twins	Antipholus (2), Dromio (2)
Crucible,The	Arthur Miller
Cyrano De Bergerac	Edmond Rostand
Cyrano's Affliction	Large nose
Cyrano's Love	Roxane
Death of a Salesman	Arthur Miller
Salesman	Willy Loman
Doctor Faustus	Christopher Marlowe
Doll's House,A	Henrik Ibsen
Doll	Nora
Nora's Husband	Torvald Helmer
Electra	Sophocles, Euripides (different plays)
Entertainer,The	John Osborne
Title	Archie Rice
Entertaining Mr Sloane	Joe Orton
Equus	Peter Schaffer
Psychiatrist	Dysart
Stableboy	Alan Strang
Father,The	Strindberg
Faust	Goethe
Frogs,The	Aristophanes
Glass Menagerie,The	Tennessee Williams
Family	The Wingfields
Hamlet	Shakespeare
Courtiers	Rosencrantz and Guildenstern
1st Actor to play	Richard Burbage
Hamlet's Love	Ophelia
Hamlet's Mother	Gertrude
Hamlet's Uncle	Claudius (new King)
Set in	Elsinore Castle, Denmark
Skull	Yorrick (Jester)
Stabbed by mistake	Polonius (Chancellor)
Sword Fight with Hamlet	Laertes
Hay Fever	Noel Coward
Hedda Gabler	Henrik Ibsen
Hedda's Husband	Professor George Tessman
Henry V	Shakespeare

Set in	Agincourt
Henry VIII	Shakespeare
Iceman Cometh,The	Eugene O'Neill
Salesman	Hickey
Set in	Harry Hope's, New York
Importance of Being Ernest,The	Oscar Wilde
Ernest	Jack Worthing (real and assumed name)
Governess	Miss Prism
Jack found in	Handbag at station
Left in baby's place	A novel
In Camera	Jean-Paul Sartre
Characters	Garcin, Estelle, Inez
Set in	Hell
Inspector Calls,An	J.B.Priestley
Inspector General,The	Nikolai Gogol
Imposter	Khlestakov
Jew of Malta,The	Christopher Marlowe
Jew	Barabas
Journey's End	R.C.Sheriff
Theme	WWI
Julius Caesar	Shakespeare
Caesar stabbed by	Casca (1st), Brutus (last)
Caesar warned of	Ides of March (stabbed on)
Noblest Roman	Brutus
Where stabbed	Senate
Jumpers	Tom Stoppard
Professor	George Moore
George's Wife	Dotty
Juno and the Paycock	Sean O'Casey
Paycock	Jack Boyle
King Lear	Shakespeare
Lear's Daughters	Goneril, Regan, Cordelia
Disinherited	Cordelia
Lady Windermere's Fan	Oscar Wilde
Lady Windermere's Mother	Mrs Erlynne
Lady's Not for Burning,The	Christopher Fry
Set in	Cool Clary
Le Bourgeois Gentilhomme	Molière
Title	Monsieur Jourdain
Long Days Journey into the Night,A	Eugene O'Neill
Family	The Tyrones
Look Back in Anger	John Osborne
Central Character	Jimmy Porter (Angry Young Man)
Wife	Alison
Love's Labours Lost	Shakespeare
Lower Depths,The	Maxim Gorki
Lysistrata	Aristophanes
Macbeth	Shakespeare
Macbeth	Thane of Glamis, then Thane of Cawdor
Macbeth killed by	Macduff
Macbeth murders	Duncan (King)
Witches' prophecy	Macbeth not overthrown till Birnam wood shall come to Dunsinane
Maids,The	Jean Genet
Title	Claire, Solange
Major Barbara	G.B.Shaw
Man and Superman	G.B.Shaw

Man for all Seasons,A	Robert Bolt
Marriage à la Mode	John Dryden
Measure for Measure	Shakespeare
Central Character	Duke of Vienna
Duke leaves as Ruler	Angelo
Imprisoned	Claudio's sister, Isabella
Medea	Euripides
Merchant of Venice,The	Shakespeare
Bassanios's Friend	Antonio
Couples	Bassanio and Portia, Lorenzo and Jessica
Lawyer at Antonio's trial	Portia
Moneylender	Shylock
Shylock's Requirement	Pound of flesh
Why unable to obtain pound of flesh	Can't spill any blood
Merry Wives of Windsor,The	Shakespeare
Central Character	Falstaff
Sequel to	*Henry IV*
Title	Mistress Ford and Mistress Page
Midsummer Night's Dream,A	Shakespeare
Actors	Bottom (Weaver), Quince (Carpenter), Snug (Joiner)
King of Fairies	Oberon
Oberon's Servant	Puck
Play	*Pyramus and Thisbe*
Puck, Other Name	Robin Goodfellow
Queen of Fairies	Titania
Season takes place in	Spring
Set in	Athens
Misanthrope,The	Molière
Title	Alceste
Mother Courage	Bertold Brecht
Mourning becomes Electra	Eugene O'Neill
Based on	Oresteia (Aeschylus)
Much Ado About Nothing	Shakespeare
Lovers	Claudia and Hero, Beatrice and Benedict
Murder in the Cathedral	T.S.Eliot
No Sex Please, We're British	Anthony Marriott, Alistair Foot
Norman Conquests,The	Alan Ayckbourn
Odd Couple,The	Neil Simon
Oedipus the King	Sophocles
Oedipus' Father	Laius
Oedipus' Wife/Mother	Jocasta
Seer	Teiresias
Oresteia Trilogy,The	Aeschylus
Orestes	Euripides
Othello	Shakespeare
Accuses Desdemona of Infidelity	Iago
Full Title	Othello, the Moor of Venice
Othello's Wife	Desdemona
Our Lady of the Flowers	Jean Genet
Written in	Prison
Peter Pan	James Barrie
Captain	Hook
Children	John, Michael, Wendy
Dog	Nana

Fairy	Tinkerbell
Family	The Darlings
Ship	*Jolly Roger*
Written for	Llewellyn Davis
Phèdre	Racine
Based on	Hippolytus (Euripides)
Picture of Dorian Gray,The	Oscar Wilde
Artist	Basil Hallward
Playboy of the Western World,The	J.M.Synge
Title	Christie Mahon
Private Lives	Noel Coward
Written for	Gertrude Lawrence
Prometheus Bound	Aeschylus
Pygmalion	G.B.Shaw
Flower Girl	Eliza Doolittle
Higgin's House	In Wimpole Street
Professor	Henry Higgins
Scandal because	Uses 'Bloody'
Quare Fellow,The	Brendan Behan
Set in	Irish Jail
Riders to the Sea	J.M.Synge
Rivals,The	Richard Sheridan
Lady	Lydia Languish
Lydia's Aunt	Mrs Malaprop
Set in	Bath
Title	Captain Absolute (using name Ensign Beverley), Sir Lucius O'Trigger, Bob Acres
Romeo and Juliet	Shakespeare
Juliet; Family	The Capulets
Love Scene setting	Balcony
Romeo; Family	The Montagues
Set in	Verona
Roots	Arnold Wesker
Central Character	Beatie Bryant
Set in	Norfolk
Rose Tattoo,The	Tennessee Williams
Rosencrantz and Guildenstern are dead	Tom Stoppard
Royal Hunt of the Sun,The	Peter Schaffer
School for Scandal,The	Richard Sheridan
Seagull,The	Anton Chekhov
Characters	Irina,Nina
Novelist	Trigorin
Second Mrs Tanqueray,The	Sir Arthur W.Pinero
Title	Paula Ray
Sergeant Musgrave's Dance	John Arden
Seven against Thebes	Aeschylus
Shadow of a Gunman,The	Sean O'Casey
She Stoops to Conquer	Oliver Goldsmith
Central Character	Marlow
Marlow woos	Miss Hardcastle
Six Characters in Search of an Author	Luigi Pirandello
Sleuth	Anthony Shaffer
St Joan	G.B.Shaw
Streetcar Named Desire,A	Tennessee Williams
Blanche's Sister	Stella
Central Character	Blanche Du Bois

Set in	New Orleans
Stella's Husband	Stanley Kowalsky
Taming of the Shrew,The	Shakespeare
Katherina's Husband	Petruchio (Who tames her)
Shrew	Katherina
Tartuffe	Molière
Tempest,The	Shakespeare
Duke of Milan	Prospero
Prospero's Daughter	Miranda
Prospero's Slave	Caliban
Spirit	Ariel
Three Sisters,The	Anton Chekhov
Title	Olga, Masha, Irina
Travesties	Tom Stoppard
Set in	Zurich
Trojan Women,The	Euripides
Twelfth Night	Shakespeare
Couples	Duke Orsino and Viola, Sebastian and Olivia
Olivia's Steward	Malvolio
Olivia's Uncle	Sir Toby Belch
Subtitle	*What you will*
Twins	Viola, Sebastian
Two Gentlemen of Verona	Shakespeare
Title	Valentine, Proteus
Ubi Roi	Alfred Jarry
Uncle Vanya	Anton Chekhov
Volpone	Ben Jonson
Volpone's Servant	Mosca
Voyage Round my Father,A	John Mortimer
Waiting for Godot	Samuel Beckett
Tramps	Vladimir (Didi), Estragon (Gogo)
Waiting for Lefty	Clifford Odets
Title	Lefty Costello
Way of the World,The	William Congreve
Characters	Mirabell, Millamant, Lady Wishfort
What the Butler Saw	Joe Orton
Set in	Psychiatrist's clinic
Who's Afraid of Virginia Woolf?	Edward Albee
Winslow Boy,The	Terence Rattigan
Based on	Archer–Shee case
Winter's Tale,A	Shakespeare
King of Bohemia	Polixenes
King of Sicilia	Leontes

Poetry

By: Title → Author, General

Abou Ben Adhem	James Leigh Hunt
Absalom and Achitophel	John Dryden
Adonais	Percy Bysshe Shelley
In memory of	John Keats
Aeneid,The	Virgil
Alexander's Feast	John Dryden
Annabel Lee	Edgar Allan Poe
Written to	Wife

Annals	Tacitus
Ash Wednesday	T.S.Eliot
Babi Yar	Yevgeny Yevtushenko
Barbara Frietchie	John Whittier
Beowulf	Unknown
Monster	Grendel
Set in	King Hrothgar's Danish Kingdom
Title	Swedish Prince (slays monster)
Book of Nonsense,The	Edward Lear
Written For	Children of Lord Derby
Bridge,The	Hart Crane
Bucolics,The	Virgil
Cantos,The	Ezra Pound
Cautionary Tales	Hilaire Belloc
Charge of the Light Brigade,The	Alfred, Lord Tennyson
Childe Harold	Lord Byron
Child's Garden of Verses,A	R.L.Stevenson
Christabel	Samuel Taylor Coleridge
Courtship of Miles Standish,The	Henry Wadsworth Longfellow
Curfew must not ring tonight	Rose Thorpe
Deserted Village,The	Oliver Goldsmith
Divine Comedy,The	Dante
'Do not go gently into that good night'	Dylan Thomas
Don Juan	Lord Byron
Elegy Written in a Country Churchyard	Thomas Gray
Endymion	John Keats
England,My England	William Henley
Excelsior	Henry Wadsworth Longfellow
Faerie Queene,The	Edmund Spenser
Four Quartets,The	T.S.Eliot
Georgics,The	Virgil
Gitanjali	Rabrindranath Tagore
Gunga Din	Rudyard Kipling
Hiawatha	Henry Wadsworth Longfellow
Tribe	Ojibwas
Wife	Minnehaha
Highwayman,The	Alfred Noyes
Howl	Allen Ginsberg
Hudibras	Samuel Butler
Hunting of the Snark,The	Lewis Carroll
'I wandered lonely as a cloud'	William Wordsworth
Iliad,The	Homer
In Flanders Field	John McCrae
In Memoriam	Alfred, Lord Tennyson
Written to	Arthur Hallam (sister's fiancé)
Intimations of Immortality	William Wordsworth
Jaberwocky	Lewis Carroll
Kubla Khan	Samuel Taylor Coleridge
Sacred River	Alph
Set in	Xanadu
La Belle Dame sans Merci	John Keats
Lady of Shalott,The	Alfred, Lord Tennyson
Leaves of Grass	Walt Whitman
Locksley Hall	Alfred, Lord Tennyson
Lotos Eaters,The	Alfred, Lord Tennyson
Love Song of J.Alfred Prufrock,The	T.S.Eliot
Mandalay	Kipling

Matilda	Hilaire Belloc
My Heart Leaps Up	William Wordsworth
Ode on A Grecian Urn	John Keats
Odyssey,The	Homer
Old Vicarage, Grantchester,The	Rupert Brooke
Owl and the Pussycat,The	Edward Lear
Buy ring from	Pig
Dine on	Mince and slices of quince
Eat with	Runcible spoon
Married by	Turkey
Ring costs	Shilling
Sailed for	Year and a day
Ozymandias	Percy Bysshe Shelley
Paradise Lost	John Milton
Paradise Regained	John Milton
Paul Revere's Ride	Henry Wadsworth Longfellow
Piers Plowman	William Langland
Prelude	William Wordsworth
Prometheus Unbound	Percy Bysshe Shelley
Queen Mab	Percy Bysshe Shelley
Railway Bridge of the Silvery Tay,The	William McGonagall
Rape of Lucrece,The	Shakespeare
Rape of the Lock,The	Alexander Pope
Raven,The	Edgar Allen Poe
Rime of the Ancient Mariner	Samuel Taylor Coleridge
Theme	Shoots albatross and suffers thereby
Rubaiyat	Omar Khayyam
Translated by	Edward Fitzgerald
Samson Agonistes	John Milton
Sea Fever	John Masefield
Shropshire Lad,A	A.E.Housman
Sohrab and Rustom	Matthew Arnold
Soldier,The	Rupert Brooke
Solitary Reaper,The	William Wordsworth
Tam O'Shanter	Robert Burns
Tintern Abbey	William Wordsworth
To a Nightingale	John Keats
To his Coy Mistress	Andrew Marvell
Traveller,The	Oliver Goldsmith
'Twas the night before Christmas	Clement Moore
Twelve,The	Aleksandr Blok
Tyger	William Blake
Village Blacksmith,The	Henry Wadsworth Longfellow
Walrus and the Carpenter,The	Lewis Carroll
Wasteland,The	T.S.Eliot
Wreck of the Hesperus,The	Henry Wadsworth Longfellow

The Living World

Contents

Animals	269	Land Animals	286
Animal Sounds		Male and Female	
By: Animal	269	By: Animal	291
Animal Life, General	269	Other Names	
Animals, Products from		By: Animal	292
By: Product	271	Scientific Names	
Birds	271	By: Scientific Name	293
Breeds		Young	
By: Breed	274	By: Animal	293
Collections		**Biology**	**294**
By: Animal	277	**Plants**	**295**
Dogs	277	Common Names	
Families		By: Scientific Name	295
By: Animal	278	Other Names	295
Famous Animals		Plant Families	
By: Animal/Description	280	By: Plant	296
Fish and Sea Creatures	282	Plant Varieties and Types	
Habitations		By: Variety	297
By: Animal	284	Plants, General	298
Horses	284	Plants, Products obtained from	
Insects (and Related Creatures)	285	By: Product	300

ANIMALS
Animal Sounds

By: Animal → Sound

Ape	Gibber
Ass	Bray
Bittern	Boom
Cat	Meow
Cow	Low/Moo
Crow	Caw
Deer	Bell
Dove	Coo
Duck	Quack
Goose	Hiss
Hen	Cackle
Jay	Chatter
Lion	Roar
Magpie	Chatter
Owl	Hoot/Screech
Pig	Grunt
Swallow	Twitter
Turkey	Gobble
Wolf	Howl

Animal Life, General

By General

Notes: *Covers information not identified with more specific sections.*

Abundant; Most   Nematode Sea Worm

Animal grouping (Phylum); Largest	Arthropods
Asian – Australian Geographical Divide	Wallace's Line
Baby; Biggest	Whale
Backbones; With	Vertebrates
Backbones; Without	Invertebrates
Believed Extinct previously	Coelocanth (Fish). Discovered alive, 1939
Birth to Live Young; Gives; Term for	Viviparous
Blood; Shoots jet of, from eyes	Horned Toad
Boxer; Named after	Jack Dempsey Fish
Brain(s);-	
11	Silkworm
Heaviest	Sperm Whale
Largest as body proportion	Ant
Coral; Biggest reef	Great Barrier Reef, Australia
Dictionary; 1st animal in	Aardvark
Egg;-	
Biggest for size	Kiwi
Gives Birth from; Term for	Ovoviviparous
Group, laid at one time	Clutch
Largest	Ostrich
Largest; Extinct	Aepyornis (Roc)
Male; Carried by	Sea Horse
Expeditions; 'Bring 'em back alive'	Frank Buck
Eye(s);-	
Largest	Giant Squid
Move separately	Chameleon
Third, on top of head	Tuatara
Fly; Artificially; 1st	Sheep, Cock, Duck in balloon, 1783
Flying Animal; Largest	Quetzalcoatlus (Pterosaur)
Foot; One	Molluscs (Snails)
Gas Leaks; Trained to detect	Dog
Gestation Period;-	
Longest	African Elephant
Shortest	Dasyurus Vivverinus (Marsupial Cat), 8 days
Ink Screen; Produces as defence	Cuttle-fish, Octopus, Squid
Invertebrate; Largest	Giant Squid
Jump; Highest	Whale
Land and water; Lives on; Term for	Amphibian
Largest	Blue Whale
Law; Animal's evidence admissible, US	Bloodhound
Legs:-	
Crab	10
Lobster	10
Shrimp	10
Spiders	8
Starfish	5
Littoral Animals; Habitat	Sea shore
Longest	Bootlace Worm
Longest Life;-	Tortoise
Mammal	Man
Mammal; 2nd	Elephant
Male; Gives birth	Seahorse
Meat Eating; Term for	Carnivore
Mermaid; Resembles	Manatee
Migratory Animal; Largest	Whale

Pets; Minimum legal age of buyer	12
Pinnipeds; Meaning	Mammals with flippers (Walrus, Seal, Sea-lion)
Plant and Animal Eating; Term for	Omnivore
Plant Eating; Term for	Herbivore
Psittacosis; Other name	Parrot Fever
Reproduces without developing to adulthood	Axolotl
Reproduction without sex; Term for	Parthenogenesis
Sexes; Alternates between annually	Oyster
Sight Behind without turning head	Giraffe
Simplest Form of animal life	Protozoa
Sleep;-	
At Night; Term for	Diurnal
During the Day; Term for	Nocturnal
On Back, regularly; Only species	Humans
Standing up	Horse
Stomach; Can turn inside out	Starfish
Strongest Natural Object for its weight	Feather
Suckles Young; Animal type	Mammal
Sunburn; Only non human to suffer	Pig
Surgery; Used in	Ants (as stitches)
Tail; Can grasp things; Term for	Prehensile
Tail; Sheds to escape predators	Lizard
Teeth; Largest	Elephant (tusks)
Temperature; Hottest	Goat
Tongue; Fastened at front	Toad
Twins; Always give birth to	Armadillo (Identical), Salamander
Upside Down; Turns head to eat	Flamingo
Valuable; Most	Race Horse
War Medals: Have Won	Carrier Pigeons, Dogs
Washes Food	Raccoon
White; Turns in winter	Arctic Fox, Ptarmigan, Stoat
World Wildlife Fund; Symbol	Giant Panda
Zoo; 1st	Regent's Park, London

Animals, Products from

By: Product → Source

Ambergris	Whale intestine
Catgut	Sheep or Horse
Cochineal	Powdered insect
Guano	Dried bird droppings (fertiliser)
Lanolin	Sheep's wool
Mohair	Angora Goat
Musk	Civet
Nutria Fur	Coypu
Pearl	Oyster (made of Nacre)
Tyrian Purple	Murex (shell)

Birds

By: General

Arctic Tern; Migrates to	Antarctic
Backwards; Can fly; Only one	Hummingbird

Barricades itself in tree cavity with eggs	Hornbill
Beak;-	
Insect eating; Characteristic	Pointed
Meat eating; Characteristic	Hooked
Bill;-	
Never closes	Open Bill Stork
Turned up; Most	Avocet
Bird of Paradise; From	New Guinea
Bird of Prey;-	
Largest	Harpy Eagle
Largest; UK	Golden Eagle
Blackbird; Female; Colour	Brown
Budgerigar;-	
Originates from	Australia
Wild; Colour	Green
Buries Acorns	Jay
Canaries;-	
Name from	Canary Islands
Singing	Only males
Cassowary; From	Australia, New Guinea
Chicken;-	
Bird Order	Galliforme
Castrated Male	Capon
Under 1 year	Pullet
Claws on wing tips	Hoatzin
Colour; Changes to white in Winter	Ptarmigan
Commonest	Red-billed Quelea
Cuckoo; Baby; Characteristics	Pushes other young out of nest
Deepest Diving	Emperor Penguin
Descended from	Reptiles
Dodo;-	
Extinct; When	1681
From	Mauritius
Domestic Bird; Commonest	Chicken
Drinks without having to hold head back	Pigeon
Drops Bones on rocks to break	Lammergeier (Bearded Vulture)
Duck;-	
Bird Order	Anseriforme
Commonest; Britain	Mallard
Eggs; When laid	Morning
Quack	Females
Earliest	Archaeopteryx
Egg;-	
Incubates using decomposing vegetable matter	Megapode
Lays in other birds' nests	Cuckoo
Smallest	Hummingbird
Emu; From	Australia
Enclosure for	Aviary
Extinct; Once most numerous in US	Passenger Pigeon
Fastest;-	
Level Flight	Spine-tailed Swift (106 mph)
Running	Ostrich
Stooping	Peregrine Falcon
Fish; Catching, Trained for	Cormorant
Flightless; Can swim	Penguin

Flying; Largest	Kori Bustard
Food; Ground in	Gizzard
Food; Keeps stuck on thorns	Shrike
Gas in Mines; Used to detect	Linnet, Budgerigar
Great Auk;-	
Extinct	1844
Other Name	Atlantic Penguin
Hangs Upside Down	Bird of Paradise
Harpy Eagle; Feeds on	Capuchin Monkey
Heaviest;-	Mute Swan, Kori Bustard
Heron; Flying; Distinguishing feature	Holds head back, not extended
Hummingbird;-	
African Equivalent	Sunbird
Food	Nectar from flowers
Noise from	Wings
Impales Prey on sticks	Shrike
Kingfisher; Nest	Built at end of tunnel in riverbank
Kiwi; Original name	Apteryx
Largest;-	
Ever	Moa
Flying	Kori Bustard
Living	Ostrich
Living; 2nd	Emu
Wing Span	Albatross
Migrates furthest	Arctic Tern
Nest;-	
In water; British	Crested Grebe
Near the ground; Term for	Gallinaceous
Stitches	Weaver Bird
Non-flying; Largest	Ostrich
Nostrils at tip of beak	Kiwi
Nuts; Wedges into rocks to open	Nuthatch
Owl; Smallest	Elf Owl
Painter of US species; Renowned	J.J.Audobon
Parrot;-	
Attacks sheep	Kea
Largest	Macaw
Toes	Two forwards, two backwards
Penguin;-	
King; Holds eggs in	Abdominal fold
From	Antarctic
Largest	Emperor
Uses wings for	Swimming
Pink	Flamingo
Ptarmigan; Winter; Change	Grows white plumage
Puffin; Feet; Colour	Red: Summer. Yellow: Winter
Raced with jockeys	Ostriches
Rhea; Found in	South America
Running; Fastest	Ostrich
Sacred;-	
Aztec	Quetzal
Egyptian	Ibis
Secretary Bird; Name from	Quill shaped crest
Shells; Breaks by hammering with	
stones	Thrush
Shrike; Nickname	Butcher Bird
Slowest; Flying	American Woodcock

Smallest;-	Bee Hummingbird
European	Goldcrest
Smell; Best sense of	Kiwi
Sonar; Equipped with	Guacharo (Oilbird)
Stationary; Can stay in the air; Only	Hummingbird
Steals Food from other birds in flight	Skua
Stupid; Most	Turkey
Swan;-	
Australian; Colour	Black
Queen's; Identified by	Nick in beak
Take off from water; Method	Runs along water first
Takes other birds' fish	Skua
Tallest (ever)	Moa
Thrush; Snail Shell; Breaks with	Stone
Torch; Used as	Fulmar (Petrel)
Total Darkness; Can fly in	Guacharo
Traps Mate in nest	Hornbill
Underwater; Walks	Dipper
Web-footed; Smallest	Petrel
Wing Span; Largest	Albatross
Wings; Largest	Andean Condor
Woodpecker;-	
Doesn't peck trees for food	Flicker (eats ants)
Nest	Tree trunk
Pecking; Reason	To reach insects

Breeds

By: Breed → Animal

Notes: Includes Breed used together with animal name, e.g., Tiger Moth.

Aberdeen Angus	Cattle
Airedale	Terrier
Alderney	Cattle
Angora	Cat, Goat, Rabbit
Appaloosa	Horse
Arabian	Camel, Horse
Archangel	Cat
Arctic	Fox, Hare, Tern
Australorp	Chicken
Aylesbury	Duck
Ayrshire	Cattle (dairy)
Barbet	Dog
Basenji	Dog
Bearded	Lizard, Tit
Beltsville	Turkey
Berkshire	Pig
Birdwing	Butterfly
Black Norfolk	Turkey
Blackface	Sheep
Blue Orpington	Chicken
Bluefin	Tuna
Bonito	Tuna
Border	Terrier
Borzoi	Dog

Brahman	Cattle
Briard	Dog
Brimstone	Butterfly
Brittany	Spaniel
Broad-breasted Bronze	Turkey
Buff Orpington	Duck
Cairn	Terrier
Cape	Buffalo, Zebra
Charolais	Cattle
Chester White	Pig
Cheviot	Sheep
Chinese	Goose
Clun	Sheep
Clydesdale	Carthorse, Terrier
Coal	Tit
Cocker	Spaniel
Colbred	Sheep
Copper	Butterfly
Cornish	Chicken
Corriedale	Sheep
Dale and Fell	Pony
Dark Cornish	Chicken
Dorking	Chicken
Duroc	Pig
Embden	Goose
English Romney	Sheep
Faverolle	Chicken
Friesian	Cattle (dairy)
Friesland	Sheep
Galloway	Cattle (beef)
Grant's	Gazelle
Grey Headed	Albatross, Wagtail
Greylag	Goose
Griffon	Dog
Guernsey	Cattle (dairy)
Hampshire	Pig
Hartmann's	Zebra
Havana Brown	Cat
Hen	Harrier
Hereford	Cattle (beef)
Highland	Cattle, Pony
Hobby	Falcon
Holstein	Cattle
Houdon	Chicken
Humpbacked	Whale
Husky	Dog
Irish	Setter, Terrier, Wolfhound
Jersey	Cattle (dairy)
Jersey White Giant	Chicken
Kentish Glory	Moth
Khaki Campbell	Duck
Killer	Whale
King Charles	Spaniel
Kuvasz	Dog
Landrace	Pig
Large Black	Pig
Large White	Pig

Leghorn	Chicken
Leicester	Sheep
Light Sussex	Chicken
Lippizaner	Horse
Long Horn	Cattle
Mangolitza	Pig
Manx	Cat, Shearwater
Merino	Sheep
Mexican Hairless	Dog
Milkweed	Butterfly
Monarch	Butterfly
Montague's	Harrier
Muscovy	Duck
New Forest	Pony
Painted Lady	Butterfly
Papillon	Dog
Percheron	Carthorse
Peregrine	Falcon
Persian	Cat, Lamb
Plymouth Rock	Chicken
Poland China	Pig
Puss	Moth
Red Admiral	Butterfly
Rhode Island Red	Chicken
Rottweiler	Dog
Rouen	Duck
Russell's	Viper
Russian Blue	Cat
Saluki	Dog
Samoyed	Dog
Schnauzer	Dog
Sealyham	Terrier
Shetland	Pony, Sheepdog
Siamese	Cat, Fighting Fish
Skipjack	Tuna
Skye	Terrier
Southdown	Sheep
Sperm	Whale
Spitz	Dog
Springer	Spaniel
Suffolk Punch	Carthorse
Swaledale	Sheep
Tamworth	Pig
Thompson's	Gazelle
Tiger	Beetle, Moth, Shark
Tortoiseshell	Cat, Butterfly, Turtle
Toulouse	Goose
Turnopit	Dog
Viceroy	Butterfly
Vizsla	Dog
Wandering	Albatross
Welsh Cob	Pony
Wessex Saddleback	Pig
Wyandotte	Chicken
Yellowfin	Tuna
Yucca	Moth

Collections

By: Animal → Collective Name

Badgers	Cete
Bears	Sloth
Bees	Swarm
Cats	Cluster
Cattle	Herd
Chickens	Brood
Choughs	Chattering
Coots	Covert
Crows	Murder
Deer	Herd
Dogs	Kennel
Ducks	Team, Flight
Foxes	Skulk
Frogs	Army
Geese	Gaggle (Skein – in flight)
Hares	Down
Hawks	Cast
Horses	Herd
Kangaroos	Mob
Kittens	Kindle
Leopards	Leap
Lions	Pride
Monkeys (Chimpanzees)	Troop
Partridges	Covey
Peacocks	Muster
Penguins	Rookery
Pigs	Drove
Rhinoceroses	Crash
Sheep	Flock
Swans	Bevy
Toads	Knot
Whales	School

Dogs

By: General

Afraid of dogs; Animal	Jaguar
Alsatian; Former name	German Shepherd Dog
Ancestor	Tomarctus
Awarded Titles in Ancient China	Pekinese
Banned from city streets	China
Bark; Can't	Basenji, Dingo
Bites Humans most	Alsatian
Borzoi; Other name	Russian Wolfhound
Bred for; Originally:-	
Borzoi	Wolf hunting
Boxer	Bull baiting
Bull Terrier	Bull and Bear baiting
Bulldog	Bull baiting
Dachshund	Badger hunting

Dalmatian	Running beside stage coaches
Giant Schnauzer	Cattle herding
Great Dane	Wild Boar, Bear hunting
Harrier	Hare hunting
Husky	Sledge pulling
Mastiff	Bear baiting
Pomeranian	Sledge pulling
Poodle	Duck shooting, Gun dog
Yorkshire Terrier	Rat catching
Chihuahua;-	
Descended from	Techichi (Central American Indian Dog)
Origin	Mexico
China; Sacred Dog	Pekinese
Colour Vision	None
Dog show; Most important	Crufts
Eyesight; Best	Greyhound
Fastest	Greyhound
Heaviest	St Bernard
Identification; Used for	Nose print
Indian; Wild	Dhole
Lying Down; Does before	Turns around
Moult; Doesn't	Poodle
Smallest	Chihuahua
Spaniel; Name origin	Spain
Sweats	Through paws
Tallest	Great Dane, Irish Wolfhound
Tax Collector; Name from	Doberman
Tongue; Blue-black	Chow

Families

By: Animal → Family

E.g.: What type of animal is a . . .?
Notes: Includes general (e.g. Bird) and Specific Categories.
See Also: Breeds

Ai	Sloth
Ant Lion	Insect
Axolotl	Salamander
Aye Aye	Primate (Squirrel-like)
Beluga	Whale
Basilisk	Lizard
Besang	Goat
Blind Snake	Lizard
Bongo	Antelope
Booby	Gannet
Capercaillie	Grouse
Capybara	Rodent
Chipmunk	Squirrel
Coati	Raccoon
Condor	Vulture
Copperhead	Snake
Corkwing	Fish
Cottontail	Rabbit
Crossbeak	Finch
Dik Dik	Antelope
Duiker	Antelope
Egret	Heron

Eland	Antelope
Firefly	Beetle
Flicker	Woodpecker
Flying Dragon	Lizard
Flying Fox	Fruit Bat
Fritillary	Moth
Gar	Fish
Gecko	Lizard
Genet	Civet
Gharial	Crocodile
Giant Panda	Raccoon
Gila Monster	Lizard
Glass Snake	Lizard
Glow worm	Beetle
Goby	Fish
Goldfish	Carp
Gourami	Fish
Grampus	Dolphin
Griffon	Vulture
Grunt	Fish
Gudgeon	Carp
Guppy	Fish
Hammerkop	Bird
Harlequin	Duck
Hartebeest	Antelope
Horned Toad	Lizard
Ibex	Goat
Impala	Antelope
Jack Rabbit	Hare
Jaeger	Gull
Jay	Crow
Jubiru	Stork
Kea	Parrot
Kestrel	Falcon
Kinkajou	Raccoon
Kittiwake	Gull
Klipspringer	Antelope
Kookaburra	Kingfisher
Krait	Snake
Kudu	Antelope
Loon	Bird
Loris	Primate
Lory	Parrot
Macaw	Parrot
Mandrill	Baboon
Markhor	Goat
Marmoset	Monkey
Marmot	Squirrel
Marten	Weasel
Mollie	Fish
Mouflon	Sheep
Mudskipper	Fish
Muntjac	Deer
Nautilus	Mollusc
Nightingale	Thrush
Nilgai	Antelope
Noddy	Tern

Nyala	Antelope
Okapi	Giraffe
Onager	Ass
Oriole	Bird
Oryx	Antelope
Phoebe	Bird
Pika	Rabbit
Pipistrelle	Bat
Platy	Fish
Polecat	Weasel
Potto	Primate
Prairie Dog	Rodent
Ptarmigan	Grouse
Quagga	Zebra (extinct)
Quetzal	Bird
Robin	Thrush
Rorqual	Whale
Sable	Marten
Saiga	Antelope
Serval	Cat
Siamang	Gibbon
Skink	Lizard
Slow Worm	Lizard
Snapper	Fish
Snook	Fish
Springbok	Antelope
Tarsier	Primate
Tasmanian Devil	Marsupial (dog-like)
Teal	Duck
Tenrec	Mammal (spiny)
Terrapin	Turtle
Thrasher	Bird
Tinamou	Bird
Titmouse	Bird
Tuatara	Lizard
Wahoo	Fish
Wanderoo	Monkey
Waterboatman	Insect
Whippoorwill	Bird
Widgeon	Duck
Wolverine	Weasel
Woolly Bear	Tiger-moth Caterpillar
Yak	Cattle
Yellowhammer	Finch
Zebu	Cattle
Zorilla	Weasel

Famous Animals

By: Animal/Description → Name

Bear;-

Michael Bond created	Paddington
Checked Trousers	Rupert
Jellystone Park; Lives in	Yogi, Boo boo
Jungle Book	Baloo
A.A.Milne created	Pooh

Cats;-
Chases after Jerry	Tom
Chases after Tweetie Pie	Sylvester
Kattomeat Advertisement; Star of	Arthur
Don Marquis story	Mehitabel
Old Possum's Book of Practical Cats	
(and Musical *Cats*)	Macavity, Mr Mistoffelees,
	Skimbleshanks, Mungojerrie
Postman Pat's	Jess
3 lives; Has (film)	Thomasina
Chimpanzee; Tarzan's	Cheta
Chipmunk; Cartoon	Chip 'N Dale
Cockroach; Don Marquis poems	Archy
Deer; Walt Disney cartoon	Bambi

Dog;-
Alexander the Great's	Peritas
Little Orphan Annie's	Sandy
King Arthur's	Cavall
Beryl the Peril's	Pearl
Biggest in the World (film)	Digby
Blondie's	Daisy
Elizabeth Barrett Browning's	Flush
Lord Byron's	Boatswain
Darling family's (*Peter Pan*)	Nana
Dennis the Menace's	Gnasher
Dorothy (*Wizard of Oz*)	Toto
Famous Five (member)	Timmy
Female, played by male	Lassie (played by Pal)
Grave, Owner's; Watches over, for	
14 years	Greyfriars Bobby
Guards Hades	Cerberus
Jean Harlow's Arms; Dies in	Rin Tin Tin
His Master's Voice	Nipper
Isaac Newton's (upset candle burning	
work)	Diamond
John Noakes' (*Blue Peter*)	Shep
Llewelyn's	Gelert
Magic Roundabout	Dougal
Nixon's; Used in 1952 campaign	Checkers
Peanuts, in	Snoopy (Beagle)
Perishers (Cartoon) in	Boot
Punch's	Toby
Queen's (breed)	Corgis
Rescues over 40 people; St Bernard	Barry
Saves Hollywood (film)	Won Ton Ton
Secret Seven's	Scamper
Space; 1st dog in	Laika (Fox Terrier)
Thin Man series	Asta
Three Men in a Boat	Montmorency
Tin Tin's	Snowy
Trench; German; Discovered in	Rin Tin Tin
Ulysses'	Argos
Dr Who's	K9
Dolphin; TV series	Flipper
Eagle; Escapes from London Zoo, 1965	Goldie

Elephant;-
Babar	Creator: Jean De Brunhoff. Wife: Celeste

Barnum and Bailey's Circus	Jumbo. Killed by: Train
Flying	Dumbo (Disney)

Horses;-

Achilles'	Xanthus
Alexander the Great's	Bucephalus
Gene Autry's	Champion
Buddha's	Kantanka
Caligula's	Incitatus
Cisco Kid's	Diablo
Cortez'	El Morzillo
Don Quixote's	Rosinante
Duke of Wellington's (at Waterloo)	Copenhagen
El Cid's	Babieca
Flying; Mythical	Pegasus
Garibaldi's	Marsala
Hercules'	Arion
Hoppalong Cassidy's	Topper
Little Big Horn; Only survivor	Comanche
Lone Ranger's	Silver
Mohammed's	Al Borak
Napoleon's	Marengo
Odin's (eight-legged)	Sleipner
Roman Consul; Made	Incitatus
Steptoe and Son	Hercules
Dick Turpin's	Black Bess
William III's (Dies of fall from)	Sorrel
Wonder Horse,The	Champion
Leopard; Film about	Baby (*Bringing up Baby*)

Lion;-

Daktari; In	Clarence (Cross-eyed)
Born Free; In	Elsa
Magpies; Cartoon	Heckle and Jeckle
Mongoose; *Jungle Book*	Rikki Tikki Tavi
Mouse; Cartoon	Jerry
Mule; Mohammed's	Fadda
Otter; *Ring of Bright Water*	Tarka
Panda; London Zoo attempts to mate	Chi Chi (with An An)

Parrot;-

George V's	Charlotte
Long John Silver's	Captain Flint

Rabbit;-

Beatrix Potter created	Peter
Uncle Remus	Brer Rabbit

Rat;-

Films about	Ben, Willard
Superstar	Roland
Swan; Hans Christian Andersen story	*The Ugly Duckling*

Whale;-

Herman Melville story	Moby Dick
Killer (film)	Orca

Fish and Sea Creatures

By: General

'Bait' on line; Uses	Angler Fish
Blood; Drinks, through sucker	Lamprey
Breath through	Gills

Breathes Air	Lungfish
Catfish; Name from	Whiskers
Climbing	Mudskipper
Crabs; Jaws	6 Pairs
Crayfish	Freshwater Lobster
Dolphin; Eyes when sleeping	One eye always open
Eels; Where born	Sargasso Sea (North Atlantic)
Eggs;-	
Floating; Term for	Pelagic
Sinking; Term for	Demersal
Term for	Spawn
Fastest	Cosmopolitan Sail Fish
Ferocious; Most; Freshwater	Piranha
Fin; Types	Dorsal, Pectoral, Tail, Anal
Freshwater; Study of	Limnology
Green Bones	Garfish
Hermit Crab; Lives in	Whelk or Winkle Shell
Inflates body when taken from water	Puffer
Jawless	Hagfish, Lamprey
Jellyfish;-	
Brain	None
Type	Primitive animal
Jet Propulsion; Uses	Cuttle Fish
Kissing	Gourami
Knots itself when eating	Hagfish
Largest;-	Whale Shark
Freshwater (not current)	Catfish
Freshwater; UK	Sturgeon
Sea Mammal	Blue Whale
Lobster;-	
Colour	Bluish (red when cooked)
Eyes	On stalks
Nest;-	
Bubbles; Made of	Fighting Fish
Stones; Made of	Lamprey
Wood; Made from, glued together	Stickleback
Octopus; Hearts	3
Oyster; Produces pearls because	Irritant in shell
Oyster Catcher; Food	Mussels
Piranha; Where from	South America
Poisonous;-	
Most	Stone Fish
Most around Britain	Weever
Prehensile Tail	Sea Horse
Pressure Detecting Organ	Lateral Line
Sardine	Young Herring
Sea Lion; Mane	Yes
Shark;-	
Biggest	Whale Shark
Dangerous; Most	Great White Shark
Longest tail	Thresher
Skeletons made from	Cartilage
Ships; Sticks to	Barnacle
Shoots Prey with water squirt	Archer Fish
Slowest	Sea Horse
Smallest	Goby
Starfish; Eyes	At end of arms

Teeth cleaned by other fish	Barracuda
Whale;-	
Horned (ivory tusks)	Narwhal
Nasal Opening	Spiracle
Prehistoric	Basilosaurus
Spends summer in	Polar regions
Substance from used in perfumes	Ambergris
Tongue; Weight	About 4 tons
Type	Mammal, not fish

Habitations

By: Animal → Habitation

Badger	Set
Beaver	Lodge
Bee	Hive
Eagle	Eyrie
Fox	Earth, Burrow
Hare	Form
Horse	Stable
Lion	Den
Otter	Holt
Penguin	Rookery
Rabbit	Burrow/Warren
Squirrel	Drey
Wolf	Lair

Horses

Horses

By: General

Age told by	Teeth
Ages:-	
Female; 1 to 4	Filly
Female; 5 and over	Mare
Male; 1 to 4	Colt
Male; 5 and over	Stallion
Under One	Foal
Ancestor;-	
Prehistoric	Eohippus
Post Ice Age	Przewalski's horse, Tarpan
Arousal, sign of	Ears back
Circus; Breed used in	Lippizaners
City named after	Bucephalus (Bucephalia)
Colours:-	
Bay	Brown with black mane and legs
Chestnut	Reddish-brown
Dun	Sandy with black mane
Palomino	Golden with pale mane
Piebald	Patches of black and white
Skewbald	Patches of brown and white
Strawberry Roan	Chestnut with white hairs
Draft; Earliest breed	Shire
Oldest Breed	Arabian
Parts:-	
Croup	Rump
Dock	Fleshy part of tail

Fetlock	Projection on lower leg
Hock	Ankle
Withers	Base of neck
Sleep; Usual position	Standing up (breath easier)
Smallest Breed	Falabella
Teeth; Number	Male: 40. Female: 36
Toes	1

Insects (and Related Creatures)

By: General

Ants;-	
Have 'Slaves'; Type	Amazon Ants
Milk for Honey-dew	Aphids
Noses	5
Bee;-	
Beats Wings in Summer to	Blow air to cool hive
Beats Wings in Winter to	Warm hive
Enclosure for hives	Apiary
Eyes	5
Gathers	Nectar (sweet liquid from flowers), Pollen
Larvae fed by workers with	Royal Jelly
Legs	6
Sex	Drones: Male. Workers: Female
Wings	2
Beetle; Sacred to Egyptians	Scarab
Butterfly, Moths; Difference	Butterfly: Smooth, fly during day, wings spread when landing. Moth: Cannot close wings vertically
Butterfly;-	
Develops without chrysalis	Satyr, Panessian
Largest	Queen Alexandra's Birdwing
Largest; UK	Monarch
Life Cycle	Egg, Larva (Caterpillar), Pupa, Butterfly
Migrates	Monarch
Tastes with	Back feet
Tongue usually kept	Coiled
Centipede;-	
Legs per segment	2
Millipede; Difference from	Millipede: 4 legs per segment
Chirping Sound; Makes	Cicada, Cricket
Cotton Crop, Pest	Boll Weevil
Cricket;-	
Chirping, sound from	Wing covers rubbed together
Ears	On front legs
Daddy Long Legs; Proper name	Crane Fly
Deaths; Human; Most responsible for	Malarial Mosquito
Death-Watch Beetle; Ticking sound caused by	Knocking head against wood
Destructive; Most	Locust
Dies after stinging	Bee
Dragonfly; Type	Not true fly
Dye from	Cochineal (from ants)
Firefly;-	
Produces light	Male

285

Type	Beetle, not fly
Flea; Jump	100 times its length
Fly;-	
Laboratories; Most used in	Drosophila (Fruit Fly)
2nd pair of wings	Halteres
Walking upside down; Method	Sticky secretion
Wings	4
Glow Worm;-	
Glow; Reason	To attract mates
Male, Female; Difference	Female light flashes faster
Type	Beetle
Heaviest	Goliath Beetle
Honeycomb; Cells; Sides	6
Ladybird; Importance	Eats Greenfly
Largest;-	Goliath Beetle
Ever	Dragonfly
Largest Section	Coleoptera (Beetles and Weevils)
Legs (true insects)	6
Locust; Type of	Grasshopper
Mayfly;-	
Eating ability	Can't – no mouth or stomach
Life span	1 day
Millipede; Legs per segment	4
Mosquito: Bites	Female only
Moth;-	
Clothes; Damage to, caused by	Larvae, not moths
Largest	Hercules Moth
Largest; Europe	Emperor Moth
Largest; UK	Death's Head Hawkmoth
Parts of an insect	Head, Thorax, Abdomen
Potato Crops; Damages	Colorado Beetle
Scorpion's sting	On its tail
Silk Worm Moth; Brains	11
Silkworm; Food	Mulberry leaves
Sleeps for 17 years, awake 5 weeks	Cicada
Spider;-	
Creates Trap with lid	Trapdoor Spider
Eyes; Normal	8
Hour Glass shaped markings	Black Widow
Largest; UK	Cardinal Spider
Throws Line to catch prey	Bolas Spider
Type	Arachnid, not insect
White Ants; Type of	Termite
Woodlouse; Legs	14

Land Animals

By: General

Notes: Includes Mammals, Amphibians.

Abominable Snowman; Local name	Yeti
Agouti; Found in	South America
Amphibian; Largest	Chinese Giant Salamander
Ape; Anthropoid; Distinguishing features	No tail
Ape; Smallest	Gibbon
Arboreal Animals; Live in	Trees

Armour Plated	Armadillo
Babies; Smallest relative to adult; Mammal	Kangaroo
Bat;-	
Flies in dark using	Sonar
Sleeps	Hanging upside down
Smallest; UK	Pipistrelle
Beak; Has nostrils	Kiwi
Bear; Biggest	Kodiak (Alaskan Brown) Bear
Beats Chest	Gorilla
Bottom; Red and blue	Mandrill
Brontosaurus; Other name	Apatosaurus
Bull; Effect of red on	None, as colourblind
Camel;-	
Hump; Contains	Fat, not water
1 humped	Dromedary
2 humped	Bactrian Camel
Capybara; From	South America
Carnivore;-	
Largest	Tyrannosaurus Rex
Largest; Now	Kodiak (Alaskan Brown) Bear
Largest; UK	Badger
Cat;-	
Blue eyes	Siamese
Breed; Usually deaf	Angora
Legs when walking	Same side together
Origin	Egypt. Killing punishable by death
Tailless	Manx
Cat Family;-	
Jumper; Best	Puma
Largest	Siberian Tiger
Retractable Claws; Without	Cheetah
Cattle;-	
Ancestor	Auroch
Beef; Most widespread breed	Shorthorn
Largest	Gaur
Stomachs	4
Sweats	Through nose
Cheetah; Difference from other cats	Non-retractable claws
Colour; Changes	Chameleon
Crocodile;-	
Bird eats insects infesting	Egyptian Plover
Difference from Alligator	4th tooth of lower jaw protrudes
Egg; How broken	Young have point on head
Cud Chewing animals; Term for	Ruminants
Dam; Builder	Beaver
Deer;-	
Antlers; New; How often	Annually
Antlers, when new	Covered in Velvet
Barks	Muntjac
Largest	Alaskan Moose
Largest; UK	Red Deer
Smallest	Musk Deer
Dinosaur;-	
Food	Meat and plants
Heaviest	Brachiosaurus
Horned; Biggest	Triceratops

Longest	Diplodocus
Meaning	Terrible lizard
Plates on back	Stegosaurus ('Roof Lizard')
Sail on back	Dimetrodon
Dormouse; Used by Romans for	Food
Droppings;-	
Deer	Crotties
Hare	Currants
Otters	Spraints
Drown in large numbers when	
migrating	Lemming
Elephant;-	
African, Indian; Difference	African larger and big ears
Drinking; Method	Sucks up water in trunk, squirts into mouth
Largest	African Bush Elephant
Teeth; Number	4 (including tusks)
Toes; Hind Feet	African: 3. Indian: 4
Trunk; Muscles	About 40,000
Ermine; Source	Stoat
Faster: Horse or Greyhound	Horse
Fastest;-	Cheetah
UK	Roe Deer
Fiercest; Per weight	Wildcat
Fire; Believed could live in	Salamander
1st on land	Amphibians
Fish; Catches	Jaguar, Raccoon, Leopard
Food; Stores in cheek pouch	Chipmunk
Footprints; Human-like	Raccoon
Fox; Tail	Brush
Frog;-	
Eggs, coating	Jelly
Largest	Goliath Frog
Toad; Difference from	Frog: Soft moist skin. Toad: Hard dry skin, toothless
Tree; Grip	With suckers
Winter; Where spent	Pond bottoms
Fur; Most expensive	Chinchilla
Giant Tortoise; Found on	Galapagos Islands
Giraffe;-	
Birth	Standing up
Bones in neck	7 (same as Humans and other mammals)
Closest Relation	Okapi
Original Name	Camelopard
Run	Moves legs on same side at same time
Goat;-	
Largest; Wild	Markhor
Sleeping; Characteristic	Doesn't close eyes
Great Dane; From	Not Denmark
Guinea Pig;-	
Descended from	Cavy
First kept by	Incas
Introduced in Europe for	Food
Hamsters; Descended from	Syrian family found in 1930
Heaviest; Land;-	Elephant
Ever	Brachiosaurus
2nd	Hippopotamus

Hinny	Male Horse/Donkey Cross
Hippopotamus;-	
Gives Birth	Underwater
Name from	River-horse
Hoofed animal; Smallest	Mouse deer
Horns;-	
Largest	Cape Buffalo
Longest	Indian Buffalo
Jaguar; From	South America
Kangaroo;-	
Family; Smallest member	Potoroo
Name from	Aborigine 'I don't understand'
Size at birth	About ¾ inch
Koala;-	
Name from	Aborigine 'No drink' (Doesn't drink)
Food	Eucalyptus leaves
Kodiak Bear; From	Alaska
Komodo Dragon; From	Indonesia
Legs; Raise hind first when standing	Ruminants only
Lemming; Characteristic	Drown in large numbers while migrating every 4 years
Lemur;-	
Name from	'Ghost'
Wild; From	Madagascar
Leopard; Other name	Panther
Lions; Hunting	Females usually
Litter of 4 always	Peba, 9 Banded Armadillo
Lizard;-	
Largest	Komodo Dragon
Poisonous	Gila Monster, Bearded Lizard
Llama; Family; Other members	Guanaco, Alpaca
Longest (Ever)	Diplodocus
Mammal;-	
Causes most deaths	Cape Buffalo (after Man)
Distinguising Feature	Produces milk for young
Egg Laying	Platypus, Echidna (Spiny Anteater)
Flying; Only one	Bat
Hair lies towards head	Sloth
Kneels on 4 legs (4 knees, only one)	Elephant
Land; Largest (ever)	Baluchitherium
Longest Living	Man
Longest Living; 2nd	Elephant
Male tends babies	Marmoset
Rarest; UK	Pine Marten
Sea Living	Cetaceans
Slowest	Sloth
Smallest	Etruscan Shrew
Toothless	Aardvark, Anteater, Echidna, Pangolin
Marsupial; North and South America; Found in	Opossum
Mastodon; Related to	Elephant
Moles; Sight	Not blind
Monkey;-	
Difference from Apes	Have a tail
Dog-like Features	Baboon
Europe; Wild; Only	Gibraltar (Barbary Ape)
Large Nose	Proboscis Monkey

Largest	Mandrill
Lion-like Ruff	Wanderoo
Nocturnal	Owl Monkey (South American)
Pet; Most common (West)	Capuchin
Prehensile Tails	South American Monkeys
Sacred	Rhesus, Hanuman
Smallest	Marmoset
Moss grows on fur	Sloth
Mule	Horse/Male Donkey cross
Nimblest	Chamois
Orangutang; Meaning	'Man of the Forest'
Panda;-	
Cubs; When born	January
Food	Bamboo leaves
Panther; Type of	Leopard
Platypus; Young; Means of feeding	Through pores in stomach (no nipples)
Primate;-	
Largest (living)	Gorilla
Most primitive	Lemur
Rabbit;-	
Disease	Myxomatosis
Difference from Hare	Rabbit: Born bald, smaller, smaller ears
Paw Marks; Order	Hind feet first if running
Warning of danger	Stamp on ground
Rats; Brown, Black; Difference	Black Rats vegetarian
Rattlesnake; Finds prey in dark by	Heat-sensitive organ
Rattlesnake; Rattle	At end of tail
Reptile;-	
Blood	Cold
Largest	Salt Water Crocodile
Study of	Herpetology
Rhinoceros;-	
Horn; Made of	Hair
1 Horn	Indian, Javan
2 Horns	White, Black, Sumatran
Rodent;-	
Bred for meat	Capybara
Largest	Capybara (South American Water Hog)
Largest; European	Beaver
Largest; UK (Wild)	Coypu
Ruminant;-	
Stomachs (Most have)	4
Without 4 stomachs	Camel, Chevrotain
Sheep; Effect of weather on wool	Uncurls if stormy
Skunk; Scent glands	Under tail
Sloth; Teeth	None
Sloth; Two toed	Ai
Slowest	Three Toed Sloth
Smallest	Bumblebee Bat
Snail; Eating, method	Scrapes tongue against
Snails; Eyes	At end of horns
Snake;-	
Bones	Has
British	Grass Snake, Adder, Smooth Snake
Deaths; Causes most human	Cobra
Detects movement and noise by	Tongue
Eye Covering	Spectacle

Eyelids	None
Feet; Vestigial	Pythons, Boa Constrictors
Heaviest	Anaconda
Ireland	None
Killed by	Mongoose
Lacks (most)	Left lung
Longest	Regal Python
Means of travel	Horizontal oscillations
Poisonous; Most	Sea Snake
Skin, why shed	Skin can't grow
Squirts venom	Black Necked Cobra
Tongue, Moves; Reason	To help smell
Squirrels; UK types	Grey, Red
Stereoscopic Vision; Only animals	Monkey, Man, Ape
Tail Wagging – Cats, Dogs; Difference	Cats: Warning. Dogs: Welcome
Terrapin	Freshwater Tortoise
Toilet; Digs hole for	Badger
Tortoise; Difference from Turtle	Tortoise: Land dwelling. Turtle: Sea dwelling
Tortoiseshell; Source	Hawkesbill Turtle
Triplets; Always has	Madagascan Dwarf Lemur
Turtle;-	
Largest	Leatherback Turtle
Lays eggs	In sand on sea shore
Teeth	None
Weasel; Tail; Distinguishing feature	Black end
Whiptail Lizards; Sex	All female
White Rhinoceros; Colour	Grey
Wombat; From	Australia
Wool; South American small animal noted for	Vicuna
Zebra; Extinct	Quagga

Male and Female

By: Animal → Name

Bear;-	
Female	Sow
Male	Boar
Bee; Male	Drone
Cat; Male	Tom
Deer;-	
Female	Doe, Hind
Male	Buck, Hart, Stag
Dog; Female	Bitch
Donkey;-	
Female	Jenny
Male	Jack
Duck; Male	Drake
Elephant;-	
Female	Cow
Male	Bull
Ferret;-	
Female	Jill
Male	Hob
Fox; Female	Vixen

Goat;-	
Female	Nanny
Male	Billy
Goose; Male	Gander
Horse;-	
Female	Mare
Male	Stallion
Kangaroo; Male	Boomer, Buck
Lion; Female	Lioness
Pig;-	
Female	Sow
Male	Boar
Rabbit;-	
Female	Doe
Male	Buck
Salmon;-	
Female	Hen
Male	Cock
Sheep;-	
Female	Ewe
Male	Ram
Tiger; Female	Tigress

Other Names

By: Animal → Alternate Name

Anableps	4 eyes
Beluga	Russian Sturgeon
Blowfly	Bluebottle
Bush Baby	Galago
Caracal	Persian Lynx
Cockchafer	May Bug
Coypu	Nutria
Dabchick	Little Grebe
Daphnia	Water Flea
Devil Fish	Manta
Dugong	Sea Cow
Echidna	Spiny Anteater
Ermine	Stoat, Weasel
Finback Whale	Rorqual
Flounder	Fluke, Turbot
Galago	Bush Baby
Gnu	Wildebeest
Grampus	Killer Whale
Groundhog	Woodchuck
Grunion	Smelt
Guacharo	Oilbird
Hagfish	Slime Eel
Hamadryas	Sacred Baboon
Hawksbill	Tortoiseshell Turtle
Kangaroo Rat	Dipodomys
King Cobra	Hamadryad
Kingfish	Whiting
Kookaburra	Laughing Jackass
Langur	Leaf Monkey
Lapwing	Peewit, Green Plover

Moose	Elk
Mouse Deer	Chevrotain
Muntjac	Barking Deer
Nematode	Roundworm
Ocelot	Painted Leopard
Oryx	Gemsbok
Pangolin	Scaly Anteater
Plaice	Flounder
Puma	Cougar, Mountain Lion
Ratel	Honey Badger
Reindeer	Caribou
Serval	Bush Cat
Shrike	Butcher Bird
Tarpon	Bigscale
Termite	White Ant
Tern	Sea Swallow
Thylacine	Tasmanian Wolf
Viper	Adder
Wapiti	American Elk
Wild Cat	Red Lynx
Wolverine	Glutton

Scientific Names

By: Scientific Name → Common Name

Arachnid	Spider
Aves	Birds
Bos taurus	Cattle
Cetacea	Whales, Dolphins
Chiroptera	Bats
Gorilla gorilla	Gorilla
Latemeria	Coelacanth
Lepidoptera	Butterflies and Moths
Monotremes	Platypus, Echidna
Mus musculus	House Mouse
Musca domestica	Fly
Pinnipedia	Seal, Walrus, etc.
Proboscidae	Elephant
Puffinus puffinus	Manx Shearwater
Rattus rattus	Black Rat
Struthio camelus	Ostrich
Troglodytes troglodytes	Wren
Vulpes vulpes	Fox

Young

By: Animal → Name

Ass	Foal, Hinny
Bear	Cub
Beaver	Kitten
Cat	Kitten
Cod	Codling
Cow	Calf, Heifer
Crane-fly	Leather Jacket

Deer	Fawn
Duck	Duckling
Eagle	Eaglet
Eel	Elver
Elephant	Calf
Fish	Fry
Fox	Cub
Frog	Tadpole
Gnat	Bloodworm
Goat	Kid
Goose	Gosling
Grouse	Poult
Hare	Leveret
Hippopotamus	Calf
Horse	Foal
Kangaroo	Joey
Lion	Cub
Otter	Whelp
Pig	Piglet
Pigeon	Squab
Pike	Jack
Rabbit	Kit
Roe Deer	Kid
Salmon	Parr, Smolt
Seal	Pup
Sheep	Lamb
Squirrel	Kitten
Swan	Cygnet

BIOLOGY

By: General

Cell; Single, most primitive life form	Protozoa
Classification; Biological; Originator	Linnaeus
'Darwin's Bull Dog'; Nickname	Thomas Huxley
Evolution;-	
Animal Species that demonstrated to Darwin	Finches
Based on inheritance of acquired characteristics; Theory	Lamarck
Developed theory independently of Darwin	Alfred Russel Wallace
Island where Darwin observed	Galapagos Islands
Pioneer	Charles Darwin
Genes; Thread-like bodies containing	Chromosomes
Genetic Code; Bearer of	DNA
Geneticist; Attempted to use Lamarckian ideas in Soviet agriculture	Lysenko
Genetics; Founder	Gregor Mendel (Austrian monk)
Mutation; Introduces idea	Hugo De Vries
Oxygen; Organism that can live without	Anaerobic
Protein; Constituent parts	Amino Acids

PLANTS
Common Names

By: Scientific Name → Common Name

Aconite	Monkshood, Wolfsbane
Aesculus	Horse Chestnut
Agave	Century Plant
Ailanthus	Paradise Tree/Tree of Heaven
Antirrhinum	Snapdragon
Aquilegia	Columbine
Bellis	Daisy
Calendula	Marigold
Calluna	Heather
Camellia Sinensis	Tea
Campanula	Bellflower
Cheiranthus	Wallflower
Chile Pine	Monkey Puzzle
Chlorophytum	Spider Plant
Common Mullein	Aaron's Rod
Convallaria	Lily of the Valley
Delphinium	Larkspur
Dianthus	Carnation
Ficus Robusta	Rubber Plant
Galanthus	Snowdrop
Gypsophila	Baby's Breath
Hevea Brasiliensis	Rubber
Helianthus	Sunflower
Impatiens	Busy Lizzy
Monstera Deliciosa	Swiss Cheese Plant
Myosotis	Forget-me-not
Prunus Domestica	Plum
Quercus Suber	Cork
Scilla	Squill
Sparaxus	Harlequin
Tradescantia	Wondering Jew
Vitis Vinifera	Grape

Other Names

By: Plant → Alternative Name

Blackberry	Bramble
Bluebell	Harebell
Cassava	Manioc
Charlock	Wild Mustard
Courgette	Zucchini
Deadly Nightshade	Belladonna
Eggplant	Aubergine, Brinjal
Egyptian Thorn	Gum Arabic Tree
Endive	Chicory
Forsythia	Golden Bells
Furze	Gorse
Garbanzo	Chick Pea
Groundsel	Ragwort

Hazelnut	Filbert
Hibiscus	Mallow
Jimson	Thorn Apple
Lucerne	Alfalfa
Millet (African)	Sorghum
Okra	Gumbo
Peanut	Monkey Nut, Groundnut
Persicaria	Lady's Thumb
Pimento	Allspice
Pimpernel	Shepherd's Clock
Pumpkin	Squash
Rosebay Willowherb	Fireweed
Rowan	Mountain Ash
Sorrel	Dock
Sycamore	Buttonwood
Thrift	Sea Pink
Veronica	Speedwell
Wild Arum	Cuckoo Pint, Lords and Ladies
Wild Clematis	Old Man's Beard
Wild Pansy	Heartsease
Wood Anemone	Granny's Nightcap
Woodbine	Common Honeysuckle

Plant Families

By: Plant → Family (Common Name)

Apple	Rose
Asparagus	Lily
Bamboo	Grass
Banana	Ginger
Blackberry	Rose
Bluebell	Lily
Broccoli	Cabbage
Brussel Sprout	Cabbage
Camellia	Tea
Carrot	Parsley/Carrot
Cauliflower	Cabbage
Celery	Parsley/Carrot
Cherry	Rose
Chives	Lily
Cinnamon	Laurel
Clove	Pink
Coffee	Madder
Cork	Oak
Cotton	Mallow
Eggplant	Nightshade
Elder	Honeysuckle
Fig	Mulberry
Garlic	Lily
Gooseberry	Saxifrage
Hemlock	Parsley/Carrot
Hyacinth	Lily
Jasmin	Olive
Jerusalem Artichoke	Sunflower
Leek	Lily
Lemon	Rue

Lettuce	Daisy
Lilac	Olive
Lupin	Legume
Marijuana	Mulberry
Mustard	Cabbage
Onion	Lily
Orange	Rue
Peach	Rose
Pear	Rose
Plum	Rose
Potato	Nightshade
Radish	Cabbage
Raspberry	Rose
Rhubarb	Dock
Strawberry	Rose
Tobacco	Nightshade
Tomato	Nightshade
Tulip	Lily
Turnip	Cabbage
Vanilla	Orchid
Wheat	Grass

Plant Varieties and Types

By: Variety → Plant

Arthur Turner	Apple
Bartlett	Pear
Beefsteak	Tomato
Bramley	Apple
Cabernet Sauvignon	Grape
Cantaloupe	Melon
Casaba	Melon
Chantenay	Carrot
Chardonnay	Grape
Comice	Pear
Conference	Pear
Cos	Lettuce
Cox's Orange Pippin	Apple
Desirée	Potato
Discovery	Apple
Duncan	Grapefruit
Elberta	Peach
Gamay	Grape
Golden Delicious	Apple
Granny Smith	Apple
Grenache	Grape
Honeydew	Melon
Iceberg	Lettuce
James Grieve	Apple
King Edward	Potato
Laxton's Superb	Apple
Maris Piper	Potato
Marsh Seedless	Grapefruit
Merton Pride	Pear
Montmorency	Cherry
Morello	Cherry

Muscat	Grape
Pentland (Crown, etc.)	Potato
Peregrine	Peach
Pinot Noir	Grape
Sauvignon Blanc	Grape
Semillon	Grape
Victoria	Plum
Walters	Grapefruit
William's	Pear
Worcester Pearmain	Apple

Plants, General

By: *General*

Agriculture; Soilless	Hydroponics
Alexander the Great's Army; One tree sheltered	Banyan tree
Almond; Bitter; Poison contained in	Prussic acid
Aspidistra pollinated by	Snails
Banana; Type	Plant, not tree
Blooms once in 150 years	Puya plant of Mexico
Blue; Only fruit	Irish Bilberry
Botanists; Named after	Dahlia, Fuchsia, Gardenia
Carnivorous Plants	Venus Fly Trap, Sundew, Pitcher Plant
Carrot; Native to	Afghanistan
Chrysanthemum; From	Japan
Clementine; Cross of	Orange, Tangerine
Coconut;-	
Dried	Copra
Eyes	3
Fibre; Name for	Coir
Commonest	Grass
Conifer; Deciduous	Larch, Swamp Cypress
Cotton; Pest	Boll Weevil
Crop; Biggest area; Britain	Barley
Dandelion; Name from	Dent de lion (Lion's tooth)
Disraeli; Favourite flower	Primrose
Dye; Red, produced from roots	Madder
Fibre; Oldest cultivated	Flax
Flower;-	
Female Part	Pistil
Largest	Rafflesia
Leaf-like Appendage	Sepal
Male and Female Parts; Contains; Term for	Perfect
Male Part	Stamen
Pistil; Base	Ovary
Pistil; Mouth	Stigma
Pistil; Neck	Style
Pollen; Contained in	Anther
Smallest	Brazilian Duckweed (Wolfia)
Stamen; Parts	Anther, Filament
Flowering Plant; Most ancient	Ginko (Maidenhair tree)
Flowers every 120 years	Bamboo
Food Production using sunlight	Photosynthesis
Freesia; Seed	Corm

Fruit; Largest	Jackfruit
Fuchsia; Name from	Leonard Fuchs (naturalist)
Fungi; Most poisonous	Death Cap
Grapefruit; Developed from	Shaddock
Grass; Largest	Bamboo
Gravity; Effect on plants; Term for	Geotropism
Green Colouring; Plants	Chlorophyll
Growing; Fastest	Bamboo (15 inch/day)
Grows Underwater	Rice
Hardwood; Trees from	Deciduous
Hops; Dried in	Oast house
Jumping Bean; Reason	Moth grub avoiding heat
Largest;-	
Living Thing	Sequoia Tree ('General Sherman')
Plant without trunk	Banana
Leaf;-	
Largest	Raffia Palm
Openings for breathing	Stomata
Outer Layer	Epidermis
Lichen	Fungus and algae in symbiotic association
Loganberry; Name from	J.H.Logan (US Judge)
Monkey Puzzle tree; From	Chile
Mushroom;-	
Most poisonous	Death Cap
Toadstool; Difference	No scientific one
Nettle, sting,-	
Antidote	Dock leaves
Caused by	Formic acid
Nitrogen; Absorbs from air; Plant type	Legumes
Oak Apples; Caused by	Wasp eggs
Oats; Fungus disease affecting	Smut
Orange; Small Japanese variety	Kumquat
Orchid Family; Member with commercial use	Vanilla
Photosynthesis;-	
Substance responsible for	Chlorophyll
Where takes place	Chloroplast
Pineapple; Type of	Berry
Plant Breeding; US Pioneer	Luther Burbank
Plant Parts;-	
Food distributed by	Phloem
Woody tissue	Xylem
Plant Types;-	
Seed bearing; Division	Angiosperms, Gymnosperms
Seeds enclosed in ovary	Angiosperms
Seeds on open scales	Gymnosperms
Plant Life, most found in	The Sea
Poisonous Plant; British: Most	Deadly Nightshade
Pomegranate; Varieties	Wonderful, Paper-shell, Spanish Ruby
Rose;-	
Breeder; Renowned	Harry Wheatcroft
Cultivated; Types	Summer (Single bloom), Perpetual
Wild; Petals	5
Rubber;-	
Distributed abroad; 1st Method	Smuggled to Kew Gardens
Name from	Original use as eraser

Origin	Brazil
Original liquid	Latex
Rye; Fungus disease affecting	Ergot
Sacking; Fibre used for	Jute
Seaweed; Colour types	Brown, Green, Red
Seed;-	
Largest	Coco de Mer (Seychelles)
Leaf Part	Cotyledon
Tissue surrounding developing	Endosperm
Smell; Plant that can	Sundew
Strawberry; Grows off	Runners
Sugar Beet;-	
Developed from	Beetroot
Development; Reason	Napoleon prohibited sugar imports
Sweet Pea; From	Sicily
Toadstool; Most poisonous	Death Cap
Tomato;-	
Introduced as	Ornamental plant
Original Name	Love Apple
Tree;-	
Age; Method of telling	By counting rings
Coverage; Biggest	Banyan
Cultivation for decoration	Arboriculture
Dwarf Cultivation	Bonsai
Heaviest	Sequoia
Largest	Sequoia tree ('General Sherman')
Oldest	Bristlecone Pine ('Old Methuselah')
Smallest	Dwarf Willow
Tallest	Douglas Fir
Trunk; Biggest	Baobab
Trunk; Square	Cottonwood tree
Trunks; Many grow from branches	Banyan tree
Water holding leaves	Travellers' tree
Tulip;-	
Name from	Turban (Turkish)
Originally from	Turkey
Vegetables; Perennial	Asparagus, Rhubarb
Water Absorption; Principle	Osmosis
Willow; Flowers	Catkins
Wood; Densest	Black Ironwood
Yucca Tree; Pollinated only by	Pronuba Moth

Plants, Products obtained from

By: Product → Plant

Agar Agar	Seaweed
Amber	Pine tree resin
Aspirin	Willow tree (originally)
Atrophine	Deadly Nightshade
Cocaine	Coca plant
Copra	Coconut
Digitalis	Foxglove
Frankincense	Resin from tree bark
Hessian	Jute
Linen	Flax
Madder	Root of plant

Quinine	Cinchona bark
Tapioca	Root of Cassava (Manioc)
Turmeric	Curcuma plant
Turpentine	Coniferous trees

People

Contents

Biography 305
Awards and Prizes 305
Biographical Quotations
  By: Quotation 306
Brothers and Sisters 306
Children
  By: Name 307
Death
  By: Description 308
Death, After
  By: Description 311
Diseases and Disabilities
  By: Disease/Disability 311
Executions
  By: Description 312
  By: Name 313
Last Words
  By: Words 313
Marriages
  By: Name 314
Miscellaneous
  By: Attribute, Description 319
Nationality and Origin
  By: Name 321
Occupations
  By: Occupation 322
Pairs and Partnerships
  By: Name 325
Parents

By: Name 325
Relations
  By: Name 326
Relationships
  By: Name 327
Suicide
  By: Name 328
Names 329
Christian Names
  By: Name 329
Initials
  By: Name 330
Maiden Names
  By: Name 331
Middle Names
  By: Name 331
Names, General
  By: Name 331
Nicknames
  By: Category/Nickname 332
Real (First) Names
  By: Current Name 336
Real Names
  By: Category/Original Name 337
Surnames
  By: First Name 345
Titles
  By: Name 345
  By: Title 346

BIOGRAPHY
Awards and Prizes

By: General

See Also: Specific Topics, e.g. Entertainment, Science and Technology, Society and Politics

Nobel Peace Prize winner;-
  Organisation awarded — ILO, 1969
  Youngest — Martin Luther King

Nobel Prize winner;-
  1st — Dr Emil Behring, Medicine (1901)
  Mother and Daughter — Marie Curie, Irene Joliot-Curie
  Physics; 1st — Roentgen
  2 Awards; Different subjects — Linus Pauling (Chemistry and Peace – only dual sole winner), Marie Curie (Chemistry and Physics)
  2 Awards; Same subject — John Bardeen (Physics), Frederick Sanger (Chemistry)
  Youngest — William Bragg, Physics

Nobel Prizes — Chemistry, Economics (from 1969), Literature, Medicine, Peace, Physics

Victoria Cross;-
　Founded　　　　　　　　During Crimean War
　Youngest　　　　　　　　Andrew Fitzgibbon (15)

Biographical Quotations

By: Quotation → Person Described, Source

'Age cannot wither her, nor custom stale her infinite variety'	Cleopatra (by Shakespeare)
'Brilliant to the top of his army boots'	General Haig (by Lloyd George)
'Can't act, can't sing, slightly bald, can dance a little'	Fred Astaire (by a talent scout)
'A Desiccated calculating machine'	Gaitskell (by Aneurin Bevan)
'(Ears) made him look like a taxi cab with both doors open'	Clark Gable (by Howard Hughes)
'Half naked fakir'	Gandhi (by Winston Churchill)
'Indomitable in retreat; invincible in advance; insufferable in victory'	Montgomery (by Churchill)
'It required but a moment to sever that head, and perhaps a century will not be sufficient to produce another like it'	Lavoisier (by Lagrange)
'A Modest little man with much to be modest about'	Attlee (by Churchill)
'A Sheep in sheep's clothing'	Attlee (by Churchill)
'Simply no brains, all character and temperament'	Henry Irving (by G.B.Shaw)
'Very clever, but his brains go to his head'	Earl of Birkenhead (by Margot Asquith)
'Would you buy a second-hand car from this man?'	Richard Nixon (by Mort Sahl)
'You care for nothing but shooting, dogs and rat catching'	Charles Darwin (by his father)

Brothers and Sisters

By: Name → Sibling

Duane Allman	Gregg
Attila the Hun	Bleda (brother)
Lionel Barrymore	Ethel, John
Warren Beatty	Shirley MacLaine
David Broome	Liz Edgar
David Carradine	Keith
Bobby Charlton	Jackie
Ray Davies	Dave
Catherine Deneuve	Francoise Dorleac
Lawrence Durrell	Gerald
Edward IV	Richard III
Joan Fontaine	Olivia De Havilland
Edward Fox	James
Naum Gabo	Antoine Pevsner
George IV	William IV
George Gershwin	Ira
Lillian Gish	Dorothy
Hannibal	Hasdrubal
Sir Michael Havers	Nigel
Henry VIII	Son (only legitimate): Edward VI.

Henry James	William
Emperor Franz Joseph	Maximilian
John Kennedy	Robert, Edward
Charles Lamb	Mary Ann
Louis XVIII	Charles X
Loretta Lynn	Crystal Gayle
Marky Mark	Donnie Wahlberg
Wynton Marsalis	Branford
Liza Minnelli	Lorna Luft
Stirling Moss	Pat Moss-Carlsson
Napoleon	Joseph, Louis
Mike Oldfield	Sally
Sir Walter Raleigh	Sir Humphrey Gilbert (half brother)
Peter Sarstedt	Eden Kane, Robin Sarstedt
Pete Seeger	Peggy
Charlie Sheen	Emilio Estevez
Norma Talmadge	Constance Talmadge
Titus	Domitian
Ernie Tyrell	Jean (The Supremes)
Andrew Lloyd Webber	Julian
John Wesley	Charles

Children

By: Name → Child

Princess Alexandra	James, Marina
Woody Allen	Satchel (Mia Farrow)
Kingsley Amis	Martin
Prince Andrew	Beatrice, Eugenie Victoria
Princess Anne	Peter, Zara
Rodrigo Borgia	Cesare, Lucrezia
David Bowie	Zowie
Lloyd Bridges	Beau, Jeff
Pieter Brueghel	Jan, Pieter
Lord Byron	Ada Lovelace
David Carradine	Free
Joseph Chamberlain	Austen, Neville
Charlie Chaplin	Geraldine
Prince Charles	William, Henry (Harry)
Charles II	Duke of Monmouth (illegitimate)
Cher	Chastity
Eric Clapton	Connor
Cleopatra	Caesarion
Nat 'King' Cole	Natalie
Tony Curtis	Jamie Lee Curtis
Francis Duvalier (Papa Doc)	Jean Claude Duvalier (Baby Doc)
Duncan I	Malcolm III, Donald Bane
Edward III	Edward, the Black Prince
Elizabeth II	Charles, Anne, Andrew, Edward
Eric the Red	Leif Ericson
Henry Fonda	Jane, Peter
Henry Ford	Edsel
Indira Gandhi	Sanjay, Rajiv
Bob Geldof	Fifi Trixibelle, Peaches, Little Pixie
George VI	Elizabeth II, Margaret
Princess Grace of Monaco	Caroline, Albert, Stephanie
Woodie Guthrie	Arlo
George Harrison	Dhani

Sir Michael Havers	Nigel
Henry VIII	Son (only legitimate): Edward VI. Daughters: Mary, Elizabeth
Gustav Holst	Imogen
John Huston	Angelica
Mick Jagger	Jade, Elizabeth Scarlett, James
Shah Jehan	Aurangzeb
Emperor Franz Joseph	Crown Prince Rudolf
John Lennon	Julian (Cynthia). Sean (Yoko Ono)
Princess Margaret	David (Viscount Linley), Lady Sarah Armstrong-Jones
Charles Martel	Pepin the Short
Prince Michael of Kent	Frederick, Gabriella
John Mills	Hayley, Juliet, Jonathan
Robert Morley	Sheridan
Mohammed	Fatima
Napoleon Bonaparte	Francois (Napoleon II)
Nicholas II (Tsar)	Anastasia (youngest)
Aristotle Onassis	Christina, Alexander
Emmeline Pankhurst	Christabel, Sylvia
Cecil Parkinson	Flora (Sarah Keays)
Elvis Presley	Lisa Marie
Michael Redgrave	Vanessa, Lynn, Corin
Vanessa Redgrave	Joely, Natasha Richardson
Auguste Renoir	Jean
Debbie Reynolds	Carrie Fisher
Shakespeare	Son: Hamnet. Daughter: Judith, Sussanah
Martin Sheen	Charlie Sheen, Emilio Estevez
Stalin	Svetlana Alliluyeva
Sylvester Stallone	Sage Moonblood
Ringo Starr	Zac
Stephen	Henry II (adopted)
Margaret Thatcher	Carol, Mark (twins)
Feliks Topolski	Daniel
Vespasian	Titus
Victoria	Daughter (eldest): Victoria. Sons: Edward VII, Alfred, Arthur, Leopold (haemophiliac)
Frank Zappa	Moon Unit

Death

By: Description → Name

See Also: Executions, Suicide, Society and Politics; Assassination and Murder

Addison's Disease	Jane Austen
Aids	Rock Hudson, Freddy Mercury
Airship explosion (R101)	Lord Thompson (Air Minister)
Alcohol poisoning	Bon Scott (AC/DC), Dylan Thomas
Anorexia related	Karen Carpenter
Arrow in the New Forest while hunting	William II (Rufus)
Bath; While in	Agamemnon, Marat
Battle	Sir Philip Sidney (Siege of Zutphen), Richard III (Bosworth Field)
Cancer	Ingrid Bergman, Gary Cooper, Sammy Davis Jnr (Throat), Diana Dors, Engels, George VI (lung), Charles

	Laughton, Bob Marley, Steve McQueen, Eva Peron, Strindberg, Humphrey Bogart
Car crash	Marc Bolan, Eddie Cochran (in taxi), James Dean (in Porsche Spyder), Grace Kelly, Bessie Smith
Carbon Monoxide Poisoning	Emile Zola
Childbirth	Mumtaz Mahal
Chill caught when stuffing chicken with ice to demonstrate refrigeration	Francis Bacon
Choking on a sandwich	(Mama) Cass Elliott
Choking on vomit	Jimi Hendrix
Cholera	Tchaikovsky
Cliff; Thrown off	Aesop
Clubbed to death	Captain Cook
Coffee, Excessive drinking of	Honore de Balzac
Cricket ball	Frederick, Prince of Wales (George II's son)
Crossbow Wound in shoulder	Richard I
Decapitated in a car crash	Jayne Mansfield
Drowning	Barbarossa, Harold Holt, Amy Johnson, Brian Jones (in swimming pool), Mary Jo Kopechne (at Chappaquidick), King Ludwig of Bavaria, Shelley (sailing off Italian coast), Dennis Wilson, Natalie Wood
Drowning in Malmsey	George, Duke of Clarence (brother of Edward IV)
Drug abuse	Lowell George, Paul Kossoff, Janis Joplin, Jack London, Keith Moon, Dante Gabriel Rossetti (Chloral Hydrate)
Duelling	Galois (at 20), Alexander Hamilton (by Aaron Burr), Mikhail Lermontov, Pushkin
Dysentery	Francis Drake (in the West Indies), Henry V, King John
Eddystone Lighthouse, when it is swept away	Winstanley (Builder)
18th Century; Last moment	George Washington
Electrocution; While playing guitar	Keith Relf
Fall on stairs	James Bruce (explorer)
Fever	Lord Byron (in Missolonghi)
Fire	Barbara Hepworth
Gout	Milton
Hammer; Beaten to death with	Joe Orton
High Wire; Fall from	Karl Wallenda
Horse; Fall from	Genghis Khan, William the Conqueror (impaled on pommel), William III (caused by molehill)
Insect Bite; Septic	Alban Berg
Lampreys; Surfeit of	Henry I
Laughing	Philemon (Greek writer)
Leprosy	Robert the Bruce
Leukaemia	Bartok, Sonja Henjie, George Raft, Frank Worrell

Lung Abscess	Karl Marx
Malaria	Caravaggio, Oliver Cromwell
Malnutrition	Howard Hughes
Mob Attack	Joseph Smith
Monkey (pet) Bite	Alexander of Greece (1920)
Motor-cycle Accident	Lawrence of Arabia
Multiple Sclerosis	Jacqueline Du Pré
Mushrooms; Poisonous	Alexander I
Newspaper over face at his club	Michael Faraday
Nose Bleed	Attila the Hun
Overeating (supposed)	King John
Peritonitis, from perforated ulcer	Rudolph Valentino
Piles	David Livingstone
Plague	Giorgione
Plane Crash	Big Bopper (with Buddy Holly), Yuri Gagarin, Sanjay Gandhi, Dag Hammarskhold, Graham Hill, Buddy Holly (1959, Iowa), Carol Lombard, Samora Machel, Rocky Marciano, Rick Nelson, Otis Redding (Lake Monona, Wisconsin), Jim Reeves, Mike Todd, Richie Valens (with Buddy Holly)
Pleurisy	Charlemagne
Pneumonia	Jim Henson, Liszt
Poisoning, from thorn prick	Rainer Maria Rilke
Poker; Red hot	Edward II
Pregnancy	Charlotte Bronte
Pub Brawl	Christopher Marlowe
Punch in stomach when unprepared, causing peritonitis	Harry Houdini
Radiation	Marie Curie (1st victim)
Rescuing drowning woman	William Gilbert
Roasted on grid iron	St Lawrence
Russian Roulette (by accident)	Terry Kath (Chicago)
Scarlet Fever	Johann Strauss (the Elder)
Scrofula	Louis XVII (at 10)
Ship Torpedoed	Lord Kitchener
Shot;-	
By military policeman during curfew	Anton Webern
In hotel	Sam Cooke
While committing suicide by poison	Hitler (by Eva Braun)
Smallpox	Mary II
Stabbed in foot with conductor's baton	Lully
Strangled when scarf caught in car wheel	Isadora Duncan
TB	Aubrey Beardsley, Chekhov, Chopin, Edward VI, Franz Kafka, Keats (in Rome), D.H.Lawrence, Vivien Leigh
Tile, thrown	Pyrrhus
Toilet Seat; Fall from	George II
Tortoise dropped on head	Aeschylus (story about)
Typhoid	Prince Albert, Arnold Bennett (after drinking Paris water to show safe), Prince Henry (son of James I), Schubert

Umbrella Point, containing poison Ricin	Georgi Markov
Venereal Disease	Baudelaire, James Boswell, Al Capone, Lord Randolph Churchill, Delius, Gauguin, Nell Gwyn (caught from Charles II), Heine, Guy De Maupassant, Nietzsche, Bram Stoker
Vesuvius erupting, while investigating	Pliny the Elder
Window; Fall from	Jan Masaryk

Death, After

By: Description → Person

Bones disinterred and burnt	John Wycliffe
Buried;-	
Standing up in Westminster Abbey	Ben Jonson
With a telephone	Aimee Semple McPherson (evangelist)
Burnt at stake, 80 years after death	Wycliffe
Funeral; Late for own	Duke of Wellington
Head carried in bag	Sir Walter Raleigh (by widow)
Head stuck on roof of Parliament after body exhumed	Oliver Cromwell
Heart buried separately from body	Voltaire, Shelley
Hijacked and burnt	Gram Parsons
Hung upside down	Mussolini
Moved from Italy to Spain to Argentina	Eva Peron
Preserved;-	
In brandy	Nelson
In jar of honey	Alexander the Great
Stolen, later returned	Charlie Chaplin
Stuffed body in case at University College, London	Jeremy Bentham
Tried and executed by throwing body in Tiber	Formosus (Pope)

Diseases and Disabilities

By: Disease/Disability → Name

See Also: Death

Alzheimer's Disease	Rita Hayworth
Asthma	Marcel Proust
Blind	Jorge Luis Borges, Ray Charles (at 6), Delius (last 9 years), George III, Homer, John Metcalf, Milton, James Thurber (last 20 years), Stevie Wonder
Breast Cancer	Ingrid Bergman
Club Foot	Byron, Goebbels, Dudley Moore
Deaf	Beethoven
Epilepsy	Julius Caesar, Gustave Flaubert, Edward Lear, Van Gogh, Wagner, Duke of Wellington
Gout	Alexander the Great, Calvin, Charlemagne, Darwin, Luther, Michelangelo
Haemophilia	Tsarevich Alexis

Hodgkin's Disease	Roger Tonge
Huntington's Chorea	Woody Guthrie
Insane	Beau Brummell, George III, (Porphyria) Henry VI, Guy De Maupassant, Schumann, Vincent Van Gogh
Lame	Tamburlaine (Timur the Lame)
Leprosy	Robert the Bruce
Multiple Sclerosis	Ronnie Lane
Nose, false	Tycho Brahe (golden)
One armed	Nelson, Cervantes
One Eyed	Joe Davis, Moshe Dayan, Sammy Davis Jnr., Peter Falk, John Ford, Rex Harrison, Marconi, Leo McKern, Colin Milburn, Nelson
One Legged	Sarah Bernhardt, Peter Stuyvesant, Josiah Wedgwood
Parkinson's Disease	Michael Redgrave
Polio	Ian Dury, F.D.Roosevelt
Scrofula	Samuel Johnson
Skin Infection	Marat
Speech Defect	Claudius
Stammer	Aneurin Bevan, Charles I, Demosthenes, George VI, Charles Lamb, Somerset Maugham

Executions

By: Description → Name

See also: Society and Politics; Crime

Adultery; By Henry VIII	Anne Boleyn, Catherine Howard
Burnt at Stake;-	
By the Inquisition for questioning earth-centred universe	Giordano Bruno
By Queen Mary, at Oxford	Cranmer, Ridley, Latimer
For witchcraft and heresy, at 19	Joan of Arc
Crucified	Jesus
Crucified upside down	St Peter
Desertion; WWII; US private	Eddie Slovik
Germany; 1918; Socialist leaders	Karl Liebkneckt, Rosa Luxemburg
Guillotined;-	
Chemist	Lavoisier
French revolutionary leaders	Danton, Robespierre (1794)
Hand that signed recantation first to burn; Says	Thomas Cranmer
Hanged; 3 times, as rope breaks	William Kidd (pirate)
Heart doesn't burn (reputedly)	Joan of Arc
Irish Independence leader; For leading 1916 Easter Rising	James Connolly
Nurse; British; By Germans in Belgium, 1915	Edith Cavell
Minorca; Shot for failing to relieve	Admiral Byng (1756)
Spying; By French, 1917	Mata Hari
Strangled (then burnt); For heresy	William Tyndale
Treason;-	
Anglican priest, under Charles I	William Laud
Broadcasts from Germany in WWII	William Joyce (Lord Haw Haw)
Former House of Commons Speakers; By Henry VIII	William Empson, Edmund Dudley

French Vichy Government leader	Pierre Laval
Irish nationalist leader and author, 1921	Erskine Childers
Norwegian Nazi leader	Vidkund Quisling
Refused to accept Henry VIII as leader of Church	Sir Thomas More
Two shirts; Wore at execution	Charles I
US Labour leader, by firing squad	Joe Hill
Witchcraft; Witchfinder executed for	Matthew Hopkins

Executions

By: Name → General
See Also: Society and Politics; Crime

Zulfiqar Ali Bhutto	(Former Pakistani PM) By: General Zia Al Haq government (1979)
Anne Boleyn	(Henry VIII's 2nd wife) Beheaded for: Adultery (1536)
King Charles I	By: Parliamentarians (1649)
Caryl Chessman	Sentenced 1948 as 'Red Light Bandit' for indecent assault (charge kidnapping carries death penalty). Writes: *Cell 2455 Death Row*. Executed in: Gas chamber (May 1960)
Damiens	By: Quartering, for attempted assassination of King Louis XV (1757)
Lady Jane Grey	By: Queen Mary
Catherine Howard	(Henry VIII's 5th wife). Beheaded for: Adultery (1542)
King Louis XVI	(and Marie Antoinette) By: Guillotine (1793)
Mary, Queen of Scots	By: Elizabeth I (1587)
Benito Mussolini	Shot by: Italian Partisans (1945). Hung upside down with mistress Clara Petacci
Tsar Nicholas I	(and Russian Imperial Family) In: Ekaterinburg (1918). Controversy surrounds claim that daughter Anastasia survived
Sir Walter Raleigh	By: James I (1618)
Socrates	With: Poison hemlock (self-administered), for moral and social views (399 BC)

Last Words

By: Words → Person

'And still it moves'	Galileo
'Die, my dear doctor, why that's the last thing I shall do'	Lord Palmerston
'Don't turn down the light, I'm afraid to go home in the dark'	O.Henry
'Either that wallpaper goes or I do'	Oscar Wilde (reputed)
'Et tu Brute'	Julius Caesar

'God will pardon me, it's his trade'	Heine
'I am dying as I lived, beyond my means'	Oscar Wilde
'I am just going outside and I may be some time'	Captain Lawrence Oates
'I go from a corruptible to an incorruptible crown'	Charles I
'I have opened it'	Tennyson
'I regret that I have but one life to give for my country'	Nathan Hale
'I shall hear in heaven'	Beethoven
'I should never have switched from Scotch to Martinis'	Humphrey Bogart
'I think I could eat one of Bellamy's pork pies'	Pitt
'If this is dying, I don't think much of it'	Lytton Strachey
'I've had 18 straight whiskies, I think that's a record'	Dylan Thomas
'Last words are for fools who haven't said enough'	Marx
'Let not poor Nelly starve'	Charles II
'Let us now relieve the Romans of their fears by the death of a feeble old man'	Hannibal (committing suicide)
'Monsieur, I beg your pardon'	Marie Antoinette (tripping over executioner)
'More light'	Goethe
'Nonsense, they couldn't hit an elephant at this dist . .'	John Sedgwick (US General)
'O liberty! What crimes are committed in thy name'	Madame Roland
'Oh I'm so bored with it all'	Churchill
'So little done, so much to do'	Cecil Rhodes
'Thank God I have done my duty'	Nelson
'This is a sharp medicine, but it will cure all diseases'	Sir Walter Raleigh (being executed)
'Wait till I have finished my problem'	Archimedes (to Roman soldier)
'We shall this day light such a candle, by God's grace, in England as I trust shall never be put out'	Hugh Latimer
'What an artist the world is losing in me'	Nero
'What an irreparable loss'	Auguste Comte
'Why should I see her, she will only want to give a message to Albert'	Disraeli (asked whether he wants to see Queen Victoria)
'You will show my head to the people, it is well worthwhile'	George Danton

Marriages

By: Name → Spouse

Ahab (King of Israel)	Jezebel
John Alden	Priscilla Mullers (Pilgrim Father Alden wooed her for Miles Standish)
John Alderton	Pauline Collins
Alexander the Great	Roxana
Princess Alexandra	Angus Ogilvy

Woody Allen	Louise Lasser
Julie Andrews	Blake Edwards
Queen Anne	George, Prince of Denmark
Lauren Bacall	Humphrey Bogart, Jason Robards
David Bailey	Catherine Deneuve, Marie Helvin
Lucille Ball	Desi Arnaz
Brigitte Bardot	Roger Vadim, Jacques Charrier, Gunther Sachs
Daniel Barenboim	Jacqueline Du Pré
Hywel Bennett	Cathy McGowan
Candice Bergen	Louis Malle
Claire Bloom	Rod Steiger
Boadicea	King Prasutagus
Humphrey Bogart	Lauren Bacall (4th wife)
Valeri Borzov	Lyudmila Turischeva
Kenneth Branagh	Emma Thompson
Charles Bronson	Jill Ireland
Mel Brooks	Ann Bancroft
Robert Browning	Elizabeth Barrett (Browning)
George Burns	Gracie Allen
Richard Burton	Elizabeth Taylor (twice), Susan Hunt, Sally
Lord Byron	Annabella Milbanks
Michael Caine	Shakira Baksh
Leslie Caron	Sir Peter Hall
Princess Caroline of Monaco	Pierre Junot, Stephano Casiraghi
Paul McCartney	Linda Eastman
Johnny Cash	June Carter
Catherine II (Of Russia)	Peter III
Catherine of Aragon	Henry VIII, Arthur – Henry's brother (previously)
Catherine of Valois	Henry V, Owen Tudor
Charlie Chaplin	Paulette Goddard, Oona O'Neil
Charlemagne	Hildegarde
Charles I	Princess Henrietta Maria of France
Charles II	Catherine of Braganza
Keith Chegwin	Maggie Philbin
Cher	Sonny Bono, Gregg Allmann
Agatha Christie	Sir Max Mallowan (archaeologist)
Eric Clapton	Patti Boyd
Claudius	Agrippina
John Cleese	Connie Booth
Cleopatra	Ptolemy XII (brother), Mark Antony
Clovis I	Clotilda
Joan Collins	Maxwell Reed, Anthony Newley
Sean Connery	Diane Cilento
Billy Connolly	Pamela Stephenson
Shirley Conran	Sir Terence Conran
Jilly Cooper	Leo
Cicely Courtneidge	Jack Hulbert
Joan Crawford	Douglas Fairbanks Jnr.
Tom Cruise	Nicole Kidman
Tony Curtis	Janet Leigh
Roald Dahl	Patricia Neal
Bebe Daniels	Ben Lyon
Sammy Davis Jnr.	Mai Britt
Peter Davison	Sandra Dickinson
John Derek	Ursula Andress, Linda Evans, Bo Derek

Angie Dickinson	Burt Bacharach
Diana Dors	Alan Lake
Lesley-Anne Down	William Friedkin
Isadora Duncan	Sergei Essenin
Bob Dylan	Sarah Lowndes
Clint Eastwood	Sondra Locke
Edward I	Eleanor of Castile
Edward II	Isabella
Edward VII	Princess Alexandra of Denmark
Eleanor of Aquitaine	Louis VII, Henry II
Elizabeth II	Philip Mountbatten (1947)
Ethelbert	Bertha
Trevor Eve	Sharon Maughan
Chris Evert	John Lloyd
Douglas Fairbanks Jnr	Joan Crawford
Douglas Fairbanks Snr	Mary Pickford
Mia Farrow	Frank Sinatra, André Previn
Federico Fellini	Giulietta Masina
Albert Finney	Anouk Aimée
F.Scott Fitzgerald	Zelda Sayre
Errol Flynn	Lili Damita (1st)
Jane Fonda	Roger Vadim, Tom Hayden, Ted Turner
Lynn Fontanne	Alfred Lunt
Michael Foot	Jill Craigie
Anna Ford	Mark Boxer
Bruce Forsyth	Anthea Redfern
David Frost	Lynne Frederick, Lady Carina Howard
Clark Gable	Carole Lombard
Ava Gardner	Mickey Rooney, Artie Shaw, Frank Sinatra
Bob Geldof	Paula Yates
George IV	Maria Fitzherbert, Princess Caroline of Brunswick
George V	Princess Mary of Teck
George VI	Elizabeth Bowes-Lyon (the Queen Mother)
Liza Goddard	Colin Baker, Alvin Stardust
Paulette Goddard	Charles Chaplin, Erich Maria Remarque, Burgess Meredith
Lady Godiva	Leofric (Earl of Mercia)
Mikhail Gorbachev	Raisa
Cary Grant	Barbara Hutton, Dyan Cannon
Lady Jane Grey	Lord Guilford Dudley
George Harrison	Patti Boyd, Olivia Arias
Rita Hayworth	Orson Welles, Aly Khan
David Hemmings	Gayle Hunnicut
Henry II	Eleanor of Aquitaine
Henry III	Eleanor of Provence
Henry V	Catherine of Valois
Henry VIII	Catherine of Aragon (divorced), Anne Boleyn (executed for adultery), Jane Seymour (died), Anne of Cleves (marriage annulled), Catherine Howard (executed for adultery), Catherine Parr (outlived him)
Audrey Hepburn	Mel Ferrer, Dr Dotti
Hitler	Eva Braun (for 1 day)
Buddy Holly	Maria Elena Santiago

Howard Hughes	Jean Peters
Attila the Hun	Ildico
Jill Ireland	David McCallum, Charles Bronson
Jeremy Irons	Sinead Cusack
Hattie Jacques	John Le Mesurier
Mick Jagger	Bianca de Macia, Jerry Hall
Jean-Michel Jarre	Charlotte Rampling
Elton John	Renata Blauel
Al Jolson	Ruby Keeler
Tom Jones	Linda
Josephine	Viscount De Beauharnais, Napoleon
Justinian	Theodora
Jacqueline Kennedy	John F.Kennedy, Aristotle Onassis
John F.Kennedy	Jacqueline Bouvier
Ludovic Kennedy	Moira Shearer
Carole King	Gerry Goffin
Kris Kristofferson	Rita Coolidge
D.H.Lawrence	Frieda Von Richthofen
Vivien Leigh	Laurence Olivier
John Lennon	Cynthia Powell, Yoko Ono
Abraham Lincoln	Mary Todd
Charles Lindbergh	Anne Morrow
Maureen Lipman	Jack Rosenthal
Carole Lombard	William Powell, Clark Gable
Sophia Loren	Carlo Ponti
Louis VII	Eleanor of Aquitaine
Louis XVI	Marie Antoinette
Mahler	Maria Schindler
Lee Majors	Farrah Fawcett
Jayne Mansfield	Mickey Hargitay
Ferdinand Marcos	Imelda
Princess Margaret	Anthony Armstrong-Jones
Karl Marx	Jennie Von Westphalen
Mary Queen of Scots	Francis II, Lord Darnley, Earl of Bothwell
Paul McCartney	Linda Eastman
John McEnroe	Tatum O'Neal
Steve McQueen	Ali McGraw
John McVie	Christine Perfect
Melina Mercouri	Jules Dassin
Cliff Michelmore	Jean Metcalfe
Sarah Miles	Robert Bolt
Mohammed	Aisha (favourite of 12)
Marilyn Monroe	Jim Dougherty, Joe Di Maggio, Arthur Miller
Yves Montand	Simone Signoret
Dudley Moore	Suzy Kendall, Tuesday Weld, Brogan Lane
Roger Moore	Dorothy Squires (1st)
Mozart	Constanze Weber
Nefertiti	Akhnaton
Nero	Agrippina, Poppaea
Paul Newman	Joanne Woodward
Robert De Niro	Diahnne Abbott
Richard Nixon	Thelma
Laurence Olivier	Jill Esmond, Vivien Leigh, Joan Plowright
Aristotle Onassis	Jackie Kennedy
John Osborne	Jill Bennett
Oswald Mosley	Cynthia Curzon, Diana Mitford
Peter O'Toole	Sian Phillips

Ann Packer	Robbie Brightwell
Peter the Great	Catherine I, Eudoxia
Pat Phoenix	Anthony Booth
Harold Pinter	Vivien Merchant, Lady Antonia Fraser
Sylvia Plath	Ted Hughes
Jacqueline Du Pré	Daniel Barenboim
Elvis Presley	Priscilla Beaulieu
Andre Previn	Dory Previn, Mia Farrow
Charlotte Rampling	Jean-Michel Jarre
Esther Rantzen	Desmond Wilcox
Ronald Reagan	Jane Wyman, Nancy Davis
Vanessa Redgrave	Tony Richardson
Debbie Reynolds	Eddie Fisher
Burt Reynolds	Judy Carne, Loni Anderson
Richard I	Berengaria
Richard II	Anne of Bohemia
Roy Rogers	Dale Evans
John Rolfe	Pocahontas
Mickey Rooney	Ava Gardner (1st)
Franklin D.Roosevelt	Eleanor Roosevelt
Dante Gabriel Rossetti	Elizabeth Siddal
Rubens	Helena
Leonard Sachs	Eleanor Summerfield
Victoria Sackville-West	Harold Nicholson
Prunella Scales	Timothy West
Alma Maria Schindler	Mahler, Kokoschka, Walter Gropius
George C. Scott	Colleen Dewhurst (twice)
Peter Sellers	Anne Hayes, Britt Ekland, Miranda Quarry, Lynne Frederick
Shakespeare	Ann Hathaway
Norma Shearer	Irving Thalber
Frank Sinatra	Ava Gardner, Mia Farrow, Barbara Marx
Socrates	Xanthippe
Phil Spector	Ronnie (Veronica) Bennett
Earl Spencer	Raine (2nd wife)
Barbara Stanwyck	Robert Taylor
Ringo Starr	Maureen Cox, Barbara Bach
R.L.Stevenson	Fanny Osbourne
Dave Stewart	Siobhan Fahey
Rod Stewart	Alana Hamilton, Kelly Emberg
Sting	Frances Tomelty
John Stonehouse	Sheila Buckley
Tom Stoppard	Miriam
Barbara Streisand	Elliott Gould
Gloria Swanson	Wallace Beery (1st)
Elizabeth Taylor	Conrad Hilton, Michael Wilding, Mike Todd, Eddie Fisher, Richard Burton (twice), John Warner, Larry Fortensky
James Taylor	Carly Simon
Tammie Terrell	Ernie
Denis Thatcher	Margaret Kempson, Margaret Roberts
John Thaw	Sheila Hancock
Daley Thompson	Frances Morgan
Sybil Thorndike	Lewis Casson
Jeremy Thorpe	Marion Harewood
General Tom Thumb	Lavinia Warren
Pierre Trudeau	Margaret

Donald Trump	Ivana
Mao Tse Tung	Chiang Ching (4th wife)
Lana Turner	Lex Barker
Queen Victoria	Albert
Robert Wagner	Natalie Wood (twice)
Wagner	Minna Planer, Cosima Von Bülow
George Washington	Martha
Denis Waterman	Rula Lenska
Sidney Webb	Beatrice Potter
Andrew Lloyd Webber	Sarah Brightman
Kurt Weill	Lotte Lenya
Orson Welles	Rita Hayworth
May Whitby	Ben Webster
Andy Williams	Claudine Longet
Bruce Willis	Demi Moore
Stevie Wonder	Syreela Wright
Victoria Wood	Geoff Durham (The Great Soprendo)
Virginia Woolf	Leonard Woolf
Bill Wyman	Mandy Smith

Miscellaneous

By: Attribute, Description → Name

Notes: *Covers descriptions not relating to a more specific topic.*

Amputated Leg given full burial	Peter Stuyvesant
Bear; Refused to shoot	Theodore Roosevelt
Birthday; Bequeathed to girl born on Christmas Day	R.L.Stevenson
Born;-	
In Ladies' Cloakroom	Churchill
On Carpet	Napoleon
Burnt poor who ask for food. Eaten by mice	Bishop Hatto
Castrated; French philosopher	Pierre Abelard
Cheese; Ate only	Zoroaster
Cheque; Personal, for $23 Million; Wrote	Howard Hughes (buying RKO)
Chief Justice; Former thief	Sir John Popham (16th Century)
Choked on a half sovereign	I.K.Brunel
Cleanliness; Obsession with; Millionaire	Howard Hughes
Desert; Lost in, during Paris–Dakar Car Rally	Mark Thatcher
Devils of Loudon; Priest	Urbain Grandier
Disappeared	Ambrose Bierce, Buster Crabbe, Amelia Earhart, Jimmy Hoffa, Leslie Howard, Lord Lucan, Glenn Miller
Dung; Threw in House of Commons	Yana Mintoff
Epitaph;-	
'Here lies one whose name was writ in water'	John Keats
'On the whole I'd rather be in Philadelphia'	W.C.Fields
Explorer; Became delegate to League of Nations	Fridtjof Nansen
Fly; Held funeral for	Virgil
Flying Saucers; 1st to see (and gives name to)	Kenneth Arnold

Halley's Comet; Born and died during	Mark Twain
Homosexual/Bisexual	Leonard Bernstein, David Bowie, Graham Chapman, Cocteau, Leonardo da Vinci, Diaghilev, Edward II, E.M.Forster, Hadrian, Gilbert Harding, Richard I, Virginia Woolf, Elton John, Charles Laughton, T.E.Lawrence, Pasolini, Proust, Rimbaud, Tom Robinson, Gertrude Stein, Tchaikovsky, Bill Tilden, Verlaine, Oscar Wilde
Illegitimate	Borodin, Willy Brandt, Cézanne, Eric Clapton, Leonardo da Vinci, Erasmus, Larry Grayson, T.E.Lawrence, Sophia Loren, Charles Manson, Ramsay MacDonald, Rod McKuen, Marilyn Monroe, Juan Peron, Pat Phoenix, Wagner, William the Conqueror
Income;-	
Highest; US; 1920s	Al Capone
Highest; US; 1930s and 40s	Louis B.Mayer
Judgement between two women claiming the same baby	King Solomon
Kleptomaniac	King Farouk of Egypt
Landlord;-	
Private; Richest; UK	Duke of Westminster
Private; Largest; UK	Duke of Buccleuch
Left Handed	Chaplin, Leonardo da Vinci, George II, George IV, Jimi Hendrix, Jack the Ripper, James I, Harpo Marx, Paul McCartney, Michelangelo, Cole Porter, Queen Victoria
Masochist	Henri Rousseau
Mecca; Made pilgrimage to disguised as Muslim	Sir Richard Burton
Millionaire;-	
1st	Cornelius Vanderbilt
1st; US	George Washington
Youngest; US	Jackie Coogan
Minstrel; Searched for Richard I through Europe	Blondel
Miser; Richest US woman at death	Hetty Green
Nose; Insured	Jimmy Durante
Nude Centrefold; 1st; UK	Marilyn Cole
Oranges; Sold outside Theatre Royal	Nell Gwynn
Orchid; Always wore in button hole	Nubar Gulbenkian
Pet Owl; Always carried in pocket	Florence Nightingale
Pie; Served in, to Charles I	Jeffrey Hudson (dwarf)
Prohibitionist; Used hatchet to destroy bars	Carry Nation
Public Speech; Fastest	J.F.Kennedy
Red Headed	Sarah Bernhardt, Churchill, Cromwell, Elizabeth I, Henry VIII Rod Laver, Napoleon, Shakespeare, Shaw, Vivaldi, George Washington, William the Conqueror

Richest;-	
Individual	Sultan of Brunei
Individual; Ordinary	Sam Moore Walton
Individual; UK	Queen
Woman	Queen
Seclusion; Millionaire's obsession with	Howard Hughes
Short	Attila the Hun, Alexander Pope, Christopher Wren
Tallest	Robert Wadlow
Taxi; Millionaire's car modelled on	Nubar Gulbenkian
Three Legged	Lentini
Twins; Had	Cleopatra, Mia Farrow, Margaret Thatcher
Vegetarian	G.B.Shaw
Water; Offered in battle, gave to another	Sir Philip Sidney at Zutphen
Waves; King tried to turn back	Canute
Whale; Swallowed by, for 2 days, lived	James Bartley
Who's Who; Youngest (non peer)	Yehudi Menuhin
Wolf Children; Indian	Amala and Kamala
Words; Mixed up parts of when speaking	Reverend Spooner

Nationality and Origin

By: Name → Nationality, Origin

Hans Christian Andersen	Denmark
Marie Antoinette	Austria
Miguel Angel Asturias	Guatemala
Lord Beaverbrook	Canada (born)
David Ben-Gurion	Poland
Irving Berlin	Russia (Siberia)
Sarah Bernhardt	France
Simon Bolivar	Venezuela
Katie Boyle	Italy
Constantin Brancusi	Romania
Yul Brynner	USSR (Sakhalin Island)
John Calvin	France
Charlie Chaplin	UK (born)
Christopher Columbus	Italy
Copernicus	Poland
Eamonn De Valera	Father: Spanish. Born in: New York
Dvorak	Czechoslovakia
Adolf Eichmann	Austria
Errol Flynn	Tasmania
Garibaldi	US (became)
Tony Grieg	South Africa
Che Guevara	Argentina
Handel	Britain (naturalised, born German)
Laurence Harvey	Lithuania
Haydn	Austria
Bob Hope	UK (born)
Bianca Jagger	Nicaragua
Al Jolson	Russia
Kiri Te Kanawa	New Zealand
Kandinsky	Russia
Henry Kissinger	Germany
Ivan Lendl	Czechoslovakia
Doris Lessing	Zimbabwe

321

Ferdinand Magellan	Portugal
Magnus Magnusson	Iceland
René Magritte	Belgium
Michael Marks (Marks and Spencer)	Poland
Robert Maxwell	Czechoslovakia
Cardinal Mazarin	Sicily (originally)
Leo McKern	Australia (born)
Golda Meir	Ukraine
Yehudi Menuhin	US
Carmen Miranda	Portugal
Joan Miro	Spain
Mozart	Austria
Edvard Munch	Norway
Rupert Murdoch	Australia
Napoleon	Corsica
Ilie Nastase	Romania
Martina Navratilova	Czechoslovakia (now US)
Merle Oberon	Tasmania
Bernardo O'Higgins	Chile
Gary Player	South Africa
Ferdinand Porsche	Austria
Anthony Quinn	Mexico (born)
Keke Rosberg	Finland
Helena Rubinstein	Poland
Andrew Sachs	Germany (born)
Schubert	Austria
Jacob Schweppe (Schweppes)	Switzerland
Jean Sibelius	Finland
Bedrich Smetana	Czechoslovakia
Tom Stoppard	Czechoslovakia
Joan Sutherland	Australia
Sophie Tucker	Russia (born)
P.G.Wodehouse	US (became)
W.B.Yeats	Ireland

Occupations

By: Occupation → Name

Notes: Included are unusual or interesting past occupations of people
famous for other reasons.

Accountant	Bob Newhart
Acrobat	Cary Grant
Actor	Shakespeare
Aircraft Designer	Nevil Shute
Archaeologist	André Malraux
Architectural Assistant	Thomas Hardy
Army Officer	David Niven
Army Officer (Crimean War)	Tolstoy
Army Swimming Instructor	Clint Eastwood
Artist	Samuel Morse
Baby Photographer	Gary Cooper
Bank Clerk	Gauguin, Terry Wogan
Bank Employee (Lloyd's)	T.S.Eliot
Bank of England, Secretary to	Kenneth Grahame
Barber	Perry Como
Barrister	William Gilbert
Beautician	Tammy Wynette

Biochemist	Chaim Weizmann, Isaac Asimov
Bookseller	Michael Faraday
Boxer	Arthur Mullard, Bob Hope
Brewer	James Prescott Joule
Bricklayer	Freddie Starr
Brickmaker	Daniel Defoe
British Army Colonel	George Washington
British Army Sergeant	Idi Amin
Building Labourer	Sean O'Casey
Bus Driver	Fangio
Butcher	Frank Finlay
Candlemaker	Garibaldi
Cartoonist	William Gilbert
Circus Acrobat	Burt Lancaster
Civil Servant	James Callaghan, Mussorgsky, Tchaikovsky
Coffin Polisher	Sean Connery
Court Stenographer	Charles Dickens
Criminal	Jean Genet
Customs Controller for Wool	Geoffrey Chaucer
Customs Office Clerk	Henri Rousseau
Customs Official	Herman Melville
Decorator	Syd Little
Dentist	Zane Grey
Doctor	Hastings Banda (in Liverpool), Roger Bannister, Galileo, Graeme Garden, Gatling (Machine Gun Inventor), W.G.Grace, Che Guevara, St Luke, Jonathan Miller, David Owen, Rabelais, Roget
Electrician	Rod Hull, David Jason, Eddie Large, Lech Walesa
Embassy Official	Dante
Engineer	Andres Courreges
Excise Officer	Robert Burns
Film Extra	Fidel Castro
Fire Chief	Goethe
Fisherman	St Andrew, St Peter
Football Goalkeeper	Julio Iglesias
Foreign Minister	Goethe
Glove Salesman	Sam Goldwyn
Gravedigger	Rod Stewart
Gun Runner	Arthur Rimbaud
Haberdasher	Harry S. Truman
Hairdresser	Delia Smith
Hat Unpacker/Hat Model	Greta Garbo
History Professor	Charles Kingsley
Hollywood Scriptwriter	F. Scott Fitzgerald
Horse Guardsman	Tommy Cooper
Hospital Porter	Ludwig Wittgenstein
Hotel Worker (Carlton, London)	Ho Chi Minh
Inspector of Mines	A.J.Cronin
Insurance Clerk	Leonard Rossiter
Intelligence Agent	Ian Fleming
Jazz Clarinettist	Woody Allen
Jockey	George Formby
Laboratory bottle washer	Michael Faraday
Labourer on Panama Canal	Gauguin

Lawyer	Wassily Kandinsky, Lenin, Sir Walter Scott, Margaret Thatcher
Librarian	Casanova
Lion Tamer	Alex Harvey
Lottery Director	Casanova
Lumberjack	Clark Gable
Male Model	Gerald Ford
Marine	Harvey Keitel
Market Porter	John Thaw
Mathematics Lecturer	Lewis Carroll
Merchant	Arthur Rimbaud
Milkman	Benny Hill, Jimmy Tarbuck
Miner	Harry Worth, Robert Mitchum
Mining Commissioner	Goethe
Mint, Warden of	Isaac Newton
Monk	Gregor Mendel, Stalin (Trainee)
Motor Racing Driver	Paul Newman
MP	Geoffrey Chaucer, Hilaire Belloc, Richard Sheridan, Isaac Newton
Music Teacher	William Herschel
Naturalist	James Robertson Justice
Naval Officer (when writing book)	Dr Spock
Newsboy	Thomas Edison
Newspaper Correspondent (*New York Tribune*)	Karl Marx
Novelist	Benjamin Disraeli
Nutritionist	Magnus Pyke
Oil Company Employee	Walter De La Mare
Opthalmologist	Arthur Conan Doyle
Ornamental Mason	Auguste Rodin
Painter and Decorator	Brendan Behan
Pastry Cook (Escoffier – in France)	Ho Chi Minh
Patent Office Clerk	Einstein
Peanut Farmer	Jimmy Carter
Pharmacist	Ibsen
Picador	Orson Welles
Playwright	John Vanbrugh
Policeman	John Arlott, Christopher Dean, Dave Dee, Bob Harris (DJ), George Orwell
Post Office Employee	Anthony Trolloppe
Postcard Painter	Adolf Hitler
Postman	Terry Griffiths
Postmaster	William Faulkner
Priest	Henry Armstrong, Franz Liszt, Little Richard, Jonathan Swift
Printer	Benjamin Franklin
Professor of Art	Samuel Morse
Professor of Astronomy	Sir Christopher Wren
Professor of Chemistry	Borodin
Professor of English (Oxford University)	J.R.R.Tolkien
Professor of Greek	Enoch Powell
Publisher	Harold Macmillan
Research Chemist	Margaret Thatcher
Royal Navy Sailor	Sean Connery
Seaman	Gareth Hunt, Tommy Steele
Shipyard Worker	Billy Connolly, Peter the Great
Shoe Black Factory Worker	Charles Dickens

Shopkeeper	Daniel Defoe
Slave	Aesop
Social Worker	Clement Attlee
Soldier	Cervantes, Chaucer
Solicitor's Clerk	Arnold Bennett
Speech teacher to deaf	Alexander Graham Bell
Spy	Somerset Maugham, Casanova
Stamp Distributor	Wordsworth
Stockbroker	Gauguin
Swimsuit Model	James Garner
Tax Collector	Lavoisier, St Matthew
Tax Official	James Callaghan
Teacher	Russell Harty
Telegraph Operator	Thomas Edison
Toilet Paper Salesman	John Mills
Tugboat Worker	Billy Fury
Undertaker	Strowger
University Lecturer	Kingsley Amis
Veterinary Surgeon	John Boyd Dunlop

Pairs and Partnerships

By: Name → Partner

Abbott	Costello
Bill	Ben
Cannon	Ball
Damon	Pythias
Dante	Beatrice (Portinari)
George	Mildred
Hero	Leander
Hinge	Bracket
Rod Hull	Emu
Laurel	Hardy
Little	Large
Morecambe	Wise
Roland	Oliver
Sooty	Sweep
Steptoe	Son

Parents

By: Name → Parent

Alexander the Great	Philip II
Queen Anne	James II
Marie Antoinette	Francis I, Maria Theresa (Austria)
Lionel, Ethel, John Barrymore	Maurice Barrymore
Candice Bergen	Edgar
Cesare Borgia	Pope Alexander VI
Charlemagne	Pepin the Short
Winston Churchill	Lord Randolph Churchill, Jennie Jerome
Jamie Lee Curtis	Janet Leigh, Tony Curtis
Princess Diana	Earl Spencer, Mrs Shand Kydd
Duke of Edinburgh	Prince Andrew of Greece, Princess Alice of Battenburg
Edward VI	Henry VIII, Jane Seymour
Elizabeth I	Henry VIII, Anne Boleyn

325

Ethelred the Unready	Elfthryth
Mia Farrow	Maureen O'Sullivan
Carrie Fisher	Debbie Reynolds, Eddie Fisher
Lady Antonia Fraser	Lord Longford
Indira Gandhi	Nehru
George III	Frederick, Prince of Wales. Charlotte of Mecklenburg
Larry Hagman	Mary Martin
Hannibal	Hamilcar
Nigel Havers	Sir Michael
Henry II	Matilda
Henry III	King John
Henry IV	John of Gaunt
Henry VII	Edmund Tudor, Margaret Beaufort
John Huston	Walter
James I	Mary, Queen of Scots
John Kennedy	Joseph
Nastassia Kinski	Klaus
Paul Kossoff	David
Richard Leakey	Louis
Queen Mary	Henry VIII, Catherine of Aragon
Mary Queen of Scots	James V of Scotland, Mary of Guise
Matilda	Henry I
Liza Minnelli	Judy Garland, Vincente Minnelli
Napoleon III	Louis (Napoleon's brother)
Marco Polo	Niccolo
Richard I	Henry II
Queen Victoria	Edward (Duke of Kent), Victoria of Saxe Coburg
William I	Robert I of Normandy (illegitimate son)
Shirley Williams	Vera Brittain
Virginia Woolf	Leslie Stephen

Relations

By: Names → Relation

Notes: Order is Relation of 1st person to 2nd.

Augustus Caesar, Julius Caesar	Grandnephew (and Adopted Son)
Augustus, Tiberius	Stepfather
Juan Carlos I, Alfonso XIII	Grandson
Charlie Chaplin, Eugene O'Neill	Son-in-law
Neville Chamberlain, Austen Chamberlain	Half Brother
Charlemagne, Charles Martel	Grandson
Charles II, Mary (William and Mary)	Uncle
Cecil B.De Mille, Anthony Quinn	Father-in-law
Princess Diana, Barbara Cartland	Step Granddaughter
Duke of Edinburgh, Queen Victoria	Great Great Grandson
Elizabeth I, Mary Queen of Scots	Cousins
Elizabeth II, Queen Victoria	Great Great Granddaughter
Clement Freud, Sigmund Freud	Grandson
George V, Kaiser Wilhelm	Cousins
Hadrian, Trajan	Adopted Son
Henry VIII, Catherine of Aragon (before marriage)	Brother-in-law
Alec Douglas Home, Charles Douglas Home	Uncle
Whitney Houston, Dionne Warwick	Cousins

T.H.Huxley, Aldous and Julian Huxley	Grandfather
Julius Caesar, Pompey	Father-in-law
Kublai Khan, Genghis Khan	Grandson
Christopher Lee, Ian Fleming	Cousins
Lord Lichfield, Queen	Cousins
Walter Lindrum, Horace Lindrum	Uncle
Franz Liszt, Richard Wagner	Father-in-law
Thomas Mann, W.H.Auden	Father-in-law
Patrick McNee, David Niven	Cousins
Napoleon III, Napoleon I	Nephew
Ginger Rogers, Rita Hayworth	Cousins
Roland, Charlemagne	Nephew
Franklin Roosevelt, Theodore Roosevelt	5th Cousins
Lord Rothermere, Lord Northcliffe (1st)	Brother
Bertrand Russell, Lord John Russell	Grandson
Lord Salisbury, Arthur Balfour	Uncle
Martin Scorsese, Ingrid Bergman and Roberto Rosselini	Son-in-Law (Former)
Stephen, Henry I	Nephew
Queen Victoria, Albert	Cousins
Queen Victoria, George III	Granddaughter

Relationships

By: Name → Partner

Notes: Includes Mistresses, Affairs, Engagements, Names Romantically Linked, etc.

Abelard	Heloise
Woody Allen	Diane Keaton, Mia Farrow
Paddy Ashdown	Tricia Howard
Ingmar Bergman	Liv Ullmann
Ingrid Bergman	Roberto Rossellini
Brahms	Clara Schumann
Byron	Lady Caroline Lamb, Augusta Leigh (Half Sister)
Calamity Jane	Wild Bill Hickok
King Carol of Romania	Magda Lupescu
Catherine II (Russia)	Grigori Potemkin
Charles II	Nell Gwyn
Chopin	George Sand
Cleopatra	Julius Caesar, Mark Antony
Jimmy Connors	Chris Evert
Gabriele D'Annunzio	Eleonora Duse
Catherine Deneuve	Roger Vadim, Marcello Mastroianni
Charles Dickens	Ellen Ternan
Edward II	Piers Gaveston
Edward III	Alice Perrers
Edward IV	Jane Shore
Edward VII	Lillie Langtry
George Eliot	George Lewes
Brian Ferry	Jerry Hall
Anna Ford	Jon Snow
Edward Fox	Joanna David
Greta Garbo	Mouritz Stiller
Goya	Duchess of Alba
Hadrian	Artinous

William Randolph Hearst	Marion Davies
Lillian Hellman	Dashiell Hammett
Henry II	Rosamund Clifford
Henry II (France)	Diane of Poitiers
Hitler	Eva Braun
Catherine Howard	Thomas Culpepper, Francis Dereham
Chrissie Hynde	Ray Davies
Queen Isabella	Roger De Mortimer
Mick Jagger	Marianne Faithfull, Jerry Hall
John Keats	Fanny Browne
Louis XIV	Madame De Montespan, Madame De Maintenon
Louis XV	Madame Du Barry, Madame De Pompadour
Princess Margaret	Group Captain Peter Townsend, Roddy Llewellyn
Lee Marvin	Michelle Triola (sued for half his earnings)
John McCarthy	Jill Morrell
Paul McCartney	Jane Asher
John McEnroe	Tatum O'Neal
David Mellor	Antonia de Sancha
Lola Montez	Ludwig I of Bavaria
Mussolini	Clara Petacci
Nelson	Lady Hamilton
Stevie Nicks	Lindsay Buckingham
Joe Orton	Kenneth Halliwell
Cecil Parkinson	Sarah Keays
Vanessa Redgrave	Franco Nero, Timothy Dalton
Linda Rondstadt	Gerry Hall
Lillian Russell	Diamond Jim Brady
George Sand	Chopin, Alfred de Musset
Romy Schneider	Alain Delon
Percy Bysshe Shelley	Mary Godwin
Jean Shrimpton	David Bailey, Terence Stamp
Grace Slick	Paul Kantner
Rod Stewart	Britt Ekland
Jeremy Thorpe	Norman Scott
Twiggy	Justin De Villeneuve
Paul Verlaine	Arthur Rimband
Alan Whicker	Olga Deterding
William IV (when Duke of Clarence)	Mrs Jordan (Dorothy Bland)
William Wordsworth	Annette Vallon

Suicide

By: Name → General

Fred Archer	By: Shooting (during Typhoid attack)
Dr Gareth Bennett	After article attacking Archbishop of Canterbury
Cassius	Reason: Mistakenly believed Battle of Phillipi lost
Lord Castlereagh	By: Penknife
Cato the Younger	Reason: Army surrounded by Julius Caesar
Cleopatra	By: Asp bite (supposedly)
Robert Clive	By: Shooting (had attempted twice before)
Hart Crane	By: Jumping off ship

George Eastman	By: Shooting
Emily Davison (suffragette)	By: Trampled by King's horse, Derby, 1913
Brian Epstein	By: Drug overdose
Judy Garland	By: Drug overdose
Tony Hancock	By: Drug overdose. In: Sydney (1968)
Hannibal	Reason: To avoid capture by the Romans (183 BC)
Ernest Hemingway	By: Shooting (1961)
Himmler	By: Poisoning
Hitler	In Berlin bunker. By: Cyanide. Also shot by Eva Braun (1945)
Elton John	Attempted
Arthur and Cynthia Koestler	Together
Carole Landis	By: Drug overdose
Jack London	By: Poisoning
Mark Antony	Reason: Mistakenly believed Cleopatra dead
Masada	Mass suicide by Jewish fortress (AD 73)
Vladimir Mayakovsky	By: Shooting
Yukio Mishima (Japanese Poet)	By: Harakiri (1970)
Mithridates (King of Pontus)	Reason: Son revolted against
Marilyn Monroe (Supposed suicide)	By: Overdose of barbiturates (1962)
Nero	By: Stabbing (AD 68). Reason: Sentenced to death by Roman Senate
Captain Lawrence Oates	With Scott's Antarctic expedition. Crippled and not wanting to delay return, walked out into a blizzard (1912)
Jan Palach	By: Self Immolation. Reason: Russian Invasion of Czechoslovakia
Sylvia Plath (Poet)	By: Gas fumes (1963)
Reverend Jim Jones (and other members of People's Temple)	In: Guyana, 1978. By: Cyanide. Largest mass suicide
Rommel	By: Shooting
Mark Rothko	By: Slashing wrists
Crown Prince Rudolf	(After shooting lover Maria Vetsera.) At: Mayerling Hunting Lodge
Romy Schneider	(Supposed suicide)
Robert Schumann	Attempted
Seneca	Reason: Nero forces
Wolfe Tone	(Irish Revolutionary Leader) Reason: Facing execution. By: Cutting throat with penknife
Vincent Van Gogh	By: Shooting (1890)
Harriet Westbrook (Shelley's 1st Wife)	By: Drowning in Serpentine
Virginia Woolf	By: Drowning (1941)

NAMES
Christian Names

By: Surname → Christian Name(s)

Lord Baden Powell	Robert Stephenson Smyth
Brunel	Isambard Kingdom

Lord Byron	George Gordon
J and P Coats	James and Peter
Gandhi	Mohandas Karamchand
Mrs Gaskell	Elizabeth Cleghorn
Gilbert and Sullivan	William Schwenck, Arthur
Gillette	King Camp
Gluck	Christoph Wilibald
Brothers Grimm	Jacob, Wilhelm
Lady Hamilton	Emma
Marks and Spencer	Michael, Tom
Princess Michael of Kent	Marie-Christine
Miro	Joan
Mussorgsky	Modest
Colonel Sanders	Harland
Smetana	Bedrich
Stock, Aitken, Waterman	Mike, Matt, Peter
Madame Tussaud	Marie
Woolworth	Frank Winfield
Sheikh Yamani	Ahmad

Initials

By: Name → Initials

W.H. Auden	Wystan Hugh
W.E.B. Du Bois	William Edward Burghardt
G.K. Chesterton	Gilbert Keith
Arthur C. Clarke	Charles
A.J. Cronin	Archibald Joseph
E.E. Cummings	Edward Estlin
R.F. Delderfield	Ronald Frederick
T.S. Eliot	Thomas Stearns
W.C. Fields	William Claude
F. Scott Fitzgerald	Francis
C.S. Forester	Cecil Scott
E.M. Forster	Edward Morgan
W.E. Gladstone	William Ewart
B.F. Goodrich	Benjamin Franklin
W.G. Grace	William Gilbert
D.W. Griffith	David Wark
H.J. Heinz	Henry John
Jerome K. Jerome	Klapka
J.M. Keynes	John Maynard
R.D. Laing	Ronald David
D.H. Lawrence	David Herbert
C.S. Lewis	Clive Staples
L.S. Lowry	Laurence Stephen
Cecil B. De Mille	Blount
A.A. Milne	Alan Alexander
J.B. Priestley	John Boynton
O.J. Simpson	Orenthal James
B.F. Skinner	Burrhus Fredric
W.H. Smith	William Henry
C.P. Snow	Charles Percy
R.L. Stevenson	Robert Lewis (changed to Louis)
J.R.R. Tolkien	John Ronald Reuel
Harry S. Truman	S (nothing)
Booker T. Washington	Taliaferro
H.G. Wells	Herbert George

| P.G. Wodehouse | Pelham Grenville |
| W.B. Yeats | William Butler |

Maiden Names

By: Name → Maiden Name

Evonne Cawley	Goolagong
Agatha Christie	Miller
Marie Curie	Sklodowska
Princess Diana	Spencer
Mrs Gaskell	Stevenson
Lady Emma Hamilton	Lyon
Bianca Jagger	Macias
Ann Jones	Haydon
Billy Jean King	Moffitt
Princess Michael of Kent	Von Reibnitz
Mary Rand	Bignal
Eleanor Roosevelt	Roosevelt
Mrs Wallis Simpson	Wallis Warfield
Margaret Court	Smith
Margaret Thatcher	Roberts
Madame Tussaud	Grosholtz

Middle Names

By: Name → Middle Name

Humphrey Bogart	De Forest
Charlie Chaplin	Spencer
Sebastian Coe	Newbold
Charles Dickens	John Huffam
Walt Disney	Elias
Thomas Edison	Alva
David Frost	Paradine
Oliver Hardy	Norville
Elton John	Hercules (names himself)
Neil Kinnock	Gordon
John Lennon	Winston (changed to Ono)
Harold Lloyd	Clayton
John Major	Roy
Nelson Mandela	Rolihlahla
Ferdinand Marcos	Edralin
Bob Marley	Nesta
Paul McCartney	James
Robert McNamara	Strange
Glenn Miller	Alton
Richard Nixon	Milhous
Arthur Pinero	Wing
Ronald Reagan	Wilson
Percy Shelley	Bysshe
Norman Tebbit	Beresford
Margaret Thatcher	Hilda
Daley Thompson	Francis
Oscar Wilde	Fingal O'Flahertie Wills

Names, General

By: General

| Christian Name;- | |
| France, Germany; How chosen | From official list (formerly) |

Most common; Britain; Female	Elizabeth
Most common; Britain; Male	John
Nicknames for Surnames:-	
Clark	Nobby
Martin	Pincher
Miller	Dusty
Murphy	Spud
White	Snowy, Knocker
Surname;-	
English; Longest	Featherstonehaugh (Pronounced Fanshaw)
'Fitz' means	Son of
'Mc/Mac' means	Son of
Most Common	Chang
Most Common; Britain and US	Smith
Most Common; 1st letter; UK	B
Most Common; Korea	Kim
Most Common; UK; 2nd	Jones
Most Common; US; 2nd	Johnson
'O' means	Grandson of

Nicknames

By: Category/Nickname → Name

Categories: Crime, Literature, Music, Others, Politics, Sport, Stage and Screen
See Also: Real (First) Names

Crime	
Acid Bath murderer,The	John George Haig
Birdman of Alcatraz,The	Robert Franklin Stroud
Boston Strangler,The	Albert De Salvo
Cambridge Rapist,The	Peter Cook
Candy Man Killer,The	Ronald O'Bryan
French Bluebeard,The	Henri Landru
Monster of Dusseldorf,The	Peter Kurten
Papillon	Henri Charrière
Son of Sam	David Berkowitz
Yorkshire Ripper,The	Peter Sutcliffe
Literature	
Bard of Avon,The	Shakespeare
Bard of Ayrshire,The	Robert Burns
Gidget	Frances Lawrence (fiction)
Great Cham,The	Samuel Johnson
Great Unknown,The	Walter Scott
Master,The	Noel Coward
Music	
Bird	Charlie Parker
Boss,The	Bruce Springsteen
Father of the Blues,The	W.C. Handy
Flash Harry	Sir Malcolm Sargent
King of Hi de Ho,The	Cab Calloway
King of Swing,The	Benny Goodman
Lady Day	Billie Holliday
Last of the Red Hot Mamas	Sophie Tucker
Little Sparrow,The	Edith Piaf
March King,The	John Sousa
Mother of the Blues,The	Ma Rainey

Pearl	Janis Joplin
Pelvis,The	Elvis Presley
Satchmo	Louis Armstrong (from: Satchel Mouth)
Singing Nun,The	Soeur Sourire
Sweetheart of the Forces,The	Vera Lynn
Swedish Nightingale,The	Jenny Lind
Two Ton Tessie	Tessie O Shea
Voice,The	Frank Sinatra
Yog	George Michael

Others

Angelic Doctor,The	Thomas Aquinas
Apostle of the Indies,The	Francis Xavier
Calamity Jane	Martha Jane Canary (later Bierke)
Divine Pagan,The	Hypatia
Father of Modern Chemistry,The	Lavoisier
King of Clowns,The	Grock
Lady with the Lamp,The	Florence Nightingale
Last of the Dandies,The	Count D'Orsay
Lone Eagle,The	Charles Lindbergh
Lord Porn	Lord Longford
Lucky	Lord Lucan
Madame Sin	Cynthia Payne
Man who broke the Bank at Monte Carlo,The	Joseph Holson Jagger
Soapy Sam	Bishop Samuel Wilberforce
Thunderthighs	Christina Onassis
Typhoid Mary	Mary Mallon
Wickedest Man in the World,The	Aleister Crowley
Wizard of Menlo Park,The	Thomas Edison
World's Most Perfectly Developed Man,The	Charles Atlas

Politics

Barbarossa	Frederick I (Holy Roman Emperor), also 2 Pirates
Beast of Bolsover,The	Dennis Skinner
Beauclerc	Henry I
Black Prince,The	Edward Prince of Wales (eldest son of Edward III)
Bloody Mary	Mary I (Mary Tudor)
Bluff Prince Hal	Henry V
Bonnie Prince Charlie	Charles Edward Stuart
Bravest of the Brave,The	Marshal Ney
Brenda (*Private Eye*)	The Queen
Butcher,The	Duke of Cumberland
Chingford Skinhead,The	Norman Tebbit
Cicero	Elyesa Bazna (spy)
Citizen King,The	Louis Philippe
Conqueror,The	William I
Cunctator (the Delayer)	Quintus Fabius (Roman General)
Danny the Red	Daniel Cohn-Bendit
Desert Fox,The	Rommel
El Cid	Ruy Diaz De Bivar
El Libertador (the Liberator)	Simon Bolivar
Empress Maud	Matilda
Face that Launched a Thousand Ships,The	Helen of Troy
Farmer George	George III

Flanders Mare,The	Anne of Cleves (called by Henry VIII)
Genghis Khan (Mighty Warrior)	Temujin
Glubb Pasha	Sir John Glubb
Goldenballs (*Private Eye*)	Sir James Goldsmith
Grand Old Man,The	William Gladstone
Great Commoner,The	William Pitt the Elder
Great Elector,The	Frederick William, Elector of Brandenburg
Handsomest Man in the World,The	Philip IV (the Fair) of France
Harefoot	Harold I
Hotspur	Sir Henry Percy
Iron Chancellor,The	Bismarck
Iron Duke,The	Duke of Wellington
Iron Lady,The	Margaret Thatcher
Ironside	Edmund II
King Maker,The	Richard Neville, Earl of Warwick
Lackland	King John
Lawrence of Arabia	Thomas Edward Lawrence
Lion Heart,The	Richard I
Longshanks	Edward I
Lord Haw Haw	William Joyce
Mahatma (Great Lord)	Gandhi
Maid of Orleans,The	Joan of Arc
Man Who Never Was,The	Major William Martin (body with false documents used to fool Germans in WWII)
Merry Monarch,The	Charles II
Molly Pitcher	Mary McCauley
Moonshine Philosopher,The	Thomas Jefferson
Old Blood and Guts	General Patton
Old Buddha,The	Empress Tzu Hsi
Old Chevalier,The	James Stuart
Old Hickory	Andrew Jackson (US President)
Old Ironsides	Oliver Cromwell
Old Pretender,The	James Stuart (son of James II)
Old Rowley	Charles II
Pam	Lord Palmerston
Pandit (Wise Man)	Nehru
Princes in the Tower,The	Edward V and (brother) Richard
Red Baron,The	Baron Manfred Von Richthofen
Red Eminence,The	Cardinal Richelieu
Red Robbo	Derek Robinson
Restorer of the World,The	Aurelian (Roman Emperor)
Rufus	William II
Scourge of God,The	Attila the Hun
Sea Green Incorruptible,The	Robespierre
Silent Cal	Calvin Coolidge
Silent,The	William I, Prince of Orange
Silly Billy	William IV
Stonewall	General Jackson (from: Battle of Bull Run)
Sun King,The	Louis XIV
Supermac	Harold Macmillan
Tarzan	Michael Heseltine
Tiger	Georges Clemenceau
Tricky Dicky	Richard Nixon
Tumbledown Dick	Richard Cromwell
Unready,The	Ethelred II

Wisest Fool in Christendom,The	James I
Wonder of the World,The	Frederick II
Young Pretender,The	Charles Edward Stuart

Sport

Ambling Alp,The	Primo Carnera
Arkle	Derek Randall
Big Bird	Joel Garner
Big Bill	William Tilden
Black Panther,The	Eusebio
Bounding Basque,The	Jean Borotra
Brockton Bomber,The	Rocky Marciano
Brown Bomber,The	Joe Louis
Chilly	Chris Old
Clockwork Mouse,The	Niki Lauda
Clones Cyclone,The	Barry McGuigan
Doc,The	Tommy Docherty
Eagle,The	Eddie Edwards
Fiery Fred	Fred Trueman
Flo Jo	Florence Griffith-Joyner
Flying Finn,The	Paavo Nurmi
Galloping Major,The	Ferenc Puskas
Gazza	Paul Gascoigne
Gentleman Jim	Jim Corbett (Boxer)
Golden Bear,The	Jack Nicklaus
Great White Shark,The	Greg Norman
Gorgeous George	George Wagner (Wrestler)
Grinder,The	Cliff Thorburn
Homicide Hank	Henry Armstrong
Hurricane	Alex Higgins
King,The	Barry John
Little Miss Poker Face	Helen Wills Moody
Louisville Lip,The	Muhammed Ali
Manassa Mauler,The	Jack Dempsey
Marvellous	Marvin Hageler
Muscles	Ken Rosewall
Nonpareil,The	Jack Dempsey
Orange Juice	O.J. Simpson
Orchid Kid,The	Georges Carpentier
Pine Tree	Colin Meads
Rabbi,The	Jimmy Hill
Red Fox,The	Chris Chataway
(Rockhampton) Rocket,The	Rod Laver
Shoe,The	Willie Shoemaker
Skeets	Renaldo Nehemiah
Sultan of Swat,The	Babe Ruth
Superbrat	John McEnroe
Super-Mex	Lee Trevino
Typhoon	Frank Tyson
Whirlwind	Jimmy White
White Lightning	Alberto Juantorena
Wizard of Dribble,The	Stanley Matthews

Stage and Screen

America's Sweetheart	Mary Pickford
America's Sweethearts	Nelson Eddy, Jeanette Macdonald
Biograph Girl,The	Florence Lawrence
Boop a Doop Girl,The	Helen Kane
Brazilian Bombshell,The	Carmen Miranda
Cheeky Chappie,The	Max Miller

Duke	John Wayne
Great Profile,The	John Barrymore
Great Stoneface,The	Buster Keaton
Hollywood's Mermaid	Esther Williams
It Girl,The	Clara Bow
Italian Stallion,The	Sylvester Stallone
Man of 1000 Faces,The	Lon Chaney Senior (title of biographical film with James Cagney)
Million Dollar Legs	Betty Grable
Parrot Face	Freddie Davies
Prime Minister of Mirth,The	George Robey
Schnozzle	Jimmy Durante
Sooty	Russell Harty
Stone Face	Buster Keaton
Sweater Girl,The	Lana Turner
Thinking Man's Crumpet,The	Joan Bakewell
Uncle Mac	Derek McCulloch
Vagabond Lover,The	Rudy Vallee
Voice,The	Richard Burton
Wolfman Jack	Bob Smith

Real (First) Names

By: Current Name → Original Name

Notes: Includes Nicknames which relate to first names.

Bud Abbott	William
Red Adair	Paul Neal
Cannonball Adderley	Julian
Paddy Ashdown	Jeremy
Count Basie	William
Chuck Berry	Charles
Bix Biederbecke	Leon Bismarck
Beau Bridges	Lloyd
Capability Brown	Lancelot (Landscape Gardener)
Beau Brummell	George Bryan
Max Bygraves	Walter
Cab Calloway	Cabell
Al Capone	Alphonse
Coco Chanel	Gabrielle
Perry Como	Pierino
Sean Connery	Thomas
Gary Cooper	Frank James
Bing Crosby	Harry
Bebe Daniels	Phyllis
Bette Davis	Ruth Elizabeth
Dixie Dean	William Ralph
Jack Dempsey	William
Legs Diamond	Jack (John) Thomas
Babe Didrikson	Mildred
Fats Domino	Antoine
Duke Ellington	Edmund
Buster Edwards	Ronald
Moss Evans	Mostyn
Mia Farrow	Maria
Pretty Boy Floyd	Charles
Barry Gibb	Douglas
Dizzy Gillespie	John Birks
Che Guevara	Ernesto

Rex Harrison	Reginald
Heinrich Heine	Harry (changed)
Jimi Hendrix	Johnny Allen (renamed James Marshall when 4)
Woody Herman	Woodrow
Benny Hill	Alfred
Lightnin Hopkins	Sam
Stonewall Jackson	Thomas
Bianca Jagger	Blanca
Casey Jones	John Luther
Kiri Te Kanawa	Janette
Buster Keaton	Joseph Frank
Machine Gun Kelly	George
B.B.King	Riley (stands for: Blues Boy)
Jonathan King	Kenneth
Evel Knievel	Robert Craig
Lillie Langtry	Emily
Chico Marx	Leonard
Harpo Marx	Arthur
Groucho Marx	Julius
Barry McGuigan	Finbar
Melina Mercouri	Maria Amolia
Jelly Roll Morton	Ferdinand
Len Murray	Lionel
Baby Face Nelson	George
Kim Novak	Marilyn
Kid Ory	Edward
Ozzy Osbourne	John
Marie Osmond	Olive
Jesse Owens	James Cleveland (nickname from initials)
Evita Peron	Eva
Debbie Reynolds	Marie Francis
Smokey Robinson	William
Babe Ruth	George Herman
George Savalas	Demosthenes
Telly Savalas	Aristoteles
Leo Sayer	Gerald
Peter Sellers	Richard Henry
Eddy Shah	Selim Jehan
Sissy Spacek	Mary Elizabeth
Koo Stark	Kathleen
Meryl Streep	Mary Louise
Turnip Townsend	Charles
Rudy Vallee	Hubert Prior
Gore Vidal	Eugene
T.Bone Walker	Aron
Fats Waller	Thomas
Tuesday Weld	Susan
Tennessee Williams	Thomas Lanier
Sonny Boy Williamson	John
Googie Withers	Georgina

Real Names

By: Category/Original Name → Changed Name

Categories: Crime, Literature, Music, Others, Politics, Sport, Stage and Screen
E.g. Who was . . . better known as?

Notes: Includes Name Changes, Stage-names, Pseudonyms, Pen Names.
See Also: Nicknames/Titles/Real (First) Names

Crime

William Bonney	Billy the Kid
Charles Bottom	Black Bart
Arthur Fiegenheimer	Dutch Schultz
Lester Gillis	Baby Face Nelson
Henry Longbaugh	The Sundance Kid (jailed in Sundance, Wyoming)
No-name Maddox	Charles Manson
Robert LeRoy Parker	Butch Cassidy
Edward Teach	Blackbeard

Literature

Francois Marie Arouet	Voltaire
Acton/Currer/Ellis Bell	Anne/Charlotte/Emily Bronte
Marie Henri Beyle	Stendhal
Eric Arthur Blair	George Orwell (from river)
Karen Blixen	Isak Dinesen
Charles Farrar Browne	Artemus Ward
Hablot K. Browne	Phiz (Dickens Illustrator)
Alfred Caplin	Al Capp
Samuel Clemens	Mark Twain (means: Two Fathoms, from Mississippi boatman's call)
David Cornwell	John Le Carré
Frederic Dannay and Manfred Lee	Ellery Queen
Guillaume De Krostrovitzky	Guillaume Apollinaire
Charles Dickens	Boz
Rev. Charles L. Dodgson	Lewis Carroll
William Donaldson	Henry Root
Amandine Dupin	George Sand
Marian Evans	George Eliot
Daniel Foe	Daniel Defoe
Theodore Seuss Geisel	Dr Seuss
John Griffith	Jack London
Romain Kacev	Romain Gary
Francis Kane	Harold Robbins
Count Teodor Korzeniowski	Joseph Conrad
Erich Maria Kramer	Erich Maria Remarque
Charles Lamb	Elia
Publius Vergilius Maro	Virgil
Herman Cyril McNeile	Sapper
H.H.Munro	Saki
Neville Norway	Neville Shute
Max Peshkov	Maxim Gorky. (means: Maxim 'The Bitter')
Jean Baptiste Poquelin	Molière
William Sidney Porter	O.Henry
Q	Sir Arthur Quiller-Couch
Francoise Quorez	Francoise Sagan
Harold Rubin	Harold Robbins
John Stewart	Michael Innes
Edward Stratemeyer	Franklin W. Dixon, Laura Lee Hope, Carolyn Keene
Tom Straussler	Tom Stoppard
Anatole Thibault	Anatole France
Arthur Sarsfield Ward	Sax Rohmer

Music

Nathaniel Adams	Nat King Cole
Marvin Lee Aday	Meat Loaf

Roberta Joan Anderson	Joni Mitchell (married name)
William Ashton	Billie J.Kramer
Michael Barratt	Shakin Stevens
Antonio Dominick Benedetto	Tony Bennett
John Beverly	Sid Vicious
William Broad	Billy Idol
Annie Mae Bullock	Tina Turner
Frederick Bulsara	Freddy Mercury
Chester Arthur Burnett	Howling Wolf
Stanley Kirk Burrell	(MC) Hammer
Buster Campbell	Prince Buster
Robert Walden Cassotto	Bobby Darin
Frank Castellucio	Frankie Valli
James Chambers	Jimmy Cliff
Leslie Charles	Billy Ocean
Maddonna Ciccone	Madonna
Eric Clap	Eric Clapton
Allison Clarkson	Betty Boo
Alfred Cocozza	Mario Lanza
David Cook	David Essex
Vincent Craddock	Gene Vincent
Susan Dallion	Siouxsie
August Darnell	Kid Creole
David Ivor Davies	Ivor Novello
Henry John Deutschendorf Jnr.	John Denver
Autry DeWalt	Junior Walker
Otis Dewey	Slim Whitman
Derek Dick	Fish
Arnold Dorsey	Engelbert Humperdinck (from German Composer's name. Also sang as Gerry Dorsey)
Reginald Dwight	Elton John (from Elton Dean, Long John Baldry of band Bluesology. Also takes middle name Hercules)
Norma Egstrom	Peggy Lee
Dave Evans	The Edge
Ernest Evans	Chubby Checker
Eleanora Fagan	Billie Holliday
Mark Feld	Marc Bolan
Fabiano Forte	Fabian
Concetta Franconers	Connie Francis
Vincent Furnier	Alice Cooper
Paul Gadd	Gary Glitter (also sang as Paul Raven)
La Donna Andrea Gaines	Donna Summer
Edith Gassion	Edith Piaf
Brenda Gail Gazzimos	Crystal Gayle
Steven Georgiu	Cat Sevens (now named Yusuf Islam)
Stuart Goddard	Adam Ant
Sandra Goodrich	Sandie Shaw
Peter Greenbaum	Peter Green
Christopher Hamill	Limahl
Stevland Morris Hardaway	Stevie Wonder
Stephen Harrington	Steve Strange
Paul Hewson	Bono
Thomas Hicks	Tommy Steele
Charles Hardin Holley	Buddy Holly
George Ivan	Van Morrison
Harold Jenkins	Conway Twitty

Bernard Jewry	Alvin Stardust (also sang as Shane Fenton)
Steveland Judkins (later Morris)	Stevie Wonder
David Jones	David Bowie (from Bowie knife)
Herbert Khaury	Tiny Tim
Ian Kilminister	Lemmy (Motorhead)
Carole Klein	Carol King
Cherilyn Sarkisian La Pierre	Cher
Marie Laurie	Lulu
Donovan Leitch	Donovan
Wladziu Valentino Liberace	Liberace
Michael Lubowitz	Manfred Mann
John Lydon	Johnny Rotten
Pauline Matthews	Kiki Dee
Ellas McDaniel	Bo Diddley
Declan McManus	Elvis Costello
Graham McPherson	Suggs (Madness)
John Mellencamp	John Cougar
Felix Mendelssohn-Bartholdy	Felix Mendelssohn
Helen Mitchell	Dame Nellie Melba
McKinley Morganfield	Muddy Waters
Terry Nelhams	Adam Faith
Prince Rogers Nelson	Prince
Mary O'Brien	Dusty Springfield
George O'Dowd	Boy George
James Jewel Osterberg	Iggy Pop
Raymond O'Sullivan	Gilbert O'Sullivan (from Gilbert and Sullivan)
Yorgos Panayioutou	George Michael
Richard Penniman	Little Richard
Bill Perks	Bill Wyman
Clive Powell	Georgie Fame
Wynette Pugh	Tammy Wynette
Malcolm Rebennach	Dr John
Keith Richards	Keith Richard (after Cliff Richard)
J.P.Richardson	The Big Bopper
Ray Charles Robinson	Ray Charles
Lynsey Rubin	Lynsey De Paul
Sealhenry Samuel	Seal
James Smith	P.J.Proby
Kim Smith	Kim Wilde
Reginald Smith	Marti Wilde
Robert Smith	Wolfman Jack (D.J.)
Richard Sarstedt	Eden Kane
Richard Starkey	Ringo Starr (from wearing many rings)
Yvette Stevens	Chaka Khan
Sylvester Stewart	Sly Stone
Gordon Sumner	Sting (from a jumper coloured like a wasp)
Brenda Tarpley	Brenda Lee
Doug Trendle	Buster Bloodvessel
Guiseppe Uttini	Verdi
Robert Velline	Bobby Vee
Don Van Vliet	Captain Beefheart
Robert Van Winkle	Vanilla Ice
Mark Wahlberg	Marky Mark
Eunice Wayman	Nina Simone
Gary Webb	Gary Numan

Harry Webb	Cliff Richard
Vera Welch	Vera Lynn
Charles Westover	Del Shannon
Toyah Wilcox	Toyah
Thomas Woodward	Tom Jones
Ronald Wycherly	Billy Fury
Robert Zimmerman	Bob Dylan (after: Poet Dylan Thomas)

Others

George Baker	Father Divine
Guiseppe Balsame	Count Cagliostro
Giovanni de Bernardone	St Francis of Assisi
Agnes Bojaxhin	Mother Teresa
Martha Jane Canary/Burke	Calamity Jane
Giorgio da Castelfranco	Giorgione
John Chapman	Johnny Appleseed
Jean Chauvin	John Calvin
Elizabeth Cochrane	Nellie Bly
Cristobel Colon	Christopher Columbus
Sandra Daly	Soraya Khashoggi (married Adnan Khashoggi)
Nigel Davies	Justin De Villeneuve
Willie Donaldson	Henry Root
Giovanni de Fiesoli	Fra Angelico
Allessandro dei Filipepi	Botticelli (means: Little Barrel)
Roland Fuhrhop	Tiny Rowland
Claude Gellee	Claude Lorrain
Gheraerd Gheraerd	Erasmus
Florence Nightingale Graham	Elizabeth Arden
Ludvik Hoch	Robert Maxwell
Lesley Hornby	Twiggy
Cyril Henry Hoslan	Tuesday Lobsang Rampa
Charles Jeanneret	Le Corbusier
Edward Zane Judson	Ned Buntline
Amy Lyon	Emma, Lady Hamilton
Phoebe Anne Oakley Mozee	Annie Oakley
Denis Pratt	Quentin Crisp
Anna Mary Robertson	Grandma Moses
Jacopo Robusti	Tintoretto (from father's occupation – dyer)
Sami Rosenstock	Tristan Tzara
John Rowlands	Sir Henry Stanley
Pablo Ruiz	Pablo Picasso (from mother's maiden name)
Rafaello Sanzio	Raphael
Angelo Siciliano	Charles Atlas
Simon	St Peter
Charles Stratton	Tom Thumb
Domenikos Theotocopoulos	El Greco
Tiziano Veceli	Titian
Andrew Warhola	Andy Warhol
Adrien Wettach	Grock
Karol Wojtyla	Pope John Paul II

Politics

Lucius Domitius Ahenobarbus	Nero
King Albert	George VI (name not used, in deference to Queen Victoria's wishes)
Amenhotep IV (Pharaoh)	Ikhnaton
Dovoteo Arango	Pancho Villa

Lev Davidovitch Bronstein	Trotsky (after a Jailer)
Josip Broz	Marshal Tito
Bonnie Prince Charlie	Betty Burke (Irish Spinning Maid, when escaping)
Jeanne Darc	Joan of Arc
Josef V. Dzhugashvili	Stalin (means: Man of Steel)
Karl Herbert Frahm	Willy Brandt
David Green	David Ben-Gurion
Joel Hagglund	Joe Hill
Grace Kelly	Princess Grace of Monaco
Mustafa Kemal	Kemal Ataturk
Leslie King Jnr.	Gerald Ford (stepfather's name)
T.E.Lawrence	Aircraftsman Ross, Shaw
Malcolm Little	Malcolm X
Goldie Mabovitch	Golda Meir
Ras Tafari Makonnen	Hailie Selassie
Robert McGregor	Rob Roy
Mikhail Khristodoulou Mouskos	Archbishop Makarios
General Murat	King Joachim Napoleon
Octavian	Augustus Caesar
Louis Philippe, Duke of Orleans	Philippe Egalité
Sigmund Rosenblum	Sidney Reilly
Saxe-Coburg Gotha	Windsor (Royal Family) (during WWI, because of anti-German sentiment)
Vyacheslav Skryabin	Molotov (means: Hammer)
Nguyen That Thanh	Ho Chi Minh
Marcus Tullius	Cicero (from wart on nose)
Vladimir Ilyich Ulyanov	Lenin
Ahmed Zogu	King Zog

Sport

Lew Alcindor	Kareem Abdul-Jabbar
Joe Louis Barrow	Joe Louis
Manuel Benitez (Perez)	El Cordobes
Cassius Clay	Muhammad Ali (1st: Cassius X)
Rocco Marchegiano	Rocky Marciano
Edson Arantes Do Nascimento	Pele
Walker Smith	Sugar Ray Robinson (from another boxer; 'Sugar' from description of fighting as 'sweet as sugar')
Archibald Wright	Archie Moore

Stage and Screen

Edward Alden	Ted Ray
Constantin Alekseyev	Constantin Stanislavsky
Rudolpho Antognollo	Rudolf Valentino
Roscoe (Fatty) Arbuckle	William B.Goodrich (used after scandal)
Max Arenson	Bronco Billy Anderson
Frederick Austerlitz	Fred Astaire
George Balanchivadze	George Balanchine
John Eric Bartholomew	Eric Morecombe
James Baumgardner	James Garner
Shirley Beaty	Shirley MacLaine
Warren Beaty	Warren Beatty (extra 'T')
William Beedle	William Holden
Dianne Belmont	Lucille Ball
Rosine Bernard	Sarah Bernhardt
Mike Berry	Lennie Bennett
John Blythe	John Barrymore

Lionel Blythe	Lionel Barrymore
George Booth	George Formby
Gerald Bright	Geraldo
John Henry Brodribb	Sir Henry Irving
Angeline Brown	Angie Dickinson
Charles Buchinski	Charles Bronson (appeared under original name in early films)
James Byron	James Dean
Margarita Cansino	Rita Hayworth
Harlean Carpentier	Jean Harlow
Daniel Carroll	Danny La Rue
Maria Ceciarelli	Monica Vitti
Appolonia Chalupek	Pola Negri
Lily Chauchoin	Claudette Colbert
Maurice Cole	Kenny Everett
Cathleen Collins	Bo Derek
Lynda Crapper	Marti Caine
Louis Cristillo	Lou Castello
Dino Crocetti	Dean Martin
Robert Davies	Jasper Carrott
Barbara Deeks	Barbara Windsor
Marchesa Caterina De Francabilla	Katie Boyle
Lady De Frece	Vesta Tilley
Joan De Havilland	Joan Fontaine
Issar Danielovitch Demsky	Kirk Douglas
William Claude Dukenfield	W.C.Fields
Michael Dumble-Smith	Michael Crawford
Carlos Estevez	Charlie Sheen
Ramon Estevez	Martin Sheen
Cicily Fairfield	Dame Rebecca West
Stephania Federkiewicz	Stephanie Powers
W.C.Fields	Mahatma Kane Jeeves (wrote as)
Roy Fitzgerald	Rock Hudson
Susannah Fletcher	Susannah York
Joyce Frankenberg	Jane Seymour
Arthur Gellen	Tab Hunter
Maria Eliza Gilbert	Lola Montez
Edna Gillorly	Ellen Burstyn
Emanuel Goldenberg	Edward G. Robinson
Sam Goldfish	Sam Goldwyn
Elliott Goldstein	Elliott Gould
Frances Gumm	Judy Garland
Natasha Gurdin	Natalie Wood
Greta Gustafsson	Greta Garbo
Diane Hall	Diane Keaton
Vivien Hartley	Vivian Leigh
Derek Harris	John Derek
Avrom Hirsch-Goldbogen	Mike Todd
Thomas Terry Hoare-Stevens	Terry Thomas
Margaret Hookham	Margot Fonteyn
Leslie Townes Hope	Bob Hope (to avoid nickname Hope, Les)
Rose Louise Hovick	Gypsy Rose Lee
Edward Iskowitz	Eddie Cantor
Annemarie Italiano	Anne Bancroft
Lee Jacob	Lee J. Cobb
Camille Javal	Brigitte Bardot
Arthur Jefferson	Stan Laurel

Richard Jenkins	Richard Burton (from school Drama Teacher)
Carol Diahann Johnson	Diahann Carroll
Joseph Jule	Mickey Rooney
Cecilia Kalageropoulos	Maria Callas
Simone Kaminker	Simone Signoret
Melvin Kaminsky	Mel Brooks
Dorothy Kaumeyer	Dorothy Lamour
Taidje Khan Jnr.	Yul Brynner
Hedwig Kiesler	Hedy Lamarr
Allen Konigsberg	Woody Allen
Benjamin Kubelsky	Jack Benny
Archibald Leach	Cary Grant
Lee Yuen Kam	Bruce Lee
Lucille Le Sueur	Joan Crawford
Ivo Levi	Yves Montand
Joseph Levitch	Jerry Lewis
Marion Levy	Paulette Goddard
Laszlo Loewenstein	Peter Lorre
Maxwell Lorimer	Max Wall
Alice Marks	Alicia Markova
Walter Matuschanskavasky	Walter Matthau
Eddie McGuinness	Eddie Large
Virginia McMath	Ginger Rogers
Cyril Mead	Syd Little
Morris Micklewhite	Michael Caine (from hoarding for Bogart film, The Caine Mutiny)
Joan Molinsky	Joan Rivers
Jeanette Morrison	Janet Leigh
Marion Morrison	John Wayne
Norma Jean Mortenson	Marilyn Monroe (original surname sometimes given as Baker)
Jimmy Mulgrew	Jimmy Cricket
Natassja Nakszynski	Natassia Kinski
Yootha Needham	Yootha Joyce
Jim Noir	Vic Reeves
Sean O'Fearna	John Ford
Ann-Margret Olsson	Ann Margret
Tynian O'Mahoney	Dave Allen
Pal	Lassie (note sex change)
Betty Joan Perske	Lauren Bacall
Jane Peters	Carole Lombard
William Henry Pratt	Boris Karloff
John Rajan	Jack Lord
Harry Relph	Little Tich
Dennistoun Franklyn John Rose-Price	Dennis Price
Harold Sargent	Max Miller
Shirley Schrift	Shelley Winters
Roy Scherer Jnr.	Rock Hudson (from Rock of Gibraltar, Hudson River)
Bernard Schwartz	Tony Curtis
Alfred Schweider	Lenny Bruce
Sophia Scicolini	Sophia Loren
Michael Shalhoub	Omar Sharif
Magnus Sigursteinnson	Magnus Magnusson (father: Sigursteinn)
Jerome Silberman	Gene Wilder
Michael Sinnott	Mach Sennett

Larushka Mischa Skikne	Laurence Harvey
Leonard Slye	Roy Rogers
Gladys Smith	Mary Pickford
Harold J. Smith	Jay Silverheels
David Solberg	David Soul
Francoise Sorya	Anouk Aimée
Charles Springall	Charlie Drake
Leslie Stainer	Leslie Howard
James Stewart	Stewart Granger
Cheryl Stoppelmoor	Cheryl Ladd
Lynne Stringer	Marti Caine
Josephine Swenson	Gloria Swanson
Jacques Tatischeff	Jacques Tati
Raquel Tejeda	Raquel Welch
Esteile Thompson	Merle Oberon
Reginald Truscott-Jones	Ray Milland
Lawrence Tureaud	Mr T
Douglas Ullman	Douglas Fairbanks
Edda Hepburn Van Heemstra	Audrey Hepburn
Bernard Vinogradsky	Bernard Delfont
Doris Von Kappelhoff	Doris Day (from the song 'Day by Day')
Magdalene Von Losch	Marelene Dietrich
Jack Waters	Jack Warner
Chaim Weintrop	Bud Flanagan
Erich Weiss	Harry Houdini (from French magician, Robert Houdin)
Julia Wells	Julie Andrews
William White	Larry Grayson
Walter William	Bill Maynard
Ernie Wiseman	Ernie Wise
Harvey Lee Yeary 2nd	Lee Majors
Joe Yule Jnr.	Mickey Rooney

Surnames

By: First Name → Surname

Notes: *Covers People better known by their first names.*

St Bernadette (of Lourdes)	Soubirous
Dante	Alighieri
Galileo	Galilei
Empress Josephine	De La Pagerie (later Beauharnais)
Michelangelo	Buonarroti
Napoleon	Bonaparte
Rembrandt	Van Rijn
Sade	Adu
Vangelis	Papathanassiou

Titles

By: Name → Title

Max Aitken	Lord Beaverbrook
Harold Alexander	Earl Alexander of Tunis
Herbert Asquith	Earl of Oxford and Asquith
Francis Bacon	Lord Verulam, Viscount St Albans
Tony Benn	Viscount Stansgate (Renounced title)
Richard Bingham	Lord Lucan
Thomas Bruce	Earl of Elgin (Elgin Marbles)

James Brudenell	Lord Cardigan
John Buchan	1st Baron Tweedsmuir
Patrick Campbell	Baron Glenavy
John Churchill	Duke of Marlborough
Anthony Ashley Cooper	Lord Shaftesbury
Benjamin Disraeli	Earl of Beaconsfield
John Douglas	Marquess of Queensberry
Sir Alec Douglas-Home	Earl of Home (Renounced title)
Anthony Eden	Earl of Avon
Hugh Foot	Lord Caradon
George Gordon	Lord Byron
Alfred Harmsworth	Lord Northcliffe
Harold Harmsworth	Lord Rothermere
Quintin Hogg	Lord Hailsham
Anthony Armstrong Jones	Lord Snowdon
Bernard Law	Viscount Montgomery (Field Marshal)
W.H.Lever	Lord Leverhulme
David Lloyd George	Lord Dwyfor
Harold Macmillan	Lord Stockton
George Molyneux	Lord Caernarvon
Bernard Montgomery	Lord Montgomery of Alamein
Laurence Olivier	Baron Olivier of Brighton
Francis Pakenham	Lord Longford
William Pitt the Elder	Earl of Chatham
Jeanne Antoinette Poisson	Marquise de Pompadour
Frederic Rolfe	Baron Corvo
Bertrand Russell	3rd Lord Russell
Edward Short	Lord Glenamara
Fitzroy Somerset	Lord Raglan
Robert Stewart	Lord Castlereagh
Henry John Temple	Lord Palmerston
George Thomas	Lord Tonypandy
Benjamin Thompson	Count Rumford
William Thomson	Lord Kelvin
Hugh Trevor-Roper	Lord Dacre
Arthur Wellesley	Duke of Wellington
Thomas Wentworth	Earl of Strafford, Baron Ruby

Titles

By: Title → Family Name

Argyll	Campbell
Beaufort	Somerset
Bedford	Russell
Buccleuch	Montagu-Douglas-Scott
Devonshire	Cavendish
Marlborough	Spencer-Churchill
Northumberland	Percy
Somerset	Seymour
Wellington	Wellesley
Westminster	Grosvenor

Science and Technology

Contents

General 349
Chemical Names
  By: Chemical Name 349
Chemistry and Materials 350
Communications 353
Computers 354
Discoveries and Theories
  By: Discovery 354
Energy Technology 355
Inventions
  By: Invention 356
Mathematics 358
Measurement 359
Miscellaneous 360
Ores
  By: Ore 361
Physics 362
Printing 363
Rocks and Gems 364
Sciences and Studies
  By: Subject 365
Scientific Instruments
  By: Instrument 366
Scientists and Inventors 366
Time and Calendars 367

Weapons and Military Technology 368
Weapons, Famous
  By: Name 369
Transport 370
Air Transport 370
Aircraft, Famous Models
  By: Model 372
Airlines, National
  By: Airline 373
Cars, Countries from
  By: Make 374
Cars, Famous Models
  By: Model 374
Motorcycles, Famous Models
  By: Model 375
Other Transport 375
Rail Transport 376
Road Transport 377
Roads 379
Sea and Water Transport 380
Ships, Famous
  By: Description, Owner 381
Trains and Engines, Famous
  By: Description 382

GENERAL
Chemical Names

By: Chemical Name → Common Name

Acetic Acid (dilute)	Vinegar
Adenosine Triphosphate	ATP
Aluminium Potassium Sulphate	Alum
Ammonium Carbonate	Sal Volatile
Ammonium Chloride	Sal Ammoniac
Calcium Carbonate	Chalk
Calcium Hydroxide	Slaked Lime
Calcium Oxide	Quick-lime
Carbolic Acid	Phenol
Carbon Dioxide (solid)	Dry Ice
Deoxyribonucleic Acid	DNA
Deuterium Oxide	Heavy Water
Dichloro-Diphenyl-Trichloroethane	DDT
Ethyl Alcohol	Alcohol
Ethylene Glycol	Antifreeze
Hydrated Aluminium Silicate	China Clay
Hydrochloric Acid	Spirits of Salt
Hydrocyanic Acid	Prussic Acid
Iron Pyrites	Fools Gold
Magnesium Sulphate	Epsom Salts
Mercurous Chloride	Calomel
Mercury	Quick Silver

Methyl Salicylate	Oil of Wintergreen (contains)
Nitric Acid	Aqua Fortis
Nitrous Oxide	Laughing Gas
Poly-Tetra-Fluoro-Ethylene	PTFE, Teflon
Polyethylene	Polythene
Polyvinyl Chloride	PVC
Potassium Bitartrate	Cream of Tartar
Potassium Nitrate	Saltpetre
Potassium Quadroxalate	Salts of Lemon
Silicon Carbide	Carborundum
Sodium Bicarbonate	Baking Soda
Sodium Borate	Borax
Sodium Carbonate	Washing Soda
Sodium Chloride	Salt
Sodium Hydroxide	Caustic Soda
Sodium Sulphate	Glaubers Salts
Sodium Thiosulphate	Hypo
Sulphur	Brimstone
Sulphuric Acid	Oil of Vitriol
Trinitrotoluene	TNT
Triplumbic Tetroxide	Red Lead

Chemistry and Materials

By: General

Acid; Opposite	Base (Alkali)
Acidity, Alkalinity; Measure of	pH value
Air; Main Components	Nitrogen (78%) and Oxygen (21%)
Air; Composition of; 1st determined	Joseph Priestley
Alloys; Composition of:-	
Alnico	Aluminium, Nickel, Cobalt
Brass	Copper, Tin
Britannia Metal	Tin (mainly), Antimony, Copper
Bronze	Copper, Zinc
Gunmetal	Copper, Tin, Zinc
Nickel Silver	Copper, Nickel, Zinc
Pewter	Tin, Lead (Normally)
Solder	Tin, Lead
Steel	Iron, Carbon
Ancient Greeks; Elements	Earth, Air, Fire, Water
Antifreeze; Main constituent	Ethylene Glycol
Atomic Theory; Formulator; Modern	John Dalton
Atomic Theory; Originator; Ancient	Democritus
Balloons; Gas used in	Helium, Hydrogen
Benzene Ring; Discoverer	Kekulé (In a dream)
Bones and Teeth; Constituent	Calcium
Calcium Carbide, with water, produces	Acetylene
Car Exhaust; Poisonous gas	Carbon Monoxide
Carbon Compounds; Chemistry of	Organic (Non-Carbon: Inorganic)
Cement; Made from	Chalk, Clay
Chemical Formulae:-	
CO_2	Carbon Dioxide
C_2H_4	Ethylene
C_6H_6	Benzene
CH_4	Methane

CO	Carbon Monoxide
H_2O	Water
H_2SO_4	Sulphuric Acid
H_2O_2	Hydrogen Peroxide
HNO_3	Nitric Acid
NaCl	Salt
NH_3	Ammonia
Chemical Reaction; Changes speed of, without being affected	Catalyst

Chemical Symbols:-

Ag	Silver
Au	Gold
Fe	Iron
Hg	Mercury
K	Potassium
Na	Sodium
Pb	Lead
Sb	Antimony
Sn	Tin
W	Tungsten

Chemistry;-

Early mystical form	Alchemy
Main division	Organic, Inorganic
China Clay; Other name	Kaolin
Compound; Same formula, different physical properties	Isomer
Compound; Union of many simple molecules	Polymer
Copper; Rust on	Verdigris
Crystal; Types of; Number	7
Diamond; Made of	Carbon
Ekasilicon; Was the name for	Germanium
Electricity; Reaction caused by passing through liquid	Electrolysis

Element(s);-

Artificially Produced; 1st	Technetium
Commonest; On Earth; 1st	Oxygen
Commonest; On Earth; 2nd	Silicon
Commonest; Universe	Hydrogen (75% by mass)
Commonest; Universe; 2nd	Helium
Electricity; Best conductor	Silver
Forms most compounds	Carbon
Heat; Best Conductor	Silver
Lightest	Hydrogen
Liquid at room temperature	Mercury, Bromine
Melting Point; Highest	Carbon
Melting Point; Lowest	Helium
One Letter difference in name	Hafnium, Hahnium
Radioactive, Gas	Radon
Rarest Naturally Occurring	Astatine
Same atomic number, different atomic weight	Isotope

Elements, Names from;-

Asteroid, Ceres	Cerium
Charcoal	Carbon
Copenhagen	Hafnium
Cyprus	Copper

4 from 1 place	Yttrium, Terbium, Erbium, Ytterbium, from Ytterby, Sweden
France	Gallium, Francium
Germany	Germanium
Goblin	Cobalt
Moon	Selenium
Paris	Lutetium (Roman name)
Person; Only naturally occurring element named after	Gadolinium
Poland	Polonium
River Rhine	Rhenium
Scottish Village	Strontium (Strontian)
Stockholm	Holmium
Sun	Helium (1st seen in Sun's spectrum)
Thor	Thorium
Town in Turkey, 2 elements	Manganese, Magnesium (Magnesia)
Uranus	Uranium
Elements; Uses:-	
Anti-knock Petrol Additives	Lead
Cigarette Lighter Flints	Cerium
Electroplating	Chromium
Flash Bulbs	Magnesium
Galvanizing Steel	Zinc
Heart Pacemakers	Polonium
Kitchen Utensils	Aluminium
Light Bulb Filaments	Tungsten
Luminous Watch Dials	Radium
Matches	Phosphorus
Microchips	Silicon
Pen Nibs	Osmium
Plating Steel for Containers	Tin
Swimming Pools	Chlorine
Torch Battery Casings	Zinc
War (Poison Gas)	Chlorine
Wiring	Copper
Father of Modern Chemistry; Called	Antoine Lavoisier
Fireworks, colours from;-	
Green	Barium, Copper
Red	Strontium
Orange	Calcium
Purple	Lithium, Potassium
Yellow	Sodium
Galvanised Iron; Coating	Zinc
Gases; Don't form compounds easily	Inert Gases
Glass;-	
Darkens in light	Photochromic
Dissolved by Acid	Hydrofluoric Acid
Manufacturing; Main constituent	Sand
Gold;-	
Dissolved by	Aqua Regia (concentrated Nitric and Hydrochloric Acid)
Supposed to transmute base metals to	Philosopher's Stone
Gunpowder made of	Charcoal, Sulphur, Potassium Nitrate
Haber process manufactures	Ammonia
Hardness; Scale of	Moh's Scale
Lead in Pencil	Graphite (Carbon)

Liquid Absorption, as by plants through roots	Osmosis
Litmus Paper; Colour change	Acid (red), Alkali (blue)
Mercury; Alloy with other metals	Amalgam
Metal;-	
Commonest on Earth	Aluminium
Densest	Osmium
Lightest	Lithium
Strongest for weight	Titanium
Thinnest film; Can be beaten into	Gold
Microscopic Droplets of one liquid in another	Emulsion
Mineral; Softest	Talc
Mineral; Weavable into fabric	Asbestos
Molecules, Joined together in chains	Polymer
Oxygen; Discoverers	Priestley, Scheele (independently)
Ozone	Form of Oxygen
Periodic Table; Originator	Mendeleev
Philosopher's Stone	Alchemists believed would turn base metal into gold
Plastic; 1st	Bakelite
Radioisotopes; Well known;-	
Carbon; Used in dating objects	14
Cobalt; Radioactive	60
Strontium; Radioactive	90
Uranium; Most abundant	238
Uranium; Naturally fissile	235
Reaction; Heat absorbed	Endothermic
Semiconductors; Most important	Silicon, Germanium
Silver; Main use	Photography
Solid becoming Gas without liquid phase	Sublimation
Solid; Element; Lightest	Lithium
Solution; Solid formed in, due to chemical reaction	Precipitate
Synthetic Dyes; Inventor	William Perkin
Tin Cans; Material	Iron coated with tin (Tinplate)
Tungsten; Alternative name	Wolfram
Water;-	
Gaseous state of	Water Vapour
Removal of, from substance creates	Anhydride

Communications

By: General

Love Letters; Cheap rate; 1st	Venezuela (pink envelopes)
999 Calls;-	
Introduced	1937
US equivalent	911
Penny Post; Responsible for	Rowland Hill (introduced 1840)
Pillar Boxes; Original colour	Green
Radio;-	
AM; Stands for	Amplitude Modulation
FM; Stands for	Frequency Modulation
Radio Transmission, Transatlantic;-	
Message; 1st	Letter 'S'

Location	Poldhu, Cornwall, Britain to St John's, Newfoundland
Royal Mail; 1st	Bath to London
Stamp; Adhesive; 1st	Penny Black, Twopenny Blue (1840)
Telephone Directory; British; 1st	1880 (255 names)
Television:-	
Lines, UK	625
Lines; UK; Former	405
Lines; US	525
Transmission standard; UK	PAL
Transmission standard; US	NTSC
UHF; Stands for	Ultra High Frequency
Video Recording; Main standards	VHS, Betamax

Computers

By: General

Ada; Name from	Countess Lovelace, Babbage's assistant
BASIC; Stands for	Beginners' All-purpose Symbolic Instruction Code
Bit; Short for	Binary digit
Byte	8 Bits
COBOL; Stands for	Common Business Oriented Language
Computer; Mechanical pioneer	Charles Babbage
Computer Programmer; 1st	Ada, Countess Lovelace (Babbage's assistant)
Computers; Main types	Mainframe, Minicomputer, Micro
Department of Defence, US; Language sponsored by	Ada
1st; Totally electronic	ENIAC (1945)
FORTRAN; Stands for	Formula Translation
Microprocessor; 1st	Intel 4004
Models; Makers:-	
Amiga	Commodore
BBC Micro	Acorn
Macintosh	Apple
PDP Series	Digital Equipment Corporation
Pet	Commodore
Spectrum	Sinclair
360 Series	IBM
ZX80	Sinclair
Modem; Short for	Modulator – Demodulator
Number Base; Computers use	2
Program Error; Caused space failure	Mariner I, Venus Probe (1962)
Punched Card; Pioneer	Hollerith

Discoveries and Theories

By: Discovery → Discoverer, Pioneer

See Also: Inventions

Antisepsis	Semmelweiss
Antiseptic surgery	Joseph Lister
Atomic Theory of Matter	John Dalton
Bacteriology	Pasteur
Circulation of the blood	William Harvey

DNA Structure	Crick and Watson
Earth spinning on axes, Proving	Jean Foucault
Electromagnetic Induction	Faraday
Electromagnetic Waves	Heinrich Hertz
Electron	J.J. Thomson
Evolution	Darwin
Gas Pressure/Volume Relation	Robert Boyle
Genetics	Gregor Mendel
Gravitation, Law of	Newton
Information Theory	Claude Shannon
Insulin	Frederick Banting (with Best and Macleod)
Light as Electromagnetic Waves	James Clerk Maxwell
Neutron	James Chadwick
Oxygen	Priestley, Scheele
Penicillin	Alexander Fleming
Periodic Table of Elements	Dimitri Mendeleev
Pluto	Clyde Tombaugh (1930)
Polio Vaccine	J. Salk
Proton	Rutherford
Radioactivity	Antoine Becquerel
Radium	Pierre and Marie Curie
Relativity	Einstein
Splitting the Atom	Cockcroft and Walton (1932)
Time and Motion Study	Frederick Taylor
Tuberculosis Bacteria	Robert Koch
Uranium	Martin Klaproth
Uranus	William Herschel (1781)

Energy Technology

By: General

Fluid; Conductive; Used to generate electricity	Magnetohydrodynamics (MHD)
Gaslit street; 1st	Pall Mall
North Sea Gasfields; Names	Ann, Audrey, West Sole
North Seal Oilfields; Names	Cora, Ruth, Anne, Bray, Andrew, Forties, Tartan, Brent
Nuclear Accident;-	
Worst	Chernobyl (April 1986)
Worst; US	Three Mile Island, Harrisburg (1979)
Nuclear Power Station;-	
1st	Obrusk, USSR
1st; UK	Calder Hall (1956)
Nuclear Reactor; Disintegration, Term for	Melt down
Oil Centre; USSR	Baku
Oil Rig Accident; Worst	Piper Alpha, North Sea (1988)
Oil Refining; Process to break up into constituents	Cracking
Oil Well; 1st drilled	Colonel Edwin Drake, Titusville, US
Petrol;-	
Anti-knock ingredient	Tetraethyl Lead
Knock; Rating	Octane Rating
Sellafield; Former name	Windscale

Pears: Ultimate Quiz Companion

Inventions

By: Inventions → Inventor, Other

Aeroplane	Wright Brothers
Air Pump	Otto Von Guericke
Aqualung	Jacques Cousteau, Emile Gagnan
Assembly Line	Samuel Colt
Ball-point Pen	John T. Loud
1st practicable mass produced model	Lazlo Biro
Barbed Wire	Lucien Smith
Barometer	Torricelli
Bicycle	Kirkpatrick Macmillan
Bifocal Lens	Benjamin Franklin
Brassière	Mary Jacobs
Canning	Nicholas Appert
Wins prize for from	Napoleon
Carpet Sweeper	Melville Bissell
Cash Register	James Ritty
Cat's-Eye	Percy Shaw
Celluloid	Alexander Parkes
Developed and trademarked by	J.W.Hyatt
Centigrade Thermometer	Anders Celsius
Chronometer	John Harrison
Cigarette	Turkish troops at Battle of Acre
Cloud Chamber	C.T.Wilson
Coat Hanger	Albert Parkhouse
Coca Cola	Dr John Pemberton
Called	Esteemed Brain Tonic and Intellectual Beverage
Condensed Milk	Gail Borden
Crossword Puzzle	Arthur Wynne
DDT	Paul Muller
Double Entry Bookkeeping	Fra Luca Parioli
Doughnut (with hole)	Hanson Gregory
Dynamite	Alfred Nobel
Electric Battery	Alessandro Volta
Electric Bell	Joseph Henry
Electric Chair	Alphonse Rockwell
Electric Shaver	Jacob Schick
Frisbee	Fred Morrison
Frozen Food	Clarence Birdseye
Geiger Counter	Hans Geiger
Glider	Sir George Cayley
Gramophone	Thomas Edison
1st recording	'Mary had a little lamb'
Work done by	Assistant Dickson
Gun Cotton	Schonbein (mopping up acid from kitchen table)
Gunpowder	The Chinese
Gyroscope	Leon Foucault
Holography	Dennis Gabor
Hovercraft	Christopher Cockerell
Jeans	Levi Strauss
Jet Engine	Frank Whittle

Jigsaw Puzzle	George Spilsbury
Name from	Saw used to make
Kaleidoscope	Sir David Brewster
Lie Detector	John Larson
Lift	Elisha Otis
Demonstrated by	Having lift rope cut with him inside
Lightning Conductor	Benjamin Franklin
Logarithms	John Napier
LP	Peter Goldmark
Mackintosh	MacIntosh (No "K")
Margarine	Hippolyte Mege-Mouries
Match	John Walker
Metronome	N. Malzel
Microphone	Hughes
Microwave Oven	Percy Spencer (of Raytheon)
Miners' Safety Lamp	Sir Humphrey Davy
Motorcar	Karl Benz
Motorcycle	Gottlieb Daimler
Nylon	Dr Wallace Carothers
Paper	The Chinese
Penicillin	Alexander Fleming
Photocopier	Chester Carlson
Piano	Bartolome Cristofori
Potato Crisps	George Crum
Pressure Cooker	Denis Papin
Radio Communications	Mahlon Loomis
1st transatlantic transmission	Gugliemo Marconi
Railway Airbrake	George Westinghouse
Roller Skates	Joseph Merlin
1st demonstration	Crashed through mirror
Roulette Wheel	Blaise Pascal
Safety Pin	Walter Hunt
Safety Razor	King Gillette
Saxophone	Adolph Sax
Shoe Lace	Harvey Kennedy
Shorthand (Roman times)	Tiro
Spinning Jenny	James Hargreaves
Spinning Mule	Samuel Crompton
Steam Engine	Thomas Savery
1st steam piston engine	Thomas Newcomen
Stethoscope	Rene Laennec
Submarine	Cornelius Van Drebbel
Telegraph	Samuel Morse
1st message	'What hath God Wrought'
Telephone	Alexander Graham Bell
1st message	To assistant, 'Mr Watson, come here, I want you'
Telephone Exchange (Automatic)	Strowger
Reason	Thought operators diverted calls to rival undertakers
Telescope	Hans Lippershey
Television	John Logie Baird
1st person on	William Taynton, Office Boy
Toothbrush	William Addis (when in jail)
Top Hat	John Hetherington
1st wearing caused	Fine for disturbance
Torpedo	G.Luppis

Transistor	John Bardeen, Walter Brittain
Vaccination	Edward Jenner
Vacuum Flask	James Dewar
Vulcanised Rubber	Charles Goodyear
Wheel	The Mesopotamians
X-rays	Wilhelm Röntgen
Zip Fastener	Whitcomb Judson

Mathematics

By: General

Angle;-	
Less than 90 degrees	Acute
More than 90 degrees	Obtuse
Calculus; Pioneers	Newton and Leibnitz
Chain; Suspended; shape of	Catena
Circle; Ratio of circumference to diameter	Pi
Collective Name for French mathematician's work	Bourbaki
Complex Number; Parts	Real and imaginary
Coordinate;-	
X	Abscissa
Y	Ordinate
Curve;-	
Lamp Reflectors; Ideal for	Parabola
Rolling Wheel; Point of moves in	Cycloid
Sum of distances from two points constant	Ellipse
Fraction;-	
Lower number	Denominator
Upper number	Numerator
Game Theory; Pioneer	John Von Neumann
Geometry;-	
Non Euclidean	Riemann, Lobachevskian
Pioneer	Euclid
Inca Counting Device	Quipu
Logarithms; Inventor	John Napier
Mathematician; Famous 'Last Theorem'	Fermat
Number;-	
Base 2; Term	Binary
Base 8; Term	Octal
Base 16; Term	Hexadecimal
Cannot be expressed as a fraction	Irrational
Equal to the sum of all numbers it's divisible by	Perfect number
Numbers:-	
Billion	UK: Million million. US: Thousand million
Crore	10 million
Googol	One followed by a 100 noughts
Googolplex	One followed by googol noughts
Lakh	100,000
Myriad	10,000 (original meaning)
Polygons; Sides:-	
5	Pentagon

6	**Hexagon**
7	**Heptagon**
8	**Octagon**
9	**Nonagon**
10	**Decagon**
12	**Dodecagon**
20	**Icosagon**
Quadrilaterals (4 sides)	
All sides same length, no right angles	**Rhombus**
1 pair of sides parallel	**Trapezium**
Opposite sides parallel	**Parallelogram**
Regular Solids (faces the same)	**5**
4 sides	**Tetrahedron**
6 sides	**Cube**
8 sides	**Octohedron**
12 sides	**Dodecahedron**
20 sides	**Icosohedron**
Roman Numerals:-	
50	**L**
5	**V**
500	**D**
100	**C**
Longest date to present	**1888**
Number can't be represented	**0**
10	**X**
1000	**M**
'Rubber Sheet' Geometry; Called	**Topology**
Set Theory; Algebra of	**Boolean algebra**
Solid; Biggest volume for given surface area	**Sphere**
Star of David; Points	**6**
Statistical relationships between variables	**Correlation**
Tiling patterns; Identical tiles; number of different	**17**
Triangle;-	
All sides different	**Scalene**
Right Angled; Longest side	**Hypotenuse**
Right Angled; Relation between length of sides	**Pythagoras theorem**
3 Sides equal	**Equilateral**
2 Sides equal	**Isosceles**

Measurement

By: General

Standards; British HQ	National Physical Laboratory, Teddington
Systems; Used for:-	
Apothecaries	Drugs
Avoirdupois	General goods
Troy	Precious metals
Units; Equivalents:-	
Barleycorn	1/3rd inch
Barrel (oil)	35 gallons
Cable	240 yards

Carat	.2 gram
Chain	22 yards
Cubit	18 inches
Fathom	6 feet
Furlong	220 yards
Gallon	8 pints
Hand	4 inches
Hectare	1/100th square kilometre
Hundredweight	112 pounds
League	3 miles (nautical)
Micron	Millionth of a metre
Mile	1760 yards
Point	1/72nd inch (printing), 1/100th carat (jeweller's weight)
Span	9 inches
Square Mile	640 acres
Stone	14 pounds

Units; Quantity measured:-

Ampère	Electric current
Angstrom Unit	Distance (e.g. light wavelength)
Bar	Atmospheric pressure
Bushel	Grain Volume
Candela	Luminous Intensity
Cran	Fish weight
Drachm	Apothecaries' weight
Farad	Capacitance
Gauss	Magnetic flux density
Henry	Inductance
Hertz	Frequency
Joule	Energy
Kelvin	Temperature
Light Year	Distance
Lux	Illuminance
Mach Number	Speed (in relation to speed of sound)
Millibar	Atmospheric pressure
Newton	Force
Ohm	Electric resistance
Parsec	Distance
Pascal	Pressure
Pennyweight	Troy weight
Quire	Paper Weight
Radian	Angle
Scruple	Apothecaries' weight
Steradian	Solid angle
Watt	Power
Weber	Magnetic flux
Yard; Origin	Henry I, nose to finger

Miscellaneous

By: General

| Ammonia; Process for converting atmospheric nitrogen to | Haber process |

Disaster:-

| Chemical; Worst | Bhopal, India (1984). Gas: Methyl Isocyanate |

Chemical; UK	Flixborough, Nypro works (1974)
Chicago Fire	1871
Explosion destroyed town	Halifax, Nova Scotia (1917)
Mollases Flood	Boston (1919)
Seveso; Chemical released	Dioxin
Engine;-	
Fuel and air mix in	Carburettor
Fuel ignited by compression	Diesel
4 Stroke Engine Cycle; Other name	Otto cycle
Gold; Refinery; Largest	Germinston, South Africa
Mining; Surface	Open cast or strip mining
Rotary Engine; Triangular rotor	Wankel engine
Rubber; Heating with sulphur to improve qualities	Vulcanization
Steam engine; James Watt's innovation	External condenser
Steel; 1st mass production method	Bessemer process
Tin mines; Cornwall; 1st dug by	Phoenicians

Ores, Metals from

By: Ore → Metal

Argentite	Silver
Bauxite	Aluminium (main)
Bismite	Bismuth
Calamine	Zinc
Carnallite	Potassium
Cassiterite	Tin (main)
Cerussite	Lead
Chalcocyte	Copper
Chalcopyrite	Copper (main)
Cinnabar	Mercury (main)
Dolomite	Magnesium
Galena	Lead (main)
Haematite	Iron
Heavy Spar	Barium
Ilmenite	Titanium
Kernite	Boron
Magnesite	Magnesium
Magnetite	Iron
Massicot	Lead
Mispickel	Arsenic
Orpiment	Arsenic
Pentlandite	Nickel (main)
Pitchblende	Uranium
Pyrolusite	Manganese
Realgar	Arsenic
Rutile	Titanium
Scheelite	Tungsten
Siderite	Iron
Smaltite	Cobalt
Smithsonite	Zinc
Stibnite	Antimony
Sylvite	Potassium
Witherite	Barium
Wolframite	Tungsten

Physics

By: *General*

Absolute Zero	−273 Degrees C (approximately)
Atom;-	
Parts	Electron (negative), proton (positive), neutron (neutral)
Parts; Relative weights	Electron lightest, neutron heaviest
Splitting; 1st	Cockcroft and Walton
Atomic Number	Number of protons (or electrons)
Atomic Weight; Base unit	Carbon 12 (1/12th mass of)
Capacitor; Old name	Condenser
Cavendish Laboratory; Location	Cambridge
Charge; Ability to store	Capacitance
Cloud Chamber; Inventor	C.T.R.Wilson
Current and Voltage; Relationship	Ohm's Law
Cyclotron; Inventor	James Lawrence
Density; Relative to water	Specific gravity
Echo free room	Anechoic chamber
Electricity; Voltage; Device that changes	Transformer
Electrode;-	
Negative	Cathode
Positive	Anode
Electromagnetic Induction; Discoverer	Faraday
Electron; Discoverer	J.J.Thomson
Ether; Experiment proving non-existence	Michelson-Morley
Experiment; Failure led to major advance	Michelson–Morley experiment (led to Relativity)
Forces; Fundamental	4. Electromagnetic, gravity, strong and weak nuclear
Gas;-	
Temperature and volume relation	Charles' Law
Pressure and volume relation	Boyle's Law
Gravity; Experiment at Leaning Tower of Pisa	Galileo
Heat; Types of transfer	Conduction, convection, radiation
Light;-	
Bending when passing through a lens, etc.	Refraction
Diffraction Spectrum produces	Diffraction grating
Particle of	Photon
Speed; 1st determination	Claus Roemer
Spreading of, when passing through narrow opening	Diffraction
Wave Theory; Pioneer	Christian Huygens
Liquid;-	
Skin-like effect on	Surface tension
Thickness; Technical term for	Viscosity
Matter to Energy; Conversion formula	$E = MC^2$
Microwave Cookers; Wave generator	Magnetron
Momentum	Mass multiplied by velocity
Narrow Tube; Rise of liquid up	Capillary action

Neutron; Discoverer	James Chadwick
Plug Hole; Direction water goes down	Anticlockwise in the Northern Hemisphere
Police Speed Trap; Principle used	Doppler effect
Pressure on Crystals; Electricity produced by	Piezoelectricity
Radiation; Types of;-	
Alpha	Least penetrative; 2 protons, 2 neutrons
Beta	Electrons
Gamma rays	Most penetrative; Electromagnetic waves
Radiation; Wavelength	Gamma rays (shortest), x-rays, ultraviolet, light, infra-red, radio (longest)
Rainbow; Colours	Violet, indigo, blue, green, yellow, orange, red (from inside out)
Random motion of dust and other small particles	Brownian motion
Rotating Body;-	
Inward force	Centripetal
Outward force (apparent)	Centrifugal
Snowflake; Sides	6
Solid; Change to gas without liquid phase	Sublimation
Sound;-	
Intensity measured in	Decibels
Pitch Change due to movement	Doppler effect
Waves; Frequency above range of human ear	Ultrasonic
Strain and Stress in materials; Relationship between	Hooke's Law
Telescope;-	
Largest	Zelenchuleskaya, USSR
Main types	Reflecting, refracting
Temperature;-	
Lower Limit	Absolute Zero
Same Fahrenheit as Centigrade	−40 degrees
Scale; Fahrenheit; Reference points	Freezing point of specified ice and salt mixture; Body temperature
Scale; Starts at absolute zero	Kelvin
Very High; State of matter at	Plasma
Thermodynamics;-	
Law; 1st	Conservation of energy
Law; 2nd	Entropy increases
Uncertainty Principle; Originator	Heisenberg
Water; Behaviour; 0–4 Degrees C	Contracts on heating
Wave Frequency; Change in, due to motion	Doppler effect

Printing

By: General

Engraved plates; Printing technique using	Gravure, Photogravure
1st;-	
Europe	John Gutenberg, Mainz, Germany

UK	Thomas Caxton
Ink; Indian; From	China
Light and Dark; Provided by dots	Half tone process
Paper Roll; Continuous	Web
Papier Mâché; Type impression made with	Flong
Silk Screen Printing; Other name	Serigraphy
10 Point; Term for	Elite
12 Point; Term for	Pica
Type; Printing technique using raised	Letterpress
Water Rejection of ink; Printing technique using	(Offset) Lithography

Rocks and Gems

By: General

Diamond;-	
Blue; Famous	Hope diamond
Company controls majority of production	De Beers
Curse on (supposed)	Hope diamond
Cut; Type of	Brilliant
Facets; Normal	58
Kept in Tower of London	Kohinoor
Largest found	Cullinan Stone
Major use	Industrial cutting, grinding, etc.
Fool's Gold	Iron pyrites
Gem; Animal origin; Only	Pearl
Gems; Colours:-	
Amethyst	Violet
Aquamarine	Blue-green
Emerald	Green
Lapis Lazuli	Blue
Moonstone	White
Peridot	Green
Ruby	Red
Sapphire	Blue
Topaz	Yellow
Turquoise	Blue
Hardness; Scale of	Mohs scale
Jade; Types	Jadeite, nephrite
Jet	Variety of coal
Pearl;-	
Cultured; Meaning	Artificially induced by inserting object into oyster
Material	Nacre
Origin	Secretions around foreign matter in oyster
Precious Stones; Most expensive	Rubies
Rocks; Types of	Igneous, Sedimentary, Metamorphic
Stalactite	Hang from roof
Stalagmite	Grow up from the ground
Stone; Can float	Pumice stone

Stones; Precious   Diamond, emerald, ruby, sapphire,
                                (others semiprecious)

Sciences and Studies

By: Subject → Name

Notes: Includes Non-scientific Studies.
See Also: Health and the Body; Medical Specialities

Air in Motion	Aerodynamics
Aircraft Operation	Aeronautics
Animal Behaviour	Ethology
Animals	Zoology
Birds	Ornithology
Birds' Eggs	Oology
Caves	Speleology
Cells	Cytology
Codes	Cryptology
Earth; Physical properties	Geophysics
Earth; Size and shape of	Geodesy
Earthquakes	Seismology
Elections	Psephology
Environment and Living Things	Ecology
Fish	Ichthyology
Fluids	Hydraulics
Forests	Silviculture
Fossilised Animals and Plants	Palaeontology
Fruit Growing	Pomology
Fungi	Mycology
Handwriting	Graphology
Hormones	Endocrinology
Inheritance	Genetics
Knowledge; Theory of	Epistemology
Lakes	Limnology
Light	Optics
Living Things	Biology
Low temperatures	Cryogenics
Lubrication and Friction	Tribology
Maps	Cartography, topography
Measurement	Metrology
Medicines	Pharmacology
Mosses	Bryology
Physical Laws applied to living things	Biophysics
Plants	Botany
Poisons	Toxicology
Projectile Motion	Ballistics
Reptiles	Herpetology
Rocks and Minerals	Petrology
Skull (shape, influence on character)	Phrenology
Speech; Sound of	Phonetics
Stars; Composition	Astrophysics
Tissues of Organisms	Histology
Tree rings; Historical dating with	Dendrochronology
Universe; Origin of	Cosmology
Upper Atmosphere	Aeronomy
Words; History and derivation	Etymology
Words; Meaning	Semantics

Scientific Instruments
By: Instrument → Quantity Measured, Use

Notes: Unless otherwise stated, quantity measured is given.

Instrument	Quantity Measured, Use
Altimeter	Altitude
Ammeter	Electric current
Anemometer	Wind speed
Barometer	Atmospheric pressure
Bourdon Gauge	Pressure
Calorimeter	Heat
Chronometer	Time
Clinometer	Angle of elevation
Craniometer	Skull size
Dynamometer	Engine torque and power
Endoscope	Examining body interior
Extensometer	Ductility
Galvanometer	Electric current
Goniometer	Crystal angles
Gravimeter	Gravity
Hydrometer	Density (liquid)
Hygrometer	Humidity
Lactometer	Density of milk
Manometer	Pressure
Micrometer	Small distances
Microscope	Magnifying small objects
Odometer	Distance
Pyrometer	High temperatures
Seismometer	Earthquakes
Sextant	Latitude
Spectroscope	Analysing light spectrum
Speedometer	Speed
Sphygmomanometer	Blood pressure
Stethoscope	Listening to heart, etc.
Tachometer	Rotational speed
Telescope	Magnifying distant objects
Thermometer	Temperature
Voltmeter	Voltage

Scientists and Inventors

By: General

Apple falling inspired	Isaac Newton
Marie Curie; Died of	Effects of radiation
Dream on a Bus; Inspired discovery	Kekule (benzene ring)
Duel; Killed in, when 20	Evariste Galois
Edison Research laboratory	Menlo Park
Einstein; Nobel prize for	Discovery of photoelectric effect
Eureka; Ran naked shouting	Archimedes
Frogs' Legs; Experimented with effect of electricity on	Luigi Galvani
Heresy; Tried by inquisition for	Galileo
Husband and Wife Team	Pierre and Marie Curie
Kettle; Holding spoon over spout inspired invention	James Watt
Lectures for Children; Started series of	Michael Faraday
Midwife Toad; Experiments with alleged fabricated	Paul Kammerer
Mirror Writing; Wrote notes in	Leonardo da Vinci

Monk; Pioneering biologist	Gregor Mendel
Musicians on Train; Used in experiment	Doppler
Paralysed almost totally	Stephen Hawking
Patents; Held over a 1000 at death	Edison
Pendulum; Deduced Theory from lamp in Pisa Cathedral	Galileo
Presidency of Israel; Offered	Einstein
Price on his head by Nazis	Einstein
Road building pioneer; Blind	John Metcalf
Schoolboy; Made pioneering chemical invention	William Perkin
Socks; Didn't wear	Einstein
2 Years Schooling; Became President of the Royal Society	T.H.Huxley

Time and Calendars

By: General

Big Ben; Hour stroke	1st
Calendar;-	
Greek	From 1st Olympic Games
French Revolutionary	10 day weeks. 12, 30 day months
Gregorian	Introduced by Pope Gregory III
Islamic	From Hegira (AH). AD 622 is 1 AH
Julian	Introduced by Julius Caesar
Julian; Still used; UK	Foula, Shetland Islands
Chinese Calendar; Cycle	12 years
Chinese Calendar; Year of:-	
1988	Dragon
1989	Serpent
1990	Horse
1991	Sheep (Goat)
1992	Monkey
1993	Rooster
1994	Dog
1995	Pig
2000	Dragon
Dates that didn't exist; UK	September 3rd to 13th, 1752 (when Gregorian replaced Julian calendar)
Days; Name origin:-	
Sunday	Sun
Monday	Moon
Tuesday	Tiw (Norse god)
Wednesday	Woden (Odin – Norse god)
Thursday	Thor (Norse god)
Friday	Freya (Norse goddess)
Saturday	Saturn
Harvest Moon	Full moon nearest Autumn Equinox
Ides of March	15th
Months; Name origin:-	
January	Janus (Roman god)
February	Februus (Roman god)
March	Mars (Roman god)
April	Aprilis
May	Maia (Roman goddess)
June	Juno (Roman goddess)

July	Julius Caesar
August	Augustus Caesar
September	Seven (Latin)
October	Eight (Latin)
November	Nine (Latin)
December	Ten (Latin)
1 BC; Year following	AD 1
Same Days for Dates; Years with;-	
1970s	1973, 1979
1980s	1981, 1987
1990s	1993, 1999
Time Zones; International; Introduced	1884
21st Century; Starts on	1st January, 2001

Weapons and Military Technology

By: General

Atom Bomb;-	
Exploded; 1st	Alamogordo, New Mexico (June 16th, 1945)
US Development Project; Code name	Manhattan Project
Use; 1st	Hiroshima (1945). Plane: Enola Gay. Bomb: 'Little Boy'
Use; 2nd	Nagasaki (1945). Bomb: 'Fat Man'
Ballistic Missile; 1st	V2
Bazooka; Name from	Musical instrument of Bob Burns (comedian)
Big Bertha	German gun used to shell Paris in WW1. Name from: Bertha Krupp
Bow; Traditionally made of	Yew
Bren Gun; Name from	Brno (Czechoslovakia), Enfield
Brown Bess	Smooth bore gun, standard weapon from Elizabethan times to 19th Century
Bullet; Expanding	Dum dum. Name from: Arsenal near Calcutta
Chemical and biological warfare research centre; UK	Porton Down
Crossbow-like; Large ancient weapon	Ballista
Dynamite; Made from	Nitroglycerin absorbed in Kieselguhr
Gun;-	
Nickname; 'That won the West'	Colt .45
Slow burning match ignites powder	Matchlock
Spark from flint ignites powder	Flintlock
Hydrogen Bomb;-	
Exploded; 1st	Eniwetok Atoll, Pacific (1952)
USSR; Developed	Andrei Sakharov
Irish Club; Traditional	Shillelagh
Mulberry	Code name for artificial harbour used in D-Day landings
Neutron Bomb	Kills, with limited effect on property
Nitrocellulose; Common name	Guncotton
Poisoned Arrows; Substance used to tip, by South American Indians	Curare
Snrapnel; Name from	Henry Shrapnel (inventor)
Siege Weapon; Mediaeval; Lever and counterweight	Trebuchet, Mangonel

Spear; Zulu warriors use	Assegai
Sten Gun; Name from	Sheppard and Turpin (designers), Enfield
Stones linked by string	Bola
Sword; Roman	Gladius
Tank:-	
1st	No 1, Lincoln
Use; 1st	Somme (1916)
Use; Mass attack; 1st	Cambrai, France (1917)
Tommy Gun; Name from	Thompson (make)
U Boat; Stands for	Unterseeboot
V2; Meaning	Revenge weapon – 2

Weapons, Famous

By: Name → Type

AK47 (Kalashnikov)	Automatic rifle
AR18 (Armalite)	Automatic rifle
Beretta	Semi-automatic pistol
Big Bertha	Howitzer
Bofors	Anti-aircraft gun
Bowie	Knife
Browning FN	Automatic pistol
Browning M2	Machine gun
Carl–Gustaf RCL	Recoilless anti tank gun
Chieftain	Tank
Colt .45 (Peacemaker)	Revolver
Derringer	Pistol
Dum dum	Bullet (expanding)
Erma MP	Submachine gun
Exocet	Air/sea to sea missile
FN (Belgium)	Automatic rifle
Gatling	Machine gun
Honest John	Surface to surface missile
Lee–Enfield	Rifle
Leopard	Tank
Lewis	Machine gun
Luger P'08	Semi-automatic pistol
M1 (Garand)	Rifle
M16	Automatic rifle
M60	Tank
Mills Bomb	Hand Grenade
Minuteman	Ballistic missile
Patriot	Anti-missile missile
Pershing	Ballistic missile
Polaris	Ballistic missile (submarine)
Poseidon	Ballistic missile (submarine)
Schmeisser	Sub-machine gun
Scud	Surface to surface missile
Sherman	Tank
Sidewinder	Air to Air missile
Smith and Wesson	Magnum Revolver
Springfield	Rifle
SS20	Ballistic missile
Sten	Sub-machine gun
Sterling	Sub-machine gun
T34	Tank

Thompson	Sub-machine gun
Titan	Ballistic missile
Tomahawk	Cruise missile
Trident	Ballistic missile
V1	Flying bomb (pilotless aircraft)
V2	Rocket
Walther PPK	Semi-automatic pistol
Winchester	Rifle
Wombat	Recoilless Anti-tank gun

TRANSPORT
Air Transport

By: *General*

See Also: *The Universe and Space Exploration; Space Exploration*

Aircraft;-	
Fastest; Passenger	Concorde
Largest	Boeing 747
Largest; Wing span	Howard Hughes 'Spruce Goose' (made 1 flight only)
Air Hostess(es);-	
1st	Ellen Church
Occupation; 1st	Nurses
Airline;-	
Largest	Aeroflot
Largest; UK	British Airways
National; Oldest	KLM
Airport;-	
Busiest	O'Hare, Chicago
Busiest; International flights	Heathrow
John F.Kennedy; Former name	Idlewild
Largest	King Khalid, Riyadh, Saudi Arabia
Largest; UK	Heathrow
Largest; UK; 2nd	Gatwick
Airports; Location;-	
Bromma	Stockholm
Ciampino	Rome
Dum Dum	Calcutta
Fornebu	Oslo
Haneda	Tokyo
Heathrow	London
John Foster Dulles	Washington
John F.Kennedy	New York
Kloten	Zurich
La Guardia	New York
Le Bourget	Paris
Logan	Boston
Melsbroek	Brussels
Narita	Tokyo
O'Hare	Chicago
Orly	Paris
Santa Cruz	Bombay
Schipol	Amsterdam
Tempelhof	Berlin
Airship; Flight; 1st	Henri Giffard (1852)

Atlantic Crossing; 1st;-
Balloon | Double Eagle II (1978)
Non stop | Alcock and Brown in Vickers Vimy (1919)

On (not in) an aircraft | Jaromer Wagner (1980)
Solo; 1st | Charles Lindbergh in Spirit of St Louis (1927)

Solo; 1st; Woman | Amelia Earheart (1932)
Atom Bombs dropped from | Boeing Super-Fortress
Bankruptcy; US aircraft company narrowly saved from | Lockheed
Britain – Australia; 1st;- | Ross and Keith Smith (1919)
Solo; Woman | Amy Johnson in Jason (1930)
British Airways; Formed from | BEA, BOAC
Civil Aircraft Markings:-
Britain | G
Netherlands | PH
Spain | EC
US | N
West Germany | D
Crashes and Disasters;-
Fatal; 1st | Thomas Selfridge (Orville Wright – pilot)

Fatal; 1st; UK | Charles Rolls
Hindenburg | Zeppelin explodes in US (1937)
Iranian Aircraft, shot down by USS Vincennes | Iranair Airbus A300, Flight 655 (1988)
Korean Aircraft, shot down by Russian fighter | Flight KAL 007 (1983)
Manchester United team, 7 members killed | Munich (1958)
R101 | Beauvais, France (1930)
Worst | Tenerife (1977)
Worst; Single aircraft | Near Tokyo, JAL Flight 123 (1985)
Cross Channel Flight; 1st;-
Aircraft | Louis Bleriot in Type XI
Aircraft; Man-powered | Gossamer Albatross (1979). Pilot: Bryan Allen

Douglas Aircraft Company; Taken over by; 1967 | McDonnell
Fighter Bomber; UK; Cancelled 1964 | TSR2
Flight; 1st;-
Man-powered (over 1 mile) | Gossamer Condor (1977). Pilot: Bryan Allen

Powered | Orville Wright (December 17th, 1903). Aircraft: Flyer I. At: Kitty Hawk

Helicopter blades (unpowered) on aircraft | Autogiro
Hiroshima Bombing; Aircraft | Enola Gay. Pilot: Colonel Paul Tibbets
Hot Air Balloon;-
Atlantic Crossing; 1st | Richard Branson (1987)
Manned Flight; 1st | Pilatre de Rozier (1783). Balloon built by: Montgolfier Brothers

Hypersonic; Meaning | Over Mach 5
Jet;-
Aircraft; 1st | Heinkel He 178

371

Engine; Inventor	Frank Whittle
Passenger; 1st	De Havilland Comet I
MiG; Stands for	Mikoyan and Gurevich
Nickname;-	
Foxbat	MiG 25
Jumbo Jet	Boeing 747
Whispering Giant	Bristol Brittania
Night Passenger Service; 1st	Lufthansa
Pacific; Flight; 1st	Charles Kingsford Smith (1928)
Parachute Descent; 1st	André Garnerin (1797)
Parachute Jump, from aircraft; 1st	Captain Albert Berry (1912}
Radar; US bomber, invisible to	Stealth
Red Square; Flight from Helsinki	Mathias Rust (1987)
Round the World Flight; 1st;-	L.Smith and Erik Nelson (1924)
Non-stop	James Gallagher in Lucky Lady II (1949)
Non-stop; Without refuelling	Voyager (1986)
Solo	Wiley Post in Winnie Mae (1933)
Sky Train; Associated with	Freddy Laker
Solar Powered Aircraft; 1st	Solar Challenger
Speed;-	
1,000 MPH; 1st to exceed	Fairey Delta I
Relative to speed of sound	Mach number
Sound Barrier; 1st to exceed	Bell X1. Pilot: Chuck Yeager. Book and film about: The Right Stuff
Too slow; Condition	Stall
Spitfire;-	
Designer	R.J.Mitchell
Engine	Rolls Royce Merlin
Supersonic;-	
Regular passenger service; 1st	Concorde, 1976
Transport; 1st	TU144
Turn; 180 Degrees, while climbing	Chandelle
Vapour Trail; Composition	Ice crystals
Wright Brothers; Occupation	Printers and bicycle makers

Aircraft, Famous Models

By: Model → Maker

Anson	Avro
B-1	Rockwell International
Bird Dog	Cessna
Camel	Sopwith
Canberra	English Electric, BAC
Caravelle	Sud Aviation
Cherokee	Piper
Chipmunk	De Havilland
Comanche	Piper
Comet	De Havilland
Concorde	BAC/Sud Aviation
Constellation	Lockheed
Cub	Piper
DC-3 (Dakota)	Douglas
DC-8	Douglas
DC-10	(McDonnell) Douglas
Delta 2	Fairey
F111	General Dynamics

F-15 Eagle	(McDonnell) Douglas
Flying Fortress (B-17)	Boeing
Foxbat	MiG
Galaxy (C5A)	Lockheed
Harrier	Hawker Siddeley
Hercules	Lockheed
Hunter	Hawker
Hurricane	Hawker
Javelin	Gloster
JU 52/3m	Junkers
Jumbo (747)	Boeing
Lancaster	Avro
ME 262	Messerschmitt
Meteor	Gloster
Mirage	Dassault
Mosquito	De Havilland
Nimrod	BAC
One-Eleven (111)	BAC
Sea King	Westland
Seminole	Piper
Spitfire	Vickers
Starfighter	Lockheed
Stealth F117A Fighter	Lockheed
Stealth B2 Bomber	Northrop
Stirling	Short
Stratofortress (B-52)	Boeing
Superfortress (B-29)	Boeing
Supermarine	Vickers
Tomcat	Grumman
Tornado	Panavia
Trident	Hawker Siddeley
Tristar	Lockheed
TSR2	BAC
TU-144	Tupolyev
U-2	Lockheed
VC-10	BAC
Vimy	Vickers
Viscount	Vickers
Vulcan	Avro
X1	Bell
Yak-25	Yakovlev

Airlines, National

By: Airline → Country

Aer Lingus	Ireland
Aeroflot	USSR
Alia	Jordan
Alitalia	Italy
Avianca	Colombia
Cathay Pacific Airways	Hong Kong
DETA	Mozambique
El Al	Israel
Garuda	Indonesia
Iberia	Spain
Interflug	East Germany
JAT	Yugoslavia

KLM	Netherlands
LOT	Poland
Lufthansa	Germany
Malev	Hungary
Olympic Airways	Greece
PIA	Pakistan
QANTAS	Australia
Sabena	Belgium
SAS	Denmark, Norway, Sweden
TAP	Portugal
THY	Turkey
Varig	Brazil

Cars, Countries from

By: Make → Country from

Bugatti	France
Duesenberg	USA
Facel Vega	France
Hindustan	India
Hispano Suiza	Spain (originally)
Holden	Australia
Hyundai	South Korea
Lagonda	UK
Lamborghini	Italy
Lancia	Italy
Marcos	UK
Maserati	Italy
Moskvich	USSR/Russia
Saab	Sweden
Seat	Spain
Skoda	Czechoslovakia
Stutz	USA
Volvo	Sweden
Wartburg	(East) Germany
ZCZ	Yugoslavia
Zil	USSR/Russia

Cars, Famous Models

By: Model → Make

Alfonso	Hispano Suiza
Alpine	Sunbeam
Arrow	Pierce
Batmobile	BMW
Bearcat	Stutz
Boxer	Ferrari
Carrera	Porsche
Corniche	Rolls Royce
Cortina	Ford
Corvette	Chevrolet
Countach	Lamborghini
Dauphine	Renault
DB Series	Aston Martin
Diablo	Lamborghini
E Type	Jaguar

Elf	Riley
Elite	Lotus
Escort	Ford
Esprit	Lotus
Hornet	Wolseley
Interceptor	Jensen
Javelin	Jowett
Jeep	Willys
Mangusta	De Tomaso
Minor	Morris
Model T	Ford
Mustang	Ford
MX-5	Mazda
Phantom	Rolls Royce
Plus 4	Morgan
Quattro	Audi
Royale	Bugatti, Maserati
Scimitar	Reliant
Silver Cloud	Rolls Royce
Silver Ghost	Rolls Royce
SS	Jaguar
Steamer	Stanley
Testarossa	Ferrari
Thunderbird	Ford
2 CV	Citroen
Uno	Fiat
XK Series	Jaguar

Motorcycles, Famous Models

By: Model → Make

Bonneville	Triumph
Commando	Norton
Daytona	Triumph
Dominator	Norton
Electra Glide	Harley-Davidson
Gold Wing	Honda
International	Norton
Manx	Norton
Pantah	Ducatti
Square Four	Ariel
SS100	Brough Superior
Super Glide	Harley-Davidson
Trident	Triumph

Other Transport

By: General

Escalator;-	
1st; UK	Harrods (1898)
1st; UK underground	Earls Court, London
Hovercraft;-	
Original name	Ripplecraft
Passenger flight; 1st	Saunders-Roe SRN1 (1959)
Human Powered; Pulled	Rickshaw
Wheelless Land Transport; Early type	Sedan chair

Rail Transport

By: General

Accident;-	
1st	William Huskisson (by the Rocket)
UK; Worst	Gretna Green (1915)
Bridge; Longest; Britain	Tay Bridge
Chicago; City rail system	The El (Elevated)
Disaster; Bridge collapsed in storm	Tay Bridge (1879)
Express Train; 1st	London to Brighton
France; High speed train	TGV
Gauge;-	
Ireland	5 foot 3 inches
Narrowest; Britain	15 inches (Ravenglass and Eskdale; Romney, Hythe and Dymchurch)
Spain	5 foot 6 inches
Standard; Origin	Stephenson's Mine Railway
Three main; Country with	Australia
Train with changing facility	Talgo (Spanish)
Longest	Trans Siberian Railway (Moscow – Nakhodka)
National Railway Museum; Location	York
National Railways;-	
France	SNCF
Spain	RENFE
Public Railway; 1st (steam)	Stockton and Darlington Railway
Railway System; Largest	USSR
San Francisco; Rail system	BART (Bay Area Rapid Transit)
Signal; Arm	Horizontal for 'Stop'
Sleeping Cars; Company running, Europe	Wagons Lits
Standard Gauge	4 foot 8½ inches
Station;-	
Largest	Grand Central, New York
Largest; UK	Clapham Junction
Platforms; Most; UK	Waterloo
Station, Locations;-	
Anhalter	Berlin
Charing Cross	London
Connolly	Dublin
Euston	London
Gare Du Nord	Paris
Grand Central	New York
King's Cross	London
Lime Street	Liverpool
Liverpool Street	London
New Street	Birmingham
Paddington	London
Parkway	Bristol
Piccadilly	Manchester
Queen Street	Cardiff, Glasgow
Saint Lazare	Paris
Spa	Bath
St Davids	Exeter
Temple Meads	Bristol
Union	Washington
Victoria	London, Manchester, Bombay

Waterloo	London
Waverley	Edinburgh
Steam Route; British Rail; Only	Vale of Rheidol
Straight Line; Longest	Nullarbor Plain, Australia
Tank Engine; Advantage	No tender needed
Third Class; Abolished	1956
Timetable; National; 1st	Bradshaw's
Tunnel; Longest; UK (Discounting Underground Railways)	Severn Tunnel
Underground;-	
Berlin; Called	U-Bahn
Britain	London, Glasgow, Liverpool, Tyne and Wear (Metro)
Line; 1st	Metropolitan, London (1863)
London; Lines	Bakerloo, Central, Circle, District, Jubilee, Metropolitan, Northern, Piccadilly, Victoria, (Waterloo & City)
London; Newest	Jubilee (1979)
Longest	London
Most Passengers	Moscow
Most Stations	New York
Oldest	London
Paris; Called	Metro
Rome; Called	Metropolitana
Stockholm; Called	T-Bana
US; Passenger rail system; Operating company	Amtrak
USSR; Term for 1st and 2nd class	Soft and Hard Class
Wheel Designation; Steam engine	Front idle wheels, coupled wheels, rear idle wheels

Road Transport

By: General

See Also: Sports and Leisure; Motor Racing

A.A; Formed	1909
Aston Martin; Founder	David Brown (DB stands for)
Belfast Car company; Failed 1982	De Lorean
Belisha Beacons; Introduced	By Leslie Hore-Belisha (Minister of Transport)
Bicycle; Large front wheel	Penny farthing
Biggest Selling Model	Volkswagen Beetle (20 Million)
British	Mini
2nd	Ford Model T
Breathalyser; Introduced	1967
Car Manufacturer; Biggest	General Motors
Car; Offered to Britain as WWII reparations	Volkswagen
Cars; Country banned till 1948	Bermuda
Cars; Famous;-	
Donald Campbell; Record breaking car	Bluebird
Flop; Famous, US	Ford Edsel
James Bond; Goldfinger	Aston Martin DB-5
Love Bug (Disney)	Herbie, VW

Saint's	Volvo P1800S
Cars; Name derivations;-	
BMW	Bayerische Motoren Werke
British Leyland	Leyland, Lancashire
Fiat	Fabrica Italiana Automobile Torino (Turin Italian Automobile Works)
Edsel	Henry Ford's son
JCB	J.C.Bamford
Jeep	GP (general purpose)
Mercedes Benz	Daughter of Emil Jellinek, financier
MG	Morris Garages
Oldsmobile	Olds, founder
Saab	Svenska Aeroplan Aktiebolaget (Swedish Aeroplane Company)
Vauxhall	1st made in Vauxhall, South London
Volvo	Latin – I Roll
Chrysler; Brands	De Soto, Dodge, Plymouth
Driving; Left to Right; Changed	Sweden (1967)
Driving Test; 1st	1935
Drunk Driver; Britain; 1st	London taxi (electric)
Fastest	Richard Noble, Thrust II
Fiat; Owners	Agnelli family
1st, Motor car;-	
Petrol Driven	Benz (1885)
Petrol Driven; UK (4 wheel)	Lanchester
Ford; Company base	Dearborn, Michigan
Green Goddess; Type of	Fire Engine
International Number Plates:-	
CH	Switzerland
D	Germany
E	Spain
GBA	Alderney
GBG	Guernsey
GBJ	Jersey
GBM	Isle of Man
GBY	Malta
GBZ	Gibraltar
IRL	Ireland
Jaguar; Founder	William Lyons
L Plates; Introduced	1935
Lotus; Founder	Colin Chapman
Million Seller; 1st; UK	Morris Minor
Mini; Designer	Alec Issigonis
Mini; Introduced	1959
Model T; Successor	Model A
MOT; 1st	1960
MOT; When required	Annually after 3 or more years (7 – Northern Ireland)
Motor Oil; Viscosity measure	S.A.E. number
Motorcycle; 1st	Daimler (1885)
Nicknames:-	
Model T	Tin Lizzie
Volkswagen	Beetle
Austin 7	Baby
Morris Cowley	Bull Nose
Fiat 500	Tipolino
Number Plates; Can use without	Reigning sovereign

Number Plates; 1st; UK	A1, to Lord Russell (1903)
Omnibus; Meaning	For everyone
Parking Meters; 1st	1958
Petrol; Anti-knock index	Octane number
Petrol Pumps; 1st; UK	1919
Rear Wheels; Allows to corner at different speeds	Differential
Red Flag Act (1st)	1831
Registration; Letter A; Year	1963 and 1983
Road Builder; 1st; UK	John Metcalfe

Road Signs

Diagonal black line on white background	National speed limit applies
Number; On blue background	Minimum speed limit
Over motorway; Zero	End of speed restriction
Red and black car in red circle	No overtaking
Red Circle; Nothing inside	No vehicles
Red Circle; Red diagonals on blue background	No stopping
Red Circle; Motorcycle over a car inside	No motor vehicles
White arrow pointing up on blue rectangular background	One way
Rolls Royce Mascot; Name	Spirit of Ecstasy
70 mph limit; Introduced	1965

Speed;-

60 mph; 1st car to reach	Electric
100 mph; 1st car to reach	Gobron–Brillie (Louis Rigolly)
300 mph; 1st car to reach	Bluebird (Malcolm Campbell)
Speed Limit; 1st	4 mph country, 2 mph town (1865)
Tarmac; Word origin	Tarmacadam – John McAdam

Traffic Lights;-

1st (red–green)	Cleveland, US
1st; What happened	Exploded
Traffic Wardens; 1st	London (1958)
Tram; 1st; UK	Blackpool
Veteran Car Run; Course	London to Brighton
Veteran; Cars termed	(Up to the end of) 1918
Vintage; Cars termed	1919–30
Volkswagen; Designer	Ferdinand Porsche
Wheel Clamp; Other name	Denver boot

Roads

By: General

Motorway; 1st; UK	Preston Bypass (1958)
Road; Longest	Pan American Highway (Alaska to Brazil)

Roads; Famous:-

Appian Way	Rome to Brindisi
Carnaby Street	London, centre of 1960s fashion
Ermine Street	London to York
Fosse Way	Lincoln to Exeter
High, The	Oxford

Karl Marx Allee	East Berlin
Lanes, The	Brighton
Petticoat Lane	London Market, officially Middlesex Street
Pilgrim's Way	Winchester to Canterbury
Princes Street	Edinburgh
Rotten Row	Riding track in Hyde Park
Route 66	Chicago to Los Angeles
Royal Mile	Edinburgh
Sauchiehall Street	Glasgow
Sixth Avenue	New York. Official name: Avenue of the Americas
Watling Street	Dover via London to St Albans and Wroxeter
Spaghetti Junction; Official name	Gravelly Hill Interchange

Sea and Water Transport

By: General

Atlantic Crossing; Regular service; 1st company	Cunard
Fastest	Virgin Atlantic Challenger II
Fastest; Ship	SS United States
Boats, countries from;-	
Dhow	Arab countries
Felucca	Mediterranean (especially Greece)
Ferilia	Malta
Gondola	Venice, Italy
Goolet	Turkey
Junk	China
Kayak	Eskimo
Circumnavigation of the Globe; 1st;-	Magellan. Boat: *Vittoria*
Non-stop	Robin Knox-Johnston. Boat: *Suhaili* (1969)
Solo	Joshua Slocum. Boat: *Spray* (1898)
Solo; Woman	Krystyna Choynowska-Liskievicz. Boat: *Mazurek* (1978)
Distress Signal	SOS (Morse), Mayday (Voice)
Hull; Butted planks	Caravel
Hull; Overlapping planks	Clinker
Lighthouses; UK Authority	Trinity House
Lights	Starboard: Green, Port: Red
Lloyd's Designation for First Rate	A1
Maximum Loading Mark	Plimsoll Line
Nautical Terms:-	
Bells	Every half hour. Repeated 4 hourly. 12 o'clock is 8 bells
Ceremony when Royalty arrive or leave battleship	Piping the side (using boatswain's pipe)
Compass Housing	Binnacle
Compass Points, repeating in order	Boxing the compass
Floating Objects	Flotsam
Kitchen	Galley
Left	Port

Objects thrown overboard	Jetsam
Right	Starboard
Sling used for rescues	Breeches buoy
Watches	7. 1st from 8 pm. 4 hourly except 4pm–6pm, 6pm–8pm, 2 dog watches
Norway; Former name	*France*
P & O, stands for	Peninsular and Oriental
Port;-	
Athens	Piraeus
Biggest	New York
Busiest	Rotterdam
Largest; Inland	Montreal
London	Tilbury
Rome	Ostia
PT Boat; Stands for	Patrol Torpedo Boat
Queen Mary; Intended name	*Queen Victoria*
Ships; Register of	Lloyds
V Shaped Hull; Pioneer	Uffa Fox
Venice; Powered water bus	Vaporetto

Ships, Famous

By: Description, Owner → Name

See Also: Geography; Exploration
Accidents and Sinkings;-

After Fire; Hong Kong harbour	*Queen Elizabeth* (1972)
By French Agents in Auckland, New Zealand	*Rainbow Warrior*
By German Submarine	*Lusitania*
By Hitting Iceberg	*Titanic*. Date: April 15th, 1912. Band played: 'Nearer my God to thee'. Captain: Edward Smith
Car Ferry, Zeebrugge disaster	*Herald of Free Enterprise* (1987). Operator: Townsend Thoresen
Italian, collided with Swedish	*Andrea Doria* (1956)
Nuclear Submarine, US	*Thresher* (1963)
Oil Tanker, off Brittany	*Amoco Cadiz* (1978)
Oil Tanker, off Land's End	*Torrey Canyon* (1967)
Swedish	*Wasa* (1628). Now at: Stockholm
Aircraft Carrier; 1st	*Argus*
Aristotle Onassis; Yacht	*Christina*
Battleship; Largest; German, WWII	*Bismarck*
Battleship; Largest; UK	*Vanguard*
Battleship Class; Ship gave name to	*Dreadnought*
Blackbeard	*Queen Anne's Revenge*
Captain Cook	*Adventure, Discovery, Endeavour, Resolution*
Columbus	Flagship: *Santa Maria*. Others: *Pinto, Nina*
Darwin	*Beagle*. Captain: Robert Fitzroy
Deepest Descent	*Trieste* (Jacques Cousteau)
Edward Heath	*Morning Cloud* (3; all sank)
Found Abandoned, unsolved mystery	*Mary Celeste* (1872)

Francis Chichester	*Gypsy Moth IV*
Francis Drake	*Golden Hind.* Original name: *Pelican.* Replica at: Brixham
Sir Humprey Gilbert	*Squirrel*
Sir Richard Grenville	*Revenge*
Harold Wilson, Ian Smith talks held on	*Tiger*
Henry VIII; Main ship	*Mary Rose.* Sunk: 1545. Raised: 1982. Now at: Portsmouth
Hijacked by Palestinian terrorists, Mediterranean	*Achille Lauro* (1985)
Jacques Cousteau	*Calypso*
John F.Kennedy; Torpedo Boat	*PT 109*
Magellan	*Vittoria* (1st Circumnavigation of Globe)
Nansen	*Fram*
North Pole; 1st ship to reach	*Arktika* (1977)
Nuclear Powered;-	
Aircraft Carrier; 1st	*Enterprise*
Ship; 1st	*Savannah*
Submarine; 1st	*Nautilus*
Old Ironsides, nickname for	*Constitution*
Panama Canal; 1st ship through	*Ancon*
Passenger Ship; Largest	*Norway*
Passenger Ship; Largest; UK	*Queen Elizabeth*
Pearl Harbour; Survived; Sunk in Falklands War	*General Belgrano*
Polar Ice Cap; 1st under	*Nautilus*
Sir Alec Rose	*Lively Lady* (round the world yacht)
Screw Propelled Ship; 1st (large)	*Great Britain.* Builder: Brunel. Now at: Bristol
Scuttled near Montevideo	*Graf Spee* (German pocket battleship) (1939)
Sir Ernest Shackleton	*Endurance* (Antarctic exploration ship) Now in: Dundee
Shelley; Boat drowned in	*Don Juan*
Spanish Armada; Flagship against	*Ark Royal*
Spy Ship, US, seized off North Korea	*Pueblo* (1968)
Tea Clipper; Last	*Cutty Sark.* Now at: Greenwich. Record held: China to England
Thor Heyerdahl;-	
Balsa raft, sailed Peru to Polynesia on	*Kon Tiki*
Papyrus boat, sailed Africa to America on	*Ra II*
Transatlantic Cable Layer; 1st	*Great Eastern.* Builder: Brunel
Turbine Engine; 1st	*Turbinia.* Builder: Parsons. Demonstrated at: Spithead (1897), Queen Victoria's Diamond Jubilee review where it steamed past fleet
Wreck; Found 1985	*Titanic*

Trains and Engines, Famous

By: Description → Name

Calais to Rome	*Blue Train*
Cape Town to Pretoria	*Blue Train*

Casey Jones; Associated with	*Cannonball Express*
Cincinnati to New Orleans	*Chattanooga Choo Choo*
Fastest; Steam train	*Mallard*. Designer: Nigel Gresley
London to Edinburgh	*Flying Scotsman*
London to Inverness	*Clansman*
London to Paris	Golden Arrow
Moscow to Vladivostok	*Tran-Siberian Express*. Now called: The Russia
Paris to Istanbul	*Orient Express*. Journey now: London to Venice
Paris to Monte Carlo	*Blue Train, Golden Arrow*
Tokyo to Osaka	*Bullet Train*
US Civil War; Confederate engine hijacked by Union soldiers	*The General*. Film about by: Buster Keaton. Chased by: *The Texas*

Society and Politics

Contents

Crime **387**
Assassination and Murder
  By: Victim 387
Assassination and Murder, Attempted
  By: Intended Victim 390
Crime Detection and Punishment 390
Crime, Other 391
Fraud and Forgery 392
Gangs and Gangsters
  By: Name, Organisation 393
Kidnapping 394
Law 395
Murderers
  By: Description 396
  By: Name 396
Pirates 397
Robbery and Robbers 397
Wild West, Outlaws and
  Highwaymen 398
Economics and Business **399**
Advertising Slogans
  By: Slogan 399
Companies and Business 400
Currencies
  By: Country 402
Currency, Slang
  By: Slang Term 402
Economics and Finance 403
Occupations, Traditional
  By: Name 404
Politics and History **404**
Archaeology 404
Colonies, Former
  By: Country 404
Customs and Superstitions 405

Education 405
Espionage 406
Heraldry 407
International Politics and
  Institutions 407
Military 408
Parliaments, Names of
  By: Country 410
People
  By: Name 411
Royalty
  By: Country 413
  By: Description 414
Royalty, UK
  By: Description 415
  By: Name 417
Rulers, Names for
  By: Place 419
Social and Welfare Issues 419
Society, Other 420
Trade Unions 420
Treaties 421
United Kingdom
  By: Description 422
  By: Term, Name 426
United States 428
Wars and Battles
  By: Description 431
  By: Name 432
World Politics and History
  By: Country/Description 437
  By: Description 446
  By: Term 448

CRIME
Assassination and Murder

By: Victim → Murderer, General

Agamemnon	Clytemnestra and Aegisthus
Method	Axed in bath
Alexander the Great's family	Cassander
Tsar Alexander II	Sophia Perovskaya (led by), for the Narodnaya Volya (People's Will) Organisation (1881)
Benigno Aquino	A Government-backed assassin
At	Manila Airport (August, 1983)
Atahualpa	The Spanish
Method	Strangling
Thomas Becket	(Archbishop of Canterbury) Barons Fitzurse, De Tracy, De Morville, Le Breton (1170)

Incited by	Henry II. 'Will no one rid me of this turbulent priest?'
Billy the Kid	Sheriff Pat Garrett (1881)
Grace Brown	Chester Gillett (1906)
Book based on	*An American Tragedy*
Gaston Calmette	Madame Caillaux
Reason	Calmette, Editor of *Le Figaro* had accused Joseph Caillaux of fraud
Roberto Calvi	Found hanging from Blackfriars bridge (1982). Head of *Banco Ambrosiano*, linked with Italian P2 scandal
President Sadi Carnot of France	Santo Caserio (1894)
Claudius	Agrippina (wife)
With	Poison mushrooms (AD 54)
Commodus	Narcissus (Wrestler)
Method	Strangling
Dollfuss (Austrian Chancellor)	The Nazis (1934)
Edward (The Martyr)	Elfthryth (conspiracy organised by)
Edward II	De Gournay and Maltravers
Method	Red hot poker
King Faisal	(Saudi Arabia) Nephew, Prince Faisal (1975)
Archduke Franz Ferdinand	Gavrilo Princip. Helped to precipitate WW1
Date	June 28th, 1914
In	Sarajevo
Indira Gandhi	2 Sikh members of bodyguard, Satwant Singh and Beant Singh (October 1984)
Rajiv Gandhi	Sri Lankan Tamil Tigers (suspected) (1991)
Gandhi	Nathuram Godse (1948)
President Garfield	Charles Guiteau (1881)
Kitty Genovese	Nobody answered calls for help. Became cause célèbre
In	New York
Henry IV of France	Ravaillac
Henry VI	Richard of Gloucester (reputedly)
In	Tower of London
Reinhard Heydrich	Kubis and Gabcik (Czech Partisans). Lidice population massacred in retaliation
Wild Bill Hickok	Jack McCall (1876)
Hickok held	'Dead Man's Hand' at poker (2 aces, 2 eights)
King Umberto of Italy	Bresci (1900)
Jesse James	Fellow outlaw Bob Ford (in the back of the head) for the reward money (1882)
James I of Scotland	Earl of Atholl (and others)
Jean Jaures	Raoul Villain
Julius Caesar	Conspirators led by Cassius and Brutus
Date	The Ides (15th) of March (44 BC)
President John F.Kennedy	Lee Harvey Oswald (supposedly)
Car	Lincoln Continental
Commission investigating	The Warren Commission (rejected a conspiracy)

Date	November 22nd, 1963
Oswald assassinated by	Jack Ruby
In	Dallas
Shooting filmed by	Abraham Zapruder
Robert Kennedy	Sirhan Sirhan (Jordanian) (1968)
Martin Luther King	James Earl Ray (1968)
Kirov (Communist Party Leader in Leningrad)	Leonid Nikolayev (1934). Great Purges ensued
John Lennon	Mark David Chapman
At	Outside New York apartment
Date	December 9th, 1980
Abraham Lincoln	John Wilkes Booth (actor) (1865)
At	Ford's Theatre, Washington
Booth said	'Sic Temper Tyrannis, the South is avenged'
Gun	Derringer
While watching	*Our American Cousin*
Macbeth (King of Scotland)	Malcolm
Marat	Charlotte Corday (1793)
Where	In the bath
Georgi Markov (Bulgarian defector)	Bulgarian Secret Service (supposedly), London (1978)
Method	Pellet containing the poison ricin dispensed from an umbrella
Maria Marten	William Corder
Where	In the Red Barn (1827). Forms basis of numerous melodramas
President McKinley (US)	Leon Czogolz
At	The American Exposition (1901)
Rachel McLean	John Tanner
Harvey Milk	(with San Francisco Mayor, George Moscone) Dan White. Lack of police action led to riots by gay rights protesters
Aldo Moro (former Italian PM)	The Red Brigades (1978)
Lord Mountbatten	The IRA (1979)
While	Fishing in County Sligo, Ireland
Hilda Murrell	Found stabbed in a wood (1984). Link with General Belgrano documents caused controversy over Secret Services involvement
Airey Neave (Tory MP)	The INLA (1979)
Method	Car bomb outside Parliament
Joe Orton	Kenneth Halliwell
Method	With hammer
Olof Palme (Swedish PM)	In: 1986
Chung Hee Park	Kim Jae Kyu, Head of Korean CIA
Pier Paulo Pasolini	Giuseppe Pelosi (1975)
Spencer Perceval (British PM)	John Bellingham (1812). Only British PM to be assassinated
Peter III of Russia	Aleksei Orlov
Francesco Pizzarro	Diego de Almagro (under direction of)
Princes in the Tower (Edward V and the Duke of York)	Sir James Tyrell (under direction of)
Method	Smothering
Ordered by	Richard III (supposedly)

Rasputin	Prince Yussupoff and others (1916)
Method	Poisoned, bludgeoned, and drowned in the River Neva
Sandra Rivett	Lord Lucan (supposedly – Inquest verdict)
David Rizzio (Mary, Queen of Scots' Aide)	Earls of Morton and Lindsay under Henry Darnley's direction
Archbishop Oscar Romero	In: El Salvador (1980)
Anwar Sadat (Egyptian President)	4 Muslim fundamentalists (1981)
During	Military parade
Karen Silkwood	Car suspected forced off road (1973)
Reason (supposedly)	Investigating plutonium safety at workplace
Peter Tosh	In: 1987
Trotsky	Ramon Mercader (1940)
Place	Mexico
Method	With an ice pick
Wat Tyler	William Walworth
Henrik Verwoerd (South African PM)	Dimitric Tsafondas (1966)
Pancho Villa	In: 1923
William of Orange	Balthasar Gerard

Assassination and Murder, Attempted

By: Intended Victim → Responsible

Gerald Ford	Lynette (Squeaky) Fromme, member of Charles Manson's 'family' (1975)
Henry Frick (Steel Magnate)	Alexander Berkman
King George III	James Hadfield (1800), acquitted as insane
Hitler	Bomb planted by: Colonel Von Stauffenberg (1944)
Pope John Paul II	Mehmet Ali Agca (1981)
Lenin	Fanny Kaplan (1918)
Napoleon III	Felice Orsini
Ronald Reagan	John W.Hinckley (1981)
Margaret Thatcher	IRA, Grand Hotel bombing in Brighton (October, 1984)
George Wallace	Arthur Bremer (1972). Left paralysed
Andy Warhol	Valerie Solinas

Crime Detection and Punishment

By: General

See Also: Law

APB; Stands for	All Points Bulletin
Beheading; Last UK	Lord Lovat, Tower Hill (1747)
Central Criminal Court, London	Old Bailey
Death Penalty;-	
Abolished; 1st country	Liechtenstein (1798)
Abolished; UK	1965
Last Execution; UK	Peter Allen, John Walby (1964)
Last Execution; UK; Woman	Ruth Ellis (1955)

Still exists for	Treason, Piracy, Arson in HM Dockyards, Military Offences
Death Sentence; Judge wears before pronouncing	Black Cap
Detective Agency; Prominent; US	Pinkertons
Electric Chair; Execution; 1st	William Kember (1890)
Execution; By injection; 1st; US	Ronald O'Bryan (1982)
Execution; Last; Public; UK	Michael Barrett (1868)
FBI; Head, 1924–1972	J.Edgar Hoover
Fingerprints; Patterns	4. Arch, Loop, Whorl, Composite
Fingerprints; Pioneer of use	Francis Galton
Gendarmes	Not police, soldiers doing police duty
Headgear; Original Police	Top Hat
Lie Detector; Other name	Polygraph
Metropolitan Police; Headquarters	New Scotland Yard
Metropolitan Police; Highest position	Commissioner
National Detective Force; Founded by former criminal	French Sûreté (by Vidocq)
Police; Predecessor, London	Bow Street Runners
Prison;-	
Dartmoor; Land owned by	Prince Charles
Island in San Francisco Bay, closed 1963	Alcatraz
Maze, Belfast; Blocks	H-blocks
Sing Sing	New York
Singapore	Changi
Spandau; Only inhabitant (at his death, 1987)	Rudolf Hess
Prison Reform; Campaigner	Elizabeth Fry
Radio Transmission; 1st criminal arrested because of	Dr Crippen
Tower of London; Last prisoner held in	Rudolf Hess
Truncheons, Wooden; Made of	Cocus Wood

Crime, Other

By: General

Jeffrey Archer; Libel against	*Daily Star* newspaper for allegation of paying prostitute Monica Coghlan
Damages awarded	£500,000 (1987)
Arson;-	
Rome (supposedly)	Nero
Temple of Artemis at Ephesus	Herostratus
Bribery: Lord Chancellor impeached for	Francis Bacon
Car Manufacturer; Arrested on cocaine smuggling charges	John De Lorean (1982)
Conspiracy; Sentenced to execution for; Reprieved	Dostoyevsky
Drug Dealing; Steroids; US	David Jenkins
Heresy; Imprisoned for	Roger Bacon
Hijacking; Palestinian female terrorist, jailed in London	Leila Khaled (1970)
Libel Action; Against accusation of being boring	William Roache
Queen; Talked to after gaining access to the Royal bedchamber	Michael Fagan (1982)
Railway Ticket; Not buying; Fined for	C.E.M.Joad

Rape; William Kennedy Smith acquitted of	Patricia Bowman
Scopes Monkey Trial	Teacher Scopes tested law against teaching evolution. Found guilty, but moral victory (1925)
Defence	Clarence Darrow
Prosecution	William Jennings Bryan
Scottsboro' Boys	9 negro youths falsely accused of rape (1931). 8 sentenced to death. Agitation leads to retrials
Shoplifting; Committed suicide after found guilty	Lady Isobel Barnett
Subway Vigilante; Acquitted of shooting muggers	Bernard Goetz
Whistler (v Ruskin)	Whistler sued Ruskin for insulting his paintings, 'Flinging a pot of paint in the public's face' (1875)
Damages awarded	A farthing
Oscar Wilde (v Lord Queensberry)	Sued for: Homosexuality allegations with Queensberry's son, Alfred Douglas (1895). Lost
Wilde jailed in	Reading Jail

Fraud and Forgery

By: General

Construction Company, US, involved in financial corruption	Credit Mobilière (1860s)
Diamond Necklace; Affair of	Cardinal De Rohan bought for Marie Antoinette
Cheated by	Countess De Lamotte
Disappearance; MP attempted to fake	John Stonehouse
Caught in	Australia
Former Ministerial post	Postmaster General
Married	Mistress, Sheila Buckley, after jail term
MP for	Walsall
Used name	Joseph Markham
Vanished at	Miami Beach (1973)
French Speculator set up fraudulent companies	Serge Stavisky. Scandal causes fall of government
Hitler Diaries	Reporter Gerd Heidemann and dealer in Nazi memorabilia Konrad Kajau attempted to defraud Stern magazine (1983)
Authenticated by	Lord Dacre and other specialists
Howard Hughes' Autobiography; Forged	Clifford Irving (1972)
Insurance Company, Fire, Auto and Marine; Collapsed	Emil Savundra (owner)
Jewish Plot for World Domination; Documents purported to show	Protocols of the Elders of Zion
Jockey; Jailed for tax fraud	Lester Piggott
Mississippi Scheme	Scotsman John Law took over French National Debt
Multiple Share Applications; British Telecom; Tory MP	Keith Best

Piltdown Man	Charles Dawson claimed to discover 'missing link' on Piltdown Common in Sussex (1912). Exposed as fake in 1953
Religious Leader; Jailed for tax fraud	Reverend Moon (1982)
Rolls Razor Domestic Appliance Company; Collapsed 1964	John Bloom (owner)
Rowley (15th Century Monk); Wrote works pretending to be by	Thomas Chatterton
Samuel Palmer Paintings; Forger of	Tom Keating
Shakespeare plays; Claimed to discover new	William Henry Ireland (18th Century)
Shroud of Turin	Mediaeval forgery, exposed as fake by carbon 14 dating in 1988
South Sea Bubble	South Sea Company, founded 1710, took over part of national debt. Collapsed, 1720
Spanish Coupons, exchanged in US; Fraud involving	Ponzi Scheme
Swedish Match Magnate; Committed suicide after fraud uncovered	Ivor Kreugar
Tichborne Claimant	Arthur Orton claimed to be the missing Sir Roger Tichborne. Jailed for perjury (19th Century)
Vermeer Paintings; Forger of	Hans Van Meegeren
Victory Bond Swindle; MP and Journalist jailed for fraud	Horatio Bottomley (1922)

Gangs and Gangsters

By: Name, Organisation → General

Ma Barker	Head of Barker–Karpis gang, which included her children. Killed 1935
Song about	Ma Baker (Boney M)
Bonnie and Clyde	Bonnie Parker and Clyde Barrow
Killed in	Police ambush (1934)
Camorra	Criminal brotherhood based in Naples
Al Capone	
Base	Chicago
Convicted of	Tax evasion
Died from	Syphilis
Former bodyguard of	Johnny Torrio
Income	World's highest private
On business card	'2nd hand furniture dealer'
Vincent 'Mad Dog' Coll	1930s psychopathic gangster
Gunned down in	A telephone booth (1932)
'Legs' Diamond	Leads Bootlegging gang, rival to Luciano
Killed	1931
John Dillinger	Prolific bank robber
Dubbed	'Public Enemy No.1' by FBI
Killed	Outside the Biograph cinema in Chicago by FBI agents (1934)
Tip-off by	'Woman in red' – girlfriend's landlady
'Pretty Boy' Floyd	Bank robber

Shot by	FBI (1934)
The Krays	Ronald and Reginald, leading London (East End) gangsters
Sentenced to	30 years imprisonment (1969)
Gang	The Firm
Lucky Luciano	US underworld leader following Capone. Jailed 1936 and later deported
Mafia	
Comes from	Sicily
Later known as	Cosa Nostra ('Our Thing')
Later leaders include	Vito Genovese, Carlo Gambino
Leader after Capone	Lucky Luciano
Other leaders include	Meyer Lansky, Bugsy Siegel, Dutch Schultz
Testified against	Joe Valachi (1960)
Murder Incorporated	Contract killers
Headed by	Louis 'Lepke' Buchalter, executed 1944
Chief Executioner	Albert Anastasia
'Baby Face' Nelson	Pathological killer
Member of	Dillinger's gang
The Richardsons	Charles and Eddie, leading South London gangsters and rival of the Krays
St Valentine's Day Massacre	Al Capone's gunmen eliminated 6 members of the rival 'Bugs' Moran gang
Took place in	Chicago garage
Date	February 14th, 1929
Triads	Chinese secret criminal society
Based in	Hong Kong
Union Corse	
Now centred in	Marseilles
Originally from	Corsica
Particularly active in	Drug trafficking
Yakuza	Japanese equivalent of the Mafia

Kidnapping

By: General

British Ambassador in Uruguay	Geoffrey Jackson
By	Tupamaros Guerillas (1971)
Chiang Kai Shek	By: Chang Hsueh-Liang (Sian Incident – 1936)
Ear cut off after kidnapping in Italy	J.Paul Getty III
Gypsies; Kidnapped by, at 4 years old	Adam Smith
Italy; Kidnapped in, when 2 years old	William Gilbert (of Gilbert and Sullivan)
Lindbergh Baby	Son of Charles Lindbergh kidnapped and murdered in 1932
Executed for crime	Bruno Hauptmann
Mormon Missionary	Kirk Anderson
By	Joyce McKenney
Richard I	By: Duke Leopold
Shergar (Racehorse)	By: IRA (1983). Never found
Stansted Airport; Found in crate	Umaru Dikko (Nigerian politician)

The Law

By: *General*

See Also: *Crime Detection and Punishment*

Abortion; Britain	1968 Act
Abortion; First country to legalise	USSR (1920)
Age of majority, 18	1970
Betting Shops; Legalised	1960
Chewing Gum; Banned	Singapore
Chief Justice; Former thief	Sir John Popham (16th Century)
Children; Illegal to spank	Sweden
Clergy; Special court	Ecclesiastical Court till 1827 (no death penalty)
Copyright; Time for	50 years after death
Coroner; Scottish equivalent	Procurator Fiscal
Damages for injuries; Law of	Tort
Decree Nisi; Meaning	'Unless', doesn't take effect (Absolute) for 6 months
Deemster	Isle of Man special judges (2)
France; Civil law code	Code Napoleon
Habeas Corpus; Meaning	'Thou may have the body'; Commands person to be brought before a court
Heir Apparent; Meaning	Apparent as no heir legally allowed during lifetime
Heir Presumptive; Meaning	One who would be heir but whose status may change e.g., a female if a male is born later
High Court; Divisions	Chancery, Queen's Bench, Family
Homosexuality; Report recommending law relaxation	Wolfenden Report (1956)
Infanticide; Who can be charged with	Mother only (Others – Murder)
Inns of Court	Lincolns Inn, Gray's Inn, Inner Temple, Middle Temple
Function	To admit Barristers
International Law; Pioneer	Hugo Grotius
Judge; Senior Civil	Master of the Rolls
Lawyers; Types	Solicitors, Barristers
Legal Officer; Highest	Lord Chancellor
Marriage; Morganatic	Between high rank (e.g. Royal) man and a commoner where she doesn't inherit
Oldest	Code of Hammurabi
Oldest; Britain	Statute of Marlborough (1267)
Prostitution; Soliciting made illegal	Street Offences Act (1959)
Queen's Counsel; Becoming; Term for	Taking silk
Riot; Number needed for	3 or more
Royalty; Impersonation on stage legalised	1968
Scottish Court; Not guilty; Term for	Not proven
Slander; Libel; Difference	Libel written
Solicitors; New; Signs certificate	Master of the Rolls
Statute of Limitations; Meaning	Limits time after which an action can be brought
Trespassers; Prosecution	Not possible as a civil offence
Will;-	
Dying without; Term for	Intestate
Witnesses needed	2

Murderers

By: Description → Name, General

A6 Murder; Accused of, 1961	James Hanratty
Bambi Murders	Jeremy Bamber (1985)
Originally suspected	Murdered sister, Sheila Cafell
Birds; Became authority on in prison	Robert Franklin Stroud (The Birdman of Alcatraz)
Body Snatchers, later murderers; Scottish	Burke and Hare
Bodies for	Dr Knox
Hung	Burke
Turned King's evidence	Hare
Disappeared after Nanny found murdered	Lord Lucan
Drains Blocked; Caused discovery	Dennis Nilsen
Hungarian Countess; Murdered young girls and bathed in blood	Countess Bathory
Sentence	Entombed alive
Hungerford Massacre	Michael Ryan (August 1987)
Marshal of France; Sadistic murderer	Gilles De Rais
Moors Murderers	Ian Brady, Myra Hindley
Town applied to change name over	William Palmer (Rugeley)

Murderers

By: Name → General

Lizzie Borden	Acquitted (1893) of axe murder of stepfather and mother in Massachusetts
Nursery rhyme based on	'Lizzie Borden took an axe . . .'
The Boston Strangler	Albert De Salvo. Found guilty of 13 sex murders and sentenced to life imprisonment (1967)
Occupation	Plumber
John Christie	Murdered wife and other inhabitants of house
Falsely convicted and hung for murder	Arthur Evans
House	10 Rillington Place, Notting Hill, London
Hanged	1953
Dr Crippen	
Arrested using	Wireless message (1st time used)
False name	John Philo Robinson
Fled to	Quebec
Hanged	1910
Mistress	Ethel Le Neve (dressed as a boy)
Poisoned wife with	Hyoscine
Ship	*SS Montrose*
John George Haigh	'Acid Bath Murderer' (1949)
Neville Heath	Sex murderer, hanged October 1946

Jack the Ripper	
Murdered	(Prostitutes) Mary Nicholls, Annie Chapman, Elizabeth Stride, Catherine Eddowes, Marie Kelly in East London (1888)
Signed 1st note	'Yours truly, Jack the Ripper'
Peter Kurten	'The Monster of Dusseldorf', 'The Dusseldorf Ripper', convicted of 9 sex murders and executed (1931)
Henri Landru	'The French Bluebeard', murdered at least 11 women. Executed 1922
Charles Manson	Killed Sharon Tate and 3 guests (1969)
Group	The Family
Dennis Nilsen	Murdered up to 16 people. Convicted 1983
Houses	Cricklewood (Melrose Avenue) and Muswell Hill (Crackley Gardens)
Discovered after	Drains blocked with remains
Carl Panzram	Multiple motiveless murderer, executed 1930
Autobiography	*Killer, a Journal of Murder*
Quote	'I hate the whole darn human race'
Papillon	(Butterfly), Henry Charrière, French murderer
Escaped from	Devil's Island to British Guiana (1941)
George Joseph Smith	'Brides in the Bath' murderer, hanged 1915
Son of Sam	Multiple murderer (1976–7), in New York, David Berkowitz
Sentenced to	365 years imprisonment
Wayne B. Williams	Convicted of Atlanta, Georgia, child murders (1979–1981)
The Yorkshire Ripper	Sex murderer, Peter Sutcliffe, convicted 1981
Killed	13 women
Occupation	Lorry driver

Pirates

By: General

American War of Independence; Fought for Americans	Jean Lafitte
Blackbeard	Edward Teach. British pirate, died 1718
Female; Noted	Anne Bonny (partner – John 'Calico Jack' Rackham), Mary Read
Captain Kidd	Scottish pirate, hanged 1701
Knighted by Charles II and became Governor of Jamaica	Sir Henry Morgan

Robbery and Robbers

By: General

Ronald Biggs	Great Train Robber
Arrived to arrest	Chief Superintendent Jack Slipper
Couldn't be deported because	Girlfriend pregnant
Escaped to	Australia, then Brazil

Film, appears in	Sex Pistol's film *The Great Rock'n'Roll Swindle*
Kidnapped to	Barbados
Cricket Pitch dug up by demonstrators protesting innocence	George Davis
Crown Jewels	By: Colonel Thomas Blood (1675). Pardoned
Dr Bridget Rose Dugdale	Ex debutante, with others robbed Russborough House, Blessington of pictures worth 8 million (1974). Sentenced to 9 years
Escaped 3 times protesting innocence	Alfred Hinds (1950s)
Great Train Robbery	
Date	August 8th, 1963
Gang leaders	Bruce Reynolds, 'Buster' Edwards, Charles Wilson, Douglas Goody
Hideout at	Leatherslade Farm
Place	Bridego Bridge, near Cheddington, Buckinghamshire
Train	Glasgow–London Mail
John McVicar	Armed robber
Autobiography filmed with	Roger Daltrey
Escaped from	Durham Jail
Mona Lisa	By: Vicenzo Perrugia from the Louvre (1911)
Security warehouse at Heathrow robbed of £25 million	Brinks Mat (1984)
Jack Sheppard	18th Century criminal, famous for escaping 4 times

The Wild West, Outlaws and Highwaymen

By: General

Armour; Wore	Ned Kelly
Butch Cassidy	Died in (supposedly): Bolivia
Dalton Brothers Gang	Names: Robert, Emmett, Gratton
Claude Duval	
Famous for	Dancing with wives of victims
From	France (came to England)
Hanged	1670
Gunfight at OK Corral	Wyatt and Virgil Earp with Doc Holliday v Clanton Gang (1881)
Location	The OK Corral near Tombstone, Arizona
Jesse James	Bank robber with James Gang, including brother Frank
Shot by	Bob Ford (1882)
Ned Kelly	Australian bushranger, hanged 1880
Painted by	Sidney Nolan
Robin Hood of Texas; Known as	Sam Bass
Dick Turpin	Highwayman
Hanged in	York (1739)
Horse	Black Bess
Legendary ride	London–York
Younger Brothers	Members of: The James Gang

ECONOMICS AND BUSINESS
Advertising Slogans

By: Slogan → Product
Notes: Includes Non-commercial Slogans.

'Ahh'	Bisto
'All human life is there'	*News of the World*
'All the news that's fit to print'	*New York Times*
'And all because the lady loves'	Milk Tray
'The Appetiser'	Tizer
'Beanz meanz'	Heinz beans
'The Beer that made Milwaukee famous'	Schlitz
'Bet he Drinks . . .'	Carling Black Label
'B.O.'	Lifebuoy
'Brandy of Napoleon'	Courvoisier
'Builds bonny babies'	Glaxo
'Can you tell . . . from butter'	Stork margarine
'Chocolates with the less fattening centres'	Maltesers
'Clunk click, every trip'	Seat belt wearing campaign (featuring Jimmy Savile)
'Cool as a mountain stream'	Consulate cigarettes
'Don't ask the price, it's a penny'	Marks and Spencer (original)
'Don't be vague, ask for'	Haig
'Don't forget the fruit gums, mum'	Rowntrees Fruit Gums
'Don't say brown, say'	Hovis
'The Effect is shattering'	Smirnoff Vodka
'Fifty-seven varieties'	Heinz (always more)
'Fingerlickin' good'	Kentucky Fried Chicken
'Fortifies the over forties'	Phyllosan
'Full of eastern promise'	Fry's Turkish Delight
'Gives a meal man appeal'	Oxo
'Go to work on an'	Egg
'(Is) Good for you'	Guinness
'Good to the last drop'	Maxwell House coffee
'Grow on you'	Rose's chocolates
'Have a break, have a'	KitKat
'It beats as it sweeps as it cleans'	Hoover carpet sweepers
'It's a man's life'	Army
'Keep your schoolgirl complexion'	Palmolive
'The Listening bank'	Midland
'Looks good, tastes good and by golly it does you good'	Mackeson stout
'Make tea bags make tea'	Tetley's
'Makes exceedingly good cakes'	Mr Kipling
'Means happy motoring'	Esso (sign)
'Melts in your mouth, not in your hand'	Treets
'Milk from contented cows'	Carnation
'Mint with the hole'	Polo
'Nothing acts faster than'	Anadin
'One degree under'	Aspro
'Put a tiger in your tank'	Esso
'Puts the 'T' in Britain'	Typhoo Tea
'Refreshes the parts other beers can't reach'	Heineken

'The Right One'	Martini
'Simply years ahead'	Philips
'Snap! Crackle! Pop!'	Kellogg's Rice Krispies
'Someone isn't using'	Amplex deodorant
'Spreads straight from the fridge'	Blue Band margarine
'Stop me and buy one'	Wall's ice cream
'Sweet as the moment when the pod went pop'	Birds Eye peas
'The Sweet you can eat between meals'	Milky Way
'Tell Sid'	British Gas (Privatisation Share Issue)
'Things go better with'	Coke (Coca Cola)
'Things happen after a'	Badedas bath
'Too good to hurry mints'	Murraymints
'Top people take'	*The Times*
'Watch out there's a Humphrey about'	Milk
'We try harder'	Avis rent-a-car
'Wodka from Warrington'	Vladivar
'Works wonders'	Double Diamond
'Wot a lot I got'	Smarties
'You know it makes sense'	Road safety
'You know who'	Schweppes
'You press the button, we do the rest'	Kodak
'You too can have a body like mine'	Charles Atlas body building course
'You'll look a little lovelier each day'	Camay
'You'll wonder where the yellow went'	Pepsodent
'Your country needs you'	Army recruitment poster (WWI, with Lord Kitchener pointing)
'You're never alone with a'	Strand cigarette

Companies and Business

By: General

A and P, name from	Atlantic and Pacific (Tea) Company
Advertising Agency; Tory Party campaign run by	Saatchi and Saatchi
Advertising Campaigns; People associated with;-	
Henry Cooper	Brut
James Coburn	Schlitz
William Franklin	Schweppes
Maureen Lipman	British Telecom
Sir Robert Mark	Goodyear Tyres
Leo McKern	Lloyds Bank
Jimmy Savile	Car Seat Belts
Norman Vaughn	Rose's Chocolates
Orson Welles	Domecq Sherry
Advertising Jingle; Pioneer	Pepsi Cola
American Express; Created by	Wells, Fargo and Company
Amstrad, name from	Alan M.Sugar Trading
Apple Computers; Founders	Steve Jobs, Steve Wozniak
Auctioneers; London; Major	Christies, Sotheby's
BASF, name from	Badische Anilin und Soda Fabrik
Birds Eye Foods; Founder	Clarence Birdseye
Black Horse; Symbol	Lloyds Bank

Boots;-	
1st chemist shop	Nottingham
Founder	Jesse Boot
British Airways formed from	BEA, BOAC
BSA;-	
Originally produced	Guns
Stands for	Birmingham Small Arms
Chemicals Company;-	
Largest	Du Pont
Largest; UK	ICI
Cigarette Advertising; TV ban	1965
Coca Cola;-	
Invented by	Dr John S.Pemberton
1985 change	New Formula
Company;-	
Largest Turnover; UK	British Petroleum
Manufacturing; Largest; UK	ICI
Department Store;-	
1st	Marshall Field, Chicago
1st; UK (large)	Selfridges, Oxford Street
Detergent; Household; 1st	Persil
Dewhurst Butchers; Owner	Lord Vestey
Griffin; Symbol	Midland Bank
Hitler; Kept photograph of and vice versa	Henry Ford
HMV; Trade mark	Dog: Nipper
India; Company; Largest	Tata Group
Japan; Large conglomerates	Zaibatsu
Kentucky Fried Chicken; Founder	Colonel Sanders
Kleenex; Original name	Celluwipes
Marks and Spencers; Founders	Michael Marks, Thomas Spencer
McDonald's; Owner	Ray Kroc
NBC; Founder	David Sarnoff
Odeon; Founder	Oscar Deutsch
Package Tour; 1st	Thomas Cook's to Paris
Pawnbrokers' sign from	Medici coat of arms
Penguin Books; Founder	Allen Lane
Pepsi Cola, name from	Intended to relieve dyspepsia
RCA; Stands for	Radio Corporation of America
Restaurant Chain; Largest	McDonald's
Revlon; Founder	Charles Revson
RKO stood for (originally)	Radio – Keath – Orpheum
Rubber Factory; 1st	Akron, Ohio
Scotch Tape; Name from	Derogatory criticism for stinginess
Shell; Founder	Marcus Samuel
Sony; Original name	Tokyo Tsushin Kogyo
SR, name from	Sodium Ricinoleate
St Michael (Marks & Spencer), name from	Michael Marks
Tesco, name from	T.E. Stockwell (Tea Supplier), Jack Cohen
3M stands for	Minnesota, Mining and Manufacturing Company
Toyshop; Largest	Hamleys, Regent Street, London
Travel Bureau; Soviet	Intourist
Travel Company; 1st excursion	Leicester to Loughborough for a Temperance Society, Thomas Cook

Travellers' Cheques; 1st	Thomas Cook
Unilever:-	
Created from	Lever Brothers, Anton Jurgens (Dutch)
Original location	Port Sunlight
Vernon's Pools; Owner	Robert Sangster
Virgin Records; Owner	Richard Branson
Winfield (Woolworths); Name from	Frank Winfield Woolworth
Woolworths; 1st shop	Utica, New York
Xerox; Name from	Xerography, Dry (Greek: Xeros) copying

Currencies

By: Country → Currency

Albania	Lek, Qindarka
Argentina	Austral. Was: Peso
Australia	Dollar
Austria	Schilling, Groschen
Bhutan	Ngultrum
Brazil	Cruzado
Bulgaria	Lev
Burma	Kyaz
China	Yuan
Czechoslovakia	Koruna
Denmark	Krone
Egypt	Pound
Finland	Markka
France	Franc
Germany	Mark, Pfennig
Greece	Drachma
Guatemala	Quetzal
Hungary	Forint
India	Rupee, Paise
Indonesia	Rupiah
Israel	Pound
Italy	Lira
Japan	Yen
Korea	Won
Mexico	Peso
Netherlands	Guilder
Poland	Zloty
Portugal	Escudo
Russia	Rouble, Kopeck
Saudi Arabia	Riyal
South Africa	Rand
Spain	Peseta
Switzerland	Franc
Turkey	Lira
Yugoslavia	Dinar
Zaire	Zaire

Currency, Slang

By: Slang term → currency

Bob	1 Shilling
Buck	1 Dollar

Copper	1 (Old) Penny
Dime	10 Cents
Grand	1000 Pounds/1000 Dollars
Greenback	Any US note
Monkey	500 Pounds/500 Dollars
Nickel	5 Cents (US)
Nicker	1 Pound
Pony	25 Pounds
Quarter	25 Cents
Quid	1 Pound
Sawbuck	10 Dollars
Tanner	6 (Old) Pence
Two Bits	25 Cents

Economics and Finance

By: *General*

Bank of England;-	
Established by	William III
Nationalised	1946
Banks;-	
English; Big Four	Barclays, Lloyds, Midland, National Westminster
Scottish	Royal Bank of Scotland (largest), Bank of Scotland, Clydesdale Bank
Settle mutual accounts through	Bankers' clearing house
Bear	Speculator who sells expecting a fall in share price
Bond; Without mortgage backing	Debenture
Bull	Speculator who buys expecting a rise in share price
Dutch Auction	Price comes down till sold
Futures Market; Largest	Chicago
Gold;-	
Largest store	Federal Reserve Bank, New York
US Reserve; Main store	Fort Knox
Gresham's Law	'Bad money drives out good money'
Income Tax; 1st UK	1799, by William Pitt
Inflation; Worst	Hungary (1946)
Lloyds; Originally	Coffee House
Monetarism; Theoretician	Milton Friedman (Chicago School)
Paper Money; 1st	China
Physiocrats; Leader	François Quesnay
Royal Mint; Location	Llantrisant (since 1968)
Royal Mint; Location; Former	Tower Hill, London
Say's Law	Supply creates its own demand
Stock Exchange;-	
Indexes	US: *Dow Jones*. Japan: *Nikkei*. UK: *Financial Times* ('Footsy')
Oldest	Amsterdam
Paris	Bourse
UK; 1986 change	'Big Bang'
UK; Number	8
Stocks; Secure, government	Gilt edged securities
Tax; Non religious; 1st	To pay Richard the Lion Heart's ransom
Two metals; Exchange in terms of	Bimetallism

Unemployment and Inflation; Theory describing relationship	Phillips Curve
World Bank; Proper name	International Bank for Reconstruction and Development (IBRD)

Occupations, Traditional

By: Name → Meaning

Chandler	Candle maker, also General goods merchant
Cobbler	Shoe maker
Cooper	Barrel maker
Cordwainer	Shoe maker
Fletcher	Arrow maker
Mercer	Textile dealer
Vintner	Wine merchant

POLITICS AND HISTORY
Archaeology

By: General

Dating Organic Objects; Method used	Carbon 14
Dead Sea Scrolls	Found near: Qumran, Palestine, by an Arab Shepherd (1947)
Indus Valley; Prominent archaelogist involved	Sir Mortimer Wheeler
Jade Princess; Name	Dou Wan
Kitchen Midden; Meaning	Prehistoric waste heap
Knossos; Discoverer	Sir Arthur Evans
Linear B; Deciphered by	Michael Ventris
Machu Picchu; Discoverer	Hiram Bingham
Mycenae; Excavated by	Heinrich Schliemann
Pottery Fragment	Potsherd
Rosetta Stone; Significance	Allowed Jean Champollion to decipher hieroglyphics. Discovered: Near Nile Mouth
Troy; Discoverer	Heinrich Schliemann
Tutankhamun; Age at death	18
Tutankhamun's Tomb; Discoverers	Howard Carter and Lord Caernavon (1922)
Ur (Sumeria); Discoverer	Charles Woolley

Colonies, Former

By: Country → Colonizer

Notes: Excludes British only colonies. Multiple answers are in
historical order.

Algeria	France
Angola	Portugal
Brazil	Portugal
Crete	Venice, Turkey
Goa	Portugal
Guyana	Holland, Britain

Indonesia	Holland
Jamaica	Spain, Britain
Kampuchea	France
Laos	France
Libya	Italy
Madagascar	France
Mali	France
Malta	France, Britain
Mozambique	Portugal
Newfoundland	Britain (till 1949)
Niger	France
Philippines	Spain
South America (except Brazil)	Spain
Sri Lanka	Portugal, Holland, Britain
Surinam	Britain, Holland
Trinidad	Spain, Britain
Tunisia	France
Vietnam	France
Zaire (Congo)	Belgium

Customs and Superstitions

By: General

Bull Running	Pamplona, Spain in July
Christmas Tree; Origin	From Germany; Prince Albert popularized
Death; Cremation; Proportion, UK	Two-thirds
Destruction and giving away of goods; American Indians	Potlatch
Foot Binding	China, for upper class girls, to render useless
India; Widow burnt with husband	Suttee
Inheritance:-	
Firstborn son inherits	Primogeniture
Sons shared equally in estate; Saxon custom	Gavelkind
Kissing; Bestows powers of persuasion	Blarney Stone
Kissing under Plant	Mistletoe
Mayor weighed on initiation and leaving office	High Wycombe
Mistletoe; Used in church decorations; Only place	York Minster
Mourning Colour; China	White
New Year; First footer; Requirement	Dark
Pancake Race: Run since 15th Century	Olney, Buckinghamshire
Saint Swithin's Day; Rain on	Will rain for 6 weeks after
Suicide; Ritual; Japan	Hara-Kiri (strictly Seppuku)
Swans; Annual marking	Swan-Upping

Education

By: General

Birmingham University; Founder	Joseph Chamberlain
Blue; Oxford and Cambridge	Oxford: Dark. Cambridge: Light
Cambridge University:-	
Designation on degree	Cantab (Cantabrigienses – Latin name)

Honours degree examination	Tripos
Christ's Hospital (School); Alternate name	Bluecoat School
Comprehensive School; 1st	Holyhead, Wales (1949)
Degree Awarded when too ill to sit exam	Aegrotat
Delinquents; Schools for; Former	Approved Schools
Dinner at Oxbridge for past students	Gaudy
Eton; Founder	Henry VI
Exams; Solitary confinement for	Chinese Mandarins
Free Secondary Education; UK; Date	1944 (Universal)
Harrow;-	
Former pupils	Byron, Churchill
Founder	John Lyon
Hilary Term; Meaning	Oxford expression for Lent Term
Kindergarten; Pioneer	Friedrich Froebel
Open University; Opened	1970
Oxford University;-	
Designation on degree	Oxon (Oxonia – Latin name)
Library	Bodleian
Rhodes Scholarship	Oxford, for British, German, US
School Meals; Legislation	1906
Summerhill	
Founder	A.S.Neill (1923)
Location	Suffolk
Teachers; Salary scale	Burnham
University;-	
Oldest; Britain	Oxford University
Oldest; Northern Ireland	Queens University, Belfast
Oldest; Scotland	St Andrews
Oldest; US	Harvard
Winchester College; Students at	Wykehamists (Founder: William of Wykeham)

Espionage

By: General

Ace of Spies; Known as	Sidney Reilly
Willy Brandt; Personal assistant to	Günther Guillaume (caused resignation when found)
Burgess and Maclean;-	
Defected	1951
Warned by	Kim Philby
CIA;-	
1st Director	Allen Dulles
Predecessor	OSS (Office of Strategic Services)
Coding Machine; Germany used in WWII	Enigma
Communications Monitoring Service; US	National Security Agency
Couple executed 1953 amid controversy; US	Julius, Ethel Rosenberg
Drag; Wore	Chevalier D'Eon
Fourth Man	Anthony Blunt
Full Stops; Messages disguised as	Microdots
GCHQ Spy; Sentenced 1982	Geoffrey Prime

MI5; Director General, suspected of being a Russian agent	Sir Roger Hollis
MI6; Head of; Called	C
National Agencies;-	
Britain	MI6 (Military Intelligence 6) – based abroad. MI5 – based in Britain
France	SDECE
Israel	MOSSAD
South Africa	BOSS (Bureau of State Security)
US	CIA (Central Intelligence Agency)
USSR (Former)	KGB (Committee of State security)
Nuclear Spy; British of German origin	Klaus Fuchs
Gary Powers; Exchanged for	Rudolf Abel
Signals Intelligence; Headquarters	GCHQ, Cheltenham
SMERSH	Part of KGB
'Spycatcher'; Author	Peter Wright
Surveyor of the Queen's Pictures	Anthony Blunt
U2 Incident; Shot down over USSR	Francis Gary Powers
USSR; Master Spy; Died in Japan	Richard Sorge
Valet of British Ambassador to Turkey in WW11, stole D-Day plans	Cicero
Whittaker Chambers; Passed secrets to (US)	Alger Hiss

Heraldry

By: General

Animals; Positions;-	
Lying with Head erect	Couchant
On Hind Legs	Rampant
Sleeping	Dormant
Walking	Passant
Background; Term for	Field
College of Arms; Lowest officers	Pursuivants
Colours;-	
Black	Sable
Blue	Azure
Green	Vert
Purple	Purpure
Red	Gules
Colours; Term for	Tinctures
Furs	Ermine, Vair
Lion; Not rampant	Leoparde
Main Item	Charge
Metals	Or (Gold), Argent (Silver)
Organisation in Charge of	College of Arms/Herald's College

International Politics and Institutions

By: General

Amnesty International; Founder	Peter Benenson
EEC;-	
Britain joined	1973 (under Edward Heath)

Headquarters	Brussels
Joined with Britain	Denmark, Ireland
Left 1985	Greenland
Members; Additional	Denmark, Ireland, UK (1973), Greece (1981), Portugal, Spain (1986)
Members; Original	Belgium, France, Italy, Luxemburg, The Netherlands, West Germany
Treaty creating	Treaty of Rome (1957)
European Court of Justice; Headquarters	Luxemburg
ILO; Headquarters	Geneva
IMF; Headquarters	Washington
IMF, World Bank; Conference establishing	Bretton Woods (1944)
International Court of Justice; Headquarters	The Hague
League of Nations; Founded	1920
NATO;-	
Headquarters	Brussels
Withdrew from, 1966	France
Oil Producing Countries; Organisation	OPEC
Red Cross; Founder	Henri Dunant. Battle that prompts: Solverino
UN; Secretary Generals;-	
1946	Trygve Lie (Norway)
1953	Dag Hammarskjold (Sweden)
1961	U Thant (Burma)
1972	Kurt Waldheim (Austria)
1982	Javier Perez de Cuellar (Peru)
1992	Boutros Boutros-Ghali (Egypt)
United Nations;-	
Founding; Date	October 24th, 1945
Predecessor	League of Nations
Referendum voted against joining	Switzerland
Security Council; Permanent members	Britain, China, France, USSR, US (15 members in all)
Warsaw Pact; Official name	Eastern European Mutual Assistance Treaty
World Bank; Official name	International Bank for Reconstruction and Development
World Bank President; Former US Secretary of Defence became	Robert McNamara

Military

By: General

See Also: Wars and Battles/Science and Technology; Weapons and Military Technology

Air Ace; WWII; German	Baron Manfred Von Richthofen (the Red Baron). Team: The Flying Circus
Airforce;-	
German	Luftwaffe

Officer; Ranks	Pilot Officer, Flying Officer, Flight-Lieutenant, Squadron Leader, Wing Commander, Group Captain, Air Commodore, Air Vice-Marshal, Air Marshal, Air Chief Marshal, Marshal of the RAF
Officer training school; UK	Cranwell
Ranks	Aircraftsman, Flight Sergeant

Army;-

European country; None	Liechtenstein
Largest	China
Officer; Ranks	2nd Lieutenant, Lieutenant, Captain, Major, Lieutenant-Colonel, Colonel, Brigadier, Major-General, Lieutenant-General, General, Field Marshal
Officer training school; UK	Sandhurst
Oldest regiment	Royal Scots
Ranks	Private, Lance Corporal (1 stripe), Corporal (2 stripes), Sergeant (3 stripes), Company Sergeant Major
Top rank; US	General of the Army (5 Star General)
Units	Section, Platoon, Company, Battalion Regiment, Brigade, Division, Corps (largest)

Bugle Call;-

1st	Reveille
Last	Lights Out
Last but one	Last Post
Concentration Camp; 1st	British in Boer War
Continued fighting WWII till 1974; Japanese Soldier	Hiroo Onoda

Decoration;-

Highest; Civilian; UK	George Cross
Highest; Military; UK	Victoria Cross
Foreign Legion; Headquarters; Former	Sidi Ben Abbas (Algeria)
General, US; Parents Pacifists	Eisenhower

Guards;-

Distinguishing feature	Tunic button arrangement (among others)
Regiments	Scots, Coldstream, Grenadiers, Irish, Welsh
Gurkhas; From	Nepal
Home Guard; Original name	Local Defence Volunteers
Household Cavalry; Regiments	Life Guards, Blues and Royals
Marines; Which service	Soldiers, under Admiralty control
Military Hero; US; WWI, Originally conscientious objector	Sergeant York
Military Academy; US	West Point
Monty's Double	Clifford James
National Service; Abolished	1960

Navy;-

Officer; Ranks	Sub-Lieutenant, Lieutenant, Lieutenant Commander, Commander, Captain, Commodore, Rear-Admiral, Vice Admiral, Admiral, Admiral of the Fleet

Officer training school; UK	Dartmouth
Ranks	Ordinary Seaman, Able Seaman, Leading Rating, Petty Officer, Chief Petty Officer
Nuclear Weapons; Treaty Restricting	Non Proliferation Treaty (1968)
Parachute Regiment; Nickname	Red Devils
Pilot;-	
Lost both legs	Douglas Bader
WWI; Most victories	Baron Von Richthofen (the Red Baron). Plane: Fokker Triplane
WWI; Most victories; US	Eddie Rickenbacker
Private Army; Allowed	Duke of Atholl (Highlanders)
RAF;-	
Aerobatics team	Red Arrows
Base; Anti-Nuclear Campaign focus	Greenham Common, Berkshire
Formed	1918 (Royal Flying Corp – 1912)
Roman Army; Units	Century (100 men – commanded by a Centurion), Cohort (600 men), Legion (4000–6000 men)
Royal Engineers; Nickname	Sappers
Royal Highland Regiment; Nickname	Black Watch
Salutes;	Queen's Birthday: 62 guns. Opening of Parliament: 42 guns
SAS; Founder	David Stirling
Sick and Wounded; Rules governing	Geneva Conventions
Siege; SAS; 1st publicly involved	Iranian Embassy (1980)
Special Forces;-	
US	Delta Force
USSR (Former)	Spetsznaz
Supplies; In charge of	Quartermaster
Swiss Guard; Uniform; Designed by	Michelangelo
Underwater Expert; Disappeared investigating Russian ships	Buster Crabbe
Vatican; Army	Swiss Guard
Victoria Cross;-	
Made from	Gunmetal, originally from guns captured at Sebastopol, Crimean War
Most in one action	Rorke's Drift, Zulu war
Refused (and Knighthood)	T.E.Lawrence

Parliaments, Names of

By: Country, Territory → Name

Austria	Nationalrat, Bundesrat
Britain	House of Commons, House of Lords
Denmark	Folketing
Finland	Eduskunta
Germany	Lower House: Bundestag. Upper House: Bundesrat
Iceland	Althing
India	Lower House: Lok Sabha. Upper House: Rajya Sabha
Iran	Majlis
Ireland	Oireachtas. Lower House: Dail

Isle of Man	Tynwald. Elected part: House of Keys
Israel	Knesset
Japan	Diet
Jersey, Guernsey, Alderney	The States
Netherlands	States General
Northern Ireland (former)	Stormont
Norway	Storting
Poland	Sejm
Sark	Court of Chief Pleas
Spain	Cortes
Sweden	Riksdag
US	Congress (House of Representatives, Senate)

People

By: Name → *General*

Alexander the Great	
Died when	32
Fought over Kingdom after death	Diadochi
Horse	Bucephalus
King of	Macedon
Tutor	Aristotle
Steve Biko	South African student leader. Killed in prison
Bonnie Prince Charlie	Charles Edward Stuart, Pretender to the throne
Borgia Family	
Rodrigo	Pope Alexander VI
Rodrigo's daughter	Lucrezia
Rodrigo's son	Cesare
John Brown	Anti-slavery campaigner. Executed
Freed slaves at	Harper's Ferry, Virginia
Jimmy Carter	From: Plains, Georgia
Charlemagne	Founder of Holy Roman Empire
Winston Churchill	
Posts (included)	Home Secretary, First Lord of Admiralty (Liberal – when WWI breaks out), Chancellor of the Exchequer, First Lord of Admiralty (Conservative – when WWII breaks out), Prime Minister
Cinque	Slave revolt leader on ship *Amistad*. Set free
Croesus	
Known for	Wealth
Last King of	Lydia
Overthrown by	Cyrus
Darling, Grace	
Daughter of	Lighthouse keeper
Rescues survivors of	Wrecked *Forfarshire* on Farne Islands (1838)
Adolf Eichmann	Head of Gestapo's Jewish section
Executed in Israel	1962
Kidnapped from	Argentina

Kitty Fisher	18th Century prostitute
Anne Frank	Writer of WWII diary
Lived in	Amsterdam
Gandhi	English accent: Irish
Garibaldi	Member of Young Italy movement
Conquered	Sicily and Naples
Che Guevara	Killed in: Bolivia (1967)
Helen of Troy	Called: 'The Face that launched a 1000 ships'
Hereward the Wake	Saxon rebel against William I
Headquarters	Isle of Ely
Hitler	Born at: Braunau um Inn, Austria
Joan of Arc	
Birthplace	Domremy
Burnt at stake	1431
Captured at	Compiègne
Defeats English at	Orléans
Executed at	Rouen
Judge Jeffries	Tried Duke of Monmouth's supporters after attempt to overthrow James II (Bloody Assize)
Julius Caesar	River crossed to fight Pompey: Rubicon
Edward Kennedy	
Car crash at	Chappaquidick (1969)
Killed in crash	Mary Jo Kopechne
Henry Kissinger	Nobel Peace Prize winner (1973)
Secretary of State under	Nixon and Ford
Luther	Decree Outlawing: Edict of Worms
Flora MacDonald	Helped Charles Edward Stuart escape after the 1745 rebellion
Metternich	Austrian Chancellor
Bridey Murphy	Past life of Irish woman described by Virginia Tighe (US)
Mussolini	Executed at: Como
Napoleon	
Birthplace	Corsica
Died	St Helena
Exiled to	Elba, St Helena
Period after escape from Elba	100 days
Alexander Nevski	Name from: Victory on Neva River
Florence Nightingale	
Born in	Florence
War known for	Crimean
Nostradamus	16th Century Seer
Hiroo Onoda	Japanese soldier who continued fighting WWII till 1974
Pocohontas	American Indian princess
Father	Chief Powhatan
Saved life of	Captain John Smith
John Profumo	Secretary of State for War. Resigned after disclosure of involvement with prostitute, Christine Keeler
Keeler's Lover	Soviet Naval Attaché, Ivanov
Profumo introduced to Keeler by	Stephen Ward, Osteopath
Paul Revere	Rides from: Boston to Lexington
Cardinal Richelieu	Chief Minister to: Louis XIII
Roland	Killed at: Roncevalles

Albert Schweitzer	Missionary Hospital at: Lambarene, Gabon
Sir Philip Sidney	Killed at: Zutphen
Lambert Simnel	Pretender to throne of Henry VII
Became	Scullery Boy, Falconer
Margaret Thatcher	School: Kesteven and Grantham Girls School
Harold Wilson	Influential Private Secretary: Lady Falkender

Royalty

By: Country → Monarch

Belgium	King Baudouin
Bhutan	King Jigme Singye Wangchuck
China (last)	Emperor Pu Yi
Dynasty	Ching (Manchu)
Denmark	Queen Margrethe II
Consort	Prince Henrik (Count Henri Montpetot)
France (last)	Charles X (Louis Phillippe was 'King of the French', Louis Napoleon was Emperor)
Germany (last)	William II (Kaiser Wilhelm)
Iran (last)	Shah of Iran
Dynasty	Pahlavi
Italy (last)	Umberto II
Dynasty	Savoy
Japan	Emperor Hirohito
Jordan	King Hussein
Dynasty	Hashemite
Libya (last)	King Idris
Liechtenstein	Prince Franz Josef II
Luxemburg	Grand Duke Jean
Monaco	Prince Rainier III
Dynasty	Grimaldi
Morocco	King Hassan II
Nepal	King Birendra
Netherlands	Queen Beatrix
Consort	Prince Bernhard
Norway	King Olav V
Portugal (last)	Manuel II
Dynasty	Braganza
Russia (last)	Tsar Nicholas II
Dynasty	Romanov
Saudi Arabia	King Fahd
Spain	King Juan Carlos I
Dynasty	Bourbon
Sweden	King Carl Gustav
Dynasty	Bernadotte
Thailand	King Bhumibol
Tonga	King Taufa
UK	Queen Elizabeth II
Dynasty	Windsor

Royalty

By: Description → Monarch, General

Notes: Excludes UK.

Abolished by referendum, 1946	Italy
Affair with King's son; Queen	Elizabeth of Valois, married to Philip II of Spain. Son: Carlos
Ballet; Performed in many	Louis XIV
Castles; Obsession with	Ludwig II of Bavaria
China; Longest dynasty	Chou
Congo; Atrocities in; Accused of responsibility for	Leopold II of Belgium
Crowned; 35 years after death	Czar Peter III
Deformity; Hapsburg	Lip
Dirty Button; Ordered bodyguard to march to Siberia because of	Tsar Paul I
Dynasty; Longest reigning	Japan
Electric Chair; Used as throne	Emperor Menelik I of Ethiopia
Emperor;-	
Crowned himself	Napoleon
Retires	Diocletian, Charles V (Holy Roman)
Father; Donkey Driver	Shah of Iran
France;-	
Orléanist King; Only one	Louis Philippe
Throne; Heir to; Name	Dauphin
Greece; Monarchy abolished	1973
Heart Eaten by English Dean	Louis XIV
Heaviest	King of Tonga
Houses of Parliament; Foreign Monarch; 1st to address both	Juan Carlos (1986)
Japan;-	
Emperor; Ancient title	Mikado
1st to marry commoner	Crown Prince Akihito
Killed Son	Ivan the Terrible (1580)
Lockheed Bribery Scandal; Involved in	Prince Bernhard (Netherlands)
Lover murdered by father, while Crown Prince	Peter I of Portugal
Marine Biology; Authority on	Hirohito
Maroon; Only Royal family can have car in	Japan
Most Countries; Ruler of (in Europe)	Charles V (Holy Roman Emperor)
Name; Most popular; European Kings	Charles
Napoleon's Marshal; Descended from	Sweden (Marshal Bernadotte)
National Anthem; Had man to notify when played	Alfonso XIII of Spain
Never ascended throne; French King	Louis XVII
Paratroop Sergeant; Former; Emperor	Bokassa, Central African Empire
Peasant Shooting; Daily (Mock) ceremony	King Otto of Bavaria
PM; Became King	Ahmet Zogu – King Zog (Albania)
Portugal; 1st King	Alfonso I
Reign;-	
Longest	Pepi II (Pharaoh)
Longest; Europe	Louis XIV (72 years)
Satirist and Patron of arts	Catherine II
Shipyards; Worked in	Czar Peter the Great

Soap Commercials; Appeared in	Grace Kelly (later Princess Grace of Monaco)
Spider; Saved life by falling in poisoned drink	Frederick the Great
Swedish King; 1st with name Charles	Charles VII
Tall Guardsmen; Obsession with	Frederick William I of Prussia
Tattoo; 'Death to all Kings'	Charles XIV of Sweden (formerly General Bernadotte)
Wealth; Known for	Croesus

Royalty, UK

By: Description → Monarch, General

Abdicated; 1st	Richard II
Anti-smoking Tract; Wrote	James I
Bald at 31; Queen	Elizabeth I
Baldness revealed at execution; Queen	Mary Queen of Scots
Bathed every 3 months, 'Whether she needed it or not'	Elizabeth I
Battle;-	
Died in; Last	Richard III
Led troops in; Last	George II, Battle of Dettingen
Bigamist; King	George IV
Bodyguard; Royal, Resigned after homosexuality scandal	Commander Michael Trestrail
Buckingham Palace; 1st monarch to live in	Victoria
Burnt the cakes (legend)	King Alfred
Catholic Succession to throne; Act barring	Declaration of Rights and Bill of Rights
Cherry Brandy; Drank large amounts of	George IV
Children;-	
Most	Henry I
Most; Legitimate	Edward I (18)
Christian; 1st	Ethelbert
Commoner; 1st to marry	Henry IV
Cornwall; Duke of	Prince Charles
Coronation; Rolled down steps at	Lord Rolle at Queen Victoria's
Crowned;-	
On Battlefield	Henry VII
Twice	Charles II
Defender of the faith; 1st applied to	Henry VIII (by the Pope)
Deposed	James II
Divorce;-	
1st	Henry VIII
King attempted to	George IV (Caroline of Brunswick)
2nd	Princess Margaret
Duchy of Cornwall; Held by	Monarch's eldest son
Dukes: Royal	Cornwall (Prince Charles), Edinburgh, Gloucester, Kent, York (Prince Andrew)
Fat; Required machinery to use stairs	Henry VIII
Father dead 3 months when born; King	Henry VII
Fattest; King	George IV
Film; Acts in	Edward VIII (when Prince of Wales)
Finger; Extra	Anne Boleyn

1st to write name	Richard II (King John sealed Magna Carta)
Hanoverian Monarch; 1st	George I
Head covered; Right to Appear before Monarch with	Baron Kingsale, Archbishop of Canterbury
Heirs to throne	Male: Apparent. Female: Presumptive
Hitler had tea with	Duke and Duchess of Windsor
Honours; When awarded	New Years Day, Queen's Official Birthday
Hunchback; Popularly portrayed as	Richard III
Illegitimate	William I (The Conqueror)
'King over the water'	Jacobite term for Pretenders
Lancaster; House of; Kings	Henry IV, V, VI
Mad;-	
King	George III (Porphyria)
Queen; Considered	Caroline of Brunswick
Madness; Had Bouts of	Henry VI
Married Kings of England and France	Eleanor of Aquitaine (Louis VII, Henry II)
Mother 14 when born; King	Henry VII
Mountbatten; Originally	Battenberg (changed during WWI)
Murdered by Queen and her lover; King	Edward II
Never Crowned	Edward VIII
Never in England; Queen	Berengaria (Richard I)
Newspaper; Wrote letter to (*Times*)	Queen Victoria
Norman Monarch;-	
1st	William the Conqueror
Last	Stephen
Oak Tree; Found talking to	George III
Oldest;-	
At death	Queen Victoria (81)
Coming to throne	William IV (64)
Parent not a Monarch; Last	Queen Victoria
Parliament; 1st; In the reign of	Henry III
Pawned Crown Jewels to pay for marriage	Richard II
Plantagenet Monarch;-	
1st	Henry II
Last	Richard II
Plantagenets; Origin	Angevins (from Anjou, France)
Pretenders to Throne (Henry VII)	Perkin Warbeck, Lambert Simnel
Prince of Wales; Welsh; Last	Llewelyn
Prince Regent	George IV, while George III was alive (1811–1820)
Proposed to husband; Queen	Queen Victoria
Queen; In own right; Number	5
Refused Entrance to King's Coronation, Queen	Caroline of Brunswick (Queen of George IV)
Reign;-	
Longest	Queen Victoria (63 years)
Longest; King	George III
Shortest	Lady Jane Grey (13 days)
Shortest; King	Edward V
Richard; Kings with name; Similarity	All (3) died violently
Royal Family; Allowance	Civil List

Royal Household; Highest office	Lord Chamberlain
Royal Residence; Oldest	Windsor Castle
Royal Standard; Coats of Arms on	English, French, Scottish
Royal Toast: Drink when sitting	Royal Navy
Saxe Coburg; Only King	Edward VII
Shortest; Queen	Matilda (wife of William the Conqueror)
Sister-in-Law; Married	Henry VIII (Catherine of Aragon)
Spider; Inspired by, to fight English	Robert the Bruce
Spoke no English	George I
Stone; Kept under coronation chair	Stone of Scone. Stolen: 1950–1952
Stuart Monarch; 1st	James I
Stuart Monarch; Last	Anne
Submarine; 1st in	James I (supposed)
Teeth; Black	Elizabeth I
Toilet; Died on	George II
Tudor Monarch;-	
1st	Henry VII
Last	Elizabeth I
Two Queens; Father of; King	James II (Mary, Anne)
Urinated in Font	Ethelred the Unready
US; 1st to go to	George VI
Waves; Ordered to turn back	Canute
Welsh; Promised Prince who didn't spoke a word of English	Edward I (Gave infant Edward II)
Westminster Abbey; Coronation; 1st	William the Conqueror (1066)
Widowed; Remarried; Queen (last)	Catherine Parr
Wife;-	
Didn't meet till marriage ceremony	George III (Princess Charlotte)
Prisoner	George I
Wimbledon; Played at	George VI
'Wisest Fool in Christendom'; Described as	James I
York, House of; Kings	Edward IV, V, Richard III
Youngest;-	Mary, Queen of Scots (7 days)
King	Henry VI

Royalty, UK

By: Name → General

Alfred	
Daughter	Ethelfleda
Defeated Danes at	Edington
Escaped to when Danes invade	Athelney
King of	Wessex
Charles I	
Executed	1649
Wore at execution	2 shirts so as not to shiver and appear frightened
Charles II	
Chief Minister	Thomas Darby, Earl of Clarendon
Plot against	Rye House Plot
Duke of Edinburgh	
British subject; Became	1947
Naval Rank	Commander
Surname	Mountbatten

Edward IV	Younger brother: Duke of Clarence
Edward VII	
Age ascending throne	59
Prince of Wales at	1 month
Edward VIII	
Abdicated	December 1936
During WWII	Governor of Bahamas
Elizabeth I	
Favourite	Robert Dudley, Earl of Leicester
Plot to assassinate	Babbington, Ballard and others
Elizabeth II	
Birthday	Real: 21st April. Official: Saturday in mid June
Children's surname	Windsor
Coronation day	June 2nd, 1953
Heard she was Queen when in	Kenya
Marriage	November 1947
Position in war	Second Subaltern in ATS
Ethelred the Unready	Meaning: 'Without counsel'
George I	Spoke with Walpole in: Latin
George IV	Dandy; Friend of: Beau Brummell
George V	Elder Brother: Albert (Died)
George VI	
1st name	Albert (didn't use in deference to Queen Victoria)
Died of	Lung cancer
Henry I	
Legitimate son drowned in	White Ship disaster
Henry II	
Ordered murder of	Thomas Becket
Henry III	Defeated by: Barons under Simon De Montfort at Lewes
Henry VI	Rebellion against; Leader: Jack Cade
Henry VII	
Rebellion against; Pretenders	Lambert Simnel, Perkin Warbeck
Stepfather	Earl of Derby
Henry VIII	
Chancellor, had executed	Wolsey
Divorced from Catherine of Aragon	Thomas Cranmer
Met Francis I of France on	Field of the Cloth of Gold
James I	1st Stuart. 1st King of England and Scotland (James VI)
Called	'The Wisest fool in Christendom'
Mary, Queen of Scots	Kidnapped by: Earl of Bothwell
Mark Phillips	Father's occupation: Sausage manufacturer
Prince Andrew	
Married	Sarah Ferguson (July 1986)
Military college	Dartmouth Naval College
School	Gordonstoun
Ship in Falklands war	HMS *Invincible*
Prince Charles	
Houses	Highgrove, Chevening (formally)
Investiture	Caernarvon (1969)
Married	Lady Diana Spencer (1981)
Schools	Cheam, Gordonstoun, Timbertop (Australia)
University	Trinity College, Cambridge

Princess Anne
  Became Princess Royal   1987
  Married   Mark Phillips (1973)
  Separated   1989
Princess Margaret
  Born in   Glamis Castle
  Married   Antony Armstrong-Jones, Earl of Snowdon (1960)
Queen Anne   Last reigning Stuart. 1st Monarch of England and Scotland
  Favourites   Sarah (Duchess of Marlborough), Abigail Masham
Richard I
  Archbishop of Canterbury under   Hubert Walter
  Imprisoned at   Durenstein Castle
  Imprisoned by   Leopold of Austria
Richard III
  Killed by   Henry VII at Battle of Bosworth
  Rebellion against   Henry Stafford, Duke of Buckingham
The Queen Mother
  Born in   St Pauls Walden Bury
  Maiden name   Elizabeth Bowes-Lyon
Victoria
  Age at coronation   19
  Children   9
  Controversy over highland servant   John Brown
  Names   Alexandrina, Victoria
William II   Killed: In the New Forest
William III   Joint Ruler: Mary II (William and Mary)
William IV   Before becoming King: Duke of Clarence

Rulers, Names for

By: Place → Name

Algiers	Dey
Baghdad	Caliph
Buganda	Kabaka
Ethiopia	Negus
Hyderabad	Nizam
Persia	Shah
Russia	Tsar
Tibet	Dalai Lama
Tunis	Bey
Venice	Doge

Social and Welfare Issues

By: General

Census; 1st	1801
National Health Service;-	
1st Health Minister	Aneurin Bevan
Set up	1948
National Insurance; 1st	1911
Old Age Pensions;-	
1st	Germany (1889)

1st; UK	1908
Suicides;-	
Sex/Ratio; Attempted	Mainly female
Sex Ratio; Successful	60% men
Successful	5–10%
Welfare State; Report formulating	Beveridge Report

Society, Other

By: General

Cultures; Comparative study of	Ethnology
Historian;-	
Ecclesiastical of England	The Venerable Bede, at Jarrow
Jewish people	Josephus
19th Century English	Thomas Macaulay
Peloponnesian War	Thucydides
Roman; Described German tribes and	
history of the Empire	Tacitus
Marriage;-	
One Man, Several Women	Polygyny
One Woman, Several Men	Polyandry
Rule; Types of;-	
Military	Stratocracy
Nobility	Aristocracy
The Old	Gerontocracy
One person	Autocracy
The People	Democracy
Priests	Hierocracy, Theocracy
Wealthy	Plutocracy
Social Anthropology; Pioneer	Bronislaw Malinowski
Sociology; Name coined by	August Comte
Structural Anthropology: Leading	
proponent	Claude Levi-Strauss
Suicide; Pioneer study of	Emile Durkheim

Trade Unions

By: General

Actors' Union	Equity
AFL; President; 1st	Samuel Gompers
Chartist Movement; Union	Grand National Consolidated Trade Union
Dorset Farm Labourers; Transported for forming union	Tolpuddle Martyrs (1834)
France; Largest TU Confederation	CGT
GPMU; Formed from	SOGAT, NGA
Grape Union and Boycott Organiser, California	Cesar Chavez
Illegal; Law making Trade Unions	Combination Acts (1799/1800)
Initials;-	
ASLEF	Associated Society of Locomotive Engineers and Firemen
BALPA	British Airline Pilots Association
BIFU	Banking Insurance and Finance Union

COHSE	Confederation of Health Service Employees
CPSA	Civil and Public Services Association
GPMU	Graphical Paper Medium Union
ISTC	Iron and Steel Trades Confederation
MSF	Manufacturing, Science and Finance Union
SCPS	Society of Civil and Public Servants
UCATT	Union of Construction, Allied Trades and Technicians

Largest;-	
Ever	Solidarity (Poland)
UK	Transport and General Workers Union
US	Teamsters Union
MSF; Formed from	ASTMS, TASS
Non Union Firm; Largest	IBM
SOGAT 82; Made up of	SOGAT, NATSOPA
Strike; 1st	Egypt, Rameses III tomb workers
Strike over Union Recognition, photograph processing factory	Grunwicks
Strikes; Allows Unions to be sued for damages over	Taff Vale Decision (1901)
Teamster Leader; Jailed for corruption	Jimmy Hoffa
Terrible Twins; Known as	Jack Jones, Hugh Scanlon
TGWU; General Secretary 1920s and 30s	Ernest Bevin
TUC;-	
Founded	1868
General Secretary	Norman Willis
General Secretary; Previous	Len Murray
US;-	
Formed 1869	Knights of Labour
Main Union Federation	AFL-CIO
Steel strike at Carnegie Steel Works	Homestead (1892)
White Paper on Trade Unions; 1964–1970 Labour Government	*In Place of Strife*

Treaties

By: Name → War

Adrianople	Russo–Ottoman War (1829)
Aix La Chapelle	Austrian Succession (1748)
Amiens	(During) Napoleonic Wars (1802)
Berlin; Congress of	Russo–Turkish War (1878)
Brest–Litovsk	Russia, Germany after WW1 (1918)
Frankfurt	Franco–Prussian War (1871)
Lausanne	Greece, Turkey after WW1 (1923)
Paris	American War of Independence (1783)
Shimonoseki	Sino–Japanese War (1895)
Tilsit	Napoleon with Russia and Prussia (1807). Venue: Middle of River Niemen

Versailles	WWI (1919)
Westphalia	Thirty Years War (1648)

United Kingdom

By: Description → Name, General

Act;-

Allows temporary release from prison to prevent starvation	Cat and Mouse Act
Compels all office holders to take Church of England communion	Test Act (1673)
Henry VIII's children with Ann Boleyn made royal line	Act of Succession
Restricts trade by non English Ships	Navigation Acts
Act of Parliament; Procedure establishing	Royal Assent
Agricultural Workers Riots, 1830s mythical leader	Captain Swing
Alderman; Former Scottish equivalent	Baillie
Ambassadors, accredited to	Court of St James
Antagonism; 19th Century politicians famous for	Disraeli, Gladstone
Architecture; Tax influences	Window Tax (1695–1851)
Attempted Murder of homosexual lover; Liberal leader acquitted of	Jeremy Thorpe
Bill; Number of readings	3
Bowls; Finished game before sailing to fight Armada	Sir Francis Drake
Brothel, West End; Exposed with Prince of Wales client	Cleveland Street scandal (1889)
Budget; Usually presented on	Tuesday

Cabinet;-

Member in both World Wars	Churchill, Lord Beaverbrook
Most positions held	Winston Churchill
Senior member without specific function	Lord Privy Seal
Cabinet Minister; Woman; 1st	Margaret Bondfield, Minister of Labour (1929)
Catholics; Allowed to stand for Parliament from	1829
Chancellor; Resigned after budget details leaked	Hugh Dalton
Child Labour; Prominent campaigner against	Lord Shaftesbury
Civil Service; Head of Government department	Permanent Secretary
Civil War; Royalist HQ	Oxford
Cloak; Put in puddle in front of Queen Elizabeth	Sir Walter Raleigh
Common Land; Fencing of	Enclosure

Constituency;-

Historical; Tiny population	Rotten Boroughs
No Voters	Old Sarum
Under water	Dunwich
Co-op; 1st	Rochdale Society of Equitable Pioneers (Weavers)

County; Royal representative	Lord Lieutenant
Dictator; Only	Oliver Cromwell
Duel; Foreign and War Ministers	George Canning, Lord Castlereagh
Duke; Premier	Duke of Norfolk
Election Slogan; 'You've never had it so good'	Macmillan (1959)
Embassy Siege; SAS released hostages	Iranian Embassy (1980)
Empire; Outside Europe; 1st territory	St John's, Newfoundland (founded by Sir Humphrey Gilbert)
Father of the House	(Traditionally) MP with longest continuous membership
Fenian Bomb Attack on jail	Clerkenwell (1867)
Fire Brigade; Highest rank	Chief Officer
Fishing Fleet Fired on, 1904	Russian Fleet off Hull, believing Japanese Fleet
Food Shipments; US WWII scheme	Lend Lease
Forged Letter; Used to discredit Labour, 1924	Zinoviev letter
General Belgrano Sinking; Civil Servant prosecuted for revealing information	Clive Ponting
General Strike; 1926, Miners' slogan	'Not a penny off the pay, not a minute on the day'
Grouse Shooting; Shot beater	Lord Whitelaw
Hangman; Offered to act as, if capital punishment reintroduced	Peter Bruinvels
Holy Roman Emperor; Henry III's brother became	Richard of Cornwall
House of Commons;-	
Forbidden to enter	Monarch
Number that can be seated	About 456
Quorum	40
Term used for Lords (and vice versa)	Another place
Voting; Sides	Ayes, Noes
House of Lords;-	
Bishop; Equivalent rank to	Baron
Black Rod; Special duty	To summon Commons to Lords to hear the Queen's Speech
Life Peer's status	No Vote
Members; Types	Lords Spiritual and Temporal
Quorum	3
Speaker	Lord Chancellor
Speaker's seat	Woolsack
Usher and official messenger	Black Rod
Voting; Sides	Contents, Not Contents
Julius Caesar; Landed at	Deal
Knight; Dubbing of; Term for	Accolade
Knighthood;-	
Highest order	Garter, Thistle (Scotland)
Oldest order	Garter
Labour Government; 1st	1924. PM: Ramsay MacDonald
Labour Party;-	
Constitution; Socialist clause	Clause 4
Norma Levy Scandal; Tory Minister involved in	Lord Lambton
Libyan People's Bureau; Policewoman shot from	Yvonne Fletcher (1984)

Life Peerages; Instituted	By Macmillan (1958)
Lord Chancellor; Seat	Woolsack
Lord Protectors	Oliver Cromwell, Richard Cromwell
Majority; Largest	Liberals (1832)
Mayor;-	
London; Official residence	Mansion House
Scottish equivalent	Provost
Miners' Strike, 1984–85; Coal Board Chairman	Ian McGregor
Minister of Information; 1st	Lord Beaverbrook
Minister without Portfolio; Office	Chancellor of the Duchy of Lancaster
MP(s);-	
Asian; 1st	Dadabhai Naorogi (1892)
Atheist; 1st	Charles Bradlaugh
Heaviest	Cyril Smith
Jewish; 1st	Lionel Rothschild (1858)
Labour; 1st	Keir Hardie
Make sure they attend important votes	Whips
Means of resignation	Applying for Chiltern Hundreds
Named by Speaker	Has to leave House
Not office holder	Back Bencher
Number	650
Only speech recorded: Request for window open	Isaac Newton
People not eligible to stand as	Peers, Priests, Public Office Holders, Members of Armed Forces, Felons, Insane
Salaries; Introduced	1911
Tory then Labour MP, later Fascist leader	Oswald Mosley
Woman; 1st	Countess Markievicz (1918)
Woman; 1st to take seat	Nancy Astor (1919)
Youngest	Edmund Waller (16)
Youngest; Woman	Bernadette Devlin (22)
National Health Cuts; Resigned from Cabinet over	Harold Wilson
Nuclear Base; Extended Women's sit in at	Greenham Common
Ombudsman; Official name	Parliamentary Commissioner (for Local Administration)
Order of Merit; Holders; Number	24
Order of the Garter; Established by	Edward III
Parliament;-	
Act to end session	Prorogation
Maximum Term	5 years
Opening day	Tuesday
Public gallery	Strangers' Gallery
Shortest	1 Day (Edward I, 1306)
Parliamentary Debates; Record of	Hansard (from first printer)
Peer(s);-	
Allowed to renounce titles	1963
Jewish; 1st	Nathan Rothschild
Removing rights of, for crimes	Attainting
Poor Law; Introduced at	Speenhamland
Poulson Affair caused resignation	Reginald Maudling

Prime Minister;-

Assassinated	Spencer Perceval (1812)
Country residence	Chequers (Court)
Cricket; 1st Class, played	Alec Douglas Home
Divorce case; Cited in at 78	Lord Palmerston
Fear of opening letters	Lord Liverpool
1st	Robert Walpole (1721)
Illegitimate	Ramsay MacDonald
Labour; 1st	Ramsay MacDonald (1924)
Liberal; Once Tory Chancellor	Gladstone
Longest term	Robert Walpole (20 years)
Longest term; 20th Century	Margaret Thatcher
Longest term; Without break	William Pitt the younger (18 years)
Oldest	William Gladstone (84)
Publisher; Former	Harold Macmillan
Re-elected after full term	Lord Salisbury, Margaret Thatcher
Renouncing title allows to become	Alec Douglas Home
Residence	10 Downing St. No 11: Chancellor. No 12: Whip's Office
Shortest term; Single period	Duke of Wellington, 22 days. (Earl of Bath's 3 days normally discounted)
Shortest term; Total	George Canning (4 months)
Shortest term; 20th Century	Bonar Law (7 months)
Suez Crisis led to resignation	Sir Anthony Eden
Suicide, Committed	Lord Castlereagh
Tallest	James Callaghan
Without seat in Commons or Lords	Alec Douglas Home (1963)
Youngest	William Pitt the younger (24)
Youngest; 20th Century	Harold Wilson (48)
Private Army; Allowed to keep by Royal Warrant	Duke of Atholl
Privy Council; Full meeting; Occasion	Death or intended marriage of Sovereign
Privy Councillors; Addressed as	Right Honourable
Queen's Speech; Read in	House of Lords
Referendum; 1st	EEC (1975)
'Rivers of Blood' Speech	Enoch Powell
Robert Owen; Model Community	New Lanark, Scotland
Roman Colony; 1st	Colchester
Roman Invasion; 1st	55 BC by Julius Caesar
Romans; Revolt against	Boadicea, Queen of the Iceni
Salamanders; Keeps	Ken Livingstone
Saxon Invaders; 1st	Hengist and Horsa
Saxon Parliament	Witan
Scotland;-	
King; 1st	Kenneth
Kings crowned at, 12th–15th Century	Scone Palace
Slavery abolished	1807
Spanking of Young Boys; MP resigned over	Harvey Proctor
System of Relief for agricultural labourers	Speenhamland System
Tax to buy off Danish raiders	Danegeld
Taxation; 1st	Under Pitt the Younger (1799)
Terrorist Group; 1960s; Carry out London Bomb attacks	Angry Brigade

Title; Oldest	Earl
Towers; Built against Napoleonic invasion	Martello Towers
Voting; Excluded from	Peers, Lunatics, Criminals
Voting Age; 18; Introduced	1969
Wales; Independence leader 15th Century	Owain Glyndwr (Owen Glendower)
Walpole (Prime Minister); Formal post	First Lord of the Treasury
William the Conqueror; Landed at	Pevensey Bay
Women's vote	1918 (over 30), 1928 (universal)

United Kingdom

By: Term, Name → General

Act of Settlement	Stipulates future Monarchs must be Church of England (1701)
Act of Supremacy	Makes Sovereign head of Church of England
Act of Union	
England and Scotland	1707
Britain and Ireland	1800
Bedchamber Crisis	Queen Victoria refused change to Ladies of household nominated by Peel's Government
Bevin Boys	Men 'conscripted' into mines, WWII
Name from	Ernest Bevin, Minister of Labour
Bloody Assizes	Against supporters of Monmouth's rebellion
By	Judge Jeffreys
Cato Street Conspiracy	Plot to kill Ministers and overthrow Lord Liverpool's government (1820)
Leader	Arthur Thistlewood
Chartists	Name from: People's Charter
Cinque Ports	Hastings, Romney, Hythe, Dover, Sandwich (later – Winchelsea, Rye)
Co-operative Movement	Founded: Rochdale (1844)
Corn Laws	Stop grain imports to Britain (1815)
Coupon Election	1918
Domesday Book	Survey for tax purposes (1086)
Fabian Society	Prominent members: G.B.Shaw, Sidney and Beatrice Webb
General Strike	In defence of miners (1926)
Glencoe Massacre	Campbells massacred Macdonalds
Glorious Revolution	Overthrow of James II and succession of William and Mary
Gordon Riots	Anti-Catholic ('No Popery', 1780)
Leader	Lord George Gordon
Great Exhibition	Crystal Palace, Hyde Park (1851)
Great Fire of London	1666
Started	Pudding Lane
Great Plague	1665
Gunpowder Plot	November 5th, 1605
Conspirators included	Guy Fawkes, Robert Catesby, Thomas Percy
King	James I

Heptarchy	7 Anglo-Saxon Kingdoms, 4th–9th Century, England
Ironsides	Cromwell's soldiers
Jacobite Rebellion	1645
Defeated at	Culloden
Jacobites won at	Prestonpans
Jacobites	Supporters of the House of Stuart
Name from	Jacobus – James
Khaki Election	1900
Levellers	Radical Civil War group
Leader	John Lilburne
Lollards	Followers of: John Wycliffe (1834)
Long Parliament	1646–1660
Purge of	Pride's Purge (1648)
Remnant	Rump
Luddite Riots	Machine breaking movement (1811)
Possibly named after	Ned Ludd
Magna Carta	
Imposed by	Barons
Location	Runnymede
Sealed by	King John (1215)
Why not signed	King John couldn't write
Mohocks	18th Century aristocratic gangs
Monmouth's Rebellion	
Defeated at	Battle of Sedgemoor
Landed at	Lyme Regis
Mutiny; At Spithead, Nore	Against conditions (1797)
Mutiny on the *Bounty*	1789
Bounty carries	Breadfruit trees
Captain	Bligh
Mutineers go to	Pitcairn Island
Mutineer's leader	Fletcher Christian
National Government	Coalition (1931)
Old Contemptibles	British Expenditionary Force Soldiers, WW1
Peasant's Revolt	1381
Leaders	Wat Tyler, John Ball
Peterloo Massacre	Soldiers attack meeting at St Peter's Field, Manchester (1819)
Pilgrimage of Grace	Roman Catholic Uprising (1536)
Leader	Robert Aske
Poor Law	Established Workhouses (1834)
Popish Plot	(Claimed) Jesuit to kill Charles II
Alleged by	Titus Oates
Pride's Purge	1648, Purge of Long Parliament
Protectorate	Period of Cromwell's rule as Lord Protector (1653–1659)
Reform Act (1st)	1832
Restoration	Charles II becomes King (1660)
Rump	Remains of Long Parliament after Pride's Purge
Short Parliament	1640
Length	3 weeks
Six Acts	Curtail Public Meetings, etc. (1819)
Star Chamber	Tribunal under the Tudors
Suffragettes	Movement for women's vote
Prominent leaders	The Pankhursts

Taff Vale decision	Allowed TUs to be sued for damages over a strike (1901)
Tolpuddle Martyrs	Dorset farm labourers transported for forming a union
Westland Affair Resigned over	Helicopter Company takeover Michael Heseltine
Winter of Discontent	Winter of industrial unrest (1978–9)

United States

By: *General*

Act; Provided land free	Homestead Act (1862)
American Revolution; Frenchman played prominent role in	Marquis De Lafayette
Anti-Communist Witch-hunt; Organiser; 1950s	Senator Joseph McCarthy
Back to Africa Movement; Leader	Marcus Garvey
Black Muslims Official name Former Leader	Nation of Islam Elijah Muhammed
Black Panthers Former Leader	US Black Power Group Stokely Carmichael
Boston Tea Party	Protest against: British Tea Tax
Burglary of Democratic HQ in Washington	Watergate
Bus Boycott	Rosa Parks refusing to give seat up started (1955)
Child; 1st born of English parents in America	Virginia Dare (1587)
Civil Rights Demonstration; Federal Troops called in to protect	Selma, Alabama (1956)
Civil War; States	11 Southern, 23 Northern
Congress; Women; 1st	Jeanette Rankin (1916)
Constitutional amendments	13th: Abolishes slavery. 18th: Prohibition. 19th: Women's vote
Declaration against European interference; 19th Century	Monroe Doctrine
Declaration of Independence; Date	July 4th, 1776
Democratic Party; Chicago Boss	Boss Tweed
Desegregation; University of Mississippi; 1st black to enter	James Meredith
Emancipation Proclamation By	Declaration freeing slaves during US Civil War Abraham Lincoln
Executed for Terrorism; Italian immigrants; Pardoned 1977	Sacco and Vanzetti
Fireside chats; Radio broadcasts	F.D.Roosevelt
Georgia; Marched through	General Sherman
Gettysburg Address	Lincoln's speech (1863)
Gold; Discovery on land caused gold rush	John Sutter
Gold Rush; Starts	1849
Good Neighbour Policy	Introduced by Roosevelt towards Latin America (1928)
GOP; Stands for	'Grand Old Party' – The Republicans
Grape Workers Union Leader; Organised boycott	Cesar Chavez (1968)

Haymarket Massacre	US Police fire on crowd after explosion at May Day Rally (1886)
Honorary Citizen; Only	Churchill
Indian Chief; Surrendered to General Miles	Geronimo
Intolerable Acts	British Legislation to punish US colonists after Boston Tea Party
Invited to become King	Prince Henry of Prussia (1786)
Irangate Scandal	US government implicated in providing arms for Iran in return for funds to Nicaraguan Contras
Testimony, Famous	Oliver North
J.F.Kennedy; Attorney General	Robert Kennedy
Kitchen Cabinet	President Andrew Jackson's unofficial advisers
Louisiana Purchase	USA buys Mississippi Valley from France
Manhattan Island	
Purchased from Indian Tribes for	60 Guilders
Purchaser	Governor, Peter Minuit
Mason–Dixon Line	Boundary between north and south in pre-civil war America
Massacre; Police fire at Chicago demonstration	Haymarket Massacre (1886)
National Guard, Ohio shot 4 students during anti-war demonstration	Kent State University (1970)
New Deal	Franklin Roosevelt's recovery program in the US (1930s)
Oil Bribery Scandal involving Albert Fall under President Warren Harding	Teapot Dome Affair
Pilgrim Fathers	Settlers in America
Established	Plymouth Colony
1st to land	John Alden
Landed in	Massachusetts
Ship	*Mayflower*
President:-	
Appeared in shirt advertisement	Ronald Reagan
Assassinated	Lincoln, Garfield, McKinley, Kennedy
Bachelor (only)	James Buchanan
Bald	Eisenhower, Van Buren
Bath; Got stuck in	Taft
British Knight	Eisenhower
China; 1st to visit	Ulysses Grant
Confederate states	Jefferson Davis
Democrat turned Republican; 1st	Ronald Reagan
Divorced; 1st	Ronald Reagan
Duel; Killed opponent in	Andrew Jackson
Elected for 4 terms	F.D.Roosevelt
Elected unanimously (by Electoral College)	George Washington
Elected with 1 vote against (by Electoral College)	Monroe
Ex-President re-elected; Only	Grover Cleveland (22nd & 24th)
Father and son	John Adams, John Quincy Adams
Father, UK Ambasssador	J.F.Kennedy

1st 5	Washington (1st), Adams, Jefferson, Madison, Monroe
For 1 day	David Atchison (Zachary Taylor wouldn't be sworn in on a Sunday)
Hospital; 1st born in	Jimmy Carter
Illegitimate child; Accused of	Grover Cleveland
Impeachment; Avoided by 1 vote	Andrew Johnson
Imprisoned by British during War of Independence	Andrew Jackson
Longest term	F.D.Roosevelt (12 years)
Male model; Former	Gerald Ford
Not elected as President or Vice President; Only	Gerald Ford
Occupation; Most common	Lawyer
Offered Democratic and Republican nominations	Eisenhower
Oldest to take office	Ronald Reagan (69)
Only child	None
President of Columbia University	Eisenhower
Quaker	Nixon
Qualifications	Natural born, 14 years residence, at least 35 years old
Residence	White House
Resigned	Richard Nixon
Roman Catholic; 1st	John Kennedy
Terms; Limit (currently)	2
Unelected; Longest	Gerald Ford (3 years)
WW1; During	Woodrow Wilson
Youngest	Theodore Roosevelt (on McKinley's assassination)
Youngest; Elected	John Kennedy (43)
Presidential Campaign; Cried on TV during	Edmund Muskie
Presidential Candidate;-	
Democratic; 1988	Michael Dukakis
Ran from prison	Eugene Debs (1912)
Presidential Slogan;-	
'Full Dinner Pail'	McKinley
'Great Society'	Lyndon Johnson
'New Deal'	F.D.Roosevelt
'New Frontier'	John Kennedy
'Would you buy a used car from this man?'	(Anti-) Nixon
Prohibition	18th Amendment banning alcohol, in force 1917–1933
Act enforced	Volstead Act
Ride; To warn American forces of British troops	Paul Revere
Riots, Los Angeles	Watts (1965)
Roosevelt; 1930s recovery programme	New Deal
School Integration; Federal Troops enforced	Little Rock, Arkansas (1957)
Secretary of State;-	
Eisenhower's	John Foster Dulles
Nixon's	Henry Kissinger
Senator; Black; 1st	Edward Brooke
Size of US; Doubled	Louisiana Purchase (1803)

Slave; Former; Prominent abolitionist	Harriet Tubman
Slave Uprising in Virginia	Nat Turner Insurrection (1831)
Slavery;-	
Abolished	1863
Escape network to the north	Underground Railroad
Slogan during dispute over taxation	
with Britain	'No taxation without representation'
State; 1st	Delaware
Symbol;-	
Democratic Party	Donkey
Republican Party	Elephant
Tammany Hall	US, New York Democratic Party HQ
Townshend Acts	Taxes on America by Britain, sparked off revolt
Traitor; For British in War of Independence	Benedict Arnold
Unemployed March to Washington, 1894	Coxey's Army
Vice Presidents;-	
Carter	Walter Mondale
Eisenhower	Nixon
Ford	Nelson Rockefeller
Johnson	Hubert Humphrey
Kennedy	Johnson
Nixon	Spiro Agnew, Gerald Ford
Reagan	George Bush
Bush	Dan Quayle
Vice President; Resigned after income tax evasion charge	Spiro Agnew
Vice Presidential Candidate; Woman; Major Party; 1st	Geraldine Ferraro (1984)
Vietnam; Secret documents of US involvement	Pentagon Papers
Revealed by	Daniel Ellsberg (1971)
Witchcraft; Trials; 17th Century	Salem
Wobblies	Industrial Workers of the World, US General Union

Wars and Battles

By: Description → War

Atom Bomb; 1st used	Hiroshima: August 6th, 1945. Nagasaki: August 9th, 1945
Britain; Last land battle	Culloden (1746)
Casualties; Most; Military	Somme
Ear; Allegedly caused	War of Jenkin's ear
Football; British troops advanced kicking	Battle of Loos (1915), Somme (1916)
Football Match; War provoked by	Honduras against El Salvador (1969)
Last Land Battle; England	Sedgemoor (1685)
Left Boots Only; British Army supplied with	Crimean War
Maine; Sinking of; Starts war	Spanish–American War (1898)
Nelson puts telescope to blind eye	Battle of Copenhagen. Signal from: Admiral Hyde Parker

Pears: Ultimate Quiz Companion

Organised to boost newspaper circulation	Cuban–US War (by W.R.Hearst)
Poison Gas (Chlorine); 1st use	Second Battle of Ypres (1915)
Shortest	Britain v Zanzibar (1896) (38 minutes)
Spartans, 300; Hold out against Persians	Thermopylae
Tanks; 1st used	Somme (1916)
Telegram; Caused	Franco–Prussian War (1870) (Ems Telegram)

Wars and Battles

By: Name → Adversaries, General

Actium	Augustus Caesar defeated Mark Antony and Cleopatra
Agincourt	Henry V defeated French (1415). Normandy captured
Alamo	Mexican General Santa Ana besieged Texas Fortress (1836)
Killed	Davy Crockett
American Independence	
1st major battle	Bunker Hill
Treaty ended	Paris
Washington wintered at	Valley Forge
Appomattox	General Lee surrendered to General Grant in US Civil War
Arab/Israeli Wars	
1948	1st
1956	Suez War
1967	'Six Day War'
1973	'Yom Kippur War'
1978 Peace	'Camp David Agreements'
Austerlitz	Napoleon's victory over Russia (Marshal Kutuzov) to take Moscow (1812)
Austrian Succession	Over Maria Theresa's accession to throne. Treaty ended; Aix La Chapelle (1748)
Balaklava	In Crimean War. Charge of the Light Brigade took place during (1854)
Bannockburn	Robert the Bruce defeated Edward II (1314)
Battle of Britain	Air battle (1940)
Blenheim	Duke of Marlborough against French under Marshal Tallard
Boer War	
Sieges	Ladysmith, Mafeking, Kimberley
British Commander	Lord Kitchener
Bosworth Field	Ended War of the Roses. Richard II killed, Henry VII King
Location	Leicestershire
Boyne	William III defeated James II in Ireland (1690)
Bulge, Battle of the	Last German offensive of WWII. Patton defeated Germans

Bunker Hill	US v British. 1st major battle of American Revolution
Cannae	Hannibal defeated Romans
Caxamarco	Spanish (Pizarro) against Incas. Atahualpa captured
Chalons	Final defeat of the Huns
Charge of the Light Brigade	During Battle of Balaklava, Crimean War
Cod War	Iceland–UK dispute over Fishing Rights (1976)
Coral Sea, Battle of	US defeated Japan in Pacific (1942)
Crecy	Edward III defeated French under Philip VI (1346)
Crimean War	Turkey, Britain and France against Russia
Achieved fame in	Florence Nightingale
Treaty ended	Treaty of Paris
Crusades	
Number	8
Saladin seized Jerusalem	3rd
Culloden	Defeat of Bonnie Prince Charlie by Duke of Cumberland
Dambusters Raid	
Bouncing bomb designer	Barnes Wallis
From	Scampton
Leader	Guy Gibson
Planes	Lancasters
D-Day Landings	Allied invasion of France (June 6th, 1944)
Beaches	Omaha, Utah, Gold, Sword, Juno
Code name	Overlord
Dien Bien Phu	Vietnamese under Vo Nguyen Giap defeat French (1954)
Dunkirk	Evacuation of British and French forces (1940)
Eighty Years War	Dutch independence struggle against Spain
El Alamein	General Montgomery defeated Rommel (1942)
Entebbe, Raid on	(Uganda) Israeli Commandos freed hostages (1976)
Falkland Islands, Battle of (WWI)	Sir Frederick Sturdee (Britain) defeated Graf Spee (Germany). Scharnhorst sunk
Falklands War	
Argentina Ruler	General Galtieri
Argentinian Air Force; Head of	Lami Dozo
Argentinian ship sunk; Biggest	*General Belgrano*
British airfield; Nearest	Ascension Islands
British destroyers sunk	*Sheffield, Coventry*
British frigates sunk	*Ardent, Antelope*
Exocet sinks	HMS *Sheffield*
Islands seized	April 1982
Task Force Commander	Admiral John Woodward
Flodden Field	Earl of Surrey defeated James IV of Scotland
Football War	Honduras and El Salvador (1969)

Gallipoli	Attempted landing in Turkey, WW1, by allies, especially Australia and New Zealand
Gettysburg	Union forces under Meade defeat Robert E.Lee (US Civil War, 1863)
Glorious 1st of June	Lord Howe, Britain defeated French Fleet at Ushant (1794)
Green Mountain Boys Leader	US Force in Independence War Ethan Allen
Gulf War	Against Iraq after Kuwait Invasion
Hastings	William the Conqueror's victory over Harold II
Fought at	Senlac Hill
Tapestry depicts	Bayeux
Hiroshima	1st atom bomb
Code name	Little Boy
Date	August 6th, 1945
Pilot	Paul Tibbets
Plane	Enola Gay
Hundred Years War	England v France
Major battles	Crecy, Poitiers, Agincourt
Duration	116 years
Indo–Pakistan	Over Kashmir (1965)
Iwo Jima	US v Japan
Flag raised on	Mount Suribachi
Jenkin's Ear	England against Spain over alleged injury to English Captain
Jutland	British Navy under Jellicoe against Germany under Scheer (1916)
Khartoum, Siege of	General Gordon killed at 10 month siege by Mahdists
Korean War	North Korea, China against South Korea and UN Forces
Allied Commander	Douglas Macarthur
Border	38th Parallel
Talks ended	Panmunjom talks
Lepanto	Christians against Turks (Naval). Last major battle with galleys
Little Big Horn	General Custer's 'Last Stand'
Lucknow, Siege of	Raised by: Sir Colin Campbell
Mafeking; Relief of	British under Baden Powell v Boers under General Cronje. Ended after 217 days (1900)
Marathon	Athens defeated Persians under Darius
Marengo	Napoleon defeated Austrians (1800)
Metaurus	Romans defeated Carthaginians
Mulberry	Floating Harbour used in D-Day landings
My Lai Massacre	Vietnam War 1968. Troops under Lieutenant Calley destroyed village
Nagasaki	2nd Atomic Bomb
Bomb called	Fat Man
Date	August 9th, 1945
Nations; Battle of	European powers against Napoleon. Exiled to Elba after defeat

Navarino	English, French, Russian Fleets defeated Turkish and Egyptian Fleet (1827)
Nile	Nelson defeated French Fleet
Alternative name	Aboukir Bay
Nore	Mutiny (1797)
Omdurman, Battle of	Kitchener defeated Khalifa of Sudan
Operation;-	
Avalanche	Allied invasion of Italy
Barbarossa	WWII, German invasion of USSR
Bernhard	German plan to debase the currency with forged notes
Dynamo	Dunkirk evacuation
Overlord	Allied invasion of Europe (D-Day landings)
Sea Lion	WWII, planned German invasion of Britain
Opium War	Britain against China (1840)
Pearl Harbour	Japanese suprise attack on Hawaii (1941)
Japanese code name	Operation Z
Leader	Admiral Yamamoto
Peloponnesian Wars	Athens against Sparta and Corinth
Peninsular War	Britain, Spain, Portugal against France
Philippi	Mark Antony, Octavian defeated Brutus, Cassius
Plassey	Clive defeated Nawab of Bengal
Pluto (Pipeline under the Ocean)	Cross-channel fuel lines in WW11
Poitiers	Edward, the Black Prince defeated John II of France (1356)
Punic Wars	Rome v Carthage. Three wars. Carthage defeated at Zama
Quebec; Siege of	James Wolfe defeated Montcalm to establish British rule of Canada
Roses; War of	York (White) against Lancaster (Red)
Salamis	Greeks (Themistocles) Victory over Persians (Xerxes)
Somme	Most casualties in a modern battle. French Field Marshal Joffre and British General Douglas Haig v Germans (1916)
Spanish–American War	Started with: Sinking of US Ship *Maine* in Havana
Spanish Armada; Defeat of	1588
British Commander	Admiral Howard
British 2nd in Command	Sir Francis Drake
Earlier attack called	'Singeing the King of Spain's Beard'
Spanish Commander	Duke of Medina Sidonia
Spanish Civil War	Nationalists (under Franco) against Republicans
Spanish Succession	
Main battles	Blenheim, Ramillies, Oudernarde, Malplaquet
Treaty ended	Utrecht, Rasstatt
Spithead	Mutiny (1797)
Stalingrad	Decisive defeat of Germany by USSR on the Eastern front (1942)

Star Wars	Popular name for Strategic Defence Initiative
Tet Offensive	Attack by Vietcong during Vietnam War (1968)
Thermopylae	Spartans under Leonidas against Persians. 1 of 300 Spartans survived
Thirty Years War	
Began when	Czechs threw Hapsburg representatives out of window (Defenestration of Prague) (1618)
European war ended by	Treaty of Westphalia (1648)
Tours	Franks (Charles Martel) defeated Muslims
Trafalgar	Nelson v France and Spain (Villeneuve)
Message to Fleet	'England expects every man will do his duty'
Tsushima	Japanese Fleet defeated Russians (1905)
Vietnam War	
Ended	1975
US Resolution approving intervention	Tonking Gulf Resolution
Waterloo	Wellington defeated Napoleon (1815)
Location	Belgium
Whiskers; War of	Henry II against Louis of France
WWI	
Allied Commander (at end of war)	Marshal Foch
Armistice signed in	Railway Carriage at Compiègne
German Fleet scuttled at	Scapa Flow, Orkneys
German Navy; Head	Admiral Tirpitz
Naval Battle; Largest	Jutland (Jellicoe v Scheer, 1916)
Telegram intercepted offering Mexico 3 US states if allied with Germany	Zimmerman Note
Treaty after	Versailles
WWII	
Commander in Palestine	Viscount Allenby
Commander of Egyptian and Libyan Campaign	Earl Alexander of Tunis
Conference after	Potsdam (1945)
Conference to plan final stage of war	Yalta (Crimea). Present: Stalin, Roosevelt, Churchill (1945)
Ended in Europe	VE Day (May 8th, 1945)
Ended in Japan	VJ Day (September 2nd, 1945)
Final German offensive	Battle of the Bulge
German fortifications along Western Border	Siegfried Line
Japanese major naval defeat	Midway
Japanese surrender; Location	On USS *Missouri* in Tokyo Bay
Parachuted to Scotland on peace mission	Rudolf Hess
Started	September 3rd, 1939
Yorktown	George Washington defeated British under Cornwallis (ending American War of Independence)
Zulu War	British stand: Rorke's Drift

World Politics and History

By: Country/Description → General

Notes: Excludes UK, US.

Africa;-
Independence; 1st	Liberia (1847)
Independence; 1st (modern – south of Sahara)	Ghana (1957)
Only non colonised country	Ethiopia
Akkadians; Ruler of	Sargon

Albania;-
Former King	King Zog
Leader for 40 years	Enver Hoxha

Algeria;-
Independence movement	FLN
Anti-independence French force	OAS

Argentina;-
Cowboys	Gauchos
Populist leader	Juan Peron

Australia;-
1st convict settlement	Botany Bay
Governor General dismissed Labour government	Sir John Kerr (1975)
PM; Longest serving	Sir Robert Menzies

Austria;-
Fascist Chancellor	Seyss-Inquart
President; Former UN Secretary General	Kurt Waldheim

Aztecs;-
From	Mexico
Capital	Tenochtitlan (on Lake Texcoco)
Last King	Montezuma II, captured by Cortez

Babylon;-
1st King	Hammurabi
Jews; Took into captivity	Nebuchadnezzar
Law; Codifier	Hammurabi
Baghdad; Caliph; Most powerful	Harun-Al-Rashid

Bangladesh;-
Independence from Pakistan	1971 (formerly East Pakistan)
Leader at Independence	Sheikh Mujibur Rahman
Major party	Awami League
Barbados; 1st Post-independence PM	Errol Barrow
Benin; Ancient Kingdom, now part of	Nigeria
Berlin; Administered by	Britain, France, US, USSR
Botswana; President; 1st	Sir Seretse Khama

Byzantine Empire;-
Empress; 1st	Irene
Justinian; Military Commander	Belisarius
Revolt against Justinian	Nika Insurrection

Cambodia;-
Prince who became Prime Minister	Sihanouk
'Year Zero'	1975

Canada;-
Nova Scotia granted to, by James I	Sir Alexander Stirling (for penny rent)
PM; Elected 6 times	William Mackenzie King
PM; 1970s	Pierre Trudeau
Central African Republic; Emperor	Bokassa proclaimed himself (1976)

Chile:-

Coup, 1973	Allende overthrown by General Pinochet
Independence leader	Bernardo O'Higgins

China;-

Artistic liberalisation; 1956	Hundred Flowers Movement
Coup attempted in 1970, General died in air crash	Lin Piao
Dowager Empress; Led Boxer Rebellion	Tzu Hsi
Economic spurt; 1958 attempt	Great Leap Forward
Emperor; 1st	Qin Shi Huangdi
Emperor; Last	Pu Yi
Great Wall builder	Qin Shi Huangdi
Japanese puppet state in from 1930s	Manchukuo
Military Leaders of regions	Warlords
Mongol Dynasty; Founder	Kublai Khan
Nationalist leader	Chiang Kai Shek
Ports opened to trade after	Opium War Treaty Ports
President of the Republic; 1st	Sun Yat Sen (1911)
Prime Minister; Post-revolution; 1st	Chou En Lai
Pro Democracy Movement crushed at	Tiananmen Square (1989)
Retreat to the North by the Communists	The Long March (1934)

Crete; Early civilization — Minoan

Cuba:-

Dictator overthrown by Castro	Batista
Invasion attempt, backed by US	Bay of Pigs invasion (1961)
Missile Crisis, 1962	Over siting of Russian missiles in Cuba
Independence from Spain: 'Apostle' of	José Marti

Cyprus;-

Division	Kypros (Greek), Kibris (Turkish – north)
EOKA; Leader	George Grivas
Invasion	By Turkey (1974)
President; 1st	Archbishop Makarios
Union with Greece; Name for	Enosis

Czechoslovakia;-

Disputed area with Germany	Sudetenland
Invasion	By Soviet Troops (1968)
Leader deposed by Soviet forces, 1968	Alexander Dubcek
Town; Male population murdered WWII	Lidice (for assassination of Gestapo General Heydrich)

Dominican Republic; Dictator (1936–61) — Rafael Trujillo

Egypt;-

Dynasty formed by former slaves	Mamelukes
King; Last; Overthrown	King Farouk by Nasser (1952)
Leaders massacred at feast	Mamelukes by Mohammed Ali
Ptolemaic Dynasty; Origin	Greece
Union with Syria	United Arab Republic (1958)

Ethiopia;-

Emperor; Former	Haile Selassie, deposed 1974

Italy invaded	1935
Wars	Eritrea, Ogaden (with Somalia)
Fiji; Became Republic	October 1987
France:-	
Carolingian Dynasty; Founder	Charlemagne
Carolingian Dynasty succeeded by	Capetian Dynasty
Charlemagne; Paladin	Roland
Charles X overthrown by	July Revolution (1830), Louis Philippe King
Dynasties; Main	Carolingian, Capetian, Valois, Bourbon
Emperor, 1852	Louis Napoleon
English territory in; Last	Calais (till 1558)
Fortifications built against German invasion	Maginot Line
Gauls; Leader of; Defeated by Julius Caesar	Vercingetorix
Huguenots; Guarantee of security	Edict of Nantes (1598)
Huguenots; Massacre of	St Bartholomew's Day Massacre (1572)
Judicial Courts before Revolution	Parlements
Kings crowned	Rheims
Louis XIV; Chief Minister	Mazarin
Merovingian Dynasty; Founder	Clovis
Napoleon proclaimed Emperor	1804
Negotiators with US demanded bribes, scandal over	XYZ Affair (1797)
Order of Chivalry; Only	Legion of Honour
Paris insurrection, 1871	Paris Commune
Paris; Means of Escape from during 1869 siege	By Balloon
President; 1960s	General De Gaulle
Presidential term	7 years
Pro-German regime in WWII	Vichy Government
Resistance movement, WWII	Maquis
Revolution; Action which began	Storming of the Bastille (July 14th, 1789)
Revolution; Conspiracy of Equals; Leader	Gracchus Babeuf
Revolution; Estates	Nobility, Clergy, Third Estate
Revolution; Radical group	Jacobins (Robespierre, Danton)
Revolution; Removed Robespierre	Thermidoreans
Revolution; Replaced religion after	Cult of Reason
Revolution; Third estate swore to meet at	The Tennis Court, Versailles
Ruling body, 1795	The Directory
Split with Popes, 14th Century	Great Schism
Uprising against arrest of magistrate	The Fronde (1648)
Village massacred by Germans, WWII	Oradour
WWII; Vichy Government Head	Marshal Pétain
Gabon; President	Omar Bongo
Germany:-	
Berlin Airlift	1948. To beat Soviet Blockade
Catholic Church; Attempt by Bismarck to subordinate to state	Kulturkampf
Chancellor, 1949–63	Konrad Adenauer
Fascism; Concept of expansion	Lebensraum
Fascist Laws depriving Jews of rights	Nuremberg Laws (1935)

Fascist; Secret Police	Gestapo
Gestapo; Head	Hermann Goering, (later) Heinrich Himmler
Hitler; Attempted coup, 1923	Munich (Beer Hall) Putsch
Hitler; Came to power	1933
Hitler; Eliminated radical wing of Nazi Party	Night of the Long Knives
Hitler; Meeting place with Chamberlain	Bad Godesberg (1938)
Hitler; Successor, Surrendered to Allies	Admiral Karl Doenitz
Joined with in plebiscite, 1935	Saar
Landed aristocracy and military elite	Junkers
Naval mutiny	Kiel (1918)
Nazi anthem	Horst Wessel Lied
Nazi doctor, known as the 'Angel of Death'	Josef Mengele
Nazi Minister of Air	Hermann Goering
Nazi Minister of Propaganda	Joseph Goebbels
Plan to restructure economy after WWI	Dawes Plan
Republic set up after WWI	Weimar Republic
Reunification	1990
SS; Head of	Heinrich Himmler
Territory disputed with Denmark	Schleswig–Holstein
Terrorist Group; Prominent in 1960s	Baader–Meinhof Gang. Leaders: Andreas Baader, Ulrike Meinhof
Trial of leaders after WWII	Nuremberg Trials
Ghana; President; 1st	Kwame Nkrumah
Gibraltar; Treaty ceding to Britain	Treaty of Utrecht
Greece;-	
Ancient; Athenian lawgiver, known for severity	Draco
Ancient; Law maker; Drafted constitution	Solon
Ancient; Oracle at	Delphi
Coup, 1967; Leader	George Papadopoulos
Military coup	1967
Grenada; US Invasion	1983
Guinea; President; 1st	Sékou Touré
Haiti;-	
Dictatorship, overthrown 1987	'Papa Doc' (later Baby Doc) Duvalier
Leader of Independence struggle	Toussaint L'Ouverture
Secret Police under Duvalier	Tonton Macoutes
Holland; King; Napoleon's brother	Louis
Holy Land; Ruler of; 1st	Godfrey of Bouillon
Holy Roman Empire: Buyer	Jacob Fugger
Hong Kong;-	
Chinese rule scheduled for	1997
Ceded to Britain by	Treaty of Nanking (1842)
Hungary;-	
Independence Leader 19th Century	Lajos Kossuth
Revolution, crushed by USSR	1956
Huns; Leader, 5th Century	Attila
Incas;-	
From	Peru
Last King	Atahualpa, captured by Francisco

	Pizarro. Brother: Huascar
Written language	None
India;-	
British Supremacy established by	Battle of Plassey
Indira Gandhi; Succeeded by	Rajiv Gandhi
Governor General; 1st	Warren Hastings
Governor General; Last	Mountbatten
Independence	1947
Massacre by British troops, 1919	Amritsar
Mogul Emperor; Last great	Aurangzeb
Mogul Empire; Centre	Oudh
Mogul Empire; Founded by	Babar
Non-violent movement; Leader	Mahatma Gandhi
Prime Minister; 1st	Jawaharlal Nehru
Queen Victoria made Empress at	Durbar (1877)
Sikh Temple; Troops entered, 1986	Golden Temple, Amritsar
Indonesia;-	
Annexed, 1976	East Timor
President; 1st	Sukarno
Iran;-	
Leader, after Shah	Ayatollah Khomeini
Ruling Dynasty, 3rd–7th Century	Sassanian
Ireland;-	
Affair with MP's wife used to discredit Independence movement	Charles Parnell
Attempted uprising, 1916	Easter Rising
Executed for treason for landing from German submarine	(Sir) Roger Casement
Famine	Potato Famine (1840s)
Murder of Ministers by Fenians	Phoenix Park Murder (1882)
PM: Longest serving	Eamon De Valera
President; Woman; 1st	Mary Robinson
Protestant conquest; Completed	Battle of the Boyne (1690)
Rebellion against England, 1803; Leader	Robert Emmet
Royal Irish Constabulary forces, known for brutality	Black and Tans
Shooting of 13 Roman Catholics by British Troops	Bloody Sunday (January 1972)
Unifier	Brian Boru
United Irishman: Founder	Wolfe Tone
Israel;-	
Area occupied after 1967, Palestinian refugee centre	Gaza Strip
British statement supporting creation of	Balfour Declaration
Presidency offered to when formed	Einstein
President; 1st	Chaim Weizmann
Prime Minister; 1st	David Ben Gurion
Syria; Disputed area with	Golan Heights
Terrorist groups; Prominent in formation of state	Stern Gang, Irgun
Italy;-	
Abolished Monarchy	1946
Fascist leader	Benito Mussolini (Il Duce)
Florence, Ruling family, 15th–18th Century	Medicis

Invaded 1935	Ethiopia
King; Last	Umberto II
Leader after Mussolini's fall	Marshal Badoglio
Milan; Rulers 15th Century	Sforza Family
Monk; Reforming; Burnt at Stake	Savonarola
Naples; King of; Napoleon's brother	Joseph
Naples; King of; Napoleon's General	Murat
National Unification movement; 19th Century	Risorgimento
Pre-Roman civilization in Tuscany	Etruscans
Socialist Deputy, murdered by fascists, 1924	Matteotti
Terrorist group	Red Brigades
Unifier	Giuseppe Garibaldi
Vatican City; Treaty recognising sovereignty	Lateran Treaty
Young Italy Unification movement; Leader	Mazzini
Ivory Coast; President; 1st	Houphouet-Boigny
Japan;-	
Local feudal rulers	Daimyo
Military rulers, 12th–19th Century	Shoguns
Opened up to the West by	Commodore Perry
Overthrow of Shogunate, 1868	Meiji restoration
Prime Minister; During WWII	Hideki Tojo
Ruling family, 17th–19th Century	Tokugawa
Samurai code	Bushido
Judaea; Revolt against Syria, 167 BC; Leader	Judas Maccabeus
Kashmir; Nationalist leader	Sheikh Abdullah
Kenya;-	
President; 1st	Jomo Kenyatta
Revolt in 1950s	Mau-Mau rebellion
Korea, North; Leader	Kim Il Sung
Korea, South;-	
City occupied by workers, suppressed by troops, 1980	Kwangju
President: 1st	Synghman Rhee
Lebanon, Refugee camps; Slaughter, 1982	Sabra, Shatila
Lesotho; PM; 1st	Chief Jonathan
Liberia;-	
Coup leader, 1980	Master Sergeant Samuel Doe
President; 1st	Joseph Roberts
Libya;-	
Former King	Idris
Leader	Muammur Qadhafi
Malawi; President	Hastings Banda
Mali; Empire; 14th Century Ruler	Mansa Musa
Malta; Order of Knights rule	Knights of St John
Mayas; Empire in	Central America
Mexico;-	
Austrian Emperor	Archduke Maximilian (1863)
Aztec ruler, overthrown by Spanish	Montezuma
Peasant leader of 1910 revolution	Emiliano Zapata
Spanish Conqueror of	Hernando Cortez

Mozambique; Post-independence President	Samora Machel
Nicaragua;-	
Dictator till 1956	Somoza
Government	Sandinistas
President 1856, US adventurer	William Walker
Nigeria; State that attempted secession	Biafra (1967)
Norway;-	
Puppet ruler in WWII	Vidkund Quisling
Separation from Sweden	1905
Unifier .	Harold Fairhair
Ottoman Empire; Founder	Osman I
Pakistan;-	
Governor-General; 1st	Jinnah
Independence; Dominant Party	Muslim League
Military leader; died 1988	General Zia Al-Haq
PM in 1988	Benazir Bhutto, daughter of executed Zulfiqar Ali Bhutto
President; 1958–69	Ayub Khan
Secession of East Pakistan	1971
Persian Empire; Founder	Cyrus the Great
Peru; Spanish Conqueror of	Francisco Pizarro
Philippines;-	
Former Dictator	Ferdinand Marcos. Wife: Imelda
Post-war rebellion	Huks
President after Marcos	Corazon (Cory) Aquino
Poland;-	
Eastern frontier set after WWI	Curzon Line
Independence leader, 18th Century	Kosciusko
Nationalist leader and Dictator, 1920s–30s	Jozef Pilsudski
WWII uprising against Germans	Warsaw uprising (1944)
Portugal;-	
Dictator till 1968	Salazar
Empire in Asia; Established	Albuquerque
Romania;-	
King; 1st	Carol I
Leader, deposed 1989	Ceausescu
Rome;-	
Bridge over Tiber; Defended	Horatius Cocles
Capital moved to	Byzantium, AD 330 (became Constantinople)
Caracalla; Name from	Hooded tunic he popularized
Chief magistrates	Consuls (2)
Citizenship extended to all free males by	Caracalla
Citizenship granted to all Empire; Statute	Constitutio Antomniana
Clan; Term for	Gens
Conspiracy to seize power, 63 BC	Catiline Conspiracy
Dictator for 2 weeks	Cincinnatus
Emperor; Abdicated	Diocletian
Emperor; African	Septemius Severus
Emperor; Bodyguard	Praetorian Guard
Emperor; Colour of robes	Tyrian Purple

Emperor; 1st	Augustus (Original name Octavian)
Emperor; 1st; Eastern	Arcadius
Emperor; Last; (of United Empire)	Theodosius
Emperor; Last; Western	Romulus Augustulus
Emperor; Murdered mother, brother and wife	Nero
Emperor; Non Roman; 1st	Trajan
Empire auctioned; Buyer	Didius Julianus
Founders of; Legendary	Romulus and Remus
General; Known for lavish feasts	Lucullus
Heliogabalus; Name from	Syrian Sun King
Invasion by Huns; Leader	Attila
King; Last (traditional)	Tarquin the Proud
Nero's tutor, forced to commit suicide	Seneca
Orator, executed for opposing Antony	Cicero
Ostrogoth Leader, captured	Totila
Population kept happy by	Bread and Circuses (Juvenal)
Reforming brothers assassinated	Tiberius and Gaius Gracchus
Representatives elected to protect Plebeians	Tribunes
Republic; Division of people	Patricians and Plebeians
Slave uprising	Spartacus rebellion, crushed by Crassus
Triumvirate; 1st	Crassus, Pompey, Julius Caesar
Triumvirate; 2nd	Lepidus, Mark Antony, Octavian
Visigoth King, invaded	Alaric
Sarawak; White Rajahs of	Brooke family (ruled till 1945)
Saudi Arabia;-	
King; 1st	Ibn Saud
Princess executed for adultery	Princess Mishaal
Sumer	
Capital	Ur
Pyramids	Ziggurats
Writing	Cuneiform
Singapore;-	
Founder	Sir Stamford Raffles
Leader	Lee Kuan Yew
South Africa;-	
Boer migration from the Cape	Great Trek
Leader; Imprisoned 1963, Released 1990	Nelson Mandela
Massacre, 1960	Sharpeville
Parliament; Location	6 months each in Pretoria and Cape Town
Secret society; Powerful	Broederbond
Student leader, died in custody, 1977	Steve Biko
Student rising; 1976	Soweto
Tribal homeland; 'Independent'; 1st	Transkei
Union Confederation, formed 1985	COSATU
WWII leader	General Smuts
Zulu leader, 19th Century	Shaka
Zulu War; British stand	Rorke's Drift
South America;-	
Feudal labour system; Introduced by Spanish	Encomienda
Liberator from the Spanish	Simon Bolivar

Spain;-
Civil War; International Republican Volunteers	International Brigades
Grand Inquisitor; Spanish Inquisition	Torquemada
King; Napoleon's brother	Joseph
National hero, 11th Century	El Cid
Socialist Party Prime Minister	Felipe Gonzalez
Sparta: Slaves	Helots
Sudan; Leader of 19th Century religious revolt	Mahdi
Taiwan; Post-war leader	Chiang Kai Shek
Tanzania; President; 1st	Julius Nyerere
Tibet; Former ruler	Dalai Lama
Tunisia; President; 1st	Habib Bourguiba

Turkey;-
Government; Historic name for	Sublime Porte
Kemalist revolution	Abolishes Veil, Fez, Changes to Roman alphabet (1923)
Ottoman Empire; Constantinople made capital	1453
President; 1st	Kemal Ataturk
Westernizer; Founder of Modern Nation	Kemal Ataturk

Uganda;-
Dictator; 1970s	Idi Amin
Post-independence PM; 1st	Milton Obote
Raid to free Israeli hostages	Entebbe
Uruguay; Dominant parties	Blanco, Colorado

USSR/Russia;-
Anarchist; Prominent 19th Century	Bakunin
Defeated Swedes and Teutonic Knights	Alexander Nevski
Democratic revolt in 1825	Decembrists
Economic programme, 1921–28	New Economic Policy (NEP)
Emancipated Serfs	Tsar Alexander II (1861)
Exile; Post-revolution; 1st	Trotsky
Gorbachev; Position	President and Secretary of Communist Party
Gorbachev; Policy	Glasnost ('Openness'), Perestroika ('Reform')
Khruschev; Denunciation of Stalin	20th Party Congress (1956)
Khruschev; Successor	Brezhnev
Model worker, 1930s	Stakhanov
Naval Mutiny, 1921	Kronstadt
Priest led demonstration fired on by troops, 1905	Father Gapon
Secret Police Chief under Stalin	Lavrenti Beria
Tsar; 1st	Ivan the Terrible
Tsar; Last	Nicholas II
Vandals; Leader in North Africa	Gaiseric

Vietnam;-
Anti-Japanese Independence movement	Vietminh
Chinese refugees from, 1970s	Boat People
Leader; War; North	Ho Chi Minh
Vietcong offensive, New Year, 1968	Tet Offensive
Yugoslavia; Post-war Leader	Marshal Tito

Zaire;-
Attempted secession	Katanga province
Leader murdered	Patrice Lumumba
PM; 1st	Patrice Lumumba
Zambia; Post-independence leader	Kenneth Kaunda

Zimbabwe;-
Leader	Robert Mugabe
Matabele leader at conquest	Lobengula
Pre-independence agreement	Lancaster House Agreement
President; 1st	Dr Canaan Banana
UDI declared	1965, Under Ian Smith

World Politics and History

By: Description → Names, General

Notes: Covers cases where the Country is not implied.

Aid programme;-
To Europe after WWII, by US	Marshall Plan
US in Latin America, 1960s	Alliance for Progress
Banking Family; Dominant financial power, 16th Century	Fuggers
Baptised troops after invoking wife's god for victory	Clovis
Bath; Sat in because of skin disease	Marat
Broom; Fastened to ship mast as symbol	Admiral Van Tromp (Holland)
Burghers; 6 offered lives to save city	Calais
Caliph; 1st	Abu Bakr
Cats; Frightened of; Military Leader	Napoleon
Cherry Tree; Chopped down (myth)	George Washington
Churchill and Roosevelt; Agreement, 1941	Atlantic Charter
Colony; Former British; Never member of Commonwealth	Burma
Conference; Discussed African colonization	Conference of Berlin (1884)
Dead; Left for and awarded honour, WWI	De Gaulle
Deported; Nation, by Turkey	Armenia (1915)
Duel; Opponent chose weapon of sausages, one poisoned	Bismarck
Elephants; Crossed Alps with	Hannibal
Fly Whisk; Known for carrying	Jomo Kenyatta
Freezer contained bodies of political opponents (reputed)	Idi Amin
French General, became Governor of Isle of Wight	Jean Cavalier
German Bombing; City not warned, to pretend German code not cracked (claimed)	Coventry (1940)
Governor General; Deposed government	Australia (1975)
Holy Roman Emperor; 1st	Charlemagne
Homosexuality; Accused of in attempt to discredit	Sir Roger Casement
Horse Owner; Religious leader	Aga Khan

Inquisition; Country condemned to death	Netherlands
Killed Eldest Son in fit of rage	Ivan the Terrible
King; Legendary Christian ruler	Prester John
Leader; Replaced as, but not told	Salazar (Portugal, 1968)
Leopold of Belgium, personally owned	Congo
Lifeguard, saved over 70 people	Ronald Reagan
Lockheed Scandal; Convicted for receiving bribes	Tanaka (Japan)
Man in the Iron Mask	In Bastille (velvet mask)
Married Uncle; Murdered him	Agrippina (uncle: Claudius)
Marx; Close collaborator with	Friedrich Engels
Massacre; Polish officers by Russians, 1940	Katyn
Murdered Nephew, married nephew's wife to gain throne	Andronicus Comnenus I (Byzantine Emperor)
Nazi Past; President accused of	Kurt Waldheim
Nobel Prize for Literature awarded; British Statesman	Winston Churchill
Non-Aligned Conference; 1955	Bandung Conference (Indonesia)
Oldest Representative Assembly	Iceland (Althing)
Olympic Games; Palestinian group killed Israeli athletes	Munich Massacre (1972). Group: Black September
Organisation; Members spied on each other	Illuminati
Orient Express; Fell off in pyjamas	Paul Deschanel (French PM)
Peace; Longest, Europe	Sweden
Pearl; Dissolved in drink	Cleopatra
Pirates:-	
Base on North African Coast	Barbary Coast
Captured by in youth	Julius Caesar
PM:-	
Concert pianist	Jan Paderewski, 1st Polish PM
Woman; 1st	Sirimavo Bandaranaike, Sri Lanka (1960)
Woman; Margaret Thatcher; Which	5th
President:-	
Became King	Ahmet Zogu in Albania became King Zog (1928)
Woman; 1st	Isabel Peron, Argentina (1974)
Woman; Elected; 1st	Vigdis Finnbogadottir, Iceland (1980)
3 in 1 day	Bolivia (1970)
Priest; Studied to become	Stalin
Recited Gray's *Elegy* before battle	General Wolfe
Rug; Presented to Julius Caesar rolled in	Cleopatra
Sea; Ordered to be lashed after storm	Xerxes
Sewers; Forced to hide in	Marat
Shoe:-	
Hit table with during conference	Khruschev (1960)
Used as symbol of conquest	Aurangzeb (Mogul Emperor)
Slavery:-	
Abolition; Prominent Campaigner	William Wilberforce
1st to abolish	Denmark
Slept fully clothed	George Clemenceau
Smoking; Servant threw water over when saw	Sir Walter Raleigh

447

Tea; Drinking banned	US (1775)
Treaty; Signed on raft	Treaty of Tilsit; Napoleon and Alexander I of Russia
Votes for Women;-	
1st	New Zealand (1893)
Last; Europe	Liechtenstein (1984)
Voting age; Highest; Western country	Andorra
Voting; Compulsory; Western country	Australia
Wedding Night; Died on	Attila the Hun
WWII; Fought on both sides	Italy
Zionist Movement; Founder	Theodor Herzl

World Politics and History

By: Term → General

Notes: Covers all Non UK and Non US Events, Groups, etc.

Anschluss	German union with Austria (1938)
Anzacs	Australia and New Zealand forces in WWI
Anzus Pact	Treaty between Australia, New Zealand, US
Arab Legion	Commander: General Sir John Glubb (Glubb Pasha)
Axis	Germany, Italy, Japan in WWII
Bayeux Tapestry	Embroidery depicting Norman Conquest
Beer Hall Putsch	Hitler attempted to sieze power in Munich (1923)
Berlin Airlift	To supply West Berlin after East German blockade (1948–1949)
Berlin Wall	Built: 1961. Ended 1990
Bilderberg Group	Top statesmen, businessmen, etc. from Western Powers
Black and Tans	Irregulars enlisted to fight for Britain against Irish independence (1920)
Black Hole of Calcutta	Responsible: Nawab of Bengal
Black Shirts	Italian Fascists (originally, later other fascists groups)
Bolsheviks	Meaning: Majority men
Boxer Rebellion	Chinese peasant uprising (1900)
Name from	Society of Harmonious Fists
Camp David Agreement	Egypt–Israel Peace Treaty (1978)
Catiline Conspiracy	Plot against Rome (64 BC)
Defeated by	Cicero
Children's Crusade	Leaders: Stephen (France), Nicholas (Germany)
Chindits	Allied forces in Burma behind Japanese lines, WWII
Commander	Wingate
Comintern	Other name: Third (Communist) International
Dissolved	1943
Congress of Vienna	After Napoleon's defeat
Main Statesmen	Metternich, Talleyrand, Castlereagh
Contras	US backed Counter Revolutionary forces in Nicaragua
Crusade; 1st	Crusader elected King in Jerusalem: Godfrey of Bouillon

Defenestration of Prague	Governors thrown out of window; Started 30 years war
Diet of Worms	Conference of Holy Roman Empire under Charles V (1521). Outlawed Luther
Dragonades	Persecution of Huguenots in France by Louis XIV
Dreyfus Affair	Alfred Dreyfus convicted incorrectly of spying
Sent to	Devil's Island
Edict of Emancipation	Freed serfs in Russia (1861)
By	Alexander II
Edict of Nantes	Henry IV guaranteed security to French Huguenots (1598)
Edict of Worms	Edict outlawing Luther (1521)
Falange	Spanish Fascist Party
Fashoda Incident	Britain–France dispute over control of the Nile (1898)
Fenians	Irish Nationalist Secret Society
Field of the Cloth of Gold	Meeting place of: Henry VIII and Francis I of France (1520)
Fianna Fail	Irish Political Party
Meaning	Warriors of Destiny
Foreign Legion	HQ: Sidi-ben-Abbas, Algeria, then Corsica/France
Fourteen Points	Woodrow Wilson's plan for WWI peace
Great Schism	14th Century split in Papacy with Rome and Avignon Popes
Great Trek	March to North by Boers of South Africa
Guelphs	Dukes of Bavaria, supported the Pope
Ghibelines	German House of Hohenstauffen
Hanseatic League	Northern European Confederation. Lubeck, Hamburg and Bremen prominent
Holy Alliance	Austria, Prussia and Russia at Congress of Vienna (1815)
Huks	Filipino peasant revolutionary movement after WWII
Hundred Days, The	Napoleon's period from leaving Elba to abdicating
Hussite Rebellion	In Bohemia
Indian Mutiny	1857
Cause	Indian troops refused to handle cartridges coated in cow and pig grease
IRA	Factions: Officials, Provisionals
Irgun	Zionist Terrorist Group
Iron Guard	Romanian Fascist Organisation
Iwo Jima	US Flag raised on Pacific Island during WWII, became classic photograph
Jacquerie	Peasant revolt in N.E.France (1358)
Leader	Guillaume Carle
Janissaries	Army of the Ottoman Empire
Kalmar Union	Union of Denmark, Norway, Sweden (15th–16th Century)

Knights; Military Orders of	Templars, Hospitallers (St John of Jerusalem), Teutonic Order
Ku Klux Klan	US Anti-black organisation
Leader	Imperial Wizard
Kuomingtang (KMT)	Chinese Nationalist Party
Leader	Chiang Kai Shek
Land League	Irish tenants organisation
Founder	Michael Davitt
League of Nations	Founded after WWI, predecessor to UN
Little Entente	Czechoslovakia, Yugoslavia, Romania (1920s)
Long March, The	Chinese Communist retreat to the North under Mao Tse Tung (1934)
Marshall Plan	Post WWII Economic Aid Programme for Europe
Mensheviks	Russian Political Party
Meaning	Minority men
Molly Maguires	Irish, later US terrorist group
Montagnards	French Revolutionary group
Muldergate	South Africa. Misappropriation of public funds for propaganda use by Connie Mulder. Caused Vorster's resignation (1979)
Munich Agreement	Neville Chamberlain met Hitler and Mussolini. Announced 'Peace in our time'
Nuremberg Laws	Germany laws against Jews (1935)
New Jewel Movement	Grenadan Party
Night of the Long Knives	Hitler eliminated Rohm and radical wing of Nazi Party
Nuremberg Trials	Trials of Nazi Leaders for war crimes (1945/6)
Orange Order	Irish Protestant Society
Plantagenet	Name from: Geoffrey of Anjou wearing genet (sprig of broom) in hat
PLO (Palestine Liberation Organisation)	Leader: Yasser Arafat
Reagan–Gorbachev summit	1986 – Reykjavik, 1985 – Geneva (1st)
Sian Incident	Chiang Kai Shek kidnapped and forced to make deal with Communists against Japan
Sinn Fein	Irish Nationalist Movement
Means	Ourselves Alone
Socialist Revolutionary Party	Russian Peasant Party in the revolution
Solidarity	Polish Trade Union
Leader	Lech Walesa
Spanish Inquisition	Grand Inquisitor: Torquemada
SS	Elite Nazi organisation
Modelled on	Jesuits
Full time members	Waffen SS
St Bartholomew's Day Massacre	Massacre of Huguenots in France (1572)
Stern Gang	Zionist Terrorist Group
Suez Crisis	Israel, Britain, France invade Egypt after threat to nationalize Suez Canal (1956)
Taiping Rebellion	Civil War in China (1850–64)

Third Reich	Hitler's rule in Germany
Third Republic	French Government (1870–1940)
Tonton Macoutes	Haitian Secret Police
Tupamaros	Uruguayan Terrorist Group
United Irishman Leader	Nationalist Group Wolfe Tone
Vestal Virgins	Priestesses (6) at Temple of Vesta in Rome
Waldensian Movement	Founder: Peter Waldo
Warsaw Pact	Russian and East European Alliance
Weimar Republic	German Republic set up after WWI; Abolished by Hitler, 1933
Yalta Conference	Meeting of Roosevelt, Stalin, Churchill (1945)

Sport and Leisure

Contents

Leisure	**455**	Cricket	481
Coins	455	Cycling	483
Cookery, Dishes		Darts	484
By: Description	456	Equestrian Events	484
By: Dish	456	Fencing	484
Cookery, Food	459	Golf	485
Cookery, Terms		Greyhound Racing	486
By: Term	461	Gymnastics	486
Drink	462	Horse Racing	487
Drink, Cocktails	463	Motor Racing	489
Drink, Made from		Motorcycle Racing	491
By: Name	464	Olympic Games	491
Fashion and Dress	464	Other Sports	495
Games	465	Rowing	497
Games, Terms from		Rugby League	497
By: Term	467	Rugby Union	498
Holidays and Festivals	467	Sailing	500
Leisure Activities and Skills	468	Skating	500
Stamps	469	Skiing and Winter Sports	501
Sport	**470**	Snooker	501
American Football	470	Speedway	502
Association Football	470	Sport, General	
Athletics	474	By: Description	502
Awards and Trophies		Sporting Terms	
By: Award	477	By: Term	503
Badminton	477	Sportspeople	
Baseball	478	By: Description	506
Basketball	478	By: Name	506
Bowling (Ten pin)	479	Squash	508
Bowls	479	Swimming	508
Boxing	479	Table Tennis	509
Bullfighting	481	Tennis	509

LEISURE
Coins

By: General

See Also: Society and Politics; Currencies

Britannia; Original	Frances Stewart, Duchess of Richmond
Decimalisation; Date	February 15th, 1971
Dollar Note; Picture on	George Washington
Farthing;-	
Bird on	Wren
Withdrawn	1960
FD; On Coins; Stands for	Defender of the Faith
Guinea; Amount	21 shillings
Head, Tail; Proper name for	Obverse and reverse sides
Highest Value	£1 million (Bank of England, internal use)
King; Head not on coins	Edward VIII
Largest	Yap Islands (Pacific)

Maundy Money;-	
Values	1p, 2p, 3p, 4p
When presented	Maundy Thursday
Monarch; Distributed by	Maundy Money
Numerical Indication; None on coins;	
Major Country	US
£1000 Note; Withdrawn	1943
Pound, (Old); Pennies in	240
Rarest; UK	1952 George VI half crown, 1954 Queen Elizabeth penny
Reverse; Picture on;-	
£1	Sir Isaac Newton
£5	Duke of Wellington/George Stephenson
£10	Florence Nightingale/Charles Dickens
£20	William Shakespeare/Michael Faraday
£50	Sir Christopher Wren
Reverse Two Pence Piece	Prince of Wales Feathers
Sides;-	
Fifty pence	7
Threepenny piece	12
Twenty pence	7
UK; Omitted from coins after 1948	Ind Imp (Emperor of India)

Cookery, Dishes

By: Description → Dish

Ballerina; Named after	Pavlova
Composer; Named after (by Escoffier)	Tournedos Rossini
Napoleonic Battle; Named after	Chicken Marengo
Opera Singer; Named after	Peach Melba (by Escoffier), Melba Toast
Pie; Italian word for; Name from	Pizza
Salad; Named after hotel first made in	Waldorf Salad (Waldorf–Astoria)
Saliva of Bird; Made from	Birds Nest Soup
Skewer; On; Name means	Kebab

Cookery, Dishes

By: Dish → Main Ingredients, Country From, General

Aioli	Garlic mayonnaise
Angels on Horseback	Oysters wrapped in bacon
Artsoppa	Sweden. Dried pea soup with ham
Avgolemono	Greece. Sauce made with egg and lemon
Babka	Poland. Fruit bread/cake
Baklava	Pastry filled with nuts
Biltong	South Africa. Dried meat
Bird's Nest Soup	Constituent: Saliva of swiftlet
Bisque	Creamy soup
Black Pudding	Pig's blood and fat
Blanquette	France. Meat stew
Blini	Russia. Stuffed pancakes
Blintz	Stuffed pancake
Blutwurst	Germany. Blood sausage
Boeuf Bourguignon	France. Beef in red wine sauce
Bombe	Spherical ice cream dish

Bordelaise	Sauce of red wine and shallots
Borsht	Russia. Beetroot soup
Bouillabaisse	France. Fish stew
Bourride	Fish soup
Bratwurst	Germany. Fried sausage
Braxelloise	Sauce of butter, asparagus and eggs
Bubble and Squeak	Cabbage and potatoes
Calamares	Fried squid or cuttlefish
Cannelloni	Pasta stuffed with meat in cheese sauce
Carpetbag Steak	Australia. Steak stuffed with oysters
Cassata	Italy. Ice cream dish
Cassoulet	Casserole with haricot beans, meat and vegetables
Chapatti	India. Bread pancake
Charlotte Russe	Jelly and cream pudding
Chasseur	Sauce of white wine, mushrooms and onions
Chateaubriand	Thick steak
Chilli Con Carne	Minced beef with chilli and beans
Chop Suey	Invented in: US
Chorizo	Spain. Spiced sausage
Chow Mein	Fried noodles
Chowder	Fish or seafood soup
Cocido	Spain. Chicken and vegetable stew
Cock a Leekie	Scotland. Leek, prune and chicken stew
Colbert	Sauce with lemon and madeira
Colcannon	Ireland. Potato and cabbage stew
Coleslaw	US. Shredded cabbage salad
Consommé	France. Clear Soup
Couscous	North Africa. Steamed hard wheat
Crêpes Suzette	France. Pancakes with orange syrup and liqueur
Cumberland Sauce	Redcurrant-based
Devils on Horseback	Stuffed prunes wrapped in bacon
Dhall	India. Lentil dish
Dolmades	Vine leaves stuffed with meat and rice
Doner Kebab	Skewered mince meat
Duchesse	Baked mashed potatoes
Enchiladas	Mexico. Fried meat-stuffed pancakes
Entrecôte	Steak from between two ribs
Falafel	Chick pea patties
Fettucine	Italy. Ribbon shaped pasta
Financière	Sauce made with madeira and truffles
Fondue	Switzerland. Melted cheese in white wine
Fricasée	Meat stew in white sauce
Frikadelle	Meat ball
Fritto Misto	Italy. Seafood, etc., fried in batter
Gado Gado	Indonesia. Vegetables in peanut sauce
Galantine	Chopped meat in calves-head jelly
Gazpacho	Spain. Cold vegetable soup
Gnocchi	Italy. Savoury dumplings
Goulash	Hungary. Paprika-flavoured meat stew
Granita	Italy. Water ice
Gravlax	Scandinavia. Salmon with mustard sauce
Guacamole	Mexico. Avocado dip

Gumbo	Stew with okra and rice
Haggis	Scottish. Sheep's stomach filled with offal
Halva	Sesame seed sweet
Hoisin Sauce	Made from: Soya beans
Hollandaise	France. Sauce with egg yolk, vinegar, lemon juice
Hot Dog	Frankfurter in bun. Name from: Cartoon with dachshund in bun
Hummus	Chick pea and sesame purée
Kedgeree	India. Rice and fish dish
Lasagne	Flat pasta dish with minced meat and white cheese sauce
Luau	Hawaii. Steamed meat or fish with plant leaves
Lobscouse	Stew
Lyonnaise	Sauce with white wine and onions
Madeleine	Small sponge cake
Maitre D'Hotel	Sauce with butter, parsley and lemon
Marrons Glacé	Candied chestnuts
Meringue	Egg white and sugar baked pudding
Mortadella	Italy. Sausage from Bologna
Moussaka	Greece. Minced lamb and eggplant pie
Mulligatawny	India. Curried soup
Nasi Goreng	Indonesia. Meat and fried rice dish
Nougat	France. Sweet made from almonds and honey
Osso Buco	Italy. Braised veal dish
Paella	Spain. Baked saffron rice with meat and seafood
Pâté de Foie Gras	Goose liver pâté
Pavlova	Fruit, cream and meringue dessert. Named after: Anna Pavlova
Peach Melba	Ice cream with peaches and raspberry sauce. Named after: Dame Nellie Melba
Perigueux	Sauce with madeira and truffles
Pesto	Italy. Sauce of basil, garlic and cheese
Petit Four	Small cake
Piperade	Tomatoes and peppers with egg
Piroshki	Russia. Small pies with filling
Pissaladière	France. Pastry with onion and anchovy covering
Pizza	Italy. Flat-baked dough with various coverings. Name means: Pie
Profiteroles	Choux pastry puffs with sweet filling
Proscuitto	Italy. Smoked ham
Pumpernickel	Germany. Malted rye bread
Quiche Lorraine	France. Savoury tart
Ragout	Stew of meat and vegetables
Raita	Yoghurt-based salad
Ratatouille	France. Aubergine, courgette, pepper and tomato dish
Ravioli	Italy. Small pasta casings with stuffing
Rhum Baba	Small sponge cake soaked in rum and syrup. Inventor: King Stanislaus (Polish)

Rijsttafel	Indonesia. Collection of dishes
Risotto	Italy. Rice with saffron
Rissole	Fried minced meat ball
Roghan Ghosh	Kashmir. Lamb curry with yoghurt
Rollmop	Herring with onion or gherkin
Sacher Torte	Austria. Chocolate sponge cake
Sambal	Spiced Pickle
Sashimi	Japan. Raw fish
Satay	Malaysia. Grilled skewers of meat
Saltimbocca	Italy. Veal and ham dish
Sauce Bearnaise	Sauce of egg and butter
Sauce Bechamel	Butter, flour and milk sauce
Sauce Bigarade	Orange-flavoured, served with duck
Sauce Mornay	Cheese-flavoured
Sauce Veloute	Butter, flour and meat or fish stock
Sauerkraut	Germany. Pickled cabbage
Scotch Woodcock	Anchovies and eggs on toast
Shish Kebab	Skewered meat pieces
Smorgasbord	Scandinavia. Buffet with various dishes
Smorrebrod	Denmark. Open sandwich
Solyanka	Russia. Cucumber soup
Sorbet	Water ice
Soufflé	Light egg dish
Stollen	Germany. Fruit loaf
Stroganoff	Russia. Beef in sour cream
Strudel	Thin pastry with various fillings
Sukiyaki	Japan. Beef and vegetables in soy sauce
Sushi	Japan. Vinegared rice with raw fish
Tabouleh	Cracked wheat with lemon and mint
Taco	Mexico. Stuffed fried pancake
Tagliatelle	Italy. Ribbon shaped pasta
Tapas	Spain. Appetizers served in bars
Taramasalata	Greece. Mullet roe dip
Tartare	Sauce with gherkins, vinegar and mustard
Tempura	Japan. Fish fried in deep fat
Thousand Year Old Eggs	Buried in ground for months
Toad in the Hole	Sausage (toad) in batter
Tortillas	Mexico. Pancakes
Tourtière	Pork pie
Tzatziki	Greece. Cucumber in yoghurt
Veal Escalope	Veal fried in breadcrumbs
Vichyssoise	Potato and leek soup
Vindaloo	India. Vinegary pork curry
Vol Au Vent	Puff pastry shell with filling
Welsh Rarebit	Cheese on toast
Wiener Schnitzel	Austria. Breaded veal cutlet
Wonton	China. Meat-filled dumplings
Zabaglione	Egg yolks with marsala

Cookery, Food

By: General

Abalone	Shellfish
Allspice; Other name	Pimento

Associated with a place;-

Arbroath	Smokies
Bakewell	Tart
Banbury	Cake
Bath	Bun
Chelsea	Bun
Eccles	Cake
Kendal	Mint Cake
Lancashire	Hot-Pot
Melton Mowbray	Pie
Pontefract	Cake
Worcester	Sauce
Yorkshire	Pudding
Baine Marie	Double walled pan
Banana; Cooking variety	Plantain
Bombay Duck	Fish
Bouquet Garni	Parsley, thyme, bay leaf
Brazil Nuts; From	Bolivia
Brisling	Small herring-like fish
Caviar	Roe of sturgeon
Charcuterie	Pork products and shop selling these

Cheese;-

Largest producer	US
Used to curdle milk for	Rennet, from calf's stomach

Cheese; Types of;-

Feta	Greek salted, sheep or goat's milk based
Gorgonzola	With blue veins, made from ewe's milk
Mozzarella	Originally made from buffalo milk
Parmesan	Made from skimmed milk
Ricotta	Sweet cottage cheese
Roquefort	Made from sheep and goat's milk
Stilton	Add cream of one day to milk of next

Chef;-

'Architect of French Cuisine'	Carème
Larousse Gastronomique; Author	Prosper Montagne
Chewing Gum; Original base	Chicle
Cinnamon; From	Bark of tree
Coffee; Source	Pips of fruit (not beans)
Condensed Milk; Inventor	Gail Borden

Consumption;-

Beer; Most	West Germany
Tea; Most	Ireland
Wine; Most	France
Croissant	France. Crescent-shaped Roll
Croutons	Toast pieces, fried in butter
Eggs; Brown or white, most nutritious	Same
Endive; English word for	Chicory
Escargots	Snail (French)
Fines Herbes	Chopped chives, parsley, tarragon, etc.
Five Spice Powder	Anise, pepper, cinnamon, cloves, fennel
Flageolets	Small beans
Garam Masala	Mixed spices used in curries
Garbanzos	Chick peas

Ghee	Clarified butter
Guinea Pig; Where eaten	Peru
Herring; Canned as	Sardine
Honey;-	
Classification	White, golden, amber, dark
Nectar for 1 lb	From 2 million flowers
Insect; Most eaten·	Grasshopper
Kipper	Smoked herring
Langouste	Crayfish
Licence; Chefs require to prepare	Fugu (Puffer fish) in Japan
Margarine; 1st ingredients	Chopped sheep intestine, cow's udder, beef suet
Meat; Cholesterol free	Kangaroo, possum
Milk; U.H.T.; Stands for	Ultra High Temperature
Miso	Fermented soya bean paste
Naan	Indian flat bread
Noisette	Hazelnut (French)
Oysters; When to eat; Saying	'When 'r' in the month'
Petit Pois	Green peas (French)
Pitta	Flat bread
Potato; Poisonous part	Leaves and fruit (tuber eaten)
Prosciutto	Italian smoked ham
Prunes; Made from	Plums (dried)
Puri	Indian deep fried puffed bread
Raisins; Made from	Grapes (Dried)
Ramequin	Small casserole dish
Restaurant;-	
1st	Boulangers, Paris (1765)
Guide; 1st European	Michelin
Sago; Source	Pith of a palm
Spam; Name from	Spiced ham
Spice(s);-	
From same plant	Nutmeg, Mace
Most expensive	Saffron
Sweetbread	Pancreas
Tabasco; Name from	Mexican State
Tapioca; Source	Root of cassava (manioc)
Tofu	Bean curd
Tripe	Cow or sheep's stomach lining
Truffles; How found	Detected by trained pigs
Turmeric; Obtained from	Curcuma plant
Vegetable; Oldest known	Broad bean
Wok	Hemispherical Pan used in Chinese Cookery
Worcester Sauce; Origin	India

Cookery Terms

By: Term → Meaning

Armoricaine	In the Breton fashion, with wine, brandy and tomato sauce
Beurre, Au	Cooked in butter
Blanquette	With a white sauce
Bonne Femme	In country style
Bretonne, A La	Garnished with beans
Brouillé	Scrambled

461

Chantilly	With whipped cream
Crécy, A La	Garnished with carrots
Croûte, En	In pastry
Daube, En	Braised with vegetables
Diablé	Devilled
Doré	Brushed with egg yolk
Espagnole	With a brown sauce
Farci	Stuffed
Florentine	With spinach
Forestière	With bacon and mushrooms
Forno, Al	From the oven (roasted, etc.)
Garni	Garnished
Gratin, Au	Browned with cheese and breadcrumbs
Greque, A La	Cooked in oil and lemon juice
Indienne	Curried
Jardinière	With garnish of fresh vegetables
Julienne	Cut in fine strips
Lyonnaise	With a garnish of fried onions
Macédoine	Diced
Mocha	Flavoured with coffee
Montmorency	Flavoured with asparagus
Mornay	Served with cheese sauce
Papillotte, En	Cooked in a paper bag
Parisienne	With potatoes and leeks
Paysanne	In peasant style
Plat du Jour	Dish of the day
Poivre, Au	With pepper
Red Cooked	Braised in soy sauce and wine
Soubisé	With onion
Tandoori	Grilled in clay oven (tandoor)
Terrine, En	Potted

Drink

By: General

Alcohol; Coffee effect on	Makes worse
Angostura Bitters; From	Tree bark
Beer; Highest alcohol content	Barley Wine
Bottle Sizes:-	
Balthazar	16 bottles
Jeroboam	4 bottles
Magnum	2 bottles
Methuselah	8 bottles
Nebuchadnezzar	20 bottles
Rehoboam	6 bottles
Salmanazar	12 bottles
Champagne; Designations	
Brut	Very dry
Demi-Sec	Sweet
Extra-Sec	Very dry
Sec	Dry
Coca Cola; Original constituent	Cocaine (until 1903)
Drink; Drinking once could cause excommunication	Chocolate (Central America, 18th Century)
Port; Name from	Oporto, Portugal
Sherry; Name from	Jerez, Spain

Sparkling Wine; Monk invented	Dom Perignon
Tea;-	
Categories	Black (fermented), Green (unfermented), Oolong (semi-fermented)
Grades	Orange Pekoe (highest), Pekoe, Pekoe Souchong, Congou, Pekoe Dust, Dust (lowest)
Original use	Medicine
Used as a currency	Siberia (in blocks)
Wine; Types;-	
Amontillado	Sherry
Amoroso	Sherry
Asti Spumante	Sparkling Italian wine
Bull's Blood	Hungarian wine
Chianti	Italian red wine
Claret	Red Bordeaux wine
Fino	Dry, light sherry
Hock	German Rhine wine
Liebfraumilch	Type of Hock
Manzanilla	Sherry
Marsala	Sicilian fortified wine
Moselle	German white wine
Oloroso	Dark sherry
Retsina	Greek wine
Tokay	Hungarian wine
Vinho Verde	Portuguese white wine
V.S.O.P.	Very Special Old Pale

Drink, Cocktails

By: Name → Constituents

Black Russian	Vodka, Kahlua
Black Velvet	Champagne, Stout
Bloody Mary	Vodka, tomato juice
Bucks Fizz	Champagne, orange juice
Champagne Cocktail	Champagne, brandy
Cuba Libre	Rum, Coke
Daiquiri	Rum, lemon
Dry Martini	Gin, Vermouth
Gimlet	Gin, lime juice
Harvey Wallbanger	Vodka, orange juice, Galliano. Named after: Tom Harvey (surfer)
Manhattan	Rye Whisky, Sweet Vermouth, Angostura Bitters. Named after: Manhattan Club, New York. Inventor: Jenny Jerome (Churchill's mother)
Pina Colada	Rum, pineapple juice, coconut milk
Rob Roy	Scotch Whisky, Sweet Vermouth, Angostura Bitters
Screwdriver	Vodka, orange juice
Whisky Mac	Whisky, Ginger Wine

Drink, Made from

By: Drink → Made from, Flavouring

Absinthe	Flavoured with: Wormwood
Aquavit	Grains or potatoes (flavour: Caraway)
Arrack	Coconut
Beer	Barley (flavoured with: Hops)
Brandy	Grapes
Calvados	Apples
Cassis	Blackcurrant-flavoured spirit
Chartreuse	Orange liqueur
Cider	Apples
Gin	Corn (flavoured with: Juniper berries)
Kirsch	Cherries
Kumiss	Mare's milk
Kummel	Cummin-flavoured liqueur
Kvass	Barley
Maraschino	Cherry liqueur
Mead	Honey
Pernod	Aniseed-flavoured spirit
Pulque	Agave
Rum	Molasses (from sugar cane)
Sake	Rice
Slivovitz	Plums
Southern Comfort	Orange-flavoured spirit
Tequila	Agave
Tia Maria	Coffee-flavoured liqueur
Vodka	Grains or potatoes
Whisky, Grain	Corn
Whisky, Malt	Barley
Wine	Grapes

Fashion and Dress

By: General

Astrakhan Wool; From	Karakul (sheep)
Batik; Originates in	Malaya
Beads; Used by American Indians	Wampum
Biba; Founder	Barbara Hulanicki
Bikini; Designer	Louis Reard
Blazer; Name from	HMS *Blazer*, ship first used on
Body Shop; Founder	Anita Roddick
Cardigan; Name from	Earl of Cardigan
Clothes; Hire	Moss Bros
Colours, Unusual, Uses	Schiaparelli
Designer; Died 1985	Laura Ashley
Dior; House of; Head from 1957	Yves St Laurent
Dress Designer; British; Longest Established	Norman Hartnell
Ermine; Source	Stoat (winter coat)
Fair Isle Knitwear; From	Shetland Islands
Farthingale	Gave shape to women's dress, 16th Century
Gannex Raincoats; Associated with	Harold Wilson
Hair; Men's; Short	From Henry VIII

Hat;-
  Bowler; US Name   Derby
  North Africa   Fez or Tarboosh
  Panama; Where made   Ecuador
  Ten Gallon; Capacity   6 pints (approximately)
  Ten Gallon; Name from   Ribbons on first ones
Jeans;-
  Inventor   Levi Strauss
  Material; Original   Canvas
  Originally made for   Gold prospectors
Jewellery; Pure gold   24 Carat
Little Girl Look   Yves St Laurent
London; 1960s fashion centre   Carnaby Street
Mini Skirt; Associated with   Mary Quant
Muslin; Word origin   Mosul (Iraq)
New Look; 1950s   Christian Dior
Nylon; Word origin   New York, London
Perfume;-
  Eau De Cologne, invented for   Plague Protection
  Fixatives; Used as   Ambergris, Musk, Civet
  Marilyn Monroe; Only thing she wore
    to bed (Quote)   Chanel No 5
Pigtail; Outlawed   China (1911)
Princess Diana; Dress designers   David and Elizabeth Emanuel
Sack Dress; 1950s; Designer   Cristobal Balenciaga
Shift; Introduced   Balenciaga
Spanish Headdress   Mantilla
Sweaters; Made fashionable   Coco Chanel
Tennis Wear; Famous designer   Teddy Tinling
Trousers; For women   Yves St Laurent
Vests; Sales slump 1930s; Reason   Because Clark Gable appears without
                                                      in *It Happened one Night*

Wedding Rings; Finger worn on
    formerly   Thumb (16th and 17th Centuries)

Games

By: General

See Also: Darts
Acrostic   Words formed from 1st letter of
                                                      lines of a poem

Australian Gambling Game   Two Up
Baccarat; Object   Hold cards with value as close to
                                                      nine

Backgammon;-
  Dice; Number   5
  Pieces   15 per player
  Points   12 on each side
Bezique; Cards; Number   32 per person playing
Bingo; Former name   Housey-Housey
Bingo; Numbers;-
  10,20, etc.   Blind
  11   Legs
  21   Key of the door
  22   Two little ducks
  66   Clickety click

88	Two fat ladies
Blackjack; Aim	21 points or less
Bridge;-	
No Card over 9	Yarborough
Open Championship; Trophy	Bermuda Bowl
Women's Championship; Trophy	Venice Trophy
World Team Championship; Most wins	Italy
Cards; Queens; Model for	Elizabeth of York (15th Century)
Charades; Actions;-	
Name	Pat on head
Number of syllables	Fingers on arm
Sounds like	Tug on ear
Chemin de Fer; Meaning	Railway
Chess;-	
Castle; Other name	Rook
Grandmaster; Youngest	Bobby Fischer (14)
International Grandmaster; UK; 1st	Tony Miles
King; Colour on	Opposite to its own colour
Pawns; Each side	8
Pieces always on same colour squares	Bishop
Right-hand corner, colour	White
World Champion; Longest	Emanuel Lasker (27 years)
World Champion; Oldest	Steinitz (58)
World Champion; Regained title (twice)	Mikhail Botvinnik
World Champion; US; Only	Bobby Fischer
World Champion; Youngest	Garry Kasparov (22)
Cluedo;-	
Characters	Colonel Mustard, Professor Plum, Reverend Green, Mrs Peacock, Miss Scarlet, Mrs White
Weapons	Knife, revolver, spanner, lead pipe, rope, candlestick
Conkers; Strikes per turn	3
Craps; Player; Name for	Shooter
Crossword;-	
Author investigated for spying	1944 Daily Telegraph contained Normandy invasion code words
1st	Arthur Wynne, *New York World* (1913)
1st; Britain	*Sunday Express* (1924)
Dominoes;-	
Pips; Total	168
Set; Number	28
Euchre; Cards; Number	32
Frisbee; Original name	Pluto Platter
Gambling; Illegal in	Sweden
Games; Authority on	Edmund Hoyle
Gin Rummy; Cards per player	10
Go; Intersections	361
Mah Jongg;-	
Craze	1922, US
Suits	3
Tiles	Rectangular (144), suit (108), honour (28), flower (8)

Monopoly;-	
1st verdict	52 fundamental playing errors (Parker Bros)
Inventor	Charles Darrow (heating engineer)
Most valuable property	Mayfair (Boardwalk – US)
Towns	London, Atlantic City (US version)
Pinochle	
Cards	48
Pinochle	Jack of Diamonds, Queen of Spades
Poker;-	
Best hand	Royal flush (AKQJ10)
Full House	3 of a kind and a pair
Types	Stud, draw
Premium Bonds; Winner-selecting computer	ERNIE
Roulette; Numbers	1–36,0 (Double 0 in US)
Scrabble;-	
Inventor	James Brunot
Letter values	Q,Z: 10. J,X: 8. K: 5. Blank: 0

Games, Terms from

By: Term → Game

Box-up	Craps
Castling	Chess
Checkmate	Chess
Double	Bridge
Dummy	Bridge
En Passant	Chess
Full House	Poker
Giucco Piano	Chess
Grand Slam	Bridge
Lay Off	Gin Rummy
Meld	Rummy
Natural	Craps
Peg Out	Cribbage
Queen's Gambit	Chess
Redouble	Bridge
Royal Flush	Poker
Ruy Lopez	Chess
Shooter	Tiddlywinks
Stick	Pontoon
Taw	Marbles
Twist	Pontoon
Yarborough	Bridge

Holidays and Festivals

By: General

See Also: Ideas and Beliefs; Christianity

Armistice Day	November 11th
Bank Holiday;-	
1st; UK	Whit Monday
Instituted; UK	1871
Bastille Day	July 14th

Goose Fair; Famous	Nottingham
Hallowe'en; Name from	All Hallows Eve
Hogmanay	New Year's Eve (Scotland)
Mardi Gras	Shrove Tuesday
May Ball; Cambridge University; When	June
Mother's Day;-	
UK	4th Sunday in Lent (Mothering Sunday)
US	2nd Sunday in May
Pancake Day	Shrove Tuesday
Quarter Days	Lady Day, Midsummer Day, Michaelmas, Christmas
Queen's Official Birthday	Saturday in mid June
St Valentine's Day	February 14th

Leisure Activities and Skills

By: *General*

Birthstones;-	
January	Garnet
February	Amethyst
March	Aquamarine
April	Diamond
May	Emerald, agate
June	Pearl, moonstone
July	Ruby, onyx
August	Sardonyx, carnelian
September	Sapphire
October	Opal, beryl, tourmaline
November	Topaz
December	Turquoise, ruby, zircon
Boy Scouts;-	
Founder	Robert Baden-Powell (1908)
Highest grade	Eagle Scout
Types	Cub Scouts, Scouts, Venture Scouts
Collectors; Most	Stamps
Domestic Accidents; Most	Kitchen
Embroidery; Stitches	Lazy daisy, outline, blanket, buttonhole
Flower Show; British; Major	Chelsea Flower Show
Girl Guides; Founder	Robert Baden-Powell (1910)
Hobbies; Names of;-	
Bell Ringing	Campanology
Books; Collecting	Biblicphily
Butterflies; Collecting	Lepidoptery
Caving	Spelunking
Cheese Labels; Collecting	Fromology
Cigarette Cards; Collecting	Cartophily
Coins,Medals; Collecting	Numismatology
Dwarf Plant Growing	Bonsai
Flower Arranging	Ikebana
Hedge Shaping	Topiary
Matchbox Labels; Collecting	Phillumeny
Paper Folding	Origami
Picture Postcards; Collecting	Deltiology
Shells; Collecting	Conchology
Stamps; Collecting	Philately
Holiday Camp; 1st	Dodd's, Caister-on-Sea, Norfolk

Knitting; Stitches; Basic	Knit, Purl
Knots;-	
Lasso; Used for	Honda
Tying ropes to a post; Used for	Hitch
Tying ropes together; Used for	Bend
Needlework; Stitch; Most common	Running Stitch
Park; National; 1st	Yellowstone Park (1872)
Shell; Most expensive	Glory-of-the-Seas
Signature; Most expensive	Julius Caesar
Smoking; King size cigarette; 1st	Pall Mall
Weaving;-	
Crosswise threads	Weft,Woof
Lengthwise threads	Warp
Wedding Anniversaries;-	
10th	Tin
20th	China
25th	Silver
30th	Pearl
40th	Ruby
50th	Gold
60th	Diamond
70th	Platinum
Women's Institute; Britain; 1st	Llanfair PG, Anglesey
World's Fair 1962; Location	Seattle
YMCA; 1st organised	London, 1844. By: Sir George Williams
YWCA; 1st organised	London, 1855. By: Lady Kinnaird

Stamps

By: General

Actress; 1st on	Grace Kelly
Actress; British; 1st on	Sybil Thorndike
1st (prepaid stick on)	Penny Black, Twopenny Blue, Britain (1840)
Never appears on; British	Living person, apart from Monarch
No Country Name on	Britain
Place; Inscriptions;-	
Bayern	Bavaria
Cambodge	Cambodia
Drzava	Slovenia (Yugoslavia)
Eesti	Estonia
Helvetia	Switzerland
Hrvatska	Croatia
Island	Iceland
Hetuva	Lithuania
Magyar	Hungary
Nippon	Japan
Norge	Norway
Persanes	Iran
Romana	Romania
Shqiperia	Albania
Sverige	Sweden
Rarest; British	Sixpenny Purple (1904)
Valuable; Most	British Guiana, 1 cent, Black on Magenta (1856)

SPORT
American Football

By: General

Game; Length	1 hour
Pitch; Called	Gridiron
Player;-	
Key	Quarterback
Most valuable; Award	Jim Thorpe Trophy
Players; Number	11
Points;-	
Field goal	3
Safety touch	2
Touchdown	6
Rules	Harvard Rules
Rushing; Most yards gained	Walter Payton
Superbowl;-	
Contestants	Winners of National and American Football Conferences
Most wins	Pittsburgh Steelers, San Francisco 49ers
Trophy	Vince Lombardi trophy
When played	January
Winners 1988	Washington Redskins
Winners 1989/90	San Francisco 49ers
Winners 1991	New York Giants
Winners 1992	Washington Redskins
Teams;-	
Dallas	Cowboys
Green Bay	Packers
Miami	Dolphins
Washington	Redskins
Chicago	Bears
Los Angeles	Rams
San Francisco	49ers
Buffalo	Bills
New York	Giants, Jets
Houston	Oilers
Denver	Broncos
Minnesota	Vikings
Cleveland	Browns
Indianapolis	Colts
Pittsburgh	Steelers
Touchdowns; Most	Jim Brown

Association Football

By: General

Artificial Turf; 1st	QPR (1981)
Ball; Size	27–28 inch circumference
Black; 1st English International	Viv Anderson (1978)
Cap; Youngest; UK	Norman Whiteside (17)
Celtic/Rangers; Traditional support	Catholic/Protestant
Clubs; Nicknames;-	
Blades	Sheffield United

Bluebirds	Cardiff City
Canaries	Norwich City
Dons	**Aberdeen**
Gunners	**Arsenal**
Hammers	**West Ham**
Lions	Millwall
Magpies	Notts County
Owls	Sheffield Wednesday
Pensioners	Chelsea
Pilgrims	Plymouth Argyle
Reds	Liverpool
Robins	Bristol City
Saints	Southampton
Seagulls	Brighton and Hove Albion
Sky Blues	Coventry
Toffees	Everton
Wolves	Wolverhampton
Clubs; UK; Names;-	
Academical	Hamilton
Albion	West Bromwich, Brighton and Hove, Stirling
Alexandra	Crewe
Argyle	Plymouth
Athletic	Oldham, Wigan, Charlton, Dunfermline, Forfar
Forest	Nottingham
North End	Preston
Rangers	Queen's Park, Berwick, Glasgow
Rovers	Bristol, Blackburn, Doncaster, Tranmere, Albion, Raith
Thistle	Partick, Meadowbank
Wanderers	Bolton, Wolverhampton
Wednesday	Sheffield
Cup Winner's Medal; English, Scottish, Irish	J.Delaney
Disaster; Bradford Fire	During match with Lincoln (May 1985)
Division 1;-	
Champions, 1992	Leeds
Championships; Most	Liverpool
Most seasons in	Everton
3 consecutive wins	Huddersfield Town, Arsenal, Liverpool
Double, League and FA Cup	Preston North End (1889), Aston Villa (1897), Spurs (1961), Arsenal (1971), Liverpool (1986)
England–US, 1950 World Cup Match	England lost 1–0
European Cup;-	
English winners; 1st	Manchester United
1992	Barcelona
Scottish Club	Celtic (1967)
3 consecutive wins	Ajax Amsterdam, Bayern Munich
Winners; Most	Real Madrid (6)
European Cup Winner's Cup; 1992	Werder Bremen
European Footballer of the Year;-	
1st	Stanley Matthews
Most wins	Cruyff, Platini (3)

Most wins; UK	Kevin Keegan
3 consecutive years	Michel Platini
European Trophy; UK winners; 1st	Tottenham Hotspur (Cup Winner's Cup, 1963)
FA; Set up at	Freemason's Tavern, Lincoln Inn Fields
FA Cup;-	
1st	1872
Most wins	Tottenham Hotspur (8)
1988	Wimbledon (1–0, over Liverpool)
1989	Liverpool (3–2, over Everton)
1990	Manchester United (1–0, over Crystal Palace
1991	Tottenham Hotspur (2–1, over Nottingham Forest)
1992	Liverpool (2–0, over Sunderland)
Non-English club wins	Cardiff City (1927)
Non-League club wins	Tottenham Hotspur (1901)
Score; Highest	26–0, Preston North End v Hyde United
2nd Division Winner; Last	West Ham (1980)
Stanley Matthews Winner's Medal	1953, Blackpool
Stolen	1895, from Birmingham shop
3 consecutive wins	Wanderers, Blackburn Rovers
FA Cup Final;-	
Broken Neck; Kept goal with	Bert Trautmann, Manchester City (1956)
1st	Royal Engineers v Wanderers at Oval (1872)
Goalkeeper, not scored against in 3	Dick Pym, Bolton Wanderers
Horse cleared pitch	1923
Player sent off; 1st	Kevin Moran (1985, Manchester
Replay; 1st	1970
Replay; Last	1990
Scored for both sides	Tommy Hutchison (1981 – only goals), Gary Mabutt (1987)
Spurs; 1st defeat	1987
Team all Full Internationals	Manchester United (1985)
Wembley; 1st	1923
Youngest Player	Paul Allen, West Ham, 1980 (17)
FA Cup winners v League winners; Match	FA Charity Shield
Field; Length	100 to 130 yards
FIFA; President, 1961	Sir Stanley Rous
1st Class Matches; 1000; 1st	Pat Jennings
Former Names;-	
Ardwick	Manchester City
Clapton Orient	Leyton Orient
Leicester Fosse	Leicester City
Newton Heath	Manchester United
Small Heath	Birmingham City
Woolwich Arsenal	Arsenal
4th Division player; 1st Cap	V.Rouse (1959, Wales)
Goal;-	
Height	8 feet
Width	8 yards
Goals; Most;-	
International	Pele
International; England	Bobby Charlton
International; UK	Bobby Charlton (49)
League	Arthur Rowley

Match (Highest score)	Arbroath v Bon Accord (36–0) (1885)
Match; Individual	Joe Payne, Luton (10)
Match; Individual (1st Class); UK	John Petrie (13)
Match; League	**13–0 (Stockport v Halifax, Newcastle v Newport)**
Season	Dixie Dean (60)
Golden Boot Award	European top scorer
Governing Body; International	FIFA
Grounds;-	
Benfica	Stadium of Light
Brighton and Hove Albion	Goldstone
Cardiff City	Ninian Park
Celtic	Parkhead
Chelsea	Stamford Bridge
Coventry City	Highfield Road
Derby County	Baseball Ground
Dundee United	Tannadice Park
Everton	Goodison Park
Fulham	Craven Cottage
Glasgow Rangers	Ibrox Park
Leeds United	Elland Road
Liverpool	Anfield
Manchester City	Maine Road
Millwall	The Den
QPR	Loftus Road
Rangers	Ibrox Stadium
Sheffield United	Bramall Lane
Sheffield Wednesday	Hillsborough
Southampton	The Dell
Sunderland	Roker Park
Tottenham Hotspur	White Hart Lane
West Bromwich Albion	The Hawthorn
West Ham	Upton Park
Wolverhampton Wanderers	Molineux
Hat Tricks; Most;-	Pele
UK; International	Jimmy Greaves (6)
UK; League	Dixie Dean
UK; Season, Post war	Jimmy Greaves
Ian Botham; Football, Player for	Scunthorpe United
International Caps;-	
England; Most	Peter Shilton
100, 1st	Billy Wright
UK; Most	Pat Jennings
International Match; 1st	England v Scotland (Draw, 1883)
Knighthood; 1st	Stanley Matthews (1965)
League Champions; 3 consecutive years	Huddersfield Town, Arsenal, Liverpool
League Cup;-	
Division 3 winners	QPR, Swindon Town
1st	1961
Names	Milk Cup, Littlewoods Cup, Rumbelows Cup, Coca Cola Cup
1992	Manchester United
League Matches without defeat; 1st Division; Most	Nottingham Forest (42)
Liverpool Ground, Terrace; Nickname	The Kop
Match; Length	45 minute halves
Munich Air Disaster; Team	Manchester United (1958)

Peer; Played League football	Lord Kinnaird, Wanderers
Pele;-	
Brazilian Club	Santos
Played for Brazil	110 times
US Club	New York Cosmos
Penalty Spot; Distance from goal	12 yards
Playboy activities forced retirement	George Best
Player; Most valuable	Diego Maradona
Riot; Heysel Stadium, Brussels	European Champions Cup Final. Liverpool v Juventus (May 1985)
Scotland; National Stadium	Hampden Park, Glasgow
Scottish FA Cup; Most wins	Celtic
Scottish League;-	
Divisions	Premier, 1, 2
Most wins	Rangers
Soccer; Name; Derivation	Association Football
War; Caused by football match	El Salvador, Honduras (1969)
World Cup;-	
Double winners	Argentina, Uruguay, West Germany
Final; Hat Trick	Geoff Hurst (1966)
Hosted twice	Mexico
Most tournaments	5. Antonio Carabajal, Mexico (Goalkeeper)
Most wins	Brazil, Italy, West Germany (3)
Original trophy	Jules Rimet Trophy
Sent off: Argentinian Captain	Antonio Rattin (1966)
Top scorer	Just Fontaine, France (13 in 1958)
Top scorer; 1990	Schillaci (6)
Youngest player	Norman Whiteside (1982) (17)
World Cup; Winners;-	
1930 (1st)	Uruguay (in Uruguay)
1966	England (in England)
1970	Brazil (in Mexico)
1974	West Germany (in Germany)
1978	Argentina (in Argentina)
1982	Italy (in Spain)
1986	Argentina (in Mexico). (3–2 over West Germany)
1990	West Germany (in Italy). (1–0 over Argentina)

Athletics

By: General

See Also: Olympics for Athletic events at the Olympic Games

American Women's Team Championship; Won single handed	Babe Didrickson
Backwards; Running; Record	Bill 'Bojangles' Robinson
Cancer; Died of at 22 years	Lillian Board
Chariots of Fire; Athletes; About	Harold Abrahams, Eric Liddell (1924 Olympics)
Children; One of 43	John Akii-Bua
Decathlon; Events	100 m, 400 m, 1500 m, 110 m Hurdles, High Jump, Long Jump, Pole Vault, Discus, Javelin, Shot
Discus;-	
Circle; Diameter	2.5 m

Weight	Men: 2 kg. Women: 1 kg
Drugs; 1st UK life ban for	Jeff Gutteridge, Pole Vault (1988)
European Championship; 4 consecutive wins	Janis Lusis, Javelin
Field Event; Women don't participate in	Hammer, Pole Vault, Triple Jump
5000 m; Under 13 minutes; 1st	Said Aouita
400 m; Record holder; Women; For 7 years; Never competed in Olympics	Sin Kim Dan (North Korea)
Hammer; Weight	16 lb
Heptathlon; Events	100 m Hurdles, 200 m, 800 m, High Jump, Long Jump, Javelin, Shot
High Jump;-	
Backward; Style	Fosbury Flop
2 m; 1st; Women	Rosie Ackermann
6 ft; 1st	Marshall Jones Brooks (1876)
6 ft; 1st; Women	Debbie Brill (1970)
7 ft; 1st	C.Dumas (1956)
8 ft; 1st	Javier Sotomayor (1989)
Styles	Fosbury Flop, Scissors, Straddle, Western Roll
Hurdles;-	
110 m; Height; Men	3 ft 6 in
100 m; Height; Women	2 ft 9 in
110 m; Strides between	3
400 m; Height	Men: 3 ft. Women: 2 ft 6 in
400 m and 100 m; Number	10
Javelin;-	
100m; 1st over	Uwe Hohn (1984)
World Record; UK; 1st	Fatima Whitbread
Weight; Mens	800 g
London Marathon; 3 times winner; Women	Ingrid Kristiansen
Long Jump;-	
1930s record	Jesse Owens, lasted 25 years
Record	Mike Powell
Record holders; 20th Century; Number	12
US term	Broad Jump
Marathon;-	
Distance	26 miles 385 yards
Distance; Origin	Additional 385 yards to finish in front of Royal Box (Edward VII, 1908)
Origin	Run by Pheidippides to convey news of Battle of Marathon
Mile;-	
In 4 minutes; 1st (Exactly)	Derek Ibbotson (1958) (Bannister 1st under 4 minutes)
Under 3 minutes 50 seconds; 1st	John Walker (1975)

Under 4 minutes; 1st	Roger Bannister (May, 1954). Number
	    on shirt: 41. Time: 3 minutes 59.4
	    seconds. Venue: Iffley Road. Oxford

Under 4 minutes; 2nd	John Landy
Under 5 minutes; Women; 1st	Diane Leather (1955)

World Record Holders; UK	Sydney Wooderson, Roger Bannister,
	    Derek Ibbotson, Sebastian Coe,
	    Steve Ovett, Steve Cram

100 m;-

Biggest margin knocked off record
10 seconds; 1st   Florence Griffith-Joyner (1988)

10 seconds; 1st   Armin Hary (1960)

100 yd; Under 10 seconds; 1st   J.P.Tennent (1868)

110 m Hurdles; 13 seconds; 1st
under   Renaldo Nehemiah

Pentathlon;-

Events; Ancient   Running, Jumping, Discus, Javelin, Wrestling

Events; Modern   Cross-country Riding, Fencing, Pistol Shooting, Swimming, Cross-country Running

Events; Women   200 m, 100 m Hurdles, Shot, High Jump, Long Jump

Pole Vault;-

6m; 1st over   Sergey Bubka (1985)

19ft; 1st over   Terry Vigneron

20ft; 1st over   Sergey Bubka (1991)

Polio, Born with; Became sprint
champion   Wilma Rudolph

Professional record; Better than
amateur for 13 years   Shot, Brian Oldfield (1975–1988)

Racehorse; Runner won race with   Jesse Owens

Relay; Last runner   Anchorman

Shot;-

Circle; Diameter   7 ft

Methods   O'Brien Shift, Rotational

Weight; Men   16 lb

Sisters; Record Holders   Tamara Press (Shot, Discus), Irina Press (Decathlon)

Steeplechase;-

Waterjump; Depth (deepest)   2.5 ft

Waterjump; Times in Race   7

Sunday; Refused to compete on   Eric Liddell

Throwing events; Dual record holder   Tamara Press (Shot, Discus)

Top 10 Times in Event; Held   Ed Moses, 400 m Hurdles

Track Event; Men only   Steeplechase

Track Events; Direction   Anticlockwise

Unbeaten;-

Men; 1977–1987   Ed Moses, 400 m Hurdles

Women; 1956–1966   Iolanda Balas, High Jump

World Championship; 1987; Gold;
British; Only   Fatima Whitbread, Javelin

World Championship; 1991; Gold;
British; Only   Liz McColgan, 10000 m

World Record(s);-

5 in one day   Jesse Owens (1935)

Greatest achievement; Considered   Bob Beamon, Long Jump (1 ft 9½ in over record – 1968)

Longest held   Jesse Owens, Long Jump (25 years)

Mens; Never set at Olympics   Discus

Oldest holder   John Flanagan, Hammer (41)

Set 17, won only Bronze Medal   Ron Clarke

Women's better than Men's   Discus (Weights different)

'Worsens' significantly   Javelin (New Standard – 1987)

World Record Breaking run; Fell during
race   Lasse Viren, 10000 m (1972)

World Record Holder; UK; Became MP   Chris Chataway

Awards and Trophies

By: Award → Sport

Air Canada Silver Broom	Curling
America's Cup	Yachting
Ashes,The	Cricket
Bowring Bowl	Rugby Union
Britannia Cup	Rowing
Calcutta Cup	Rugby Union
Corbillon Cup	Table Tennis
Courtney Trophy	Rugby League
Curtis Cup	Golf
Davis Cup	Tennis
Eisenhower Trophy	Golf
Espirito Santo Trophy	Golf
Federation Cup	Tennis
Gordon Bennett Cup	Ballooning
Grand Challenge Cup	Rowing
Grey Cup	Canadian Football
Harry Sunderland Trophy	Rugby League
Jules Rimet Trophy	Football
King George V Gold Cup	Show Jumping
Lance Todd Award	Rugby League
Leonard Trophy	Bowls
Lonsdale Belt	Boxing
Lugano Trophy	Walking
MacRobertson International Shield	Croquet
Peall Trophy	Car Rallying
Prince Philip Cup	Rowing
Prince Philip Trophy (formerly President's Trophy)	Show Jumping
Princess Elizabeth Cup	Rowing
Queen Elizabeth II Cup	Show Jumping
Russell-Cargill Trophy	Rugby Union
Ryder Cup	Golf
Sam McGuire Trophy	Gaelic Football
Sheffield Shield	Cricket
Stanley Cup	Ice Hockey
Stewards Cup	Rowing
Swaythling Cup	Table Tennis
Thomas Cup	Badminton
Uber Cup	Badminton
Volvo World Cup	Show Jumping
Walker Cup	Golf
Waterloo Cup	Bowls, Greyhound Racing
Wightman Cup	Tennis

Badminton

By: General

All England Championship;-	
Men; Most wins	Rudy Hartono (Indonesia)
Most wins	Judy Devlin/Hashman (10)
7 successive years	Rudy Hartono (Indonesia)
Singles; UK winner; Last	Gillian Gilks (1978)
Family; Won 35 All-England titles	Frank Devlin, daughters Judy and Sue

International Team Events	Men: Thomas Cup. Women: Uber Cup
Name; origin	Badminton, Duke of Beaufort's house (1st played in UK at)
National Sport of Origin;-	Malaysia, Indonesia
Game	Shuttlecock and Battledore
Place	India
Points to win	15

Baseball

By: *General*

Field; Term for	Diamond
Home Base; Sides	5
Home Runs;-	
Most	Hank Aaron
Record for 40 years	Babe Ruth
Innings; Game (professional)	9
Inventor; Popularly known	Asner Doubleday
New York to Los Angeles; Team moved	Brooklyn/Los Angeles Dodgers
New York Yankees; Nickname	Bronx Bombers
Perfect Game; 1st Pitcher	Cy Young (1904)
Pitcher and Catcher; Term for	Battery
Rules	Cartwright Rules
Runs; Most	Ty Cobb
Team; Number in	9
Teams;-	
Baltimore	Orioles
Boston	Red Sox
New York	Yankees, Mets
Chicago	White Sox, Cubs
Philadelphia	Phillies
Pittsburgh	Pirates
Houston	Astros
Los Angeles	Dodgers
San Francisco	Giants
Cincinnati	Reds
St Louis	Cardinals
World Series	National League against American League Champions
Most wins	New York Yankees

Basketball

By: *General*

Baskets; 1st	Peach baskets
Highest Score in a Game	Wilt Chamberlain (100)
HIV Positive; Announces and retires	Magic Johnson
Inventor	Dr James Naismith (1892)
Kareem Abdul-Jabbar (Formerly Lew Alcindor); Team	Los Angeles Lakers
Most Popular Team	Harlem Globetrotters
Olympic Final; USSR beat US in last second	1972 (50–51), (1st US defeat)
Olympics;-	
Champions, 1992	CIS

Non US Winners	USSR, Yugoslavia
Points; Record	Kareem Abdul-Jabbar
Team; Number on court	5
Teams;-	
Boston	Celtics
Los Angeles	Lakers
New York	Knicks
Philadelphia	76ers
Wilt Chamberlain; Nickname	The Stilt

Bowling (Ten Pin)

By: General

Ball;-	
Holes in; Number	3
Weight	16 lb
Machine to pick up pins	Pin Spotter
Maximum Score possible in a game	300
Origin	To circumvent US ban on 9 pin bowling
Pins knocked down;-	
One ball	Strike
Two balls	Spare

Bowls

By: General

French Equivalent	Boules
Round; Term for	End
White Ball	Jack
World Champion;-	
Indoor; 3 times	David Bryant
Men; 3 times	David Bryant

Boxing

By: General

Notes: Unless otherwise stated, Championships refer to Undisputed World Titles.

Amateur Championship; US	Golden Gloves
Champion;-	
At most weights	Thomas Hearns (6)
British; Award	Lonsdale Belt
British; Held title for 64 days	Randol Turpin, Middleweight
Longest reign	Joe Louis (1937–49)
Most successful defences of title	Joe Louis
Murdered	Stan Ketchel (1910)
Oldest	Archie Moore, Light Heavyweight (48)
Undefeated as professional	Rocky Marciano (49 fights)
Youngest	Wilfred Benites, Light Welterweight (17)
Championship; Title fights; Most	Joe Louis
Eastern Europe; 1st professional	Laszlo Papp
Featherweight Champion; British; Last	Barry McGuigan (WBA)
Film; Subject of; With Robert De Niro	Jake Le Motta (*Raging Bull*)
Heavyweight Champion;-	
Bareknuckle; Last	John L.Sullivan

Black; 1st	Jack Johnson
British; Only	Bob Fitzsimmons (1897)
Brothers	Michael (IBF Champion) and Leon Spinks
Heaviest	Primo Carnera
Jailed for robbery, previously	Sonny Liston
Jumped bail for Immmorality Charge	Jack Johnson
Lectured on Shakespeare	Gene Tunney
Lightest	Bob Fitzsimmons
Longest Reign	Joe Louis (1937–49)
Non Black; Last	Ingemar Johansson (1959)
Oldest	Jersey Joe Walcott (37)
Olympic Champion at same weight	George Foreman, Joe Frazier
Regained Title; 1st	Floyd Patterson (beating Ingemar Johansson)
Regained Title; Twice	Muhammed Ali
Tallest	Primo Carnera
Undefeated	Rocky Marciano (49 fights)
Youngest	Mike Tyson
Heavyweight Champion; British; Longest Reign	Henry Cooper
Heavyweight Championship;-	
British; Father and Son (post-War)	Jack and Brian London
Father and Son fought for	Joe, Marvis Frazier (not together)
Gloves; 1st fought with	Jim Corbett defeated John L.Sullivan (1892)
Won on foul	Max Schmeling
Henry Cooper; Left hook called	'Ennery's 'ammer
Light-Heavyweight; Former name	Cruiserweight
Lightweight Champion; British	Freddie Welsh, Ken Buchanan (1970), Jim Watt (1979 – WBC)
Long Count; Fight known for	Dempsey v Tunney – count delayed and Tunney eventually won
Middleweight Champion; British	Bob Fitzsimmons (1891), Randolph Turpin (1951), Terry Downes (1961), Alan Minter (1980)
Million Dollar Gate; 1st	Dempsey v Carpentier (1921)
Muhammed Ali	
Defeated for title	Sonny Liston, George Foreman, Leon Spinks
Floored but saved by the bell	By Henry Cooper (1963)
Manager	Angelo Dundee
1974 Foreman Fight location	Kinsasha, Zaire
1975 Frazier Fight location	Manila
Olympic Victory	Light Heavyweight (1960)
Stopped; Only time	Last fight v Larry Holmes (1980)
Taunt to Ernie Tyrell	'What's my name?'
Title removed	1967 – for refusing Vietnam draft
Olympic Games;-	
Brothers; Gold Medals	Leon and Michael Spinks (1976)
Heavyweight Champion; Triple	Laszlo Papp (Hungary), Teofilio Stevenson (Cuba)
Losing Finalist disqualified for not trying	Ingemar Johansson (1952)
Queensbury Rules; 1st match under	Jim Corbett beat John L.Sullivan (1892)
Referee stopping fight; Term (US)	Technical Knock Out
Right hand; Leads with; Fighter	Southpaw

Round; Length	3 minutes (1 minute break)
Rules; Original	Queensbury
Titles; Most simultaneously	Henry Armstrong (3)
Weights; Professional	Fly, Bantam, Feather, Light, Junior Light, Junior Welter, Welter, Junior Middle, Middle, Light-Heavy, Heavy
Welterweight Champion;-	
5 times	Sugar Ray Robinson
British	Ted Kid Lewis (1915), Lloyd Honeyghan (1986)

Bullfighting

By: *General*

Barbed sticks	Banderillas
Bulls Killed; Number; Normal Bullfight	6
Matador;-	
Award	Tail or Ears
Cape	Muleta. Colour: Red one side, yellow other
Highest Paid	El Cordobes
Number	3
On Horses	Picadors
Passes; Term for	Veronicas
Stab bull with lances	Picadors

Cricket

By: *General*

Appeal; Call	How's That
Ashes; Term from	Mock obituary after Australia beat England
Bails; Number	2
Ball; Weight	5½ to 5¾ ounces
Bat; Weight; Limit	None
Benson & Hedges Cup;-	
2 consecutive wins	Somerset
Bishop; Former Test Cricketer	David Sheppard
Bodyline Controversy;-	
Bowler	Harold Larwood
Captain	Douglas Jardine
Ian Botham; Resigned from Somerset over	Sacking of Viv Richards, Joel Garner
Bowling;-	
Spin; Left Hander, off break	Chinaman
Spin; Reversed	Googly
Bradman; Score needed in last match for 100 Test Average	4 (out for a duck)
Brothers;-	
Australian; Played for country	Greg and Ian (later Trevor) Chappell
Pakistani; Played for country	Hanif, Mushtaq, Sadiq, Wazir Mohammed
7; Played for Worcestershire	Foster
South African; Played for country	Graeme, Peter Pollock

Captain;-
England; Olympic Boxing Champion	J.W.H.T.Douglas
Oldest; Test	W.G.Grace (50)

Century;-
And 10 wickets; Test	Ian Botham, Imran Khan
Double; Both Innings (First Class Cricket)	Arthur Fagg
Fastest	Percy Fender, Steven O'Shaugnessy (35 minutes)
Fewest Balls; Test	Viv Richards (56)
Most; Test	Sunil Gavaskar

County Champions;-
John Player League winners, same season	Essex (1984)
Most	Yorkshire
7 consecutive years; Post-War	Surrey
Creases	Return, Popping
Debut; Scores Ducks in; Test	Graham Gooch
Development; Village associated with	Hambledon, Hampshire
Dismissal; Ways	Bowled, Caught, Handling the ball, Hitting the ball twice to score, Hit wicket, LBW, Obstructing field, Run out, Stumped, Time out (recent)

England v Australia; Test;-
1st	1876
Trophy	The Ashes
FA Cup Medal; Test Cricketer	Dennis Compton

Fielding Position;-
Close behind wicket	Slip
Designates close in	Silly
Football International; Test Cricketer	Viv Richards, Dennis Compton (special match)
Football World Cup Medal; Played county cricket match	Geoff Hurst
4 Wickets without scoring; Test	India (against England, 1952)

Googly;-
Australian term	Bosie
Inventor	Nicholas Bosanquet

Highest Score;-
First Class Cricket	Hanif Mohammed (499)
Individual; Test	Garfield Sobers (365 not out)
Team; Test	903 for 7, England (1938)
Illegal Delivery	No ball
Illegal; England; Cricket made	By Edward IV, 1477 (till 1748)
Innings; Longest; Test	Hanif Mohammed
International Governing Body	ICC (International Cricket Conference)
Lords; Location	St John's Wood, London
Lowest Score; Test	New Zealand (26)

Matches; Most; Test;-
Captain	Sunil Gavaskar
England	Clive Lloyd
	Colin Cowdrey. 2nd: Geoff Boycott
MCC; Stands for	Marylebone Cricket Club
No Ball; Batsman dismissed from	Run out only
Obstructing the Field; 1st dismissal for, Test Cricket	Len Hutton
Oldest; Test Cricketer	Wilfred Rhodes
Olympics: Champions	Britain

Oval; Location	Kennington, London
Over;-	
Balls in	6
No runs scored	Maiden
Peer; West Indian	Learie Constantine
Players; Side	11
Prince; Indian; Played for Sussex	Ranjitsinhji
Record Book; Standard	Wisden
Run; Without touching bat	Bye, Leg Bye
Runs;-	
Highest Average; Test	Donald Bradman
Most; (First Class Cricket)	Jack Hobbs
Most; Test	Sunil Gavaskar
One Over; 36; (First Class Cricket)	Garfield Sobers (bowler: Malcolm Nash), Ravi Shastri
Season; 1st 1000 runs and 100 wickets	W.G.Grace
South African born player; Playing for England caused tour cancellation	Basil D'Oliviera
Sri Lanka; Test Victory; 1st	Against India (1986)
Stumps;-	
Distance between	22 yards
Height	28 inches
Width	9 inches
Test; Stopped as team's ship sailing	England v South Africa (1939)
Three W's; West Indian Cricketers, known as	Weekes, Worrell, Walcott
Throwing; Bowler in controversy over	Charlie Griffith, West Indies
Tied; Test	Australia v West Indies (1960), Australia v India (1986)
Umpire; Pakistani; Swore at	Mike Gatting. Umpire: Shakoor Rana
Umpire Signals;-	
4	Arm waved across body
Out	Finger up
6	Hands in air
W.G.Grace; County	Gloucestershire
West Indies; Spin Bowlers; 1950s	Sonny Ramadhin, Alf Valentine
Wickets; All in an innings; Test	Jim Laker (1956)
Wickets; Most;-	
England; Test Cricket	Ian Botham
First Class Cricket	Wilfred Rhodes
Test Cricket	Richard Hadlee
Test Match	Jim Laker (19–90 runs)
Women; English Captain; Famous	Rachel Heyhoe-Flint
World Cup;-	
Winners; 1983	India (beating West Indies)
Winners; 1987	Australia (beating England)
Winners; 1992	Pakistan (beating England)
Winners; Twice	West Indies
Youngest;-	
Test Cricketer	Mushtaq Mohammed, Pakistan (15)
Test Cricketer; England	Brian Close (18)

Cycling

By: General

Milk Race; Former name	Tour of Britain
Pursuit; Start	Opposite sides of track

Sprint; Professional; Champion;-

10 times consecutively	Koichi Wakano
UK; 54 year old	Reg Harris
Standing out of the saddle; Term	Honking
Teams of 2 riders; One racing	Madison, Americaine

Tour De France;-

Drugs test; Wins after positive	Pedro Delgado (1988)
Exhaustion, after drug taking, caused death	Tom Simpson, UK (1967)
1st Non European winner	Greg Le Mond, US (1986)
5 times winners	Jacques Anquetil, Eddy Merckx, Bernard Hinault
4 consecutive wins	Jacques Anquetil, Eddy Merckx
Leader wears	Yellow Jersey
1987 winner	Stephen Roche, Ireland
1988 winner	Pedro Delgado
1989/1990 winner	Greg LeMond
1991/1992 winner	Miguel Indurain
Track; Indoor; Length (common)	333 m
Wins; Most; Classic Races	Eddy Merckx

Darts

By: General

Bottom of Board	3
Bull (Inner); Points	50
Championship Games; Points	501
Highest Score; One dart	60
Next to 20	5 and 1
301; Minimum darts needed	6
Two Figure Number; Can't finish from with 2 darts	99
World Cup; Non England winner	Wales
World Masters Champion; Most wins	Eric Bristow

World Professional Champion;-

1st	Leighton Rees
Most	Eric Bristow (5)
Scottish	Jocky Wilson (1982)
Welsh	Leighton Rees

Equestrian Events

By: General

See Also: Horse Racing

Badminton, Winner;-

1st and 2nd same year	Ian Stark (1987)
Most	Lucinda Prior-Palmer/Green (6)
Most; 2nd	Mark Phillips (4)
3 Consecutive	Sheila Willcox/Waddington
Brothers; Italian; Olympic Gold and Silver	Raimondo, Piero D'Inzeo
European Championship winner, 1971	Princess Anne
Eventing; Sections	Dressage, Cross-Country, Show Jumping (in order)
Fence; Made of poles and a hedge	Oxer

Horses; Riders;-

Doublet	Princess Anne

Foxhunter	Colonel Harry Llewellyn
Mattie Brown	Harvey Smith
Mister Softee	David Broome
Priceless	Ginny Holgate/Leng
Sir Wattie	Ian Stark
King George V Gold Cup and Queen Elizabeth II Cup; Winner (horse)	Sunsalve
King George V Gold Cup; Winner; Most	David Broome (5)
Olympics;-	
Gold Medals; Most	Hans-Gunter Winkler (5)
Gold Medals; Most; Individual	Pierre D'Oriola (2)
Gold Medals; Most; UK	Richard Meade (3)
Show Jumping; Woman; 1st	Pat Smythe
Queen Elizabeth II Cup; Winner; Most	Liz Edgar
Trot; On the spot; Term for	Piaffer
V-Sign; Famous for	Harvey Smith
World Team Championship; Trophy	Prince Philip Trophy

Fencing

By: General

Guard; Foil or Epee	Coquille
Hit; Acknowledgement	Touché
Olympics;-	
Cheating; Caught	Boris Onischenko, USSR (Modern Pentathlon fencing event – 1976)
Gold Medal; UK; Only	Gillian Sheen
Scoring; Detected by (not Sabre)	Electrical contact
Target Area	Foil: Body only. Sabre: Over waist. Epée: No restriction
Weapons	Foil, Epée, Sabre
Women; Weapon	Foil only

Golf

By: General

Amateur Team Championship	Eisenhower Trophy
Army; Supporters called	Arnold Palmer (Arnie's Army)
Balls; UK–US	British smaller than US
British and US Open and Amateur Championships; Winner; 1st	Bobby Jones (1930)
British Open; Venue; 1990	St Andrews
British Open; Winner;-	
Most	Harry Vardon (6)
1991	Ian Baker Finch
1992	Nick Faldo
3 Consecutive; Last	Peter Thomson (1954–6)
UK; Last 5	Tony Jacklin (1969), Sandy Lyle (1985), Nick Faldo (1987/90/92)
Youngest; 20th Century	Seve Ballesteros (22)
Club;-	
Carrier	Caddie
Most can be used (professionals)	14
Used on the green	Putter
Used to drive from tee	Wood
18 Hole Course; 1st	St Andrews, Scotland

Grips; Normal	Interlocking, overlapping, two-handed
Headquarters	Royal and Ancient Club, St Andrews
Holes; Major Tournament played over	72
Millionaire; 1st	Arnold Palmer
Money; Biggest winner	Jack Nicklaus
Par; Terms for;-	
One over	Bogey
One under	Birdie
Three under	Albatross
Two over	Double Bogey
Two under	Eagle
Ryder Cup; Loses on final putt	Bernhard Langer (1991)
Suntory World Matchplay Championship; Winner; UK; 1st	Ian Woosnam (1987)
UK–US;-	
Biennial Women's Amateur Tournament	Curtis Cup
Men's; Amateur; Trophy	Walker Cup
Professional Competition; Trophy	Ryder Cup
US Masters;-	
Held at	Augusta, Georgia
Winner; Youngest	Seve Ballesteros
Wins; Most	Jack Nicklaus
US Open;-	
Amateur; 4 times Winner	Bobby Jones
Winner; Non US; Last	David Graham (Australia, 1981)
Winner; UK	Harry Vardon, Edward Ray, Tony Jacklin (1970), Sandy Lyle (1988)
US Women's Open; Winner; UK; 1st	Laura Davies
Warning Shout	'Fore'
Woman Golfer; 1st (reputed)	Mary, Queen of Scots
World Cup; Former name	Canada Cup

Greyhound Racing

By: General

Colours	1: Red. 2: Blue. 3: White. 4:Black. 5: Orange. 6: Black and White (Striped)
Distance; Standard	525 Yards
Dogs; Number	UK: 6. US: 8
Greyhound Derby;-	
Double Winner	Mick the Miller, Patricia's Hope
Held at	Wimbledon (since 1985)
Greyhound Grand National;-	
Held at	Hall Green, Birmingham (since 1985)
Wins; Most	Sherry's Pride (3)
Race; 1st	Hendon, London (1876)
Waterloo Cup; Held at	Attcar, Lancashire
Wins; Consecutive; Most	Ballyregan Bob (32)

Gymnastics

By: General

Beam	5 ft 4 in from ground, 4 in wide

Exercises;-
   Men   Floor exercises, Horizontal bar, Parallel bars, Pommelled horse, Rings, Vaulting horse

   Men and Women   Floor exercises, Vaulting horse
   Women   Assymetric bars, Beam, Floor exercises, Vaulting horse

Handspring; Backward   Flic-flac
Olympics;-
   Gold Medals; Most   Larissa Latynina (9)
   Gold Medals; Most; Individual   Vera Caslavska
   Gold; Youngest   Nad²a Comaneci (1976)
   Medals; Most   Larissa Latynina, USSR (18)
   Perfect Score; 1st   Nadia Comaneci (1976) (7 marks of 10)
   Perfect score; 1st; Men   Alexander Dityatin (1980)
   Slipped on Assymetric bars, 1972   Olga Korbut
   Team Championship; Men; Most   Japan
   Team Championship; Women; Most   USSR
World Champion: Youngest   Olga Bicherova (15)

Horse Racing

By: General

Ascot;-
   Month held in   June
   Racecourse owner   The Queen
Australia; Most important race   Melbourne Cup
Autumn Double   Bet on Cesarewitch and Cambridgeshire
Becher's Brook; Name from   Captain Becher fell at (1st Grand National, 1839)

Bookmakers' Sign Language   Tic Tac
Cesarewitch; Name from   Tsarevitch (later Tsar) Alexander II of Russia

Bob Champion; Grand National; Won on   Aldaniti
Champion Jockey;-
   Flat; Most times   Gordon Richards
   National Hunt; Most times   Gerry Wilson, John Francome
   13 consecutive seasons   Fred Archer
   26 times   Gordon Richards
Cheltenham Gold Cup;-
   3 consecutive wins; Post War   Cottage Rake (jockey: Aubrey Brabazon), Arkle (jockey: Pat Taffe)

   5 consecutive wins   Golden Miller
Classics   Oaks, Derby, St Leger, 1000 guineas, 2000 guineas. All for 3 year olds (and therefore can only be won once)

Controlling Body;-
   Flat Racing   Jockey Club
   National Hunt   National Hunt Committee
Derby;-
   Biggest winning distance   Shergar (1981, 10 lengths)

Distance	1.5 miles
1st run	1780
Inaugurated by	Earl of Derby and Sir Charles Bunbury
Jockey; 3 consecutive wins	Steve Donoghue
Most wins; Jockey	Lester Piggott
Suffragette killed at	Emily Davison (1913)
3 consecutive wins; Jockey	Steve Donoghue (1923–1925)
Toss coin to choose name	Earl of Derby, Sir Charles Bunbury
Winner; 1st	Diomed
Winner; 1988	Kahyasi
Winner; 1989	Nashwan
Winner; 1990	Quest for Fame
Winner; 1991	Generous
Winner; 1992	Dr Devious
Winner; Reigning monarch's horse	Minoru (1909 – Edward VII's)
Winner; Teenage jockey	Lester Piggott (1954)
Grand National;-	
Brooks	Bechers Brook, Valentines Brook
Distance	About 4.5 miles
Fences jumped once only	The Chair, Water Jump
Jockey; Most wins	George Stevens (5)
Jumps	30
Month held in	March or April
Ploughhorse won	Rubio (1908)
100-1 winner	Foinavon (1967)
Road crossing course	Melling Road
Royal horse collapsed	Devon Loch (1956) (Jockey: Dick Francis)
Trainer; Most Wins; Post war	Fred Rimell (4)
Triple winner	Red Rum
Winner; 1988	Rhyme and Reason
Winner; 1989	Little Polveir
Winner; 1990	Mr Frisk
Winner; 1991	Seagram
Winner; 1992	Party Politics
Woman jockey; 1st	Charlotte Brew (1977)
Woman jockey; 1st to complete course	Geraldine Rees
Harness Racing;-	
Gaits	Trotting, Pacing (same side legs together)
Trotting Classic; US	Hambletonian
Vehicle	Sulky
Horses; Measured in	Hands (4 inches)
Horseshoe; Nails in	8
Irish Classics; Run at	Curragh
Irish Grand National; Winner; Woman; 1st	Ann Ferris
Jockey;-	
Author after retiring	Dick Francis
Knighted; 1st	Gordon Richards
Most winners	Willie Shoemaker
Most winners; Flat racing; UK	Gordon Richards
Most winners; National Hunt; UK	Peter Scudamore
Retired, 1985; Returned 1990	Lester Piggott
Kidnapped; 1983; Horse	**Shergar**
Last Race, run 1916	**Blagdon Races**

Oaks; Distance	1.5 miles
1000 Guineas; Distance	1 mile
Pedigree; Listing	General Stud Book
Prix De L'Arc De Triomphe; Winner; 3 consecutive	Pat Eddery
Race Courses;-	
Cambridgeshire	Newmarket
Cesarewitch	Newmarket
Derby	Epsom
Grand National	Aintree
Kentucky Derby	Churchill Downs, Louisville
Melbourne Cup	Flemington Racecourse, Melbourne
Oaks	Epsom
1000 Guineas	Newmarket
Prix De L'Arc De Triomphe	Longchamp
Scottish Grand National	Ayr
St Leger	Doncaster
Steward's Cup	Goodwood
Sussex Stakes	Goodwood
2000 Guineas	Newmarket
Welsh Grand National	Chepstow
Racecourse; Largest	Newmarket
Spring Double	Bet on Lincoln Handicap and Grand National
Steeplechaser; Greatest; Considered	Arkle
Thoroughbred;-	
Ancestry	All thoroughbreds from 3 horses imported to England (Darley Arabian, Byerly Turk, Godolphin Arabian)
Birthday; (Northern Hemisphere)	January 1st
Definition	Registered in General Stud Book showing pedigree
Tote; French; Term	Pari Mutuel
Triple Crown	2000 Guineas, Derby, St Leger
Last winner	Nijinsky (1970)
US	Belmont Stakes, Kentucky Derby, Preakness Stakes
12 Winners in a row	Gordon Richards
Woman Jockey; 1st race won by	Eileen Joel, Newmarket Town Plate (1925)

Motor Racing

By: *General*

Accident; Worst	Le Mans (1955)
British Grand Prix;-	
4 times consecutive winner	Jim Clark (1962–65)
Most wins	Jim Clark (5)
Clay Pigeon Shooting Champion	Jackie Stewart
Drag Racing; Distance	1/4 mile
Grand Prix;-	
Champion;-	
Car designed himself	Jack Brabham
1st	Giuseppe Farina
Most times	Fangio (5)

Most times successively	Fangio (4)
1991	Ayrton Senna
1992	Nigel Mansell
Oldest	Fangio (46)
Posthumously awarded	Jochen Rindt
UK; British car; 1st	Graham Hill, BRM (1962)
UK; 1st	Mike Hawthorn (1958)
UK; Last	Nigel Mansell (1992)
US	Phil Hill, Mario Andretti
Wins; Most; UK	Nigel Mansell
Youngest	Emerson Fittipaldi (25)
Championship;-	
Most Grand Prix victories; Never won	Stirling Moss
2nd in 4 successive years	Stirling Moss
Championship points; Most in 1 year	Alain Prost
Constructor's Championship;-	
Most wins	Ferrari
UK winner; 1st	Vanwall
Flags;-	
Danger, no overtaking	Yellow
Disqualification of a driver	Black
End	Chequered Black and White
Oil on track	Yellow and Red Diagonal Stripes
Overtake; Car about to	Blue
Premature end	Red
Start	National Flag
Front position at start	Pole position
Governing Body; International	FIA
Oldest	French
Town circuit	Monaco
Wins; Most	Alain Prost
Wins; Most consecutive	Alberto Ascari (9)
Woman Driver; 1st	Lella Lombardi (1975)
Grand Prix Circuits;-	
Argentinian	Buenos Aires
Australian	Adelaide
Austrian	Osterreichring
Belgian	Spa-Francorchamps, Zolder
Brazilian	Rio De Janeiro
British	Silverstone, Brands Hatch
Canadian	Montreal
Dutch	Zandvoort
French	Dijon
German	Hockenheim, (New) Nurburgring
Italian	Monza
Mexican	Mexico City
Monaco	Monte Carlo
Portuguese	Estoril
San Marino	Imola (Italy)
Spanish	Montjuich
US	Detroit, Long Beach
Indianapolis 500;-	
Distance	200 laps
Non US Winners	Jim Clark (1965), Graham Hill (1966)
Started with	'Gentlemen, start your engines'

Wins; Most	A.J.Foyt, Al Unser (4)
Land and Water Speed Record Holder	Sir Henry Seagrave (1st), Malcolm Campbell (Bluebird), Donald Campbell
Land Speed Record;-	Richard Noble, Thrust II
Father and son	Malcolm, Donald Campbell
Last wheel driven holder	Donald Campbell, Bluebird (1964)
Over 100 mph; 1st	Louis Rigolly (1904)
Last rites; Given; Later Champion	Niki Lauda
Le Mans;-	
Film Star; Comes 2nd	Paul Newman
Manufacturer; Winner; 1981–87	Porsche
Manufacturer; Winner; 1988	Jaguar
Manufacturer; Winner; 1991	Mazda
Most wins	Jacky Ickx (6)
Monaco Grand Prix; 5 times winner	Graham Hill
Monte Carlo Rally;-	
Most wins	Sandro Munari, Walter Rohl (4)
Top 4 cars disqualified	1966
RAC Rally; Most wins	Hannu Mikola
Race;-	
1st Major	Paris–Rouen (1894)
1st UK	Gordon Bennett Race (1903)
Racing Circuit; 1st; UK	Brooklands
Rally; Longest; Annual	Safari Rally (East Africa)
Rallying; Champions; Nationality; Most	Finnish
Road Race; Italy; Closed down 1957	Mille Miglia

Motorcycle Racing

By: *General*

Champion;-	
Double (350 cc and 500 cc); 5 consecutive years	Giacomo Agostinhi
500 cc, 250 cc; Same season; 1st	Freddie Spencer (1985)
500 cc; UK; Last	Barry Sheene (1977)
Most times	Giacomo Agostinhi
7 consecutive years	Giacomo Agostinhi (500 cc)
500 cc; Manufacturers' Championship;-	
Last non Japanese bike	M.V.Agusta (1974)
17 consecutive years	M.V.Agusta
Isle of Man TT;-	
Fatalities	Over 130
Most wins	Mike Hailwood (14)
Motocross; World Champion; 5 consecutive years (250 cc)	Joel Robert

Olympic Games

By: *General*

Notes: Includes Athletic Events at the Olympics. Other Events under individual sports.

Ancient; Location	Olympia
Appearances;-	
Most	Raymondo D'Inzeo (8)
Most; Athletics	Lea Manolini (6)

Biathlon	Cross Country Skiing, Rifle Shooting
Black Power; Salute	Tommie Smith, John Carlos (1968)
Brazil; Gold; 1st	J Cruz, 800 m (1984)
Cancelled	1916, 1940, 1944
Cheating; Discovered	Boris Onischenko, in Modern Pentathlon, Fencing Section (1976)
China; Competes	1984. Previous time: 1952
Collision; Zola Budd – Mary Decker	3000 m (1984)
Colours; Chosen because	At least one in every flag
Competitor; British; Oldest	Hilda Johnstone, Dressage (70)
Country; In all Summer and Winter Olympics	UK
Decathlon; Gold; Twice	Bob Mathias (1948, 1952), Daley Thompson (1980, 1984)
Drugs Test;-	
Athletics medallist failed; 1st	Martti Vainio, 10000 m (1984)
Disqualification; 1st	Danuta Rosani (1976)
Disqualification; Athletics Gold Medallist; 1st	Ben Johnson, 100 m (1988)
800 m, 1500 m; Gold;-	
Men; Post-War	Peter Snell (1964)
Women	Tatyana Kazankino (1976)
Emblem	5 rings (representing the continents). Colours: Black, Blue, Red, Green, Yellow. Colour of upper left: Blue
Equestrian Events held in different country	Melbourne, 1956 (held in Stockholm)
Event;-	
Longest distance	Cycling Road Race (about 200 km)
Longest time	50 km walk
Extra Lap; Run by Mistake	Steeplechase (1932)
Father and Son; Gold Medallists	Imre Nemeth (Hammer), Miklos Nemeth (Javelin)
1500 m; Gold; Men; Twice	Sebastian Coe (UK)
1st Olympics; Greek winner	Spyridon Louis, Marathon
5000 m; Gold; Men; Country; Most	Finland
5000 m, 10000 m; Gold; Twice	Lasse Viren
5000 m, 10000 m, Marathon; Gold	Emil Zatopek, Czechoslovakia (1952)
400 m; 800 m; Gold; Only	Alberto Juantoreno, Cuba (1976)
400 m Hurdles; Gold; UK	Lord Burghley (1928), David Hemery (1968), Sally Gunnell (1992)
Games; Years;-	
1940 Olympics; 1st scheduled for	Tokyo
1944; Planned location	London
1984; Medals; Multiple; UK	Sebastian Coe (Gold and Silver)
1984; New sports	Sail-boarding, Synchronised Swimming
1988; New sport	Tennis
Gold Medal (Winners);-	
Athletic Event; Youngest	Ulrike Mayfarth, High Jump (16)
Athletics; Women; 4	Fanny Blankers-Koen (1948)
Athletics; Women; UK; 1st	Mary Rand (1964)
Disqualified, later reinstated; UK	Chris Brasher (1956)
Emulates Jesse Owens	Carl Lewis (1984)
Fell over during race	Lasse Viren, 10000 m (1972)
4 Consecutive games	Al Oerter, Discus (1956–68)

Host Country failed to win	Canada, Montreal (1976)
King (Former)	Constantine of Greece, Yachting (1960)
Made of	Over 90% Silver
Medals forfeited for receiving professional payments	Jim Thorpe
Most	Including 1906 Games: Ray Ewry (10). Otherwise: Larissa Latynina, Paavo Nurmi, Mark Spitz (9)
Most; Individual; UK; Year	1964
Most; 1 Games	Mark Spitz, 7 (1972)
Most; 1 Games; Athletics	Paavo Nurmi, 5 (1924)
Most; 1 Games; Athletics; Women	Fanny Blankers Koen, 4 (1948)
Most; 1 Games; Individual	Eric Heiden (5)
Most; 1 Games; Women	Kristin Otto, 6 (1988)
1984; UK; Athletics	Tessa Sanderson (Javelin), Daley Thompson (Decathlon), Sebastian Coe (1500 m)
1984; 4	Carl Lewis (100 m, 200 m, Long Jump, 100 m Relay)
1988; UK	5 (none in athletics)
1992; UK	5
Oldest	Oscar Swahn, Shooting (64)
Oldest; Men; Track Event	Miruts Yifter
Paralysed as a child	Ray Ewry
Priest	Robert Richards, Pole Vault (1952–56)
3 Consecutive Games; Women	Dawn Fraser (Swimming), Sonja Henjie (Skating)
Track; Women; UK; 1st	Ann Packer, 800 m (1964)
Winner; 1st	James Connolly, Triple Jump
Without winning	Nero (Ancient Games)
Women; Won by Man	100 m, Stella Walsh (1932)
Youngest; Individual	Marjorie Gestring, Diving (13)
Youngest; Men	Bob Mathias, Decathlon (17)
High Jump; Gold; Youngest and oldest winner	Ulrike Mayfarth (16, 28)
Highest Altitude	Mexico City
Husband and Wife, Gold on same day	Emil Zatopek, Dana Zatopekova (1952)
IOC (International Olympic Committee); President	Avery Brundage (1952–1972), Lord Killain, Juan Samaranch
Israeli Athletes; Massacre of	Munich, by Black September guerillas (1972)
Javelin;-	
Gold Medals; 2 Consecutive; Women; Only	Ruth Fuchs
Gold; UK; Only	Tessa Sanderson (1984)
Location;-	
Continent never held in	Africa
Twice at the same	Paris, London, Los Angeles
2 in 1 country	St Louis, Los Angeles (US)
Locations;-	
1948	London
1952	Helsinki
1956	Melbourne
1960	Rome
1964	Tokyo
1968	Mexico City

1972	Munich
1976	Montreal
1980	Moscow
1984	Los Angeles
1988	Seoul
1992	Barcelona
1996 (planned)	Atlanta

Long Jump;-

| Gold; Treble Winner; Only | Carl Lewis |
| Gold; UK | Lynn Davies, Mary Rand (1964) |

Marathon;-

Committed suicide when didn't win	K.T.Suburaya (Japan). Committed Hara-kiri after Tokyo Olympics (1964)
Double winner	Abebe Bikila (1960, 1964), Waldemar Cierpinski
1st; Helped across tape, disqualified	Dorando Pietri (1908)
Ran barefoot	Abebe Bikila (1960)
Winner; Never run before	Emil Zatopek (1952)
Women; 1st held	1984. Winner: J Benoit (US)

Marry; US and Czech Gold Medallists — Harold Connolly, Olga Fikotova

Mascot; 1980 — Misha (Bear)

Medal(s);-

50 years late	Anders Haugen got skiing bronze, 1974 after 1924 scoring error discovered
Most	Larissa Latynina, Gymnastics (18)
Most; UK; Individual	Sebastian Coe (4)
Reinstated after 61 years (1973)	Jim Thorpe
Summer and Winter Games	Edward Eagan (US)

Modern;-

1st	Athens (1896)
1st; Winter	Chamonix, France (1924)
Initiator	Baron Pierre De Coubertin

Olympic Flame; Woman; 1st lit by — 1968

Olympic Oath;-

| Athlete holds when taking | Corner of national flag |
| Woman; 1st | Heide Schuller (1972) |

100 m;-

Gold; Men; UK	Harold Abrahams (1924), Allan Wells (1980), Linford Christie (1992)
Gold; Men; Twice	Carl Lewes (US)
Gold; Women; Twice	Wyomia Tyus (US)

100 m; 200 m, 400 m; Gold Medals — Betty Cuthbert (in different Games)

100 m; 200 m; Gold; Men; Post-War — Bobby Joe Morrow (US – 1956) Valerie Borzov (USSR – 1972), Carl Lewis (US – 1984)

Parade;-

| Last | Host country |
| Leader | Greece |

Pole Vault; Gold; 1st Non US — Wolfgang Nordwig, East Germany (1972)

Scoreboard unable to correctly display score — Nadia Comaneci's perfect score (Gymnastics, 1976)

Sex Test;-

| 1st | 1968 |
| Woman not given; 1976 | Princess Anne (reputedly) |

Summer and Winter; Same country — France (1924), US (1932), Germany (1936)

Walkover, win by	Wyndham Halswelle, 400 m (1908)
Winter Locations;-	
1948	St Moritz
1952	Oslo
1956	Cortina d'Ampezzo, Italy
1960	Squaw Valley
1964	Innsbruck, Austria
1968	Grenoble
1972	Sapporo, Japan
1976	Denver
1980	Lake Placid
1984	Sarajevo
1988	Calgary
1992	Albertville
Women; 1st	1900 (Track and Field – 1928)
World Record;-	
Broke in heats, semi-final, final	Ludmila Bragina, 1500 m
1984; Only Track	Mens 4 × 100 m relay (US)
1992; Track	Mens 4 × 100 m/400 m relay (US)
	Mens 400 m hurdles (Kevin Young)

Other Sports

By: General

Angling; World Championships; Most wins	France
Archery	
Rings	Gold (centre), Red, Blue, Black, White (outer)
Target centre; Term	Gold
Australian Rules Football	
Inventor	George Ligowsky
Team; Number	18
Biathlon; Event	Cross Country Skiing, Rifle Shooting
Billiards; Balls	White (plain), White (spot), Red
Bobsleigh;-	
2 person Bobsleigh	Boblet
Number	2 or 4
Boules; Other name	Petanque
Canadian Football; Team; Number	12
Canoeing	
Canoes; Types	Canadian, Kayak
Flat water; Types	Sprint, Marathon
Olympics; Gold; Most	Gert Fredriksson
Righting capsized; Technique	Eskimo Roll
Rough water; Types	Slalom, Wild Water
Clay Pigeon Shooting; Clays released by	Trap
Croquet	
Balls	One side: Black and Blue. Other side: Red and Yellow
Titles; Most	John Solomon
Curling	
Ice area and team	Rink

Sweeping ice; Term for	Sooping
Team Captain	Skip
Diving	
Olympics; Golds; 4	Pat McCormick, Greg Louganis
Olympics; Golds; 3 successive	Klaus Dibiasi
Olympics; Head hits board	Greg Louganis (1988)
Olympics; Perfect score (twice)	Pete Desjardus (1928)
Grouse Shooting Season	
End	10th December
Start	Glorious Twelfth (12th August)
Hockey	
Olympic Champions, 1992	Germany
Olympic; Gold; 6 successive wins	India
Ice Hockey	
Game started or restarted with	Face Off
NHL; Most goals; Season	Wayne Gretzky
NHL; Most valuable player; 7 consecutive seasons	Wayne Gretzky
Olympic Champions; 1992	CIS
Olympic Championships; Most	USSR
Team; Number	6
Judo	
Olympics; Open winner; 1st	Anton Geesink
203 successive wins	Yasuhiro Yamashita
World Champion (Open); Only non Japanese	Anton Geesink, Holland (1961)
Karate; Meaning	Empty hand
Kung Fu; Meaning	Leisure time
Modern Pentathlon; Events	Cross Country Riding, Cross Country Running (4000 m), Fencing, Pistol Shooting, Swimming (300 m)
Netball	
Game; Length	4, 15 minute Quarters
Team; Number	7
Pheasant Shooting Season	1st October–1st February
Polo	
Originated in	Persia
Team; Number	4
Time	Up to 8 Periods (Chukkas) of 7 minutes
Pool	
8 Ball; Colour	Black
US name	Pocket Billiards
Rifle Shooting; Famous UK range	Bisley, Surrey
Rodeo; Professional; Duration required	8 seconds
Sports Aid; Date	May 25th, 1986
Tobogganning	
Course; Main	Cresta Run, St Moritz
Number	Luge: 1 or 2. Skeleton: 1
Rider feet first	Luge
Rider head first	Skeleton Tobogganning
Triathlon; Events	Swimming (3.8 km), Cycling (18 . . . Marathon
Volleyball; Team; Number	6
Water Polo	
Colours (caps)	Dark Blue, White, (Goalkeepers: Red)
Team; Number	7 (+ 4 Substitutes)

Water Skiing
  Titles; 4 individual, simultaneously   Liz Shetter
  World Champion; Men; 3 times   Sammy Duvall
Weightlifting
  Heaviest Weight Lifted   Paul Anderson
  Olympic; Lifts   Clean and Jerk, Snatch
  Power set of lifts   Bench Press, Dead Lift, Squat
Wrestling
  Amateur; Olympic styles   Freestyle, Graeco–Roman
  Amateur; Titles; Most   Aleksandr Medved
  Professional; Death after fight with
    Big Daddy   Mal Kirk

Rowing

By: General

Bumping   Object to bump boat in front
    (used at Oxford and Cambridge)

Cambridge; Reserve crew   Goldie
Club; Oldest; UK   Leander
Head of the River Race; Direction   Opposite to the Boat Race
Henley; Sculling event   Diamond Sculls
International Governing Body   FISA
Oarsman;-
  1 oar   Rowing
  2 oars   Sculling
Oxford; Reserve crew   Isis
Oxford–Cambridge Boat Race;-
  Course   Putney to Mortlake
  Dead heat   1877
  Distance   4¼ Miles
  1st   1829
  1st Woman in team   Susan Brown (1981)
  Number in boat   9 (8 Rowers, 1 Cox)
  6 winning teams   Boris Rankov
  Winner; 1992   Oxford
  Wins; Longest run of   Oxford (1976–85)
  Wins; Most   Cambridge
Pace Setter   Stroke
Race; Sculling; Oldest   Doggetts Coat and Badge
Race;-
  Length; Standard   Men: 2000 m, Women: 1000 m
  Longest   Boston Marathon, Lincolnshire
Regatta; Main; UK   Henley Royal Regatta
Steers boat   Cox (Swain)

Rugby League

By: General

Australia; Team nickname   Kangaroos
Broken Arm; Played international with   Alan Prescott
Challenge Cup; 4 consecutive years   Wigan
Challenge Cup Final; Man of the Match;
  Award   Lance Todd Award
Countries Playing; Important   Australia, Britain, France, New Zealand
Divisions   2

Lance Todd Award; Dual winner	Gerry Helme
New Zealand; Team nickname	Kiwis
Nickname;-	
Chemics	Widnes
Wires	Warrington
Original name	Northern Rugby League
Originates	George Hotel, Huddersfield (1895)
Players; In Rugby Union, not in League	Flank Forwards
Players; Team; Number	13
Points;-	
Most; Career	Neil Fox
Most; Match; International	Jim Sullivan
Premiership Final; Man of the Match; Award	Harry Sunderland Trophy
Premiership Trophy;-	
And National Champions, same year	Hull Kingston Rovers, Wigan
Former name	Championship Playoff
Scored in Every Game; 2 consecutive seasons	David Watkins
Tournament;-	
Knockout; Main	Challenge Cup
Top League Clubs; Award	Premiership Trophy
Tries;-	
Most; Career	Brian Bevan
Most; International	Mick Sullivan
World Cup; Most wins	Australia

Rugby Union

By: General

All Blacks; Dance	Haka
British Lions; South African Tour, 100% record	1974. Captain: Willie John McBride
Caps, Most;-	Mike Gibson, Ireland
England	Rory Underwood
Scotland	Andy Irvine, Jim Renwick
Wales	J.P.R.Williams
Captain; France; Most	Jean-Pierre Rives
Colours (Jerseys);-	
Australia	Gold
Barbarians	Black and White (Hoops)
England	White
France	Blue
Ireland	Green
New Zealand	Black
Scotland	Blue
Wales	Red
County Champions; 1992	Lancashire
Debut for Wales; Equalled scoring record	Keith Jarrett
Drop Goal; Longest	Gerry Brand, South Africa (90 yards)
Emblems;-	
England	Red Rose
Ireland	Shamrock
New Zealand	Silver Fern

Scotland	Thistle
South Africa	Springbok
Wales	Fleur De Lys
England–Scotland; Trophy	Calcutta Cup
England; South Africa; 1st victory	1969. England Captain: Bob Hiller
Five Nations Competition;-	
Champions; Most	Wales
Champions; 1991/1992	England
Five Way Tie	1973
Winning all matches	Grand Slam
Flank Forward; Other name	Wing Forward
Fly Half; Other name	Stand-Off Half
Grounds, International;-	
England	Twickenham
France	Parc Du Prince
Ireland	Lansdowne Road
Scotland	Murrayfield
Wales	Cardiff Arms Park
Home International Competition;	
Winning all matches	Triple Crown
Internationals;-	
Captains on 1st	Mike Watkins, Wales. Nigel Melville, England. J. S. Ritchie, Ireland
Prince (Russian)	Alexander Obolensky, England (1936)
Player sent off; 1st; Post-War	Colin Meads
Union and League	David Watkins (Lions/Great Britain), Keith Fielding (England), Jonathan Davies (Wales)
John Player Cup; Winners 1984–87	Bath
Lions;-	
Defeated All Blacks; 1st	1971
Official Name	British Isles Rugby Union team
Match; Length	2 × 40 minute halves
Nicknames;-	
Argentina	Pumas
Australia	Wallabies
New Zealand	All Blacks
South Africa	Springboks
Olympic Champions	US (last played 1924)
Originator (supposed)	William Webb Ellis of Rugby School (1823)
Oxford, Cambridge; Trophy	Bowring Bowl
Place Kick; Longest; International	Paul Thorburn, Wales (70 yards)
Players; Number	15
Points;-	
Conversion	2
Penalty	3
Try	4
Points; Most;-	
First Class Matches; Career	Dusty Hare
First Class Matches; Season	Sam Doble
International	Michael Lynagh
International; England	Dusty Hare
International; Ireland	Olly Campbell
International; New Zealand	Don Clarke
International; Scotland	Andy Irvine
International; Wales	Phil Bennett

Pontypool Front Row; Legendary	Graham Price, Bobby Windsor, Charlie Faulkner
Streaker; Twickenham	Erika Roe
Tries:-	
First Class Matches; Most	Alan Morley, Bristol
International; Most	David Campese, Australia
Varsity Match; Most wins	Cambridge

Sailing

By: General

See Also: *Science and Technology; Sea Transport*

Admiral's Cup	Fastnet, Britannia Cup, + two
America's Cup;-	
Location	Off Newport, Rhode Island
Non American Winner; Only	Australia (1983), Skipper: John Bertrand. Boat: *Australia II*
Winner; 1987	US. Boat: *Stars and Stripes*
Atlantic Crossing; Fastest	*Virgin Atlantic Challenger II* (1986) Skipper: Richard Branson
Australia; Main races	Southern Cross Series
Change Course;-	
Away from wind	Gybe
Towards wind	Luff
Compass Housing	Binnacle
Deck; Raised part of rear	Poop
Fastnet Race; Course	Ryde, Round Fastnet Rock, Portsmouth
Hulls;-	
3	Trimaran
2	Catamaran
Olympic Classes;-	
Biggest	Soling (only 3 man crew)
Fastest	Tornado (Catamaran)
Smallest	Finn (only solo class)
Olympics;-	
Flying Dutchman Class; Double winner; UK	Rodney Pattison. Boats: *Superdocious, Superdoso*
4 consecutive wins	Paul Elvstrom
Race; Longest regular	Whitbread Round the World Race
Sail;-	
Forward	Jib
Ropes for hoisting	Halyards
Ropes for trimming	Sheets
Single-handed Transatlantic Race; Double winner	Francis Chichester, Eric Tabarly
Whitbread Round the World Race; Double winner	Cornelius Van Rietschoten
Wind; Sail against in zigzag course	Tack
Yacht Designers; US brothers	Olin, Rod Stephens

Skating

By: General

Champions; World, British, European; 4 successive years	Bernard Ford, Diane Towler (1966–1969)

Grand Slam;-	World, European, Olympic Titles
Individual; Double; Men	Karl Schafer
Individual; Double; Women	Sonja Henjie
Individual; UK	John Curry (1976)
Pair; UK	Torvill and Dean (1984)
Olympics;-	
Figure Skating; Men; UK winners	John Curry, Robin Cousins
Figure Skating; Women; UK winners	Madge Cave/Syers, Jeanette Altweg
Ice Dance; UK winners	Torvill and Dean
Pairs; 3 consecutive wins	Irina Rodnina (with Ulanov, Zaitsev)
Speed Skating; All medals in one Games	Eric Heiden (1980)
Titles; 5 in one year	Dick Button
World Championships; Most wins;-	
Ice Dance	Pakhomova and Gorshkov
Men (Individual)	Ulrich Salchow
Women (Individual)	Sonja Henjie (10 consecutive)

Skiing and Winter Sports

By: General

Alpine Skiing; Events	Downhill, Giant Slalom, Slalom
Downhill Race; Longest	The Inferno
Everest; Skied down	Yuichiro Muira (Japan)
Olympics;-	
Alpine and Nordic events; Gold; Only	Birger Ruud
Gold; Triple (all events)	Toni Sailer (1956), Jean-Claude Killy (1968)
Sisters; Gold and Silver; Slaloms	Christine, Marielle Goitschel (1 Gold each)
Twins; Gold and Silver; 1984	Phil, Steve Mahre
Race; Long Distance; Most famous	Vasaloppet
Ski-jumping;-	
Came last; 1988 Olympics	Eddie Edwards
Landing	Telemark position
World Championship; All events; Winner	Toni Sailer, Jean-Claude Killy
World Cup;-	
Brother and Sister winners	Andreas, Hanni Wenzel (Liechtenstein)
Most wins	Ingemar Stenmark
Most wins; Men; Downhill racing	Franz Klammer
Most wins; Men; Slalom	Ingemar Stenmark
Most wins; Women	Annemarie Proll/Moser

Snooker

By: General

Balls;-	
Made of	Crystallate
Number	21 + Cue ball

Values	Red: 1. Yellow: 2. Green: 3. Brown: 4. Blue: 5. Pink: 6. Black: 7
Break, Maximum;-	
1st in World Championship	Cliff Thorburn
1st on TV	Steve Davis
Pots needed	36
Score (no fouls)	147
Brothers; World Champions	Joe, Fred Davis
Father and Son: Partners in major Championship	Geoff, Neal Foulds
1st played	Jubbulpore, India
Head Butting; Fined for	Hurricane Higgins
Pot Black Competition; Winner; 1st	Ray Reardon
Table Bed; Made of	Slate
UK Open; Venue	Guild Hall, Preston
World Champion;-	
Amateur; Youngest	Jimmy White (1980)
1st	Joe Davis
1st after Joe Davis	Walter Donaldson
Most wins	Joe Davis (15)
1986	Joe Johnson
1987	Steve Davis
1988	Steve Davis
1989	Steve Davis
1990	Stephen Hendry
1991	John Parrott
1992	Stephen Hendry
Non UK	Horace Lindrum, Australia (1952), Cliff Thorburn, Canada (1980)
3 consecutive years; Last	Steve Davis
Youngest	Stephen Hendry

Speedway

By: General

Champion;-	
3 consecutive years	Ivan Mauger
Individual, Pairs, Long Track, Team; Simultaneously	Erik Gundersen
Most years	6. Ivan Mauger, New Zealand
UK; Last	Gary Havelock (1992)
UK; Twice	Peter Craven
Club; UK; Most Championships	Belle Vue
Laps in a race	4
Races in a meeting; Usual number	20

Sport, General

By: Description → Sport

Afghanistan; National game	Bushkazi
Backwards; Competitors travel	Tug of War, Rowing, Backstroke Swimming
Ball Game; Fastest	Jai Alai
Ball; Hit with gloves	Fives

Earnings;-

Most; Men (estimated)	Muhammed Ali
Most; Women	Martina Navratilova
Eton; Played only at	Eton Wall Game
Fatalities; Leisure activity; Most; UK	Fishing
Loser sacrificed	Mayan Ball Game
Minoan Crete; Played in	Bull Leaping
Nickname; 'Sport of Kings'	Horse Racing
Popular; Most	Football
Trophy; Dog finds after stolen	World Cup (1966)

Sporting Terms

By: Term → Sport

Adolph	Trampolining
Albatross	Golf
Assist	Basketball
Axel	Skating
Back Alley	Badminton
Balestra	Fencing
Barani	Trampolining
Besom	Curling
Bib	Netball
Birdie	Golf
Blind Side	Rugby
Bogey	Golf
Bonspiel	Curling
Boston Crab	Wrestling
Brakeman	Bobsleigh
Bunt	Baseball
Burgee	Yachting
Button	Curling, Rowing
Buttonhook	Basketball
Bye	Cricket
Calx	Eton Wall Game
Caman	Shinty
Cannon	Billiards
Catalina	Synchronized Swimming
Catch a Crab	Rowing
Chicane	Motor Racing
Chinaman	Cricket
Christie	Skiing
Chukka	Polo
Circle	Dressage
Close-hauled	Yachting
Cover	Cricket
Cover Point	Cricket
Crampit	Curling
Cross Buttock	Wrestling
Crucifix	Gymnastics
Dig	Volleyball
Ditch	Bowls
Dog Leg	Golf
Down	American Football
Drop Out	Rugby
Dropped Goal	Rugby
Dunk	Basketball

Eagle	Golf
Eastern Grip	Tennis
Egg Position	Skiing
English	Pool
Eskimo Roll	Canoeing
Extras	Cricket
Face Off	Ice Hockey
Fine Leg	Cricket
Flèche	Fencing
Flic-Flac	Gymnastics
Fliffus	Trampolining
Flying Mare	Wrestling
Follower	Australian Rules Football
Free Throw	Basketball
Gaff	Yachting
Garryowen	Rugby
Genoa	Yachting
Goal Crease	Lacrosse
Googly	Cricket
Goosewinged	Yachting
Gully	Cricket
Gybe	Yachting
Half Nelson	Wrestling
Halyard	Yachting
Hand In	Squash
Hash Marks	American Football
Hecht	Gymnastics
Herringboning	Skiing
Hog	Curling
Hog's Back	Show Jumping
Hooker	Rugby
Hoop	Croquet
House	Curling
Hurley	Hurling
In Touch	Rugby
Irish Whip	Wrestling
Jack	Bowls
Jib	Yachting
Jump Off	Show Jumping
Keyhole	Basketball
Kiggle Kaggle	Curling
Kip	Gymnastics
Knock-on	Rugby
Laundry, Hand Out	Drag Racing
Line Out	Rugby
Lock	Rugby
Long Hop	Cricket
Loop	Skating
Luff	Yachting
Lutz	Skating
Maiden	Cricket
Mallet	Croquet
Mashie	Golf
Maul	Rugby
Mid Off/On	Cricket
Miller	Trampolining
Monkey Climb	Wrestling

Niblick	Golf
No Ball	Cricket
Oxer	Show Jumping
Painter	Yachting
Parallelogram,The	Gaelic Football
Pebble	Curling
Penholder Grip	Table Tennis
Penthouse	Real Tennis
Pike	Gymnastics
Pinch Hitter	Baseball
Piste	Fencing, Skiing
Planche	Gymnastics
Plastron	Fencing
Poop	Yachting
Popping Crease	Cricket
Prop	Rugby
Randolph (Randy)	Trampolining
Repechage	Rowing
Riposte	Fencing
Rocker	Skating
Roquet	Croquet
Rover	Australian Rules Football, Croquet
Ruck	Rugby
Rudolph (Rudy)	Trampolining
Salchow	Skating
Schuss	Skiing
Scissors	Rugby
Scrimmage	American Football
Scrum	Rugby
Sell a Dummy	Rugby
Serpentine	Dressage
Short Leg	Cricket
Shroud	Yachting
Shuttlecock	Badminton
Silly Point	Cricket
Sliothar	Hurling
Slip	Cricket
Snap	American Football
Soop	Curling
Spider	Darts, Snooker
Spike	Volleyball
Spinnaker	Yachting
Spoon	Golf/Angling
Stealing Bases	Baseball
Stutz	Gymnastics
Sulky	Harness Racing
Surf Board	Wrestling
Tack	Yachting
Tee	Golf, Curling
Third Man	Cricket
Three	Skating
Tice	Croquet
Tinsica	Gymnastics
Toucher	Bowls
Trapeze	Yachting
Triangle and Sausage	Yachting
Tsukahara	Gymnastics

Up and Under	Rugby
Vortage	Skiing
Votte	Dressage
Walkover	Gymnastics
Wedge	Golf
Wind up	Baseball
Wipe Out	Surfing
Wired	Croquet
Yamashita	Gymnastics
Yorker	Cricket

Sportspeople

By: Description → Name

Notes: Covers only descriptions not specific to a single sport.

Brothers; Both County Cricketers, 1st Division Footballers	Leslie, Dennis Compton
Cricketer; 1st President of English Bowls Association	W.G.Grace
England International;- Football and Cricket	Charles Fry (also World long jump record holder), Denis Compton
Rugby and Cricket;	M.J.K.Smith
International Competitor;- Youngest	Anita Jokiel, Polish Gymnast (11)
Youngest; UK	Magdalena Colledge, Skater (11)
King; Offered position of	Charles Fry (by Albania)
Knighthood; Professional Sportsman; 1st	Jack Hobbs
Motor Racing, Motocycling; World Champion	John Surtees
Sportswoman of the Year, 1971	Princess Anne
Winnings; Over $100,000; Woman; 1st	Billie Jean King
World Champion; Cycling; Speed Skating	Sheila Young (US – 1973)
World Record(s);- Most broken	Vasily Alexeev, USSR (Weight Lifting)
Youngest holder	Gertrude Ederle, 880 yards Swimming (12)

Sportspeople

By: Name → Sport

Notes: Mainly covers less well known sports.

Kareem Abdul-Jabbar	Basketball
Vasily Alexeev	Weightlifting
Jacques Anquetil	Cycling
Earl Anthony	Ten Pin Bowling
Alberto Ascari	Motor Racing
Viktor Barna	Table Tennis
Jonah Barrington	Squash
Billy Boston	Rugby League
David Broome	Show Jumping
Jim Brown	American Football
David Bryant	Bowls

Beryl Burton	Cycling
Erik Carlsson	Rally Driving
Wilt Chamberlain	Basketball
Ty Cobb	Baseball
Fausto Coppi	Cycling
Joe Dimaggio	Baseball
Christian D'Oriola	Fencing
Desmond Douglas	Table Tennis
Joey Dunlop	Motor Cycle Racing
Sammy Duvall	Water Skiing
Paul Elvstrom	Yachting
Juan Manuel Fangio	Motor Racing
Gert Fredriksson	Canoeing
Anton Geesinck	Judo
Gillian Gilks	Badminton
Lucinda Green	Eventing
Wayne Gretzky	Ice Hockey
Jill Hammersley	Table Tennis
Ellery Hanley	Rugby League
Reg Harris	Cycling
Rudy Hartono	Badminton
Bernard Hinault	Cycling
Gordie Howe	Ice Hockey
Geoff Hunt	Squash
V.Ivanov	Rowing
Karin Enke/Kania	Speed Skating
Peritti Karppinen	Rowing
John B.Kelly	Rowing
Jahangir Khan	Squash
Meadowlark Lemon	Basketball
Virginia Leng	Eventing
Joe Lydon	Rugby League
Mickey Mantle	Baseball
Pat McCormick	Diving
Heather McKay	Squash
Aleksandr Medved	Amateur Wrestling
Eddy Merckx	Cycling
Dally Messenger	Rugby League
Eugenio Monti	Bobsleigh
Pat Moss-Carlsson	Rally Driving
Nedo Nadi	Fencing
Koichi Nakano	Cycling
Joe Namath	American Football
Tazio Nuvolari	Motor Racing
Jerzy Pawlowski	Fencing
William 'The Refrigerator' Perry	American Football
Don Ritchie	Long Distance Running
Stephen Roche	Cycling
Aleksandr Romankov	Fencing
Bill Russell	Basketball
Babe Ruth	Baseball
Nolan Ryan	Baseball
Neum Shalamanov/Suleymanoglu	Weightlifting
O.J.Simpson	American Football
Harvey Smith	Show Jumping
Pat Smythe	Show Jumping
John Solomon	Croquet

Ian Stark	Eventing
Goose Tatum	Basketball
Joe Theissman	American Football
Aleksandr Tikhonov	Biathlon
Daniel Topolski	Rowing
Johnny Unitas	American Football
John Whitaker	Show Jumping
Yasuhiro Yamashita	Judo

Squash

By: General

Ball Boy; Became World Champion	Hashim Khan
British Open Champion;-	
Most times; Men	Jahangir Khan (10, consecutive)
Most times; Women	Heather Blundell/McKay, Australia
UK; Men; Last	Jonah Barrington (1973)
Champion, Open;-	
5 years in succession	Jahangir Khan (1981–85)
1991	Rodney Martin
Youngest	Jahangir Khan
Family; Most dominant	Khans (Hashim, Azam, Mohibullah, Roshan, Jahangir)
Origin	Harrow School
Rivals; Famous, 1970s	Jonah Barrington, Geoff Hunt
Undefeated;-	
5 years	Jahangir Khan
Woman; 16 years	Heather Blundell/McKay

Swimming

By: General

Backstroke; Men; Unbeaten for 7 years	Roland Matthes
Butterfly; Established	1952
English Channel, Swimming;-	
Both Ways; Woman; 1st	Florence May Chadwick
1st; Man	Captain Matthew Webb (1875)
1st; Woman	Gertrude Ederle (1926)
Youngest	Marcus Hooper (12)
1500 m; 15 minutes; 1st under	Vladimir Salnikov (1980)
400 m; 4 minutes; 1st under	Rick De Mont
International Governing Body	FINA
Olympic Pool; Lanes	8
Olympics, Gold;-	
Black Swimmer; 1st	Anthony Nesty, Surinam (1988)
Disqualification for drugs (taken for asthma)	Rick De Mont (1972)
Most	Mark Spitz, 9 (8 World Records)
Most; 1 Games	Mark Spitz, 7
Most; 1 Games; Women	Kristin Otto, 6
Slower time than Silver Medallist	John Devitt, 100 m (1960)
3 individual titles in 1 Games; 1st	Debbie Meyer
3 successive Games (same event)	Dawn Fraser, 100 metre Freestyle
UK; Individual; Men (Post-War)	David Wilkie (1976), Duncan Goodhew (1980), Adrian Moorhouse (1988)

UK; Individual; Women	Lucy Morton (1924), Judy Grinham (1956), Anita Lonsbrough (1960)
Olympics; Medals; Most	Mark Spitz, 11
100 m;-	
1 minute; 1st under	Johnny Weismuller (1922)
1 minute; 1st under; Women	Dawn Fraser
50 seconds; 1st under	Jim Montgomery (1976)
Strokes; Speeds	Crawl (fastest), Butterfly, Backstroke, Breaststroke (slowest)
200 m; 2 minutes; 1st under	Men: Don Schollander. Women: Kornelia Ender
World Records; 5 Freestyle simultaneously	Shane Gould

Table Tennis

By: *General*

Champion;-	
1st 5 times; Women	Maria Mednyanszky
Most times; Men	Viktor Barna
Most times; Women	Angelica Rozeanu, 6 (in successsion)
Singles, Doubles, Mixed; Twice	Viktor Barna
Team; Most; Men	Hungary
3 times in succession; Post-War; Men	Chuang Tse-Tung
2 Countries; Men	Richard Bergmann (Austria, England)
UK; Men	Fred Perry, Richard Bergmann, Johnny Leach (1951)
Men's Team Championship; Trophy	Swaythling Cup
Net; Height	6 inches
Twins; Won 2 World Championships	Diane, Rosalind Rowe
Women's Team Championship; Trophy	Corbillon Cup
World Titles; Most; Men	Viktor Barna

Tennis

By: *General*

Battle of the Sexes	Billy Jean King defeated Bobby Riggs (1973). (Riggs had beaten Margaret Court)
Davis Cup;-	
Most wins	US
6 consecutive years	France
Four Musketeers	Jean Borotra, Jacques Brugnon, Henri Cocket, René LaCoste
French Open; Venue	Stade Roland Garros
Grand Slam;-	Holding Wimbledon, US, Australian and French titles simultaneously (originally winning all in 1 year)
Men	Don Budge, Rod Laver (twice)
Singles and Doubles	Martina Navratilova (Current definition)
Singles, Doubles, Mixed Doubles	Margaret Court

Singles; Never beaten	Maureen Connolly
Women	Maureen Connolly, Margaret Court, Steffi Graf, Martina Navratilova (Current definition)
Grand Slam Events; Wins; Most	Margaret Court
Grand Slam Events; Wins; Most; Men	Roy Emerson
Homosexual Scandal; Involved in; 1946	Bill Tilden
Men's Team Championship	Davis Cup
Money;-	
Most made	Martina Navratilova
Most made; Men	Ivan Lendl
Net; Height in middle	3 feet
Olympics; Gold; 1992	
Men	Marc Rosset
Women	Jennifer Capriati
Original Name; Tennis patent	Sphairistike
Point replayed; Term	Let
Riding Accident forced retirement	Maureen Connolly
Service Winner not touched	Ace
Unbeaten; 1920–1925	Bill Tilden
US Open; Venue	Flushing Meadow (Forest Hills 1967–77)
US Open Champion;-	
Black; 1st	Althea Gibson
6 years in a row; Men; 20th Century	Bill Tilden
Youngest; Women	Maureen Connolly
US–UK; Women's Team Championship	Wightman Cup
Wimbledon;-	
Boycott, because of suspension of Pilic	1973
Disqualification for arriving late	Suzanne Lenglen
1st opened as	Croquet Club
Longest match	Pancho Gonzales v Charles Pasarell (1969)
Wimbledon Champion;-	
Amateur; Last; Men	John Newcombe
Black; 1st	Althea Gibson
Black; Men	Arthur Ashe (1975)
Czech; Men	Jan Kodes
Doubles; Most	Elizabeth Ryan, 12 + 7 Mixed
Egyptian (Czech Born); Men	Jaroslav Drobny (1954)
1st	Spencer Gore
1st; Women	Maud Watson
Mixed Doubles; Brother and Sister	John and Tracy Austin (1981)
Most; 20th Century; Men	Bjorn Borg
Most Consecutively; Men	Bjorn Borg, 5 (1976–80)
Most; Men	William Renshaw, 7
Most	Martina Navratilova, 9
1990; Men	Stefan Edberg
1990; Women	Martina Navratilova
1991; Men	Michael Stich
1991; Women	Steffi Graff
1992; Men	Andre Agassi
1992; Women	Steffi Graff
Oldest; Men	Arthur Gore (41)
Professional; 1st	Rod Laver (1968)

Singles, Doubles, Mixed Doubles Titles; Women	Doris Hart (1951), Billy Jean King (1967)
9 times; Women	Martina Navratilova
3 events in same year; 1st	Suzanne Lenglen (1920)
Titles; Most	Billy Jean King, 20
2 events in same year; UK; Post-War	Ann Jones
UK; Last; Men	Fred Perry (1936)
UK; Last; Women	Virginia Wade (1977) (beating Betty Stove)
Unseeded Player	Virginia Wade (1977), Boris Becker (1985)
World Table Tennis Champion	Fred Perry
World Table Tennis Championship Finalist	Ann Jones
Youngest	Lottie Dod (15)
Youngest; And US Champion	Maureen Connolly
Youngest; Men	Boris Becker (17)
Wimbledon Final;-	
Appearance; Singles; Greatest Span	Ken Rosewall (20 years)
3; Lost in same year	Betty Stove (1977)
UK Players only; Last	Angela Mortimer, Christine Trueman (1961)
Unseeded Player; Men	Chris Lewis (1983)
Women's Team Championship	Federation Cup

511

The Universe and Space Exploration

Contents

Astronomy and the Universe   515   By: Name   517
Constellations   Space Exploration   517

Astronomy and the Universe

By: General

Asteroids;-	
Largest	Ceres
Position	Orbit between Mars and Jupiter
Astronomer;-	
Astronomer Royal; 1st	John Flamsteed
'Canals' on Mars; Proposed	Percival Lowell
Well; Fell into while studying stars	Thales
Big Bang Theory; 1st advanced by	Georges Lemaitre
Comet;-	
Closest collision escape known	Hermes (1937)
Halley's; Period	Every 76 years (1986 last)
Smallest known orbit	Encke's Comet
Tail when moving away from Sun	Tail first
Constellation;-	
Largest	Hydra
Number classified	83
Earth;-	
Axis; Tilt	23½ degrees
Distance to Sun	93 million miles
Orbit	Ellipse
Shape	Oblate spheroid (flattened at the Poles)
Eclipse;-	
Most in a year	7
Solar, Total; Frequency in one place	About every 360 years
Evening Star	Venus
Expanding Universe;-	
Caused by, theory	Big Bang
Discoverer	Edwin Hubble
Pioneer Theoretician	Arthur Eddington
Galaxy;-	
Earth in	Milky Way
Nearest	Andromeda
Ratio of speed of recession to distance	Hubble's Constant
Receding; Spectral effect	Red Shift
Jodrell Bank;-	
Location	Cheshire, UK
Official name	Nuffield Radio Astronomy Laboratories
Meteorite	Meteor that falls to Earth
Moon;-	
Distance	About 240,000 miles
Gravity on	⅙th Earth
Waxing and Waning; Crescent	Waxing – right handed crescent
Planet(s):-	
Closest to Sun	Mercury

Coldest	Pluto
Furthest from Sun	Pluto normally, Neptune (1979–1999)
Heaviest	Jupiter
Hottest	Venus
Inner	Mercury, Venus, Earth, Mars
Largest	Jupiter
Moon; Largest	Ganymede (Jupiter), larger than Mercury
Moons; None	Mercury, Venus
Musician discovered	Uranus (by William Herschel)
Named by teenager	Pluto. By: Venetia Burney (13) from Oxford
Nearest to Earth	Venus
Orbits; Order	Mercury (closest to Sun), Venus, Earth, Mars, Jupiter, Saturn, Uranus, Neptune, Pluto
Red Spot	Jupiter
Rings	Saturn
Smallest	Pluto
Spin; Backwards	Venus (East to West)
Table showing Positions	Ephemeris
Year; Shorter than a day	Venus
Planet Moons;-	
Earth	1. Moon
Jupiter	Largest: Ganymede. Include: Io, Europa
Mars	2. Phobos, Deimos
Mercury	None
Neptune	Largest: Triton
Pluto	Only known: Charon
Saturn	Largest: Titan
Uranus	Include: Ariel, Miranda, Oberon, Titania
Venus	None
Planetary Motion; Laws of; Discoverer	Kepler
Quasar; Abbreviation of	Quasi Stellar (Radio) Source
Radiation belts around Earth	Van Allen
Radio waves from Space; Discoverer	Karl Jansky
Satellite Orbit;-	
Point closest to Earth	Perigee
Point furthest from Earth	Apogee
Spectroscopy; Pioneer	Fraunhofer
Star(s):-	
Brightest	Sirius
Brightness; Measurement unit	Magnitude
Collapse; Result of (Possible)	Black Hole
Emits regular radio pulses	Pulsar
Nearest	Proxima Centauri (apart from Sun)
Visible to the naked eye; Number	About 5700
Saturn; Rings; Composition	Ice and rock
Sun;-	
Main constituent	Hydrogen
Outer atmosphere; Visible in Eclipse	Corona
Surface temperature	About 6000 Degrees Centigrade
Sun-Centred Planetary System; Pioneer	Copernicus
Sunspots; Cycle	11 years
Uranus; Originally called	Georgian
Venus; Previous names	Phosphorus, Hesperus

Constellations

By: Name → Meaning

Aquarius	Water Carrier
Aquila	Eagle
Argo	Ship
Aries	Ram
Auriga	Charioteer
Bootes	Herdsman
Cancer	Crab
Canis Major	Great Dog
Capricornus	Goat
Cetus	Whale
Corvus	Crow
Crux	Southern Cross
Cygnus	Swan
Draco	Dragon
Gemini	Twins
Leo	Lion
Lepus	Hare
Libra	Scales
Pegasus	Winged Horse
Pisces	Fish
Sagittarius	Archer
Scorpio	Scorpion
Taurus	Bull
Ursa Major	Great Bear
Virgo	Virgin

Space Exploration

By: General

Animals;-	
1st in Space	Dog Laika, USSR (1957). Died
1st to Return Safely	Dogs Belka and Strelka, USSR
Others	USSR uses mainly dogs. US, chimpanzees, e.g., Abel and Baker (1959)
Artificial Satellite;-	
1st	Sputnik 1, USSR (October 4th, 1957). Sputnik means: 'Travelling Companion'
Astronaut;-	
British; 1st	Helen Sharman
Former occupation; Main	Test Pilot
Russian name	Cosmonaut
Communications;-	
Commercial; 1st	Early Bird (1965). Renamed: Intelsat
Predicted	Arthur C.Clarke (1945)
Transatlantic TV; 1st	Telstar (1962). Instrumental hit named after: The Tornados
Earth Resources Satellites; 1st	ERTS (renamed Landsat) (1972)
Fatality; 1st (known)	Soyuz II (1971)
Joint US–Soviet Venture; 1st	Apollo–Soyuz (1975)

Launching Site; Main US	Cape Canaveral, Florida. Known as Cape Kennedy (1963–1973)
Man in Space;-	
1st (Successful)	Yuri Gagarin. In: *Vostok 1* (April 12th, 1961). Vostok means: 'East'
1st; US; Orbital	John Glenn. In: *Friendship 7* (1962). Glenn became: US Senator
1st; US; Non Orbital	Alan Shephard. In: *Liberty Bell 7* (1961)
Manned Space Programmes; US	Mercury, Gemini, Apollo
Meteriological Satellite; 1st	*Tiros 1* (1960)
Moon;-	
Golf ball; 1st to hit on	Alan Shepherd
Last men on	Cernan and Schmitt. In: *Apollo 17* (1972)
Man on; 1st	Neil Armstrong. In: *Apollo 11* (July 21st, 1969). Location of landing: Mare Tranquillitatis
Man on; 2nd	Edwin 'Buzz' Aldrin. (Michael Collins in orbital craft didn't land)
Man on; 3rd	Charles Conrad, *Apollo 12* (1969)
Manned flight round; 1st	*Apollo 8* (1968) – Borman, Lovell, Anders
Other landings	6 Missions, 12 US Astronauts land
Soft landing; 1st	*Luna 9*, USSR (1966)
Time of flight	About 3 days
Vehicles on	Lunar Roving Vehicle (US), Lunokhod (USSR)
Words on; 1st	'That's one small step for (a) man, one giant leap for mankind' (omitted 'a' by mistake)
National Agency; US	NASA (National Aeronautics and Space Administration)
Non Russian or American in Space; 1st	Czech
Ordinary Person; 1st in Space Programmme	Christa McAuliffe, Teacher, killed in Shuttle *Challenger* (1986)
Pictures from another Planet; 1st	*Venera 9* (1975)
Pioneers;-	
US; 'Father of Space Travel'	Robert Goddard
US; Former German Developer of V1, V2	Werner Von Braun
USSR	Konstantin Tsiolkovsky
Planets	
Jupiter; 1st	*Voyager 1* (flew past)
Landing on another; 1st	Venus, USSR (1966)
Mars; 1st	*Viking 1* (landed on)
Mercury; 1st	*Mariner 10* (flew past)
Neptune; 1st	*Voyager 2* (flew past – due 1989)
Saturn; 1st	*Voyager 1* (flew past)
Uranus; 1st	*Voyager 2* (flew past)
Principles of;-	
Leaving Earth	Velocity greater than the escape velocity (7 miles/second) needed
Rocket propulsion	Newton's 3rd Law governs
Rocket Programme; UK; 1st	Blue Streak

Rockets;-
  For Space Exploration, 1st to
    Suggest   Tsiolkovsky, Russia (1903)
  Invented by   Chinese
  Liquid propelled; 1st   Robert Goddard (1926)
Shuttle (Re-usable Space Vehicle);-
  1st (in operation)   *Columbia* (1981) (earlier *Enterprise*
                                       never in orbit)
  Disaster   *Challenger* (January 28th, 1986). 7
                                        killed
Skylab crashed in   Australia
Solar System; Man-made object; 1st
    to leave   *Pioneer 10* (1983)
Space Station;-
  Concept; Pioneer   Tsiolkovsky
  1st   *Salyut*, USSR (1971). Salyut means:
                                        'Salute'
  1st; US   *Skylab* (1973)
Walk;-
  1st   Alexei Leonov (1965)
  Woman; 1st   Svetlana Savitskaya
  Untethered; 1st   Bruce McCandless (1984)
Woman
  1st in Space   Valentina Tereshkova (1963)
  1st; US   Sally Ride (1983)

Subject Index

Abbreviations, 205
Abbreviations, Trade Unions, 420
Accidents, Air, 371
Accidents, Nuclear, 355
Accidents, Sea, 381
Actors/Actresses, 99
Actors/Actresses, Nicknames, 335
Actors/Actresses, Real Names, 342
Acts of Parliament, 422
Advertising Campaigns, 400
Advertising Slogans, 399
Affairs, 327
Air Transport, 370
Aircraft, Famous Models, 372
Airforce, Ranks, 409
Airlines, 370
Airlines, National, 373
Airports, 370
Alcoholic Drinks, 462
Alloys, 350
American English, 207
American Football, 470
Animal Life, General, 269
Animals, Alternative Names, 292
Animals, Breeds, 274
Animals, Collections, 277
Animals, Families, 278
Animals, Habitations, 284
Animals, Land, 286
Animals, Male and Female, 291
Animals, Products from, 271
Animals, Scientific Names, 293
Animals, Sounds, 269
Animals, Young, 293
Archaeology, 404
Architects, 8
Architectural Terms, 3
Army, Ranks, 409
Art, Craft and Architecture, 1
Art Terms, 4
Artistic Movements and Schools, 5
Artists, 6
Assassination and Murder, 387
Assassination and Murder, Attempted, 390

Association Football, 470
Astronomy, 515
Athletics, 474, 491
Atlantic Crossings, 371
Atom Bomb, 368
Atoms, 362
Attempted Murder, 390
Authors, 224, 226
Authors, Real Names, 337
Autobiography, 226
Awards and Prizes, 305
Awards and Trophies, Sporting, 477
Backing Groups, 56
Badminton, 477
Ballet Terms, 96
Ballets, 96
Banks, 403
Baseball, 478
Basketball, 478
Battles, 431
Bays and Gulfs, 133
BBC, 106
Bears, Famous, 280
Bees, 285
Bible, The, 187
Biographical Information, 305
Biographical Quotations, 306
Biography, 227, 305
Biology, 294
Birds, 271
Birthstones, 468
Blood, 173
Boats, Countries from, 380
Body, The, 173
Bones, 174
Booker Prize, 254
Books, 229, 252
Bottle Sizes, 462
Bowling (Ten pin), 479
Bowls, 479
Boxing, 479
Brain, The, 174
Breeds of Animal, 274
Bridges, 128
Brothers and Sisters, 306
Buddhism, 199

Buildings and Constructions, 128, 130
Buildings, Architects of, 8
Bullfighting, 481
Business, 399
Butterflies, 285
Calendars, 367
Canals, 132
Capes, 134
Capitals, 149, 152
Capitals, Former, 152
Cars, 374, 377
Cars, Countries from, 374
Cars, Famous, 377
Cars, Famous Models, 374
Cars, Name Derivations, 378
Cars, Nicknames, 378
Cartoons, 227
Castles, 128
Catchphrases, 100
Cathedrals, 128
Cats, 287
Cats, Famous, 281
Characters from Fiction, 242, 248
Characters from Films, 17
Chemical Formulae, 350
Chemical Names, 349
Chemistry, 350
Chess, 466
Children, 307, 325
China, Politics, 438
Christian Names, 329
Christianity, 189
Churches, 128
Cinema, 17, 21
Circumnavigation of the Globe, 380
Circus, 99
Cities, 152, 153
Cities on Lakes, 153
Cities on Rivers, 154
Classical Music, General, 57
Cocktails, 463
Codes and Ciphers, 208
Coins, 455
Collections, Animal, 277
Colonies, Former, 404
Comics, 227
Communications, 353
Companies and Business, 400
Company Names, Origin, 400

Composers, 57, 60
Computers, 354
Conductors, Musical, 62
Constellations, 517
Continents, 142
Cookery, Dishes, 456
Cookery, Food, 459
Cookery, Terms, 461
Counties, UK, 170
Countries, 155, 157
Country of Origin, People, 321
Crafts, 9
Crashes, Air, 371
Cricket, 481
Crime, 387, 391
Crime Detection and Punishment, 390
Criminals, 393
Criminals, Nicknames, 332
Criminals, Real Names, 337
Currencies, 402
Currency, Slang, 402
Customs and Superstitions, 405
Cycling, 483
Dance and Ballet, 96
Darts, 484
Days, Name Origins, 367
Death, 308
Death, After, 311
Derivations, Word, 209
Deserts, 134
Detectives, Fictional, 249
Diamonds, 364
Dinosaurs, 287
Directors, Film, 52, 54
Disabilities, 311
Disasters, Air, 371
Disasters, Chemical, 360
Disasters, Natural, 141
Disasters, Nuclear, 355
Disasters, Sea, 381
Discoveries and Theories, 354
Disease and Medicine, 178
Diseases and Disabilities, 311
Diseases, Common Names, 181
Diseases, Effects, 182
Divination, Means of, 197
Dogs, 277
Dogs, Famous, 281
Dress, 464
Drink, 462

Drinks, Alcoholic, 462
Drinks, Cocktails, 463
Drinks, Made from, 464
Drugs, Common Names, 179
Drugs, Medical, 179
Earthquakes, 141
Economics and Business, 399
Economics and Finance, 403
Education, 405
EEC, 408
Eggs, 272
Elements, Chemical, 351
Elements, Chemical Symbols, 351
Elements, Names from, 351
Elements, Uses, 352
Energy Technology, 355
Entertainment, 15
Equestrian Events, 484
Espionage, 406
Evolution, 294
Executions, 312, 313
Exploration and Discovery, 158
Extremities, Geographical, 159
Eyes, 175
FA Cup, 472
Famous Animals, 280
Fashion and Dress, 464
Fencing, 485
Festivals, 467
Festivals, Christian, 190
Festivals, Musical, 57
Fiction, Books, 229
Fiction, Plays, 258
Fictional Characters and Things,
   242, 248
Fictional Detectives, 249
Film Directors, 52, 54
Film Quotes, 49
Film Stars, 54
Films, 23, 26
Films, Songs from, 51
Films, Themes, 50
Finance, 403
Fish and Sea Creatures, 282
Flags, 160
Flowers, 298
Food, 459
Football, American, 470
Football, Association, 470
Football Grounds, 473
Foreign Phrases, 210

Forgery, 392
Formulae, 350
France, Politics, 438
Fraud, 392
Galleries and Collections, 10
Games, 465
Games, Terms from, 467
Gangs and Gangsters, 393
Gems, 364
Geographical Terms, 134
Geography and Places, 125
Geology, 134
Germany, Politics, 439
Gods and Goddesses, 192
Golf, 485
Grand Prix Circuits, 490
Greek Gods and Goddesses, 192
Greyhound Racing, 486
Gulfs, 133
Guns, 368
Gymnastics, 486
Habitations, 284
Health and the Body, 171
Heraldry, 407
Highwaymen, 398
Hinduism, 199
Historians, 420
Historical Territories, 160
History, 404
History, World, 437, 446, 448
Hobbies, Names of, 468
Holidays and Festivals, 467
Homosexual/Bisexual People,
   320
Horse Racing, 487
Horses, 284
Horses, Famous, 282
Horses, Riders, 484
House of Commons, 423
House of Lords, 423
Houses, Famous, 133
Husbands, 314
Ideas and Beliefs, 185
Illegitimate People, 320
Inhabitants of Places, 161
Initials, People's, 330
Insects, 285
Instruments, Scientific, 366
International Number Plates, 378
International Organisations, 407
International Politics, 407

Inventions, 356
Inventors, 356, 366
Ireland, Politics, 441
Islam, 200
Islands, 136, 137
Italy, Politics, 441
Judaism, 200
Kidnapping, 394
Kings, 413
Labours of Hercules, 195
Lakes, 139
Lakes, Cities on, 153
Land Animals, 286
Language and Literature, 203
Languages, 211, 212
Last Words, 313
Latitude and Longitude, 168
Law, 395
Law Enforcement, 390
Legendary Characters and
    Things, 250
Legs, Animal, 270
Leisure, 455
Leisure Activities and Skills, 468
Libraries, 254
Light, 362
Literary Movements, 251
Literature, 224
Literature, Themes and Plots, 252
Magazines, 255
Maiden Names, 331
Mammals, 289
Man Made Constructions, 128
Manias, 183
Marriages, 314
Materials, 350
Mathematics, 358
Measurement, 359
Medical Specialities, 183
Medicine, 178
Mental Illnesses and Conditions,
    183
Metals, 353
Metals, Ores From, 361
Meteorology, 148
Middle Names, 331
Military, 408
Military Technology, 368
Mistresses, 327
Money, 402
Monkeys, 289

Months, Name Origins, 367
Moon, Man on, 518
Motor Racing, 489
Motorcycle Racing, 491
Motorcycles, Famous Makes, 375
Mottoes, 213
Mountain Ranges, 139
Mountains, 139, 140, 141
MPs, 424
Murder, 387
Murderers, 396
Muscles, 176
Muses, 196
Music, 56
Music Hall, 99
Music, Notes, 59
Music, Tempo, 59
Musical Instruments, 58
Musical Terms, 58
Musical Themes, Film, 50
Musical Works, 59, 60
Musical Works, Common Names,
    61
Musicals, 97
Musicals, Songs from, 99
Musicians, 62
Musicians, Instruments Played,
    62
Musicians, Nicknames, 332
Musicians, Real Names, 338
Mythical Animals, 196
Mythological Gods and
    Goddesses, 192
Mythology, 194
Name Changes, People, 337
Name Changes, Places, 164
Names, 329, 331
National Anthems, 161
National Symbols, 162
Nationality and Origin, People,
    321
Natural Disasters, 141
Natural Features, 133
Natural Sites and Places, 142
Nautical Terms, 380
Navy, Ranks, 409
News Agencies, 255
Newspapers, 255
Nicknames, Football Clubs, 470
Nicknames, People, 332
Nicknames, Places, 167

Nobel Prizes, 305
Non-Fiction, 256
Number Plates, International, 378
Numbers, Large, 358
Nursery Rhymes, 257
The Occult, 197
Occupations, People, 322
Occupations, Traditional, 404
Oceans, 145
Olympic Games, 491
Opera Characters, 63
Operas, 65
Operations, Medical, 180
Ores, 361
Oscars, 22
Outlaws, 398
Paintings, 10, 12
Pairs and Partnerships, 325
Parapsychology, 197
Parents, 307, 325
Parliament, UK, 424
Parliaments, Names of, 410
Partners, 327
Patron Saints, 191
Pen-Names, 337
People, 303, 411
Peoples and Tribes, 163
Periodicals, 255
Philosophers, 198
Philosophy, 198
Phobias, 184
Photographers, 12
Phrases and Terms, 213
Physics, 362
Pirates, 397
Place Name Changes, 164
Place Name Derivations, 166
Place Name Parts, Meaning, 167
Place Names, Roman, 168
Place Nicknames, 167
Places, 149, 162
Places, Latitude and Longitude, 168
Planets, 515, 518
Plants, 295
Plants, Alternative Names, 295
Plants, Common Names, 295
Plants, Families, 296
Plants, General, 298
Plants, Products obtained from, 300

Plants, Varieties and Types, 297
Plays, 258
Poetry, 263
Police, 391
Political Figures, Nicknames, 333
Political Figures, Real Names, 341
Politics, 404
Politics, International, 407
Politics, World, 437, 446, 448
Polygons, 358
Pop Groups, 67, 68
Pop LPs/Albums, 80
Pop Music, Other, 82
Pop Records, 83
Pop Singers, 67, 68
Pop Singles, 84
Popes, 191
Population, 156
Ports, 381
Precious Stones, 364
Presidential Slogans, US, 430
Presidents, US, 429
Prime Ministers, British, 425
Printing, 363
Prisons, 391
Pseudonyms, 337
Psychiatry, 184
Psychology, 184
Publicity Blurbs, Film, 49
Queens, 413
Quotations, 214, 215
Quotations, Biographical, 306
Quotations, Catchphrases, 100
Quotations, Film, 49
Quotations, Last Words, 313
Quotations, Literary, 214
Radiation, Types of, 363
Radio, 102, 353
Radio Isotopes, 353
Radio Programmes, 102
Radio Stations, Local, 102
Rail Transport, 376
Real (First) Names, 336
Real Names, 337
Regular Solids, 359
Relations, Famous People, 326
Relationships, 327
Religion, 199
Rhyming Slang, 222
Rivers, 144

Rivers, Cities on, 154
Road Signs, 379
Road Transport, 377
Roads, 379
Roads, Famous, 379
Robbery and Robbers, 397
Rocks, 364
Roman Gods and Goddesses, 192
Roman Numerals, 359
Roman Place Names, 168
Rome, Ancient, 443
Rowing, 497
Royalty, 413, 414
Royalty, UK, 415, 417
Rugby League, 497
Rugby Union, 498
Rule, Types of, 420
Rulers, Names for, 419
Sailing, 500
Saints, 192
Science and Technology, 347
Sciences and Studies, 365
Scientific Instruments, 366
Scientists, 366
Sculptors, 13
Sculptures, 13
Sea and Water Transport, 380
Sea Creatures, 282
Seas and Oceans, 145, 146
Security Agencies, 407
Ships, 380
Ships, Famous, 381
Showjumping, 484
Singers, Classical, 94
Sisters, 306
Skating, 500
Skiing and Winter Sports, 501
Skills, 468
Slang, 222
Sleep, Animal, 271
Slogans, Advertising, 399
Snakes, 290
Snooker, 501
Social and Welfare Issues, 419
Society and Politics, 385
Sociology, 420
Songs and Tunes, 94
Songs from Films, 51
Space Exploration, 517
Speedway, 502
Spiders, 286

Spies, 406
Sport, 470, 502
Sporting Terms, 503
Sports Commentators, 107
Sports, Other, 495
Sportspeople, 506
Sportspeople, Nicknames, 335
Squash, 508
Stage Entertainment, 96
Stage Names, 337
Stage Partnerships, 325
Stamps, 469
Stars, 516
Stars, Film, 52, 54
Stars, Radio and TV, 107, 108
States, US, 170
Stations, Railway, 376
Stock Exchange, 403
Straits, 146
Suicide, 328, 420
Superstitions, 405
Surnames, 332, 345
Swimming, 508
Table Tennis, 509
Television, 354
Temperature, Geography, 148
Temperature, Physics, 363
Tennis, 509
Territories, Sovereignty, 169
Theatre, 99
Theories, Scientific, 354
Time and Calendars, 367
Titles, 345, 346
Trade Unions, 420
Trains, 376
Trains and Engines, Famous, 382
Transport, 370
Treason, 312
Treaties, 421
Trees, 300
Triangles, 359
Tribes, 163
Trophies, 477
TV and Radio, 100
TV and Radio Characters, 104
TV and Radio Personalities, 107, 108
TV Companies, Independent, 106
TV, General, 106
TV Programmes, 108, 109
Underground Railways, 377

United Kingdom, Geography, 169
United Kingdom, Politics, 422, 426
United Nations, 408
United States, Geography, 170
United States, Politics, 428
Units of Measurement, 359
The Universe, 513
Universities, 406
USSR, Politics, 445
Valleys, 142
Variety, 99
Volcanoes, 142, 147
Wars and Battles, 431
Water Transport, 380
Waterfalls, 147
Weapons and Military Technology, 368
Weapons, Famous, 369

Weather, 148
Weather Areas, 148
Wedding Anniversaries, 469
Wild West, 398
Winds, 148
Wine, Types, 463
Winter Olympics, Locations, 495
Wives, 314
Wonders of the World, Ancient, 129
Word Derivations, 209
Words and Letters, 223
Words from other Languages, 223
World Cup, 474
World Politics and History, 437, 446, 448
WWI, 436
WWII, 436
Zodiac, Signs, 198